474 Science Activities
for Young Children

Delmar Publishers' Online Services

To access Delmar on the World Wide Web, point your browser to:

http://www.delmar.com/delmar.html

To access through Gopher:

gopher://gopher.delmar. com

For information on our products and services:
email: info@delmar.com
or call
800-347-7707

Delmar Online is part of "thomson.com", an Internet site with information on more than 30 publishers
of the International Thomson Publishing organization.

474 Science Activities for Young Children

Moira D. Green

Delmar Publishers
An International Thomson Publishing Company

Albany • Bonn • Boston • Cincinnati • Detroit • London • Madrid • Melbourne
Mexico City • New York • Pacific Grove • Paris • San Francisco • Singapore
Tokyo • Toronto • Washington

Cover Credit: Cover originally designed for the Polaroid Corporation by Can't Stop Design.

Delmar Staff

Publisher:	Diane McOscar
Senior Editor:	Jay Whitney
Associate Editor:	Erin O'Connor
Production Coordinator:	Sandra Woods
Art and Design Coordinator:	Timothy J. Conners

COPYRIGHT © 1996
By Delmar Publishers
a division of International Thomson Publishing Inc.
The ITP logo is a trademark under license

Printed in the United States of America

For more information contact:

Delmar Publishers
3 Columbia Circle
Box 15015
Albany, New York 12203-5015

International Thomson Editores
Campos Eliseos 385, Piso 7
Col Polanco
11560 Mexico D F Mexico

International Thomson Publishing Europe
Berkshire House 168-173
High Holborn
London WC1V7AA
England

International Thomson Publishing GmbH
Königswinterer Strasse 418
53227 Bonn
Germany

Thomas Nelson Australia
102 Dodds Street
South Melbourne, 3205
Victoria, Australia

International Thomson Publishing Asia
221 Henderson Road
#05-10 Henderson Building
Singapore 0315

Nelson Canada
1120 Birchmount Road
Scarborough, Ontario
Canada M1K5G4

International Thomson Publishing - Japan
Hirakawacho Kyowa Building, 3F
2-2-1 Hirakawacho
Chiyoda-ku, Tokyo 102
Japan

2   3   4   5   6   7   8   9   10   XXX   01   00   99   98   97

Library of Congress Cataloging-in-Publication Data

Green, Moira D.
    474 science activities for young children / by Moira D. Green.
        p.   cm.
    Includes index.
    ISBN 0-8273-6663-9
    1. Science—Experiments—Juvenile literature.   2. Science—Study
and teaching—Activity programs—Juvenile literature.   I. Title.
Q164.G74   1995
507.8—dc20

95-19299
CIP

CONTENTS

Full Color Feature

PREFACE

The wonderful thing about the world of science is that it is everywhere around us—in the simplest things, in the most obvious places, and in routine, everyday actions. This book uses a child-initiated, whole language approach to help you have fun exploring that world with children

The Polaroid Education Program presents the full-color feature: *Imagine A Green Tomorrow.* This is a visual learning environment project guide for students and teachers. It is filled with 17 activities to use the techniques of visual learning: exploring, recording, expressing, communicating, motivating and creating. They are designed to help students link visions with action and to make a difference in their communities.

Notice that each unit begins with an "Attention Getter." The purpose of this is to introduce each unit to children in a way that grabs their attention, stimulates their interest, and creates excitement about the discoveries you will be making together. Because they focus the group's attention, I also like to use the "Attention Getter" at the beginning of every day or session to connect with the children before they explore the activity centers, to discuss the projects which are available for the day, and to sing songs or read books which reinforce the unit. Many of the activities in this book include demonstrations of the materials that can be incorporated in your Attention Getter time.

You'll also notice that with a few of the children's books in the literature lists, I suggest that you use colored pencils to shade in diverse skin colors, expecially when illustrations show large groups or crowds of people who are all white. Even in this day and age, some publishers of children's books are quite unaware of this issue, so I don't hesitate to alter books to reflect the population, and I urge you to do the same.

Each unit is arranged according to a WHY? WHAT? HOW? format, as in the following example:

The Exploding Triangle Trick
Science

WHY we are doing this experiment: to provide children with a dramatic way of observing how soap weakens surface tension; to develop self-esteem and a sense of autonomy through use of a one-person work station.

WHAT we will need:
    Shallow tub of water
    Water refills
    Tub for emptying used water
    Three 10 cm (4") straws
    One popsicle stick
    Small container of liquid soap
    "One person may be here" sign (see
      page 3)
    Newspaper

HOW we will do it: To prepare, spread several layers of newspaper underneath your activity area. Pour a shallow amount of water in the tub, set all other materials beside it, and pin up your "One person may be here" sign.

Activities selected are from across the curriculum: science, math, music, movement, language art, multicultural diversity, dramatic play, social studies, motor and cognitive development.

I suggest, in the course of facilitating these science activities and others which you create yourself, that you refer to what you and the children are doing as "science experiments" as frequently as possible. This helps the children think of themselves as scientists, and of their daily play as legitimate scientific experimentation. It is also important that you conduct each experiment ahead of time by yourself before facilitating it with the children. This allows you to anticipate problems, to set up the activity more efficiently, and to make sure that your particular materials work as desired.

The implementation of proper safety precautions is always a primary concern when working with children. Some educators have recently expressed reservations about the use of glitter. I have included this material in my activities because in my years of teaching I have never experienced, or heard of, an injury occurring as a result of its use. However, I have also listed colored sand as an alternative to glitter, if you prefer to use it.

Finally, there is a lot of discussion these days among early childhood educators about the best approach to teaching young children. High Scope, open-ended, child-directed—these are a few of the terms commonly used. I have implemented a whole language philosophy in this guide because in my teaching experience, students thrive on this approach. There is nothing like being with children who are so enthralled with a project that they spontaneously use all parts of language—listening, speaking, reading, and writing—in the thrill and excitement of their explorations and discoveries. I have also used a child-initiated approach throughout the book because my experience has been that children who choose what they would like to do, and the length of time they would like to do it, are empowered children. That said, I would like to end this preface with the observation that regardless of our particular teaching approaches, genuinely caring for, respecting, and having fun with our children is what matters most, and is the best gift we can give them. Enjoy experiencing these science activities together, and have fun!!

Dedication

To my parents, Tom and Louise Green, with love.
To those fabulous realtors at the Stark East office in Madison, Wisconsin.
To my sister, Deirdre Green, for being who she is and then some.
And to H. S. for everything.

ACKNOWLEDGMENTS

To my Delmar editors, Jay Whitney and Erin O'Connor. Thanks also to Glenna Stanfield and Christopher Anzalone for all their help.

Special thanks to the reviewers of my manuscript who provided great ideas and advice:

Mary Henthorne
Western Wisconsin Technical College
La Crosse, Wisconsin

Judy Patchin
Black Hawk College
Genesco, Illinois

Dr. Audrey Marshall
Albany State College
Albany, Georgia

Ruth Steinbrunner
Central Virginia Community College
Lynchburg, Virginia

Etta Miller
Taylor University
Ft. Wayne, Indiana

Dr. M. Kay Stickle
Ball State University
Muncie, Indiana

Thank you to Bruce Sherwin and Linda Ayres-Demasi at Publisher's Studio for their talent and hard work. Thanks also to Jennifer Campbell for her excellent copyediting. And special thanks to Hud Armstrong for his wonderful illustrations.

INTRODUCTION

How Preschoolers Think

A few months after beginning my first teaching job, a new child, Jeremiah, was placed in my group for small group activity. One morning, our project involved propping long planks up on blocks and rolling balls and marbles down them. How fast did the objects roll? How far did they roll? What happened when the ramps were adjusted? These were the questions my children explored—all except Jeremiah. Jeremiah was more interested in smacking the blocks together, building them up into a tower and then knocking them down, and seeing what use he could make of the long plank. All the other children talked excitedly to each other about their discoveries. Involved in his own experiments, Jeremiah seemed isolated from the others. I noticed too, that I felt a little disappointed. Why was he not interested in the rolling experiment? I had thought it would be the kind of activity he would love. Not too long after this, my question was answered. We discovered that in his records, Jeremiah was younger than we had thought. He was actually an entire nine months younger than all the other children in my group—and so, naturally, was more interested in the sensory aspect of the materials, because this is the primary method employed by children his age to understand the world. This incident, which occurred early in my teaching career, was a graphic example to me of the different stages of cognitive development in children, and how vital it is to take those stages into account when planning and facilitating activities.

Piaget

Cognitive refers to the development and structure of thought processes, and how those processes affect the way individuals perceive and relate to their world. Although Jean Piaget (1896–1980) is by no means the only cognitive theorist, he is certainly the most influential. Although several of his conclusions have recently been questioned, it is safe to say that in general, his discoveries about early childhood cognition establish a firm basis for understanding how preschoolers think.

Piaget maintained that there are four primary stages of thought development in children. The table on the next page illustrates these four stages.

The term *preoperational* refers to Piaget's contention that preschoolers cannot perform operations which are the results of concepts logically related to each other. Another way to put this is that their thinking does not allow the principle of "because this happens when I do this, that will probably happen when I do that." Piaget attributed this largely to *centration*, or the inclination of preschoolers to think about one aspect of an object or situation at a time, to the exclusion of all others. He set out to prove this with his conservation experiments. When the same amounts of water, clay, or checkers were arranged differently and compared to each other, (i.e., one amount in a taller glass, longer shape, or longer line) the children did not realize that the amounts were still equal, because they focused exclusively on the appearance of the materials.

Piaget also maintained that preschoolers are primarily focused on their own perspectives, and are largely incapable of considering the perspectives of others. He called this *egocentrism*. It is important to note that those who question this theory cite experiments which produced quite different conclusions. Many developmentalists think that when preoperational children are presented with a task which makes sense to

STAGE	AGE	CHARACTERISTICS
Sensorimotor	0–2 years	The infant uses all senses, as well as motor abilities, to explore and understand the world. This stage begins with reflexes (e.g., sucking, grasping). By 18 to 24 months, the child is capable of thinking before acting, and understands the concept of object permanence.
Preoperational (Preschoolers)	2–6 years	The child often centers only on his or her own perspective, termed *egocentrism* by Piaget. (As the child moves to the next stage, s/he begins to decenter and to understand other viewpoints.) Also, the child tends to focus on one aspect of an experience to the exclusion of all others. Thought is *concrete*, that is, centered on specifics, tangibles, and appearances. The "language explosion" occurs in conjunction with the development of symbolic thought. Vocabulary expands extremely rapidly. Pretend play is very imaginative and drawings become representational.
Concrete Operational	7–11 years	The child develops an understanding of logical principles and applies them to her or his experiences and perceptions.
Formal Operational	12 years and older	The teenager thinks abstractly. Hypothetical and complex thought is applied to the questions and issues presented by his or her experiences in the world.

Piaget's four primary stages of thought development in children.

them, they are very capable of understanding viewpoints other than their own.

The Language Explosion

Almost all developmentalists believe that the ability of preschoolers to think symbolically makes possible the tremendous language explosion which characterizes this stage. Piaget believed that children must first understand an idea before they are capable of using the word which represents that idea. Jerome Burger disagrees, proposing the theory that language is an integral facet of all human experience, and that as the means of expressing experience, language also transforms that experience. For example, as children learn the difference in emotion connoted by the words *terrified* and the word *afraid*, the children are better able to

express their feelings, and this ability actually alters their experiences.

There is little dispute among theorists, however, that the growth of vocabulary among preoperational children is truly astounding. A child aged eighteen months typically has a vocabulary of fifty words. From age two to six, the average child's vocabulary numbers from eight thousand to fourteen thousand words. This means that during this stage of development children learn approximately six to ten words a day.

Other characteristics of this stage of language development include the predominance of concrete nouns and adjectives and a lack of abstract words; this is a predictable result of preoperational thinking which centers on appearances and tangibles. This also means that expressions tend to be taken literally.

As mentioned previously, preschoolers also tend to focus on one specific facet of an object or experience, to the exclusion of all others. This affects language by making it difficult for the children to understand transitions and transformations, and consequently, words that convey comparison. Preschoolers also tend to *overregularize*, meaning that they use certain rules of grammar frequently even when those rules do not apply.

Why Science?
Why Whole Language?

SCIENCE. From the moment infants enter the world, they begin to think, processing their experiences, organizing information, adjusting and reforming their schemas. (*Schema* is Piaget's term for a broad way of thinking about and interacting with objects and concepts.) Webster's New World Dictionary defines science as ". . . knowledge derived from observation, study and experimentation . . ." Clearly, children are natural scientists. Science provides children with hundreds of experiences in which to apply their existing schemas, as well as hundreds of opportunities to form new ones. In exploring fluids, the child pours honey back and forth between two different containers, fascinated by its slow, gooey flow. The exploration provides information about what happens to the same amount of fluid in differently shaped containers, or in other words, conservation of matter. In exploring gravity, the child is confronted with an "If this happens, then that will happen?" principle. She's been told that gravity pulls objects towards the center of the earth. The child discovers that no matter what object she rolls down the tube, it falls into the bucket. The experiment involves two concepts that are logically related to each other. On a chart, the child sees a soft, turquoise feather stuck above a written word and is presented with the notion that a particular combination of letters symbolizes a specific, tangible object. In using a mirror to examine different areas of the classroom, the children realize there are different views (different perspectives) not thought of before. Or as one student put it: "Now I know what the underneath of the table looks like!" These are but four examples among hundreds of how science activities provide essential experiences to the preoperational child.

Because children learn best by doing, science experimentation is tailor-made for the hands-on acquisition of knowledge. Children learn about their world by interacting with it. Child-initiated, sensory-oriented science experiments provide firsthand experiences of natural phenomena and scientific principles which become meaningful to children as they initiate and control their own exploration and discovery. The natural curiosity of young children, combined with their need to see, taste, smell, hear, and touch the world around them, makes child-directed discovery science an ideal means of satisfying children's "need to know."

LANGUAGE. The language arts program involves the development of speaking, listening, reading, and writing skills. The four steps of the scientific approach perfectly complement language arts activities for preschoolers: (1) noticing a problem (speaking, listening); (2) hypothesizing a reason for the problem and predicting "what will happen if . . ." (speaking, listening, reading, writing); (3) experimenting to find out (speaking, listening during hands-on sensorimotor experimentation); and (4) recording and/or communicating the results of the experiment (speaking, listening, reading, writing).

As noted above, preschoolers soak up new works like sponges, and in the course of facilitating science and introducing new concepts, there are a multitude of opportunities for expanding vocabulary. The whole language approach seeks to create a "print-rich" environment to aid literacy development, and this can be used to reinforce new vocabulary with tools like experience charts, graphs, language badges, writing centers, posters, activity signs, writing sheets and blank paper for recording experiment results.

Speaking and listening provide more opportunities to reinforce new vocabulary, and enable the teacher/parent to address overregularization:

Courtney:	"I need somes."
Alexander the puppet (teacher)	"You need some what?"
Courtney:	"I need some mores."

Alexander:	"You need some more what?"
Courtney:	"I need some more of baking soda."
Alexander:	"Oh—you need some more baking soda."

Science also provides a host of activities which involve comparison and introduce children to comparative and superlative forms of adjectives and adverbs, as well as the value judgments necessary in using these words.

Organizing Curriculum

In organizing curriculum, many educators find it valuable to use the webbing technique. As shown in the sample web on the next page, this method of visual organization allows you to see quickly and clearly that your plan incorporates all that it should. The web begins with the center: your topic or theme. Branching out from the center are the concepts you want to teach (goals). Branching off from your goals are your objectives, or in other words, the method you will employ to teach the concept, and the way in which the children will explore it. In whole language science, it is also valuable to include the particular language tools used, as well as the specific skills the tools are intended to develop. This allows you to make sure that all skills are practiced, and a wide variety of tools is utilized. For example, in the sample web for feathers, it is clear that reading, writing, speaking, and listening skills are all focused on many times over. The tools utilized include: language badges, a puppet, charts, a writing center, flannel board play, dramatic play, activity signs, and plenty of discussion. This is an ideal variety of language tools; however, some topics/themes lend themselves to such a variety more readily than others. The web also allows you to see that all curriculum areas have been included, that group activities are balanced with one-person and two-person work stations, and that science kits have been provided to encourage independent, individual experimentation.

To Summarize

The whole language science curriculum expands the vocabulary of the preoperational children at a time when they are most receptive to absorbing new words. It facilitates children's emerging literacy, and provides countless opportunities for self-expression and verbal interaction. Science activities provide young children with dozens of experiences which allow them to examine existing schemas and to form new ones. Child-directed, hands-on experimentation gives children the automony to initiate and control their own scientific discoveries. Whole language science caters to, encourages, and develops the natural scientist in every child!

Sample Branches of a Webbing

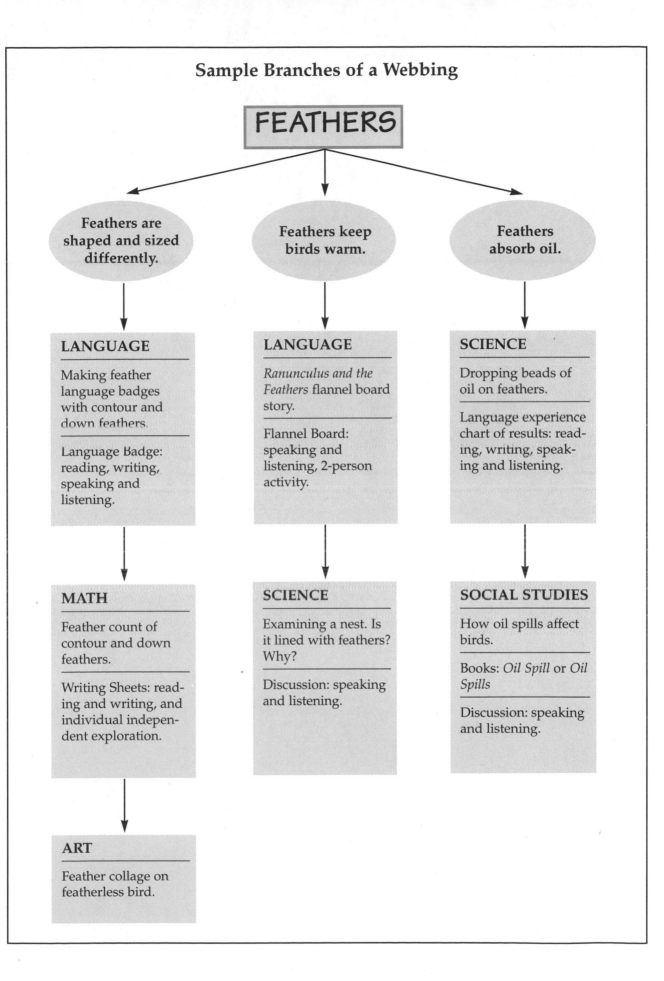

FEATHERS

Feathers are shaped and sized differently.

Feathers keep birds warm.

Feathers absorb oil.

LANGUAGE

Making feather language badges with contour and down feathers.

Language Badge: reading, writing, speaking and listening.

LANGUAGE

Ranunculus and the Feathers flannel board story.

Flannel Board: speaking and listening, 2-person activity.

SCIENCE

Dropping beads of oil on feathers.

Language experience chart of results: reading, writing, speaking and listening.

MATH

Feather count of contour and down feathers.

Writing Sheets: reading and writing, and individual independent exploration.

SCIENCE

Examining a nest. Is it lined with feathers? Why?

Discussion: speaking and listening.

SOCIAL STUDIES

How oil spills affect birds.

Books: *Oil Spill* or *Oil Spills*

Discussion: speaking and listening.

ART

Feather collage on featherless bird.

COLOR CAPERS

Attention Getter: Gather the children together before they begin exploring the activities, and have a large, clear jar of water available. If you wish, have some relaxing dream-like music playing in the background. Using food coloring and a medicine dropper, let drops of different colors fall into the jar. With the children, watch the colors diffuse while they curl and bend, making streamers in the water.

Primary Patterns
Science/Cognitive

WHY we are doing this project: to reinforce the concept of primary colors; to help children understand that red, yellow, and blue make other colors; to develop fine motor skills.

Developmental differences: Three- and young four-year-olds often do not remember the term *primary* or which colors are categorized this way, but their hands-on, child-initiated exploration of this activity will pave the way for later understanding. If you want to reinforce the concept with kindergartners, print a chart of the primary colors, with a patch of the appropriate color next to each color's name, and hang it up in your room.

WHAT we will need:
> Clear contact paper
> White cardboard or construction paper
> Medicine droppers
> Food coloring
> Muffin pans or other sectioned containers

HOW we will do it: To prepare, cut the paper in squares about 25 cm x 25 cm (5" x 5") and cover both sides with contact paper. An easy way to do this is to cut strips of contact which are about 14 cm x 28 cm (5½" x 11"), place the paper or board on one end, fold the rest of the contact over it, and seal the edges to waterproof the paper or cardboard inside.

Using medicine droppers, the children drip red, yellow, and blue food coloring on the boards. Find out what colors are produced when these original colors are mixed. If you do not have time to make the boards, children can experiment in small containers; however, they really enjoy using the boards because individual drops on plastic contact stay self-contained and retain very distinct shapes. In your muffin tins, put small amounts of water separately colored with red, yellow, and blue food coloring, and place them on the table so that all children can reach them. As you watch the children experiment, talk about the fact that they are using primary colors, and comment on the new colors they are creating. Use the words "science experiment" so that the children know *this* is science!

The Primary Song
Music/Movement/Science/Cognitive

WHY we are singing this song: to reinforce the concept of primary colors musically; to help children feel good about their singing voices; to provide a cognitive exercise in identifying red, yellow, and blue; to facilitate a memory game.

WHAT we will need:
> Construction paper (red, yellow, and blue)
> Contact paper (clear)
> Song: "THE PRIMARY SONG" (to the tune of "Twinkle Twinkle Little Star")

"THE PRIMARY SONG:"
Primary, primary what are you?
I am red or yellow or blue.
Primary, what can I do with you?
Mix us into colors that are new.
Primary, primary what are you?
I am red or yellow or blue.

HOW we will do it: First cut red, blue, and yellow shapes out of construction paper and cover with contact paper. Cut enough shapes for each child to have one of each color. Next sing this song together, singing the third and sixth lines slowly so that you have time to hold up the appropriate paper shape when that color is mentioned.

Sometimes, as time goes by and a song becomes very familiar to children, it is fun to alter the routine a little, by using variations. Here is one option: decide together on one color to leave out when you sing the song. Can everyone remember not to sing that word? You can vary the game even more by deciding to hold up the color but not sing it, and to increase the number of colors you decide to omit. Have the children make suggestions about other variations of this game, and let them take turns holding up the color shapes as you sing.

Acetate Action
Science/Cognitive

WHY we are doing this project: to reinforce the concept of secondary colors through the use of an interesting material; to develop a sense of autonomy through use of a one-person work station; to develop creativity by providing children with the opportunity to make their own colors.

WHAT we will need:
Acetate papers including red, yellow, and blue
or: transparent plastic folders (same colors as above)
"One person may be here" sign (provided below; photocopy and enlarge for your use)
Secondary color sign (directions to follow)

HOW we will do it: Acetate papers are available at graphic art supply stores. If you mention that the papers are for young children, businesses may donate supplies. If you work for a school which sends a newsletter to parents, you can sometimes offer free advertising in your publication in return for materials.

To prepare, cut the folders or acetates into single sheets, and lay them on the one-person table. Print a language chart that says: "Orange is a secondary color. Green is a secondary color. Purple is a secondary color." (Language charts should clarify, not confuse, so depending on how firmly you feel your children have grasped the concepts so far, you may wish to create a chart in the format of color equations: "Red and yellow make orange" and so forth. Or you could print a chart with this format: "Primary red and primary yellow make secondary orange." Decide which one you think will be most helpful to your students.) For all charts, put a patch of the corresponding color next to each color's name.

Hang the sign up on the wall in front of the activity table, and also put up the "One person may be here" sign. Help the children interpret/ read these signs when they have gathered together as a group, before activity exploration, and discuss the sign's meanings. (For example, ask the children: "Does that mean that two people can be there? Does that mean that three people can be there? What can you do if you want to be there and someone else is already there?") Then take acetate sheets of two primary colors and ask the children to predict what they will see when you lay one over the other. After the children have made their predictions, invite a student to lay the two sheets over each other. What happens? Tell the children that what they see is a secondary color. Point to the color chart and ask them which secondary color the two sheets created. Put only red, blue, and yellow sheets on the activity table for the first few days. As the children experiment, comment on the secondary colors they make. Use the words "science experiment" when you talk about what they are doing. After a while, lay out sheets that are secondary colors so that your students can compare them with the combined primary color sheets.

Science kits: Make experiment kits for independent, individual exploration. Collect small gift boxes with lids (or stationery boxes) and put a collection of acetate color shapes in each one. Lay them out for the children to take and use as they please.

Secondary Rhythm Chant
Music (Rhythm)/Cognitive

WHY we are saying this chant: to reinforce rhythmically the concept of secondary colors, and to help children feel rhythm.

WHAT we will need:
  Rhythm sticks
  Chant:

  "Secondary, secondary,
  tell me what it means.
  Secondary's purple and it's orange
  and it's green."

HOW we will do it: tap the rhythm sticks on the floor in time to the chant. Experiment. Tap and chant softly, loudly, quickly, slowly. See if you all stop at the same time. If possible, provide rhythm sticks that are purple, orange, and green.

Color Breakdown
Science

WHY we are doing this project: to reinforce the concept of secondary colors in reverse— that is, by enabling the children to separate them into the original primary colors that made them.

WHAT we will need:
  Coffee filters
  Markers (orange, black, purple, green)
  Saucers or very shallow containers
  Water
  Book: Aliki, *How a Book Is Made*

HOW we will do it: To prepare, cut the coffee filters into single strips about 3 cm x 8 cm (1" x 3½"). On the activity table, provide small containers of water and the orange, green, purple, and black markers. (You may want to use old markers. Sometimes during the exploration, children dip the markers in water and the pens have to be discarded after the activity because they no longer write.) Color one end of the filter strip. Dip the colored end into the water, leaving the rest of the paper on the edge of the container. Watch the color move and separate. Do this experiment yourself, first. Some markers contain ink that doesn't separate. My experience is that even if the colors do not separate, children are fascinated with how the color moves and bleeds from one end of the filter strip all the way to the other, but obviously the lesson learned is a different one.

Read *How a Book Is Made* to the children, before beginning the activity. With three- and young four-year-olds, talk them through the illustrations. Pages 18 to 24 show how the color of each picture is separated into yellow, blue, red, and black. Spend extra time discussing these pages, and then let the children know they can do their own color separation. Show them a filter strip with a patch of marker color near one end. Show them a saucer of water. Ask them to predict what will happen if they dip the colored end in the water.

Invite the children to explore the materials on the activity table. Encourage them to verbalize the results of their science experiment. (Green breaks down into blue and yellow; black breaks down into many colors; purple breaks down into red and blue; orange breaks down into yellow and red.)

Dye Delight
Science/Language

WHY we are doing this project: to facilitate an understanding of dyes; to show children through hands-on, child-initiated activity that foods contain colors which can be used as dyes; to develop an appreciation for literature by reading *The Goat in the Rug*; to promote self-esteem by enabling children to make something they can keep.

WHAT we will need:
  White sheet (cut into handkerchief squares) or: plain white handkerchiefs (about 12.5 cm x 12.5 cm [5" x 5"] but can be larger)
  Five large-sized beets
  Four large-sized onions
  Plastic margarine containers (one for each child)
  White, sticky labels (one for each child)
  Tablespoons (one for each child)
  Clothes rack or clothes line (use yarn if necessary)
  Newspaper
  Large basin
  Book: Blood, Charles L. & Link, Martin, *The Goat in the Rug*

HOW we will do it: Set aside one raw onion and beet. Boil four beets in eight cups of water to make purple water and the skins of four onions in the same amount of water to make brown. Save the cooked beets and onions. Also, set one handkerchief aside.

Read *The Goat in the Rug* before beginning the activity. Spend extra time on the pages which describe and show the wool being dyed. Show the children your raw beet and raw onion. Then show them the cooked vegetables, and the liquid they produced. Ask the children what they notice about the liquids. Hold up a handkerchief and ask the children to predict what will happen if they soak it in one of the liquids. When the children move to the activity table, invite them to use the tablespoons to ladle one of the liquids into their plastic margarine containers, and if you are working with three- and young four-year-olds, help them with this step as necessary. Use the sticky labels to put a name on each container. Encourage your students to put their handkerchiefs in their containers, and to let them soak overnight. For even dyeing, make sure all of each handkerchief is immersed in the dye. The next day, invite the children to squeeze their handkerchiefs into the basin, and to hang them on the clothesline or rack. How have the handkerchiefs changed? Are there any surprises? (The brown onion skin liquid produces a yellow dye.) Let the children compare them to the undyed handkerchief you set aside. Have new name labels ready. Some sticky labels stick onto damp fabric. If yours do not, stick the labels onto the line or rack, next to the appropriate handkerchief. When the handkerchiefs are dry, have a show-and-tell time if you like. Encourage the children to describe how they dyed their handkerchiefs, and to say what they will use them for. For an interesting variation, twist handkerchiefs tightly, secure with clothes pins, and then leave them overnight in the dyes. What result do the children observe?

Candy Colors
Science

WHY we are doing this experiment: to show that dyes are used to color food and to help children distinguish between natural and artificial colors.

WHAT we will need:
- M&M candies
- Small, shallow dishes
- Eye or medicine droppers
- Cotton swabs
- Water
- Bottles of food coloring
- Tray
- Soapy water
- Paper towels
- Green leaf
- Flowers of various colors
- Red tomato or apple
- Yellow squash
- Brown potato
- Any other natural object

HOW we will do it: On your activity table, arrange the shallow containers, cotton swabs, candies, water, and eye or medicine droppers. If you work with three- and young four-year-olds, your children may prefer to eat all the candies rather than experiment with them, so use your own judgment about doing this activity.

Arrange all your flowers and/or vegetables on the tray and have it nearby. During an Attention Getter time, pass around several candies for each child to eat. After the chocolates are eaten, ask the children to look at their hands. What do they see? Hold your own hand up so that the children can also see the color which came off on your skin and say, "The color of this candy is *artificial*. People added a dye to the candy part around the chocolate." Say the word *artificial* several times and with your fingers rub the candies as you say the syllables in order to make more dye come off. Show the children the bottles of food coloring and, together, as a group, identify each color. Explain that colors

like the ones in the bottles are often added to foods. Use the soapy water and paper towels for cleaning hands.

Next, encourage the children to touch and handle the objects on the tray. Ask them to notice what their hands look like after handling the fruits, leaves, and vegetables compared to how their skin looked after handling the candies. (Did any color come off?) Ask the children to hypothesize about why this is so, and, during the discussion, use the words *artificial* color and *natural* color. Have a discussion about the children's hair colors and whether they are natural or artificial.

Explain to the children that if they would like to experiment more with artificial colors, they can drop water drops on the candies to see what happens. Ask them what they see in the room that will help them conduct this experiment. When they discover the materials on the activity table, allow the children to explore them freely. As water is added to the candies, what happens to the dye colors? Cotton swabs can be used for mixing the colored water and making dye combinations. What happens when the same experiment is conducted on the objects from nature?

Dyeing Food
Science

WHY we are doing this activity: to enable children to use food coloring to dye their own food, and to provide more experience with mixing colors.

WHAT we will need:
- Scrambled eggs or vanilla pudding (not too yellow)
- Milk
- Plastic forks
- Food coloring
- Small containers
- Cups
- Plates
- Spoons or forks

6

HOW we will do it: If you want this project to be another experiment in mixing primary colors, then provide only yellow, red, and blue food coloring and only milk; otherwise provide other ingredients also.

Arrange all materials on the activity table. Make your scrambled eggs or pudding together as a group project, or you may choose to use instant pudding. Ask the children to predict what they will see if they add each food coloring to the foods. Help the children serve themselves. Then encourage them to dip their forks in the food coloring and to let the drops fall onto their food. (Eye and medicine droppers can pull up quite a bit of liquid, and food coloring is expensive. By using forks you ensure that the children do not use too much; however, if you work with kindergartners you may choose to use eyedroppers instead. If you do this, make sure they are thoroughly sterilized by soaking them in either weak bleach water or hot, soapy water and then rinsing well.) As the children experiment, ask: "What's happening?" Invite your students to compare what they see when a color is dropped into milk, with what they see when the same color is dropped onto scrambled eggs or yellow vanilla pudding. When the children eat their colorful snacks, does the food taste different?

Cabbage Colors
Science

WHY we are doing this project: to help children understand that chemical reactions can produce color changes; to develop all components of language arts: reading, writing, speaking, and listening; to develop fine motor skills through pouring and stirring.

The facts of the matter: Cabbage juice and other juices contain a chemical called an *indicator,* which causes the juice to turn different colors when it is mixed with an acid like vinegar or lemon juice, or a base, like soap or baking soda. In general, bases are bitter and tart, whereas acids are sour.

Developmental differences: Young children will not absorb the above information. If you are working with kindergartners, you can introduce these facts as and how you think appropriate. The important thing is that this hands-on, child-initiated experiment will lay a foundation for later knowledge; for now, making the cabbage juice turn green, red, or pink is just plain fun. Also, three- and young four-year-olds will not use the science experiment writing sheets for filling in their results, but they will scribble on them, and often they will recognize the symbols on the sheet as being associated with the project they just participated in. It is helpful to children to refer to their scribbles as "writing" when talking with them about their work.

WHAT we will need:
   Purple cabbage
   Vinegar
   Liquid soap
   Baking soda
   Water
   Plastic margarine containers
   Plastic apple sauce containers
   Spoons or medicine droppers
   Sensory table or tubs
   Small pitchers
   Blank paper
   Pens
   Crayons or markers (pink, red, and
      green)
   Activity sign and writing sheets (format
      provided on page 8; photocopy and
      enlarge for your use)

HOW we will do it: To prepare, boil purple cabbage until you have enough cabbage juice for the project. Set out the plastic margarine containers in the tubs or sensory table. Nearby, place smaller, separate containers of vinegar, baking soda, water, and liquid soap. Put medicine droppers or spoons in them. Have several extra spoons or droppers available. Put the cabbage juice in the small pitchers and place them in the tubs or sensory table. Make photocopies of the writing sheet in the text, and on a table nearby, place these, blank sheets, and pens, crayons, or markers. Make

WHAT HAPPENS WHEN YOU MIX CABBAGE JUICE WITH BAKING SODA VINEGAR AND LIQUID SOAP ??

WHAT COLOR??

CABBAGE JUICE **+** BAKING SODA **=** _____

CABBAGE JUICE **+** VINEGAR **=** _____

CABBAGE JUICE **+** LIQUID SOAP **=** _____

the activity sign, and hang it up beside the tubs or sensory table.

Before the children approach the project, help them interpret/read the activity sign and invite them to carry out its suggestions. Ask them to predict what will happen when they conduct the experiment. As the students explore the materials, discuss their results. What happens to the cabbage juice when the other materials are added to it? Invite the children to use blank paper or the science experiment writing sheets to record their results. Older children often invent their own spelling or ask to have words written down that they can copy onto the sheets, and younger children like to give dictation. When they are finished, ask the children to read their experiment results to you, or if they prefer, read the record of their experiments to them. Other ways to develop speaking and listening skills are to have a show-and-tell of experiment result sheets after the activity, a group sharing time about the experience, or use a puppet while the children are actually experimenting and have the puppet ask them questions about what they are doing. (This last method is really fun, and elicits *a lot* of language!)

Prism Project
Science

WHY we are doing this project: to help children understand that ordinary light is made up of a combination of colors; to show children that a prism breaks down these colors; to develop a sense of autonomy through use of a one-person work station.

The facts of the matter: The different colors in a beam of light travel at the same speed in air, so they stay combined and are seen as white light. When light travels through glass, however, the various colors travel at different speeds and separate from each other. One color travels faster or slower than another, and in this separation, the colors can be seen individually. The best analogy for this is a race. People in a race do not all run in the same spot at the same pace; they run at different speeds and spread out from each other.

WHAT we will need:
Prism (available at nature stores, teacher supply stores, or toy stores)
Flashlight
Cardboard (18 cm x 12.5 cm [7" x 5"])
Sturdy block
Sheet of white construction paper
Small table and one chair
"One person may be here" sign (format provided on page 3; photocopy and enlarge for your use)
Blue tack or putty

HOW we will do it: To prepare, punch a small hole in the center of the cardboard, and using blue tack or putty, secure the cardboard to the block so that it stands by itself. Hang the sheet of paper on a wall, or tape it to a book and spread the front and back of the book apart so that it is freestanding, or use a typist's stand.

Align all materials on the table so that the cardboard is nearest the chair, the paper is farthest away, and the prism is on the table, in the middle.

Make sure that when the flashlight is shining though the hole in the cardboard, it hits the prism. Ahead of time, discuss the "One person may be here" sign with the children. Ask the children to predict what they will see when they turn the flashlight on and shine it through the hole in the cardboard. As they explore the materials, talk to them about what they see on the paper (the color spectrum). After the day's activities, have a group discussion about this science experiment and what it tells us about light, as well as what it tells us about prisms. (See "The facts of the matter.")

Making Rainbows
Science

WHY we are doing this project: to reinforce the concept of the color spectrum.

The facts of the matter: A rainbow is formed by the reflection, refraction, and dispersion of sun rays in falling rain or mist. Refraction is the bending of a ray or wave of light.

WHAT we will need:
    Spray bottles on "mist" setting or hose
      with sprayer attachment (if outdoors)
    Water
    Hot, sunny day

HOW we will do it: Invite the children to spray a fine mist in the sunshine. What do they see? (They should be able to spot a rainbow.) During discussion, use the words *color spectrum* and *arc*.

Developmental differences: Three- and young four-year-olds enjoy the sensory aspect of this activity. The power of having their very own spray bottles to activate excites them and they may be most interested in spraying each other, which is fine on a hot day. Older children will be more inclined to observe and discuss the rainbows they make, and may also be inclined to spray each other.

Color Spinners
Science/Fine Motor

WHY we are doing this project: to introduce children to the idea of an optical illusion involving color (when the spinner spins, the color dots seem to merge and spread into circles); to develop self-esteem by enabling children to make something they can keep; to develop fine motor skills.

WHAT we will need:
    Cardboard (cut into circles that are 7.5 cm
      [3"] in diameter)
    Small pencils
    Markers or crayons (red, green, and blue)

HOW we will do it: To prepare, use a skewer to make a hole in the middle of each cardboard circle. Make a sample spinner by using the markers to randomly place red, green, and blue dots all over the circle. Next, push a pencil through the middle, point end down. When the children are gathered, give them the opportunity to closely examine your spinner and how it is made. Ask the children to predict what they will see when the spinner is spun, but do not actually spin it. (The children may spin it themselves though, in the course of examining it, and this is fine.) Ask them what they see in the room which will help them make their own spinners. Invite them to find out if their predictions are right by making spinners and then twirling them. As the children twirl their spinners, ask them what they see. Encourage them to compare what they observe when the spinners are moving to what the spinners look like when they are still.

Note: Some parents and teachers do not like to use adult samples when introducing a project, but my experience is that when the purpose of materials is not immediately or clearly evident, samples generate much more interest in the activity. My solution is to let the children know that my spinner (or collage or sculpture or whatever) looks the way *I* wanted it to, and that each person's will look different because each person is different, and that we all make things in our own special way. Also, it is a good idea to put the sample away before the children begin their exploration of materials.

Developmental differences: Three- and young four-year-olds sometimes have a hard time spinning spinners, and get very frustrated. You know best what level of fine motor development your children have reached, and accordingly, you can decide whether or not to do this project.

Color Spots
Gross Motor

WHY we are doing this project: to facilitate color recognition and to develop the large muscle group.

WHAT we will need:
    Construction paper to cut out large circles
    Contact paper

HOW we will do it: To prepare, take a large plate and trace circles onto a wide variety of differently colored construction paper sheets, making sure you have several of each color. Cover with contact and spread the shapes out over a large, clear space. Gather the children together and say: "Color a little, color a lot, can you find a big red spot?" (For colors with two syllables, leave out the word *big* when you say the rhyme.) As soon as you say the rhyme, the children can run to a spot which is that color and touch it. More than one person can touch a spot. After the children learn the game, let them each take a turn to say the rhyme and choose the color. Another variation of this game is to put the color circles in interesting, out-of-the-way places to see if the children can find them: under a chair, on a toy shelf, in the block bin, and so forth.

   Tip: The color circles will be even sturdier if you laminate them instead of using contact paper.

Eggsactly
Math

WHY we are doing this project: to practice rational counting; to facilitate color matching; to reinforce the names of colors for younger children; to develop reading and writing skills for older children; to develop self-esteem and a sense of autonomy through use of a one-person work station.

WHAT we will need:
    Large plastic eggs of various colors
        (available at craft, hobby, and toy stores)
    Small objects of matching colors (tiddly
        winks, small Legos, figurines, etc.)
    Tray
Older children:
    Small pencils
    Blank paper
    Writing sheets (format provided on
        page 12; photocopy and enlarge
        for your use)
    "One person may be here" sign
        (provided on page 3; photocopy and
        enlarge for your use)

HOW we will do it: To prepare, gather together the above items. If you are doing this project with older children, and you have no small pencils, ask your local library for a donation and explain that you want them for the children you teach. (Most libraries provide small pencils near the card catalogs so that patrons can write down reference numbers.) You may want to have as few as four differently colored eggs on the tray if you are short of time, because for each color of egg you have, you will need to make several writing sheets. Make photocopies of the sample writing sheet, making sure you have plenty of spares. Put a scribble of the appropriate color above the color word on each sheet. Cut out blank paper which is the same size as the writing sheets and make these available also, for children who want to create their own writing sheets.

   Next, put a variety of objects inside each egg, making sure that they correspond in color. For older children, put a small pencil and writing sheet or blank sheet inside as well. Put all the eggs out on a tray. Gather the children together and show them the eggs. Take one and shake it, and ask them to guess what is inside. Open it, and together, count the number of objects inside. If you are teaching older children, show them the pencil and writing sheet or blank paper, and write the number you counted on the paper. Also, show them the "One person may be here" sign, and discuss what it means. Replace the writing sheets and blank paper as needed.

Draw pictures that represent the objects you put in your eggs. Write the name (word) underneath. Photocopy these and put a scribble of the appropriate color above the written word which names the color.

How many **LEGOS** in the **PINK** Egg?

How many _____ in the _____ Egg?

How many _____ in the _____ Egg?

How many _____ in the _____ Egg?

How many _____ in the _____ Egg?

Developmental differences: Three- and young four-year-olds may have more fun shaking the eggs, opening and closing them, and engaging in pretend and manipulative play with the objects inside. Even if they choose not to count the objects, the concept of *things of like color* will be reinforced. Older children will be more likely to count all the objects and to write down the number counted.

Color Match
Math

WHY we are doing this project: to facilitate color matching; to reinforce the names of colors for small children; to facilitate dual matching for older children; to facilitate cooperation and communication through use of a two-person work station.

WHAT we will need:
   Pattern (provided on page 14; photocopy
      and enlarge for your use)
   Stiff board (cardboard or foam core)
   Clear contact paper
   Colored construction paper
   Double-sided tape
   Black marker
   "Two people may be here" sign
      (provided below; photocopy and
      enlarge for your use)

HOW we will do it: Foam core consists of a thin sheet of styrofoam sandwiched between two pieces of stiff paper and can be purchased at hobby, craft, and teacher supply stores. To prepare this activity, use the pattern to cut a car and garage out of each color of construction paper. If you are teaching young children, this project is a simple matching project and you will only need one of each color. For older children, make the game more challenging by also drawing stripes or dots on the cars and

garages, for more complex matching. Glue the garages onto the board, and cover the board with clear contact paper. Cover each car on both sides with contact paper. Place double-sided tape onto each car or each garage, so that as the children match the cars to the garages, they stick onto the board.

Before the children use the materials, discuss the meaning of the "Two people may be here" sign. With younger children, use the names of the colors as you talk to them about what they are doing.

A Book of Many Colors
Language

WHY we are doing this project: to develop all components of language arts and to reinforce understanding of different colors.

WHAT we will need:
Magazines with color photos
Children's scissors
Pale-colored construction paper
Glue
Crayons
Stapler

HOW we will do it: To prepare, make a blank book for each child. To do this, cut construction paper into pages that are approximately 30 cm x 45 cm (12" x 18"). For each book, put one sheet over another, and fold in half. Then staple twice along the fold.

Leaf through your magazines and tear out pages with the most colorful and interesting pictures. Older children (older four- and five-year-olds) may want to cut out their own pictures, but for younger children, it is a good idea to cut out most of the pictures yourself. Leave some scissors and pages on the table as well, so that cutting is an option. In addition to the magazine pictures, set out the blank books, glue, and crayons on the activity table.

This is one of those activities in which the children show much more interest when a sample book is read to them first. Make a sample

using photographs with good, strong color and make sure you include pictures that feature black and shades of brown. You can title your book *A Book of Many Colors* or create your own title. Print a sentence or two about each picture, for example, "I like this picture of an alligator because the green is the same color as my sweater and it's my favorite color." "This brown chocolate bar looks so good." "I picked this picture to go in my book because the purple violets are so pretty." Read the title and pages of the book to the children and encourage their comments. Ask the children what they see in the room that would help them make their own color books.

When the children have glued their pictures onto the pages, take story dictation if appropriate. Older children may want you to write their words down on a separate piece of paper so that they can copy them into their books, or they may invent their own spelling. When the books are finished, ask the children to read them to you, or if they prefer, read their books to them, or have group time show-and-tell. If you choose to have show- and-tell, have a small number of children show- and-tell their books each day, over a week or two.

Color Circle
Language/Small Group Activity

WHY we are doing this activity: to develop speaking and listening skills and to expand vocabulary.

WHAT we will need:
Construction paper shapes (one of each of the eight basic colors)
Large box or bag

HOW we will do it: To prepare, gather together your construction paper shapes. If you like, use the ones that you made for the previous Color Spots gross motor exercise. Put the shapes in your box or bag, and have the children sit in a circle. Tell them that you are going to pull a color out of the box, and that everyone who is wearing that color can stand up. Tell the children that they can also be "wearing" the color of their hair or their eyes. After you pull out a paper color shape, and those children are standing, ask each one to tell you about whatever they are wearing that matches in color. Encourage the children who are still sitting to listen to the answers. Be sure you pull out colors which give all children a chance to stand and tell about the colored item they are wearing. After a while, let the children take turns at pulling the paper color shapes out of the box and asking the questions.

Blurry Colors
Art/Cognitive

WHY we are doing this project: to facilitate creative expression and to reinforce, through art, the fact that primary colors are red, yellow, and blue, and that they make secondary colors when they are mixed.

WHAT we will need:
> Paint (primary colors—red, yellow, blue)
> Pale-colored construction paper
> Shallow pans
> Water
> Fine paintbrushes
> Containers
> Newspapers

HOW we will do it: To prepare, spread several layers of newspaper on your activity table. Mix up your paints and put them in the containers. Pour water in the shallow pans. Place all materials on the activity table.

When the children approach the table, ask them to dip a piece of paper into a pan of water, and then to hold it over the pan while the excess water runs off. Then invite the children to paint on the paper. As the primary colors blur and run together, what happens? Talk about the new colors that are made. As appropriate, reinforce the fact that the colors the children started with are primary, and the new colors that are created are secondary.

Spangles and Sequins
Art

WHY we are doing this project: to develop fine motor skills and to facilitate creative expression.

Children love using spangles and sequins for art projects, and because they come in so many vibrant colors, they are perfect for this unit. Also, they are small and are just right for fine motor development. Hobby and craft stores often sell them, or they can be ordered from teacher supply catalogs.

WHAT we will need:
> Spangles and sequins
> Glue
> Glue brushes
> Paper
> Shallow containers
> Cardboard

HOW we will do it: To prepare, pour spangles and sequins into the containers, and arrange the containers so that all children will be able to reach them easily. You do not have to use cardboard for this project, but because it is so sturdy, it lasts longer. Cut the cardboard into rectangles of 12.5 cm by 15 cm (5" x 6"). Set them out on the activity table with the spangles, sequins, glue, and glue brushes. As the children make their creations, talk about the different colors they are choosing. This is also a good opportunity to introduce the colors gold and silver. With older children, talk about which sequins and spangles are primary colors and which are secondary.

Math option: Invite older children to count how many spangles or sequins they used, and to write the number onto their cardboard pieces, or to make patterns.

Colorful Masks
Art/Multicultural

WHY we are doing this project: to facilitate creative expression; to reinforce the names of colors; to introduce children to a French custom.

The facts of the matter: Mardi Gras is held on Shrove Tuesday, the day before Lent begins, to mark the end of a long carnival period which begins on January 6. It was brought to America by French colonists in the early 1700s. Mardi Gras means "Fat Tuesday" and may refer to the custom of parading a fat ox through French villages and towns on Shrove Tuesday. Today, the New Orleans celebration of Mardi Gras is the most famous. People parade in colorful masks and fancy dress through the streets of the city. Societies called *krewes* organize and pay for festivities and parades. During the carnival season, *krewes* also give balls and parties.

WHAT we will need:
> Book: *Mardi Gras*
> Mask pattern (provided on page 18; photocopy and enlarge for your use)
> Popsicle sticks or tongue depressors
> Construction paper
> Acetate paper cut into strips
> Spangles and sequins
> Yarn or string
> Feathers (real or fake)
> Glitter or colored sand
> Any other interesting materials you have on hand

HOW we will do it: To prepare, use the mask pattern to cut out masks from different colors of construction paper. An easy way to cut the eyes and noses is to fold the mask first, as shown in the illustration, or use an Exacto knife. If you want to use real feathers, ask pet stores to save the feathers molted by birds. Avoid feathers from wild birds, as they may carry disease. Set all materials out on the activity table.

Make a sample mask by picking your favorite color of paper and decorating it with the materials. Try to put something of every color of paper on your mask. Then glue a Popsicle stick or tongue depressor onto it, so that you can hold your mask up. You may want to reinforce the back of the masks with extra Popsicle sticks so they are not too floppy to hold up. Make your sample at least two days before the children make theirs, so that the glue has time to dry. With the children, look at the photographs in the book *Mardi Gras*.

During an Attention Getter time, hold your mask up in front of your face, and tell the children that you picked your favorite color of paper and made a mask out of it. Point to the objects you glued on your mask, and as a group, say what color each one is. Tell the children that you put something of every color on your mask. Hold up the picture of Mardi Gras and use the above facts as you think appropriate to discuss this custom. Ask: "What do you think the people are doing? What are they wearing? How are they covering their faces? Which costume in the picture is your favorite and why?"

Encourage the children to make their own masks, and comment on the colors they choose as they work on their creations.

Mardi Gras
Dramatic Play/Language/Multicultural

WHY we are doing this: to reinforce names of colors; to develop speaking and listening skills; to facilitate self-expression; to facilitate social interaction; to help develop coordination of actions and words; to introduce children to a French custom.

WHAT we will need:
> Colorful masks (made in previous activity)
> Dress-up clothes (especially long jackets, skirts, and dresses)
> Hats
> Jewelry
> Music
> Children's full-length mirror

HOW we will do it: To prepare, set out the dress-up clothes, hats, jewelry, and mirror. If you have trouble collecting dress-up clothes, ask friends, parents, or neighbors for donations of old garments. Invite the children to dress up

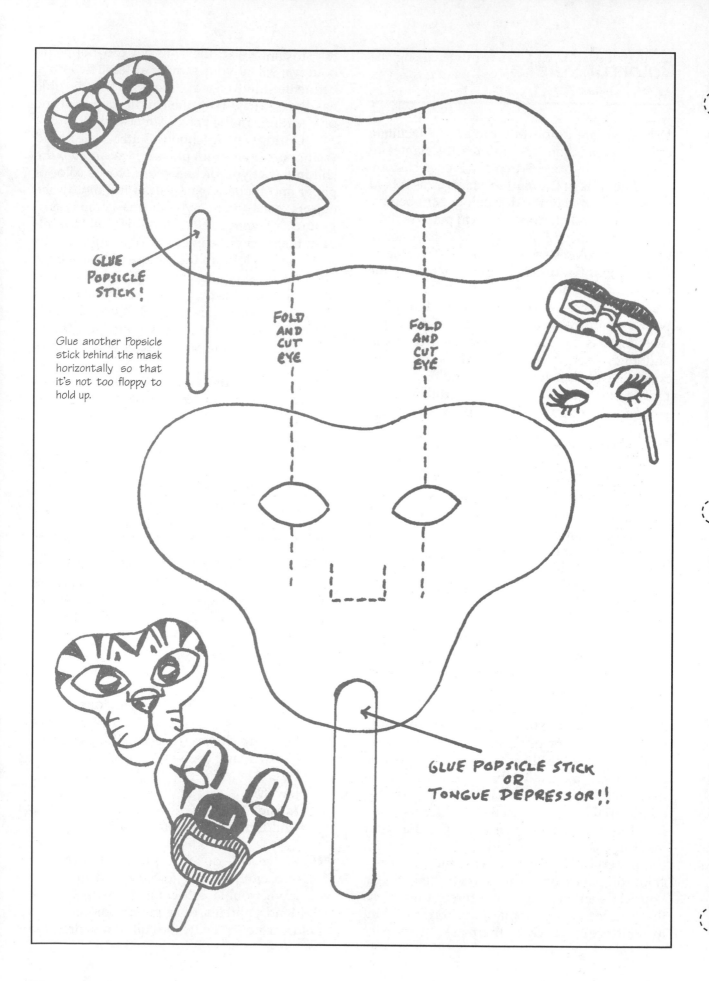

GLUE
POPSICLE
STICK!

Glue another Popsicle stick behind the mask horizontally so that it's not too floppy to hold up.

FOLD
AND
CUT
EYE

FOLD
AND
CUT
EYE

GLUE POPSICLE STICK
OR
TONGUE DEPRESSOR!!

18

for their own Mardi Gras carnival, using the masks they made themselves. You may even want to dress up yourself, to help get them in the mood. Talk about the colors each child is wearing. Give the children time to explore this dramatic play, and ask them if they would like to parade through your home, neighborhood, school, or classroom.

Skin Colors
Multicultural/Social Studies

WHY we are doing this project: to help develop appreciation of the differences between people.

WHAT we will need:
Book: Mandelbaum, Pili, *You Be Me, I'll Be You*
Flour
Instant coffee
Water
Tub of water
Paper towels
Mirror

HOW we will do it: To prepare, make a thin, paint-like substance with instant coffee and water. Set this out with the flour and the mirror. During an Attention Getter time, read *You Be Me, I'll Be You* and talk about the story. Afterward, have everyone hold one bare arm out, and put your arms next to each other. Talk about the different colors of skin you see: light brown, pink, freckled, dark brown, and so forth. Show the children the coffee liquid and the flour, and invite them to change their skin color by dabbing and painting the colors on their skin. The tub of water and paper towels can be used for clean-up time. Children enjoy this activity immensely.

Literature

Symbol Key: * Multicultural
+ Minimal diversity
No symbol: no diversity or no people

Coil, S. (1994). *Mardi Gras*. New York: Macmillan.

Dodds, D. A. (1992). *The color box*. New York: Little, Brown & Co.

Emberley, E. (1992). *Go away big green monster!*. New York: Little, Brown & Co. (The first three books in particular are terrific. The writers have utilized shapes cut out of the pages to produce ingeniously designed books. Children love them.)

Hoban, T. (1978). *Is it red? Is it yellow? Is it blue?*. New York: Greenwillow Books.*

Hoban, T. (1989). *Of colors and things*. New York: Greenwillow Books.

Jonas, A. (1989). *Color dance*. New York: Greenwillow Books.

Lionni, L. (1985). *Colors to talk about*. New York: Pantheon.

Lionni, L. (1959). *Little blue and little yellow*. New York: Astor.*

Mack, J. (Ed.). (1994). *Masks and the art of expression*. New York: Abrams. (For mask project and dramatic play:)

Mandelbaum, P. (1990). *You be me, I'll be you.* Brooklyn, New York: Kane/Miller. *

Rogow, Z. (1988). *Oranges.* New York: Orchard Books. *

Extenders

Music and Movement: Read *Color Dance* by Ann Jonas, and then let the children dance to music with differently colored scarves.

Cognitive: Distribute a variety of colors of construction paper shapes to each child, and chant:

> Color criminy color cram,
> Hold a green one in your hand.

Change the color each time you chant.

When the children understand the game, let them take turns being the one to say the rhyme and to choose the color that the other children have to hold up. With older students, say:

> Color criminy color cram,
> Let's see primary in your hand!
> or: . . .How 'bout secondary in your hand?

Math: Save small, interesting boxes (children especially love boxes with lids that snap) and on the lid of each, tape or glue a colored piece of acetate paper. Inside each box, put several pieces of the matching color of acetate, or paper cut from plastic or cardboard folders, and invite the children to count how many of each color are inside each box.

Science: After your experiments with food and food dyes, make a display from dyed foods found in the supermarket. Some ideas might include: pickles, Cheetos, colored cereal, and sweet and sour sauce. Talk about the ingredients of these foods and compare their nutritive value.

WOODWORKS

Most children love pounding nails into wood and using "grown-up" work tools. The best wood to use is pine, because it is a soft wood. Mahogany is also soft, but can be more expensive. Stay away from oak, maple, and walnut—besides being expensive, they are too hard for children. You can buy wood at a lumber yard, and if you buy pine with knot holes as opposed to clear pine, you will get the best bargain. You can also ask parents, friends, and neighbors to save pine scraps for you.

The blade of your crosscut saw should not be longer than 35 cm (14"). Some manufacturers make saws which are "tool box size"—these are perfect for children. The keyhole saw should have a blade no longer than 25 cm (10"), and the hammers should weigh no more than 340 grams (12 oz). Also, make sure your screwdrivers are an appropriate length—some are as short as 7.5 cm or 10 cm (3" or 4").

Many parents and teachers like to provide children's goggles and insist that the children wear them whenever they are working with wood and tools. If your wood is very rough, and has a lot of splinters, sweep, vacuum, or sand it to smooth it a little.

The first activity in this unit involves a demonstration of all the tools, and an opportunity for children to explore and use them. Subsequent projects involve a more in-depth focus on each tool and the science concepts and vocabulary to be understood and learned through its use. You may choose to leave all the tools out for the entire unit, and to pick two or three of the activities each day for closer focus and specific application. When you demonstrate the saws, measure a space with a tape measure and mark it off. Then draw a line between the two points with a marker and cut along this line when you use the saws. Make markers and tape measures or rulers available to the children so that they can also use them in this way.

If possible, you may want to set up a pegboard rack on which each tool can be hung at the end of the day or session. Print the name of each tool on paper, and draw a small picture of it next to its name. Place these labels beneath each tool's place on the pegboard so that the children can put the tools away themselves.

Attention Getter: Take two wooden blocks and hide them behind your back. Gather the children in a group and ask them to close their eyes. Bang the two blocks together and ask the children to guess what they are hearing. After they have done this, ask them to open their eyes and pass the two blocks around. Ask what the blocks are made from.

Hold up each woodworking tool you have. Tell the children what it is called, describe its function, and give a demonstration.

Woodworking
Science/Gross Motor

WHY we are doing this activity: to provide the children with the opportunity to explore all the woodworking tools; to allow them to become familiar and comfortable with using them; to facilitate construction with wood and tools; to develop the large muscle group.

WHAT we will need:
Hammers of varying sizes and weights
Crosscut saws
Keyhole saws
Nails
Adjustable C-clamps
Vises
Spindle-hand screw clamps
Hand drills
Nails of varying sizes
Screws (for slotted and Phillips screw-
    drivers)
Screwdrivers (slotted and Phillips)
Wooden blocks (as many sizes and
    shapes as possible)
Wooden tongue depressors (or other
    small, flat wooden pieces)
Planks (as many widths and lengths
    as possible)
Cross sections of tree trunks (if available)

HOW we will do it: Discuss safety precautions and then allow the children to explore and work with the tools freely. If the children construct creations, put them on the table for display throughout the unit. If you like, take story dictation from the children about their woodworks or invite them to write their own words (depending on their stage of language development), and then put the descriptions next to the actual constructions. Invite parents, relatives, and friends to come and see the children's woodworks display.

Weight and Force
Science

WHY we are doing this project: to help children understand the connection between the weight of a hammer and the force it delivers.

WHAT we will need:
Nails (all the same size)
Pine wood
Hammers (as many different sizes as you
    can obtain that children can easily use)

HOW we will do it: To prepare, gather your hammers together. At least two or three different sizes of hammers should be real ones from a hardware store, but it is also a good idea to provide some plastic or small toy hammers that have come with construction toys or play sets, as they provide a good basis for comparison in this activity. Set out the wood on a sturdy work surface, and set out the nails and hammers. For three- and young four-year-olds, make some starting holes in the wood by tapping nails into the wood until they stand up on their own. Do not tap them too much, though, or you will have done the children's work for them.

Together, examine the variety of hammers and ask the children to predict which hammer will be easiest to use, which one will drive a nail in fastest, which one will take the longest, which hammer will be the lightest and which one will be the heaviest. (See next project for related language activity.) Then encourage your students to experiment with the different hammers. Discuss their findings. Also, invite the children to hold a hammer in each hand and to compare how they feel.

Developmental differences: Three- and young four-year-olds will most enjoy the sensory experience of banging and hammering. Older children will be more inclined to compare the weight and force of the hammers in addition to hammering with them.

The Hammer Chart
Language

WHY we are doing this: to develop all components of language arts: speaking, listening, reading, and writing skills.

WHAT we will need:
Large piece of butcher paper
Markers (two different colors)
Tape

HOW we will do it: This activity should be done in conjunction with the Weight and Force activity above. To prepare, tape the piece of butcher paper on the wall, close to children's eye level. (If it is too low, it will be difficult for you to write on it.) As you ask the questions suggested in the above project, write down the children's comments. Draw a picture of each type of hammer, or take a photograph of it, and put comments about it next to the picture. If feasible, invite the children to draw pictures of corresponding hammers, or to trace their shapes onto the chart. Use quotation marks, and write down each child's name next to her or his words. Alternate the color of the marker you use with each observation so that your students can easily identify individual sentences. Some time after the project, read the chart back to the children. Older children may want to write their own comments on the chart and may ask you to write their words down on a separate piece of paper so that they can copy them onto the chart, or may use their own invented spelling. Younger children may make scribbles on the chart which you can refer to as their writing.

How Does a Saw Work?
Science/Language

WHY we are doing this project: to help children understand what *serrated* means and the function of serrated tools; to help develop gross motor muscles; to enable children to explore a concept through their sense of touch; to develop speaking and listening skills. (*Serrate*: having sawlike notches along the edge.)

WHAT we will need:
Pine wood
A serrated crosscut saw
Markers
Two dinner knives with a smooth edge (non-serrated)
Serrated dinner knife (Not a steak knife— plastic knives from fast-food restaurants are usually serrated and are safe to use.)
Bread knife
Loaf of unsliced bread

Box of wax paper, cling wrap, and/or aluminum foil
Scotch-tape dispenser (with tape)
Packaging-tape dispenser (with tape)
Any other serrated object
Sign (instructions follow)
Puppet
Optional:
Leaves with serrated edges

HOW we will do it: Lay out on the small table your serrated dinner knife, the tape dispensers, the food-wrap box, and any other serrated objects you have collected. Write a sign that says: "How are all these things the same?" and hang it on the wall by the table.

Set one of the non-serrated dinner knives, the bread knife, and bread on a separate work area. Make a sign that says: "Try using both of these knives to cut the bread!" Draw or trace the shape of each knife above the word "knife," and a loaf of bread above the word "bread."

A note about signs: Even though young children may not be able to read, activity signs are well worth making because they help create a print-rich environment. As children participate in activities, and encounter written words that are directly relevant to what they are experiencing, they begin to develop reading and writing skills. I find that the more symbols or pictures I draw to accompany the words on the signs, the easier it is for children to interpret them.

During Attention Getter time, encourage the children to explore the serrated objects on the table and ask them how they are all the same. (The serrated edge on wrapping paper boxes can be quite sharp, so caution the children to feel it very carefully.) If or when the children realize what the objects have in common, tell them about the word *serrated*. Print the word on a piece of paper, and hang it above the table. Ask the children if they can find anything else in the room that also has a serrated edge. If or when they mention the saws, hold them up and encourage the children to examine their serrated edges. Take your puppet out, and use its personality to talk to the children.

Note: Some teachers and parents feel self-conscious about using puppets, but if you can let yourself go, you will find that a puppet is a marvelously effective teaching tool as well as being a real kick to use. My puppet's character is always trying things that do not work, misnaming things and misunderstanding things—in other words, she constantly gives the children opportunities to be the wise, all-knowing teachers for a change!

In this activity, have the puppet look at all the objects and ask the children about them. After your students have responded, have the puppet grab a non-serrated dinner knife and try to cut wood with it. After a minute of sawing, have your puppet ask the children why the knife is not cutting the wood, and see what they say.

Before the children disperse to explore the materials, point out the bread and two knives. As a group, read/interpret the activity sign together. Invite the children to conduct the experiment. Gather together after the day's activities and discuss their experiences in using the two different knives to cut the bread.

Note: The above list of materials includes a leaf with a serrated edge. This is listed as optional because the concept is an abstract one and may confuse younger children. You know the cognitive level of your children and can decide whether or not to include this among the serrated objects on your discovery table.

More Serration
Science

WHY we are doing this activity: to allow children to use and compare a crosscut saw with a keyhole saw and to enable children to gain more experience with serrated tools.

WHAT we will need:
Keyhole saws
Crosscut saws
Vises
Blocks of wood
Preparation:
Hand drill
2.5 cm (1") drill bit

The facts of the matter: The crosscut saw has a wide blade and is used to saw through a piece of wood, from top to bottom. The keyhole saw has a narrow, thin blade and is used to cut wood out from the middle of a piece.

HOW we will do it: Use the 2.5 cm (1″) drill bit to drill a starter hole in several pieces of wood. If you like, you can have the children help prepare the wood in this manner. Attach the prepared pieces of wood securely to a work surface by using vises. Draw a line on each piece of wood, starting and ending with the starter hole, for the children to follow as they cut.

Place both the crosscut and keyhole saws near the prepared wood. As the children work, you can ask about their experiences with both kinds of saws. When appropriate, examine both saws together. How are they different? Why does the keyhole saw work better when cutting wood from the middle of a piece? Does the crosscut saw fit in the starter hole? What is it like to use a keyhole saw to saw through a piece of wood from top to bottom? How are both saws the same? Use the word *serrated* in your discussion. Ask the children why they think the keyhole saw is so called.

Measuring Marks
Math

WHY we are doing this: to introduce children to the concept of standard units; to introduce children to centimeters as standard units; to help them understand that any items which are the same size and shape can also be used as standard units; to practice rational counting.

WHAT we will need:
    Wood
    Markers
    Tape measures
    Toothpicks, dominoes, or any other
        collection of standard objects which
        could be used to measure

Note: Spindle-holed edges of computer paper make excellent measuring devices.

HOW we will do it: During an introductory Attention Getter activity, use a marker to draw a line on the wood where you will be sawing. When you are demonstrating all the tools, use a tape measure to measure this line. Show the children the centimeters and meters that are marked on the tape. Depending on the age of your children, you may choose to use builders' tape measures. The advantage to these is that they are actually used in carpentry. The disadvantage is that generally the tape winds back very quickly and can pinch fingers. You may wish to use one purely for demonstration. If so, show the children the latch that keeps the tape in place after it is pulled out.

To begin, set out your tape measures. In order to have more than one available, you may want to borrow some from friends, parents, or neighbors. Encourage the children to use them. When it seems appropriate, show them the toothpicks, dominoes, computer paper edges, or other measuring units you have collected, and invite them to use the materials for measuring. Ask your students to look around the room and see what else they might like to measure, and whether they see any other collection of objects that are all the same size and shape that could be used for this purpose. If you are teaching older children, you may want to invite them to write down their measurements.

Exploring Screws
Science

WHY we are doing this project: to help children understand that a screw is a spiral ramp; to observe that a nut or tightener ascends and descends the ramp; to help children recognize this device in everyday objects; to develop fine motor skills; to develop speaking and listening skills.

WHAT we will need:
- Vises
- Pieces of wood, including one plank
- Toy car
- Plastic jar and lid
- Glue stick, Chapstick, or empty deodorant stick
- Bolts, screws, matching nuts, and washers
- Screw-type nutcracker
- Pipes and joints (real or toy)
- Coiled spring (available at hardware stores or inside ballpoint pens)
- Any other screw-type objects you can find
- Sign (instructions below)
- Puppet

HOW we will do it: To prepare, lay out the screw-type objects on the small table and make a sign that says: "How are these things the same?" During Attention Getter time, put your plank on the floor. Say: "Right now this is just a plank." Then prop one end against the wall to make a ramp. Invite the children to roll the toy car down it. Say: "Now this plank slants, so it is a ramp. A ramp is a slanting surface." Hold up the vise and say: "A vice is a spiral ramp." Ask the children what they notice about the vise that makes it a ramp. Show them again how the vise works. What happens as the handle or knob is turned? What makes the clamp tighten? Encourage the children to touch and examine the spiral ramp of the vise. Explain that *spiral* means something which curves around and around. Move your finger in a circular, spiral motion to illustrate what you mean. Show the children the coiled spring and explain that it is shaped in a spiral.

Place the screw-type objects and your sign on a small table. Encourage the children to explore the objects. How does the inside of the jar lid look? How do the insides of the nuts and washers look? Invite the children to touch the ridges of the plastic jar, pipes, bolts, and screws. How do they feel? Read/interpret the sign together, and discuss the objects and how they screw together. Make another sign that says: "A screw is a spiral ramp. A spiral curves around and around." Glue or tape a screw onto the sign, above the word. Illustrate your sign with spirals. If you like, ask the children to help you make the sign.

Take your puppet out and use its personality to say "Hello" to the children and to ask them what they are doing. Make your puppet take two objects that do not belong together (e.g., two jars, two lids, two bolts), and have your puppet try to screw them together. Have your puppet ask the children why they will not screw onto each other.

Encourage the children to use the vises to secure the pieces of wood onto your main woodworking table. It may take the cooperation of two children to secure each vise. Children may also enjoy operating the vises without placing wood between the clamps. Encourage all types of exploration.

Exploring Clamps
Science

WHY we are doing this activity: to allow children to see how spiral ramps (screws) work in clamps.

WHAT we will need:
- Adjustable C-clamps (variety of sizes)
- Spindle-hand screw clamp
- Elmer's glue
- Blocks of wood (varying in width so that two pieces fit inside the C-clamps)
- Wooden tongue depressors (or thin pieces of wood)
- Screw-type objects (from previous activity, "Exploring Screws")

HOW we will do it: Clamps are used to hold two pieces of wood together. The C-clamps are interesting and easy for children to open and close. The spindle-hand screw clamp has two screws, which means that two knobs have to be turned simultaneously for the clamp to open or close evenly. This may frustrate your children, or on the other hand, it may encourage cooperation between children if you suggest to your students that they ask a friend to help them. Use your own judgment about whether or not your children are ready for this activity.

Set the C-clamps and blocks of wood on a table. (Include the spindle-hand screw clamp if you have one.) Set out the screw-type objects listed in the above activity to reinforce that a spiral is a curved ramp.

There are several ways to encourage children to use the clamps. Your students may enjoy simply loosening and tightening them, or they may want to put wooden pieces and blocks inside them while they open and close them. You may suggest that they use the clamps for gluing the way that carpenters do. Invite the children to spread glue between two wooden pieces, and then leave them in a clamp until the glue dries. Make sure you have enough clamps for each child, or choose a small number of children to do the project over a series of days.

Depending on which of the above options you choose, demonstrate during Attention Getter time, and then encourage your students to do their own exploration. As the children use the materials, encourage them to compare and contrast the screws in the clamps to the other screw devices. How are they the same? Invite your children to experiment with thick and thin pieces of wood in the clamps. What is the difference in how much or how little the clamps have to be screwed to press down on the wood?

The Handy Hand Drill
Science

WHY we are doing this: to facilitate observation of how the spiral ramp of a drill bit can be forced into wood to make a hole.

WHAT we will need:
    Wood
    Hand drills
    Drill bits (various sizes)
    Vises

HOW we will do it: Secure your wood to the work table with the vises. During an introductory Attention Getter activity, hold up the drill bit and turn it, without applying it to wood. Ask the children to predict what will happen if they turn the drill into the wood, and then encourage them to use the drills to find out.

Discuss what happens to the wood as the drill bit forges its way into the plank or block. What makes the drill turn around and around? Very young children may need help holding the hand drill upright. Examine the edges of the drilled hole for shreds and splinters of wood. Where did they come from? Encourage the children to experiment with different sizes of drill bits, and to compare and contrast the holes they make. Is one drill bit easier to turn than another?

More Experience with Spiral Ramps
Science/Math

WHY we are doing this experiment: to provide children with more opportunities to observe that screws are curved ramps; to gain more experience working with screws; to introduce children to Phillips and slotted screwdrivers; to practice matching skills by matching screws, drill bits, and holes.

The facts of the matter: The primary difference in function between a Phillips and slotted screwdriver is that the Phillips is easier to center; therefore, it is less likely to slip and scratch wood.

WHAT we will need:
    Screwdrivers (Phillips and slotted)
    Screws (Phillips and slotted)
    Hand drills
    Wood
    Vises
Demonstration:
    Two rulers (of equal size)
    Very large slotted nut or screw

HOW we will do it: For this activity, you will need to make sure that your screwdrivers will fit in your screws, and that your drill bits match your screws in diameter. You can check this in the hardware store when you purchase the supplies. Most hardware stores have a vast selection of screws; ask an assistant to help you match your drill bits and screws so that you can find what you need quickly. Also, make sure your screwdrivers are not too long for your children. You can buy screwdrivers which are only 6 cm to 10 cm (2" to 4") long. The shorter the tool, the easier it is for the children to manipulate.

To begin, secure your wood to the work surface with vises and encourage the children to drill holes with the hand drills, as in the above activity. During an Attention Getter time, invite the children to put the screwdrivers into the heads of the screws. Encourage them to touch the heads of the screws, and as they do, elicit observations about the differences between those with Phillips and those with slotted heads. Do the same with the screwdrivers. (When children discover this difference for themselves, it is more meaningful to them.) After your students have explored, matched, and discussed the tools and screws, collect them and put them aside. Pass around only a Phillips screwdriver and screw, and invite each child to touch and examine the screwdriver and the top of the screw once again. Explain that the tool is called a "Phillips" screwdriver. A "Phillips" screwdriver has a cross. Make a cross with the two rulers and/or draw one on paper. After all the children have examined the two objects, put them aside and pass around only a slotted screwdriver and screw. Invite the children to touch the end of the screwdriver and the top of the screw. Explain that they are called *slotted*. Take out the very large slotted nut or screw and have the children feel the indentation. Say: "Can you feel the *slot* in the top of that screw?"

Drill a hole and ask: "Do you think I could screw this screw into the hole? How do you think I could do that?" Rather than actually putting the screw into the hole, encourage the children to drill their own holes, and to use the screwdrivers and screws to drive them into the wood. Invite the children to notice how the curved ramp of each screw turns and sinks into the wood as the screwdriver turns and forces it downward.

Sandpaper and Wood: What Is Abrasion?
Science

WHY we are doing this: to help children understand, through hands-on activity, the concept of abrasion; to develop gross motor muscles.

WHAT we will need:
Sandpaper pieces
Emery boards
Wooden blocks (some with rough edges)
Magnifying glass
Large paintbrushes

HOW we will do it: Set out the sandpaper pieces, emery boards, and wooden blocks. Invite the children to close their eyes and brush their fingertips against the sandpaper. How does it feel? Tell the children that when something rough grinds against something to make it smooth, it is called *abrasion*. Provide each child with a piece of sandpaper and a block of wood, and invite them to rub the sandpaper on the wood. As you do this together, say the word *abrasion*. Rub slowly and say the word slowly. Rub quickly and say the word quickly. Then rub your fingertips across the sandpaper while you say it. Show the children how the paintbrushes can be used to brush splinters off the wooden blocks after they have been sanded.

Find a rough piece of wood and invite the children to look at it through a magnifying glass. Ask them to predict what would happen if they rubbed the sandpaper on it. Invite them to find out by using the materials. As the children do so, invite them to look at a piece of wood through a magnifier before rubbing it with sandpaper, and then again afterward. Also, encourage them to feel their wood before they rub it with sandpaper and again after they have used the sandpaper and brushed splinters away. How does the wood feel each time? How does it look? Next, ask them to compare a fresh piece of sandpaper with the piece they used to smooth the wood. How are they different? Finally, invite your students to rub their sandpaper across their blocks vigorously, and to then feel the wood. What do they notice? (The wood will feel warmer.) Introduce the word *friction* and explain that this word means the rubbing of one thing against another. Friction creates heat.

The Carpentry Song
Music/Movement/Language/Anti-Bias

WHY we are doing this activity: to help children feel rhythm and to keep time to a beat; to develop cognition through memorization of words; to help children feel comfortable with their singing voices; to expand vocabulary; to help children understand that boys and girls can be anything they want to be.

WHAT we will need:
Wooden blocks from a block set
Sandpaper pieces
Song: "THE CARPENTRY SONG"
(to the tune of "This Is the Way We Brush Our Teeth")

"THE CARPENTRY SONG"
I found some wood and that was good,
and that was good, and that was good,
I found some wood and that was good,
all on a Saturday morning.

The wood was rough, not smooth
enough,
not smooth enough, not smooth enough,
(etc.)

What have we there? Sandpaper squares,
sandpaper squares, sandpaper squares,
(etc.)

Rub a dub dub, away I rubbed,
away I rubbed, away I rubbed, (etc.)

Sounded like this: ch ch ch ch
ch ch ch ch, ch ch ch ch, (etc.)

The way it moved, it made it smooth,
it made it smooth, it made it smooth,
(etc.)

HOW we will do it: To prepare, give each child two small wooden blocks and one small piece of sandpaper. Before you attempt to sing the song, let the children simply bang their blocks for a few minutes to let off steam. When you are ready to begin, tell the children that a person who works with wood is called a *carpenter*. Ask the children who can be a carpenter (women and men). Ask if anyone knows a carpenter. Tell the children that one of the important things a carpenter has to do is to make wood smooth.

Next, ask the children if they can remember what it is called when something rough rubs against something else to make it smooth. If necessary, remind them of the word *abrasion*, and repeat the word a few times while you all rub your sandpaper pieces against your blocks. There are quite a few verses in this song, so if you are working with three- and young four-year-olds, you may want to teach them a few verses at a time, and spread the learning over a week or two. Beat your blocks in time with the music, and when you get to the "rub a dub dub" part, put down one block and use your sandpaper instead.

You may find, as time goes by, that the children become very familiar with the song. If you feel it is time to make it more interesting with a variation, leave out the word "Saturday" or "morning" to see if you can all remember not to say it, and not to make any sound with your blocks and sandpaper. Then let the children decide which word to leave out.

Levers: Using Hammer Prongs
Science

WHY we are doing this project: to help children understand that a lever lifts something; to help children compare prying an object with and without leverage; to develop the large muscle group; to help children feel competent.

WHAT we will need:
  Wood
  Hammers
  Nails

HOW we will do it: Ahead of time, hammer several nails into the wood. You may choose to hammer some nails all the way into the wood, and some partway. During an introductory Attention Getter activity, simulate each of these methods without actually pulling or prying, and ask the children to predict which will be easiest and fastest: prying a nail with the prongs of a hammer as you pull down and use the wood for leverage, or pulling the head of the nail straight upward, with no leverage.

Invite the children to experiment. Show them how the hard end of a prong can be worked underneath a nail head which has been hammered all the way into the wood. As you all discuss the results of the experiment, introduce the word *leverage*. In using leverage, why does a nail lift up even though the hammer is being pulled down?

The Nail Tin
Math

WHY we are doing this project: to practice rational counting; to help children use their sense of hearing; to develop fine motor skills; to develop self-esteem and sense of autonomy through use of a one-person work station.

Note: It is important to use very large nails in this activity so that the project is a safe one. The nails should also be clean and new, and children should sit down while they count them. That said, it is important to add that students seem to find something extremely satisfying about the metallic "clunk" the nails make when they are dropped into the can.

WHAT we will need:
  Coffee can with lid
  Very large, clean, new nails
  Tray
  Activity sign (instructions follow)

"One person may be here" sign
  (provided on page 3; photocopy and
  enlarge for your use)

HOW we will do it: Using an Exacto knife or razor blade, cut a small opening in the plastic lid of the coffee can. It should be large enough for the nails to be dropped through. Put your nails inside the coffee can, secure the plastic lid on top, and then place it on the tray. Make an activity sign that says: "How many nails are inside?" Draw or trace nails as a symbol above the word "nails," or glue or tape a nail onto the sign, above the word. Make your "One person may be here" sign, and place both signs near the tray.

During an introductory Attention Getter time, read or interpret the signs with the children, and discuss what "One person may be here" means. Shake the tin and ask the children how they know there are nails inside. Let the children know that they must sit down while they use the nail can. When your students begin to use the materials, ask them what they hear every time they drop a nail into the can.

Developmental differences: Three- and young four-year-olds will be most fascinated with dropping nails into the can to hear the noise they make, as well as shaking the cans to hear all the nails clatter inside. Older children will be more inclined to count each individual nail as it is dropped into the container.

Sorting Nails
Math

WHY we are doing this project: to facilitate classification based on size, and to develop fine motor skills.

WHAT we will need:
  Clean, new nails (large and very large)
  Sorting trays

HOW we will do it: To prepare, set out the nails and the sorting trays. It is best to put them on a table rather than on a carpeted area, so that stray nails do not get lost on the floor. If you do not have plastic sorting trays, buy cardboard or plastic divided dinner plates at the grocery store. These will serve your purpose just as well.

It has been my experience that young children do not quite know what to do with sorting materials and that they need a little help. For this reason, I usually tell the following story about whatever sorting materials I put out. Since nails are used in this activity, the story is about nails, but feel free to adapt this story for whatever material you are providing. I have been amazed at the interest the story generates:

"THE NAILS FIND A NEW HOME"

[To begin, put all the nails in one section of the sorting tray.]

Once upon a time there were a whole bunch of nail families living together, willy-nilly, all a-jumble, and it was most uncomfortable for everyone. One day, a nail from the largest nail family [take a large nail] decided to look for a new home. So she walked along and walked along [move nail around edges of sorting tray] until she found an empty space and she said, "Wow! An empty space! What a perfect place for a new home for the largest nails!" So she called over to them: "Hey, big nails! I've found a new home for you!" And so all the largest nails went to live in the new space. [Move all large nails to that section of the sorting tray.]

Well, the other nail families were also pretty fed up with living willy-nilly, all a-jumble, so one of the next largest nails decided to look for a new home, too. [Hold up one of the largest and next largest nails, side by side, and ask the children if they can see the difference.] So the nail walked along, and walked along [move one of the next largest nails along the edges of the sorting tray] and guess what he found? [Let the children answer.] And he shouted to all the other nails in his family: "Hey! Come on over here! I found us a new home!" [Have the children help you pick out all the other nails which are the next largest, and put them in the section of the sorting tray. Continue with story in the same way until all nails are sorted.]

After telling the story, show the children the nails and sorting trays, and encourage them to use the materials themselves.

Bark Rubbings
Art/Nature/Social Studies/Language

WHY we are doing this project: to facilitate artistic expression; to help children develop an understanding that different trees have different barks; to develop cooperation between partners in a two-person activity; to develop motor skills; to encourage children to explore their senses of touch; to develop speaking and listening skills.

WHAT we will need:
    Peeled crayons
    Paper
    Trees

HOW we will do it: To prepare, ask everyone to find a partner.
    Note: If you have children who can do this without problems, then great. I have usually ended up with two or three children who do not want to be each other's partners, and a few who feel sad and rejected. Then we spend ten minutes trying to resolve the situation while the rest of the children climb the walls. An easy way to get around this is to keep on hand pairs of construction paper shapes. Pass them all out, have the children find the person who holds the same shape and color, and who will then be their partner. Take back the shapes and colors to use the next time.
    After the children are paired off, ask them where wood comes from. Go to a wooded area, and ask the children if they see any trees. Point to a trunk and ask the children what that part of the tree is called. Point to the bark, and ask the children what this part of the tree is called. Ask your students to close their eyes and feel the tree's bark with their fingertips for a few seconds. Then, while one partner holds the paper, the other can rub the bark with a crayon. When the first rubbing is finished, the children can

reverse roles. Other aspects to explore: how are different barks differently textured? Invite the children to explore a variety of barks with their fingertips, and with their eyes closed. What does this tell you about how the trees are different or the same? You may also invite your students to exchange rubbings and to then match a rubbing to a tree. Afterward, have a show-and-tell of rubbings, and ask the children what it was like to help each other.

Wooden Block Prints
Art/Math

WHY we are doing this project: to facilitate creative expression with unusual materials; to develop motor skills; to develop cognition with matching activity.

WHAT we will need:
> Paint (three different colors)
> Shallow containers
> Wooden blocks (different shapes and sizes)
> Butcher paper

HOW we will do it: Cover the table with newspapers or a plastic tablecloth. Place butcher paper on top. Set out the pans of paint and the blocks. Invite the children to make block prints. When the children are finished, take a look at their work. If the prints are not distinct, make another picture yourself, using all of the blocks. When it dries, set out the (cleaned) blocks again, and invite the children to match the blocks to the corresponding prints.

"The Tree House" Flannel Board Story
Multicultural/Anti-Bias/Language

WHY we are doing this project: to develop imagination; to facilitate social interaction between children; to expand vocabulary; to develop speaking and listening skills.

WHAT we will need:
> Flannel board
> Felt
> Story: "THE TREE HOUSE"
> Flannel board pieces (patterns provided on page 33)
> "Two people may be here" sign (provided on page 13; photocopy and enlarge for your use)

HOW we will do it: To prepare, cut the story pieces out of both paper and felt. If you are short on time, just cut around the shapes in circles or ovals instead of cutting out the exact shape on the outline. If you color the pieces, they will generate more interest. Bring out all the materials and tell the story.

"THE TREE HOUSE"

Once upon a time there were three friends: Yoshi, Ladonna, and Nolberto. They wanted to build a tree house very, very badly. They talked about building a tree house, they dreamed about building a tree house, and they pretended to build a tree house, but none of it was the same as really doing it. They even knew which tree they'd build it in—a big old oak in Yoshi's backyard. But they had no tools, so they could only talk and dream about it.

But one day, something wonderful happened. It was Ladonna's birthday, and guess what her mother gave her! It was a tool box, and inside it were all the tools any carpenter could possibly want. There was a [hold up the hammer and let the children name it], and there was a [hold up box of nails and let children name it]. There was a [hold up saw and let children name it] and also a [hold up hand drill and let children name it]. Nolberto thought that

Enlarge these shapes on a photocopier before cutting out. Cut out of green felt or zig zag your scissors as you cut a green shape like this for tree leaves.

Do not cover your felt tree house with any paper, so that the children's felt pieces will stick onto the tree house at the end of the story.

Cut out of light brown felt

Cut out of dark brown felt.

NAILS

that was all there was in the tool box, but no! There was more: a [hold up tape measure and let children name it] as well as a [hold up vise and let children name it] and a [hold up cross-cut saw and let children name it] and also a [hold up keyhole saw and let children name it].

Ladonna's mother had another surprise: wooden planks from the lumberyard. She said she would help them build their tree house. Yoshi used the vise to [let children answer] and then she used the saw to [let children answer]. Ladonna used the hammer to [let children answer] and the hand drill to [let children answer]. And Nolberto used the measuring tape to [let children answer] and then he used the prongs of the hammer to [let the children answer]. Finally, after several days, their beautiful tree house was done. [Put tree house in tree.]

Yoshi, Ladonna and Nolberto sat up in the tree house and felt it was the most wonderful place in the world. Sometimes when they were up there, they pretended to be hiding from ghosts [ask the children to make ghost sounds: "Whoooo"] and sometimes they pretended to be hiding from monsters [ask the children to make monster sounds] and sometimes they just had a tea party [ask the children to pretend to sip tea]. But whatever they did, they always loved the tree house they had built themselves.

After you tell this story, leave the materials out for the children to explore. Show them the "Two people may be here" sign, and read or interpret it together. Discuss what it means. Invite the children to retell the original story and to make up new ones.

Woodwork Art
Art/Crafts

WHY we are doing this project: to develop creative expression and to develop fine motor skills.

WHAT we will need:
    Toilet paper rolls
    Toothpicks

Small styrofoam meat trays
Wooden Popsicle sticks
Wooden tongue depressors
Small boxes
Modeling clay
Markers
Construction paper (green and brown)
Small branches with leaves
Glue
Glue brushes

HOW we will do it: Set out all materials with newspaper or a tablecloth underneath. Show the students the materials and invite them to make their own creations with them. Some children may make miniature tree houses and others may take the project in different directions.

Tree House
Dramatic Play

WHY we are doing this activity: to provide children with the opportunity to act out real-life situations; to promote social interaction between children; to facilitate coordination of speech and movement; to provide children with a way of releasing emotions; to encourage children to create and fantasize.

WHAT we will need:
    An area which can be used to simulate a
        tree house (i.e., a loft area or a climber
        with a small, elevated space)
    Small tree branches
    Small box (to be overturned and used for
        a table)
    Play tools
    Dishes
    Dolls
    Other appropriate items
Optional:
    Blanket

HOW we will do it: To prepare, tape or tie the tree branches around your tree house. Use the blanket as a roof. Set out your props. During an Attention Getter time, after you have told "THE TREE HOUSE" flannel board story, show the children the dramatic play area you have set up, and ask them what it could be. The children may decide it is a tree house or something entirely different. At times when you think it is appropriate, join in their play. You could be a traveller looking for shelter, a magic tree spirit, or whatever else strikes your fancy!

Tool Time
Language/Art

WHY we are doing this project: to develop fine motor skills through cutting and gluing activities; to develop all components of language arts: writing, reading, speaking, and listening; to facilitate creative art.

WHAT we will need:
> Do-it-yourself, home improvement
>   magazines and catalogs
> Glue
> Scissors
> Butcher paper
> Markers

HOW we will do it: To prepare, set out all the materials. Tear pages out of the magazines which have photographs of tools that you have used during the unit. Older children will probably want to cut out their own pictures from these pages, but if you are working with younger children, you may want to cut out some pictures yourself. Invite your students to make a woodworking poster, and as they glue pictures of tools, lumber, and planks onto the butcher paper, ask them if they want any of their words written on the poster. Take story dictation, or with older children, encourage them to write their words onto the poster themselves and support invented spelling. When the project is finished, hang it at the children's eye level and ask them to read it back to you, or if they prefer, read it back to them.

Our Vanishing Rain Forests
Social Studies/Language

WHY we are doing this project: to help children begin thinking about social issues; to help develop speaking and listening skills; to help children feel competent in regard to problem solving; to help children understand the concept of conflicting interests.

The facts of the matter: A rain forest is defined as an area which has rainfall that is never less than 7.2 m (80") annually. (Many rain forests exceed 27 m [300"] annually.) Tree height must be at least 29 m (98'), and the average temperature of a rain forest is 75°F. Trees are integral to producing oxygen, and tree roots hold dirt in place; this dirt otherwise washes away and erodes. The earth's rain forests are vanishing at an alarming rate: between 1981 and 1990 over eight million acres were eradicated annually.

WHAT we will need:
> Book: Cherry, Lynne, *The Great Kapok Tree*
> Lengths of string (for rulers)

HOW we will do it: Read this excellent book to the children during an Attention Getter time and discuss the issues it raises.

Put containers outside to collect rain water. Use lengths of string or rulers to measure how many inches you collect. Compare this amount to the amount which falls in a rain forest.

Literature

Symbol Key: * Multicultural
             + Minimal diversity
             No symbol: no diversity or no people

Brown, A. E. (1990). *Monarchs of the forest*. Northbrook, IL: Dodd, Mead. (This book has some excellent photographs of redwood [sequoia] trees. Talk the children through the pictures, initiate discussion, and in particular, read selected parts of the chapter entitled "Man the Protector," which focuses on the devastation of our sequoia forests.)

Campbell Jackson, T. (1994). *How a house is built*. New York: Scholastic.* (In the back of this book you'll find illustrations and names of some of the most commonly used tools.)

Cherry, L. (1990). *The great kapok tree*. San Diego, CA: Harcourt Brace Jovanovich.

Cowcher, H. (1988). *Rain forest*. New York: Farrar, Straus, & Giroux. (This is an excellent picture book.)

Florian, D. (1991). *A carpenter*. New York: Greenwillow Books. (After you read this book, be sure to discuss the fact that not all carpenters are men, nor are they all white-skinned people.)

Hogan, P. (1991). *Vanishing rain forests*. Milwaukee, WI: Gareth Stevens Children's Books. (Discuss the pictures in this book, and read selected parts.)

Extenders

Rhythm and Movement: Say this rhyme with the children and do the movements:

> We are trees on a lonely hill,
> here we stand so very still.
> Suddenly wind comes with a rush;
> our leaves go shusha-shusha-shush.

For "We are trees on a lonely hill," raise your arms over your head and join your fingertips to make the shape of a hill. For "here we stand so very still," put your arms by your sides and stand straight and tall. For "Suddenly wind comes through in a rush," take your arms behind your back, and then swing them forward forcefully for the word "rush." For "our leaves go shusha-shusha-shush," move your fingers as if they are leaves being blown by the wind.

Art: When you make the block prints, tie yarn around a few blocks, or put rubber bands around others to make even more interesting prints.

Math: Invite the children to count how many times they must bang the hammer on a nail before it is driven into the wood all the way. Do this with long nails and short nails and compare the answers.

Math: As a group, build a tower or castle out of wooden blocks and then count how many blocks it took to build it. With kindergartners, make a graph. At the top of each column, trace the shape of each differently shaped or sized block you used. Together, count each kind of block, and have the children write the number on the graph.

Social Studies: Some people are professional carpenters and others enjoy carpentry as a hobby. Invite a carpenter to visit your home or classroom. Ask this person to bring in tools and completed projects to show the children.

Math: If you work with kindergartners, provide a sorting or counting activity of nails, slotted screws, and Phillips screws.

REFLECTIONS

Children enjoy experimenting with mirrors and discovering the many ways reflections can be used. Unbreakable mirrors are the best choice for most of the activities in this unit. Mirrors with frames and backs are also better than unframed mirrors because, if dropped and broken, the glass stays within the frame. A few of the activities in this unit require frameless mirrors. If you are unable to obtain unbreakable mirrors for these projects, use mirrors with beveled edges and insist that the children remain sitting at tables when they use them; this should ensure that you have no problems. I recommend beginning the theme by talking to the children about why it is very important to be careful with mirrors, and not to bang or drop them.

Attention Getter: Put a framed mirror or children's mirror somewhere in the room, before your students arrive. Gather the children together, and tell them that you are going to walk around the room to look for places where you can see yourself. Places you can look include: metal frames around windows, windows, metal door knobs, the metal part of a stapler, metal closet handles, computer screens, and other plastic objects. Look all around the room for reflections, and make sure you pass by the mirror. After your tour, talk about the reflections you saw.

Tell the children that when something gives you back a picture of what is in front of it, it is called a reflection. Say the word several times and blink, tap, or pat parts of your body while you say the syllables. Ask the children to look for things that give them reflections when they are at home. If you are a teacher, remind the children at the end of the day, or, as a group, write a note to parents telling them about the project. The next morning, ask the children about the reflections they noticed.

Comparing Reflections
Science

WHY we are doing this project: to help children become aware of how different surfaces reflect light; to help children become familiar with the properties of different materials; to facilitate scientific observation and comparison.

WHAT we will need:
    Framed mirror
    Shiny cookie pan
    Polished, silver object
    Aluminum foil
    Square of cardboard
    New stapler (one with a shiny metal part)
    Plastic picture frame with a picture
    Plastic picture frame without a picture
    Anything else which reflects
    Activity sign (format provided on
        page 41; photocopy and enlarge
        for your use)

HOW we will do it: The idea here is to provide some materials which give very blurry reflections, and others which give very clear reflections. If you do not have the exact objects listed above, just use whatever you do have. You can find inexpensive plastic picture frames in variety stores. Wrap the foil around the cardboard square so that it is sturdier. Lay out all your objects on a table. Use the symbols in the sample sign to print your own sign and place it near the table. During an Attention Getter time, show the children the activity table, and help them read or interpret the sign. When they begin to explore the objects and compare reflections, talk to them about their observations. Encourage them to look at smooth, hard surfaces in the room. Do they give reflections? How do they compare to the reflecting materials?

Reflection Chart
Language/Math/Small Group Activity

WHY we are doing this project: to facilitate scientific observation and comparison; to facilitate classification; to practice rational counting; to develop all components of language arts: speaking, listening, reading, and writing.

WHAT we will need:
    Butcher paper
    Marker
    Symbol pictures (provided for
        previous activity)

HOW we will do it: To prepare, divide your butcher paper into three columns, and glue or tape a "clear" symbol picture at the head of one column, a "blurry" symbol picture at the head of another, and "no reflection" at the head of the third. With the children, examine each object. Does it give a clear reflection, a blurry reflection, somewhere in between, or no reflection? Write the name of the object in the column where it belongs. Invite the children to draw a picture of that object next to the word. Think about the things that give reflections. How are they all the same? What things in the room give no reflection? Do all smooth, hard surfaces give a reflection? Ask the children about the surfaces in the room and how they compare and contrast to each other and to the reflecting materials.

Compare the Reflections...

CLEAR OR BLURRY?

Encourage the children to make a judgment about each item in terms of where it belongs on the chart. If you are working with kindergartners, they may want to do their own writing on the chart. When you have classified all the objects, count how many are in each column. Do your counting as a group, and write the total number at the bottom. Were there more things that gave blurry reflections, more things that gave clear reflections, or more things that gave no reflections?

Reflection Walk
Gross Motor

WHY we are going on this walk: to facilitate children's awareness of reflecting surfaces in the world around them; to develop gross motor muscles; to develop speaking and listening skills; to develop cognition by remembering the sequence of events.

WHAT we will need:
    Rope (optional)

HOW we will do it: If you would like to avoid the hassle of pairing children off before you take a walk, you may want to ask them simply to hold onto the rope instead. Before you set out on your walk, tell the children that you are all going to keep your eyes open for reflecting surfaces. As you stroll around your neighborhood, see how many reflections you can see in things like puddles, windows, and cars. Encourage the children to talk about what they see and to listen to each other. When you are back at school or home, talk about what you saw and see if the children can remember the sequence in which they saw them.

Mirrors Reflect Light
Science

WHY we are doing this activity: to facilitate hands-on discovery of how light bounces off mirrors; to promote self-esteem and develop sense of autonomy through use of a one-person work station.

WHAT we will need:
> Refrigerator box
> Mirror
> Flashlight
> "One person may be here" sign (provided on page 3; enlarge and photocopy for your use)
> Puppet

HOW we will do it: To prepare, call furniture and major appliance stores to locate an empty refrigerator box. If you cannot obtain one, just use the largest box you can find. Cut a flap for a door or opening, and if the box you are using is smaller than a refrigerator box, place it on a table.

Put the mirror and flashlight inside the box, and post the sign outside. During an Attention Getter time, take the flashlight and mirror out of the box, and shine the light on the mirror. Tell the children that they will discover something new if they do the same thing inside the dark box. (The light bounces off the mirror to make spots of light on the wall of the box.) Also discuss the "One person may be here" sign. As the children emerge from the box, ask them what they did and saw. Later, bring out your puppet and tell it that light bounces off mirrors. Your puppet does not believe you, and you turn to the children for help in explaining what they discovered with the box, flashlight, and mirror.

Bendable Mirrors
Science

WHY we are doing this project: to allow children to observe how an image changes when light hits a curved, rather than flat, mirror.

WHAT we will need:
> Reflecting paper (available in specialty paper stores, or as gift bag lining in card and gift stores)
> Mirror
> Piece of cardboard

HOW we will do it: If you cannot find sturdy silver paper, glue what you have to cardboard to make it stronger. Put your paper mirrors out on a table. During an Attention Getter time, remind and discuss with the children what was learned in the above activity—that light bounces off mirrors. Take your regular piece of cardboard and bend both edges either toward you or toward the children. Ask them to predict what they would see if they were able to bend a mirror in such a way but caution them not to actually try this. Show them the paper mirrors and encourage them to experiment with them. As the children explore the materials, discuss their findings. They may find that as they bend the mirrors away from them, their images get wider, or their faces suddenly have two noses! Invite the students to compare what they see when the light bounces off their curved (bent) mirrors with what they see when their paper mirrors are flat.

Two Halves Make a Whole
Science/Math

WHY we are doing this project: to help children understand through the use of mirrors and reflections that two halves make a whole.

WHAT we will need:
> Half-shape patterns (provided on page 43; photocopy and enlarge for your use)

Cardboard
Black construction paper
Glue or double-sided tape
Mirror

HOW we will do it: To prepare, make your half-shapes. If you are short on time, you can simply photocopy the patterns and cut them out. If you plan on using your shapes again, and want them to be sturdy, affix black construction paper onto cardboard and then cut the half-shapes out of it. Glue will make the paper wrinkle; double-sided tape or rubber cement will affix the paper smoothly.

In order to do this activity, the table surface must be at a right angle to the mirror. This can be a challenge to accomplish when all the mirrors are framed, because the margin of plastic frame around the mirror prevents the table and actual mirror from being edge to edge.

Some options: use packaging tape to tape the mirror to a wall, and then move a table up against it, or tape the upright mirror to the edge of the table, with the frame below the table's edge, and then move the table up against a wall to secure it further.

If none of these work for you, you may have to use frameless mirrors. If this is the case, tell the children ahead of time that the mirror is not to be moved. To prop the mirror up at a right angle to the table, use a typewriter stand or spread the covers of a book apart until the book is self-standing, and then prop the mirror up against it. Use clay and/or double-sided tape to secure it, if necessary.

Put the half-shapes out and encourage your students to put them up to the edge of the mirror. What do they see? (The reflection of the mirror makes a half-shape appear to be a whole.)

Making Periscopes
Science/Crafts/Fine Motor

WHY we are doing this project: to promote self-esteem and help children feel competent through the building of periscopes they can take home and use; to reinforce the fact that light bounces off mirrors; to develop fine motor skills.

The facts of the matter: If light hits a mirror at 45°, it will bounce off the mirror and reflect in another mirror at 45° also. This enables the light to make the 90° turn around a corner.

WHAT we will need:
    One-quart milk or juice cartons
    Mirrors
    Masking tape
    Glue
    Glue brushes
    Paper
Preparation:
    Scissors
    Exacto knife or razor blade

HOW we will do it: To prepare, start collecting your cartons well ahead of time. Ask neighbors, friends, and parents to help. The best thing about this project is how thrilled children are with their periscopes once they have made them. The down side is that the activity requires a little extra preparation, but if you can recruit some volunteers to help you with this, it will not be a problem.

This project requires the use of unframed mirrors. You are familiar with the maturity level of your students, and can decide about this activity accordingly. You may decide to make one periscope yourself and to supervise its use as the children take turns with it.

The least expensive way to obtain mirrors is to buy mirror tiles at an all-purpose do-it-yourself store. A pack of six to eight tiles that are 4 mm (⅛") thick and measure 36 cm x 36 cm (12" x 12") with beveled edges will cost about $15. The same set of unbeveled mirror tiles will cost about $6. You will also need a glass cutter (about $5), and sandpaper or a sanding belt

(about $2 or $3). If you are a teacher, and your school publishes a newsletter, you may be able to get some of these things donated or discounted in return for free advertising. You are going to insert the mirrors crosswise inside the quart carton boxes, so although most cartons measure 98 mm (3⅞") across, you should probably measure your cartons just to double-check. The mirrors can be about 7.5 cm (3") high. Use the sandpaper or sanding belt to smooth the edges.

To prepare the boxes, use your razor blade or Exacto knife and scissors to cut square holes that are 5 cm x 5 cm (2" x 2") on opposite sides of the carton and at opposite ends.

On one of the sides that has no square hole cut into it, cut along the sides to make a flap for a lid. This will enable the children to insert their mirrors.

Lay out all the prepared materials on an activity table, and if you are working with younger children, tear off masking-tape strips and stick them along the edge of a table, so they can use them as needed.

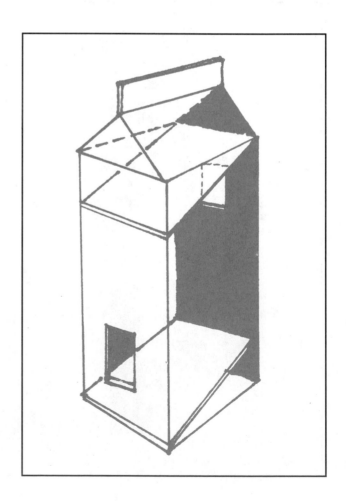

Make a periscope yourself by wedging one mirror into the bottom of the carton and one into the top so that they face each other. Each mirror should be wedged in below the square hole.

To secure the mirrors more firmly, put glue or clay along the edges, and/or wedge them with folded paper. Put just one strip of tape down on the lid, so that you can open it easily during your demonstration. After the glue has dried, use your periscope during an Attention Getter time in the following way: hide your periscope around a corner, before the children arrive. Later, gather the group together on the other side of the corner. Tell the children that you have a way of seeing them from around the corner. Go around it, poke your periscope out beyond the wall, and look at the children. Say out loud what you see them doing or wearing. When you come out from behind the corner, show the children the periscope and let them examine it. Open up the lid and let your students see how the mirrors face each other, and how they are inserted inside the box.

Show the children the materials on the table, and help them as needed. Encourage them to use the tape to seal the lids of the cartons. When the periscopes are finished, look for some corners to try them out on. This is a project children really get excited about!

Submarine!
Dramatic Play

WHY we are doing this project: to build on the interest created by the periscope construction activity above; to provide more hands-on exploration of how light that hits a mirror at 45° will also be reflected in another mirror at 45°; to provide props for imaginative play and social interaction; to expand vocabulary.

WHAT we will need:
Cardboard boxes (big enough for children to climb into)
Periscopes (made in previous activity)

Preparation:
Exacto knife or razor blade

HOW we will do it: To prepare, cut holes in the tops of the boxes, large enough for the periscopes to go through. Cut one or two in each box. Spread them out around the room, and invite the children to plunge down to the bottom of the sea in their submarines. How will they see what is outside their submarines? Might there be a giant octopus or sea serpent down there in the ocean? Encourage the children to play with the materials. Below is a list of related words and phrases which, if it seems appropriate, you may choose to introduce during the children's dramatic play.

VOCABULARY:
Navigate
Pressure
Port side
Starboard
Porthole
All sailors to their stations!
Emergency alert! Emergency alert!
All hands on deck

Backward Letters, Words, and Numbers
Science/Language Arts/Math

WHY we are doing this activity: to facilitate children's discovery that when an image is reflected, it looks different from the original image; to facilitate understanding that a reflected image looks backward, and that when a backward image is reflected, it looks normal; to facilitate reading and writing skills; to have fun with mirrors!

WHAT we will need:
Mirrors
Backward samples (provided on pages 46–48; photocopy and enlarge for your use)

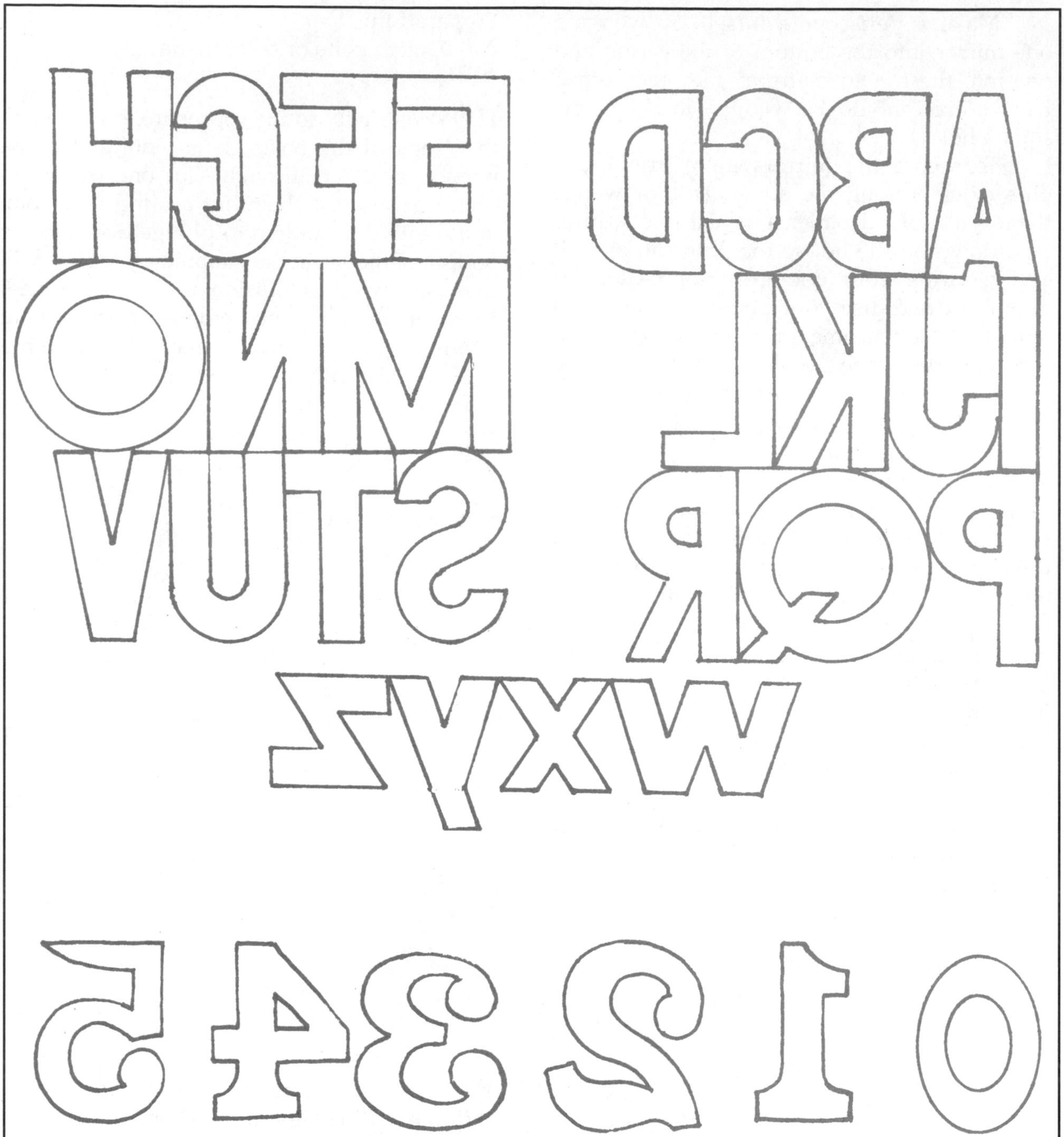

ABCD
EFGH
IJKL
MNO
PQR
STU
V
WXYZ

0123456789

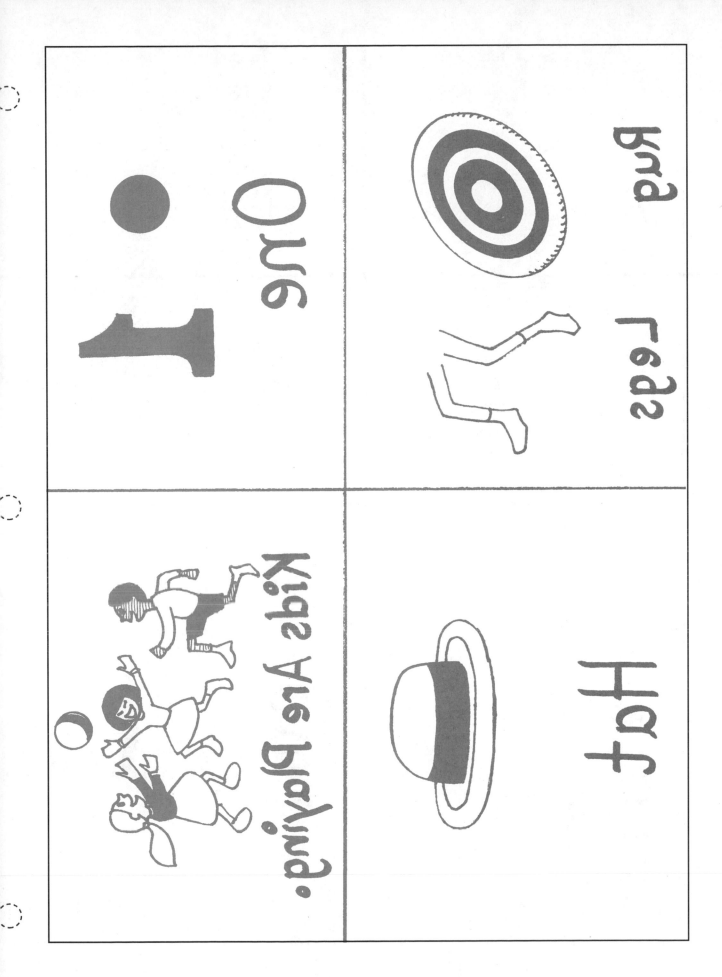

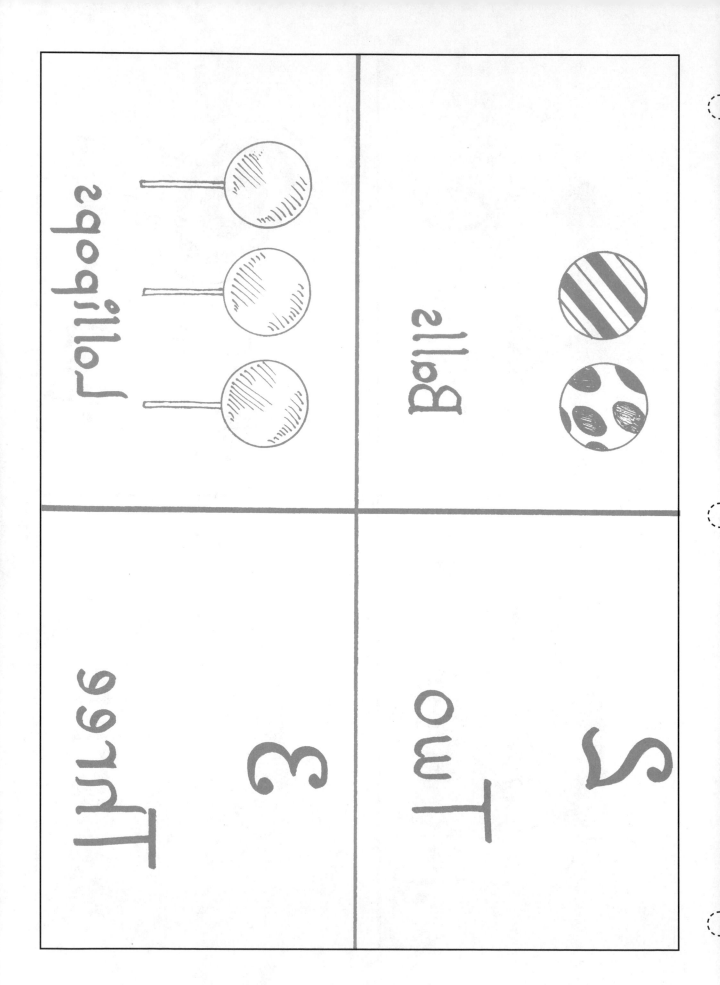

Lollipops

Balls

Three

3

Two

2

Index cards or paper squares
Markers

Optional:
Trays

HOW we will do it: To prepare, make photocopies of the backward samples and cut them out in squares or rectangles.

The mirrored surface of your framed mirrors must be perpendicular to the table or floor surface for this experiment to work. You can tape your mirrors to the wall using packaging tape, and then move the table up against them, or put the mirrors on the floor against the wall, and put thick books at their base.

Wherever you set up your mirrors, lay out the backward symbols, markers, and index cards or paper squares. You can set all the materials out on trays if you are working on the floor. During an Attention Getter time, show the children the backward pictures and ask them what they notice about them. Ask the children to predict what they will see if they put the backward pictures right up against the mirrors. When the children begin to experiment with the materials, encourage them to verbalize their findings. Why does the mirror make a backward picture "right?" What happens if you put a regular picture up against the mirror? What happens if you look at a backward picture in the mirror only? (Can you tell what it is?)

Double Reverse
Science

WHY we are doing this experiment: to facilitate an experience which proves that if an image is reversed twice, the reflection will consist of the original image.

WHAT we will need:
Two frameless mirrors (about 7.5 cm x
   10 cm [3" x 4"]
Thick towel
Packaging tape

Stickers
Mirror

Demonstration:
Piece of cardboard
Markers

HOW we will do it: To prepare, join frameless mirrors together side by side by putting strips of packaging tape on the backs. The mirrors should be attached in a V-shape so that the structure will be self-standing.

Tip: Save these joined mirrors for the next activity.

Spread a thick towel on a table and arrange the taped mirrors on top so that they are free-standing. Move the two sides of the joined mirrors until you have a perfect reflection of yourself in the corner of the two.

Hang the third mirror on the wall, making sure it is at the children's eye level. Write a word (e.g., MIRROR) in large print on the cardboard and draw a picture to symbolize the word.

During an Attention Getter time remind and discuss with the children what they learned in the previous activity: that what we see in a mirror is backward. Hold up your word card to the mirror to demonstrate this again. Pass around the stickers and invite the children to put one on one cheek. Hold up a mirror to each child and discuss which cheek in the mirror has a sticker on it.

Show the children the joined mirrors on the table. Ask them to predict what they will see if they look into the corner of the two mirrors. If the children move the sides of the joined mirrors, discuss how important it is to do it slowly and carefully so that the mirrors do not fall and break. Depending on the age of your children, you may choose to caution them not to move the mirrors at all.

As the children conduct the experiment, ask them about their findings. Which cheek has a sticker on it when they look in the single mirror hanging on the wall? What do they see when they look in the corner of the two joined mirrors? If appropriate, discuss the fact that one mirror reverses or makes an image backward once. But two mirrors reverse or make an image backward twice, until it looks the way it did in the first place.

Developmental differences: Three- and young four-year-olds will not be interested in the concept of double reverse, and will be more inclined to laugh and talk as they look into the mirrors with friends. (Two young students I once taught spent a large part of the morning peeking into a mirror together, running away, and coming back to peek again. Much giggling accompanied this activity.) Older children will be more interested in comparing their reflections in the single and double mirrors.

Corner Cube Mirror

Science

WHY we are doing this experiment: to allow children to observe that from whatever angle light hits a corner cube mirror, the corner of the three mirrors reflects the light straight back (the light does not bounce off at angles).

WHAT we will need:
Refrigerator box
Flashlights
Joined mirrors (from previous activity)
Large mirror (to be placed under joined structure)
Single mirrors
Small table (to fit in refrigerator box)
Tray or basket

HOW we will do it: Put your table in the refrigerator box, and lay the large mirror on top, reflecting surface face up. Place the joined mirrors on top, and arrange the sides of the joined mirrors until you have a perfect reflection of yourself in the corner of the three mirrors. Put the flashlights and single mirrors on the tray or in the basket, and set it on the floor in a corner.

During an Attention Getter time, shine a flashlight on a mirror and discuss again the fact that light bounces off mirrors. Show the children the corner cube mirror in the refrigerator box, and ask them to predict what will happen if they shine a flashlight into the corner of the three mirrors. Caution the children not to move the mirrors in the experimentation box. Before they conduct their experiments, show them again what happens to light when it is shone onto single mirrors. As the students emerge from the experimentation box, discuss their findings with them.

Mirror Symmetry

Math/Language Arts

WHY we are doing this activity: to help children understand that *symmetry* means opposite sides that are exactly the same in shape, size, and position; to facilitate understanding of the difference between horizontal and vertical symmetry by using certain letters; to facilitate discovery of how mirrors create symmetry; to develop all components of language arts: reading, writing, listening, and speaking.

Developmental differences: Young children may not be interested in the difference between vertical and horizontal symmetry. Even if they do not remember these terms, their experimental play with the sample pictures and mirrors will provide direct, hands-on experience with these concepts. If your children are older, you can decide how much or how little to reinforce their exploration with explanations.

In order to do this activity, children must be able to slide the half-shapes underneath the edge of a mirror. Therefore, you will have to use frameless mirrors. Once again, talk to the children beforehand about being gentle with the mirrors, sitting down at all times when they use them, and not carrying them around the room or removing them from the table.

WHAT we will need:
Mirrors (without frames)
Half-picture samples (provided on pages 51–53; photocopy and enlarge for your use)
Index cards or paper squares
Markers
Pens
One apple
One orange

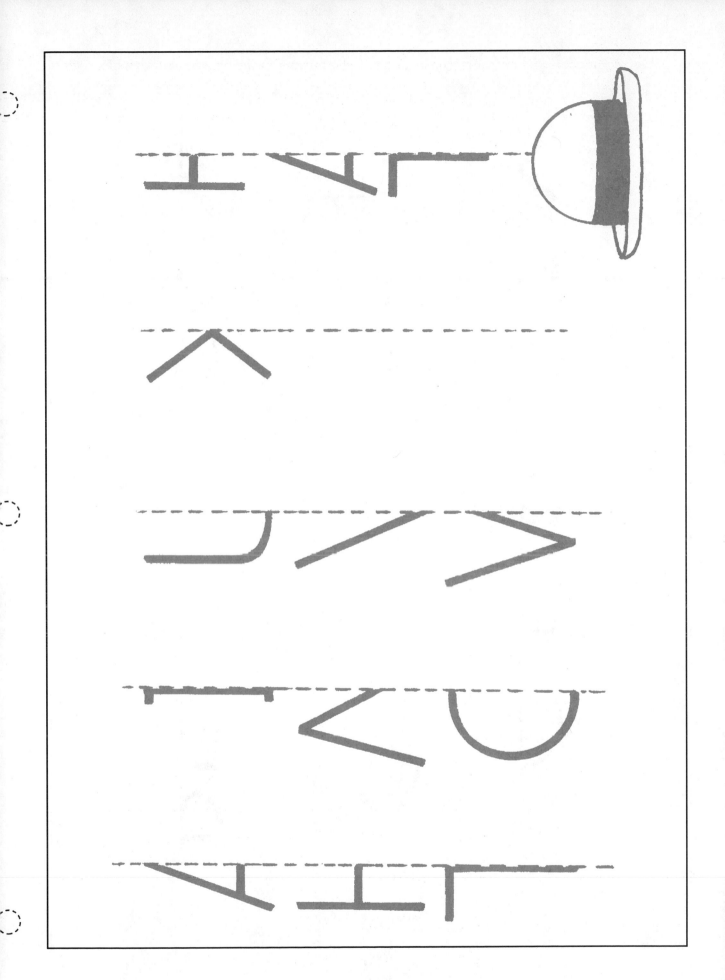

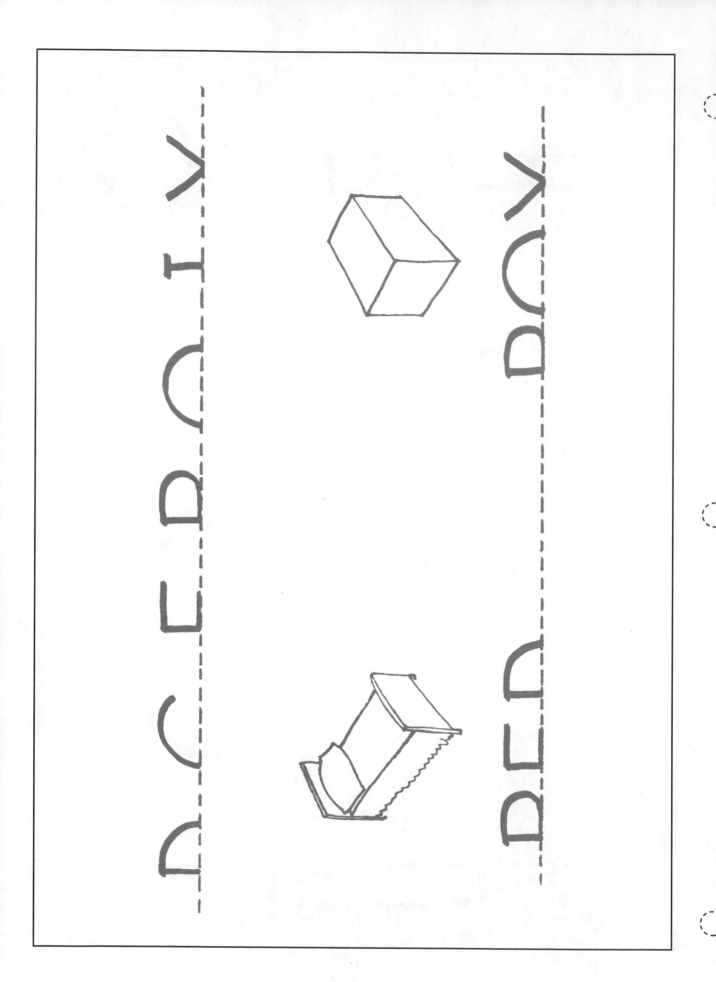

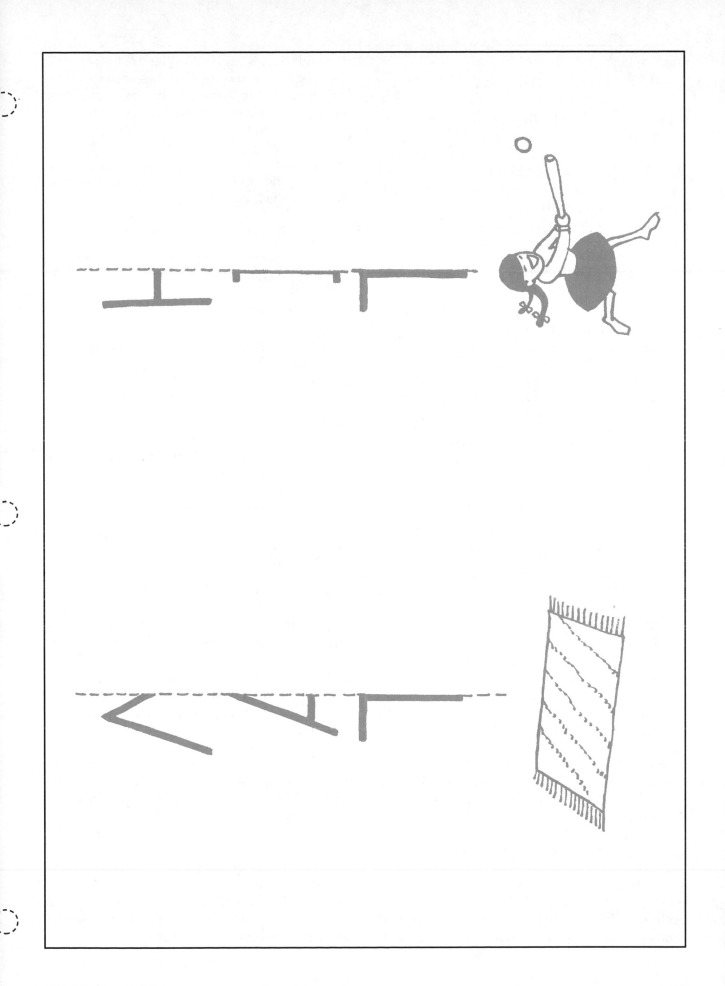

Optional:
   Trays

HOW we will do it: To prepare, set up your mirrors in the same manner as in the above activity; actual mirror parts must be perpendicular to the floor or table surface. Make photocopies of the half-picture samples and cut them out in squares or rectangles. Also, set out the writing materials on trays if you choose to use them.

The following group discussion introduces many concepts. The words in italicized print indicate the key ideas, and you may want to reinforce each one in other ways, spend varying amounts of time on different concepts, or even omit certain ones depending on the age and cognitive level of your children. You will probably want to introduce these new words and ideas over a period of days or even weeks, although, for convenience, I have listed all the demonstrations one after another.

Cut one apple in half vertically (lengthwise). When the children are gathered, hold the two halves up, facing each other, exactly opposite each other. Ask: "Do you think both sides of the apple are the same, or different? What do you notice about their size? What do you notice about their shape? What do you notice about whether they are right next to each other? Tell the children that when two sides of the same thing have the same size and shape and are *opposite* each other, they have *symmetry*. Say the word several times. Tap the syllables on your cheeks, blink the syllables, or tap the syllables on the floor with your feet. Hold the two halves of the apple up again, and this time, hold one half up higher and one half lower. Ask: "What do you notice about whether they are right next to each other now?" Let the children know that now the two sides of the apple are not symmetrical because now they are in different *positions*.

Cut the orange in half horizontally (along its width). Repeat the same procedure as above, and ask the same kinds of questions to promote group discussion and develop speaking and listening skills.

Compare the two fruits. Tell the children that when something is divided from top to bottom and both sides are the same, it has *vertical symmetry*. When something is divided

from side to side and both sides are the same, it has *horizontal symmetry*. Say these phrases several times in the same manner as above, but move your hand from top to bottom for the first phrase, and from side to side for the second. At the end of this group discussion, show the children the mirrors, sample pictures, and writing materials and invite them to find out more by exploring the materials.

Symmetry Shapes
Art

WHY we are doing this project: to reinforce the concept of symmetry through creative art and to facilitate creative expression.

WHAT we will need:
   Paper
   Paints (three or four different colors)
   Shallow containers
   Spoons
   String lengths, about 20 cm (8") long
   Mirror
Preparation:
   Scissors

HOW we will do it: To prepare, choose a shape which, when folded, will consist of two symmetrical sides, and cut all the paper out in that exact same shape. Fold all the shapes in half. Spread newspaper out on the activity table, and set out all the materials. Make a symmetry shape yourself first, by spooning paint onto one half, putting most of the string in the paint, folding one half of the paper down over the other, and then pulling the string out. After your symmetry shape has dried, show it to the children and explain how you made it. Comment on how one side of the paper is the mirror image of the other. Ask one of the children to hold one half up to a mirror, and compare the image to the actual other half.

Be sure to mention that everyone's symmetry shape will look different and put your sample away before the children approach the activity table. The children may take the project in other directions, and that is fine.

Mirrors and Mirrors and Mirrors and . . .

Science

WHY we are doing this project: to facilitate observation of what happens when two mirrors face each other; to develop self-esteem and a sense of autonomy through use of a one-person work station.

In this experiment, the light which is reflected from the toy reflects over and over again from one mirror to the other before reaching the eye.

WHAT we will need:
> Two hand mirrors
> Two large, sturdy blocks or two stacks of books
> Strong rubber bands
> Small toy with some height
> "One person may be here" sign (provided on page 3; photocopy and enlarge for your use)
> Sign which says "How many reflections do you count?"

HOW we will do it: To prepare, arrange the blocks or two stacks of books so that they face each other. Using the rubber bands, secure the mirrors to them so that they too are facing each other. Put the toy between them. Pin the "One person may be here" sign on the wall above the table, as well as the "How many reflections do you count?" sign.

During an Attention Getter time, read/interpret the signs together. Invite the children to look into one of the mirrors to see what there is to be seen. How many images of the toy can they count? How many mirrors do they count within the mirrors?

Tip: Leave this set-up intact while you do the activity which follows.

What Do I Look Like from Behind?

Social Studies

WHY we are doing this project: to show children through hands-on experimentation how mirrors can help them see new things.

WHAT we will need:
> All the materials in the above activity
> Small doll or stuffed toy which can sit up
> Two large mirrors
> Two framed medium-sized mirrors
> Pocket mirrors
> Ruler
> Meter stick or yardstick

HOW we will do it: To prepare, arrange the same set-up as in the previous project. Place the doll or toy so that it sits up between the two mirrors. In addition, secure one pocket mirror to the meter stick or yardstick and one to the ruler. Hang or prop the large mirrors up so that they are at the children's eye level and place the two medium-sized framed mirrors nearby.

During an Attention Getter time, ask the children if they can see the back of the doll as well as its front in the mirrors. Together, talk about how when two mirrors face each other, you can see the back, as well as the front, of something. Ask the children how many of them have seen what they look like from behind. Let them know that the tools they need for this are in the room. Demonstrate by looking in the big mirror and holding a framed, unbreakable mirror behind you. Let the children know that they can do the same. If they like, they can ask friends to hold the framed mirror behind them as they look into the large mirror. How does the view of their backs change as the position of the framed mirror is altered by being tilted or raised?

After the children have explored what they look like from behind, show them how mirrors can also be used to see things in some unusual spots. Use the mirrors attached to the rulers and yardsticks to take a look at places such as the bottom of their shoes, the underside of the table, or the underside of a shelf. Poke the long mirrors into out-of-the-way places to discover what can be seen. See how many unusual spots they can find in the room which they have never had a chance to see before and which, with the help of the long mirrors, they can take a look at now.

Mirror Box
Social Studies

WHY we are doing this activity: to help children develop healthy self-esteem.

WHAT we will need:
    Cigar box
    Mirror that fits inside the box

HOW we will do it: To prepare, try to find or make a box that is special in some way. Cigar boxes are perfect for this project and can sometimes be obtained at pipe and tobacconist stores. You may want to decorate the box with contact paper, fabric, stickers, or glue and glitter. Put the mirror inside, and during an Attention Getter time, tell the children that if they look in the box they will see one of the most special people in the whole world. Ask the children not to tell the box's secret after they look inside. If you do this as a small group project during an Attention Getter time, have each child come to you, lift up the lid of the box and look inside. What do they see? If you decide to put the box out for free exploration, set it on a table and post a "One person may be here" sign.

Mirror Books
Language/Social Studies

WHY we are doing this project: to develop all components of language arts: reading, writing, speaking, and listening; to develop self-esteem through appreciation of our appearance; to develop fine motor skills.

WHAT we will need:
    Pale-colored construction paper
    Glue
    Markers and/or crayons
    Mirrors
    Preparation:
    Scissors
    Stapler
    Aluminum foil or silver paper which
        gives a good reflection (sometimes
        available in specialty paper stores)
    Glue stick

HOW we will do it: To prepare, cut construction paper pieces that measure 30 cm x 20 cm (12" x 8"). Make a blank book for each child. For each book, take three pieces of the paper and fold the 30 cm (12") side over, and then staple twice along the folded edge.

Cut the aluminum foil or silver paper into small rectangles that will fit on the cover of each book. On a few books, print "The Mirror Book" above the mirror, and then below it, write: "What do I see when I look at me?" Leave several books blank with no writing and/or no mirror for children who prefer to make their own, or who wish to take the project in a different direction. Lay out all the materials on an activity table, safely hang or prop up mirrors nearby, or simply lay framed pocket mirrors on the activity table.

For Attention Getter time, make a sample mirror book yourself. Draw things about yourself—what you look like, what you are wearing—and write words on each page. Mine is as simple as: "I like the green in my eyes." "Today I'm wearing my favorite earrings. My sister gave them to me. What colors are they?" "I like my hair cut short."

During an Attention Getter time, read the sample mirror book to the children. Show them the mirrors and the materials on the table. Be sure to tell the children that this happens to be the way you made your book, but that everyone's book will be different and special because we are all different and have our own ways of making things. Put the sample away before your students begin the project. As the children look in the mirrors and draw pictures, take story dictation, write their words on separate pieces of paper for them to copy, or support invented spelling. After the day's activities, gather everyone together again and have a show-and-tell of mirror books. If you prefer, choose a few children every day to show-and-tell their books.

Alternative Snow White Story
Multicultural/Anti-Bias/Language

WHY we are doing this: to counteract the myth of women competing against each other on the basis of looks; to refashion old fairy tales into stories which present strong women cooperating with each other; to encourage children to examine gender roles; to help children become critical thinkers; to develop speaking and listening skills; to expand vocabulary.

WHAT we will need:
Book: *Snow White* (any traditional version)
Flannel board
Flannel board shapes (provided on page 58; photocopy and enlarge for your use)
Felt
Scissors
Glue
Markers or crayons
Story: "ANOTHER SNOW WHITE STORY" (provided)

HOW we will do it: To prepare, cut out and color the story shape patterns, and glue them onto felt. Set up the flannel board.

During an Attention Getter time, read the traditional fairy tale *Snow White* to the children. Invite your students to join you in saying: "Mirror, mirror on the wall, who's the fairest of them all?" If you work with three- and young four-year-olds, save the alternative Snow White flannel board story for the next day. Then, before you tell it, remind the children of the traditional story you read the day before. Who was that story about? What happened in that story? After some discussion, let the children know that there is another story about Snow White you would like to tell them.

The list of words at the end of the story are new vocabulary words you can explain and discuss as appropriate. Teach the children the new chant near the end of the story (the one that breaks the mirror's spell) and invite them to say it with you.

"ANOTHER SNOW WHITE STORY"

Once upon a time there was a Queen who sat by a window. [Put queen on flannel board.] She was using a screwdriver to fix a broken wimwacker, and I do not know if you know how tricky wimwackers are to fix, but I can tell you they are very tricky indeed. Well, she looked up for a minute to watch the snowflakes whirling around outside, and, as a result, she accidently gouged herself with the screwdriver. She said something very unqueenly and a drop of blood rolled down her finger. [Put blood drops on board.] All of a sudden, (and even now, nobody knows the reason for it,) the Queen's lady-in-waiting said, "Wouldn't it be lovely if you had a child with lips as red as blood, skin as white as snow, and hair as black as a raven?"

"Actually," the Queen said, "I have always liked redheads."

But by an amazing chance, the Queen did happen to have a baby some time later, and it was a daughter, and she did have lips as red as blood, skin as white as snow, and hair as black as a raven. [Take down other two pieces; put baby on the board.] The Queen wanted to call

Enlarge these drawings on a photocopier before cutting the shapes out of felt.

her Tawndilayo but everyone else wanted to call her "Snow White" and since Tawndilayo isn't the sort of name you can say quickly with a mouth full of peanut butter, "Snow White" is what they called her. Sadly, a few years later, the Queen got very sick and died, and the King married another Queen. [Put new queen on board.] I wonder how Snow White felt about her mother dying. What do you think? [Listen to children's comments.]

[Take baby off board; put counting picture on.] Well, the King's new Queen loved to count and she would count all sorts of things—the number of apples on the royal apple tree, the number of guards in the royal ballroom, the number of pickle juice stains on the King's royal tunic or the number of dust balls under the royal bed—it didn't matter so long as she could count them. To tell you the truth, it drove the King a little nuts [put king on board] but since the Queen said nothing to him about his habit of picking the lint out from between his toes, rolling it up into a little ball and then flicking it at the Royal Chancellor, [put up picture of King picking lint from his toes] he decided to say nothing to her about her counting. [Put original picture of King back on flannel board.] But one day, when she was counting the number of cinnamon rolls he was having for breakfast (seven, in case you are curious) he thought he'd try to give her a new interest, so he told her that there was a magic mirror in the palace. "A magic mirror!" she said. "Show it to me!"

[Take counting picture off board; put mirror on, with queen and king nearby as if they are looking at it.] So the King took her into a huge, grand hall where there hung a mirror on the wall, and he said, "Mirror, mirror on the wall, who's the fairest of them all?"

And the mirror answered, "Well, I do not know about being the fairest of them all, but you do look quite fetching in that scarlet jerkin of yours."

"Not me, you cheap piece of glass!" the King thundered to the mirror. "I'm asking for the Queen!"

"The Queen has to ask for herself," the mirror said sulkily, "and watch who you call a cheap piece of glass."

So the Queen said, "Mirror, mirror on the wall, who's the fairest of them all?"

And the mirror said, "You are, toots."

Well, if the King wanted the Queen to have a new interest, he succeeded, because after that she wouldn't do anything all day except look in that mirror. [Take king off board.] Nobody knew it, but they didn't have a straightforward, standard kind of magic mirror, which was what had been ordered. There had been a mix-up at the magic mirror factory, and they'd been sent the sneaky, crafty kind of mirror by mistake. It cast a spell over the Queen so that the more she looked into it, the more the mirror made her worry about her looks, and the more makeup she put on to try to look beautiful. The mirror cast this spell by showing her pictures all day long of women [put up advertising pictures on the board] who all looked the same in a certain way and by trying to make the Queen believe that she should look just like them. It got to the point where the Queen spent hours and hours every day, doing nothing but looking into that mirror and putting on makeup and asking who was the fairest of them all over and over again.

Now all this time Snow White was growing up [put grown up Snow White on board] and one day when the Queen asked, "Mirror, mirror on the wall, who's the fairest of them all?" the magic mirror decided to be mean to the Queen by saying: "Sorry, toots, but it is Snow White." The Queen burst into tears and when Snow White heard her crying, and found out why she was so unhappy, she gave the Queen a good talking-to.

She said, "You've got to snap out of this. You look the way you look, and I look the way I look, and one isn't better than the other—they are just different. You've got to stop spending all your time with this horrible mirror. Remember the way you used to love to count things? Remember how you used to count everything like the number of fleas on the royal dog and the number of turnips in the royal vegetable patch? Now come on—we are going to break the hold that mirror has over you!" And she dragged the Queen over to the mirror, and because the Queen was under a spell and didn't know what was good for her, she cried and whined and carried on but Snow White pretended not to notice.

They looked into the mirror and Snow White said, "Now, say after me: 'Mirror, mirror on the wall; I do not care what you think at all. I am who I want to be; and darn it, that is fine with me.'"

At first the Queen didn't want to say it, but Snow White kept poking and prodding her in the back so finally the Queen said the words: "Mirror, mirror on the wall; I do not care what you think at all. I am who I want to be, and darn it, that is fine with me." *Guess what happened?* The mirror shattered into a thousand pieces [take whole mirror off board; put broken mirror on instead] as its sneaky, crafty spell was broken.

"Aaaaaaah!" it shrieked as it shattered, "you have broken my beautiful, sneaky spell—what a world, what a world." And that was the end of that horrible magic mirror.

[Take mirror off the board.] As for the Queen and Snow White, well, they found out that Snow White loved to count things too, so they decided to open up an accounting firm together, because accountants count people's money. [Put up office picture on board.] Snow White knew of some dwarves who had no idea how much gold they had in their gold mine, [put dwarves and prince on board] and they became the first clients of "Queen & Snow White, Accountants Inc." There was also a prince in the next kingdom whose royal finances were an awful mess, and he was their second client. Soon the word got around that they were terrific accountants, so they had a booming business while the King spent the rest of his days picking the lint out of his toes. [Put picture of king picking lint out of his toes on flannel board again.] So you see, they all lived happily ever after.

Leave the flannel board materials out so that the children can retell the story, as well as invent new ones.

The children will be able to guess the meaning of some of the new words because of the context, but there are too many new words to discuss all in one sitting. If you tell the story more than once, choose a few of them to talk about each time. If you can, use those new words in your speech some time during that day in order to reinforce their meaning.

VOCABULARY:

Fetching	Gouged	Jerkin
Standard	Succeeded	Firm
Amazing	Obsessed	Sneaky
Shriek	Lint	Tunic
Habit	Ridiculous	Crafty
Flicking	Accountants	Sulkily
Curious	Clients	Thundered

Mirror Misting
Science/Art

WHY we are doing this project: to provide a sensory experience; to facilitate observation of water molecules on a mirror's surface; to experiment with unusual art utensils.

WHAT we will need:
   Mirrors
   Spray bottles (on mist setting)
   Food coloring
   Sponges
   Paper towels
   Cotton swabs
   Makeup applicators
   Cotton balls

HOW we will do it: To prepare, lay your mirrors out on the activity table. Put all the spray bottles on the mist setting. Fill them with water and add food coloring to some of them.

If you do not want your children to spray each other with the spray bottles, talk about this beforehand. You can ask: "Is it okay to spray each other with the bottles? Is it okay to spray someone in the face?"

Invite the children to spray the mirrors, and then ask them what happens if they try to draw on the mirrors with their fingers. Comment on the patterns, designs, and pictures the children make. Encourage them to use the other materials also. When the children want to create a new misting picture, show them how to wipe the mirrors with sponges and dry them with the paper towels so that they can re-mist them.

Face Painting
Art/Anti-Bias

WHY we are doing this project: to facilitate creative art through face painting; to reinforce the use of mirrors; to help children, especially boys, feel comfortable with decorating their faces.

WHAT we will need:
Face paints (commercial or homemade)
Mirrors
Water
Paper towels
Cotton swabs
Makeup applicators
Cotton balls
Small plastic containers

HOW we will do it: To make your own face paints, mix flour and water into a smooth consistency, and add food coloring or coffee for varying shades of face paints. Put the paints into the small containers, and arrange the mirrors so that the children can easily look into

them while they decorate their faces. Invite all your students, especially the boys (who may need extra encouragement), to experiment with the paints. If they would like to, let the children wear their painted faces all day. Use the water and towels to clean up.

Mirror Dances
Music/Movement

WHY we are doing this activity: to develop gross motor muscles; to help children "feel" music; to accustom children to the rhythm of music; to develop cognition by careful observation of a mirror partner.

WHAT we will need:
Open space
Music

HOW we will do it: Encourage everyone to find a partner. Put the music on, and tell the children that one person is going to pretend to be a mirror and must do whatever the partner does. You will probably want to begin with fairly simple, slow movements and gestures. As the children warm up to the game, move into slow dances. Switch roles frequently, and encourage the children to watch their partners carefully.

Literature

Symbol Key: *Multicultural
+Minimal diversity
No symbol: no diversity or no people

Davies, K., & Oldfield, W. (1989). *My mirror*. New York: Doubleday.

Hoban, T. (1990). *Shadows and reflections*. New York: Greenwillow Books.

Simon, S. (1980). *Mirror magic*. New York: Lothrop, Lee, & Shepard Books.+

Zubrowski, B. (1992). *Mirrors*. New York: William Morrow.* (This book has more activity ideas with mirrors.)

Extenders

Science: When the children participate in the Mirror Symmetry activity, discuss the fact that photographs of ourselves are *backward* to what we see in mirrors. Take a photograph of each child and invite your students to compare their photographs to their reflections in the mirror. Ask the children if they think their photographs or their reflections look most like them.

Art: When you play "submarines" in your cardboard boxes, invite the children to decorate them first with paint, markers and/or stickers. If they would like some portholes in their subs, use an Exacto knife to cut circles. If you do not cut them all the way around you will have circular flaps which the children can lift or lower. Velcro can be purchased in strips with adhesive on the back. Affix Velcro so that the porthole flaps will stick when they are lifted up.

Math: Once the children are familiar with mirrors and half-shapes, extend this to include quarter shapes. What do two quarters make? How many quarters do you see when you put one against the mirror?

Dramatic Play/Social Studies: Put out mirrors and personal dress-up items or toiletries, for example, shaving razors with no blades, empty deodorant sticks, empty plastic cologne containers, ties, make-up containers, empty skin cream bottles.

FEATHER FRENZY

A good source of clean feathers is a pet store. Stop by well in advance of when you will be needing the feathers, explain to the staff that they are for a project with children and ask if they will save the feathers their birds molt. Try to get a good variety of large, medium, and small feathers from large and small birds. Even from a small bird there is quite a variation in size between a tiny feather from a bird's face, and a large tail feather.

Attention Getter: Have the children gather in a group and ask them to close their eyes. Tell them that they are going to feel something brush against their cheeks, and to guess what it is. Take a soft feather and walk around the group, brushing your feather gently across every child's cheek. After the children have guessed, have them open their eyes and show them what you used.

Bending Feathers
Science

WHY we are doing this: to introduce the words *feather shaft*; to help children understand through hands-on experimentation the meaning of the word *pliant*; to help children understand the properties of a feather shaft.

WHAT we will need:
    Large feathers

HOW we will do it: You can either do this as a hands-on, child-initiated project or as a group activity. Hand out the feathers and ask the children to predict whether or not the feathers will break if they gently bend them. Invite them to find out. Encourage your students to take one finger and slowly bend it over their feathers. Tell the children that the hard part in the middle that holds the feathers is called the *shaft*. Ask the children to watch the shaft again as they gently bend their feathers. Explain that when something is bendable like the feather, it is *pliant*. Say the word together as you bend the shafts over with your fingers and then let the shafts bounce up again. Mention that when birds preen their feathers, they cannot reach all the way to the tip of a tail feather, so they grab the base of the feather in their beaks, and bend the feather toward them.

If you do the project so that the children approach and explore the materials on their own, lay the feathers out on a table, and tell the children they can experiment with gently bending them to see if they break.

Feather Brushes
Art/Sensory

WHY we are doing this project: to encourage creative expression through the use of unusual materials; to enable children to have a sensory experience with feathers; to develop fine motor skills.

WHAT we will need:
    Large feathers with sturdy shafts
    Feather dusters
    Paintbrushes
    Paint
    Paper

HOW we will do it: Lay out all materials and encourage the children to paint with the feathers, dusters, and paintbrushes. Notice how different the effect is when you use the tip of an individual feather, the edge of a feather, and the entire side of a feather. Which is easier or more interesting—painting with a feather, a feather duster, or a regular brush?

Feathers Come in Many Shapes and Sizes
Science

WHY we are doing this activity: to help children understand that feathers come in many different sizes, shapes, and textures; to expand vocabulary, to develop self-esteem and a sense of autonomy through the use of a one-person work station.

The facts of the matter: Small, fuzzy down feathers help keep birds warm. Tail feathers help them steer when they are flying and help them balance when they are walking, climbing, or standing. Flight feathers are found on the underside of birds' wings. The shaft of a flight feather is not precisely in the middle.

The wider feathered side bends more easily, allowing air to flow through the wing more easily as the bird beats its wings against the air.

WHAT we will need:

    Feathers (diverse in size, shape, and texture, and from all parts of birds' bodies)

    Poster board or butcher paper

    Clear contact paper

    Double-sided tape

    Tray

    Activity sign (bird outline provided below; photocopy and enlarge for your use.)

    "One person may be here" sign (provided on page 3; photocopy and enlarge for your use)

    Photographs of birds from magazines (*National Geographic, Bird Talk*)

HOW we will do it: To prepare, look at the sketch of the featherless bird with outspread wings in this text. Using this picture as a reference, draw a very large outline of the same bird on your butcher paper or poster board. Poster board is preferable because it is sturdier and easier to apply contact paper to. If you have to use butcher paper, try taping it onto a piece of cardboard from a box. After covering the picture with clear contact paper, stick double-sided tape on all parts of the bird: head, rump, wings, and body. As the children participate in the project, the double-sided tape may lose its stickiness, so place some spare pieces along the edge of a shelf so that you can easily put new strips over the old. You can put the bird poster on the floor or on the wall. Make a "One person may be here" sign, and print an activity sign that says: "Where does each kind of feather belong?" Draw a picture

of a feather above the word. Hang the sign near the activity and place the tray of feathers beside the poster. Hang your bird photographs all around the area where the children will be working. Try to include a picture of a bird with its wings outspread.

During an Attention Getter time, pass a sleek outer (contour) feather to each child. Point to one of your bird photographs and show the children the feathers on the outside of the bird (the bird's wings or back or tail). Let the children know that a smooth outer feather is called a *contour* feather. Together, stroke your smooth contour feathers as you say the words: *contour feather*. Stroke the feather slowly and say the words slowly. Stroke it quickly and say the words quickly. Pass each child an inner (down) feather and have the children brush them against their skin as you all say the words *down feather*. Brush it slowly and say the words slowly. Brush it quickly and say the words quickly. Run your fingers down the shaft in the middle of the feather while you say the word *shaft*. What would happen to a feather if there was no shaft?

Compare a soft, fluffy, down feather to a sleek outer contour feather. Ask the children why a bird needs a feather like a down feather. (Down feathers keep birds warm.) Point to one of the bird photographs. Why do we not see any down feathers on the bird in the photograph? (They are underneath the contour feathers.) Hold up a contour tail feather and ask the children which part of a bird's body it might have come from. Which feathers in the photographs look like they have the same shape? What do you think tail feathers are used for?

Take out a variety of feathers which include tiny head feathers and long tail feathers. Hold up a head feather and ask the children which part of a bird's body they think it might belong to. How can they tell it is not a tail feather? Some feathers are fluffy on one end and smooth on the other. Pass one of these around and ask: "Can you tell which end grows out of the bird's body? How?"

Look carefully at a flight feather (they make up the underside of the wings). Explain to your students that flight feathers are not from the outer wing of a bird like the outer wings seen in the pictures. Point to the picture of a bird

with its wings outspread, and show the children the flight feathers underneath. For some birds, the flight feathers are a different color than the outer contour feathers. Pass a flight feather around the group and ask the children what they notice about the position of the shaft. If they need a clue, invite them to compare the flight feather to the contour feather.

Show the children the poster and feathers and help them read/interpret the activity signs. Encourage them to explore the materials. Sometimes children like to get silly and deliberately put the feathers in odd places on the poster; silly play helps children learn too.

Feather Match
Math

WHY we are doing this project: to facilitate cognitive skills through a matching game.

WHAT we will need:
    Feathers (diverse in size, shape, and
        color)
    Double-sided tape
    Butcher paper or poster board
    Contact paper
    Bold, dark marker
    Fine, dark marker
    Tray

HOW we will do it: To prepare, arrange your feathers on your butcher paper or poster board, and using the bold marker for large feathers and the fine marker for small ones, draw each feather's outline. If you are working with kindergartners or older preschoolers and want to make the activity a little more challenging, choose a few feathers which are very close in size and shape but different in color, and use the colored markers to make the corresponding outlines match in color.

Cover the paper or poster board in contact paper, and then put double-sided tape on each feather outline. Small feathers get lost easily, so have available several extra feathers of the same size and shape with which to replace any lost feathers. Set the outline on the floor and put the feathers on the tray beside it. Invite the children to explore the materials.

Birds of a Feather
Art/Language

WHY we are doing this project: to reinforce through a sensory-oriented art project the variety in size, color, and shape of feathers; to facilitate free choice as the children choose the feathers they would like to use for the collage; to develop cooperation between children in a group project; to develop speaking and listening skills; to develop fine motor skills.

WHAT we will need:
Large piece of butcher paper
Feathers (wide variety of sizes, shapes, and colors)
Outline of a bird (provided below; photocopy and enlarge for your use.)
Glue
Glue brushes
Preparation:
Marker

HOW we will do it: To prepare, draw the outline of a large bird onto butcher paper using the drawing in the text as a reference. Lay out your materials. During an Attention Getter time, show the children the bird drawing. What is this bird missing? Let the children know that together, you are all going to cover the bird with feathers, and do this as a group project. Talk about the feathers you use as you select them. After the glue dries, put the collage up on the wall at the children's eye level. Ask the chil-

dren what they think the bird should be named, and write down all the suggestions on the side of the picture. Take a vote to see what the favorite name is. Very young children usually do not understand that they can only put their hands up for one vote, so just count all the hands that are up. Write down the number of votes next to that name. Write the name of the winner above the bird's head.

Feather Badges
Language

WHY we are doing this: to help children develop speaking and listening skills through conversation; to reinforce the difference between down and contour feathers.

WHAT we will need:
   Small contour and down feathers
   Badge pattern (provided below; photocopy and enlarge for your use)

   Double-sided tape
   Markers
   Pens
   Glue sticks

HOW we will do it: Make enough photocopies of the badge so that you have one for each child and one for yourself. Also, make several photocopies of the blank badge sample. There is a drawing of a feather on the sample badge, but it is much better to stick small, real feathers, one contour and one down, onto each badge using double-sided tape. Real feathers generate far more interest among children and are more likely to motivate them to wear a badge or to make their own. Cut out the badge shapes and stick three strips of double-sided tape on the back of each one. You can stick the prepared badges to a table edge so that they are easy to pick up. Set out the small feathers, glue sticks, markers, and pens on the table for children who decide to make their own badges. Put strips of double-sided tape along the edge of the writing table. Put a feather badge on yourself, and either wait for the children to notice and ask about it, or talk about it yourself. Show them the badges and badge-making materials.

If possible, glue or stick a real feather onto each badge.

Feather Count

Math

WHY we are doing this project: to practice rational counting; to develop reading and writing skills of letters and numbers; to reinforce the difference between contour and down feathers.

WHAT we will need:
- Small boxes
- Small contour and down feathers (to fit inside the boxes)
- Small pencils
- Tray
- Writing sheets (format provided on page 70; photocopy and enlarge for your use)
- Blank pieces of paper (same size as the writing sheets)
- Activity sign (instructions follow)

HOW we will do it: To prepare, begin gathering your small boxes ahead of time. When you are ready to do the activity, put several different kinds of feathers, a writing sheet, and/or blank paper, and a small pencil inside each one. If you are working with older children, put in twelve to fifteen feathers, or as high as your students are counting. If you are working with younger children, they may use the writing sheets/blank paper for scribbling, and that is okay. Make an activity sign that says: "How many feathers in this box?" Draw or glue feathers above the word feathers, and a box above the word box. Put the boxes on a tray and the tray near the sign. Have extra writing sheets and blank paper sheets available with which to replace used ones. Encourage the children to explore the materials, and as appropriate, talk to them about their discoveries.

Developmental differences: Three- and young four-year-olds will be more interested in sensory exploration of the feathers they find in the boxes. Older children will be more likely to count the feathers.

Feathers Close–Up

Science

WHY we are doing this activity: to enable children to observe the different parts of a feather; to allow them to examine the barbs of a feather and how they knit together.

WHAT we will need:
- Feathers (downy and smooth)
- Magnifying glasses
- Microscope

Demonstration:
- Velcro pieces

HOW we will do it: Set out all the materials on an activity table and encourage the children to explore them. They will not need help with the magnifying glasses, but if you are using a microscope, you will need to supervise. Microscopes are wonderful to have, even for very young children. When I have provided a microscope, my students have been so excited about using one that even the youngest children willingly waited for their turn. However, you can also provide magnifying glasses for waiting children if you like. There are some relatively inexpensive microscopes available from catalogs, but try to get the kind which allows you to make up your own slide—this way you can put a variety of different objects under the lens for examination. Because it is hard for a child to close one eye and keep the other eye open, you can cover one eye with a card or show the children how to do it for themselves.

As the children explore the materials, and if they look at a feather through a microscope, ask them if they see anything on the barbs. Most feathers contain an incredible amount of dust. Ask: "Where do you think all that dust comes from?" Examine the shafts for a clue. (As birds preen, the sheaths of the shafts break down so that new feathers emerge. As the shafts break, they create dust.)

Show the children the *barb* of a feather, which is the soft part that grows from the shaft. *Barbules* branch off from barbs. Invite the children to ask a friend to hold their magnifying

How many feathers in this box? _____

How many feathers in this box? _____
Take two away.
How many left? _____

How many feathers in this box? _____

How many feathers in this box? _____
Take two away.
How many left? _____

How many feathers in this box? _____

glasses while they pull some barbs apart. What happens? What happens if they smooth the barbs together again? Explain that barbs and barbules have little hooks which make them knit together, a little bit like Velcro. Invite the children to experiment with the Velcro as well as the feather barbs, in order to grasp the concept.

Try to include among your feather collection some blood feathers (those with hollow shafts). Encourage the children to examine these. Why are they hollow? (Blood flows from the bird's body through the shaft to nourish the feather.) Encourage the children to express their observations as they experiment with the materials.

The Feather Chart
Science/Language

WHY we are doing this project: to reinforce the names of the different parts of a feather learned in a previous activity and to introduce new parts; to facilitate speaking, listening, reading, and writing through use of a writing center.

WHAT we will need:
- Black construction paper
- White-colored pencil or crayon
- Feathers (contour, down, and filoplume)
- Magnifying glasses
- Small containers (for feathers)
- Pens
- Paper (lined and construction)
- Index cards
- Chart outline (provided below for reference)
- Scissors
- Crayons
- Markers
- Glue sticks
- Double-sided tape

HOW we will do it: This activity requires a chart illustrating and naming the different parts of a feather to prop on your writing center table. Children can examine the feather samples with the magnifying glasses as well as use the writing materials at the center to make

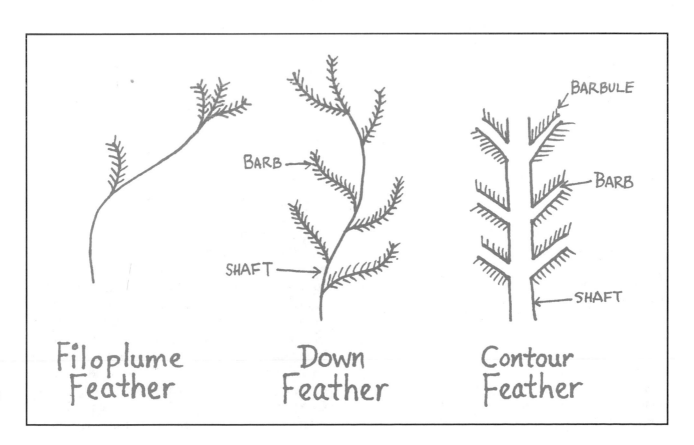

their own feather cards or to create their own projects. Speaking and listening will take place (we hope!) while the children work together at the table.

Use the chart outline in the text to make your own chart. Using glue or double-sided tape, stick several real feathers next to each corresponding illustration. It is a good idea to use black paper so that delicate filoplume feathers, which are often white or pale colored, will show up more clearly. A filoplume looks like a single long strand.

Prop your chart up on the writing table using a typewriter stand if necessary, or if the chart is propped against a wall, use modeling clay to secure it at the base. Put all other materials on the writing table. If you use double-sided tape instead of glue sticks, place some pieces onto the edge of the table for the children to take as needed.

During an Attention Getter time, show the children the chart and describe and read the names of each feather part to them. Show them the magnifying glasses and encourage the children to examine the feather samples on the chart. Show them the writing table, and let them know that if they want to make feather cards that have drawings, feathers, or words on them, the materials are waiting for them. Take story dictation, write words on paper to be copied, or support invented spelling as appropriate. When the children finish their feather cards (which may have nothing to do with feathers!), ask them to read their cards back to you.

Ranunculus and the Feathers

Language/Social Studies/Anti-Bias

WHY we are doing this activity: to stimulate children to think about superficial appearance versus the substance of personality; to develop listening and speaking skills; to help children understand that birds need feathers to stay warm; to facilitate imaginative play and cooperation between two children through use of a two-person play station; to expand vocabulary and facilitate imaginative verbal expression.

WHAT we will need:
Flannel board
Flannel board shapes (provided on page 74; photocopy and enlarge for your use)
Felt
Glue
Markers or crayons
Scissors
Down feathers from a bird
Tail feathers from a small bird
Story: "RANUNCULUS AND THE FEATHERS" (provided)

HOW we will do it: To prepare, cut out the flannel pieces in the text pattern from felt. Tail and body feather pieces are included in case you can not find real tail and down feathers, but children are thrilled when you use the real thing—it adds an extra dimension to the story. If you are using the pattern pieces instead of real feathers, color them brightly, glue them to felt, and cover the paper side with contact paper. If you are using real tail feathers, glue the feathers onto felt and cut the pieces out. Three feathers should be sufficient. Down feathers will stick onto felt directly, but you will probably want to keep them all in a small box or sandwich bag—they are easy to lose.

"RANUNCULUS AND THE FEATHERS"

Once upon a time there was a bird named Ranunculus [put colored bird on the flannel board] and Ranunculus had the most gorgeous plumage. That means he had beautiful feathers. All the other birds [put mono-colored birds on flannel board] wanted to be Ranunculus' friend because of his gorgeous feathers. They wanted to preen him and they wanted to roost next to him and they wanted to fly with him. Ranunculus' best friend was a very plain little bird called Crest-of-Red. [Put crested bird on the flannel board.] Can you guess why she was called that? [Listen to children's answers.] Ranunculus and

Crest-of-Red would spend hours together hunting for worms and flying over fields and playing tag together.

Summer was over and the days were getting colder. All the birds had to start making their nests stronger and warmer before the snow started to fall. [Put tree piece and nests on flannel board.] They began to work busily, except Ranunculus, who hated Winter and hated work.

"Come on, Ranunculus!" Crest-of-Red said. "You have to help us build up our nests. After all, you are going to be sitting inside safe and warm when the snow comes, so it is only fair that you help us work!"

But the other birds said, "Oh, Crest-of-Red, Ranunculus doesn't have to help us work on the nests. He's such a beautiful bird with such gorgeous feathers! He can take a rest and we'll build up his nest for him." They said this because they all wanted Ranunculus to be their best friend. Well, Crest-of-Red grumbled frightfully because she didn't think it was right, but there was nothing she could do. [Pretend to grumble and encourage the children to join you.]

The snow did come, and the birds all sat in their nests, safe and warm except when they went out to look for food. [Put birds in nests.] But Ranunculus hated going out in the cold, and said that because he had such beautiful feathers, and because he didn't want to ruffle them, that the other birds should get his food for him. Since they all wanted to be the friend of such a beautiful bird, they did. Crest-of-Red grumbled frightfully again because she didn't think it was right. [Pretend to grumble and invite the children to join in.]

"Ranunculus, pretty is as pretty does," Crest-of-Red said. "It is not right for you to let everyone do your work for you just because you happen to have beautiful feathers. It is fine to like your beautiful feathers and to feel good about them. But mark my words, it is not a good thing to be lazy and do nothing just because you are beautiful." But Ranunculus wasn't listening—he was too busy preening his gorgeous feathers.

Winter passed and spring came. One day Ranunculus and Crest-of-Red were out playing when they saw some big, black, shiny berries on a berry tree. [Put berry bush up on board.]

Crest-of-Red said, "Don't eat those berries, Ranunculus. I've never seen that kind before and I don't know if they're good for birds." But Ranunculus was very hungry and thought that just one wouldn't hurt, so he popped one into his beak and swallowed it.

Well, that night he began to feel very, very ill. His stomach hurt, and he felt hot and cold at the same time. But that wasn't the worst thing. The worst thing was that his feathers started to fall out. One by one his beautiful feathers fell out, and there was nothing he could do about it. [Take feathers off if feathers are detachable or put pink bird up.] Ranunculus was lucky that he'd only eaten one of the bad berries. Gradually he began to feel better, but his feathers didn't grow back. One day he tried to go out, but there was an icy wind blowing that day. [Put wind up.] Ranunculus had no feathers to keep him warm, and the wind was much too cold when it blew on his bare, pink skin. Sadly, he went back inside his nest again. But, finally, a hot summer's day arrived, and still Ranunculus' feathers had not grown back. [Take nests down and put birds up on branches of tree.] He went out to roost on a branch with the other birds but when they saw his pink skin and that he had no feathers, they said, "Oooh—get away from us you horrid thing. You look different from us and we don't want you near us." And they tried to peck him hard with their beaks (Ask the children: What do you think of the other birds for doing that? How do you think it made Ranunculus feel?)

He said, "But it is me, Ranunculus. I'm the same bird I always was—I just look different." But the other birds wouldn't listen. They nipped and bit his feet until he was forced to fly off the perch. Ranunculus flew to his nest and cried bitterly. But there was one bird who was still his friend no matter what he looked like. Can you guess who it was? (Let children answer.)

Crest-of-Red put her wing around him [put Crest-of-Red next to Ranunculus] and said, "Never mind, Ranunculus. I know those birds really hurt your feelings, but they're not worth having as friends anyway. I still like you, just the way I always have. Let's go out and look for worms." And after Ranunculus pulled himself together, that is just what they did.

There are several ways to make Ranunculus. One way, if you do not have enough real feathers, is to color the paper patterns that simulate feathers, cut them out and glue them onto felt. When you tell the story, start out with these pieces on top of Ranunculus' pink body, and then take them off when he loses his feathers. The other method is to use real feathers. Downy feathers will cling directly to the pink felt of Ranunculus' body. If you're using tail feathers that do not cling, glue them onto a piece of felt first. Children love this story even more when you use real feathers.

If you are using paper pieces instead of real feathers, use this pattern twice—once to cut one whole body out of pink felt, and once to cut three separate "feather" pieces which you will color and glue onto felt.

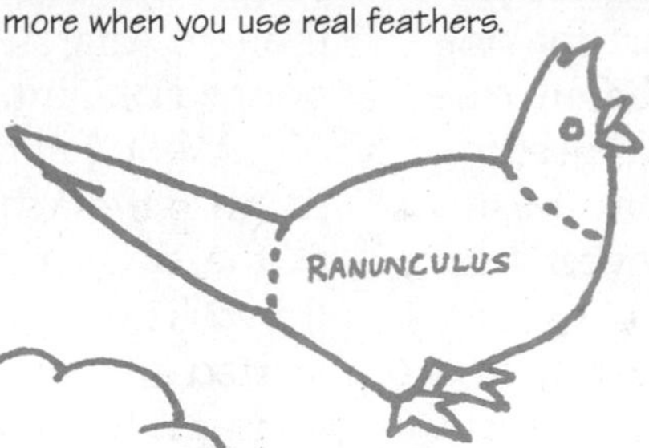

RANUNCULUS

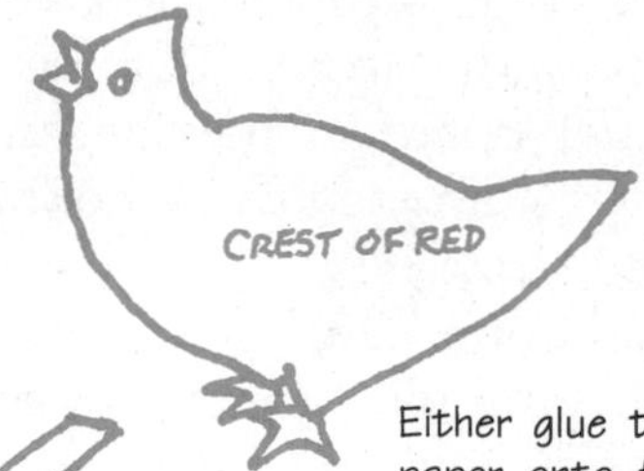

CREST OF RED

Either glue this paper onto felt and color a crest of red on it, or simply cut this shape out of felt and color a crest of red directly onto the fabric.

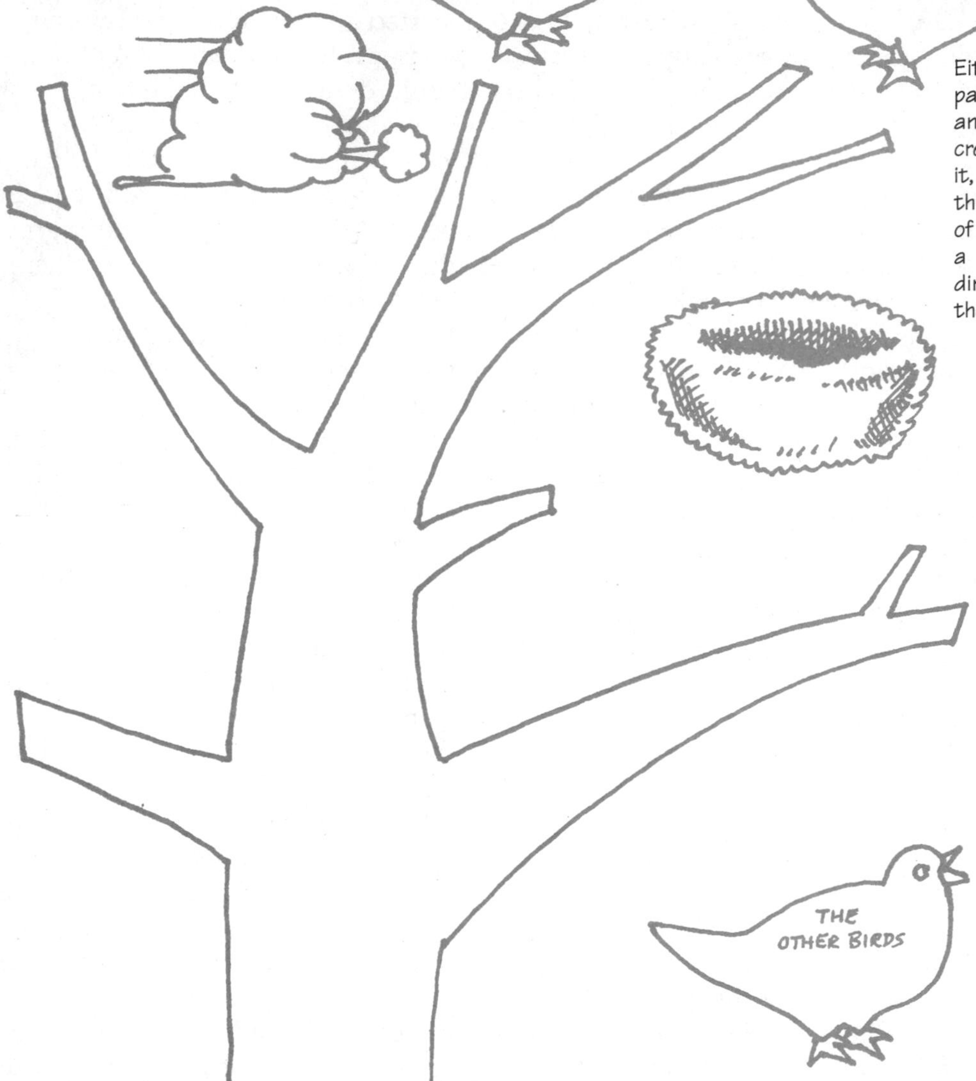

THE OTHER BIRDS

Cut out three birds using this pattern. Make each one of them a different color felt.

Blackberry bush
If you do not have time to cut out the exact outline, just cut a circular shape around it. Color this paper and glue onto felt.

A few weeks after this, Ranunculus' feathers began to grow back in again, and they were even more beautiful and gorgeous than before. When the other birds saw them, they wanted to be his friend again.

"Come and roost by me, Ranunculus!" they would say. "Is there anything I can do for you? Let me preen you!" What do you think Ranunculus answered? (Let children answer.) He and Crest-of-Red stayed best friends forever, and Ranunculus never again got carried away by his beautiful feathers and that's the end of the story.

Discussion questions: Were the other birds good friends to Ranunculus? Why do you think that? Was Crest-of-Red a good friend? Why do you think that?

Talk about people and what is on the outside—clothes, hair, skin color, eye color, jewelry—and what is on the inside—the special things your children do and say. Ask: Which do you think is more important about who a person is? Have you ever seen people be mean to someone because of how that person looked? Tell me about it. What did you think about it?

VOCABULARY:
Plumage
Ill
Gradually
Pulled himself together
Preen

After you tell the story and discuss it, show your students where the flannel board and pieces will be and invite them to use the materials.

What Is in a Bird's Nest?
Science

WHY we are doing this project: to enable children to observe the fact that birds use feathers they have molted to line their nests and make them warmer.

WHAT we will need:
Birds' nests (as many as you can collect)

HOW we will do it: Several weeks ahead of time, ask everyone you can think of—parents, friends, and family—to keep their eyes open for empty birds' nests. Sometimes, in the fall the wind blows nests down from trees. Another idea is to contact other teachers to see if anyone has nests they will let you borrow.

If you use nests which have not been part of a collection but have been taken straight from nature, you may want to keep them outdoors for examination since birds' nests often tend to be infested with insects. (I learned this the hard way!)

To begin, invite the children to examine the inside of the nests. What do they see besides sticks? If there are feathers, what have the birds done with them to make them part of the nest? Ask the children why they think the birds used the feathers in this way. Also, discuss the fact that when feathers become loose in the skin of birds, birds pull them out so that new, stronger feathers can grow. Sometimes the feathers become so loose that they fall out by themselves. This is called *molting*.

What Does a Peacock Use Its Tail Feathers For?
Science

WHY we are doing this activity: to enable children to examine peacock feathers and to help children understand that some birds, like the peacock, use tail feathers to attract mates.

WHAT we will need:
Peacock feathers
Magnifying glasses
Book: Parsons, Alexandra, *Amazing Birds*

HOW we will do it: If your local zoo has peacocks, ask about a month ahead of time if the staff can save you any molted tail feathers. Alternatively, stores like Pier One Imports sometimes sell them, or you can call other teachers to see if anyone has a few peacock feathers which you might be able to borrow. If you cannot obtain any, use the book *Amazing Birds*. You may also be able to find other books which feature peacocks.

To begin, set out the feathers and magnifying glasses. If your feathers have come from the zoo, be sure the children wash their hands after the activity.

During an Attention Getter time, examine and discuss the photographs and illustration of peacocks in *Amazing Birds*. The end pages have wonderful close-up photographs. Read the text which describes the peacock's mating ritual and discuss it with the children. Show them the feathers and magnifying glasses and talk about how the feathers should be treated gently. Invite the children to explore the materials.

Feathers and Floating
Science

WHY we are doing this experiment: to facilitate hands-on observation of how feathers are designed to be airborne; to facilitate scientific comparison; to develop speaking and listening skills.

WHAT we will need:
  Down feathers
  Scraps of tissue paper
  Scraps of regular paper
  Small boxes
  Climber (or something elevated on which
    children can climb safely)
  Puppet

HOW we will do it: To prepare, start collecting small boxes ahead of time. Inside each one, put a down feather, a scrap of tissue paper, and a scrap of regular paper. Make your paper scraps the same size as the feather. Put your boxes near the place the children will be climbing.

During an Attention Getter time, ask the children to predict which will stay in the air longest if they toss all three into the air: a feather, a piece of tissue paper, or a piece of regular paper. Show them the small boxes and the climbing place, and let them know they can conduct the experiment from this spot. Encourage your students to watch which one hits the ground first, and which one hits the ground last. When you feel the time is right, take out your puppet, and use its personality to ask the children about the results of their experiment. Have your puppet ask questions like: "What do you notice about how long each one floats? What happens if you blow on the feather while it is floating?" Later, at the end of the day's activities, gather together as a group and talk about the feather floating science experiment. What did it tell us about how birds stay up in the air?

The Feather Song
Music/Movement/Gross Motor

WHY we are doing this project: to help children feel comfortable with their singing voices; to develop cognition through memorization of words; to help children "feel" music; to help children express themselves through creative movement.

WHAT we will need:
  Down feathers
  Song: "THE FEATHER SONG" (to the
    tune of "Twinkle Twinkle Little Star"

  "THE FEATHER SONG"
  Feather floats without a sound,
  floating slowly to the ground.
  A gust of wind comes by one day,
  whirls that feather right away.
  Feather, feather in the air,
  blown away without a care.

HOW we will do it: To begin, sing the song yourself a few times, and encourage the children to join you as and when they become familiar with the words. When you feel that everyone knows the song, pass a down feather to everyone. Sing the first two lines as you hold the feather up and drop it. For "A gust of wind," blow on your feather after it lands on the ground. After you have done this a few times, stand up and spread out in a wide open space. Encourage children to become feathers. See how slowly and lazily you can float to the ground during the song's first two lines, and then see how briskly you can whirl away when the wind comes. Another variation is to divide yourselves into wind and feathers. The "wind people" blow and the "feather people" whirl away. Then switch roles.

Do Feathers Absorb Water? (Part 1)
Science

WHY we are doing this project: to help children discover through hands-on experimentation the water resistant property of feathers; to develop fine motor skills; to develop vocabulary.

WHAT we will need:
    Feathers—contour and down
    Small dishes or containers (the plastic containers from frozen foods are perfect)
    Eyedroppers
    Magnifying glasses
    Water
Demonstration:
    Sponge
    Paper towel

HOW we will do it: To prepare, set out the materials on the activity table by putting one feather in each container, and setting an eyedropper nearby. Put small containers of water all around the table so that all children will have easy access to them. Lay the magnifying glasses out as well.

During an Attention Getter time, take an eye dropper and drip a few drops of water onto a sponge. What happened to the water? Do the same with a paper towel and ask the children again what happened to the water. Use the word *absorb* as you discuss your observations. Show the children the materials on the project table, and ask them to predict whether or not the feathers will absorb water. Invite them to use the materials to find out, and as they explore, ask what they discover. What do the water drops do after they are dropped onto feathers? After you have facilitated discussion about this, say: "When water drops bounce off something, or just sit on top like the drops do on the feathers, that thing is called *water resistant*. That means the feather *resists* the water. It does not absorb it; it does not let the water soak in." Use the words *resist* and *water resistant* when you mention the experiment during the day. See Part 2 for a related language project.

Language Chart of Scientific Findings (Part 2)
Language

WHY we are doing this experiment: to develop speaking and reading skills.

Make this chart in conjunction with the feather/water experiment above to develop two components of language arts by recording the children's findings.

WHAT we will need:
    Butcher paper
    Markers (two different colors)

HOW we will do it: To prepare, pin or tape up your butcher paper at the children's eye level. As your students drop the water onto their feathers, ask them what the water does. Write down their observations or, if you are working with older students, invite them to write their observations onto the chart themselves, and facilitate this process as necessary. If you write the words yourself, use quotation marks and write down each child's name next to his or her comment. Alternate the marker colors for each sentence so that the children can easily identify each one. Sometimes children are slow to make observations. If this is the case, you can make comments of your own initially, as you watch them experiment, for example, "That water drop just rolled right off, didn't it? How does the feather feel now, if you touch it? I notice that other water drop is just sitting right on top of the feather. What happened when you dribbled other water drops on it?" This sparks conversation and also reinforces key vocabulary. Save the chart to compare your scientific results with the results of the feather and oil experiment.

More Proof That Feathers Are Water Resistant

Science

WHY we are doing this experiment: to provide children with another method of discovering that feathers are water resistant and to reinforce the words *resist* and *water resistant*.

WHAT we will need:
    Clear plastic cups
    Feathers (contour and down)
    Magnifying glasses
    Small pitchers of water
    Trays or sensory table
    Newspaper
Demonstration:
    Scrap of paper towel
    Scrap of wax paper

HOW we will do it: Spread several layers of newspaper under trays on your activity table or under your sensory table. Set out your materials.
    During an Attention Getter time, have a cup of water and the scraps of paper handy.

One of the primary purposes of this demonstration is to emphasize that the objects (in the children's case, feathers) should be plunged in water for only a second. Valuable information can also be learned by immersing the feathers into water for many seconds or even minutes, but the water-resistant property of the feathers will only be apparent when they are plunged quickly in and out of the water.
    Show the children your scrap of paper towel and ask them to predict what will happen to it if you dip it very quickly in and out of the water. Conduct this experiment and discuss the results. Ask the children to predict what will happen to the wax paper scrap if you dip it very quickly in and out of the water and follow the above procedure. Show the children the feathers on the activity table and encourage their predictions about what will happen if they conduct the same experiment with them.
    Invite them to explore the materials, and as they do so, encourage them to examine the feathers with the magnifying glasses after taking them out of the water. How does the feather feel when they brush it with their fingertips? Ask them to notice whether all parts of the feather feel and look the same. What do they notice about what is clinging to the feather? What happens when a feather is dipped into the water for a long time? Is there a difference in results when the experiment is conducted on a tail feather, a smaller contour feather, and a feather which is all down? What happens if you use very warm or very cold water; does it change the results? Together, discuss the children's findings.

Feathers and Oil

Science/Social Studies

WHY we are doing this project: to facilitate hands-on observation of the effects of oil on feathers; to encourage children to think about the effects of our way of living on the environment; to develop reading and writing skills.

WHAT we will need:
- Feathers (downy and smooth)
- Vegetable oil
- Popsicle sticks
- Small plastic containers
- Butcher paper
- Markers (two different colors)

Adult supervised:
- Motor oil

HOW we will do it: To prepare, put small amounts of vegetable oil in small containers and arrange them around the activity table so that all the children will have easy access to them. In the rest of the containers, put feathers and Popsicle sticks. Ask the children again about what they discovered with the feathers and water. Show them the oil, and ask them to predict what will happen if oil is dropped onto feathers. Show them, without conducting the experiment, how to dip the sticks into the oil, and to dribble drops of it onto their feathers. As the children experiment, ask: "What happens to the feathers? How do they feel and look after the oil is dropped on them?" Using the same procedure as in the language activity for the water absorption experiment, print the children's observations on the chart or invite them to do so.

When the children are finished experimenting, show them all the oil-sodden feathers and ask, "What do you think about whether these feathers would keep a bird warm? What do you think about whether a bird could fly with feathers like this?" At the end of the day's projects, gather together as a group, and read or have the children read the charts from both the feather/water experiment and the feather/oil experiment. Talk about the differences in the effects of the two substances on feathers. Talk to the children about oil spills. Is it the same kind of oil? As an adult-facilitated group project, let the children each drop some motor oil on a feather. Does it have the same effect on the birds' feathers as the vegetable oil? Discuss the photographs and read selected parts from either *Oil Spill* or *Oil Spills*. (See literature list.)

What Is Real? What Is Not?
Anti-Bias/Multicultural/Language

WHY we are doing this activity: to help children examine stereotypical images of Native people for purposes of comparison to photographs of real, modern Native people; to encourage children to be critical thinkers; to encourage children to question what they see in the world around them; to develop speaking and listening skills.

Food for thought: You may find that the illustrations of Native people in the majority of children's Thanksgiving books portray them with feathers in their hair, and often within a book, every Native person has the exact same clothes and headdress. The fact is that there are over 350 separate Native societies, each with its own traditional dress and customs.

WHAT we will need: In order to do this activity, you will need stereotypical images of Native people. It is a good idea to start collecting these well in advance of when you facilitate the project. You can ask friends, neighbors, or parents to help you look. Some likely sources are: books, magazines, newspapers, and children's Thanksgiving books. Thanksgiving and also Halloween can be good times for this activity since stereotypical images of Native people are particularly abundant then.

You will also need some photographs of Native people for comparison and discussion. Newspapers and magazines sometimes provide these. There is a wonderful book called *Sharing Our Worlds*, and you might also want to send a request for materials to Oyate. Pemmican Publications is another source of good children's books by and about Native people. See the literature list for addresses.

HOW we will do it: Pin up your stereotypical images together on the wall, and nearby, pin up all your photographs. Gather the children together and ask them what they notice about the people in each group of pictures. For example, in my stereotypical pictures, all of the people wear feather headdresses. In the photographs of real people, only some people wear a few feathers in their hair. In the stereotypical pictures, all the feathers stand straight up. In the real pictures, some of the feathers hang down. In the stereotypical pictures, all the people look the same. In the photographs, everyone looks different. In stereotypical pictures, the people are usually doing something like carrying corn, stringing beads or erecting a teepee. In my photographs, the people are doing things like playing soccer, giving a speech or leading a march. In stereotypical pictures, the people live in teepees that all look the same. In my photographs, the people live in houses that look different. Also consider: In the stereotypical drawings, are Native people portrayed as savage, stupid, or strange? Think about cartoons or cowboy movies you may have seen on television, and ask the children if they have seen them, too. Were Native people portrayed as inarticulate savages who grunted one-syllable words? These are the kinds of issues you can raise. If your images are in books, leaf through them and discuss the pictures with the children. Modern children's Thanksgiving books can be a particularly rich source of stereotypical images.

Feather Boas
Dramatic Play

Scour used clothes stores for some old feather boas, or if funds allow, order a few from school supply catalogs. Put them in your dramatic play area with other dress-up clothes, and provide a mirror.

Literature

Symbol Key: *Multicultural
+Minimal diversity
No symbol: no diversity or no people

Berger, M. (1994). *Oil spill*. New York: Harper Collins.

Kuipers, B. J. (1991). *American Indian reference books for children & young adults*. Englewood, CO: Libraries Unlimited.

Mainwaring, J. (1989). *My feather*. New York: Doubleday.

Patent Hinshaw, D. (1992). *Feathers*. New York: Cobblehill Books. (Leaf through the pictures and discuss them.)

Plain, F. (1989). *Eagle feather*. Winnipeg, Manitoba, Canada: Pemmican.

Pringle, L. (1993). *Oil spills*. New York: Morrow Jr. Books. (This book and Melvin Berger's *Oil Spill* both have excellent photographs of how oil spills affect birds.)

Sharing our worlds. (1980). Seattle, WA: Daybreak Star Press.

Through Indian eyes—The native experience in books for children. (1992). Philadelphia: New Society.

Excellent reference materials for this subject:

Through Indian Eyes—The Native Experience in Books for Children, New Society Publishers, 4527 Springfield Ave., Philadelphia, PA 19143.

American Indian Reference Books for Children & Young Adults, Barbara J. Kuipers, Libraries Unlimited, Inc., P.O. Box 3988, Englewood, CO 80155-3988.

Extenders

Science: Buy some fake feathers from a craft store or order them from a school supply catalog. Put out real feathers, fake feathers, and magnifying glasses. Can the children see which ones are fake and which are real? Why is it so easy to tell the difference?

Science: When you drop the water and oil on the feathers, examine a single drop of each on a feather by using a magnifying glass. What do you see?

Science: When you make feathers float in the air, toss up a large, smooth contour feather and a down feather at the same time. Which stays in the air longer? Why?

Language/Art: Collect bird and nature magazines and as a group, write your own bird book. Make a large, blank book with large pieces of construction paper by folding the pieces over and stapling on the fold. As a group, glue pictures of birds on the pages and write about them. Then read the book together.

HOT, WARM, AND COLD

Attention Getter: Find something cold, like an aluminum or silver bowl, or an ice cube wrapped in a paper towel. Gather the children together and ask them to close their eyes. Let them know that you are going to come around and put two things on their skin, and that you want them to notice how these two things feel different. Walk around the group and touch the cold object to the each child's hand, and then touch your own warm hand to each child's hand. After everyone has felt both sensations, discuss them. How did each one feel? How were they different? Let the children know that over the next few days you are going to be experimenting with hot, warm, and cold.

What Conducts Heat and Cold?
Science

WHY we are doing this project: to help children discover which materials conduct heat and cold best; to help children develop self-esteem and a sense of autonomy through use of a one-person work station; to develop reading and writing skills.

WHAT we will need:
Plastic knife
Wooden spoon
Metal utensil with a plastic handle
Wooden Popsicle stick
Metal paper clips
Bowl
Ice cubes
Water
Heating plate (yogurt maker or griddle on lowest setting)
Chart (sample provided on page 85)
Wooden clothespins
Butcher paper
Marker
Aluminum foil
"One person may be here" sign (provided on page 3; photocopy and enlarge for your use)

HOW we will do it: To prepare, use the sample outline in this text to make two separate graph charts on butcher paper. Place the graph on the wall near the place where your activity table will be. On the table, place the plastic, metal, wooden, and plastic-handled utensils, as well as the marker. String your metal paper clips together into one long strand (not a circular chain). Set out materials for a cold conducting experiment the first day, and then set out materials for the heat conducting experiment the next. If you like, set out all materials together near the end of the unit.

To facilitate the cold conducting experiment, put ice cubes and water in a bowl, and set it on the table with the utensils and a marker for drawing on the graph chart. During an Attention Getter time, tell the children that *to conduct* means to carry, and that they are going to find out which things on the activity table will carry the cold from the ice water by exploring the things on the table. Talk about the "One person may be here" sign.

Point out the graph chart and read/interpret the pictures. Show the children the marker, and then show them the "check" symbol and the "X" symbol. Which one means that something did carry the cold? Which one means that it did not? Let the children know that they can record the results of the science experiment on this chart. Hold up each object and ask the children to predict whether the utensil will feel cold in their hands when they hold it in the ice cubes. If the children record the results on the graph, write their names next to their symbols or invite them to do so.

Repeat the above procedure with a heating plate after covering its surface with aluminum foil. (Heating plates can be yogurt makers or griddles set on the very lowest setting. Set your heating plate to the lowest setting before facilitating your activity to make sure it is not too hot.) Talk to the children ahead of time about what will happen if they put their fingers directly on the heating plate. I have used one of these devices many times for melted crayon projects, and have never experienced a child burning herself or himself. The wooden clothespins can be used to hold objects. Show your students how to fasten a clothespin around each object to hold on to the heating plate, and ask them what could happen if an object does conduct heat, and they are holding it without using a clothespin.

Hold up each object and ask the children to predict whether it will conduct heat. Encourage the children to find out if their predictions are true. Talk to them about their findings and invite them to record their results on the chart. What happens when they hold the plastic-handled utensil on the heating plate? Encourage them to hold the end of the paper clip strand on the heating plate. Is the heat conducted from paper clip to paper clip? After the children have had time to make their discoveries about heat and cold conductors, compare the two graphs. Are there any surprises?

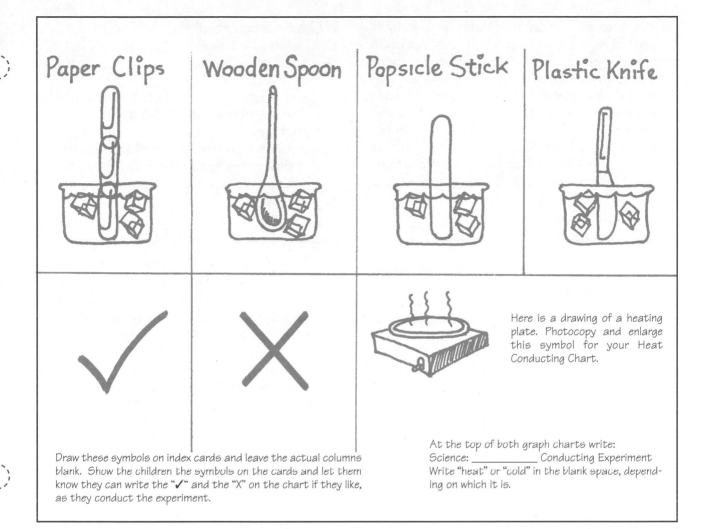

Paper Clips | Wooden Spoon | Popsicle Stick | Plastic Knife

Draw these symbols on index cards and leave the actual columns blank. Show the children the symbols on the cards and let them know they can write the "✓" and the "X" on the chart if they like, as they conduct the experiment.

Here is a drawing of a heating plate. Photocopy and enlarge this symbol for your Heat Conducting Chart.

At the top of both graph charts write:
Science: _____ Conducting Experiment
Write "heat" or "cold" in the blank space, depending on which it is.

Ice Cube Trick

Science

WHY we are doing this activity: to allow children to engage in a hands-on activity which allows them to observe that salt lowers the freezing point of water, and to develop fine motor skills.

The facts of the matter: In conducting this experiment, the surface of the ice cubes melts a little because of the lowered freezing point. Then, the water washes the salt away and the cubes refreeze. When they refreeze, the ice cubes stick to each other. It happens in a matter of seconds, but this child-initiated experiment is a fun way for children to experience this phenomenon.

WHAT we will need:
Trays or sensory table
Containers
Ice cubes
Salt
Salt shakers
Cooler

HOW we will do it: Ahead of time, make *lots* of ice cubes. It is better to make them in ice cube trays rather than to buy bags of ice, because the flat surfaces of rectangular cubes stick to each other easily, whereas commercial ice is usually cylinder shaped. On the activity table, set out the trays and salt shakers. During an Attention Getter time tell the children that you are all going to do a special trick. At the activity table, encourage them to try sticking ice cubes to each other without salt. Ask them to predict what will happen if they sprinkle salt on their cubes and then try sticking them together. Invite them to conduct this experiment. What happens? Depending on the cognitive level of your children, explain that the salt lowers the freezing point for the ice cube, and it melts a little and then refreezes. When it refreezes, the cubes freeze together. What happens when you try to pick up several stuck-together cubes by picking up one? Replace the ice cubes as necessary.

The Balloon Trick
Science

WHY we are doing this experiment: to develop reading skills and to enable children to observe that when cold and warm air meet, the air contracts and produces suction.

WHAT we will need:
Inflated balloons
Small paper cups
Ice water
Hot water from faucet (as hot as it can be and still be safe for children)
Pitchers
Activity sign (format provided below; photocopy and enlarge for your use)
Tubs or sensory table
Newspaper

Safety tip: Some brands of rubber balloons require very hot water for this experiment to work. If you determine that the water is too hot for your children, conduct a demonstration for them yourself. Three- and young four-year-olds will probably not have the necessary coordination to slap the cup on the balloon quickly. You may need to assist them or demonstrate the experiment for them.

Pour a little hot water into your paper cup. Pour cold water over your balloon. Put the cup upside down on the balloon... FAST! What happens when you hold the balloon like this?

HOW we will do it: Spread several layers of newspaper under your activity area. Use the suggested format in the text to make an activity sign, and post it by the work area. Put ice water and the hot water in pitchers and place them in the tubs or sensory table with the balloons. Take the ice out right before the children approach the work area. Encourage the children to follow the suggestions of the activity sign and to explore the materials. If appropriate, explain that when the cold balloon cools the warm air inside the cup, the air *contracts* or shrinks and this sucks the cup onto the balloon. That is why it sticks on for a few seconds.

The Frozen Water Experiment
Science

WHY we are doing this activity: to enable children to discover that frozen water expands in volume; to show that water particles move away from each other when they freeze.

WHAT we will need:
Small plastic containers with lids
Pitchers of water
Freezer
Tray
Mop or rag
Sticky labels
Markers
Sensory tub or table
Pitchers of warm water
Toy boats

HOW we will do it: To prepare, clear out space in your freezer. Place the containers on the trays, and set the pitchers nearby on a table. It is a good idea to have the table near the freezer so that you do not have too far to carry them. Encourage the children to write their names on sticky labels and to press their name labels onto their containers. Then have your students pour

water into them until the water reaches the brims. Have the children set the lids on top, without screwing them on. Ask the children to predict what will happen to the water if it is left in the freezer for a day or two. Carry the tray carefully to the freezer and set the containers inside. If you can find a safe way to do it, put a chair near the freezer and let the children take turns climbing up to help you arrange the containers inside. Fill to the top any containers that have spilled in the process, and use the mop or rag to clean up spills on the floor. Ask the children if they think the lids will still be resting on the brims of the containers when you take the water out in a day or two.

When you are ready to take the containers out, gather interested children together. (Make sure all the water is frozen solid.) What happened to the lids? Why? Explain that freezing makes water particles move away from each other. A *particle* is a tiny, tiny amount of water. Tap the word on your nose or head. Blink the word. Tap it with your foot. When the particles move away from each other, they make frozen crystals that are bigger than the water particles were. The bigger crystals take more room, and so the frozen water got bigger and pushed the lids up.

Show the children the sensory tub or table and the warm pitchers of water. Invite them to pour the warm water over the containers and slide the frozen water out. Put the plastic boats in the tubs or sensory table, and suggest they pretend the ice pieces are icebergs.

Making Popsicles
Science/Snack/Small Group Project

WHY we are doing this project: to build on information learned in the previous activity; to help children understand the scientific method of *serial dilutions*; to learn what a *control* is; to familiarize children with fraction cup measurements; to build self-esteem by enabling children to make their own snacks.

WHAT we will need:
Apple juice

Grape juice
Small paper cups
¼ cup measuring cup
½ cup measuring cup
1 cup measuring cup
Containers (large enough to hold 1 cup liquid)
Cardboard
Popsicle sticks
Water
Small pitchers
Markers
Masking tape
Tray
Freezer space

Preparation:
Skewer
Scissors

HOW we will do it: To prepare, cut circles out of cardboard which will sit on top of each paper cup. Use the skewer to poke a hole in the middle of each one so that a Popsicle stick can be inserted into the middle of the cardboard, and stand straight up as the juice freezes.

Tear off masking tape strips and stick them onto the edge of the table. Put the markers next to them. Set out small pitchers of juice, the Popsicle sticks, the paper cups, and the cardboard lids on the activity table.

During an Attention Getter time, explain what the materials are for. Invite the children to pour juice into their cups, and place the cardboard circles, with Popsicle sticks stuck in the middle, on top. They can choose between apple or grape juice. Show them the markers and masking tape strips and let them know they can use them to write their names to label their cups. They may also draw a picture to indicate whether the cup is full of grape or apple juice. (If your children are not writing yet, write their names for them.) Have the children put their prepared juice cups on the tray and ask them to predict what will happen to the juice if it is left in the freezer for a day or two. Ask the children what they think the juices will look like when they come out of the freezer. Will they all be the same?

Tell interested children that you are going to take the experiment a little farther. Have them take turns helping you measure the following amounts in the appropriate measuring cups and pouring the combinations into the larger containers: In one container, pour ¾ cup grape juice and ¼ cup water. Label the cup: "¾ juice" and draw a picture to symbolize the contents or have a child do this. Pour ½ cup water and ½ cup grape juice into the next cup, following the same procedure as before. Pour ¼ cup grape juice into the last cup with ¾ cup water. Be sure to label each cup. Tell the children that what you just did was to make *serial dilutions*, and point to each cup as you talk about it. You diluted the water with juice in graduated amounts; from a lot of juice and a little water (¾), to half juice and half water (½), to a lot of water and a little juice (¼). Encourage the children to look into the cups so that they can see the difference in color. Next, pour only water into one cup, and tell the children that this is the *control*. In all the other cups, you changed the amount of juice you put in. In the control—the cup with all water and no juice—you are going to freeze it just like the other cups, but it does not have any of the things you changed: juice. That is why it is called the control.

While the freezer is doing its work, check the serial dilution liquids every now and then by letting the children jiggle the Popsicle sticks. Which seems to be freezing the fastest? Are they freezing in the same way? (Liquid with more juice freezes as a slush; water forms ice on top and the rest freezes later.) Take the four large cups out after forty-five minutes or so and let the children inspect them. Compare them to the control and to each other. What do they notice about how the different fluids froze? Did the cold of the freezer treat them all the same?

After the Popsicles have been in the freezer for several hours, take them out and let the children enjoy their frozen fruity snacks. As they eat them, talk about the sequence of steps they followed to make them: choosing which juice to use, pouring it into the cup, putting the cardboard and Popsicle stick on, writing names and so forth. Reflect on the predictions made before the experiment, and compare them to the actual results.

Cleaning Water: Heat, Cold, and Vapor

Science

WHY we are doing this project: to enable children to discover that heat causes water to turn into vapor and that cold causes the vapor to turn back into water.

WHAT we will need:
- Soil or dirt
- Large spoons
- Small paper cups
- Clear cling wrap
- Ice cubes
- Bowls
- Stones (must be able to fit inside cups)
- Large empty basin
- Activity sign (format provided on page 90; photocopy and enlarge for your use)
- Masking tape

Teacher only:
- Boiling water

HOW we will do it: To prepare, tear off pieces of cling wrap which are big enough to cover the bowls you will be using. Put the ice, plastic cups, and containers of dirt with spoons on your activity table. Put a masking tape line down on the floor. The purpose of this is so that the children know to stand behind it and watch while you pour boiling water into their bowls.

During an Attention Getter time, tell the children that you are going to do a science experiment in which you make clean water out of dirty water. Talk about the fact that you are going to be using boiling water, and the importance of staying behind the masking tape line.

Together, interpret/read the activity sign. Ask the children to predict what will happen if they follow the sign's suggestions. Show them the materials on the table and invite them to do so. As the children assemble their experiments, take the bowls they hand you and as they watch from behind the masking tape line, peel back a little part of the cling wrap. Pour boiling water into the bowl until the water level is close to the rim, but not higher than the cup rim. Pull the cling wrap back over the bowl again and make sure the edges are secure against the outside of it. Ask the children what they see happening. Introduce the word *vapor*. What do they notice about what is collecting on the underside of the cling wrap? (The steam will condense into water.) Encourage the children to watch the process, but let it be okay if they get tired and wander off. After the boiling water has cooled substantially, invite each child to peel off the cling wrap and hold it over the cup. What happens? How does the water in the cup look compared to the dirty water? What do they notice about what was left behind when the hot water turned into vapor?

Can You Sink an Ice Cube?

Science

WHY we are doing this activity: to enable children to learn more about why ice cubes float; to provide a sensory experience; to develop self-esteem and a sense of autonomy through use of a one-person work station.

The facts of the matter: Most things contract as they get colder, but water expands if it gets colder than 39°F. It expands and increases in volume by about 9 percent. In unfrozen water, the molecules stay close together and move about quickly and at random. As water freezes, molecules move farther apart and more slowly, and become arranged in patterns. This expansion makes ice lighter than water, which is why it floats.

WHAT we will need:
- Magnifying glasses
- Ice cubes
- Tub of water
- "One person may be here" sign (provided on page 3; photocopy and enlarge for your use)

What happens when you spoon dirt into a bowl , put a cup in the middle , put stones in the cup , put cling wrap over the top of the bowl , put ice cubes over the cup , and ask your teacher to pour hot water into the bowl?

HOW we will do it: Set the tub of water on a small table, and add several ice cubes to it. Put the magnifying glass alongside it. At Attention Getter time, ask the children to predict whether or not they will be able to sink an ice cube. Next, ask them what they see in the room which might help them conduct this experiment. Discuss the "One person may be here" sign and what it means. As each child approaches the table to explore the materials, comment on how the ice cubes bob back up every time. Why? Invite the children to use the magnifying glass to examine the ice cubes. What do they notice about what is trapped inside the cubes? (Air bubbles.) Is this another clue about why the cubes float? Be prepared to replace ice cubes as they melt.

Making a Heat Trap
Science

WHY we are doing this activity: to enable children to harness the sun's heat; to help children develop self-esteem by making their own sun trap; to facilitate an understanding that certain materials attract more sun rays than others; to develop cognition by remembering the sequence of events; to develop fine motor skills.

WHAT we will need:
    Hot, sunny day
    Shoe boxes (or other boxes of
        similar size)
    Aluminum foil
    Cling wrap
    Construction paper
        (black and white)
    Plastic cups
    Sticky labels
    Markers
    Cold water
    Several 60 ml (¼ cup) measuring cups
    Jell-O mix
Preparation:
    Scissors

HOW we will do it: To prepare, cut the boxes to create an open, topless, three-sided box. Put a masking tape line down on the floor, and set a small table near it.

You can start collecting boxes and preparing them before you do this project. If you are working with younger children, put a name label on each plastic cup; otherwise, lay out the markers and blank labels on the activity table and have the children label their own cups during the experiment. Set out on your activity table the open boxes, sheets of aluminum foil, cling wrap, plastic cups, cold water, and 60 ml (¼ cup) measuring cups.

Ahead of time, make a heat trap yourself by folding tin foil over the floor and three sides of the open box.

Pour 75 ml (⅓ cup) cold water into the cup and cover it with cling wrap. During an Attention Getter time, show the children the packets of Jell-O mix, and say that you feel like eating some Jell-O today. Ask your students what else, besides the Jell-O powder, you will need to make Jell-O. If you like, read out loud the instructions on the Jell-O box. Ask the children how many different ways you could heat the water for the Jell-O. Encourage as many different ideas as you can. Then tell the children that you are going to heat your water in a heat trap, and show them the one you made. Have the children accompany you as you put the cup of water and the heat trap outside in the sun. Tell them that if they would also like to heat water for their Jell-O in a heat trap, the materials are on the activity table. Some very young children may need help folding the foil over the sides of the box. Show your students the black and white construction paper and ask if anyone would like to experiment with seeing what kind of heat trap they could make by folding and taping black or white paper to their boxes instead. If no one would like to, make one of each yourself—one covered in black and one covered in white paper. As the children set their water and heat traps outside, ask them to dip their fingers in the water to take note of how cold it is, and to predict how the water will feel after it has been in the heat trap for some time.

The length of time it will take for your water to heat up depends on how hot a day it is. Even on a very hot day, you will need to add some boiling water to each cup in order for the Jell-O powder to dissolve.

After a few hours, go outside as a group and check your water. How does it feel? Encourage your students to touch the foil on their heat traps. How does it feel? Then ask them to touch the black paper and white paper on the other heat traps. How do they feel? Is there a difference in how much the cups of water were heated? Have each child carefully carry her or his cup of water inside and continue with the next part of the activity, which follows.

Making Jell-O: Hot and Cold Water
Science/Math

WHY we are doing this project: to introduce children to the concepts of dissolving and gelling; to help them understand the former requires hot water and the latter requires cold; to enable children to observe these processes; to familiarize children with fraction cup measurements; to promote self-esteem by enabling children to make their own snack.

WHAT we will need:
Heated water (from the previous activity)
Several ¼ cup measuring cups
Bowls of cold water
0.3 oz. Jell-O powder packets—one for every two children
Popsicle sticks
Masking tape
Plastic cups (large enough to hold 1 cup liquid)
Sensory table or tubs
Ice cube trays (in different shapes, if you like)
Food coloring
Measuring cup sign (provided on page 93; photocopy and enlarge for your use)

Preparation:
Boiling water

HOW we will do it: The day before, use food coloring and water to make colored ice cubes. There are some very interesting ice cube trays available that make all kinds of differently shaped cubes, and you may want to invest in some of these trays. When you are ready to do the activity, put the ice cubes in tubs close to the Jell-O activity table, so that students have something to do while they wait their turns to make Jell-O. Label each cup with each student's name or have the children do this themselves. Put some water on to boil and set out the bowls of cold water, Popsicle sticks; and measuring cups. Take each 0.3 oz. box of Jell-O powder and pour half into a plastic cup. You are going to pour a little boiling water into each plastic cup, so put a masking tape line down on the floor near the table. The line should be close enough so that the children can clearly see what you are doing, yet far enough away so that they are well away from the boiling water. Before you begin this part of the project, tell the children what you are going to do. Let them know that they will have to stir the Jell-O powder into the hot water. Ask: "What would happen if this hot water spilled on you?" "How can we make sure no one gets hurt by the hot water?" Listen to the children's comments, and if no one else has this idea, suggest that when the children approach the table to stir their powder and water, they can leave the cups right where they are instead of picking them up.

Have the children pour their heat trap water into the cup with the powdered Jell-O, and pour enough boiling water in to make half a cup. Ask: "If you didn't know whether this was hot or cold water, what clue would tell you which it is?" (Steam.) One by one, have the children approach your table and stir the mixture with a Popsicle stick, making sure that no one moves the cups of hot water. You will probably be able to supervise three or four children at a time. Encourage waiting children to explore the colored ice cubes in the sensory tubs. While they stir the powder and water, ask questions like: "Do you remember what our water felt

Pour **..2 two quarter cups of cold water into your jell-o cup.**

like before we put it in the heat trap? When we went to get the water, was there steam coming from it? Why do you think that was? What do you notice about this water? When you look at the powder that you're stirring, what do you see happening to it?" Use the word *dissolve* as you make your Jell-O. As the children's Jell-O powder finishes dissolving, encourage them to follow the instructions on the measuring sign, and scoop two ¼ cups cold water into their plastic cups. Let them stir their liquid some more if they would like. When everyone's Jell-O mixture is prepared, put the cups on a tray and place it in the refrigerator. Follow the instructions in regard to how long the mixture should chill.

When you all sit down to eat your snack, encourage the children to touch the firm Jell-O with their fingers. What did the cold water you added, and the cold air in the refrigerator, do to the hot Jell-O water? Explain to the children that Jell-O has *gelatin* in it, and when gelatin is

chilled, it becomes a solid. As you eat your snack, talk about your sequence of actions from making the heat traps to eating your Jell-O.

Dissolving and Melting
Science/Sensory

WHY we are doing this activity: to logically extend the previous activity by showing children what happens to powder in cold water, and what happens to gelatin in warm water; to develop speaking and listening skills.

WHAT we will need:
    Warm water (as warm as possible but still
       comfortable to the touch)
    Small bowls

Tubs
Large bowl
Trays
Chilled, firm Jell-O cubes
Small pitchers
Cold water
Jell-O powder packets
Spoons
Plastic cups
Cold water
Popsicle sticks
Puppet

HOW we will do it: To prepare, fill the tubs with the warm water, and place the Jell-O cubes in the large bowl. Put these on one end of the activity center, and on the other end, place the plastic cups and Popsicle sticks. Set out pitchers of cold water and put the Jell-O powder and popsicle sticks in small bowls next to them.

During an Attention Getter time, ask the children if they remember how you made the Jell-O the previous day. Help the children remember that the Jell-O powder needed hot water to *dissolve*. If you are working with very young children, you may want to demonstrate this again quickly, before the children disperse to explore the materials. Also, help them remember that the Jell-O liquid needed cold water and cold air to gel. Ask them to predict what will happen if they try the opposite— putting cold Jell-O cubes in warm water, and Jell-O powder in cold water. Ask the children what they see in the room which might help them conduct this experiment. Invite them to use the Popsicle sticks to stir the Jell-O powder in the cold water. What happens? What happens to the Jell-O cubes in the warm water? Discuss!

After an appropriate amount of time, bring out your puppet to ask the children what they are doing. Have your puppet ask questions about what the children are doing now as well as how they made Jell-O the day before, and how they heated the water for the Jell-O. Examples: (Puppet sees a child mixing Jell-O powder with cold water.) "Oooh—Nishi! You're making Jell-O. When will it be ready to eat? Can I have some?" (Puppet sees Jell-O cube dissolving in warm water.) "Martha, why

is that Jell-O making your water red?" "Somebody told me you had a Jell-O snack yesterday. What did you do to make it?"

Aluminum Foil Mittens
Science

WHY we are doing this project: to build on the knowledge acquired in the sun trap experiment; to facilitate the discovery that heat travels in waves and will bounce off certain surfaces (in this case, aluminum foil); to develop fine motor skills.

WHAT we will need:
Aluminum foil
Marker
Scissors
Glue (in very small containers)
Cotton swabs
Bottle of sun block
Hot, sunny day

HOW we will do it: To prepare, trace one of your children's hands a few days in advance. Use this to cut a mitten shape out of foil, but make the shape larger, since the children will need room to glue around the edges. Each child will need four pieces—two for each hand.

Make aluminum foil mittens for yourself by tracing your hand, cutting out mitten shapes a little bigger, gluing around the edges, pressing them together, and letting them dry. On your activity day, set out the children's aluminum foil mitten shapes, glue, and glue brushes on an activity table. During an Attention Getter time, put on your aluminum foil mittens and ask the children to predict what will happen if you hold your mittens near your face while you are out in the sun. Ask the children what they see in the room which would help them make their own mittens and try this experiment for themselves. Tell them that you only put glue around the edges of your mittens because you wanted space for your hands. When the glue in the mittens has dried a few hours later, go outside together with your mittens on and invite the children to hold the mittens out. How do their faces feel? Talk again about how the heat waves from the sun bounce off the aluminum foil and into their faces, and compare your predictions before the experiment with the actual results.

Hold up the bottle of sun block and ask the children what it is and what it is used for. If necessary, explain that too many sun rays are bad for the skin and that sun block does just what it sounds like—it *blocks* the sun. Ask the children what would happen if they were out in the sun for a long time with no sun block. (My experience has been that most children know all about sunburn!)

What Is Dry Ice?

Language/Math

WHY we are doing this activity: to give children a chance to observe two properties of solid carbon dioxide (description follows); to facilitate comparison of regular ice and dry ice; to familiarize children with time; to develop all components of language arts: speaking, listening, reading, and writing.

The facts of the matter: Dry ice is carbon dioxide in a solid state. The only amount of water in it is actually three parts water per million parts carbon dioxide. Dry ice is 100° below zero, and is very dangerous to touch. Dry ice goes from a liquid to a gas so quickly that we do not see the liquid. When dry ice melts, it leaves nothing behind.

Young children will not understand or care about some of these facts, but they can grasp the idea that the fog that comes off dry ice is the result of the cold liquid meeting the warm air, just as warm breath is visible on a very cold day. There are quite a few concepts and activities included in the project below. Depending on the age and readiness of your children, you may choose to omit a few of the

processes in the course of the experiment. I have included them all in the activity description so that you have the option. Also, even if you choose not to do a particular part of the project, my descriptions may give you ideas for other directions in which you would like to take the activity.

WHAT we will need:
    One block of regular ice
    Two pieces of dry ice (one about the same size as the regular ice block)
    Two pans
    Large plastic jar or clear plastic box (anything under which the dry ice can be placed and still be visible such as a supermarket plastic cake covering)
    Masking or duct tape
    Grape juice
    Large pan
    Ladle
    Plastic cups
    Blank sheets of paper
    Butcher paper (three pieces)
    Markers (two different colors)
    Science experiment charts (format provided on page 96; adapt as needed)
Preparation:
    Scissors

HOW we will do it: Begin this as an adult-involved, circle activity. To prepare, cut one piece of butcher paper into a long banner, and write on it "Science Experiment Charts." Hang it on the wall and underneath, pin up your two butcher paper pieces, near the place where you will be having Attention Getter time. Using the symbols provided as a sample, draw and write "Dry Ice" at the head of one chart, and "Regular Ice" at the head of the other. Halfway down each chart write: "What happens when you leave ice/dry ice in the room for a time?" Using masking tape, make a small circle on the floor in which to put the dry ice, and to delineate a border the children must not cross. In a wider circle, a few feet away from where the dry ice will be, space masking-tape "X"s to indicate to the children where they may sit. Put

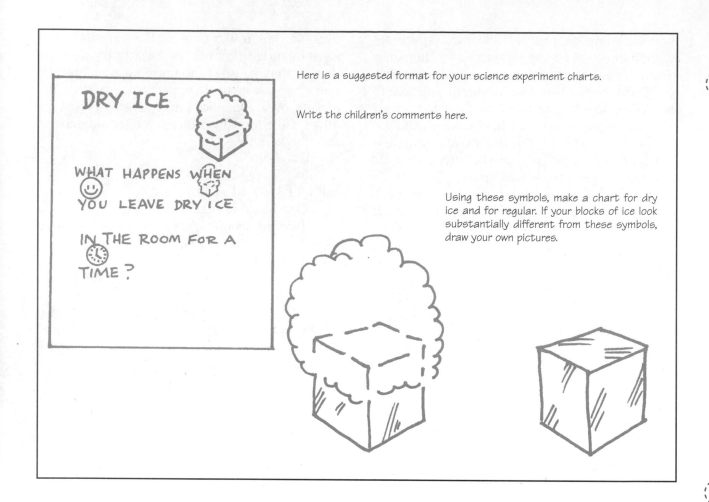

Here is a suggested format for your science experiment charts.

Write the children's comments here.

Using these symbols, make a chart for dry ice and for regular. If your blocks of ice look substantially different from these symbols, draw your own pictures.

DRY ICE

WHAT HAPPENS WHEN YOU LEAVE DRY ICE IN THE ROOM FOR A TIME?

the dry ice in the clear, plastic container, making sure not to touch it with your bare skin. Tape the container closed with masking or duct tape.

When the children are gathered for an Attention Getter time, have them sit in a very large circle. Tell them that you have something to show them that is so cold, it is 100° below zero. Let the children know that it is very important that they <u>never</u> touch dry ice, because when something is that cold, their skin could freeze onto it. Ask everyone to put their hands behind their backs since this is an "eyes only" project. Ask the children what they see in the middle of the circle, and when they mention the masking tape area, let the children know they must not reach into it after you put the dry ice there.

Walk around the circle with the dry ice so that everyone gets a good look. Put it in the middle of the circle, and ask the children what

they notice (the fog). Tell your students that this is called *dry ice* because it melts from something hard and solid so fast, that you do not see the liquid—only the fog. If you work with kindergartners, you can tell your children that dry ice is carbon dioxide in a solid state, if you think that information is appropriate.

Set out some regular ice on the floor next to the dry ice. Ask the children how the two kinds of ice are different, and write their comments about each one on the appropriate chart. Alternate marker colors to make sentences easier to distinguish, use quotation marks, and write the children's names after their remarks. Then ask: "If we let both kinds of ice sit in our room for some time, what do you predict will happen to them?" Sometimes, questions have to be asked to encourage the children to express their ideas. Some stimulating questions include: "If we let them both sit in the room for a while, what do you think we will notice about the size of both ice chunks? What do you think we will notice about how the dry ice changes? What changes do you think we will see in the regular ice? What do you think we will see in the pans that we do not see now?"

Write the children's hypotheses down on the chart in the same manner as above. Draw, or ask the children to draw, pictures of the two blocks of ice, paying particular attention to their sizes. The dry ice should be in a taped plastic container with a lid, or under a clear covering. Be sure to use the masking or duct tape to tape down the edges of the covering. Explain to the children that the dry ice must stay there. Put the dry ice up out of reach, but as it melts take it down periodically for the children to observe before putting it back up again. Supervise closely when the children are observing.

Ask the children how much time you should let the ice sit in the room, and write down on the chart the amount of time that has been decided. Talk about how many times the hands on the clock must go around before that much time has passed. When the time is up, examine both kinds of ice. Ask the children to draw new pictures of the blocks of ice and to write down their observations. Support scribbling or invented spelling. Are the blocks of ice the same sizes as before? Talk about what you see now, and compare it to the hypotheses on your experiment charts. Compare the two containers of melted ice—how are they different? (Regular ice leaves water behind after it has melted; dry ice does not. Dry ice gives off fog; regular ice does not.) Explain again that regular ice goes from a solid piece of ice to a liquid (water). Eventually, the water would evaporate into a gas. Since dry ice is so cold, it melts straight from a solid to a gas, with no water in between.

Make a special snack by putting the grape juice and dry ice in the pan. Let the children use the ladle to serve themselves making sure, once again, that they do not touch the dry ice in the juice. This makes a particularly good "witches' brew" at Halloween.

How Does Temperature Affect Melting?
Science/Sensory

WHY we are doing this activity: to facilitate hands-on experimentation with different temperatures of water to see what effect they have on ice cubes; to provide a sensory experience; to develop fine motor skills.

WHAT we will need:
   Newspaper
   Three basins or tubs
   Water
   Ice tongs
   Large spoons
   Warm water
   Cold water
   Bowls
   Bottles and scoopers
   Plastic sandwich bags
   Food coloring

HOW we will do it: The day before, use food coloring and water to make colored ice cubes. Also, place pitchers of cold water in the refrigerator overnight. When you are setting up the activity, spread newspapers on and under the activity table and put one of the following in each of the three basins or tubs: plain chilled water, chilled water with ice cubes in it, and warm water which is as warm as possible but still comfortable to the touch. In addition to the basins, set out bowls of ice cubes, ice tongs, and the large spoons. When you are all gathered for an Attention Getter time, point to your set-up, and ask the children what they see. Let them know that each of the three tubs contains water, and that they will have to feel the water in each tub to see how each one is different. Point out the bowls of ice cubes and show the children how they can put ice cubes in the sandwich bags. Wonder aloud how quickly or slowly the ice cubes will melt in each tub by using sense of touch. Encourage the children to explore the materials. Ask them what they notice about whether the ice cubes seem to melt faster in one tub than in another. Ask them why they think this is happening. Invite them to compare the temperature of the water in each tub. The large spoons come in handy for playing with cubes in the ice water. The plastic sandwich bags provide a way of immersing the ice cubes without touching the water, and seeing exactly how much of the cubes melted and how much water was produced.

Measuring Ice Water
Science/Math/Sensory/Fine Motor

WHY we are doing this activity: to extend the previous activity by providing experience with pouring and rational counting; to familiarize children, through their own child-initiated exploration, with the concept of volume and displacement; to provide a sensory experience. For kindergartners: to provide experience with subtraction.

Developmental differences: Three- and young four-year-olds may not use the math cards or participate in rational counting, but through their own free exploration of the differently sized and shaped containers they will develop a sense of the relationship between the size of the container and the volume of liquid it holds. Older children will be more likely to use the math cards.

WHAT we will need:
Ice cubes
Water
Tubs
Food coloring
Glitter or colored sand
Bottles
Funnels
Containers (distinctly different sizes and shapes)
For older children:
Pale-colored plastic folders or margarine tub lids

Math cards (provided on page 99, photocopy and enlarge for your use.)
Permanent marker
Plastic container (to hold math cards)

HOW we will do it: Using food coloring, make colored ice cubes ahead of time. Pour colored water into the tubs and sprinkle glitter or colored sand in it. Place the ice, containers, and funnels in the tubs and encourage the children to explore the materials. For young children, this is the extent of the activity.

For older children: Cut cards out of plastic folders or use the margarine tub lids to write out math problems. Use the permanent marker to write subtraction problems. I have provided some samples to give you an idea of what these problem cards could look like, but when you make your own, draw pictures and symbols that represent the actual sizes and shapes of the containers you are using. (The children will not be writing on the cards, just using them to figure out the math problems.)

Put these math problem cards in the plastic container and show them to the children. During Attention Getter time, figure out one problem together, as a group.

How Does Heat Affect Crayons?
Science/Art/Fine Motor

WHY we are doing this project: to enable children to discover the effect of heat on crayons; to experience hands-on artistic creation; to develop fine motor skills.

WHAT we will need:
Heating plate (yogurt maker or griddle on lowest setting)
Long crayons with wrappers peeled off
Aluminum foil

These are sample math problems. Draw your cards with pictures that represent the actual size and shape of your cups.

Subtraction for kindergartners.

Paper
Popsicle sticks
Graters (freestanding ones are best for
    young children)
Preparation:
Scissors

HOW we will do it: Wrap aluminum foil around your heating plate, and switch it on at low heat. Put the graters out, with some crayons near them, and make some crayon gratings yourself so that the children can see how to use the graters. The Popsicle sticks can be used by children to hold down the paper on the heating plate, so that they do not have to use their fingers. Encourage the children to grate crayons and to sprinkle the gratings onto the paper covering the hot plate. What happens? If the children press crayons directly onto the paper, examine the lengths of the crayons at the end of the activity. Are they as long as they were in the beginning? Why not?

Melted Ice Cube Pictures

Science/Art/Sensory

WHY we are doing this project: to reinforce the concept that warm air melts ice; to develop creative expression; to provide experience with an unusual art material; to develop all components of language arts: speaking, listening, reading, and writing.

WHAT we will need:
- Ice cubes
- Paper
- Tempera paint powder
- Paper towels
- Pans
- Small bowls
- Spoons
- Pens
- Popsicle sticks

HOW we will do it: Ahead of time, fill ice cube trays with water, and put a Popsicle stick in each section so that when the water freezes, the ice cubes will have handles. Put different colors of tempera paint powder, including brown and black, in small bowls with spoons. Invite the children to sprinkle the powdered paint onto their paper, and to use an ice cube to spread it around on the paper. Ask them what is happening. How does the powder turn into paint?

As the children finish making their pictures, ask them if they would like to put any words on their pictures describing how they were made. Depending on the age and readiness of your children, take story dictation, write the children's words down on a separate piece of paper for them to copy, or support invented spelling. Some questions you might ask to encourage language use include: "How did you make this picture? What did you have to do first? What did you do after that? What did you see happening? What do you think you will do with your picture?" If children want to dictate or write words that have nothing to do with the ice cube process, accept and encourage this.

Sun and Snow Woman Song

Music/Movement/Gross Motor/Cognitive

WHY we are doing this project: to help children enjoy and feel comfortable with their singing voices; to develop gross motor muscles; to provide a cognitive exercise through the memorization of the song's words; to reinforce the effect of heat on frozen water.

WHAT we will need:
- Song: "SUN AND SNOW WOMAN SONG" (to the tune of "Eency weency spider")

"SUN AND SNOW WOMAN SONG"

There stands the snow woman icy cold
and still.
Out comes the sun rising up
behind a hill.
The sun shines so hot,
slowly melts the woman down,
'til all there is to see is a puddle on
the ground.

HOW we will do it: Find a wide open space, and have the children spread out. For "There stands the snow woman icy cold and still," try to stand as much like a frozen snow woman as possible. For "Out comes the sun rising up behind a hill," move your arms in sweeping motions from below your waist to above your head. For "The sun shines so hot, slowly melts the woman down," begin to sink down to the ground slowly, and try to simulate melting snow as much as you can. For " 'til all there is to see is a puddle on the ground," make yourselves as limp and flat as possible on the ground.

As a variation of this, find a large piece of furniture to act as the hill in the song, and have half of the children hide behind it. Let them be the sun which rises slowly up and shines on the snow woman. Let the other half of the children be the melting snow people. Then switch roles.

If the children become very familiar with the song, and you feel the need to vary it a little, propose to your students that you sing the song without saying the word "sun." See if you all remember to leave that word out.

Weather: Hot and Cold
Multicultural/Language/Cognitive

WHY we are doing this activity: to provide a cognitive exercise by enabling children to make logical judgments; to expand vocabulary; to facilitate all components of language arts: reading, writing, speaking, and listening; to create multicultural awareness.

WHAT we will need:
> One side of a large cardboard box
> Contact paper (clear and also
>   pale-colored)
> Poster board
> Double-sided tape
> Markers
> Pens
> Glue sticks
> Pictures and word pictures (provided on
>   page 102; photocopy and enlarge
>   for your use)
> Index cards
> "Two people may be here" sign
>   (provided on page 13; photocopy and
>   enlarge for your use)

Optional:
> Puppet

HOW we will do it: For this activity, you will need to make a board game. A companion activity to this involves setting up a writing center with writing materials, blank paper, and photocopies of the same words and symbols used in the game. To begin, cut out one side of a large cardboard box, and cover one side of it with pale-colored contact paper. Next, cut out all the wordless pictures in the text and color them with markers. The pictures are simple

and can be quickly colored. Using double-sided tape, tape the pictures onto a piece of poster board, and cover the poster board on both sides with clear contact paper. An easy way to do this is to stick the cards face down onto a large piece of contact paper, and to then press another large piece of contact paper down on the backs of the cards, making one big contact-paper sandwich with the cards in the middle. Then cut out each one and put double-sided tape on the backs. If you do not have time to cut on the lines of the drawings, just cut around them. These will be the pictures you will need for the board game.

Next, make many photocopies of the pictures with words and glue one of each onto an index card. Cover each card on both sides with clear contact paper. You will use these covered word pictures in the game and the rest will be used in the writing center.

On a writing table, put out pens, blank index cards (whole), glue sticks, scissors, and markers. Cut some of the word pictures so that the words and pictures are separated but also leave some intact.

The idea here is to facilitate as many different writing activities as possible for the children, for example, gluing a word picture and copying the letters; gluing a symbol alone and scribbling or writing next to it; gluing a word alone and drawing next to it, creating an original word/picture card. Very young children will choose words/pictures indiscriminately and make scribbles and drawings in the same way. When you discuss their work, refer to it as their writing. Scribbling is an important part of developing writing skills.

When you are ready to do the first part of the activity (the game) with the children, bring out the board and pictures during an Attention Getter time. Here is an example of how you might play it: Put out the snow picture. Say, "What kind of weather is this? Hmmm, some children are going out to play in the snow." Put out the picture of the children in their swimming suits. Say, "There. How does that look?" When the children protest, ask: "Why wouldn't that be a good thing to wear on this kind of day? How would you feel if you did? What would happen?" (You'd be cold; you would freeze.) Put out the sun picture and the children

Sunshine

Hot

Sweaty

Gusty

Wet

Snow

Sleet

Icy

Enlarge pictures on a photocopier before cutting out.

in their winter clothes, or the sun picture and the children with their umbrella and ask the same questions. Put up as many wrong combinations as you can and have the children choose the ones they think are right. As a group, discuss the temperature of the weather in the picture, and whether your students would feel too hot or too cold or just right, depending on the dress of the children in the pictures on the board.

Variations: have the children take turns picking out combinations, right or wrong, and have the other children say if they think they go together. Or take out your puppet and have it put together wrong combinations and have the children correct the puppet.

Later, or on another day with the same activity, put up the word pictures by themselves and ask: "Would someone be hot or cold in that kind of weather, or could they be either one?" Match the word pictures to the weather/children pictures. Also, put up the children pictures by themselves, and based on how the children are dressed, ask your students to guess whether the children are in hot or cold weather or whether they could be in either one. After the game, show the children the writing materials and also let them know that two people at a time may play with the game. Take story dictation if appropriate.

Beach Day
Dramatic Play/Language

WHY we are doing this activity: to help children connect actions with words; to help children work out emotions through pretend situations; to help children develop imagination and creativity; to develop speaking and listening skills; to create a print-rich environment; to promote social interaction between children.

WHAT we will need:
Beach towels
Swimsuits

Picnic baskets/coolers
Tablecloth
Sand
Buckets
Water
Sand toys
Popsicles
Sensory table or tubs
Water
Water toys
Photographs or pictures of the beach
Butcher paper
Marker

HOW we will do it: To prepare, pin up the butcher paper at children's eye level and, several days in advance, tell the children that you are going to have a Beach Day. On this day, your classroom or home will become a beach, you will wear your swimsuits, and you will have a picnic. Talk about what you might do on Beach Day, and write down the children's suggestions. In preparation for the actual day, pin up magazine photos of beaches, sun, and water around the walls of the room. Or, if you like, have the children draw or paint a giant beach mural, and put this on your wall. Put sand and sand toys out in sensory tables. All day long, pretend with the children that the room is a beach. It is especially fun to do this in the middle of winter if the room is well heated. Have a summer picnic. If you like, buy a pack of plastic ants and scatter them on your picnic blanket when the children are not looking.

How Do People in Very Cold Climates Live?
Multicultural/Anti-Bias

WHY we are doing this activity: to enable children to learn about the lifestyle of a Yup'ik Eskimo family and to compare the reality of Eskimo life with stereotypes.

WHAT we will need:
    Stereotypical pictures of Eskimos
    Book: Jenness, Aylette, and Rivers, Alice,
      In Two Worlds: A Yup'ik Eskimo Family

HOW we will do it: Begin collecting your stereotypical pictures well ahead of time. Ask friends and family to help you with this. When you are ready for this activity, pin up your stereotypical pictures on the wall.

Before opening the book, examine these pictures with the children and discuss what you notice about them. The most blatant stereotype is usually the ice-block igloo and the dress and features of Eskimo people in cartoons and drawings. Show the children the excellent photographs in the book, and discuss them. Compare them to the stereotypical pictures. How are they different? *In Two Worlds* is too long to read in its entirety, so read selected parts and talk about them. What would it be like to live in a place that was so cold so much of the time?

Literature

Symbol Key: *Multicultural
                +Minimal diversity
                No symbol: no diversity or no people

Florian, D. (1990). *A beach day*. New York: Greenwillow Books. (Unfortunately, this book shows large groups of people on several pages who are all white. I recommend that you buy the paperback version and shade in diverse skin colors yourself.)

Jenness, A., & Rivers, A. (1989). *In two worlds: A Yup'ik Eskimo family*. Boston, MA: Houghton Mifflin.*

Keats, E. J. (1962). *The snowy day*. New York: Viking Press.* (An excellent classic.)

Maestro, B., & Maestro, G. (1990). *Temperature and you*. New York: Lodestar Books.+

Millett, P., & Rossiter, J. (1992). *Hot and cold*. New York: Franklin Watts. (Look at the pictures in this book and discuss them.)

Testa, F. (1979). *The land where the ice cream grows*. New York: Doubleday.

Extenders

Science/Math: Put regular thermometers in the water of your heat traps before you set them out in the sun. Make a note of the temperature, and compare it to the temperature after the water has been in the heat trap for several hours.

Movement/Gross Motor: After you eat your Jell-O, stand in a circle and say: "Jell-O on the plate. Jell-O on the plate. Wibble wobble wibble wobble Jell-O on the plate." Move parts of your body as if they are quivering Jell-O.

Manipulative/Science: After you do the salt and ice cube trick, try this activity again with colored cubes and make an ice cube castle or icy tower. Using the salt to stick the cubes together, how high can you build them?

Science/Math: Displacement: Some older children may be ready for this more advanced experiment: Put a cup in a bigger bowl. Fill the cup with water, and then drop in one ice cube or several. Measure the runoff of water which the ice cubes displaced. Allow that same number of ice cubes to melt in a measuring cup. Will the melted water equal the same measurement as the displaced liquid?

Math: If you live in an area where it snows, save some snow and keep it in the freezer. When summer comes, put the snow out in a sensory table with measuring cups or weighing scales.

Science/Sensory: On a cold day, have the children breathe into the cold air. Why can we see the air that comes from our lungs? The air we breathe is warm and holds quite a bit of moisture. Cold air does not hold as much moisture, so the moisture in our breath condenses into tiny droplets when it hits the cold air and cools.

SHADOW SHENANIGANS

For this unit, it is best to have several flashlights. You can usually find inexpensive ones in variety stores. Make sure that you have plenty of extra batteries on hand. Before you begin the unit, talk with the children about the proper use and care of flashlights. Open one up and show them how the batteries fit inside. If you think you will need one, also have a timer available to help your children with taking turns.

Attention Getter: Find many different objects that you think will have interesting shadows (some suggestions: a crate, a lattice-backed chair, a clothes rack, a tall container). If you need to, use a flashlight, table lamp, or standing lamp to cause these objects to cast shadows. Turn the lights off until the children are gathered. When you are all together, tell the children that you are going to turn a light on, and that when you do, they will see something that they cannot see with the light off. What they see will give them a hint about what you will be talking about and working with over the next few days. Turn the light on or walk by the objects with the flashlight and ask the children what they notice. Which one is their favorite shadow? (Crates and lattice-backed chairs cast very pretty shadows.)

Making Light and Shadow Experimentation Boxes
Art/Gross Motor

WHY we are doing this project: to generate excitement about the unit by having the children prepare the materials that will be used in it; to facilitate creative expression; to exercise large muscles by bending and stretching.

WHAT we will need:
Refrigerator boxes
Newspaper
Paints (many different colors)
Large brushes
Poster board
Marker
Preparation:
Exacto knife

HOW we will do it: To prepare, decide how many refrigerator boxes you will need according to the number of children you are working with and the available space in the room, and pick them up from furniture stores that sell large appliances. It is a good idea to call first. One or two boxes for eight children has been plenty for me, but you will also have to take into account how much space you have. Using the Exacto knife, carve a door out of each box by cutting a top, side, and bottom and then folding the door flap back.

Spread out newspaper on the floor, and put the refrigerator boxes on the paper. Set the paint and brushes on small tables nearby.

At Attention Getter time, ask the children what makes a shadow. Discuss or explain that you need light and dark to make shadows. If you need to, pick up an object and shine a flash-

light on it and ask the children what they notice—if necessary, point out the light (flashlight) and the dark (shadow). Show the children the refrigerator boxes and invite them to look inside. Explain that you need the boxes for science experiments to explore light and shadow. Ask the children what you should call the boxes and write down what they suggest. Use their suggestions to make signs and attach them to the outside of the boxes. (Some suggestions I have received: "Experiment place,""Dark box"!) Then ask: "What could we do with the paint?" If necessary, invite the children to cover the refrigerator boxes with paint.

Light in Light and Light in Dark (Part 1)
Science

WHY we are doing this project: to enable children to discover the difference between what kind of patterns light produces in light, and what kind of patterns light produces in dark; to help children understand through hands-on experimentation that light is diffused in light and concentrated in darkness; to reinforce for young children the concepts of *inside* and *outside*.

WHAT we will need:
Colanders
Flashlights
Clear wall space
Experimentation boxes (created in previous activity)
Activity signs (provided on page 109; photocopy and enlarge for your use)

HOW we will do it: Place the colanders and flashlights on a small table near the experimentation box. Hang the activity signs nearby. Encourage the children to follow the activity signs' suggestions. When they shine their lights through the colanders in the room, why don't all the holes make light spots? What happens

Shine your flashlight
through the colander
<u>outside</u> the box.

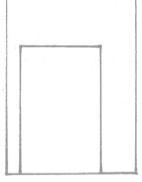

Shine your flashlight
through the colander
<u>inside</u> the box.

when they do the same thing in the experimentation box? What is the difference between the experimentation box and the room? Talk about how the light from the flashlight spills into the light in the room, but when the flashlight is used in the dark box, it is the only light, so it is forced through all the colander's holes.

Diffusion and Concentration of Light (Part 2)
Science

WHY we are doing this experiment: to build on the information learned in the previous activity and to facilitate another way of proving that light can be diffused or concentrated.

WHAT we will need:
   Cardboard
   Negative shape patterns (format
      provided on page 111; photocopy
      and enlarge for your use)
   Flashlights
Preparation:
   Exacto knife
   Scissors

HOW we will do it: To prepare, use the negative shape patterns provided to make cardboard shadow cards with these differently shaped holes in the middle. Obviously, the more interesting the shape, the more time consuming it is to cut out, so depending on the time you have available, select the simpler or more complex shapes. Make sure that you make all three sizes of whichever shape you pick. After you have made the shadow cards, lay them on the table with the flashlights. Show the children the cards and flashlights, and the experimentation box in which they can make light shapes with the materials. Ask the children to predict what difference there will be

between the three sizes of holes when light is shone through the bigger hole. As the children conduct the experiment and emerge from the experimentation box, discuss the results. Ask them to hypothesize about the difference between the smallest light shape and the biggest. Why is the smaller shape so much clearer? Explain that when light is shone through the bigger hole, the light is spread out over more space. The smaller hole has less space for the light to shine through, so that light shape is stronger and clearer.

Light and Distance
Science

WHY we are doing this experiment: to help children understand the connection between distance and the size and appearance of shadow.

WHAT we will need:
   Flashlights
   Colanders
   Fly swatters (with designs cut in the plastic)
   Construction paper
   Experimentation box
   Activity sign (format provided on
      page 112; photocopy and enlarge
      for your use)

HOW we will do it: To prepare, put a small table near the experimentation box, and set the colanders, fly swatters, and flashlights on it. Use construction paper to make the the activity sign and post it nearby. During an Attention Getter time, have the children sit together. Hold up an object, and ask them to notice whether or not it looks the same size as you hold it close to them as when you take it farther away. As you take the object further away from them, ask: "How does it look now? What about now?" Tell the children that they will have a chance to do a science experiment in the experimentation

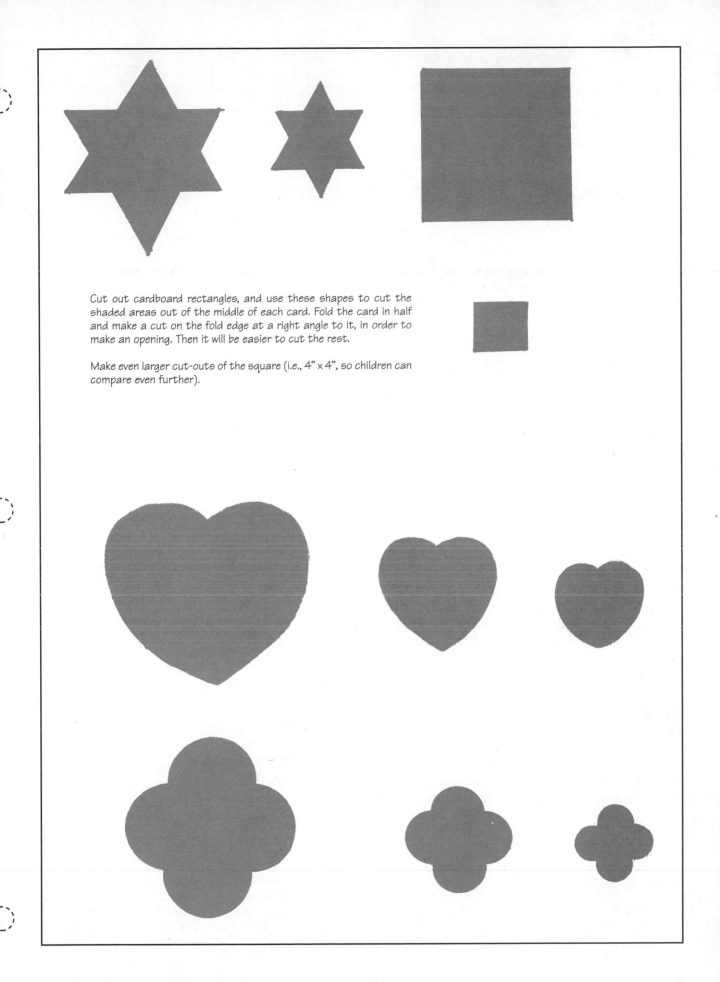

Cut out cardboard rectangles, and use these shapes to cut the shaded areas out of the middle of each card. Fold the card in half and make a cut on the fold edge at a right angle to it, in order to make an opening. Then it will be easier to cut the rest.

Make even larger cut-outs of the square (i.e., 4" x 4", so children can compare even further).

When you go into the experimentation box, hold your flashlight close to the colander , and then hold it far away.

box that will show them another way of proving that things look smaller when they are farther away, and bigger when they are close. Encourage the children to follow the suggestions of the activity sign and ask them to predict what they will see when they do. After your students conduct the experiment, discuss their findings. What is the difference between the light shadows from the holes in the colander when the colander is held close to the flashlight and the light shadows that are seen when it is held far away? Invite the children to do the same experiment with the fly swatters. Later, show them how to make different patterns by swirling and moving the colanders and fly swatters in front of the flashlight or cooperating with another person and overlapping them.

Tip: Save the refrigerator boxes to use again for the Space Unit.

Color and Shadow
Science

WHY we are doing this experiment: to allow children to observe how color fills in shadow.

WHAT we will need:
Two clip-on lamps
Acetate folder covers (red and blue)
Rubber bands
Packaging tape
Large piece of white paper

HOW we will do it: Arrange your lamps near a wall so that the lamps face each other about two feet apart. Cut out circles from the acetate, several inches larger in circumference than the lamp openings. This allows you a margin of acetate to wrap around the edges of the lamps. Use rubber bands and packaging tape to cover one of the lamp openings with the red circle and one with the blue. Pin the white paper up behind the lamps.

During an Attention Getter time, show the children the lamps and point out the colored plastic covering on each one. Invite them to switch the lamps on and ask them to predict what they will see. After the children switch the lamps on and examine the effect, discuss their observations. What do they notice about the colors cast by each lamp? (The red light floods the shadow of the blue lamp; blue light floods the shadow of the red lamp.) If you like, put different colors of acetate on the lamps throughout the unit.

Shadow Story
Anti-Bias/Language

WHY we are telling this story: to stimulate interest in the art, drama, and science activities to follow; to present different gender roles than stereotypical ones; to demonstrate shadow puppet theater; to develop speaking and listening skills; to expand vocabulary.

It can take a little extra time to set up the light and puppet theater exactly right, but children do appreciate seeing drama presented in this unusual way and then trying out shadow puppet theater themselves.

WHAT we will need:
Small table or puppet theater
Film projector, strong lamp, or
    standing light
Shadow puppet outlines (provided on
    page 114; photocopy and enlarge for
    your use)
Cardboard
Popsicle sticks
Double-sided tape
Glue
Scissors
Clear wall space

Optional:
Clear contact paper
Story:
    "TOPSY AND THE CARROT PATCH"
    (provided)

HOW we will do it: In this activity, you will need to make the characters in the shadow puppet story, and then tell the story to the children. This is intended to interest them in using the shadow puppets to retell the original story and to make up new ones, to make their own characters with the materials, and to experiment with the shapes and their shadows in the experimentation box. These activities are described below. To prepare the story, cut the character shapes out of cardboard. Glue a Popsicle stick onto all except the tree, basket, bone, acorn, and dead mouse.

The amount of time you put into making these will be determined by how often and how long you plan on using them. If you will be using them with many groups of children over a period of years, you will probably want to cover them with clear contact paper to protect them and make them sturdier. Otherwise, do not bother with contact.

Put several strips of double-sided tape on the non-Popsicle-stick side, close to the bottom of the shape. The purpose of the tape is so that each shape can be attached to the edge of the table when your hands are full of other characters. For the small bunny shape, also stick double-sided tape along its back because this character lays down to sleep. Cover one whole side of the bone, acorn, and dead mouse shapes because you will be sticking these onto the mouths of the animal characters as if they are carrying them.

If you are using a small table for a puppet theater, turn it over on its side. Arrange the table and projector or light source so that the cardboard shapes cast clear shadows on the wall. A film projector is really ideal—it is *very* effective for shadow theater. Also, think about where the children will sit to watch. It should be a place where they are facing the wall and can easily see the shadows—perhaps on either side of the table or puppet theater. A vocabulary list is provided following the story. Before you begin the story, stick the tree onto the edge of the table or puppet theater, in the middle.

TREE

BONE

DEAD MOUSE

BASKET

ACORN

Use photocopier to enlarge shapes.

114

"TOPSY AND THE CARROT PATCH"

Once upon a time there was a little bunny named Topsy whose very favorite food in all the world was carrots. She didn't much like having to dig them up out of the carrot patch however, because it was very hard work. [Hold up small bunny shape at one end of the table.] She was always making excuses to get out of digging for carrots in the carrot patch. Now one evening this little bunny's father [hold up big rabbit shape] was making carrot stew for dinner when he realized he had no carrots left.

"Topsy," he said, "Run down to the carrot patch under the tree and dig up some carrots for me."

"Oh, Daddy," Topsy said, "I'm so sleepy. Can't someone else do it?"

"No, Topsy," Daddy Bunny said. "Everyone else in the family is out digging up turnips or lettuce or parsnips for the big bunny feast tomorrow, and anyway, it's your turn to go to the carrot patch. Here's a basket [stick up basket shape] and do hurry because the stew is cooking and I need the carrots right away."

So very halfheartedly Topsy hopped and loped down to the carrot patch.

Now when she got there, what do you think she should have done? [Let children answer.] But instead that lazy little bunny lay down on the ground in the middle of the carrot patch, under a big old tree. [Stick basket on edge of table, under tree, and stick bunny shape lying down, also under same side of tree. Place it at an angle so that the shadow of the Popsicle stick is not visible.]

"Yaaawwwwn. I know Daddy needs the carrots right away, but I won't have the energy to carry a big basket of heavy carrots all the way home unless I take a little nap first." And pretty soon that naughty little cottontail was fast asleep. Do you think she made the right decision? [Let children answer.]

Well, while Topsy was sound asleep, Ms. Squirrel came along. [Move Squirrel shape along edge, toward tree, from opposite direction.] She had some acorns in the pouch of her cheek, and she was looking for a good place to hide them for the winter.

[In squeaky squirrel voice:] "I think I'll just bury my acorns under this tree. It looks like a good spot where no one would think to look." So she dug and she dug and she dug [move squirrel shape as if it is digging] and she buried those acorns until not a speck of them could be seen and then she ran away to look for more acorns.

A few minutes later Black Cat came along. [Move cat shape along edge, from same direction.] She had a half-eaten, dead mouse in her mouth. Her tummy was too full for her to finish eating it just then, but she was afraid that if she didn't hide it, someone else would steal her delectable treat.

[In drawling cat voice:] "Mmmeeeooowww," she said. "This looks like a good place to bury my tasty morsel." And so she did. [Move cat shape as if it is digging.] Do you think it was a tasty morsel you would like to eat? [Let children answer. Then move cat shape away.]

Well, a few minutes later Doggy came along [move dog shape along from same direction from which cat and squirrel came] and he had a big, stinky bone he wanted to bury so that it would get even stinkier.

[In deep, dopey dog voice:] "Duhh, this is just the place to bury my bone. Duhh, hope I remember where I hid it." And so he dug and dug and dug [move dog shape as if it is digging] and he buried that nasty, stinky bone and then he ambled away.

Well, right about then Topsy woke up. [Make yawning, stretching noises.] Suddenly she realized she must have been asleep for longer than she planned. [Make bunny shape jump around in agitation until bunny is on other side of tree where animals buried their things.] The sun was almost down and it was quite dark.

"Oh my, oh my, oh my," she said, "Tails and whiskers—Daddy's waiting for the carrots and I have been asleep for hours!" And she was in such a panic, and so afraid to go home empty-pawed, that she started digging right where she was. [Move bunny shape as if it is digging each time.] Guess what she found? [Hold up bone. Let children answer.] Yep, the first thing she found was a big, old stinky bone and because she couldn't really see what it was, she threw it into her basket. Guess what she found next? [Hold up mouse. Let children answer.] Yep, a dead, half-eaten mouse and because she was in such a hurry and couldn't see it very well, she threw that in her basket. Time was running out. It was almost completely dark and Topsy needed to get home safe and sound before the owls came out. Why do you think she was afraid of owls? [Let children answer.] So she gave one last dig, and guess what she found? [Hold up acorns. Let children answer.] Yep, instead of some juicy, fat carrots all she found were some hard, dry acorns. And because she was in such a panic, she threw the acorns into the basket without thinking and ran all the way home. When she got home, Daddy Bunny was waiting. What do you think he said to her? [Let children answer.] And what did he find when he looked in the basket? [Let children answer.] What kind of stew would you get if you put a big, stinky bone, a half-eaten mouse, and a bunch of acorns in it? Would you like to have some for dinner tonight?

VOCABULARY:
Ambled
Decision
Delectable
Energy
Excuses
Halfheartedly
Loped
Parsnips
Pouch
Realized
Tasty morsel
Turnips
Speck

Making Shadow Puppets
Art

WHY we are doing this activity: to facilitate creative expression; to develop fine motor skills; to facilitate all components of language arts: reading, writing, speaking, and listening.

WHAT we will need:
Construction paper
Markers
Crayons
Pens
Popsicle sticks
Glue
Glue brushes
Preparation:
Scissors
Flashlight or other light source

HOW we will do it: To prepare, cut out a puppet shape from construction paper and glue a Popsicle stick on the back so that the paper doesn't flop over, and so that you have a handle for the puppet. On the back, write a few sentences. For example: "This is a little ghost who lives up in the attic." Lay the materials out on your project table. After you tell the children the previous shadow puppet story, show them the materials on the activity tables. Before they approach the project table, hold your puppet up, show the children where you placed the Popsicle stick and read the words on the back. Invite the children to make their own shadow puppets and to use the flashlight or light source to see what shadows their shapes make. The markers, crayons, and pens are for the children to color the cardboard shapes if they would like to. After the children have worked on them for a while, encourage them to give story dictation or to write their own words on the back of the puppets. Ask the children to read their words back to you, or if they prefer, read the words to them. Later in the day or week, gather together and have show-and-tell of the shadow puppets the children made.

Shadow Puppet Theater
Drama/Language

WHY we are doing this activity: to facilitate pretend play; to help children develop motor and speech coordination; to help children express themselves.

WHAT we will need:
> Same theater arrangement as for puppet story
> Shadow puppets (made by children for previous activity)
> Shadow puppets from "Topsy and the Carrot Patch" story
> Experimentation box
> Two flashlights
> Duct tape

HOW we will do it: To prepare, use duct tape to tape two flashlights into the corners of the top of the experimentation box. Slant them at an angle so that the children can make shadows with their puppets at their own arm level. Encourage the children to use their shadow puppets in the theater and to make up stories with them, and also to use them in the experimentation box. What kind of shadows does each make? Are they different?

Shadow Match
Math (for three- and young four-year-olds)

WHY we are doing this activity: to facilitate matching exercise; to develop cognition through shape recognition; to help develop self-esteem and a sense of autonomy through use of a one-person work station.

WHAT we will need:
> Distinctly different objects from the classroom: manipulatives, toys, containers, etc. (many different shapes and heights)
> Black marker
> Large piece of poster board
> Container (to hold various objects)
> "One person may be here" sign (provided on page 3; copy and enlarge for your won use)
> Clear contact paper

Optional:
> Strong light source

HOW we will do it: Spread your objects out over the poster board, lay them on their sides, and trace around each with a black marker. Color each outline in to make a "shadow" for every object, and then cover the poster board sheet with contact paper. Set the paper on the floor or a table, and put the objects in the container beside it. If feasible, use a strong light source to trace the actual shadow of each object.

During an Attention Getter time, show the children the game, and explain that if they like, they can match each thing to its shadow. Discuss the "One person may be here" sign and what it means.

Shadow Lengths and the Sun (Part 1)
Science

WHY we are doing this project: to help children understand that the earth moves around the sun and to help them understand how this affects our shadows.

WHAT we will need:
> Large ball
> Small piece of cardboard
> Masking or packaging tape
> Strong light or flashlight
> Hot, sunny day
> Butcher paper
> Markers

Tip: Choose a day that is not windy for this activity, otherwise it will be difficult to keep paper in place while the children trace their shadows.

HOW we will do it: To prepare, cut out a piece of cardboard that is about 15 cm x 2.5 cm (6" x 1") and tape it to the ball so that the tab stands straight up and will cast a good shadow. Turn on your strong light or tape a flashlight to a high place so that it is shining down.

With the children, take the butcher paper and markers outside and notice the length of your shadows. Encourage your students to trace each other's shadows. Go outside again at noon and do this again. Compare the lengths of the traced shadows. Are they different? Invite the children to hypothesize about why this is.

Go back indoors, and show your students the ball and ask them to imagine for a minute that it is the Planet Earth, and that the light is the sun. Ask them to notice the shadow of the cardboard. Move the ball around the light in an approximation of the way the earth moves around the sun. At a certain point the light should be exactly above the cardboard tab. Ask the children what they noticed about how the shadow changed. Let the children take turns moving the ball around the light if they want to. If possible, go out again in the late afternoon to trace and compare your shadows one more time.

Shadow Measure (Part 2)
Science/Math

WHY we are doing this activity: to provide experience with standard measurements; to practice rational counting; to conduct scientific comparison of shadow lengths; to provide experience with writing down measurements in inches and feet; to help children cooperate with each other; to enable children to see visible proof that the earth moves around the sun, to encourage children to explore another facet of themselves and their bodies: their shadows. (For older preschoolers and kindergartners only.)

WHAT we will need:
> Three large pieces of butcher paper
> Markers
> Rulers and tape measures
> Sunny day

HOW we will do it: To prepare, gather a collection of rulers and tape measures that are child- user-friendly. For instance, are the centimeters marked in different colors than the meters? Are the numbers big? I have not succeeded in finding rulers or tape measures made specifically for children, but you can make your own by photocopying a ruler and using colored markers to write in bigger numbers. On top of one butcher paper piece print: "Shadow measurements at ___ in the morning." Write in the time you actually go outside. Make one for noon and one for late afternoon. Pin these charts up on the wall outside.

Before you go outside, as described in the previous activity, show the children the tape measures and rulers and explain what the measurements mean. When you go outside to look at your shadows, ask the children to find a partner who will measure their shadows for them. Help them read the rulers and tape measures and invite them or help them to write down the measurement on the chart. Do the same at noon and late in the afternoon. Compare the measurements. Remind the children of your demonstration with the ball, light, and cardboard tab, or do it again. Talk about the difference in shadow measurements and the reason for them.

What Is an Eclipse?
Science

WHY we are doing this project: to provide a hands-on activity in which children produce an eclipse; to develop self-esteem and a sense of autonomy through use of a one-person work station.

WHAT we will need:
> Two blocks (one large and one small)
> Strong flashlight
> "One person may be here" sign (provided on page 3; photocopy and enlarge for your use)

HOW we will do it: To prepare, arrange your light so that the object on the table will cast a shadow. Put the two blocks on the table and place the sign nearby. During an Attention Getter time, put the small block in front of the light, and ask the children if they see the block's shadow. Ask: "If I put the big block in front of the small one, do you think the small block will still have a shadow? If you would like to find out for sure, you can do this experiment yourself." Interpret or read the "One person may be here" sign together and talk about what it means. As the children explore the materials, talk to them about their discovery and use the word *eclipse*: "The big block *eclipsed* the shadow of the small block."

The shadows need to be cast on the table surface, so they can be traced. Set out the paper, objects, and markers on the table.

Ahead of time, take an object yourself and trace on paper the shadows you see when you put the same object in different positions. If you like, make another one and this time color the outlines in. During an Attention Getter time, show the children your different shadow outlines of the same object, and explain how you made it. Invite the children to make their own. Before they disperse to make their shadow outlines, make sure you say, "These are just how my outlines turned out. Everyone's will look different because we are all different individuals with our own ways of doing things." Pin up the children's pictures on your walls afterward.

Shadow Outlines
Science/Art

WHY we are doing this activity: to help children observe that when the position of an object is changed, its shadow is changed also; to promote creative expression.

WHAT we will need:
  Paper
  Markers
  Several flashlights or lights
  Objects (suggestions below)

HOW we will do it: Try to collect objects that will cast interesting shadows: fly swatters, latticed chairs, lattice-side plastic crates. Manzanita wood bird perches cast very dramatic shadows. If you know someone who has one, perhaps you can borrow it, or approach a pet store about doing so. Driftwood or gnarled branches can also achieve the same effect if they're positioned upright and secured in a base of wet sand or rocks. Arrange your lights and a long table so that several children can sit at the table and face the shadows cast by their objects. If you need to, use duct tape to attach flashlights to a surface like the edge of a shelf.

Shadow Walk
Gross Motor/Nature

WHY we are doing this activity: to sharpen powers of observation and to exercise gross motor muscle group.

WHAT we will need:
  Sunny day
Optional:
  Rope

HOW we will do it: Tell the children that we are going to go on a walk to see how many interesting shadows we can find. Use the rope for everyone to hold on to. As you take your walk, see how many interesting or pretty shadows you find, for example: the shadows cast by a chain-link fence, lattice railing, or iron gate, very small shadows (blade of grass), or very large shadows (tall building). What happens when a cloud moves in front of the sun? When you get back to home or school, talk about the shadows you saw.

Musical Shadow Tag
Music/Gross Motor

WHY we are doing this project: to exercise the large muscle group; to develop appreciation for music; to develop listening skills.

WHAT we will need:
Tape recorder
Music
Hot, sunny day
Grassy area

HOW we will do it: Play a game of musical shadow tag. The children run and dance to the music until it stops—then they must jump onto a shadow and freeze. It can be the shadow of a stationary object, or the shadow of another person. After the children learn the game, let them take turns turning the tape recorder on and off; however, young children tend not to allow much time in between so encourage them to wait each time, so that the other children have a chance to run and dance.

Literature

Symbol Key: *Multicultural
+Minimal diversity
No symbol: no diversity or no people

Anno, M. (1976). *In shadowland*. New York: Orchard Books. (This is an excellent story book.)

Bulla, C. R. (1994). *What makes a shadow?* New York: Scholastic.

Cendrars, B. (1982). *Shadow*. New York: Charles Scribner's Sons. (This is a translation of an excellent story taken from conversations with African shamans.)

Goor, R. & Goor, N. (1981). *Shadows here, there and everywhere*. New York: Thomas Y. Crowell.+

Gore, S. (1989). *My shadow*. New York: Doubleday.+

Simon, S. (1985). *Shadow magic*. New York: Lothrop, Lee & Shepard Books.*

Extenders

Science: After you conduct the Shadow Lengths and the Sun experiment, put out a flashlight and a tall object on a tray on the floor. Encourage the children to raise the flashlight over the object from one side to the other. What happens to the shadow?

Science: Set up two lights to shine on an object. How many shadows are there? If you can, set up more than two lights to shine on an object and invite the children to count the shadows again.

Math: Count the shadows in your room. Do it as a group, or invite the children to do it by themselves. If you have blinds on your windows, compare how many shadows you see when the blinds are open and when they are closed.

Language: After you count the shadows in the room, make a language chart of all the shadows. Write down the name of each object that made a shadow and invite the children to draw a picture of them. Afterward, read the chart together.

THINGAMAJIGS

For this unit, you will need to collect a variety of objects so that the children can observe their different properties and classify them accordingly. Your collections could include: cotton balls, coins (including nickles or silver coins), wooden or plastic spools, marbles, wooden blocks or beads, cork stoppers, fabric scraps, washers, buttons, pieces of sponge, Popsicle sticks, plastic milk carton lids, badges with pins removed, bottle caps, rubber bands, and frozen juice can lids. If you are working with three- and young four-year-olds, put your objects in a choke tube to make sure they are safe, or try to gather a collection of larger objects; for example, tin juice lids, wooden blocks, larger pieces of sponge and fabric scraps, and larger plastic lids.

Varied collections provide many different results in the experiments described below. For items that are more difficult to come by, like cork stoppers and pinless badges, ask for help from family and friends several weeks in advance. Make sure, after you distribute the items among the boxes, that you reserve many spare items because as the unit progresses, things are bound to get lost and for maximum fun, it is best to have one of every object for all the experiments.

You will also need boxes or tins for each child to keep her or his collection in. Ask friends, neighbors, and parents to help you find and save these as well. Cigar boxes and tea tins are ideal; tobacconists sometimes have empty cigar boxes.

Attention Getter: To prepare, put several of each object in every box or tin. When the children are gathered, give each one a box or tin. Ask your students to shake their containers and to guess what might be inside. Then invite them to open the boxes or tins. What's inside? Encourage the children to name each item. Tell the children that a *nickname* is a made-up word for something. A nickname for odds and ends like these is *thingamajigs*.

Explain that over the next few days you will be conducting science experiments on your thingamajigs to see how they are different and how they are the same.

For kindergartners, the experiments as they are described in this unit are very elementary and each experiment is really only one part of a larger goal: discovering and recording as many different results about each item as possible, and then comparing and classifying them accordingly. In other words, the scientific comparing and classifying is the main focus for kindergartners as they work through the results book, and the simple experiments are only the means by which this can be accomplished.

You might facilitate this by setting out all of the experiments for several days, giving each child an experiment results book, either blank or photocopied from the samples I have provided, and then leaving it to the children to discover and record the information as well as compare and classify it. This also encourages initiative by giving them the responsibility of conducting all the experiments in a given time. If you do not want to include every part of the experiment results book, then include and omit pages as you see fit. Pick and choose from the sample pages to create your own science experiment results book—you might decide to make one substantially shorter, or the samples may give you ideas for other experiments, resulting in a book that is even longer. You may also decide to give your children blank booklets and encourage them to design their own format for recording results. You will know what is right for your students.

If certain pictures do not match the materials your children will be using, draw your own and cut and paste them in the appropriate spaces before you make your photocopies. Another variation of this unit for kindergartners is to give the children the option of choosing a certain number of experiments from all the available centers.

Experiment Results Book for Kindergartners
Science/Language/Math

WHY we are making these books: to help children conduct experiments and record results; to help develop initiative; to practice rational counting and subtraction; to facilitate comparing and classifying; to develop all components of language arts: reading, writing, speaking, and listening.

Developmental differences: For three- and young four-year-olds, the experiments themselves are the most important process, and sorting and classifying happens as they progress from experiment to experiment. You can use parts of the science experiment results book as and how you see fit. For example, you may choose to cut out the individual pictures of thingamajigs and cover them with contact paper. Put double-sided tape on the back of each one. Using poster board and contact paper, make a sturdy chart out of the remaining experimentation sheet (the two columns with "yes" and "no"). This allows young children to stick the picture of each object in the appropriate column, and when the entire experiment is finished, there will be a graph of their results.

WHAT we will need:
Preparation:
    Pale-colored paper (letter size)
    Printed words and pictures (provided on
        pages 125–137; photocopy and enlarge
        for your use)
    Stapler
For children:
    Pens
    Markers/crayons

Thingamajigs

Science

Experiment

Results

Book

Science Experiment:
Which thingamajigs absorb water?

Thingamajigs	YES! It does absorb water. ✓	NO! It does not absorb water. ✗
Cotton ball		
Coin		
Cork stopper		
Washer		
Sponge		
Button		
Cloth		
Popsicle stick		
Badge VOTE FOR ME!		
Rubber band		
Bottle cap		

How many thingamajigs absorb water? _____

Touch them. How are they the same?

Take them away.

How many thingamajigs are left? _____

Trace or draw the thingamajigs that absorbed water.

Science Experiment:
Which thingamajigs can be picked up with a magnet?

Thingamajigs	YES! ✓ It can be picked up with a magnet.	No! ✗ It cannot be picked up with a magnet.
Cotton ball		
Coin		
Cork stopper		
Washer		
Sponge		
Button		
Cloth		
Popsicle stick		
Badge		
Rubber band		
Bottlecap		

How many thingamajigs can be picked up with a magnet? _____.

Look at them.  How are they the same?

Take all the others away.

How many thingamajigs are left?_____

Trace  or draw

the thingamajigs the magnet picked up.

Science Experiment:
Which thingamajigs Float?

Thingamajigs	YES! It does float.	NO! It does not float.
Cotton ball		
Coin		
Cork stopper		
Washer		
Sponge		
Button		
Cloth		
Popsicle stick		
Badge		
Rubber band		
Bottle cap		

How many thingamajigs float?

_____.

Touch them.   How are they
                      the same?

Take all the others away.

How many thingamajigs are left? _____

Trace   or draw

the thingamajigs   that float.

Science Experiment:
Which thingamajigs roll?

Thingamajigs	YES! It does roll. ✓	NO! It does not roll. ✗
Cotton ball		
Coin		
Cork stopper		
Washer		
Sponge		
Button		
Cloth		
Popsicle stick		
Badge		
Rubber band		
Bottle cap		

How many thingamajigs roll?

_____ .

Touch them

How are they
the same?

Take all the others away.

How many thingamajigs are left? _____

Trace   or draw

the thingamajigs   that roll.

Science Experiment:
Which thingamajigs reflect light?

Thingamajigs	YES! It does reflect light.	NO! It does not reflect light.
Cotton ball		
Coin		
Cork stopper		
Washer		
Sponge		
Button		
Cloth		
Popsicle stick		
Badge		
Rubber band		
Bottle cap		

How many thingamajigs reflect light?_____

Touch them. How are they the same?

Take all the others away.

How many thingamajigs are left?_____

Trace or draw the thingamajigs that reflect light.

Science Experiment:
Which thingamajigs conduct heat?... cold?

Thingamajigs	YES! It did conduct heat.	NO! It did not conduct heat.	YES! It did conduct cold.	NO! It did not conduct cold.
Cotton ball				
Coin				
Cork stopper				
Washer				
Sponge				
Button				
Cloth				
Popsicle stick				
Badge				
Rubber band				
Bottle cap				

How many thingamajigs conduct 🔥 heat?_____ conduct ❄️ cold?_____

Touch them.. How are they the same?

Take all the others away.

How many thingamajigs are left?_____

Trace or draw

the thingamajigs that conduct heat ...and cold .

HOW we will do it: To make the books, photocopy the provided pages, make your own if the pictures do not match the items you are using, or simply leave the pages blank. Staple them together in book format.

During an Attention Getter time, show your kindergartners an experiment results book and look through it together. Show them where the pens, markers, and crayons are.

Decorating Thingamajig Boxes
Art

WHY we are doing this project: to encourage children in artistic expression and to develop fine motor skills.

WHAT we will need:
Tissue paper scraps (many different colors)
Glue and water (or glue sticks)
Thingamajig collection boxes
Plastic sandwich bags
Newspaper or cloth (to cover table)

HOW we will do it: You can either use glue sticks or regular glue for this project. If you use liquid glue, water it down a little and put it in small containers with glue brushes. Set out the glue and tissue paper scraps on the activity table. A few days ahead of time, decorate your own collection box by gluing tissue scraps all over it. On the day of this project, show the children your collection box during an Attention Getter time. Be sure to say something like, "This is just how my thingamajig box turned out. Everyone's will look different, because we are all individuals and have our own way of making things."

If you chose to put out liquid glue for this project, be sure you or the children wipe away any glue which could cause the box lid to stick to the box. If you are working with very young children, have them empty their thingamajigs into plastic sandwich bags while they decorate

their collection boxes—otherwise, you will find more in the glue than just glue brushes.

Which Thingamajigs Absorb Water?
Science

WHY we are doing this activity: to enable children to conduct a scientific experiment in which they will discover which of their objects are absorbent and which are not; to develop fine motor skills ; to develop reading skills.

WHAT we will need:
Eye or medicine droppers
Small containers of water
Sorting trays or containers
divided into two sections
Sorting signs (provided on page 139; photocopy and enlarge for your use)
Clear contact paper
Water
Paper towels
Wax paper
Butcher paper
Marker

HOW we will do it: To prepare, make the number of photocopies of each sorting sign equal the number of sorting trays. To waterproof, cover each copy on both sides with clear contact paper. Cut out a piece of contact paper for each one that is double the width or length and a little larger than the paper, then fold the contact paper over and seal the edges together.

Place one of each sign in a section of each sorting tray. Set the sorting trays, eye or medicine droppers, and containers of water on the activity table. Pin up the butcher paper at the children's eye level.

During an Attention Getter time, bring out an eyedropper of water, a paper towel, and a piece of wax paper. Tell the children that you are going to drop some water on each type of paper and see what happens. Ask the children

138

Sorting Thingamajigs

Thingamajigs that absorbed water. ✓		Thingamajigs that did not absorb water. ✗	
Thingamajigs that were picked up with a magnet. ✓		Thingamajigs that were not picked with a magnet. ✗	
Thingamajigs that floated. ✓		Thingamajigs that did not float. ✗	
Thingamajigs that conducted heat. ✓		Thingamajigs that did not conduct heat. ✗	
Thingamajigs that conducted cold. ✓		Thingamajigs that did not conduct cold. ✗	

what they see happening as water drops fall onto the paper towel and wax paper. Which one soaks up the water? After the children comment on which paper soaks up the water and which one does not, tell them that another word for *soaking up* is *absorb*. Print the word on the butcher paper. If you work with younger students, tap and blink the word with parts of your bodies as you say the syllables together.

Show the children the "does absorb" sign and read or interpret it together. Which material belongs on it? Then hold up the "does not absorb" sign and read or interpret that. Which belongs on it?

Ask the children to predict which of their thingamajigs absorb water. Show them the materials on the activity table for conducting this experiment. Together, discuss their findings. Encourage the children to use the paper towels to dry off their thingamajigs before returning them to containers.

Which Thingamijgs Can Be Picked Up with a Magnet?
Science

WHY we are doing this project: to enable children to discover which substances are attracted to magnetic power and which ones are not; to develop reading and speaking skills.

WHAT we will need:
Magnets
Trays
Thingamajig collections
Puppet
Butcher paper
Markers
Large paper clip
Piece of paper

HOW we will do it: Set out the trays either on the floor or on a table. These help keep collections separate, and define activity space for each child. Put a magnet on each tray. (Make sure your magnets are fairly strong; weak ones are no fun to use.) Pin up your butcher paper, and draw two columns on it. Use the suggested headings on the magnet experiment page to label each column, or create your own headings. At the top of the chart, print: "Prediction Chart. Which thingamajigs can be picked up with a magnet?" Illustrate your headings in a similar manner to headings in the experiment book.

During an Attention Getter time, show the children the paper clip and paper. Try to pick up each with a magnet and see what happens. Ask the children to open up their thingamajig boxes and to predict which thingamajigs can be picked up with a magnet. Record their predictions on the chart, or invite them to do this. Then ask: "How can we find out for sure how our thingamajigs will react to magnets?" If necessary, point to the materials on the trays.

When the children have had some time experimenting with the materials, take out your puppet. Using your puppet's personality, ask the children what they are doing. Mention one of the thingamajigs that you know will not be attracted to the magnet, and guess aloud what it will be. Do the opposite with objects which you know will be attracted to the magnet. Have your puppet say, "I wonder if you have more thingamajigs that *can* be picked up with the magnet, or more thingamajigs that *can't* be?" Invite the children to record their results in their experiment books. Have your puppet engage the children in conversation about their scientific discoveries. At the end of the session or day, gather together again. Look through the thingamajigs one more time, and ask the children which turned out to be things a magnet would pick up, and which did not. Compare the results to the predictions on the chart. Discuss together.

Developmental differences: Three- and young four-year-olds will be most fascinated with the thingamajigs which are attracted to magnets, and may play with these materials for quite a while. This type of play conveys information about which materials are attracted to magnets, and which are not. Older chil-dren will also enjoy magnet play, and will be more inclined to record the results of their experiment.

Which Thingamajigs Float, and Which Ones Do Not?
Science

WHY we are doing this project: to allow children to discover which kinds of materials float and which do not.

WHAT we will need:
> Plastic tubs, preferably clear enough to see through
> Thingamajig collections
> Sorting sheets (provided for previous activity)
> Clear contact paper or plastic folder
> Permanent marker
> Water

Demonstration:
> Plastic cup
> Rock

HOW we will do it: Set out the tubs of water. You can put either newspapers or trays underneath them. Make photocopies of the sorting sheets and waterproof them in contact paper, or use permanent marker and rectangles cut from plastic folders to make waterproof sorting sheets. Put a sorting sheet down next to each tub of water. During an Attention Getter time, show the children the plastic cup and rock, and say that you are wondering whether they will float or sink when you drop them into a tub of water. Ask the children what they think. Drop one in, and then the other. Ask the children what they see. Show them a sorting sheet and read or interpret it together. On which side does the rock belong? On which side does the cup belong? Ask the children to predict which of their thingamajigs will float and which will sink. Ask the children what they see in the room that will help them conduct this experiment. Encourage exploration and, together, discuss the children's findings.

Developmental differences: Three- and young four-year-olds will enjoy seeing objects float, trying to sink them, and dropping objects into the water. They will be less interested in formally recording the results. Some older children become very engrossed in recording the results of this experiment.

Which Thingamajigs Conduct Heat and Cold?
Science

WHY we are doing this experiment: to allow children to discover which materials conduct heat and cold.

WHAT we will need:
Thingamajig collections
Very warm water
Plastic tubs
Ice cubes
Trays
Two forks
Two wooden blocks
Paper towels

HOW we will do it: Place your tubs on top of the trays to minimize mess and set them on the activity table. Put ice cubes and cold water in some of the tubs. In the others, pour water that is as warm as possible without being dangerous to the children.

During an Attention Getter time, ask the children to sit in a circle. Put a tub of ice water and a tub of warm water in the middle. Pass one fork and block around the circle, and ask the children to notice their temperatures. Do they feel very warm, very cold, or just normal? Put them both in the ice, and when you take them out a few seconds later, pat them quickly with a paper towel to dry them, if you like. Pass them around the circle, and ask all the children to feel them again. How do they feel now?

What do they notice about which one feels coldest? Talk about the fact that the fork *conducted* or carried the cold of the ice cubes. What do the children notice about how the wooden block reacted to the ice water? Next, pass around the second fork and block so that the children can feel their temperatures, and then drop them into the warm water. Pat them dry after a few seconds, and then pass them around the circle. How do they feel now? What do the children notice about which one conducted the heat? Ask your students to predict which of their thingamajigs will conduct heat and cold. Do they see anything in the room that will help them conduct this experiment? Encourage experimentation and talk to the children about their discoveries.

Developmental differences: Three- and young four-year-olds may be more interested in plunging their hands into the tubs of water and splashing their thingamajigs about. In this way, their sensory play with thingamajigs will convey information about heat and cold conducting materials. Older children will also enjoy sensory exploration in the tubs of water, but will be more inclined to take note of how their thingamajigs feel after being immersed in the tubs of water, and to record the results.

How Do Thingamajigs Look Different?
Science

WHY we are doing this experiment: to develop observation skills and to allow children to examine how the surfaces of objects differ.

WHAT we will need:
Magnifying glasses
Thingamajig collections
Optional:
Microscope (preferably the kind that allows you to put your own specimens on slides)

HOW we will do it: Set the magnifying glasses out on a table. During an Attention Getter time, ask the children what they see in the room that will allow them to get a close-up look at their thingamajigs. Invite them to use the magnifying glasses or microscope to examine their thingamajigs carefully. If you have a microscope, supervise the children as they put flat thingamajigs (e.g., fabric, a bit of cotton, a piece of sponge, a rubber band) on the lens. Help the children to cover one of their eyes while looking through the microscope with the other, or if they prefer, use a card to cover one eye for them. Some children do not like to wear blindfolds, but if your students are comfortable with them, make a blindfold with one eyehole cut out of it. As the children look into the microscope, ask them about what they see, and about how their thingamajigs look different.

Which Thingamajigs Reflect Light?
Science

WHY we are doing this experiment: to encourage children to observe which of their thingamajigs have surfaces which reflect light.

WHAT we will need:
    Flashlights
    Thingamajig collections
    Trays

HOW we will do it: To prepare, put your flashlights and trays out on an activity table. The children can spread their collections out on the trays while they conduct the experiment.

During an Attention Getter time, take a flashlight and shine the beam on a variety of objects in the room, metallic and otherwise. As you go around the room, ask the children questions like: "When I shine the flashlight on this silver water faucet, what do you notice about how it looks? When I shine the flashlight on the

wall, what do you notice? Does the wall look the same as the water faucet when the flashlight was shining on it, or does it look different? How?" If necessary, point out the small, bright beam reflected from metallic surfaces. Continue: "This window frame reflects the light. See this bright, sparkly beam on the corner of the frame right here? It looks a little bit like the brightness of the sun. Now look at how this wooden chair looks when I shine the flashlight on it. What do you notice?" Ask the children to predict which of their thingamajigs will reflect light and which ones will not. Do they see anything in the room thatwill help them conduct this experiment? Encourage experimentation and, together, discuss the children's findings.

Developmental differences: Three- and young four-year-olds seem to feel incredibly powerful with a flashlight in their hands! They may be more interested in holding the flashlights, shining them on whatever strikes their fancy, and switching them on and off. If you like, hold reflecting and non-reflecting objects and invite the children to shine the flashlights on them. This will convey the same information as the above experiment, and will still cater to the three- and four-year-olds' desire to wield the flashlight. Older children will be more inclined to pass a shining flashlight over their thingamajig collections and to notice the appearance of each object when they do so.

Which Thingamajigs Roll?
Science

WHY we are doing this experiment: to enable children to discover that a round object (one with a curved surface) rolls.

WHAT we will need:
    Long planks
    Blocks or books
    Thingamajig collections
Demonstration:
    Round or cylindrical object

HOW we will do it: To prepare, make several ramps with your planks and blocks or books. During an Attention Getter time, select a few round or cylindrical objects that are not part of the thingamajig collections, for example, a cardboard toilet roll, a plastic egg shape, a small rubber ball, or a cardboard or plastic plate. Also choose a few objects that will not roll, like a book or a box. Hold each object at the top of the ramp and ask the children to predict what each will do when you let it go on the top of the ramp. Experiment with the plate twice—once by dropping it on its edge, and once by dropping it so that it lands on its wide, flat surface.

Next, ask the children to predict which of their thingamajigs will roll. What do they see in the room that will help them conduct this experiment? With objects like coins, buttons, washers, juice can lids, and plastic lids, invite the children to let them go at the top of the ramp on their curved edges as well as their flat surfaces. What happens? What happens if you put a cork at the top of the ramp on its rounded surface? What happens if you put it on its end at the top of the ramp? Encourage experimentation.

After the children have explored the materials, invite them to touch the curved surfaces of the rolling objects with their fingertips in order to feel their rounded shapes. How are the rolling thingamajigs the same? How are the non-rolling thingamajigs the same? Talk together about the fact that objects with curved, rounded surfaces roll. Which is easier to roll: thingamajigs like corks, beads or marbles, or thingamajigs like coins, buttons, washers, and juice can lids? Encourage your students to hypothesize about why this is.

Developmental differences: Three- and young four-year-olds will most likely become engrossed in the rolling objects and may roll the roundest objects down the ramps over and over again. Older children will also enjoy rolling objects down the ramps, but may be more inclined to compare them to non-rolling thingamajigs.

Weighing Thingamajigs
Science/Math

WHY we are doing this project: to familiarize children with the different weights of different materials; to facilitate a comparative exercise.

WHAT we will need:
> Sensory table or large tub
> Weighing scales (one large and several small if possible)
> Trays
> Scoopers
> Extras of all objects in thingamajig collections

HOW we will do it: Put one small weighing scale on each tray for children to use individually. Put the extra thingamajigs into the large sensory table, and place the scoopers and large scale in it also. Encourage the children to explore the materials. If appropriate, ask questions like: "What happens if you put all of the cotton balls on one side, and one washer/some of the washers/all of the washers on the other?" Ask the children what they notice about which thingamajigs are heavy and which are light. How are objects in each group the same or different?

Sorting Thingamajigs
Science/Math

WHY we are doing this project: to facilitate sorting (separating) and grouping (joining) activities (classification exercises).

WHAT we will need:
> Egg cartons (dozen or 18-size)
> Thingamajig collections
> Sorting sheets (provided for previous activities)

HOW we will do it: There are several ways to do this activity. The first, for younger children, is simple sorting based on the appearance of objects—things that are the same go together. As mentioned in the Woodworks unit, my experience has been that younger children do not know what to do with sorting materials when they are just set out for them with no explanation. Therefore, before your children disperse to explore the projects for the day, tell them the story in the Woodworks unit called "THE NAILS FIND A NEW HOME," but instead of telling the story about nails as you sort the various objects, substitute the names of the thingamajigs. Use the egg cartons as your sorting trays.

Another way to sort the materials is to base the classification on what the children have discovered about the objects in their experiments. This is most appropriate for older children. If you are working with very young children who will not remember what object did what in which project, you can put out the sorting sheets right beside the corresponding experiment. During an Attention Getter time, use one sorting sheet together as a group, so that the children understand how to use them. With older children, you can make the sorting sheets available shortly after the experiments have been conducted, in order to encourage your students to recall the qualities and reactions of the various objects.

Thingamajig Creations
(Art)

WHY we are doing this project: to facilitate creative expression and to develop fine motor skills.

WHAT we will need:
Many extras of all objects in
  thingamajig collections
Glue
Glue brushes
Small containers

Tempera paint
Glitter or colored sand
Small boxes
Small plastic cups
Construction paper
Cardboard pieces from boxes
Any other decorating items

HOW we will do it: Put the glue and glue brushes in the small plastic cups and set them out on the activity table so that all children will have access to them. Put all the other materials on the table also. Invite the children to use the materials as they wish.

How Do They Feel?
Sensory/Language/Small-Group Project

WHY we are doing this project: to encourage children to use their senses to describe the thingamajigs; to promote all components of language arts: speaking, listening, reading, and writing.

WHAT we will need:
Butcher paper
Markers

HOW we will do it: Pin up the butcher paper at the children's eye level. During an Attention Getter time, ask the children to close their eyes and touch one item at a time. Say: "Try to find a cotton ball. How does it feel? Try to find a marble. How does it feel?" Print the name of the object and the children's words on the chart, or, if you are working with children who are writing, give them turns to write the words themselves. Younger children can also be invited to write, scribble, or draw on the chart. Words you might hear and write include: rough, shiny, smooth, cold, soft, heavy, and light. Afterward, read the chart together.

Thingamajig Toss
Gross Motor

WHY we are doing this activity: to help children develop hand–eye coordination and to help them develop the large muscle group.

WHAT we will need:
> Extras of the following thingamajigs:
> Coins, marbles, spools, washers, large buttons, badges, bottle caps, and juice can lids
> Wide, shallow containers
> Masking tape

HOW we will do it: Put a masking tape line down on the floor and set the containers a distance away from it. Decide on this distance according to the age and gross motor abilities of your children. Invite the children to stand at the masking tape line and throw a thingamajig into a container. Sincerely praise all efforts, whether or not thingamajigs land in the receptacles.

Pot Lid Game
Gross Motor

WHY we are doing this activity: to develop hand–eye coordination; to develop reflexes; to develop large muscle group in arms; because children love this game!

WHAT we will need:
> String
> Thingamajigs: spools, corks, washers, large buttons
> Plastic cup
> Nickel
> Paper
> Double-sided tape
> Markers (red and black)

> Styrofoam meat tray
> Two pot lids with handles (large and small)

HOW we will do it: Use the nickel to trace two circles. Color one black and one red. Cut these circles out, and using the double-sided tape, secure one of the colored circles to each side of the nickel. Next put the nickel in the cup and the cup on the Styrofoam meat tray. Cut lengths of string about 50 cm (20″) and tie one to each thingamajig. Provide one for each child.

To begin, children sit in a circle on the floor, with their thingamajigs in the middle. Each child holds the end of the string which is attached to his or her object. One child holds a pot lid. Another child shakes the coin in the cup and then rolls it onto the Styrofoam meat tray. (If you have a two-colored die, you can use this instead.) If the coin lands with the red side face-up, the children must snatch their thingamajigs out of the circle by jerking on their string before the pot lid can be slammed down on the objects. If the coin lands black side faceup, no one moves a muscle. Let children take turns being in charge of rolling the coin and using the pot lid. The smaller pot lid requires more coordination and skill than the larger one. Once children learn this game, they get very excited about it.

Thingamajig Shop
Dramatic Play/Language

WHY we are doing this activity: to help children explore their emotions and work out real-life situations; to facilitate interaction between children; to expand vocabulary; to develop speaking and listening skills.

WHAT we will need:
> Refrigerator box
> Extra thingamajigs
> Tubs

Scoopers
Toy cash registers
Small paper bags
Penny coins
Weighing scales
Notebooks
Pens
Baskets
Preparation:
Exacto knife
String

HOW we will do it: Using the Exacto knife, cut a flap in the side of the refrigerator box for a store front window. Punch a hole in the bottom of the flap and the top of the box, then tie the flap up with string.

Put the small table inside the box. If you do not have a refrigerator box, you can set up a shop without it, but children do enjoy going in and out of an actual structure. You may not be able to obtain all the materials in the above list, but on the other hand, you may find other things that you think the children will like. Set out the materials you have, and ask the children what the shop should be called. Together, make a big sign which displays the shop's name, and pin it up. Encourage the children to play with the materials and, when appropriate, be a customer who needs 230 g (½lb.) of thingamajigs.

Class Thingamajig Collections
Social Studies/Math

WHY we are doing this project: to encourage children to cooperate with each other as a group and to practice rational counting.

WHAT we will need:
    Very large, clear plastic container.
    Butcher paper
    Marker

HOW we will do it: During an Attention Getter time, show the children the large container. Suggest that you begin a thingamajig collection as a class, and try to fill up the container with all the thingamajigs you find. Talk about where you can look for them, what kinds of things can be included (all the things in your original collections, plus new things: shells, pebbles, old keys, crayon pieces—anything the children find and want to put in the collection), and who they could ask to help them with looking for things. If you are a teacher, send a note home to families explaining the project and asking for help. Ask the children what you should say before you write it and include their words. If you are a parent, do the same for a note to send to friends and extended family. You may continue to build up your class collection for many months after you have finished the unit.

When the container is full, bring out your personal thingamajig collection. Show it to the children and say, "Remember that each one of us had a small collection like this? This (point to big container) is the collection we all helped to create. Why does it have so many more things? When we all worked together, we were able to make a huge collection, much bigger than we could have had if we'd all been working by ourselves." Sort through the class collection and see if you remember who found various things. Ask the children for predictions of how many things there are all together, and write down their guesses on the butcher paper chart or have them do this. Then, as a class, count all the objects together, and write the total number at the bottom of your chart. Were your predictions close? Leave the collection out on a tray or small table for the children to play with and explore.

Thingamajig Shake
Music/Movement

WHY we are doing this: to help children develop a sense of rhythm; to develop cognition by memorizing words; to help children enjoy singing.

WHAT we will need:

Small thingamajigs: beads, buttons, washers

Plastic soda bottles with lids (one for each child)

Glue

Song: "THINGAMAJIG SHAKE"
(to the tune of "Pop Goes the Weasel")

"THINGAMAJIG SHAKE"

Thingamajig O-ringamajig, mixed up all a-jumble.
Shake 'em here and shake 'em there, Oh!
How they tumble!

"Thingamajig O-ringamajig, mixed up all a-jumble. Slide 'em here and slide 'em there, Oh!
How they tumble!

HOW we will do it: Put some thingamajigs in each soda bottle and glue the top on each one. When the glue has dried, sit together with your thingamajig bottles. Sing the song, and invite the children to shake and slide the thingamajigs in their bottles at the appropriate verses.

If your students become very familiar with this song, and you feel they would enjoy varying it a little, freeze when you get to the last word of each verse. Does everyone stop at the same time? Can you still hear shaking or sliding?

Literature

Symbol Key: *Multicultural
| Minimal diversity
No symbol: no diversity or no people

Lewis, B. R. (1993). *Coins and currency*. New York: Random House.

Lohf, S. (1990). *Things I can make with buttons*. San Francisco, CA: Chronicle Books.

Reid, M. S. (1990). *The button box*. New York: Dutton Children's Books.

Zweifel, F. (1994). *The make something club*. New York: Viking.

Extenders

Math: Invite the children to count how many thingamajigs are in their collections, and to write the number on a piece of paper. Keep the paper in the collection boxes.

Art/Craft: Use washers, beads, and buttons to make thingamajig necklaces and bracelets with string. For younger children, wrap masking tape around one end of the string to make a stiff end which can easily thread through objects. Only buttons with very large holes should be used for this project.

Social Studies: After you write the note to parents, family, and friends asking for help with your group thingamajig collection, walk to the nearest post office as a group to buy a stamp and mail all, some, or one of your notes. If you cannot walk to a post office, walk to a mail box. Show the children the schedule of pickup times, and figure out together when the postal worker will be putting your letter in her or his mail bag. How many hours will that be from now? What will we all be doing when the letter is picked up?

Social Studies: When you are creating your class thingamajig collection, talk about what kind of things are gathered and collected for recycling. If you like, start a class recycling project.

FLUID FORMS

In this unit, children will explore the comparative densities of different fluids. Liquids you can use for this unit include: honey, vegetable oil, dish detergent, water, syrup, hair gel, yogurt, milk, or cornstarch liquid.

Test tubes are a lot of fun to use with young children because they really evoke the feeling of being a genuine scientist. If you can find plastic test tubes in catalogs for older grades, they are a good investment. Do not forget to order a rack to hold them in, as well.

Attention Getter: Gather the children together and ask them to turn their backs to you. When they cannot see you, take out a tub and a big pitcher of water. Tell the children that they are going to hear a noise and that they have to guess what it is. Pour the water so that it flows very quickly and then pour it so that it trickles. When the children guess that they are hearing water being poured, ask them to see if they can hear another fluid being poured. Tip a bottle of vegetable oil into the tub. Ask the children how it sounded: the same as the water? Why not? Put a small container of each with pouring cups inside a sensory tub for later exploration. Tell the children that there are two other names for things that are wet and can be poured: fluid and liquid. You may want to introduce these words on different days. Tap your fingers or feet, and blink in time to the syllables as you say the words.

Pouring Fast and Pouring Slowly
Science/Sensory

WHY we are doing this experiment: to help children understand the connection between the thickness of a liquid (degree of density) and speed of motion; to provide a sensory experience; to develop fine motor coordination (specifically pouring skills); to develop all components of language arts: speaking, listening, reading, and writing.

The facts of the matter: Everything is made of *molecules*. A dense liquid, like honey or syrup, has more molecules packed together than a liquid like milk.

WHAT we will need:
Sensory table or large tubs
Newspaper
Small pitchers
Containers
Cups
Fluids (thin and thick: e.g., syrup, liquid soap, water, cornstarch liquid, honey, molasses, and milk)
Butcher paper (two pieces)
Marker

HOW we will do it: To prepare, spread newspaper underneath the work area, set out all the materials, and pin up the pieces of butcher paper close to the place where the children will be conducting the experiment. On one chart,

print: "Prediction Chart." On the other, print: "Results of Our Science Experiment." Divide both papers into two columns, each with one heading that says: "Fluids that pour quickly—runny fluids" and another which says: "Fluids that pour slowly—dense fluids." Read or interpret these headings together and discuss the meanings of *dense* and *runny*. Show the children each fluid and ask them to predict which will flow quickly and which will flow slowly. On the prediction chart, print (or have the children write) their predictions. Then ask how the children can find out for sure how the liquids flow. Encourage experimentation, and invite the children to record their findings on the results chart. After the experiment, read the charts together and compare them. Talk about how the dense or thick liquids pour slowly and how thin or runny liquids pour quickly. To reinforce the meaning of *dense*, discuss which is more dense: the honey or the water, the syrup or the milk.

The Oil Experiment
Science

WHY we are doing this experiment: to enable children to observe how oils and water-based fluids separate.

WHAT we will need:
Transparent plastic containers with lids
Vegetable oil
Sesame oil
Red vinegar
Soy sauce
Small pitchers
Funnels
Large sensory table
Small containers
Spoons

150

HOW we will do it: Put all other materials in the sensory table and spread several layers of newspaper on the floor underneath. Sesame oil is expensive so use small amounts. It is darker than vegetable oil and is easy for children to distinguish, which is why it is necessary for this experiment. Have on hand sesame oil, vegetable oil, soy sauce, and red wine vinegar (in their original bottles) for your Attention Getter demonstration.

During Attention Getter time, identify each fluid with the group, and then put some of the oils, vinegar, and soy sauce in a container and rest the lid on top of the container. Say to the children: "What do you think would happen if I shook this jar really hard right now, without screwing the lid on the container?" Talk about how important it is to screw the lid on tightly and evenly. Do this, and then pass the container around to the group of children so that each child can shake the container. Set the container on a surface and ask the children to predict what will happen to the fluids if you let the container sit still for a few minutes. Ask the children what they see in the room that would help them to conduct this science experiment for themselves.

Encourage experimentation, and together, discuss the results. Ask: "How do the oils feel? What do you notice about which fluids feel the same? What do you see after the fluids settle in the containers?" Ask the children to hypothesize why the vinegar and soy sauce remain mixed, and why the two oils do the same. Do the oils and water-based fluids all stay mixed up together?

Sinking and Floating in Different Fluids
Science

WHY we are doing this experiment: to enable children to observe that the same object may sink in one kind of fluid and float in another.

WHAT we will need:
  Water
  Syrup
  Vegetable oil
  Small pitchers or plastic cups
    (for pouring fluids)
  Clear plastic containers with lids
  Small plastic objects (e.g., manipulative
    blocks, pen caps)
  Grapes
  Corks
  Carrots cut into grape-size pieces
  Large sensory table

Note: If you work with three- and young four-year-olds and are concerned that the children may put the small objects in their mouths, you may decide to omit this activity or to facilitate it as a group project when you can supervise closely. Another option is to recruit another adult for the session to help supervise. The children do enjoy this experiment.

Some syrups separate from water after being mixed with it, and some syrups do not. Even if your syrup and water mix, you will find that the grape and carrot sink through the oil while the cork and some plastic objects float on its surface. This means that even if your syrup and water do not separate, the children will still be able to observe how the same objects sink or float in different fluids.

HOW we will do it: Spread many layers of newspaper underneath your activity area. Put all materials in the sensory table or in basins.

During an Attention Getter time, pour some oil, syrup, and water into a clear plastic container. Show the children a grape, carrot piece, cork, and plastic object. Ask them to predict what each one will do in each kind of liquid. (If you like, make a prediction chart. Draw a picture of the original container of each fluid at the head of a column, and along the sides, the floating or sinking objects. Write down the children's predictions in appropriate space or invite them to do so.) Ask the students what they see in the room that will help them conduct this experiment. Facilitate experimentation, and together, discuss the children's findings. Ask your students what happens when they screw on the container lids evenly and tightly, and shake the containers hard. Does it change how the objects sink and float?

Air and Density
Science

WHY we are doing this project: to allow children to observe how air moves through dense liquids; to help develop self-esteem and a sense of autonomy through use of a one-person work station.

WHAT we will need:
    Three plastic containers (empty peanut butter containers are perfect)
    Liquid soap
    Water
    Honey
    Straw
    "One person may be here" sign (provided on page 3; photocopy and enlarge for your own use.)
    Magnifying glass
    Flashlight
    Large, strong cardboard box
Preparation:
    Exacto knife

HOW we will do it: Pour a generous amount of honey in one container, water in the other, and liquid soap in the third. Put the magnifying glass on the table beside them, and pin up the sign on the wall above the table. Cut a three-panel divider out of your cardboard box so that it is freestanding.

Use the Exacto knife to cut a + shape in the middle panel, and push the flashlight through. Use string or duct tape to help you secure the flashlight if necessary. The light should be positioned so that it will be shining into the containers.

During an Attention Getter time, show the children the materials. Tell the children that the density of a liquid affects how quickly or slowly air bubbles move in it. Show them the magnifying glass, and tell them they may use it to observe the speed of the air bubbles in the fluids. Ask them to predict whether air bubbles will be moving quickly, moving slowly, or not moving at all in each fluid. Discuss the meaning of the "One person may be here" sign. Right before the group disperses, blow lots of bubbles into each container. Make sure there is plenty of extra space in the honey container, or the honey will overflow when you inject bubbles in it. Encourage the children to observe the fluids, and as each child observes the experiment, ask questions like: "What do you notice about which direction the bubbles are floating? What do you notice about which fluid has the most bubbles in it? What do you notice about how fast or slow the bubbles are moving?"

Force and Density
Science

WHY we are doing this project: to reinforce the concept of *density*; to give children the opportunity, through their own hands-on experimentation, to discover the connection between the degree of force needed to blow bubbles into a liquid and the degree of density of the liquid.

WHAT we will need:
    Honey
    Water
    Syrup
    Apple juice
    Small, clear plastic cups
    Small pitchers

Straws
Trays
Wastepaper basket
Popsicle sticks

HOW we will do it: Set out the trays on the activity table and, on each one, put three cups. If you can only find large plastic cups at the grocery store, cut them down with scissors. This is so that each child only uses a small amount of each fluid. Place the wastepaper basket near the table. Put a pitcher of each fluid on the table so that all children will have access to them.

During an Attention Getter time, take two cups and a straw. Ask the children if they remember observing the speed of bubbles in different fluids (previous activity). Tell them that they can try to blow bubbles into fluids themselves, and this time, you hope they will notice how hard or easy it is to blow into the different liquids. Sit on the floor so that the children can see into the cups, and pour the first one half full of juice. It is important to pour the liquids while the children watch so that they can observe the difference in density as the liquids flow quickly or slowly. Ask the children to predict whether or not they will be able to blow air through a straw into the juice. Take another cup and pour honey into it. Ask the children to predict whether or not they will be able to blow air through a straw into the honey. (The level of the honey rises quickly as air is injected into it, but it is difficult to create bubbles in it.) Ask the children what they see in the room that will help them to conduct this science experiment.

Hand a straw to each child, and then ask: "Is it okay to suck up the fluids through the straw instead of blowing bubbles into it? Why not?" (There will not be any fluids left for other children to experiment with and germs will be spread.) Children may take a taste anyway, but it is important to let them know that that is not the purpose of the activity. If you like, use the Popsicle sticks to give each child a taste of the honey and syrup before the activity.

In addition, be sure to emphasize to the children that everyone has their own straw, which should be thrown away when they are finished with the experiment. Ask: "What will happen if you leave your straw in the cup and

someone else uses it?" (Germs will spread.) "What will happen if you have a cold, and you leave your straw in the cup and someone else uses it?" (That person might get your cold.)

Encourage experimentation and communication of results. Ask the children what they notice about how easy or hard it is to blow bubbles into the different fluids. Ask why they think it is easy to blow bubbles in some fluids and not others. Say: "The honey/syrup is very *dense*." Discuss how a dense liquid has more molecules packed together than a watery liquid like the juice.

What Is a Suspension?
Science/Sensory

WHY we are doing this experiment: to provide children with a hands-on exploration of a fluid which is a suspension (they can learn that a suspension contains very small particles); to provide a sensory experience.

WHAT we will need:
Tomato juice
Strainers
Spoons
Coffee filters
Tubs or sensory table
Clear plastic containers
Demonstration:
Apple juice

HOW we will do it: To prepare, put all materials except the apple juice into the tubs or in the sensory table. During an Attention Getter time, take a clear plastic container of apple juice and a clear plastic container of tomato juice and hold them up, side by side, so that the children can clearly see both. Ask them what the difference is between them. There are several things the children may mention, but if or when someone mentions that the apple juice is clear, or see-through, and that the tomato juice is thick and cannot be seen through, tell your students that the tomato juice is a *suspension*. A suspension has tiny particles in it. Tomato juice is a suspension because it contains a lot of tiny tomato particles.

Ask the children what they see in the room that will help them prove this. Encourage exploration of the materials. What is left behind when tomato juice is forced through a strainer? What can be seen when it is poured through a coffee filter? Before you clean up for the day, invite the children to pour some tomato juice into a clear container, and leave it for a day or two. What happens? Did the particles settle?

The Liquid Book
Science/Language/Art/Fine Motor

WHY we are doing this project: to reinforce the concept of density in relation to fluids; to develop all components of language arts: reading, writing, speaking, and listening; to facilitate creative expression; to develop fine motor skills.

WHAT we will need:
   Food magazines
   Pale-colored construction paper
      (large sheets)
   Dark-colored construction paper
   Index cards
   Scissors
   Glue sticks or glue and brushes
   Markers
   Crayons
   Pens
Preparation:
   Stapler
   Aluminum foil
   Sample shapes (provided on page 155;
      photocopy and enlarge for your use)

HOW we will do it: Begin collecting food magazines well ahead of time; ask friends, family, and other parents to help. To make a blank

book, fold three sheets of construction paper over and staple along the fold.

Using the pattern provided, cut the fluid shape out of aluminum foil. Cut the pitcher shape out of dark-colored construction paper. Use a glue stick to glue the aluminum foil fluid shape onto the cover of the book, and then to glue the pitcher shape above it so that it looks like the water is being poured out of the jug. On the top write: "The Fluid Book."

Cut out enough fluid and pitcher shapes for all the children. Leaf through food magazines, and tear out pictures of any kind of fluid: juice, syrup, cream, soup, etc. If you are working with very young children, cut some of these out of the pages and leave some pages intact. Older children can cut their own shapes out of the magazine pages.

A few days ahead of time, make a sample fluid book. Cut out photographs from the magazines of fluids that appeal to you and glue them into the pages. Print words for each photograph. Your book might be as simple as: "This brown liquid is gravy. I like gravy on my mashed potatoes. This is another brown fluid, but this one is syrup. I bet it is sticky to touch." On the cover, under the pouring pitcher, write: "by (your name)."

Set the blank books, magazine pictures, pitcher and fluid shapes, glue, scissors, markers, and crayons on the activity table. Provide aluminum foil sheets and construction paper for children who want to cut their own shapes for their book covers. On the index cards, print a descriptive word on each one. Use words like: runny, sticky, drizzle, gooey, thick, and thin. Put these on the table with blank cards and pens. Children may choose to copy them, color them, or cut them out.

During an Attention Getter time, show the children the cover of your book and read what it says. Then read the rest of the book. Ask the children what they see in the room that would help them make their own fluid books. If you are working with three- and young four-year-olds, take story dictation and/or encourage their scribbling. If you are working with older children, help them in the way that is most appropriate to their needs or requests: spell words, write their words down for them to copy into their books, or support invented spelling. At the end of the day, gather together

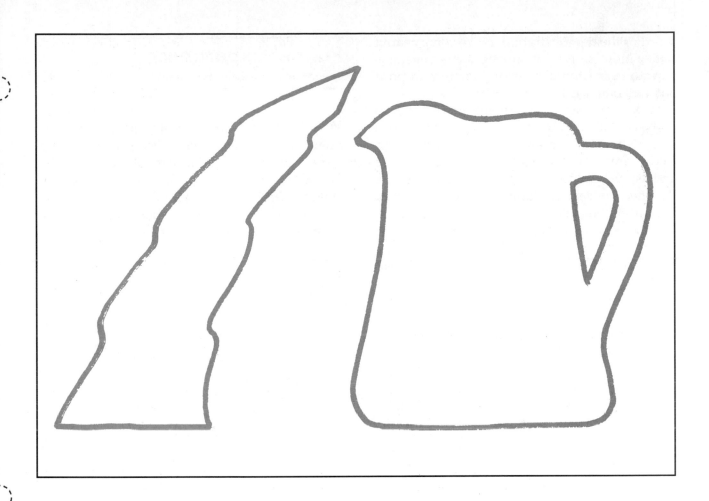

as a group, and have a show-and-tell of fluid books. If there are some children who didn't make fluid books, let them show-and-tell whatever else they prefer.

Weight, Force, and Density
Science

WHY we are doing this project: to help children understand the relationship between the density of a liquid and how that liquid absorbs a heavy, speeding object; to develop fine motor skills.

WHAT we will need:
    Clear plastic cups
    Trays
    Pitchers
    Honey
    Hair gel
    Syrup
    Water
    Small and large marbles (steel and glass)
Demonstration:
    Two large, clear, plastic containers
    Peanut butter
    Vegetable oil
    Can of clear soda (Sprite, Mountain Dew, etc.)
    Two medium-sized rocks (must fit inside containers)
    Newspaper

HOW we will do it: To prepare, put several plastic cups and marbles on each tray, and nearby, place the pitchers of fluids so that they will be accessible to all children. To control the amount of fluid each child pours, you can cut the cups down so that they are smaller in height.

For the demonstration, make some peanut butter more runny by stirring some vegetable oil into it. It should be runny enough to pour out of a pitcher, but thick enough so that the rock does not sink immediately to the bottom of the container. Spread newspaper underneath your demonstration area. During an Attention Getter time, pass your rocks around the circle and ask the children to feel the weight of them. Put the two clear containers on your tray and, in front of the children, pour the soda into one, and the peanut butter liquid into the other. It is important to pour the liquids as slowly as you can so that the children can observe their relative densities prior to the demonstration. Tell the children that you are going to drop a rock into each fluid, and that you want them to watch and see if the same thing happens to the rocks. (Beforehand, experiment with how high to hold the rock before dropping it. Getting the desired effect depends on the size of the rocks and how much liquid there is in the containers.) After you let the rock fall into the soda, ask: "What happened?" (It should sink immediately to the bottom of the cup.) Drop the other rock into the peanut butter fluid, and ask the children what they see. (It should sink very slowly to the bottom of the cup, or even stop sinking before it reaches the bottom.) What did the children notice about the speed with which the rocks travelled in the fluids? Why did one rock sink quickly and the other slowly? Which fluid is more dense?

Show the children the marbles on the activity table and pass some around the circle so that the children can feel their weight. Bring a pitcher of each substance from the project table to the circle and ask the children what is inside each one. After the group has identified the fluids, ask the children to predict how the marbles will travel when they are dropped into each fluid. Ask the children how they could find out. Invite them to discover more about weight, height, speed, and density with the materials on the activity table. Before they disperse to explore, talk about the fact that the liquids are for dropping objects into, not for drinking or tasting. Together, discuss their findings.

Funnel Experiment
Science/Sensory/Math/Fine Motor

WHY we are doing this project: to help children understand the relationship between the density of a liquid and its ease of movement; to provide a sensory experience; to familiarize children with measurement cups and their relative volume; to practice rational counting; to provide practice with pouring.

WHAT we will need:
- Sensory table
- Large basin or tub
- Honey
- Corn syrup
- Colored water
- Cornstarch liquid (cornstarch mixed with water)
- Small pitchers
- Measuring cups (several complete sets)
- Funnels
- Empty shampoo bottles (or other bottles that are tall with narrow openings)
- Tub of warm, soapy water
- Large bowl
- Writing sheets (provided on page 157; photocopy and enlarge for your use)
- Blank paper
- Markers
- Small table for one-person work station
- "One person may be here" sign (provided on page 3; photocopy and enlarge for your use)

Preparation:
- Permanent marker

HOW we will do it: To prepare, use a permanent marker to write in large numbers and words the measurement of each cup on the cup itself. I have not found measuring cups specifically made for children, and on most sets the measurements are very hard to see. By writing the measurements with a bold, permanent marker using large letters and numbers, this project provides much more of a learning opportunity for children.

Place everything in the sensory table except: one set of measuring cups, one funnel,

Science Experiment:
Liquids ⨾⨾ and Funnels 🫙🫙

Draw a bottle underneath the funnel that resembles in size and shape the bottle you are actually using. Then photocopy this master sheet.

How many quarter cups

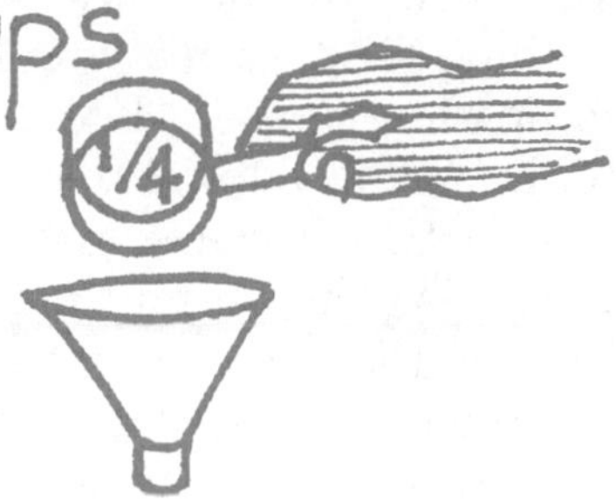

fill up the container ?

Science Experiment:
Liquids ⨾⨾ and Funnels 🫙🫙

How many third cups

fill up the container ?

Science Experiment:
Liquids ⨾⨾ and Funnels 🫙🫙

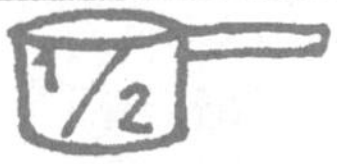

How many half cups

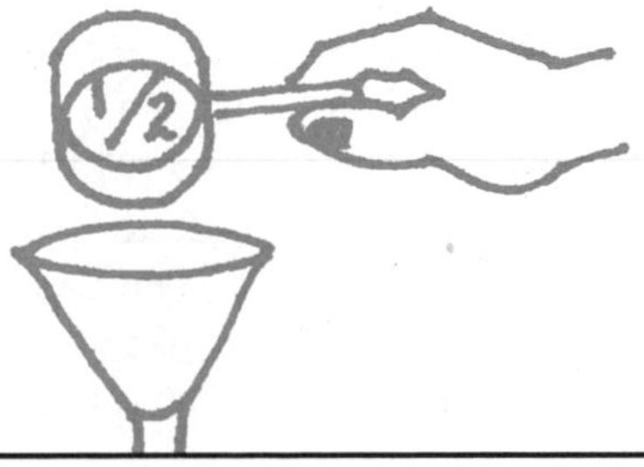

fill up the container ?

three small-sized plastic bottles, a large bowl, a pitcher of cornstarch water and a pitcher of corn syrup. Put these things in the basin or tub, and place it on the small table. Place the writing sheets, pens, and blank sheets of paper on the small table also, in order to create a one-person measuring/writing project. If you put the writing materials near the majority of materials, they can become so splattered with liquids that they are impossible to use. Also, children may dribble fluids on the floor if they have to go back and forth between a sensory table and writing materials. The writing materials, and the contents of the tub, are intended as an extension of the exploration of fluids and funnels; a one-person-at-a-time measuring/writing project. (It would be too expensive to supply several children with enough honey and corn syrup to fill several bottles.) The bowl in the tub is for emptying out the contents of the bottles so that the next child can begin the measuring project. It does not really matter whether your students use corn syrup or cornstarch water together or separately. The idea here is that they count and measure and, at the same time, notice the difference in how a thick and thin fluid pass through a funnel.

During an Attention Getter time, show the children the different fluids, funnels, and containers. Also, bring the tub with the one-person measuring/writing project to the circle. Together, read or interpret the writing sheet and show the children where the pens and sheets will be, as well as the blank paper for children who want to create their own format for recording results. Show the children how, if they choose, they can make a mark on the corresponding writing sheet for each cupful they pour. Next, use a set of measuring cups and colored water to demonstrate that it takes four ¼ cups to fill up one whole cup, two ½ cups to fill up one large cup, and so forth. Determine how complete or lengthy this explanation is depending on the age of your children. Younger children may not be interested, and older children need to have something left for them to discover for themselves.

Invite the children to explore the materials and, as appropriate, talk to them about their discoveries as they experiment. Which fluid goes through the funnel fastest? Which one passes through most slowly? Why? Show the

children the basin of soapy water for cleaning their materials when they want to begin a new experiment. Do not be surprised if this, too, becomes a material for exploration.

Density As a Barrier
Science

WHY we are doing this experiment: to provide children with a hands-on opportunity to discover that a dense liquid is "stronger" than a less dense one; to promote self-esteem and a sense of autonomy through use of a one-person work station.

WHAT we will need:
Tray (or newspaper)
Tub
Funnel
Colored hair gel
Water
Food coloring (a different color than the hair gel)
Clear container
Pitchers
Spoon
Activity sign (provided on page 159; photocopy and enlarge for your use)
"One person may be here" sign (provided on page 3; photocopy and enlarge for your use)

HOW we will do it: On a tray on the small table, place the tub, funnel, small pitcher of hair gel, small pitcher of colored water, and container. Tape the activity sign and the "One person may be here" sign prominently beside the table. During an Attention Getter time, read or interpret the signs together. Ask the children to predict what they will see when they follow the suggestions of the activity sign. As they discover that a glob of hair gel in the funnel will prevent water from passing through it, ask what they notice about the densities of the two fluids and their relationship to this discovery. There are several ways to do this: either during each child's time at the work table, or during a group gathering at the end of the day.

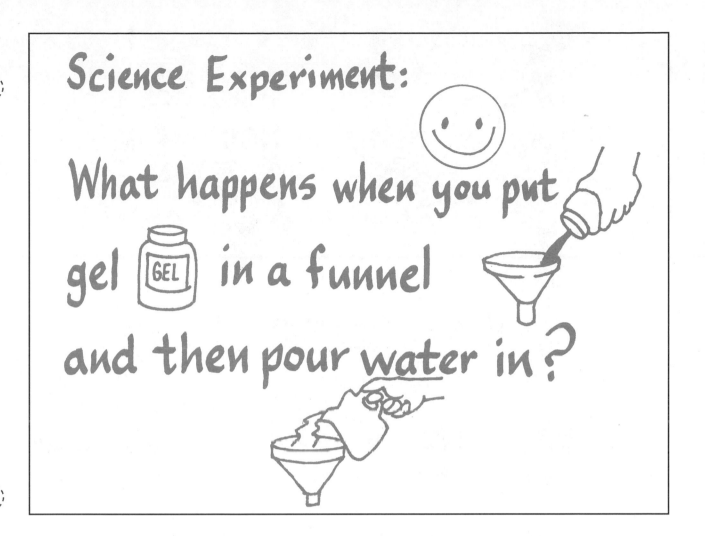

Science Experiment:

What happens when you put gel [GEL] in a funnel and then pour water in?

Liquid Drop
Science

WHY we are doing this project: to enable children to learn, through hands-on experience, that dense liquids do not disperse on impact when dropped from a height and to allow them to compare this to the reaction of watery fluids.

WHAT we will need:
- Small containers
- Medicine droppers
- Hair gel
- Honey
- Cream
- Water
- Newspapers
- Colored construction paper
- Plastic cling wrap

Activity sign (provided on page 160; photocopy and enlarge for your use)
Puppet

HOW we will do it: The key to this project, in order to avoid a catastrophic mess, is to put very small amounts of each liquid into each container, and refill them as needed. Spread plenty of newspaper out on your activity table. For this experiment, you will need a surface which does not build surface tension in water. For example, even if you drop water from a height onto wax paper, the drops will not splatter. One surface which works is plastic cling wrap wrapped over construction paper. This allows the fluid drops to be visible and does not create any surface tension. If you can find another suitable surface which lets you out of this extra work, then by all means use it. Set out the small containers of each liquid and the medicine droppers on the table as well.

Drop a drop of hair gel, + honey, cream, and water on a tray. ————— How does each drop land? _____

During an Attention Getter time, show the children the materials on the table and, together, identify each liquid. Draw up one of the fluids with a medicine dropper, and hold it over some plastic wrap. Ask the children to predict whether each one will fall with a plop, in one drop, or whether it will splatter into a lot of little drops. Rather than releasing the fluid to find out, ask the children what they see in the room that will help them conduct this experiment for themselves. Facilitate experimentation. After the children have explored for a while, take your puppet out. Use your puppet to ask your students about what they are doing and what results they notice. What happens to different fluids when they are dropped from a height? What do the results of the experiment have to do with the different densities of the liquids? Also, ask the children to notice how the suction of the medicine droppers works differently with liquids of different densities.

Note: Suction is the production of a vacuum in a cavity so that external atmospheric pressure forces the surrounding fluid into the cavity. If the children ask you what suction is, one way of explaining might be: "When you squeeze the rubber part of the medicine dropper, it forces and pushes all the air out. Then when you let go of the rubber part, because there's no air in the dropper, the air outside the dropper helps to force the fluid into the tube part. That is suction.

Fluid Roll
Science

WHY we are doing this project: to help children understand the connection between the speed with which a liquid rolls down a ramp and the density of the liquid; to develop fine motor skills; to develop self-esteem and a sense of autonomy through use of a one-person work station; to develop all components of language arts: reading, writing, speaking, and listening.

WHAT we will need:

Four long wooden planks or blocks (to be used as ramps)
Support blocks
Honey
Hair gel
Colored water
Cream
Four small containers
Four eyedroppers
Newspaper
Activity sign (provided on page 162; photocopy and enlarge for your use)
"One person may be here" sign (provided on page 3; photocopy and enlarge for your use)
Tub of warm, soapy water
Paper towels
Butcher paper
Two markers

Demonstration:

Four spoons

HOW we will do it: You can set this project out either on the floor or on a table. In either case, spread several thick layers of newspaper underneath. Make four ramps that slant downward by propping up each long block or plank with several blocks. (See illustration.)

Make sure you make each ramp exactly the same. Again, put a very small amount of each fluid in a small container to avoid too much of a mess, and put an eyedropper in each one. In a prominent place, tape up the "One person may be here" sign and the activity sign. Put a small amount of warm, soapy water in a tub and place it and several paper towels near the project. These are to be used by the children to clean and dry the ramps between experiments.

If you like, use the sample prediction chart in the text to make your own on butcher paper, or create your own headings. Your container symbols should reflect the actual size and shape of containers you have. Tape the chart up near the place where you gather at Attention Getter time.

During an Attention Getter time, show the children the original hair gel container, the cream carton, a pitcher of water, and the honey bottle or jar. Together, as a group, name the fluid in each one, and then identify the corresponding symbol for that fluid on the prediction chart. Show the children the eyedroppers and ramps. Say: "Let's predict how fast or how slow each of these fluids would roll down the ramp if you used the eye droppers to put a drop of each of the fluids on a ramp." If you are working with three- and young four-year-olds, before you write down the children's predictions about each liquid, take a spoon and spoon some of each fluid out of, and back into, the container so that the children can see their relative densities. As you do this, ask: "Is this fluid a thick, dense fluid or is it thin and watery?"

With older children, just show them the liquid containers (cream carton, honey bottle and so forth) ask about the density of each one, and elicit predictions. Ask the children to write their predictions on the chart, or do this yourself. If you print the predictions, use quotation marks and write the children's names after their comments. Use alternate marker colors to make each sentence easier to identify. Discuss the "One person may be here" sign and the purpose of the soapy water and paper towels. Show the children how to use them to clean and dry the ramps between experiments.

Invite the children, one by one, to conduct the liquid roll experiment and to make their own discoveries. Afterward, ask the children about what they found out through their experiments. Have the children read the prediction chart, or read it to them. Were there any surprises? What did they notice about which fluid rolled the slowest down its ramp? What did they notice about which one rolled the fastest? Did any of the liquids get stuck and not roll down at all? Leave the chart up on the wall for a few days.

Drop a drop of each liquid

onto a ramp.

Which rolls slowest?

Which rolls fastest?

Science Experiment Prediction Chart

Will hair gel roll quickly or slowly? 	Will honey roll quickly or slowly? 
Will water roll quickly or slowly? 	Will cream roll quickly or slowly? 

The Story of Greedy Gert

Language/Multicultural/Anti-Bias

WHY we are doing this project: to help children develop listening skills; to expand vocabulary; to help children develop their imaginations; to create multicultural, anti-bias awareness; to generate interest in the math activity immediately following.

WHAT we will need:
    Flannel board
    Flannel board shapes (provided on
        page 164; photocopy and enlarge
        for your use)
    Felt
    Glue
    Markers or crayons
    Scissors
    Clear contact paper
    Double-sided tape
    Story: "GREEDY GERT AND THE
        LIQUIDS" (provided)

HOW we will do it: To prepare, color in the flannel board story shapes, and glue them onto felt. Cut out the shapes, cover them with clear contact paper on the non-felt side, and put double-sided tape onto the front of the yoke shape so that it will stay attached to Greedy Gert.

If you work with very young children, tell the story more than once over a period of days or weeks and discuss a few of the new words each time. A vocabulary list follows the story.

"GREEDY GERT AND THE LIQUIDS"

Once upon a time there was a very wise Queen who ruled all the land. [Put queen shape on the flannel board.] And this Queen heard of a woman in her kingdom who was very, very greedy and because of this, people called her Greedy Gert. Greedy Gert cheated the people who bought things from her shop, and one hard winter, when food was very scarce, and the townsfolk were desperate for something to eat, Greedy Gert charged them very high prices for the food they bought just because she knew the people had

no choice but to pay it. So angrily they asked the Queen to make Greedy Gert leave the kingdom forever, but the Queen thought she would give Greedy Gert one more chance. The Queen called her to the palace. [Put Greedy Gert on the board.]

"Greedy Gert," the Queen said, "The people want you to leave the kingdom because of your greedy ways, but I'm going to give you one more chance. I'm sending you on a long journey to one end of the kingdom and back. And on this long journey, you must help everyone who asks you. All you may take with you is a yoke and two magic cups that are bottomless and can never be emptied. [Put up the yoke shape.] In these cups you may have water or liquid gold. Which will you choose?" Guess which one Greedy Gert chose! [Let children answer.]

The wise Queen said, "Gert, do you know that liquid gold is much heavier than water, and that you have a very long way to walk?"

But Greedy Gert only said, "Two whole bottomless cups of liquid gold!! I'm rich, I'm rich!! I'll keep this gold with me forever and when I get back from your stupid journey, I'll be the richest woman in town!! Ha ha hee hee hoo hoo ha!!" [Laugh greedily.] And she set off on her journey. [Stick yoke to Gert's shoulders; remove Queen.]

Well, Greedy Gert walked and walked and many times the liquid gold was so heavy that her shoulders ached, and many times she was so thirsty that she thought longingly of the water she could have had, but then she thought of how rich she would be when she got back to the town, and the thought of that made her greedy heart glad and kept her trudging along.

Well, on the road one day, Greedy Gert came across a man who was homeless and who held out a tin cup. [Put homeless man on the flannel board.] He looked dirty and tired and sick, and he said, "Oh please, ma'am, give me something to help me. I haven't eaten in a week, and I'm so hungry." Now Greedy Gert remembered that the Queen had said she should help everyone who asked her, but she thought the Queen would never know whether she really did or not, so Greedy Gert just walked by that man as fast as she could and pretended not to hear him even though it was hard to walk fast with those heavy, heavy cups

Enlarge these shapes on a photocopier.

Cover with contact paper and put double-sided tape on the yoke so that it sticks onto Greedy Gert when you move her.

of liquid gold. [Remove homeless man.] On she trudged, though carrying all that gold always made her back and shoulders and neck ache. Then one day, in another town, she met a little girl [put little girl on flannel board] who was weeping because her puppy was very sick, and she had no money to pay a veterinarian to help it. She asked Greedy Gert if she would lend her some money, but Greedy Gert walked by as fast as she could and pretended not to hear her. [Remove girl.]

Well, finally one day Greedy Gert came close to the end of the kingdom. At the end of the kingdom was a desert. [Put up desert scene.] Her shoulders and back were hurting badly because of how heavy the liquid gold was, and it was hard for her to walk through the sand. The air in the desert was very hot and dry, and as Greedy Gert trudged along she thought about how very soon now she would be back at home in the town again, and how she would be the richest person there. She was trying to decide what to keep all her liquid gold in—whether she should lock it in a safe or bury it in the ground—when she looked up and realized that she was lost!! She'd been so busy thinking Greedy Gert thoughts that she hadn't watched where she was going. She walked and walked, trying to find her way, and as she did, the sun in that desert burned more and more hotly and Greedy Gert got more and more tired and more and more thirsty until her throat ached and her mouth was as dry as a bone and she collapsed on the sand and was afraid she was going to die. "Oh, why didn't I choose the water?" she thought to herself. "I'm more thirsty than I have ever been in my life and I cannot drink this liquid gold. I'd give anything if only I could go back and choose the water instead!"

Well just then, the wise Queen floated down from the sky because she was a magic Queen. [Float Queen down onto the board.] It had really been she, disguised as the homeless man, who had asked Greedy Gert for help, and it had really been she, disguised as the weeping little girl, who had asked Greedy Gert to help her puppy. The wise Queen said, "Greedy Gert, I hear your wish, and if you have learned the lesson I intended, I will grant it. What have you learned?"

Well, Greedy Gert thought and thought and finally she said: "I never believed it before, but I guess there really are some things that are more important than gold."

"Like what?" the Queen asked, looking sternly at Greedy Gert.

"Well, when people are in pain and when they need help, I guess helping them is more important than being rich. I know that now because of what a horrible time I have had in this desert."

And the Queen said, "Yes, that is the lesson." And with her magic, she filled the bottomless cups with water instead of liquid gold and Greedy Gert drank and drank and drank. And when she stood up, the cups were so much lighter because now they were filled with water instead of liquid gold. Then, by magic, they found themselves back in the town. The Queen let Gert keep the bottomless cups of water to remind her forever of her journey, and Gert always thought it was the most delicious water she ever tasted. And Greedy Gert changed so much in the way that she treated people, that the townsfolk had to call her Gracious Gert and Generous Gert instead. And that is the end of that story.

VOCABULARY:
Kingdom
Scarce
Weeping
Folk
Collapsed
Desperate
Intended
Angrily
Sternly
Aware
Trudging
Generous

After telling and discussing the story, put the flannel board and pieces out for the children to retell the story and make up new ones. Put a "Two people may be here"' sign near the materials.

Weighing Liquids
Science/Math

WHY we are doing this project: to enable children to compare the weight of a dense liquid like honey to the weight of a less dense liquid like water.

WHAT we will need:
- Balancing scale
- Small paper cups
- Small coffee scoopers
- Honey or corn syrup
- Water
- Two large containers
- Sensory table

HOW we will do it: Put the honey or corn syrup in one of the large containers and do the same with the water. Place these next to the scoopers, balancing scale, and paper cups in the sensory table.

After you tell the Greedy Gert flannel board story, say: "This is our pretend liquid gold, (show them the honey or corn syrup) and this is some water." Show them the scoopers, cups, and scale and ask them to predict which one is heavier. Encourage the children to explore the materials and to verbalize their findings.

Developmental differences: Three- and young four-year-olds will not be concerned with weighing the exact same amount of each fluid, but in their sensory exploration of the materials (including the scale), they will learn, in their own way, that one fluid is heavier than the other. They may also enjoy mixing the two liquids with their fingers. Older children will enjoy scooping the liquids and will be more inclined to put both on the scale to observe what happens.

Liquid Squeeze
Science/Art/Sensory

WHY we are doing this project: to help children observe the difference in consistencies between thick and thin paint; to provide a sensory experience; to develop creative expression.

WHAT we will need:
- Paper
- Tempera paint powder
- Water
- Squeeze bottles
- Liquid starch (found in laundry supply section)
- Newspaper

Teacher:
- Funnel

HOW we will do it: Well ahead of time, start collecting small squeeze bottles like honey containers, small mustard or ketchup squeeze bottles, and lotion dispensers. To begin the activity, spread several layers of newspaper over your work area. Mix up many colors of tempera paints, being sure to include black and different shades of brown. Vary the consistency of the paints by adding more or less water and liquid starch. Some paints should be very watery and others should be fairly thick. Put *small* amounts of paints in the squeeze bottles and use the funnel to refill as necessary. Set the bottles and the paper on the table. Encourage the children to make squeeze paint pictures by squeezing paint onto paper and then using their fingers to spread the paint. Talk about how quickly or slowly the different paints flow out of the squeeze bottles and why.

Marble Roll

Science/Art

WHY we are doing this activity: to allow children to observe what happens to marbles rolling through thin and thick paint; to develop hand–eye coordination; to develop creative expression.

WHAT we will need:
Shirt boxes
Tempera paint powder
Paper
Spoons
Marbles
Water
Liquid starch
Small containers
Newspapers

HOW we will do it: Spread several layers of newspaper over your work surface. Mix your tempera paint with less or more water and liquid starch so that you have thick, pasty paints as well as more watery ones. For a medium consistency, add tempera powder directly to liquid starch. Put a small amount of paint into each container. Put a piece of paper in each shirt box, and put all the boxes on the activity table with the paint, marbles, and spoons. Invite the children to spoon paint into a box and roll marbles around. What do they notice about how the marbles roll through the thick paint? What happens when the marbles roll through watery paint? Compare the tracks made by both.

River, River

Music/Movement/Gross Motor/Language/Cognitive/
Small Group Activity

WHY we are doing this project: to reinforce, through music and movement, the difference between the movement of dense liquid and watery liquid; to develop the large muscle group; to encourage children to express themselves creatively through physical movement; to help children feel comfortable using their singing voices; to develop cognition through memorization of song words.

WHAT we will need:
Butcher paper
Markers
Song: "RIVER, RIVER" (to the tune of "Oh My Darling Clementine") (provided)

HOW we will do it: Pin up your butcher paper near the place where you gather for Attention Getter time. When the children are gathered, tell the following story, and use the markers to draw what you talk about. (Do not feel self-conscious about your pictures—I am no artist, and my drawings are always as rough as they can be, but the children still enjoy them.)

Before you begin, ask the children: "What kind of liquid do you find in a river?" When they answer, "Water," tell the story:

"THE RIVER"

Once upon a time there was a stream, and it flowed past trees and mountains and even a town. But one day the stream got very bored and decided to flow somewhere different. It met up with a mighty, rushing river that roared and tumbled its way along.

"May I join you?" the stream asked.

"As you like, as you like, but hurry along, no time to stop," the river said. So the stream joined the roaring river, but oh dear, oh dear, it didn't like it at all! They rushed and roared and tumbled along so fast that the stream had no time to look at what they were passing, and it was altogether too much. Well, as it travelled along with the huge, roaring, tumbling river, the stream saw a little creek branching off to the side. It said, "Little creek, may I join you?"

Well, the little creek said in a slow, lazy voice: "As you like, as you like, we have got all day and all night too." So the little stream branched off and joined the creek. Well, at first it was such a wonderful change not to be roaring and tumbling along all in a rush. But soon the little stream became very bored because they trickled along sooo very slowly and sooo very sluggishly and day after day there was nothing new to see and only the same old things to do. And, worst of all, the little stream noticed that it really wasn't a stream anymore. It was getting thinner and thinner until it was really just a little muddy dribble of water.

Well, luckily that night a big rain came. It rained and rained for hours and hours until it swelled up all the waterways of the land. The little stream was so swollen now that it burst the banks of the tiny creek, and branched away down a valley. And the little stream was very happy to be its old self again, splashing and gushing over rocks and stones, forming little falls and pools, and chattering and babbling away to itself under the hot, bright sun. And that is the end of that story.

After you tell the story, say: "Now we are going to be a river." Have the children line up and put their hands lightly on the shoulders of the person in front of them. Wind and twist your way around the furniture in the room as you sing this song:

"RIVER, RIVER"

Roaring river, roaring river, roaring river,
roaring free,
River rushing and a-gushing,
streaming down to meet the sea.

After the children learn the words, sing together and wind your way around the room as quickly as you can without tripping, falling, or bumping into furniture. Then say to the children: "What would a river of honey move like?" Discuss this for a while, and then suggest that you all pretend to be a river of honey. Explain that *sluggish* means slowly and lazily. Ask the children if they have ever seen a slug. How did it move? When you are ready to be a river of honey, wind your way sluggishly around the room and sing very sluggishly:

Sluggish river, sluggish river,
See it oozing sluggishly,
See it creeping and a-crawling,
slowly rolling to the sea.

Dish Wash
Science/Dramatic Play/Language

WHY we are doing this project: to help children learn to express their ideas; to develop imagination; to facilitate social interaction with other children; to help children coordinate actions with words; to enable children to compare the density of liquid dish soap to water.

WHAT we will need:
  Dramatic play kitchen furniture
  Sensory table or basins
  Play dishes
  Miniature liquid soap bottles (if possible)
  Liquid soap
  Funnels
  Strainers
  Pitcher of water

HOW we will do it: Miniature liquid soap bottles containing sample portions are sometimes available at variety stores. If you cannot obtain these, put your liquid soap in the standard-sized bottles. Spread several layers of newspaper under your sensory table or basins, fill them half or one-third full of warm water, and place them in your dramatic play kitchen area. As the children explore the materials, invite them to compare what happens when they squeeze liquid soap into a strainer to what happens when they pour water through it. How does each liquid make its way through the mesh? Invite the children to notice the speed with which each liquid flows. As the soap is mixed with the water, does it change the texture or density of the water? Discuss!

Making Lassi
Multicultural/Math

WHY we are doing this project: to develop an appreciation for the cuisine of other cultures; to enable children to make a recipe with three liquids of different consistencies; to familiarize children with cup and spoon measurements.

WHAT we will need:
- Book: Kalman, Bobbie, *India the Culture* or Ganeri, Anita, *Journey Through India*
- Plain, nonfat yogurt (one cup for each child)
- Honey
- Cinnamon
- Cold water
- Four bowls
- 1 cup measuring cup
- ⅓ cup measuring cup
- Two teaspoons
- One ½ teaspoon
- Permanent marker
- Blender
- Clear plastic cups (large enough for 1½ cups of liquid)

HOW we will do it: Set out everything on a table except the books, marker, and blender. Put the yogurt, water, honey, and cinnamon in separate bowls. Using the permanent marker, mark the measurements of the cups in clear, large numbers and letters. Put the 1 cup measuring cup in front of the yogurt, the ⅓ cup in front of the cold water, a teaspoon and the ½ teaspoon in front of the honey, and a teaspoon in front of the cinnamon.

During an Attention Getter time, look through the photographs in *India the Culture* or *Journey Through India* and talk about them together. Tell the children that it can get very, very hot in some parts of India, and that people like to drink a very cool, refreshing drink called *lassi*. Say this word together several times. Invite the children to each take a clear, plastic cup and to fill it by taking only *one* spoon or cup of each spice or liquid. If you like, walk around the table, pick up each measuring utensil, and go over this with the children before they begin.

Invite the children to put all ingredients in their cups, and as they do, ask them what they notice about how the yogurt, honey, and water are different. What did they notice about how easy or hard it was to get each fluid out of its measuring spoon or cup? Have the children bring their ingredients to you, mix them in the blender, and pour the *lassi* back into their cups to drink. You may want to sweeten your *lassi* more than is called for in this recipe. Make it to your and the children's taste.

Literature

Symbol Key: *Multicultural
+Minimal diversity
No symbol: no diversity or no people

Allen, P. (1980). *Mr. Archimedes' bath.* Lothrop, Lee & Shepard Books.

Ardley, N. (1991). *The science book of water.* San Diego, CA: Harcourt Brace Jovanovich.

Burns, D. (1990). *Sugaring season.* Minneapolis, MN: Carolrhoda Books. (This book has some excellent photographs of how maple syrup is made.)

Ganeri, A. (1994). *Journey through India.* Mahwah, NJ: Troll Associates.*

Halpern, S. (1992). *My river.* New York: Macmillan.* (Beautiful color pictures.)

Kalman, B. (1990). *India the culture*. New York: Crabtree.*

Ravzon, M. J., & Overbeck Bix, C. (1994). *Water, water everywhere*. San Francisco, CA: Sierra Club Books.* (This book has excellent photographs and does a good job of showing the effects of acid rain and water pollution.)

Turner, D. (1989). *Milk*. Minneapolis, MN: Carolrhoda Books.

Extenders

Science: Provide fluids of different densities, including hair gel. Invite the children to pour some of each into a paper cup. In which liquid does a Popsicle stick stand straight up? Why?

Science: When you conduct your liquid roll experiment down wooden ramps, let a drop of four liquids of different densities each fall on a ramp at the same time, and let them race each other. Watch as a group, and as the liquids are rolling, ask the children to predict in what order the drops will reach the end of the ramp.

Movement/Gross Motor: When you sing the "RIVER, RIVER" song, vary your movements by rolling and tumbling instead of walking. Spread gym mats out on a large open area. Have the children roll or somersault as a tumbling river, and then as a sluggish river.

Sound Makers and Conductors

Attention Getter: Collect a sock, an empty Band-Aid box, and a marble. Have the children gather together in a group and ask them to turn their backs to you. Rattle the marble in the Band-Aid box. Ask the children if they hear it. Then shake the marble in the sock. Ask the children if they hear anything. Have them turn around, and show them the marble in the sock. Why did it not make a noise? Let each child take a turn rattling the marble in the Band-Aid box. Why does it make a sound? Tell the children that you are going to be working with sound makers over the next few days. What do the children think about the sock and the Band-Aid box as good sound makers?

Rattle Boxes (Part 1)
Language/Small Group Activity

WHY we are doing this activity: to promote self-esteem and empower children by involving them in the preparation of their own materials for an activity; to develop speaking, listening, reading, and writing skills; to teach children how to work together and cooperate by participating in a group effort.

Note: Do this project several weeks ahead of unit.

WHAT we will need:
Metal Band-Aid box
Butcher paper
Markers (two different colors)
Note paper
Pens
Envelopes

HOW we will do it: In this project, the class will work together as a group to write letters to friends, neighbors, and family, asking for help in collecting a material it needs for a project: metal Band-Aid boxes or small tins with lids. Begin this project several weeks ahead of time, so that you have plenty of time to collect enough boxes.

To prepare, tape up your butcher paper pieces where you gather during Attention Getter time. During one of these gatherings, hold up the Band-Aid box you already have, and tell the children that in a few weeks, you are going to be working with things that make sound, and things that carry sound. Tell your students that you want to make rattle boxes, and that you need metal Band-Aid boxes or small tin boxes with lids for the project. Hold up your box, and explain that you only have one metal Band-Aid box, but you need one for everyone who will want to do the project. Ask: "How do you think we could get more Band-Aid boxes?" Have the children write their ideas on the chart, or print them yourself. If you print them yourself, alternate the color of marker you use so that children can distinguish between separate sentences. Use quotation marks and write the children's name next to their comments. If or when the suggestion comes up to ask other people if they have any Band-Aid boxes, say: "Who could we ask?" Write down the answers.

Suggest that you write letters to people asking for help. If you work with younger children, ask them what to say in the letter, and write down their words. Later, write their words on a regular-sized piece of paper, make photocopies, and give several copies to each child to distribute to friends and family. If you are working with kindergartners, set out the note paper and pens on a table. Instead of writing a letter on a chart, ask the children what words they might use in their letters (e.g., *Band-Aid, metal, box, please, project*) Print these words on the second piece of butcher paper, and when you can, draw a picture next to each word to illustrate its meaning. Encourage each child to write a letter asking friends and family to collect metal Band-Aid boxes to give to the class. Photocopy these letters and give each child several copies. If you need to, include a note of your own for clarification.

Rattle Boxes (Part 2)
Science/Art/Fine Motor

WHY we are doing this project: to allow children to experiment with the noises different objects make inside a metal box; to facilitate creative expression; to develop fine motor skills.

WHAT we will need:
Metal Band-Aid boxes
Tissue paper scraps
Glue
Small containers (for glue)
Glue brushes
Permanent marker
Rice
Beans
Buttons
Any other materials that will rattle
Aquarium gravel

HOW we will do it: Ahead of time, make your own rattle box by putting a variety of materials in a Band-Aid box. Put glue all around the edge, and press the lid down. Glue tissue scraps all over the outside of your box, and let it dry. (When dry, the tissue scraps will peel off if pulled, but that is okay—children enjoy decorating, as well as peeling, the boxes.) You may also want to make a few extra rattle boxes in case some children decide not to make their own—you will be using the rattles during a music time.

During an Attention Getter time, sing a song together as a group. Take out your rattle box and shake it in time to the rhythm of the song. When the song is finished, ask the children what they see in the room which will help them make their own rattle boxes. Use the permanent marker to write names on the boxes, or have your students do this. As they work on them, ask them if they remember how you collected all the Band-Aid boxes. The next day, when the rattle boxes are dry, have the children sit in a circle during an Attention Getter time and shake their rattle boxes while singing songs. Then go around the circle and have every one shake his or her rattle box. As a group, try to guess what each person put inside her or his rattle box, and whether there is a lot or a little inside.

Making Kazoos
Science/Art/Fine Motor

WHY we are doing this project: to help children understand that sound is made when something vibrates; to allow children to observe a very obvious example of vibration and the sound it creates; to facilitate artistic expression; to develop fine motor skills.

WHAT we will need:
Toilet paper rolls
Wax paper (cut into 7.5 cm (3") squares)
Crayons
Rubber bands

Preparation:
Hole puncher

HOW we will do it: To prepare, use the hole puncher to punch a hole in the toilet paper roll as far away from one end as the hole puncher will reach. Decorate your kazoo with crayons. Wrap a wax paper square on the end with the hole in it and, using a rubber band, secure it without covering the hole. Lay out the other toilet paper rolls and all other materials on the activity table.

During an Attention Getter time, show your kazoo to the children and hum into it through the uncovered end. What happens? Let the children examine it, and explain that when you hum, the paper at the other end vibrates, and makes the humming sound. *Vibrate* means to move back and forth very, very quickly. Tap, blink, and pat this word as you say the syllables together. If you can, find a tuning fork, guitar, or other instrument with vibrating parts to elaborate on this concept further. Say: "You can see quite clearly, and hear quite clearly the vibration that this kazoo makes, but did you know that *all* sound is made when something vibrates? We can't always see vibration happening, the way we can with this kazoo, but that is what makes sound."

Show the children the materials on the table and invite them to make their own kazoos. Invite them to watch each other as they use the kazoos. Can they see the wax paper vibrate?

Tip: Save your kazoos to use during Attention Getter time in the Wind and Air unit, for the wind hummer activity.

More Experiments with Vibration

Science/Sensory

WHY we are doing this experiment: to reinforce the concept of vibration and to build on information from the previous activity.

WHAT we will need:
Long, plastic rulers (or other long, flexible objects)
Table edge
Demonstration:
Pencil

HOW we will do it: During an Attention Getter time, take a pencil and put it on the edge of a table. Say: "I'm going to hit the edge of this pencil and try to make it vibrate." Did it work? Hold the pencil up to the ruler and show the children how the pencil is rigid but the ruler is flexible. Hold the ruler on the edge of the table and ask: "Do you think the end of this ruler that is sticking out over the edge of the table would vibrate if I hit it?" Instead of carrying out the demonstration, invite the children to do so. Discuss the results. Can they hear the vibrating ruler make a noise?

Invite the children to experiment with moving more and less ruler to jut out over the table edge. Does it affect the sound of the vibration? Explain that *pitch* has to do with how slowly or quickly an object vibrates. (The more slowly something vibrates, or moves back and forth, the lower the pitch. The faster it vibrates, or moves back and forth, the higher the pitch.) Why is the speed of the vibration affected by how much ruler is jutting out over the table? (The more ruler that is held to the table, the less amount of flexible ruler is available to vibrate.) Are there other things in the room that could be made to vibrate?

Developmental differences: Three- and young four-year-olds are not likely to be interested in *pitch* and *vibration*, but will have fun flicking the ruler.

How Does Thickness Affect Sound?

Science/Sensory

WHY we are doing this experiment: to enable children to discover that the thickness of an object affects the frequency of its vibrations and to provide children with a sensory experience.

WHAT we will need:
Three thick rubber bands
Three thin rubber bands
Three rubber bands of medium thickness
Six nails (6–8 cm long [2½"–3"])
Three blocks of wood
Preparation:
Hammer

HOW we will do it: To prepare one experimentation tool, hammer two nails into one block of wood so that the nails are about 12.5 cm (5") away from each other. Between them, stretch one thick rubber band, one rubber band of medium thickness, and one thin one. Keep the bands separate. Use the other materials to make two other rubber band experiment tools in the same way, and put all three on an activity table.

Show these materials to the children and ask them to predict what the rubber bands will do and how they will sound when they are plucked or pulled. Invite the children to conduct the experiment, and encourage them to verbalize their findings. What do they notice about whether the vibrating rubber bands sound the same or different? How do the rubber bands look different? What could this have to do with the way the rubber bands vibrate? Explain, when appropriate, that the thickest band is heavier, and vibrates fewer times in the same amount of time as the thin rubber band, which is lighter, and can vibrate more times in the same amount of time. The thick rubber band has the lowest frequency and the thin one has the highest. The rubber band which has medium thickness has medium frequency.

How Does Sound Travel?

Science/Small Group Activity

WHY we are doing this project: to help children understand that sound travels through the air in waves, radiating out from the source of the sound.

WHAT we will need:

A bowl of water

HOW we will do it: During an Attention Getter time, have everyone sit on the floor in a circle, and then gather as closely as possible to the bowl of water. If you are working with a small enough group, invite each child to touch the middle of the water, and ask the children to watch the surface of the water closely. Can they see the circles of ripples which spread out from the place where the water was touched? Explain that sound travels in much the same way, even though we cannot see it. Sound waves travel out away from the thing making the sound, and move through the air.

More Proof That Sound Travels through the Air

Science/Sensory

WHY we are doing this project: to provide children with a direct sensory experience which proves that sound travels through the air.

WHAT we will need:

Timer
Strong twine
Duct tape
Cardboard cylinder (from food wrap box)
"One person may be here" sign
    (provided on page 3; photocopy and
    enlarge for your use)

Preparation:

Chalk or masking tape

HOW we will do it: In this experiment, hang a ticking timer in a quiet place, and let the children discover that even when they are at a distance from the timer, or on the ground below it, the ticking is still audible. Choose a place which is removed from the rest of your activities—maybe a place outside which is visible through a window, or a room which is not normally used for children's activities, but which you can see from your main activity area.

Tie the twine around the timer and use the duct tape to affix it securely. Hang the timer from the ceiling, so that it hangs at children's ear level. Wind up the timer all the way. Find out how far away from the timer you can stand and still hear it, and draw a chalk mark at that point, or make a masking tape line.

During an Attention Getter time, show the timer, cylinder, and chalk or masking tape line to the children. Ask them to predict whether they will be able to hear the timer if they listen through the cylinder, and whether or not they will be able to hear it when they stand on the line. Invite them to experiment by listening through the cylinder in a variety of positions and at different distances. What do they notice? Afterward, discuss the children's findings. Remind them of the bowl of water, and how ripples spread out in the water when they touched it. Sound waves spread out from the timer. How did the children's experiment prove this?

Sound Travels through Water

Science/Sensory

WHY we are doing this experiment: to enable children to discover that sound travels through water and, in fact, is carried more efficiently than through air.

WHAT we will need:

    Glass aquarium
    Two rocks
    Water
    Stethoscope or a funnel and tubing
    Activity sign (format provided below;
        photocopy and enlarge for your use)

HOW we will do it: A glass aquarium, when filled with water, is normally too heavy to be knocked over by a child, but to be safe, discuss with the children the fact that the container should not be moved. Ask: "What would happen if this glass aquarium fell and broke?" For an extra precaution, make a "Please don't move the aquarium" sign and discuss it with the children after you post it above the activity. (See p. 208)

Fill the aquarium with water and put the two rocks beside it. Post the activity sign near the aquarium. To make your own stethoscope, attach plastic tubing to the narrow end of a funnel.

During an Attention Getter time ask: "Do you think sound travels in water?" Encourage the children to express what they think about this. Read/interpret the activity sign together and ask the children to predict what will happen when they follow its suggestions. Invite the children to conduct the experiment by using the stethoscope to listen while a friend knocks the rocks together in the water. Encourage your students to express their findings. Is the sound of the rocks being knocked together louder in water or air? As appropriate,

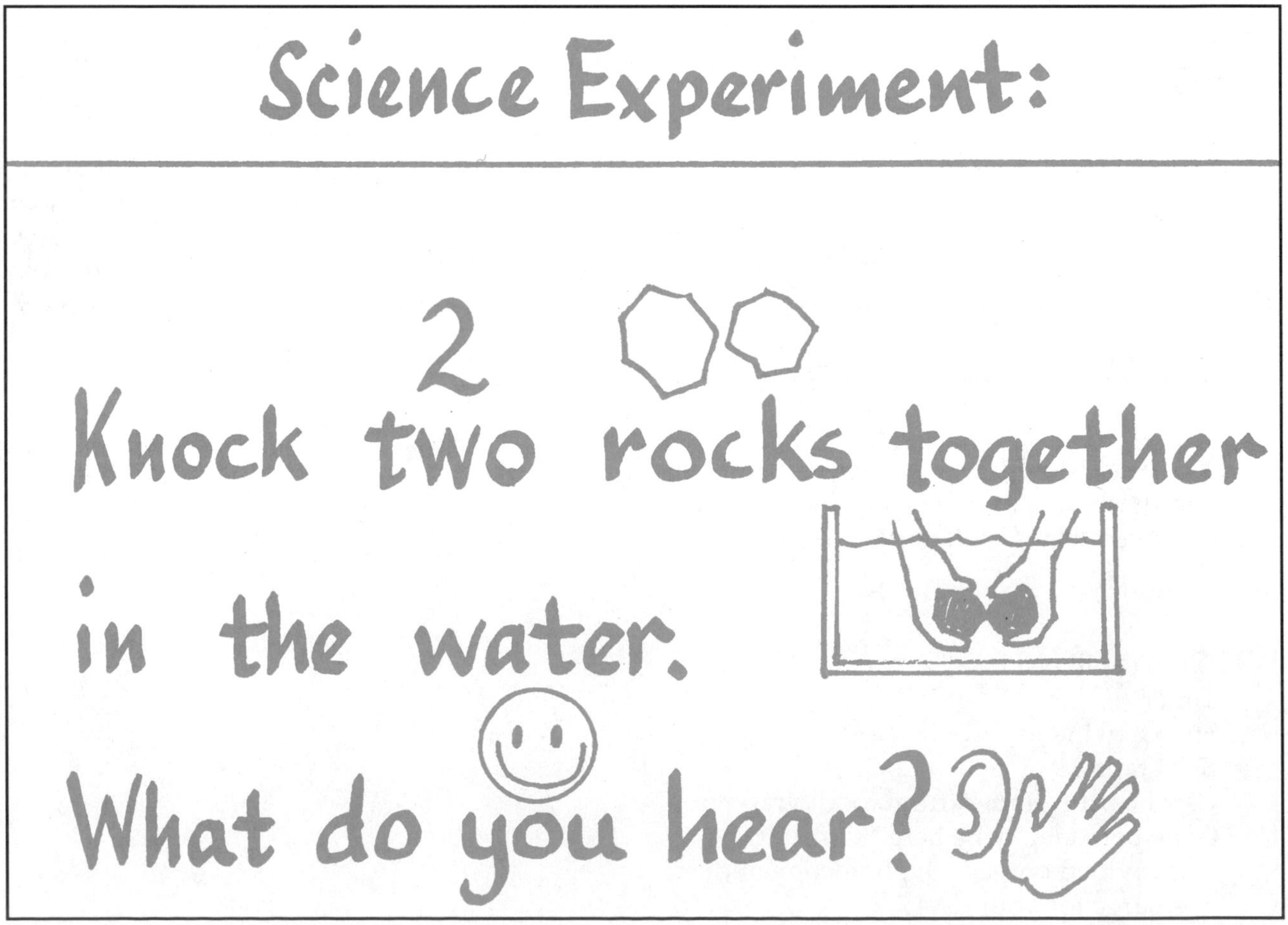

Science Experiment:

2

Knock two rocks together in the water.

What do you hear?

explain that water actually carries sound better than air does. Ask the children to look around the room and see what other objects they could use to make noise in the water to test this hypothesis further.

Musical Jars
Science/Music

WHY we are doing this project: to allow children to experiment with volume and sound and to understand how the two are related; to develop self-esteem and a sense of autonomy through use of a one-person station; to allow children to creatively explore music.

WHAT we will need:

Five large glass jars (all the same size)

Food coloring
Water
Wooden stick
"One person may be here" sign
(provided on page 3; photocopy and enlarge for your own use)
Activity sign (provided below; photocopy and enlarge for your use)

HOW we will do it: Fill each glass jar with graduated amounts of colored water, so that the first jar has the most and the last jar has the least. Make each one a different color. Arrange them in a row, and lay a stick next to them. Make the activity and "One person may be here" signs according to the suggested format in the text or create your own, and tape both signs up on the wall next to the project table.

During an Attention Getter time, read/interpret the activity sign together. Point to the jars and say to the children: "These con-

tainers are glass jars. What happens if you drop glass? Do you think it would be okay if you picked up one of these jars and tried to move it or carried it around the room? Why not?" Make sure the children understand that the jars must stay exactly where they are at all times. For an extra safety precaution, make a "Please do not move the jars" sign and discuss it with the children after you post it above the activity. (See p. 208.) Also discuss the "One person may be here" sign. Ask your students to predict whether or not the jars will all make the same sound when they are tapped with the wooden stick. Encourage them to conduct this experiment. What do they notice about the sounds the jars produce? Discuss the fact that the amount (volume) of water in each jar affects the vibration of the stick when it is tapped against it.

Sound Conductors
Science

WHY we are doing this experiment: to enable children to observe firsthand that sound waves spread in open spaces and that the walls of tubes channel or *conduct* them; to develop fine motor skills.

WHAT we will need:
    Aquarium tubing
    Funnels

HOW we will do it: Plastic tubing is available at pet or hardware stores and costs about $.20 to $.35/ft., depending on the diameter and thickness of the tubing. When you buy the tubing, make sure the ends fit securely around the narrow opening of your funnels. Put the tubes and funnels on an activity table and encourage the children to fit the tubes around the openings of the narrow funnel ends. Tell your students that they have made *stethoscopes*. Ask the children if they have ever visited a doctor who used a stethoscope. What happens when the children

put the wide funnel end on a friend's heart and listen at the other end? (Remind the children to ask their friends before placing the stethoscope on their chests.) Is the sound the same as when they try to listen to a heartbeat without a stethoscope? Explain that the tube carries or *conducts* the sound and that, without a tube, sound waves spread out and are not as easy to hear. Inform the children that as well as working with sound makers over the next few days, we will also be working with sound conductors.

Doctor's Office
Dramatic Play/Language/Science

WHY we are doing this project: to encourage the children to explore sound conductors (stethoscopes) in dramatic play; to develop reading and writing skills; to expand vocabulary; to help children learn how to put their ideas into words; to promote social interaction between children; to help children connect actions with words through pretending; to give children the opportunity to work out real-life situations through imaginative, dramatic play.

WHAT we will need:
    Stethoscopes (made in previous activity)
    Toy stethoscopes
    Band-Aids
    Toy doctor's instruments
    Notepad for prescriptions
    Pens
    Telephone
    Notebook (to simulate an appointment book)
    The following materials are sometimes donated by medical offices:
    Real stethoscopes
    White coats
    Plastic needle parts (no metal tips)
    Tongue depressors
    Gauze

HOW we will do it: Set up a doctor's office. Invite the children to play in it and, as and when appropriate, also encourage them to use all of the stethoscopes and to compare them. Ask what they notice about which ones make the best and worst sound conductors? Examine how each is made and see if they can find out why one is better than another.

Comparing Sound Conductors
Science/Sensory

WHY we are doing this experiment: to enable children to discover and compare how different materials conduct sound and to develop listening skills.

WHAT we will need:
> Cardboard tubes (from wrapping paper)
> Toilet paper rolls
> Styrofoam blocks (used as packing for appliances)
> Plastic frosting containers
> Frozen juice containers
> Metal cylinders (no sharp or rusty edges—check car maintenance businesses)
> Any other cylinders made of other materials
> Xylophone
> Timer
> Rattle
> Bell

Preparation:
> Knife
> Exacto knife

HOW we will do it: To prepare, use a knife to cut a circular core from each Styrofoam block so that they are hollow in the middle.

Cut the bottom out of each frosting container and frozen juice can so that they form cylinders. Use an Exacto knife to do this if necessary. Lay out the sound makers (xylophone, rattle, timer, and bell) on the table along with the sound conductors.

During an Attention Getter time, show the children the materials on the table, and ask them to predict which conductor will carry or conduct sound the best and which one will not conduct sound well. Ask the children how they could test each sound conductor. As the children experiment and explore, invite them to compare all three cardboard conductors: the toilet paper rolls, juice cylinders, and wrapping paper rolls. Is there a difference? What do they notice about which one is the best conductor? Encourage the children to verbalize their findings.

Superconductors
Science

WHY we are doing this experiment: to enable children to discover the connection between the length of a conductor, the distance sound waves must travel, and the sound that is heard; to facilitate cooperation between children.

WHAT we will need:
> Cardboard tubes from kitchen wraps
> Toilet paper rolls
> Vacuum cleaner hose
> Timer
> Xylophone
> Bell
> Rattle

Preparation:
> Scissors

HOW we will do it: To prepare, cut two vertical slits, each opposite the other, in both ends of all the tubes and toilet paper rolls. This allows tubes to be fitted over each other. Put the sound makers out on a table, and all the tubes out, also.

During an Attention Getter time, pass out three or four toilet paper rolls, one per child, and have the children hold the rolls to their ears while you make a noise. Repeat this until every child has had a turn. Lengthen a sound conductor by fitting three or four cardboard tubes together, so that the children can see how to do this. Ask them to predict whether or not the sound will be the same through the super-long conductor as it was through the single toilet paper roll. Ask the children if they see anything in the room that will help them conduct this experiment.

Ask: "How will you be able to hold a superlong tube and listen through it, and at the same time, make a noise with a sound maker?" Listen to the children's ideas and, if necessary, suggest that the children ask a friend to make a noise with a sound maker while they listen through a conductor. Help three- and young four-year-olds fit the tubes together. As the children experiment, ask them what they notice about whether or not the sound makers sound different through the short toilet paper rolls compared to the super-long conductors.

What do the children notice about how the super-long conductors carry sound when they are lengthened and shortened? Invite the children to compare how the vacuum hose and toilet paper rolls conduct sound and encourage them to express their findings.

Cones As Sound Conductors
Science/Art

WHY we are doing this activity: to allow children to discover how cones conduct sound and to facilitate creative expression.

WHAT we will need:
    Construction paper
    Paint (different colors, including brown and black)
    Paintbrushes
    Stapler
    Musical instruments (e.g., rhythm sticks, triangle, drum)
    Cardboard cylinders (wrapping paper tubes)

HOW we will do it: Set out art materials on the activity table. Ahead of time, make a sample sound conductor cone by painting a piece of construction paper, letting it dry, and then wrapping one end around and stapling it, to make a cone.

During an Attention Getter time, take out the cone and hold it up next to a cardboard cylinder. Ask the children what they notice about how the two are different. Remind them of the previous activities, when they experimented with how cylinders conduct sound. Invite your students to compare how cones and cylinders conduct sound by making cones of their own for the experiment. Show the children the end of your cone which is stapled, and ask them what they will need for this step when they make their own cones. What will happen if they try to staple the paper while it is still wet? The next day, after the paint has dried, assist the children with this step.

Set out the musical instruments and the cylinders to begin the experiment. Ask the children to predict whether or not sounds will be the same when heard through the cones and the cylinders. Encourage the children to verbalize their findings.

Sound Maker Song
Music/Movement/Cognitive

WHY we are doing this activity: to help children feel comfortable using their singing voices; to reinforce the concept that different materials make different sounds inside a box; to develop cognition through memorization of words and actions.

WHAT we will need:
    Song: "SOUND MAKER SONG" (to the tune of "Yankee Doodle Dandy")
    Rattle boxes (optional)

"SOUND MAKER SONG"
I have a box, a metal box and it is full of gravel.
I shake it up and shake it down and this is what it sounds like:
Ch ch ch ch ch ch ch, ch ch ch ch ch ch, Ch ch ch ch ch ch ch, and that is what it sounds like.

I have a box, a metal box, and it is full of silver.

I shake it up and shake it down and this
    is what it sounds like:
Clinky clinky clinky clink,
Clinky clinky clinky clink,
Clinky clinky clinky clink
and that is what it sounds like.

I have a box, a metal box and it is full of
    pebbles,
I shake it up and shake it down,
    and this is what it sounds like:
Rattle rattle rattle rattle,
Rattle rattle rattle rattle,
Rattle rattle rattle rattle,
that is what it sounds like.

If you sing the song without the rattle boxes, pretend to hold a box in both hands as you sing: "I have a box, a metal box, etc." For "I shake it up and shake it down, and this is what it sounds like," pretend to shake it up, then down, and then next to your ear. If the children become very familiar with the song, and you feel they would enjoy a variation, see if you can sing the song without saying a certain word, like "shake" or "box." Use your rattle boxes while you sing the song also, and see if everyone stops shaking boxes at the same time, when you reach the end of each verse.

Do We Really Need Two Ears to Listen to Sound Makers?

Science/Sensory/Small Group Activity

WHY we are doing this project: to help children become aware of the sense of hearing and to help them understand from direct experience why having two ears improves hearing.

WHAT we will need:
    Rhythm sticks
Optional:
    Blindfolds

HOW we will do it: This is a group activity appropriate for an Attention Getter time. You can either have the children cover their eyes and turn their backs, or use a blindfold, depending on how your children feel about blindfolds. Have several children at a time close their eyes, turn their backs, and cover one ear. Have one child go to another place in the room and tap the rhythm sticks together. Ask the children with one ear covered to guess where the sound is coming from. Ask the other children in the group: "Are they right?" Then repeat the exercise with both ears uncovered. Now can the children guess where the sound is coming from? Give every child a chance to conduct this experiment.

Sign Language Words

Social Studies/Anti-Bias/Language

WHY we are doing this project: to develop an appreciation for alternative methods of communicating; to introduce children to sign language; to develop cognition through memorization of words and accompanying actions.

WHAT we will need:
    Book: Charlip, Remy, Mary Beth,
    & Ancona, George, *Handtalk Birthday*

HOW we will do it: This is an *excellent* book. Read it to the children and discuss the photographs and the story. Focus on some of the words for which the hand positions are clearly shown, for example, *surprise*, *who*, *what*, and *no*. Use your hands to teach the children these sign words. Try to say these words in sign language during the course of the day.

Counting Sounds
Math/Sensory

WHY we are doing this activity: to practice rational counting; to develop reading and writing skills; to help children become aware of the sense of hearing; for older children, to facilitate a subtraction exercise.

WHAT we will need:
Four coffee cans with lids
Marbles
Buttons
Pennies
Juice can lids
Writing sheets (format provided on pages 183–184; photocopy and enlarge for your use)
Blank sheets of paper
Pens
Small containers
Colored contact paper
Four trays
Preparation:
Exacto knife

HOW we will do it: To prepare, cover all the coffee cans with contact paper. Cut a slit in each plastic lid to accommodate one of the above materials: marbles, juice can lids, pennies or buttons. Each slit should be just wide enough and large enough for the material to pass through. Set out a variety of materials (marbles, buttons, pennies, etc.) in separate small containers. The children will drop each item into a coffee can and, by listening to the "clunk" or "ping" each object makes, will count the number of objects.

You should decide how many of each material to put in the containers, according to how high your children are counting—probably below ten for three- and four-year-olds, and maybe fourteen or fifteen for kindergartners. Put the coffee cans out next to their corresponding objects.

Using the pictures on the writing sheets for "you" and "hear," print an activity sign that says: "How many do you hear?" and put it up near the materials.

Make photocopies of the writing sheets, and put these, blank sheets of paper, and pens on the trays also. Above them, tape the activity sign. During an Attention Getter time, read or interpret the activity sign and writing sheets together. Invite the children to explore the materials and to use the writing sheets or blank paper to record the number of objects they count as they hear them fall into the cans.

Sounds Around
Gross Motor/Nature/Cognitive/Sensory/Social Studies

WHY we are doing this: to develop the large muscle group; to develop awareness of the sense of hearing; to develop awareness of the sounds of nature as well as noise pollution; to develop cognition by recalling a sequence of events.

WHAT we will need:
Tape recorder
Tape
Optional:
Rope

HOW we will do it: If you work with children who have a hard time picking partners for walks, use the rope and have everyone hold onto it. This saves time and trouble.

Before you leave home or school, explain to the children that you are going to go for a walk outside to see what sound makers you find there. Ask: "What part of our bodies will we have to use?" Show the children the tape and tape recorder. Ask: "What can we use these for when we go on our walk?"

Try to walk through a noisy street, as well as a more pastoral area with trees and birds. Record the sounds you hear. Also, spend some time talking about the sounds. What do the children notice about hearing noises without seeing who or what is making them? Can they guess where they come from? Is there a place where they cannot hear themselves talk very well, because of the noise? Use the phrase *noise pollution* and talk to the children about how

Drop each marble into the can.

How many do you hear? _____

For kindergartners:

4 🙂🙂🙂🙂
Take four marbles out.
Now how many do you hear
when you drop
the other marbles in? _____

Drop each penny into the can.

How many do you hear? _____

For kindergartners:

6 ○ ○ ○
   ○ ○ ○
Take six pennies out.
Now how many do you hear
when you drop
the other pennies in? _____

Drop each button into the can.

How many do you hear?

_____

For Kindergartners:

5 ⊙⊙⊙⊙⊙

Take five buttons out.

Now how many do you hear

when you drop

the other buttons in?

_____

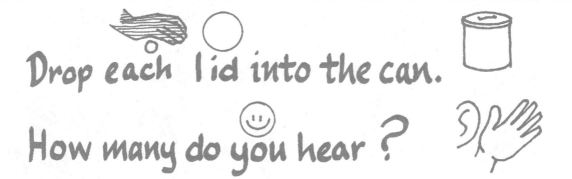

Drop each lid into the can.

How many do you hear?

_____

For Kindergartners:

3 ○○○

Take three lids out.

Now how many do you hear

when you drop

the other lids in?

_____

they feel when there is too much noise. Later, when you are back at home or school, play back the tape and talk about what made the sounds you hear. Encourage the children to recall the sequence of events that they experienced on your walk.

Literature

Symbol Key: *Multicultural
+Minimal diversity
No symbol: no diversity or no people

Bennett, D. (1989). *Sounds*. New York: Bantam Little Rooster.

Charlip, Remy, Mary Beth, & Ancona, G. (1987). *Handtalk birthday*. New York: Four Winds Press.*

Geraghty, P. (1992). *Stop that noise*. New York: Crown.

Keats, E. J. (1969). *A whistle for Willie*. New York: Viking Press.* (An excellent classic.)

Seeger, P. (1994). *Abiyoyo*. New York: Aladdin Books.* (A ukulele is instrumental [no pun intended!] in this wonderful story.)

Showers, P. (1991). *Listening walk*. New York: Harper Collins.

Wells, R. (1973). *Noisy Nora*. New York: Puffin Pied Piper.

Wise Brown, M. (1939). *The quiet noisy book*. New York: Harper Collins.

EXTENDERS

Music: Gather together as many instruments as you can, for example, drums, triangles, and maracas. Have the children play them during a music time. Compare the vibrations (sound) that each instrument makes. Have the children close their eyes while they take turns making a sound with an instrument, and see if they can guess which instrument it is.

Science/Sensory: When you have the children experiment with volume and sound using glass jars and water, add some other materials to see how they affect the sounds the jars produce, for example, a plastic knife, a spoon, or the bar that rings a triangle.

Science/Math: After the children make their own super sound conductors, make a giant one as a class, using every tube you have. Let everyone take a turn making a sound at one end and listening at the other. If you like, measure your super super sound conductor. How long is it?

Science/Sensory: When the children make their rattle boxes, make one that is one-third full, one that is one-half full, one that is three-quarters full, and one that is completely full. Seal the lids and set them out on a table. Encourage the children to shake them. How do the different volumes affect the sounds produced?

THE FIVE SENSES

Attention Getter: Cut several oranges into quarters, so that you have one quarter for each child. Have these on hand, as well as paper towels and small paper cups. Pass a cup and one orange quarter to each child. First, ask the children to lay the orange piece on the paper towel, and to look at it close-up. Ask them to pretend that they have never seen an orange before, and do not know what it is. Then ask them to close their eyes, and touch it with their fingertips. How does it feel? Next, ask everyone to squeeze the orange piece into a paper cup, and to listen carefully. Does the orange piece make a sound when it is squeezed? Ask them to close their eyes and smell the juice. Ask: "If you didn't know what was in your cup, could you tell that it's orange juice?" Last, ask everyone to drink their juice and to concentrate on the taste on their tongues.

When you have followed all the above steps, ask the children what parts of their bodies they had to use for these activities. After the children express their ideas, point to the appropriate part of your body as you mention it and say: "We used our sense of sight, our sense of hearing, our sense of taste, our sense of smell, and our sense of touch. We just used all five senses." Go back over each step you took in your discovery of the oranges, and ask the children what they remember about which senses they used with each step. Ask the children to guess what you will be talking about and working with over the next few days.

Taste: Taste Center
Science/Sensory/Language

WHY we are doing this project: to help children become aware of the sense of taste; to facilitate a sensory experience; to develop speaking and listening skills; to develop cognition by helping children learn the difference between sweet, sour, salty, and bitter; to help children understand that certain parts of the tongue are more sensitive to certain tastes.

WHAT we will need:
  Plates
  Slices of pickle
  Potato chips
  Lemon slices (very small)
  Chocolate chips
  Small paper plates
  Activity sign (provided on page 189; photocopy and enlarge for your use)
  Butcher paper
  Tongue diagram (provided on page 189; photocopy and enlarge for your use)
  Markers
  Puppet
Older children:
  Toothpicks

HOW we will do it: Cut the pickles into slices and slice the lemon into very small pieces. Put all the food out on plates, set the plates on the activity table, and put the toothpicks beside them. Make the activity sign according to the suggested format in this text, and on the butcher paper, make an enlarged chart of the tongue diagram in the text.

During an Attention Getter time, point to all the foods and ask the children to predict how each will taste. Next, ask them to predict whether parts of their tongues will be able to taste some of the foods better than other parts of their tongues. Let the children know that they can conduct a scientific taste experiment. Reinforce the part of the activity sign that says: "Please eat only one at a time." Ask: "What would happen if one person took a whole bunch of chocolate chips and ate them?" (No one else would get to try the experiment.) Also, make sure the children understand that they can put things on their paper plates, carry them back to the table, and that they must sit down while they eat.

Let the children know that it is easier to tell what parts of the tongue are tasting if they just eat a little piece of something. Show them the toothpicks, and encourage them to scrape a little bit of food onto a toothpick, and then to touch it onto different places on their tongues. If you are working with very young children, do not include the toothpicks in the activity, and encourage them to use the tips of their fingers instead. Also, if you work with three- and young four-year-olds, you will probably have to supervise this activity fairly closely. After the children have had a chance to conduct the experiment, ask them about their findings. Ask them if the lemon piece and pickle slice are sour in the same way.

When appropriate, take out your puppet and have it conduct the experiment and make wrong predictions. For example, the puppet says to one of the children: "Oooh, I'm going to try a chocolate chip. Boy, I bet it's going to be sour." Or: "I think I feel like eating something sweet now. Hand me a potato chip."

After the experiment, read the tongue chart to interested children. Did it turn out to be accurate?

Take a taste of pickle, potato chip, lemon slice, and chocolate chip.

1

Please eat one at a time!

Smell: Smelling Bottles
Science/Sensory/**Optional:** Language

WHY we are doing this project: to help children develop awareness of the sense of smell. **Optional:** to develop reading skills.

WHAT we will need:
Plastic spice bottles
Glue
Cloves
Allspice
Cinnamon
Coffee
Rubbing alcohol
Paper
Perfume or essence oil

HOW we will do it: Dip a piece of paper in rubbing alcohol, put it inside a spice bottle, and glue the perforated lid on. If the bottle has no perforated lid, glue the regular lid on and then poke holes in it with a skewer. Repeat this process with perfume or essence oil. Make smelling bottles in the same way with the rest of the materials by putting some of each item inside a bottle. The above list is really just to give you ideas; there may be other things you would like to put in your smelling bottles.

Depending on how much time you have for preparation, you may decide to make this a language development activity also. Write on sheets of paper the name of each object inside each bottle and glue a sample next to it. For rubbing alcohol and perfume, draw a picture of the original bottles beside the word. Put your activity table against a wall, and tape each sign onto the wall. Place each smelling bottle in front of its corresponding sign. Lay out blank sheets of paper, pens, and crayons for the children to scribble, write, or draw pictures. Some children may use the writing materials to write about or draw the smelling bottles; other children may use the materials to express other ideas.

Set all the bottles on an activity table and invite the children to explore. Encourage them to describe what they smell. Do they have a favorite smell? Which is their least favorite? Another variation of this is to put familiar-smelling things inside the bottles, cover the bottles so their contents cannot be seen, and encourage the children to guess what is inside them. Some ideas include: mint candy, talcum powder, a piece of orange, perfume, toothpaste, pine cone.

Smell: Making Potpourri (Part 1)
Science/Crafts/Gross Motor

WHY we are doing this: to help children become aware of the sense of smell; to help children enjoy making crafts; to develop the large muscle group; to develop speaking and listening skills.

WHAT we will need:
Commercial potpourri (small amount, the kind that consists of pure botanicals, no fillers)
Sandwich bags
Whole cloves
Cinnamon sticks
Vanilla beans
Whole allspice
Butcher paper
Marker
White labels
Clear plastic salad containers

HOW we will do it: To obtain your plastic containers, go to a deli and ask if they will donate some of these containers, or if they will sell you some; they are not expensive. The reason that these containers are ideal is because they are safe (not glass), they are transparent, and they have lids. If you come across other containers that meet these criteria, then use those. When you get your plastic containers, prepare them for the activity by using the skewer to poke several holes in the lid of each one, or if this is too difficult, cut small slits with an Exacto knife.

This allows the scent of the potpourri to be smelled even when the container is closed.

Cloves, cinnamon sticks, vanilla beans, and allspice are expensive. There are a few ways you can get the amount you need for all your children without breaking the bank. If you work for a nonprofit school, visit your local supermarket, explain your needs, and ask the store manager if she or he is willing to donate some spices. If you have a school newsletter that goes out to parents, tell the manager that you will thank the store in the newsletter (free advertising). Another option, if you are a teacher, is to ask each parent to buy one container of one of the spices.

To prepare, tape up your piece of butcher paper on the wall near the place where you gather for Attention Getter time. Write each child's name on two white labels. Apply one to the sandwich bags and reserve one for the plastic containers. During an Attention Getter time, show the children your commercial potpourri. Present it in a pretty container. Pass it around so the children can smell it and touch it. Explain to the children that it is called *potpourri* (the first syllable rhymes with "go": PO-PURR-EE) and print the word on the butcher paper. Explain that it is a French word that originally meant "stew." What is a stew? Why is the potpourri like a stew? Discuss this and say the word several times as a group. Explain that you are going to make your own potpourri, and that you will have to go out looking for things with which to make it. Go on a nature walk, and depending on the time of the year and where you are located, try to go some place where the children will be able to pick up pine cones, eucalyptus leaves, and flowers or flowering weeds. Before you set out on your walk, give each child his or her own sandwich bag. Bring home your materials and put them out to dry. An easy way to keep them separate is to have each child lay his or her materials on top of his or her sandwich bag.

When the materials are dry, have the children select cinnamon sticks, allspice, vanilla beans, and cloves to mix with the ingredients they found on the nature walk. Have the plastic containers available on the table so that each child can choose one to contain the potpourri. If you like, have the name labels on the containers already, and invite the children to find the one that has her or his name on it. At the end of the day or the session, encourage the children to pass their potpourris around to experience the scent of the different mixtures they made.

Touch: Letter and Number Boards
Science/Sensory/Language/Math/Fine Motor

WHY we are doing this project: to help children become aware of the sense of touch; to develop reading and writing skills; to practice rational counting; for kindergartners, to facilitate addition; to develop fine motor skills.

WHAT we will need:
Sandpaper
Stencils (provided on page 192;
    photocopy and enlarge for your use)
Cardboard
Small uncooked pasta shapes (or small
    beads, beans, or spangles)
Glue sticks

HOW we will do it: In this project, you're going to make cards consisting of a numeral, as well as the numeral spelled out in sandpaper letters. Children can touch and see the word and number.

To prepare, cut out the provided stencil shapes, and use them to cut out sandpaper letters and numbers. You can ask friends, family, neighbors, and other parents to help you with this several weeks in advance. Cut out cardboard rectangles about 20 cm x 10 cm (8" x 4"). Use a glue stick to attach a sandpaper word and numeral to each one. If you work with three- and young four-year-olds, also glue on a corresponding number of sandpaper circles. If you work with older children, this step is probably not necessary, though you can make that judgment yourself.

For kindergartners, make addition cards. Example: "Two and three are ____." Use the stencils to make sandpaper words and num-

bers for "two" and "three." On an activity table, set out the number cards, glue sticks, and containers of small beads, pasta shapes, or beans. Also, put out blank cardboard rectangles, sandpaper letters and numbers, and uncut sandpaper sheets for children who want to make their own number cards from scratch. If you are using glue sticks, the objects the children will attach must be small (spangles are perfect). If you plan on using liquid glue and brushes, the objects can be bigger.

Ahead of time, take a numeral card, and glue on the number of objects it specifies. During an Attention Getter time, say: "I'm going to pass something around, and I want you to touch it with your eyes closed. See if you can feel which number it is, and if you know, don't say it out loud. Keep it a secret in your head." Pass the card around and when everyone has had a chance to feel it, see what number the children think it is. Show them how you glued on that many beads (or whatever). As a

group, count the sandpaper circles on the card (which should correspond to the numeral) and then count the beads. Ask the children what they see in the room that would help them make their own number cards.

If you are working with kindergartners, comment on their addition problems as they work them out.

Developmental differences: Three- and young four-year-olds are likely to make the gluing of objects an end in itself, and will probably not match numerals with the number of objects they put on their cards. They will be using their sense of touch as they use the sandpaper, small objects, and glue. If you want to make this a math activity also, invite each child to count the total number of things glued onto the tagboard when the child is finished. Older children will be more interested in feeling the sandpaper numbers and letters, counting the number of objects designated on the cards, and also, in making their own.

Touch: Feely Box Center (Part 1)

Science/Sensory/Language

WHY we are doing this project: to help children become aware of the sense of touch.

WHAT we will need:

    Eight cylindrical oatmeal containers
    Eight knee-high stockings or socks
    Piece of velvet
    Sandpaper
    Styrofoam pieces
    Gravel
    Marbles
    Plastic bubble packing
    Wet sponge
    Plastic sandwich bag
    Two eggs
    Glue

HOW we will do it: Place one of each object inside an oatmeal container. Cut the stockings off at the ankles, and then stretch one end of a stocking over the opening of each oatmeal container so that the tube extends beyond the opening. Socks and nylons are usually tight enough to stretch across the container securely. The children will pull the stocking over their hand in order to reach inside the container. To make the egg feely box, crack open both eggs and slide the contents into a baggie. Seal the top by putting glue along the seam before you press it closed. Then put the sandwich bag in the container.

Set all these containers on an activity table and encourage the children to reach inside them and feel the contents. Can they guess what they are?

Touch: Feely Box Center (Part 2)

Science/Sensory/Language

WHY we are doing this project: to use the sense of touch in developing all aspects of language arts: speaking, listening, reading, and writing.

WHAT we will need:

    Feely boxes (from previous activity)
    Paper
    Markers
    Crayons
    Pens
    Word cards (instructions follow)
    Magazines

HOW we will do it: To prepare, make the cards by using a black marker to write words in bold, clear print: soft, rough, cold, gritty, spongy, squishy, damp, and any other words which describe the objects in the feely boxes. Cut out magazine photographs of things which can be described by one of these adjectives. Glue the picture next to the appropriate word, or, if you cannot find suitable photographs, draw a picture.

Make a writing center near the feely boxes. Set out markers, crayons, pens, blank paper, magazine photographs torn out of magazines, scissors, word cards, and glue sticks. On the wall by the writing center, tape up some of the word/picture cards you made in the paragraph above.

The materials can be explored in many variations, depending on the interests and level of language development of your children. Children can draw a picture of the object they think is in a feely box. You can take dictation of what the children felt, spell words for the children, support invented spelling or scribbling, or write down their words to be copied onto their pictures. Children can find a magazine photograph which corresponds to one of the words on the word cards, and glue the picture onto the card, or make a whole new card. Or they can glue a magazine picture onto paper and write or give story dictation which describes how it might feel. Or, if you and your children think of other ways to use the materials, go with it!

Touch: Texture Art
Art/Science/Sensory

WHY we are doing this project: to facilitate creative expression; to develop awareness of the sense of touch; to give children the opportunity to experiment with unusual art materials.

WHAT we will need:
>   Flour
>   Corn meal
>   Aquarium gravel
>   Coffee grounds
>   Ground black pepper
>   Cinnamon powder
>   Glitter or colored sand
>   Glue
>   Squeeze bottles
>   Paper
>   Newspaper
>   Small containers
>   Tub with small amount of
>   soapy water
>   Paper towels
Optional:
>   Tempera paint powder

HOW we will do it: Spread newspaper out on your activity table and put all the materials in the small containers. Put glue in your squeeze bottles, and if you like, thin it out by adding a little water. For interest, add tempera powder or food coloring to the glue as well. Put the tub of soapy water and the paper towels nearby for easy hand washing. Encourage the children to squeeze glue onto paper, and to use their fingers to sprinkle the different materials on the glue. How does each one feel? Introduce descriptive words into the conversation if necessary (e.g., *gritty*, *soft*, *coarse*), as the children make their pictures. Feel free to add other differently textured materials to this activity to make it all the more interesting. Ask the children to notice how the coffee grounds, cinnamon, and pepper smell as they use these materials.

Hearing: The Tape Recorder Game
Science/Sensory/Cognitive/Small Group Activity

WHY we are doing this project: to help children become aware of the sense of hearing; to develop competence with technology; to develop cognition through recognition of each other's voices.

WHAT we will need:
>   Tape recorder
>   Tape

HOW we will do it: This is a small group activity. Have one child leave the room (to a place which is supervised by an adult or where you can still see the child) or simply have the child go to a far place in the room, away from the group. Record one child's voice, and have the first child return. Play back the recording. Can the child guess whose voice it is? Let the children take turns with both roles, and also, show them how to operate the tape recorder. Show them the symbols on the buttons that represent *record*, *rewind*, and *play*. Let your students take turns operating the machine.

Hearing: Sounds in the World Around Us

Science/Social Studies/Small Group Project

WHY we are doing this project: to develop appreciation for nature; to make children aware of the sense of hearing; to create a restful, relaxing mood for quiet time.

WHAT we will need:

> Tapes of natural sounds (e.g., ocean, rain forest, birds, whale, or dolphin sounds)
> Tape recorder
> Paper
> Crayons

HOW we will do it: This is another group activity. Many libraries now carry tapes of natural, environmental sounds so you may want to try this as a source. Also, a recording studio called "Moods" at Gateway Recordings, P.O. Box 5087, FDR Station, N.Y., N.Y., 10022 has a wide variety of environmental tapes including "Backyard Stream," "Farm Life," "Metropolis," and "Thunderstorm Terror." You may want to send for their brochure and invest in a few tapes. Many variety stores also carry these kinds of tapes.

Gather your children together and dim the lights to create a relaxing environment. Play many different sounds from the tapes that you have, and ask the children to guess what they are hearing. In between tapes and guesses, discuss what you are hearing by asking: "Have you ever heard that noise before? Where were you? What did you see?" Provide paper, crayons, and markers and invite the children to draw what they are hearing.

Sight: Tricky Pictures

Science/Sensory/Cognitive

WHY we are doing this project: to encourage children to use their eyes in a new way; to develop awareness of the sense of sight; to develop cognition; to encourage child-to-child interaction by creating a cozy space.

WHAT we will need:
Preparation:

> Construction paper
> Hole puncher
> Clear contact paper
> Magazines
> Scissors
> Large pillows or cushions

Optional:

> Large box

HOW we will do it: To prepare, leaf through the magazines and cut out large photographs of interesting objects. Fold over the construction paper pieces to make cards. Glue a photograph on the inside of each. On the covers, write: "Can you guess what it is?" Cover your picture cards on both sides with clear contact paper. Then, using a hole puncher or scissors, cut a small circle in the cover so that only a small part of the object is visible. Make several of these picture cards.

Create a cozy space for a small number of children with the cushions or pillows. If you have a large box, you can cut a door in it, and create a cozy space inside. Otherwise, put the tricky pictures on a small box or table. During an Attention Getter time, demonstrate one of the tricky pictures for the children, and then encourage them to investigate the others.

Sight: Story Seeing, Story Telling

Sensory/Language

WHY we are doing this project: to encourage children to use the sense of sight; to facilitate cooperation and interaction between children; to develop reading, speaking, and listening skills.

WHAT we will need:

    Same cozy space created in previous project

    Wordless picture books, such as:

        Carle, Eric, *Do You Want to Be My Friend*

        Tana Hoban's photographic books

        Mercer Mayer's 'Frog' picture books

Cardboard

Activity cards (format provided below; photocopy and enlarge for your use)

Cardboard box (food packaging: 17.5–20 cm x 10 cm [7"–8" x 4"])

Contact paper (clear and colored)

"Two people may be here" sign (provided on page 13; photocopy and enlarge for your use)

Preparation:

Scissors

HOW we will do it: To prepare, photocopy both of the activity cards provided. Using glue or double-sided tape, affix them to cardboard, and cover on both sides with clear contact paper. Cut off one end of the box, and half of the front. (See activity sign for illustration.)

Cover the box with colored contact paper. Put the cards in it, and set it out near the cozy

reading area. Pin up the activity sign and the "Two people may be here" sign nearby. Then put your wordless books in the reading area as well. During an Attention Getter time, show the children the sign and the cards and read or interpret them together. Ask the children which sense they will have to use to read the books. Invite your students to explore the materials.

Sight: The Optical Illusion of the Crescent Trick
Science/Sensory

WHY we are doing this project: to help children understand that things are not always what they appear to be; to develop awareness of the sense of sight.

WHAT we will need:
Paper (*bright* green, yellow, and red)
Crescent pattern (provided below; photocopy and enlarge for your use)
Cardboard
Glue or double-sided tape
Tray
"One person may be here" sign (provided on page 3; photocopy and enlarge for your use)
Preparation:
Scissors

The facts of the matter: When the same-size crescents are arranged in this order—red, green, yellow—the green one appears to be wider than the others. When they are arranged in this order—green, red, yellow—the green one appears to be taller. The curves of the crescents interfere with the way the mind makes sense of them, and this makes the crescents appear to be different sizes.

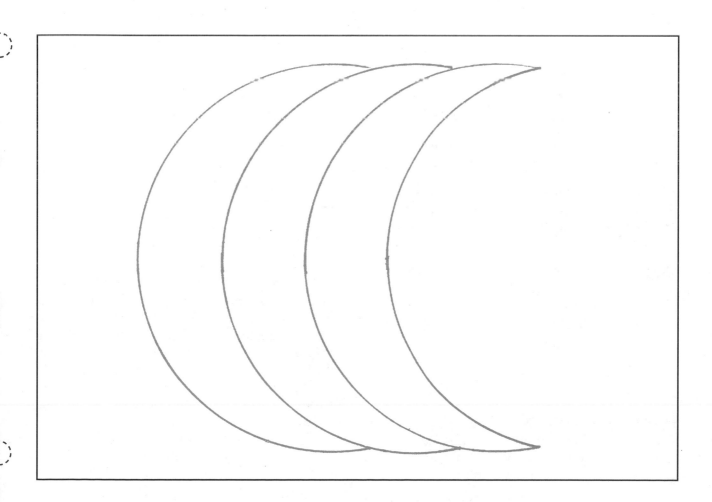

HOW we will do it: Use the crescent pattern to cut out three crescents, one from each color, all exactly the same size and shape. Using the glue or double-sided tape, affix the crescents to cardboard and cut them out; this makes them sturdier. Make the "One person may be here" sign and tape it above the area where the tray will be located.

During an Attention Getter time, stack the crescents on top of each other so that the children can clearly see they are really all the same size. Then turn the crescents upside down so that the colors are not visible and align them next to each other, so that each crescent is cradled by the curve of the next one. (See illustration.)

Ask the children to predict if, when they arrange the crescents so the colors are visible, the crescents will all look the same size and shape. Read/interpret the "One person may be here" sign together and invite the children to conduct the experiment for themselves. What do they notice?

Science kits: Make several sets of the colored crescents, and put each set in a manila envelope. Set out the envelopes for independent exploration.

Senses Working Together
Science/Sensory/Group Activity

WHY we are doing this project: to help children understand how the senses of sight, smell, and taste work together.

WHAT we will need:
>   Juice (apple, orange, grape, and
>   pineapple)
>   For kindergartners: white grape juice
>   Small paper cups
Optional:
>   Blindfold

HOW we will do it: This is a group activity for Attention Getter time. Ask the children to predict whether or not they will know what kind of juice they are drinking, when they cannot see

it. Have your students take turns tasting the juices when their eyes are covered. (Either blindfold the children, ask them to close their eyes, or cover their eyes with your hand.) Can they guess which juice it is? Let the children also taste the juices by looking at them and smelling them first. Is it easier to guess correctly? Why?

Senses Working Together: The Shaking Experiment
Science/Sensory

WHY we are doing this experiment: to help children understand how the senses of touch and hearing work together; to develop listening skills; to familiarize children with a scientific process that includes: noticing a problem, making predictions, making discoveries, comparing results, and discussing them.

WHAT we will need:
>   Four small coffee cans (or other tins—all
>   the same size with lids)
>   Gravel
>   Glue
>   Black marker
>   Butcher paper
>   Two prediction charts (format provided
>   on page 199)
>   Markers
>   Crayons

HOW we will do it: Fill two tins with a small amount of gravel, and fill the remaining two with a large amount. Label each tin with the numbers one through four. Make two copies of the prediction chart provided or create your own, and pin them up side by side. Write a heading on one that says: "Listening Only" On the other, write a heading that says: "Listening and Shaking."

During an Attention Getter time, show the children the coffee cans, and ask them to predict whether or not they will be able to guess

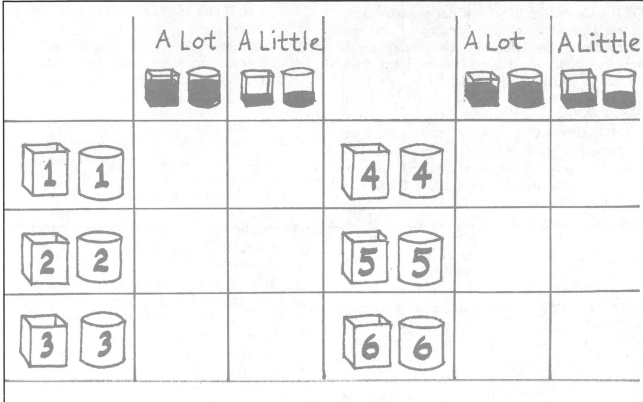

	A Lot	A Little		A Lot	A Little
1 1			4 4		
2 2			5 5		
3 3			6 6		

Use symbols that reflect the tins you are actually using.

how much is in each one only by listening to it being shaken. Have four children stand up in front of the group, and give each one a tin. Before you begin, tell the children holding the cans to zip or button their lips together, and not to tell the rest of the group whether the tin feels heavy or light, no matter how the group guesses. Have each standing child take a turn at shaking his or her can, and have the group listen carefully. After each one, have the group guess whether it has a lot of something in it, or a little, based solely on what they hear. Write down the guesses on the "Listening Only" chart by writing a check mark under the appropriate symbol for each can.

Next, pass each one around, and let each child shake it as well as listen to it. Now how do the children guess? Do the guesses for each tin change when the children can feel their weight as well as hear the contents? Write down the guesses again on the second prediction chart and compare them to the first guesses. Which was better: just hearing the cans being shaken, or hearing them shake while also

holding them? Open up the tins and let the children examine the contents. If you work with very young children, glue the lids shut. The next day, when the glue is dried, put the tins out for more exploration. Leave the charts up for several days.

What Is Braille?
Anti-Bias

WHY we are doing this project: to help children appreciate all methods of communication and to help children understand what braille is and who invented it.

WHAT we will need:
    Book: Hobart Alexander, Sally,
        Mom Can't See Me
    Children's books in braille

HOW we will do it: Most libraries carry books in braille, and anyone with a library card can check them out. There are also books which have clear, plastic inlay over the text, on which words are written in braille. Visit your local library, and check out several braille books. If you get books which are in braille only, try to get the same story in non-braille, so that your students know which story the braille book is telling. During an Attention Getter time, read *Mom Can't See Me* and talk about the braille materials in the photographs. Pass around the braille library books. As the children feel the raised bumps on the paper, explain that the bumps are arranged in patterns to form words. A man named Louis Braille invented this system and blind people all over the world use it. Ask: "Why doesn't the braille book have any pictures?" Read your non-braille book and while you do, let the children continue to pass around and touch the braille version. Afterward, put the books out on a table for the children to explore. You many want to talk about treating the books carefully while you are borrowing them.

What Do You Do with a Sour Lemon?

Music/Movement/Cognitive

WHY we are doing this: to help children feel comfortable with their singing voices; to develop cognition by: remembering movements associated with words, remembering each part of the song that went before, and connecting body parts with senses.

WHAT we will need:
   Song: "WHAT DO YOU DO WITH A SOUR LEMON?" (to the tune of *"What Do You Do with a Drunken Sailor?"*)

"WHAT DO YOU DO WITH A SOUR LEMON?"
What do you do with a sour lemon?
What do you do, oh what do you do?
Oh what do you do with a sour lemon,
I ask what do you do?

How we will do it: Sing the song with gestures. Throw your hands apart in a questioning gesture for the first three lines. for: "I ask what do you do?" point to yourself and then to the children. To answer the question, speak the line: "Smell it with your ___ (nose)." (Let the children fill in the word.) Point to your nose as you speak.

With gestures, sing the song again, follow with the spoken line, and add another: "And taste it with your ___ (tongue)." Point to your tongue as you say the line.

Repeat the song three more times, following with the previous spoken lines, and adding a new one each time: "And look at it with your ___ (eyes)." "And listen to it squirt with your ___ (ears)." "And touch it with your ___ (fingers)." Point to the appropriate body part during each line.

See if the children (and you!) can remember each sense in the list in the same order each time.

Restaurant

Dramatic Play/Language/Sensory

WHY we are doing this project: to promote child-to-child interaction; to develop speaking skills; to expand vocabulary; to facilitate imaginative, pretend play; to enable children to act out real-life situations and to work through emotions; to allow children to use all of their senses during dramatic play.

Note: The following is a list of suggestions. The more props you have to simulate a real restaurant, the more fun it will be for the children, but you may end up using very different props than the ones on this list. Use whatever you have available to you, but remember to create a print-rich environment and to provide materials that utilize all the senses.

WHAT we will need:

Large boxes (to be turned over for tables)
White butcher paper (for tablecloths)
Vases and artificial flowers
Chairs
For play kitchen—utensils that make noise:
  Whisks
  Pots
  Pans
  Wooden spoons
  Chef hats
  Children's aprons
  Plastic dishes and silverware
  Plastic trays
For menus:
  Construction paper
  Food magazines
  Scissors
  Markers
For front desk:
  Notebook (for reservations)
  Carbon paper
  Pen
  Cash register
  Play telephone
Food:
  Oranges cut in quarters
  Pickles
  Potato chips
  Paper napkins

HOW we will do it: To prepare, turn your cardboard boxes upside down and cover them with white butcher paper to simulate table cloths. Arrange chairs beside them. Arrange the materials to simulate all parts of a restaurant: hostess/host station/front desk, kitchen, and dining area.

Put paper, pens, cash register, and telephone at the front desk. Put the pots, pans, spoons, and whisks in the kitchen area. Add other cooking utensils that will create the sound of food preparation.

Make menus by cutting out pictures from food magazines, gluing them onto construction paper, and folding the paper over vertically. If you can, find and use photographs of the food you are actually using. Set a menu on each table. If you like, have the children make menus as a language and art activity.

During an Attention Getter time, ask the children how many of them have been in a restaurant. Ask: "Do you remember what you heard? (Music, kitchen noises, people talking) Smelled? (Food cooking, food being served) Saw? (Everything in a restaurant) Touched? (Silverware, seats, tablecloth) Tasted? (Food, drinks)." Talk about this together. Ask the children if they see anything in the room which they could use to play "restaurant." If you decide to use real food like oranges, pickles, and potato chips for a taste experience, have the children wash their hands before they begin to explore the materials, and let them know that they must sit down while they eat.

Literature

Aliki. (1962). *My five senses*. New York: Harper Collins.*

Hoban, T. (1984). *Is it rough? Is it smooth? Is it shiny?* New York: Greenwillow Books.

Hobart Alexander, S. (1990). *Mom can't see me.* New York: Macmillan.

Your five senses. (1984). Chicago: Children's Press.*

For young preschoolers:

Oxenbury, H. (1985). *I hear*. New York: Random House.

Oxenbury, H. (1985). *I see*. New York: Random House.

Oxenbury, H. (1985). *I touch*. New York: Random House.

For restaurant dramatic play:

Barbour, K. (1987). *Little Nino's pizzeria*. New York: Harcourt Brace Jovanovich. (There are large groups of people in the illustrations who are all white. Buy the paperback edition and shade in diverse skin colors.)

Day, A. (1988). *Frank and Ernest*. New York: Scholastic.

Rockwell, A. (1993). *Pots and pans*. New York: Macmillan.

Shaw, N. (1992). *Sheep out to eat*. Boston, MA: Houghton Mifflin.

Extenders

Music/Cognitive: Try this variation of the lemon song:
"Where do you hide a sour lemon,
where do you hide it, where do you hide it,
where do you hide a sour lemon,
where do you hide that fruit?"

Ask the children to sit in a circle. Have them take turns hiding a real lemon behind their backs while everyone sings the song. Have the children take turns sitting in the middle of the circle with their eyes covered, while the song is sung and the lemon is hidden. Can they guess where it is? If you like, and if your students feel comfortable with this, have the child who hides the lemon sing the song alone and stop as soon as the fruit is hidden, so that the child in the middle must use the sense of hearing to guess who has it.

Sensory/Science: When you conduct the shaking experiment with tin cans, vary it by putting different amounts of different materials in the tins: (e.g., marbles, beads, straw pieces, paper clips, stones), and have the children experiment with guessing whether the items are heavy and light. At first they may guess only by listening to tins being shaken, and then by listening *and* shaking.

Language/Art: Provide construction paper, scissors, magazine pictures, a hole puncher, and glue, and have the children make their own Tricky Pictures

Field Trip: Visit a restaurant. Before you go, talk about how you might use each sense once you are there.

MAGNIFICENT MAGNIFIERS

The facts of the matter: A convex lens bends light as the light enters and again as it leaves. This bending of light magnifies objects underneath the lens.

Although young children may not grasp the concept of bent light, their hands-on exploration of magnifiers in the activities below will lay the foundation for later understanding.

Several weeks ahead of time, start collecting a variety of glass jars and bottles, as well as clear plastic containers.

Throughout the unit, talk to the children about the glass in magnifying glasses, and about how important it is to use magnifiers carefully because they are breakable. Plastic magnifiers can be purchased; however, the ones I have seen have not been of very good quality in regard to their magnifying ability. Choose the magnifiers that you feel comfortable using. Also, let the children know that when you use glass jars in an experiment, the glass jars must not be moved.

Attention Getter: Pass a magnifying glass to every child. Ask them to examine their fingertips underneath the magnifier. How do their fingertips look different? Suggest that the children examine the palms of their hands. Ask the children to find a partner. Have the partner hold a magnifying glass over one palm. Compare the magnified palm with the one that is not, and ask your students what they notice. Have the children switch roles so that everyone gets a chance to make this comparison. Then show the children how to hold a magnifying glass a few inches away from their friends' faces, and examine eyes, nose, and mouth. Explain that when light passes through the magnifying glass, it bends, and then it bends again when it leaves. This makes everything under the glass look bigger, or magnified. Ask the children to guess what you will be working with over the next few days

Fingerprint Fun
Sensory/Science

WHY we are doing this project: to help children experiment with magnifying glasses; to provide a sensory experience; to enable children to discover more about their bodies; to facilitate a group project.

WHAT we will need:
    Magnifying glasses
    Ink pads (nontoxic pads)
    Butcher paper
    Masking tape

HOW we will do it: Spread the butcher paper out on your activity table and tape down the edges with making tape. Set out the ink pads and magnifying glasses. During an Attention Getter time, approach the table and make a thumbprint. Then examine it with a magnifying glass, and encourage the children to make their own explorations. Together, discuss what you notice. Use the words *magnified* and *magnifying glass* during your discussion.

Science kits: Collect some boxes or tins with lids, and several nontoxic ink pads. Put an ink pad, sheets of paper, and a magnifying glass in each box or tin. Put these science kits out for the children to explore independently. Discuss with the children that ink should be pressed only onto the paper and not on furniture or walls.

Water Magnifying Activity (Part 1)
Art/Sensory

WHY we are doing this project: to facilitate creative expression and to provide a sensory experience.

WHAT we will need:
    Tempera paints (vivid colors)
    Pieces of paper (7.5 cm x 15 cm [3" x 6"])
    Newspapers
    Children's scissors
    Plastic cup
    Clear, plastic containers (wide variety: small and large, wide and narrow)
    Glass containers (wide variety: tall vinegar bottles, fat pickle jars, small relish jars)
Preparation/Demonstration:
    Scissors

HOW we will do it: Spread newspaper on the activity table and mix up the paints. Cut out the 7.5 cm x 15 cm (3" x 6") pieces of paper, and fold them in half.

    Ahead of time, make a sample picture by finger painting on one side of the paper, folding the blank side onto it, and pressing down. Cut the paper apart in the middle after the paper has dried. You have now made two identical pictures. When one is placed behind or underneath a magnifier, you will be able to compare them and to observe how much magnification is taking place.

Push a long narrow table against a wall. Fill the plastic cup with water and set it on the table. Tape one of your identical pictures on the wall near the cup, but not directly behind it.

During your Attention Getter time, show the children the picture on the wall, near the cup of water. Show them the second, identical picture. Ask your students to compare the two pictures, noticing in particular their size and shape. Next, ask the children to predict if the second picture will still look the same when it is put behind the cup of water. Tape it there, and ask the children what they notice. How does the image look different? Why? Show your students all the other jars, bottles, and containers. Ask them to predict whether these vessels alter the image when filled with water. Suggest to the children that they make their own identical pictures to use in conducting the experiment, and ask them if they see anything in the room which will help them make their pictures.

Bring out a folded piece of blank paper, and show the children how they can paint one side, bring the other side over, and press it down on the wet paint. Use the word *identical* when you talk about the pictures. Let the children know that their identical pictures will be different from yours and everyone else's because each person has his or her own way of making things. Put your sample away before the children begin to explore the materials. When the paintings are dry, cut them along the crease lines in the middle.

Water Magnifying Activity (Part 2)
Science

WHY we are doing this project: to enable children to experiment with the magnifying ability of water.

The facts of the matter: Light that enters a glass or jar of water is bent in the same way as light that enters a magnifying glass and, therefore, magnifies.

WHAT we will need:
  Glass and plastic containers (collected for Part 1)
  Masking tape
  Identical pictures (created in Part 1)
  Water
  Small pitchers
  Duct tape
  Long, narrow table
Optional:
  Cautionary sign (provided on page 208; photocopy and enlarge for your use)
  Puppet

HOW we will do it: Using glass jars and bottles is optional, however they greatly enhance this experiment. Even if you work with very young children, you can discuss ahead of time the rule that the glass jars and bottles are not to be touched or moved. Make sure all your tall, narrow containers are plastic, and if you like, demonstrate the magnifying ability of tall, narrow glass bottles yourself during an Attention Getter time. Talk about what would happen if a glass jar or bottle was dropped. Pin up the cautionary sign beside the materials and discuss it. You know best what the listening abilities and energy levels of your children are, so use only plastic containers if you feel it is necessary—the experiment will still be an interesting one.

Move the long, narrow table up against the wall and line up your containers on it. Tape half of each identical picture made in the previous activity behind the container and jar magnifiers. Make sure you have enough jars and containers to be able to tape every child's picture to the wall.

Provide the children with small pitchers of water and ask them to fill the containers. Invite your students to find their pictures on the wall, and to tape the matching picture on the table, in front of the magnifier behind which the identical picture is placed. Ask them to compare the two identical pictures. Do the magnifiers change the way the pictures look? How?

Encourage examination and comparison of the different magnifiers. Take out your puppet to ask the following questions, or ask them yourself: What do they notice about which container is the best magnifier? What do they notice about the difference between how plastic

Please don't move the glass jars!

containers magnify and how glass containers magnify? Set out an empty container on your table also. What do the children notice when a picture is placed behind it? When experimenting with tall, short, wide, and narrow containers, what do the children notice about which ones act as better magnifiers? Encourage observations and comparisons. Explain that light bends when it passes through the water, and bends again when it leaves. This makes the pictures behind the jars of water look bigger.

Tip: Leave the containers in this arrangement for the next activity.

Another Magnifier Tester
Art/Math/Science

WHY we are doing this project: to encourage creative expression; to provide experience with creating patterns; to develop fine motor skills.

WHAT we will need:
  Inexpensive, plastic rulers (one for each child)
  Stickers (many of the same shape and color)
  Spangles (many of the same shape and color)
  Glue
  Paper
  Markers
  Containers filled with water (from previous activity—omit any tall, narrow, glass bottles)

HOW we will do it: In this project, children will design a long strip of patterned art to glue onto their rulers. When they pass the ruler behind a magnifier, they will be able to compare the magnified image with the same non-magnified image on the rest of the ruler. This will allow them to see just how much magnification the bending light in each container creates. For this experiment, make sure all the glass jars are large with wide circumferences so that they are difficult to move when filled with water. Secure them to the table with duct tape. Point again to the "Please don't move the glass jars" sign and discuss it with the children.

To prepare, cut out strips of paper that are the same size as the rulers. Set out all materials on the activity table. Ahead of time, make a sample by gluing a strip of paper onto a ruler, and then making a pattern along the strip, using glue, spangles, stickers, or your own drawings. Remove all tall, narrow, glass vessels from your collection.

During an Attention Getter time, show the children your magnifier tester and tell them that that is what it is called. Point to each shape in your pattern and encourage the group to help you identify out loud what each one is. For example (pointing to each shape in the pattern): "First there's a red heart, then a yellow star, then a red heart, then a yellow star, then a _____" After a while, stop speaking yourself and let the children speak alone. Tell the children that when something has the same shapes or colors in the same order, over and over again, it is called a *pattern*. Ask the children to predict what they will see when they put part of a magnifier tester behind each container. Ask the children what they see in the room that will help them make their own magnifier testers. (Remember to mention that everyone's pattern will be different because everyone has their own special way of doing things. Put your sample tester away before the children approach the materials.)

If children do not make patterns on their testers, let that be okay. Younger children will probably choose shapes at random for their testers, but will still see magnification when they pass them behind the containers. For older students, you can put a more complex pattern on your sample tester to challenge them; for example, make a pattern using three shapes or four. For kindergartners, you might choose to make a sample pattern that is the same in shape but not in color, or that has the same color order but not shape.

After the children make their testers and the glue has dried, encourage them to place part of their testers behind each container. Ask them to compare the size of the images that are behind the container with the images that are not. Do they notice whether any of the shapes are changed in other ways, besides being magnified (for example, twisted or distorted)? Encourage the children to express their findings.

Art kits: In large-sized sandwich bags, put a ruler, spangles, sequins, stickers, a few crayons and markers, a glue stick, and a strip of paper that is the same size as the ruler. Put these magnifier-tester art kits out for the children to use as and when they choose.

Fluids As Magnifiers
Science

WHY we are doing this project: to help children experiment with how different fluids magnify; to compare their relative magnifying power; to facilitate fine motor development through pouring.

WHAT we will need:
  Trays
  Identical, small, clear, plastic containers
    (clear, plastic cups work well)
  Funnels
  Four small pitchers
  Vinegar
  Oil
  Water
  Corn syrup
  Magnifier testers (created in previous
    activity)
  Prediction chart (format provided
    on page 210; photocopy and enlarge
    for your use)
  Butcher paper
  Markers
  Newspapers

HOW we will do it: To prepare, tape up the piece of butcher paper near the place where you gather for Attention Getter time. Use the format provided to make a prediction chart. Line up the containers on the trays. Pour a small amount of each liquid in its own pitcher.

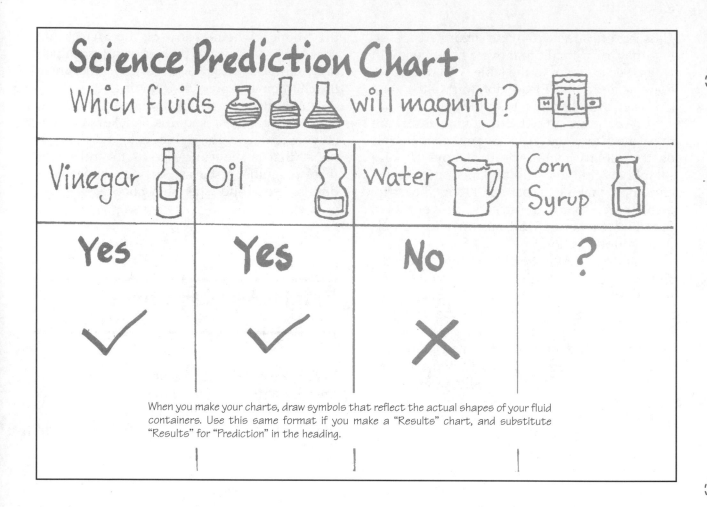

Science Prediction Chart
Which fluids 🏺🏺⚗️ will magnify?

Vinegar 🍾	Oil 🧴	Water 🫗	Corn Syrup 🫙
Yes	Yes	No	?
✓	✓	✗	

When you make your charts, draw symbols that reflect the actual shapes of your fluid containers. Use this same format if you make a "Results" chart, and substitute "Results" for "Prediction" in the heading.

Set everything on the activity table. Be sure to spread plenty of newspaper underneath, as the children will be pouring from the pitchers to the containers.

During an Attention Getter time, take out your magnifier tester, and tell the children that so far you have only used it with a magnifier made out of a container of water. Say: "You know that water is a magnifier, but do you think other liquids are too?" Show the children the original bottles that contained the vinegar, oil, and corn syrup and, together, identify the fluid in each container. Show the children the corresponding symbol for each fluid on the prediction chart. Let your students smell the liquids if they would like to.

Ask them to predict whether or not each one will magnify. Print, or have the children write, a "yes" and a check mark for each prediction that a fluid will magnify, and a "no" and an "X" mark for each prediction that it will not. Print the children's name next to their pre-

dictions or have your students do this. Show them the blank spaces on the chart, and let them know that after they conduct their experiments, they can write yes or no in these spaces. Be prepared to let younger children scribble on the chart.

After the children have poured their liquids, passed their magnifier testers behind the containers, and generally explored to their hearts' content, gather together at the end of the day or session and compare their predictions to the results. If you like, make another Science Results Chart, and record your discoveries on it. Then compare the two charts.

Making Water-Drop Magnifiers

Science/Fine Motor

WHY we are doing this project: to help children understand that drops of water are convex lenses; to help them discover that water drops bend light in the same way that magnifying glasses do and that therefore they also magnify; to develop fine motor skills.

WHAT we will need:

    Plastic cling wrap
    Cardboard
    Crayons
    Markers
    Staplers
    Eyedroppers
    Small containers
    Water
    Photocopies of design page (provided
       below) or magazine pictures

Preparation:

    Scissors
    Glue stick
    Paper

HOW we will do it: As this activity requires a lot of preparation, ask friends, neighbors, and other parents to help you with this ahead of time. To prepare, cut out cardboard squares measuring about 7.5 cm x 7.5 cm (3" x 3"). Fold each one in half, and cut out a rectangular hole out of the fold, about 13 mm (½") from the edges, so that when you unfold the cardboard, you have a frame. Make two of these for each child. Cut out photographs from magazines, especially tiny letters or pictures, and/or make photocopies of the design page, and cut and paste some of the tiny pictures onto paper. Cut out cling wrap squares which also measure about 7.5 cm x 7.5 cm (3" x 3"). To store them in preparation for the activity, it works best to lay them very loosely in a box with a lid.

Put small amounts of water in the containers, and set all materials on the activity table. Ahead of time, make a sample water magnifier. Stretch a square of cling wrap between two frames and staple around the edge. Using crayons and/or markers, decorate the frame of your magnifier. Have one of the papers with tiny pictures available.

During an Attention Getter time, ask the children what they remember about the magnification properties of water in plastic and glass containers. Ask if they remember what light does as it travels through water. (It bends.) Show the children your water magnifier and

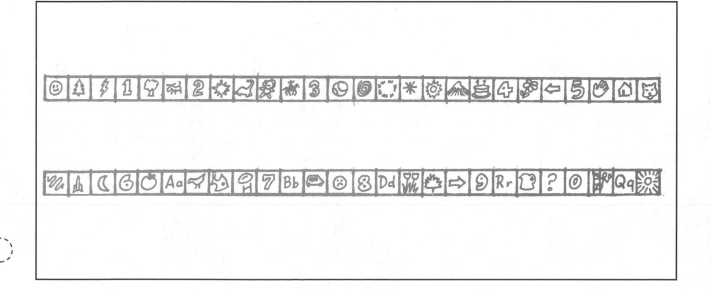

say: "This is a tool I made to test whether one drop of water will magnify." Explain how you made it, and indicate the appropriate materials on the activity table.

Use an eyedropper to drop a small bead of water onto the cling wrap. Show your students one of the miniature pictures, and without demonstrating this, ask them to predict whether the tiny bead of water will magnify the picture. Ask the children how they could conduct this experiment for themselves and after listening to their responses, invite them to use the materials on the activity table. You will probably have to help with stapling.

Encourage the children to examine the tiny pictures with their water magnifiers. What do the children notice when a picture is examined through the bead of water? What does this tell us about whether or not a single drop of water will magnify? If necessary, mention again that as light goes in the drop of water and out again, it is bent as it passes through.

What Can We See with a Magnifying Glass? (Part 1)
Science/Language

WHY we are doing this project: to enable children to watch a stain spreading with the aid of a magnifying glass; to give children an appreciation for the benefits of using a magnifier; to develop speaking and listening skills.

WHAT we will need:
    Magnifying glasses
    Medicine or eyedroppers
    Small containers
    Water
    Fabric scraps
    Mustard
    Ketchup
    Popsicle sticks
    Styrofoam meat trays
    Puppet

HOW we will do it: To prepare, set your meat trays out on the activity table. On each one, place an eye- or medicine dropper, a magnifier, and a fabric scrap. In the middle of the table, put out small containers of water, ketchup, and mustard. Put popsicle sticks into the mustard and ketchup containers so that the children can smear dabs of them onto the fabric. The containers should be arranged so that all children have access to them.

During an Attention Getter time, point out the materials to the children, and invite them to use the droppers to let small globs of mustard or ketchup fall on their fabric. Encourage them to use the magnifying glasses to watch how the stain spreads. What do they notice about whether the fabric absorbs the mustard or ketchup quickly or slowly? What happens if the children let drops of water fall onto the fabric first? What do the children notice about whether this changes how the stains spread? As the children conduct this experiment, take out your puppet and use its personality to ask your students what they are doing. Ask them to look at a spreading stain without a magnifying glass, and then with one. Which method allows them to see what is happening most clearly?

What Can We See with a Magnifying Glass? (Part 2)
Science/Language

WHY we are doing this project: to give children the opportunity to observe a chemical process with the aid of a magnifying glass; to further develop an appreciation for what magnifying glasses can do; to develop speaking and listening skills.

WHAT we will need:
    In addition to the materials from
        the previous activity:

Liquid dishwashing detergent
Liquid starch
Bar of soap
Preparation:
Grater

HOW we will do it: To prepare, grate a small amount of soap from a soap bar. After the children have used their magnifiers to watch stains spread, put out small containers of liquid starch, liquid dishwashing detergent, and grated soap. Encourage the children to watch what these soaps do to their stains under a magnifying glass. Does one type of soap work on the stains more quickly than others? What happens when the children add drops of water on top of the soap and/or on top of the stain? Use your puppet's personality to talk to the children about their experiment. Ask them how the magnifying glasses affect what they see.

Paper Textures and Magnifying Glasses
Science/Sensory

WHY we are doing this project: to expose children to different paper textures through the use of magnifiers and to provide a sensory experience.

WHAT we will need:
Embossed paper
Business cards with raised print
Aluminum foil candy wrappers
Sandpaper
Newsprint pieces
Any other interesting textured paper

HOW we will do it: To collect your paper samples, contact business offices, office supply stores, paper supply stores or photocopy shops to ask for donations of samples. Explain that

you want the materials for children. You can also ask friends, family, and other parents to help you collect these items.

On the day of the project, lay out magnifying glasses and samples of the different papers on an activity table. Encourage the children to explore, and invite them to express what they observe. Invite them also to touch the different papers with their fingertips. How do they feel different?

Science kits: Collect some small containers and/or boxes with lids. Put a magnifier and a collection of different, textured paper squares in each one. Set these out for the children to use as and when they like.

Examining Other Materials with Magnifiers
Science

WHY we are doing this activity: to enable children to closely examine a variety of everyday materials with magnifying glasses.

WHAT we will need:
Magnifying glasses
Leaves
Stamps
Alphabet noodles
Coins
Small shells
Small pebbles
Salt
Pepper
Preparation:
Poster board
Glue stick

HOW we will do it: These items are only suggestions. If you have other interesting materials you would like the children to examine in this activity, then by all means, use them. To prepare, cut out small poster board squares, and glue some salt, pepper, a stamp, and some alphabet noodles on each one. If you do not have time to do this, you can put some of each of the materials in a small plastic or Styrofoam tray. Set these and the other materials out with the magnifying glasses, and encourage the children to explore them and to verbalize their observations.

Science kits: Place a variety of these materials in several containers with lids and put a magnifier in each one so that children can engage in independent exploration.

Measuring How Much Magnifiers Magnify
Science/Math

WHY we are doing this project: to enable children to measure and compare how much a magnifying glass enlarges objects.

WHAT we will need:
    Magnifying glasses (preferably of
        varying strengths)
    Graph grids (provided below;
        photocopy and enlarge for your use)

HOW we will do it: By using the uniform grids of the graph papers, the children can compare magnified graph lines with graph lines which are not magnified. This will give them a more exact idea of just how much a magnifier enlarges

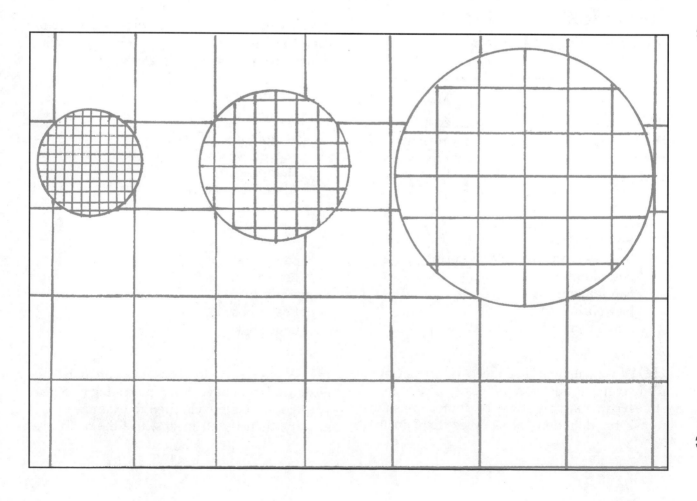

an image. If possible, invest in at least one high-quality magnifying glass. A four-power magnifier is of high quality and ranges in price from $5 to $13. Hand-held sixteen-power lenses are also available for between $10 and $15. You can find magnifying glasses in the optics section of nature stores.

Ask your students to predict how well each tool will magnify. As the children participate in this activity, encourage them to compare how much the different magnifying glasses enlarge the graph squares, and have some one- and two-power (less expensive, lower quality) magnifiers available to provide a contrast. Encourage your students to verbalize their findings as they experiment.

Magnifying Books
Science/Language

WHY we are doing this project: to develop self-esteem and initiative by encouraging children to find and choose their own materials for examining under magnifiers; to develop self-esteem by giving the children their own magnifying glasses; to develop fine motor skills; to develop all components of language arts: reading, writing, speaking, and listening.

WHAT we will need:
  Construction paper
  Glitter or colored sand
  Spangles
  Pepper
  Salt
  Magazines
  Leaves
  Fabric scraps
  Yarn
  Glue sticks
  Small, plastic magnifying glasses
  Crayons
  Markers
  Pencils
  Pens
  Scissors
Preparation:
  Hole puncher

HOW we will do it: In this project, you will provide the children with blank books and small, plastic magnifying glasses. The children will search for, choose, and glue in objects for examination with their magnifiers, and then add words about each one.

If you work with a large number of children, you can order inexpensive, small magnifying glasses from school supply catalogs. Also, they are sometimes available at toy or nature stores.

To prepare, cut the construction paper into 25 cm x 15 cm (10" x 6") pieces. Take three sheets and fold over the 25 cm (10") side. Then staple along the fold. Make one blank book for each child. Use the hole puncher to punch a hole in the upper left corner, tie yarn around the hole, and tie the other end around a magnifying glass. Make sure the yarn lengths are long enough for children to freely move the magnifier to examine objects on each page of the book.

Make a sample magnifying book. Several weeks ahead of time, begin collecting tiny and large objects which can be examined closely with a magnifier. Glue an object or objects onto each page, and write a few words about each. For example: "I found this little piece of foam on the floor, in a corner. When I look at it through my magnifying glass, I can see little holes in it." On the cover of your book, write a title and "by (your name)." Leaf through your magazines, and cut out some of the pictures you find. Also, tear out pages to put on the activity table for children who want to do their own cutting.

On the day of your activity, set out spangles, glitter or colored sand, salt, pepper, and the pictures. Cut the leaves, fabric, and yarn into pieces and set these out as well. Put out any other safe objects that could be glued into the books. Set out the blank books and glue sticks. This will be an ongoing project that begins with this activity. On a small table, make a writing center for the books the children have begun. Set out the glue sticks, scissors, and writing and drawing materials so that, as the children find materials for their books at home or in other places, they can continue to add to their magnifying books.

During an Attention Getter time, show the children the sample magnifying book and read it to them. If you like, pass it around so that the children can examine the objects in it with the attached magnifying glass. Tell the children about places you looked to find things for your book (e.g., corners, outside, in closets, under beds). Ask the children what they see in the room that would help them make their own magnifying books.

As they work on the books, take story dictation, spell words, support invented spelling or scribbling, or write words to be copied onto the book pages, depending on the needs of your students. As the children finish the project, encourage them to look in other places for things to add to their books. Together, brainstorm for places they could search. Talk about safe and unsafe places to look, as well as safe and unsafe things to touch or pick up.

Leave the books and other writing center materials on the small table for several days. If you like, have a show-and-tell of magnifying books several days later. This does not have to be formal; you can simply make a point, during the day or session, of asking each of your students to read their books to you, or if they prefer, reading the books to them.

Magnifying Boxes
Math

WHY we are doing this project: to practice rational counting; to develop reading skills; to further develop an appreciation for magnifying glasses.

WHAT we will need:
    Magnifying glasses
    Trays
Preparation:
    Small, cardboard jewelry boxes
    Glue stick
    Glitter or colored sand
    Spangles
    Small seeds (for small birds like finches)
    Small beans
    Other tiny objects
    Permanent marker

HOW we will do it: In this project, you will need to glue a small number of tiny objects inside a box. The children will then count them, using a magnifying glass. Begin collecting your jewelry boxes ahead of time.

In small, cardboard jewelry boxes, use a glue stick to smear some glue on the inside and then drop some single seeds, spangles, glitter, and so forth onto the glue. It is important that each tiny object have space around it to facilitate counting and examining. An easy way to do this is to press your finger down on the object and then let it drop onto the glue. If you work with kindergartners, drop fifteen to twenty objects in each box. If you work with younger children, drop fewer than ten in each box. On the lid of every box write: "How many?" with a permanent marker.

Put your object containers and magnifying glasses on trays and encourage the children to use the magnifiers to examine the tiny objects and to count them.

Developmental differences: Three- and young four-year-olds will be most interested in opening and closing the containers and looking at the things inside, with or without magnifiers. If you like, ask the children what they see in the boxes, and whether they would like to help you count them. Older children will be more likely to count the objects by themselves.

The Mystery of the Missing Banana Cream Pie
Language/Multicultural/Anti-Bias

WHY we are doing this activity: to develop speaking and listening skills; to present children with a different perspective on gender roles; to develop multicultural awareness.

WHAT we will need:
    Flannel board
    Flannel board shapes (provided on
        page 218; photocopy and enlarge for
        your use)

Felt
Glue
Scissors
Markers or crayons
Optional:
    Clear contact paper
    Story: "THE MYSTERY OF THE
      MISSING BANANA CREAM PIE"
      (provided)

HOW we will do it: If you can, get help coloring the flannel board shapes from friends, family, or other parents. Glue the colored pieces onto felt and cut them out. If you want to make them last longer, cover the paper side with clear contact paper. Set up your flannel board and tell this story:

"THE MYSTERY OF THE MISSING BANANA CREAM PIE"

One day a little girl named Charlotte Holmes [put Charlotte on flannel board] made a beautiful banana cream pie and set it on the kitchen table, ready to eat. [Put table with pie on board.] All of a sudden the telephone rang, and Charlotte went to answer it. [Take Charlotte off board. Take table with pie off board and replace with the table and empty pie dish.] But when Charlotte got back to the kitchen, guess what she found? [Let children answer: the pie was gone.]

"Where's my pie?" Charlotte yelled. "It took me hours to make it!! Where is it? Who took it? I can't believe this!" Charlotte was very upset. She looked under the table and on the floor but there wasn't a trace of that wonderful banana cream pie. "Hmmm," Charlotte said. "This is a real mystery. I'm going to have to use my detective tools to get to the bottom of this." [Take Charlotte off board; replace with Detective Charlotte.] A minute later Charlotte had everything she needed to unravel the mystery. [Ask children: What is Charlotte wearing on her head? (Hat) What is she wearing around her shoulders? (Cape) What is she holding in her hand? (Magnifying Glass).]

"Okay Banana Cream Pie Thief, whoever you are, look out for Charlotte Holmes, Detective Extraordinaire," Charlotte said. The first thing Charlotte did was to examine the pie plate under the magnifying glass, and she noticed that it looked as if a very large tongue had been licking it. Then the magnifying glass showed her a big white whisker in the pie dish. Do you think that whisker belonged to Charlotte? [Let children answer.] Then she looked at the floor again with her magnifying glass, and guess what she saw this time?? [Put up paw prints.] What do you think made those prints? [Let children answer.] "Hmmm," Charlotte Holmes said. "The licked pie dish, the big, white whisker, and these paw prints are all very important clues to solving this mystery."

Using her magnifier, Charlotte Holmes followed those paw prints and guess where they lead? [Put up dog in dog basket.] She found Ralph lying in his dog basket, and guess what she found all over his mouth? [Let children answer.] Ralph was so full of banana cream pie that he was lying on his side, moaning and groaning. How do you think Charlotte felt? [Discuss: Angry at Ralph? Sorry for Ralph? Disappointed that she couldn't eat the pie? All of these things?] Well, Charlotte scolded Ralph for stealing that banana cream pie, and then she wrapped him up in a blanket and let him sleep. The next morning Ralph felt better, and Charlotte made another banana cream pie. Do you think she left it on the kitchen table this time? [Let children answer.]

After telling this flannel board story ask the children for stories about their pets. Set the materials out for the children and encourage them to use them to retell the original story and to make up new ones. Make a "Two people may be here" sign and pin it up near the flannel board.

VOCABULARY:
    Trace
    Upset
    Get to the bottom of
    Mystery
    Unravel
    Detective
    Extraordinaire
    Scolded

Detective Play
Dramatic Play/Language

WHY we are doing this activity: to enable children to engage in fantasy play; to encourage child-to-child interactions; to develop language; to develop an enjoyment of acting.

WHAT we will need:
Dress-up raincoats
Dress-up hats
Plastic magnifying glasses
Notebooks
Pens

HOW we will do it: Several weeks ahead of time, start asking friends, families, and other parents if you can borrow hats and raincoats for this activity. Set out all materials in a dramatic play area. Tell the flannel board story above, or read some of the detective stories listed in the literature section. Afterward, show the children the capes, hats, and magnifying glasses and invite them to create and solve their own mysteries.

Magnifier Song
Gross/Fine Motor/Music/Movement

WHY we are doing this activity: to help children feel comfortable using their singing voices; to reinforce the function of magnifiers through music; to develop the large and small muscle groups.

WHAT we will need:
Song: "MAGNIFIER SONG" (to the tune of "Hello Operator")

"MAGNIFIER SONG"
Had a diamond in my pocket;
the pocket had a hole,
the diamond worked its way right out,
and then away it rolled.

I got my magnifier,
I scrutinized the floor,
I saw my diamond clear as day
fetched up beside the door!

HOW we will do it: Sing the song once for the children and explain the words *scrutinized* and *fetched up*. For "Had a diamond in my pocket," pretend to hold a glittering diamond between your thumb and forefinger, and put it in your pocket. For "the pocket had a hole, the diamond worked its way right out," pretend to pull out an empty pocket and make a dismayed face. For "and then away it rolled," roll your hands around each other. For "I got my magnifier," pretend to hold a magnifying glass and stand up. For "I scrutinized the floor," pretend to examine the floor through your magnifier. For "I saw my diamond clear as day, fetched up beside the door," pretend to find your diamond (by a door if possible) and pick it up with delight.

Sing the song and perform the motions together as a group. If you have an adequate number of plastic magnifying glasses, use these during the song.

Literature

Symbol Key: * Multicultural
             + Minimal diversity
             No symbol: no diversity or no people

The first three books all have several illustrations of children (or bears!) using magnifying glasses.

Berenstain, S., & Berenstain, J. (1980). *The Berenstain bears and the missing dinosaur bone*. New York: Random House.

Levy, E. (1975). *Something queer at the ball park: A mystery*. New York: Delacorte Press.

Levy, E. (1975). *Something queer on vacation: A mystery*. New York: Delacorte Press.

Norden, R. (1993). *Magnification*. New York: Lodestar. (This is an excellent pop-up book with wonderful photographs of various magnified objects.)

Extenders

Science: Encourage the children to lie on the floor and examine it with their magnifying glasses. Can they spot things they would not ordinarily see? What do they find in corners and against the walls? Invite the children to examine other objects in the room with magnifiers, for example, walls, carpet, wooden furniture, dust balls.

Science: Provide cooked and uncooked alphabet noodles for the children to examine and compare. How do they look different under the magnifying glasses?

Cognitive: Buy very small stickers and/or use the tiny pictures provided in the book. Spread butcher paper out on a table and tape it down. Affix the tiny pictures or stickers all over the butcher paper, and put matching pictures/stickers on separate index cards. Invite the children to pick a card, and to use their magnifiers to see if they can find the matching sticker or picture on the butcher paper. Make sure you pull the table away from the wall so that the children can move freely all around it. A long, narrow table is preferable to a square or circular one.

Music/Movement: As a variation of the "MAGNIFIER SONG," use a plastic bead which looks like a diamond. (These are available from craft stores.) Have one child hide it while everyone closes their eyes. Change the last line to: "I
couldn't ask for more!" As you sing the song and perform the motions, see if anyone can find the hidden diamond.

Math/Art: Let the children examine fabric pieces under a magnifying glass. Ask them what they notice about the threads, and how the individual threads are arranged to make the fabric. Introduce the word *weaving*, and then provide the children with strips of paper to weave in and out of each other.

KITCHEN KABOODLE

This unit is fun because it makes use of everyday kitchen items to teach scientific principles. One advantage of this is that children can extend the activities in their own kitchens at home. It is important to note that some educators feel extremely uncomfortable using food as a material for learning experiences, given that hunger and starvation are rampant around the world. On the other hand, whether it's Playdough on the activity table or rice in the sensory table, many teachers are reluctant to completely omit the use of food as a material from their curricula, because of the unique tactile experience it offers and how much children enjoy it. In any case, I've included this unit and these activities, and you can choose what's right for you.

Attention Getter: Ahead of time, find a home decorating magazine. When the children are gathered, leaf through the pages with them and name each room in the photographs you see (e.g., bedroom, living room, bathroom). When you come to a photograph of a kitchen, stop and discuss this room with the children. What do you do in a kitchen? What kinds of things do you find there? How many children eat in their kitchens? How many help cook in their kitchens? Let the children know that for the next few days you will be conducting scientific experiments with things you find in a kitchen.

Can You Dehydrate a Cucumber Slice with Sugar?

Science

WHY we are doing this project: to enable children to understand what *hydrate* and *dehydrate* mean; to facilitate the discovery that sugar absorbs water; to help children notice the passing of time.

WHAT we will need:

> Cucumber slices
> Brown sugar
> Spoons
> Meat trays or small, shallow containers
> Newspaper

Demonstration:

> Minced fresh parsley
> Dried parsley
> Eye- or medicine dropper
> Water

HOW we will do it: To prepare, spread several layers of newspaper over a work surface. Put sugar and cucumber slices in the meat trays. Arrange the materials on the table so that all children will have access to them. Make sure there are some empty containers so that children can scrape the sugar water into them—it will take more than one covering of sugar to dehydrate the cucumber slices.

During an Attention Getter time, show the children the fresh and dried parsley. Find out if the children know that they are the same herb.

What is the difference between the two? If necessary, mention that the fresh parsley has water in it, and the dried parsley has none. Pass them both around the circle so that each child can examine them.

Tell the children that something with water in it, like the fresh parsley, is *hydrated*. Tap or blink in time as you repeat the syllables of the word. Then show the children the dried parsley again, and say, "This parsley is *dehydrated*. That means the water in it has been taken away. Sometimes people get dehydrated. If you walked in a hot desert for a long time, you would sweat, and you would get thirstier and thirstier. Your body would become dehydrated if you didn't drink any water." Tap and blink in time to the syllables of this word as you say it.

Put a small pile of sugar on a table surface, and using the eye- or medicine dropper, drop a few drops of water onto the sugar. Ask the children what they see happening; for example, does the water run out at the bottom of the pile of sugar? Why not? Explain that the word *absorb* means to soak up. The sugar absorbs the water. Give each child a cucumber slice to eat. Does it feel wet? Ask your students to predict what will happen if they put sugar on top of the cucumber slices. Show them the experiment materials and invite them to find out what happens when they spoon sugar onto the cucumber. When the dry sugar on top of the cucumber slice is wet, that means it has absorbed water from the cucumber. When the children see this, they can scrape off the wet sugar and put a new layer of dry sugar on. The more times they do this, the more water they will take out of the cucumber. How much water can they get out of one cucumber slice? It will take a little while for the sugar to soak up the water each time. As the children conduct the experiment, encourage them to scrape the sugar water into the empty containers. At the end of the day or session, ask the children what happened to the sugar on top of the cucumber slices, as well as what happened to the slices. Use the words *hydrate*, *dehydrate*, and *absorb* as you discuss the children's findings.

Developmental differences: Three- and young four-year-olds will be more interested in the sensory aspects of this experiment. As they touch and squeeze the cucumber pieces and

222

sugar, discuss with them why the sugar feels more wet after it has been on the cucumber. If necessary, demonstrate this yourself. Older children will be more interested in the absorption capacity of the sugar.

Hydration
Science

WHY we are doing this project: to allow children to understand that many foods have had the water taken out of them (dehydration) and that it is possible to put the water back into them (hydration); to familiarize children with how to measure time.

WHAT we will need:
    Dried onions and other vegetables
        (spice section)
    Dried vegetable soup packets
    Eyedroppers
    Small containers
    Warm water
    Newspapers or trays
    Strainers
Demonstration:
    Carrot
    Onion slice

HOW we will do it: Spread newspaper out on the activity table if you do not have trays. If you do, put a container and an eyedropper on each tray. Put small amounts of water in the containers so that every child will have access to water. Save some of each dried vegetable for comparison with the hydrated vegetables the children produce.

During an Attention Getter time, show the children the regular vegetables, and then show them the dried vegetables on the table. Ask the children how they differ, and encourage them to touch both samples. Ask them to predict what would happen if they covered the dried vegetables with water. Together, agree on an amount of time that the class will let the dried vegeta-

bles sit in the water (at least twenty minutes). Talk about where the hands of the clock will be when it is time to pour the water out. If you like, draw a picture of what the clock will look like when the time has passed, so that the children can compare the picture to the real clock.

Encourage the children to put dried vegetables in their containers and to pour water over them. After the agreed-upon amount of time has passed, invite the children to pour the contents of their containers through the strainers into the sink. How have the dried vegetables changed? Have they absorbed water? Invite the children to compare how the hydrated vegetables feel (wet, soft) with how the dried vegetables feel (dry, hard, powdery, brittle). Use the words *dehydrated* and *hydrated* as you discuss the science experiment results together.

Veggie Art
Art/Fine Motor

WHY we are doing this project: to facilitate creative expression through an art project requiring unusual materials; to develop fine motor skills.

WHAT we will need:
    Dried onions and other vegetables
        (spice section)
    Dried vegetable soup packets
    Small containers
    Glue
    Glue brushes
    Small paper plates
    Crayons

HOW we will do it: Place your materials on the activity table, including some small containers of dried vegetables and other small containers of glue. Put the glue brushes on the table also, and arrange the materials so that all children will have easy access to them.

During an Attention Getter time, point to each vegetable on the table and ask the children to name it. Ask the children for ideas about what they could do with the dried vegetables and art materials. Invite them to use the Veggie Art materials.

More Proof that Sugar Absorbs Water: Sugar Tower
Science

WHY we are doing this project: to provide children with another method of observing that sugar absorbs water.

WHAT we will need:
Sugar cubes
Spoons
Food coloring
Small cups of water
Small, shallow containers
Newspapers

HOW we will do it: Spread several layers of newspaper on the activity table. Add drops of food coloring to the water and pour the colored water into the small cups. Arrange the sugar, spoons, and shallow containers on the activity table so that all children have access to them.

During an Attention Getter time, build a tower of four sugar cubes in one of the shallow containers. Show your students the cups of colored water and ask them to predict what will happen if they put spoonfuls of the water around the base of a sugar tower. Ask them what they see in the room that would help them conduct this experiment. Talk to the children about what they discover as they explore the materials.

Developmental differences: Three- and young four-year-olds will enjoy exploring the wet sugar with their fingertips, a sensory method of discovering that sugar absorbs water. Older children will observe how the sugar tower draws up the water.

Bread 'N Sugar
Science

WHY we are doing this project: to encourage children to hypothesize; to develop speaking, listening, reading, and writing skills; to allow children to observe that even dried, hard sugar will absorb moisture.

WHAT we will need:
Small plastic jars with lids (two for each child)
Pieces of fresh bread (about 5 cm x 5 cm [2" x 2"])
Brown sugar
Sticky labels
Butcher paper
Markers (two different colors)

HOW we will do it: Start collecting the plastic jars several weeks ahead of time. Ask friends, parents, and neighbors to help you save them. When you are ready to do this activity, leave some brown sugar out until it is hard—a few hours is usually adequate. Write the children's names on the labels (unless your students can do this for themselves). On an activity table, put out the lumps of hard sugar, the bread pieces, and the containers with lids.

During an Attention Getter time, pass around a piece of bread and a lump of dried sugar so that the children can feel how hard and dry the sugar is, and how soft the bread is. Ask the children if they remember what they discovered about sugar in the other sugar experiments. (Sugar absorbs water.) Ask them to predict what will happen if they put a piece of bread in a container with a hard piece of sugar. Put your hard sugar and bread in a plastic container and seal the lid. Put another lump of hard sugar in a container without a piece of bread. Ask your students what they see in the room that will help them conduct this experiment for themselves.

The next day, pin up your butcher paper at the children's level. Ask the children to feel the sugar and to compare the feeling of the sugar with the bread, and to the sugar without. How are they different? Ask them to *hypothesize* about why the sugar softened. Explain that when you hypothesize about something, you try to guess why it happened. Print the children's hypotheses on the chart or invite them to do this themselves. Let your students know they may come and write their ideas on the chart at any time during the day. At the end of the day, ask students to read the ideas on the chart to you, or read their hypotheses to them.

Remind the children about the sugar tower experiment you did, and how the sugar soaked up the water. What does this tell us about what happened to the bread in the containers? Explain that *moisture* is another word for tiny drops of water that make something wet or damp. The drops of water in the bread were too tiny to make the bread feel wet, but those tiny beads of water were there, and the sugar absorbed them. How does the bread feel after being in the containers with sugar?

Air Draws Moisture Out
Science/Language

WHY we are doing this experiment: to enable children to observe evaporation; to enable them to understand that air dries food out; to develop reading and writing skills.

WHAT we will need:
  Brown sugar
  Pieces of fresh bread
  Cake mix
  Cooked noodles
  Cooked rice
  Dozen-size egg cartons (enough for half the number of children in your group)
  Popsicle sticks
  Spoons
  Containers or bowls
  Observation pages (provided on page 226; photocopy and enlarge for your use)
  Blank paper
  Pens

Sticky labels
Plastic zip-lock sandwich bags
Preparation:
  Permanent pen
  Butcher paper
Optional:
  Food magazines

HOW we will do it: To prepare, cut the egg cartons in half. Push a long, narrow table up against a wall. On butcher paper, use the permanent marker to print words; for example, *crusty, stale, hard, dry, moist, soft,* and *crumbly.* Cut the words out and tape them on the wall above the experiment table. If you have time, cut pictures out of food magazines which fit these words and pin these up on the wall also. For example, use a cake picture for *moist,* or dried food on a dirty pot or pan for *crusty.*

Put some of each food item in the containers or bowls, and set them on the activity table. Place the spoons and halved egg cartons on the table also. Write each child's name on a sticky label (unless the children can do this for themselves).

Ahead of time, put your own name on an egg carton, and put some of each material in the cavities. Also, put some of each food item in a sealed plastic sandwich bag. During an Attention Getter time, show the children your carton and, together, identify each food item. Ask the children to predict what will happen to the food and what it will look like if it is left out in the air for a week or so. Show your students an observation sheet, and point to each word and symbol that corresponds to the food in each cavity. Read the headings aloud: Day One, Day Two, and so forth. Use a Popsicle stick to poke each item, and make sure the children have a close-up view of each one. As you poke each one, say: "This is day one of my experiment. What do you think I should write down to describe the bread (or rice or noodle, etc.) Is it soft? Moist? Crumbly?" Point to these words taped on the wall. If the children think of new ones, tape those on the wall, too. Show the children the blank paper and let them know they can also use this for recording the results of the experiment.

Put your egg carton on the experiment table and lay your observation sheet next to it.

Science Experiment: What happens when you leave food out in the air?

Kind of Food	Day One 1• ☀ ☽	Day Two 2: ☀ ☽	Day Three 3: ☀ ☽
Brown sugar			
Bread			
Cake mix			
Rice			
Noodles			

Tell the children that you are going to leave your experiment here for the next few days. Let them know that every day, you are going to poke each food with a Popsicle stick to see if it has changed, and then you will write down what you observe. Let your students know that if they would like to conduct their own experiment, the materials are on the table.

Decide on a certain time every day for the group to check the egg cartons. Young children will not record formal observations, but will use their observation sheets for scribbling—this is an important stage in developing writing skills. During your daily check of the experiment, read aloud the words on the wall and what they mean. Do any of the words describe any of the food items? As the materials get drier and harder, ask the children to hypothesize why this is so. If necessary, explain that the air is drawing the moisture out. Compare them to the food that was left in the sealed sandwich bags. Is there a difference? Why? When you decide you have left the materials out long

enough, have a show-and-tell of observation sheets if you like.

Fun with Flour
Science/Sensory/Art/Craft/Math

WHY we are doing this project: to develop self-esteem by enabling children to make their own play material; to help children understand that dough dries into a hard material because air draws moisture out; to provide a sensory experience; to familiarize children with measuring cups; to facilitate artistic expression with Playdough.

The amount of Playdough you make will depend on the number of children. The ingredients below are for one batch (enough dough for six children). Many parents and teachers already have favorite Playdough recipes—feel free to use yours instead, if this is the case.

WHAT we will need:
- 2 cups flour
- 1 cup salt
- 2 tablespoons cream of tartar
- 2 cups water
- 1 tablespoon vegetable oil
- Several large spoons
- Measuring cups
- Tablespoons

Playdough play:
- Rolling pins
- Cookie cutters
- Plastic knives
- Plastic forks

Optional:
- Kool-Aid flavors

HOW we will do it: Make the Playdough together as a small group project by combining the first three ingredients, adding the fourth and fifth, and then stirring over medium heat until the mixture thickens. Have the children help you count the amounts of each ingredient and, if you like, let them take turns filling up the cup measurements and emptying the ingredients into a big bowl. When all the ingredients have been combined, give each child a turn to stir it. If your dough is too sticky, add some flour. If it is too dry, add a little oil and water.

If you add Kool-Aid to the dough, encourage your students to smell the dough without putting their noses directly on it. When the Playdough is ready, put it out with the Playdough toys and invite the children to make shapes. If they leave their shapes out for several days, the gluten in the flour will cause them to harden, or you can bake them in a 250°F oven for three hours or until hard. If you like, have the children paint their shapes with shellac.

What Does an Acid Do? (Part 1)
Science

WHY we are doing this project: to enable children to observe the effects of an acid.

WHAT we will need:
- Clear plastic cups
- Cola
- Old pennies
- Pitchers
- Sticky labels
- Large tub or basin

Optional:
- Trays or newspaper

HOW we will do it: Arrange all materials on the activity table so that all children will have access to them. Use trays or newspaper to control spills. Designate a space for the experiment to be left overnight. Write the children's name on a sticky label or let them do this.

During an Attention Getter time, pour some cola into a cup and drop a penny into it. Ask the children to predict whether or not the penny will be changed in any way the next day. Ask your students what they see in the room which will help them conduct the same experiment.

The next day, put out the tub or basin so that the children can empty the cola into it. Encourage them to examine the pennies. Do they look different? Explain that there is an acid in the cola which is strong enough to eat away the dirt on a penny.

Acid Rain (Part 2)
Science/Social Studies/Small Group Project

WHY we are doing this activity: to build on knowledge acquired in a previous project; to develop awareness of conditions which are threatening to the environment; to develop speaking and listening skills; to develop problem-solving skills.

The facts of the matter: When oil and gas are burned, the gases diffuse into the air and mix with rain, producing sulfuric acid, carbonic acid, and nitric acid. These acids corrode stone, metal, and cement. They also kill trees and plants, and wildlife in lakes and rivers. Acid rain has already devastated thousands of lakes and thousands of miles of forest throughout the world, particularly in Eastern Europe. Possible solutions: use coal and oil which contain less sulphur, clean waste gases before they pass out of factory and power-station chimneys, fit cars with devices which clean exhaust smoke, create communities in which people can walk to their homes and workplaces. Everything has a cost. When it comes to investing in the preservation of our environment or continuing on our present course, there is disagreement about which commands the greater price.

WHAT we will need:
    Butcher paper
    Markers

HOW we will do it: Pin up your butcher paper and have your markers ready. During a group time, remind the children of how the acid in the cola ate away the dirt on the coins in the previous experiment. Tell the children that there is another kind of acid which is found when gases in the air mix with rain. The gases come from the smoke from factories and cars when oil and other things are burned. The acid smoke rises up in the air, and mixes with water drops when it rains. (On one of the butcher paper pieces, draw pictures of what you are talking about as you speak.) This is called acid rain. Remind the children how strong the acid in the cola was.

Acid rain is a strong acid, too. (Draw a picture of a normal tree with green leaves, plants, and a lake with fish in it.) When it falls, it kills fish in lakes, and it kills trees and plants. (Draw a picture of a tree trunk with no leaves.)

Ask the children: "What do you think we need to do to stop acid rain from being made?" Encourage the children's observations and ideas as you facilitate this discussion. Write down their comments using two differently colored markers, alternating a color for each sentence. Use quotation marks, and write down names of children next to their ideas. At the end of the discussion, ask the children to read the chart back to you, or read the children's comments to them. Leave the poster up for a few days.

Facilitate a discussion about what the children can do to save energy. Ask the children to brainstorm for ideas, and write them down on a chart. Some ideas you might suggest if necessary: walk or use public transportation, turn lights and the television off when they are not needed, use only as much water as you really need.

Acids and Bases (Part 1)
Science/Language

WHY we are doing this experiment: to continue building on our knowledge about acids by experimenting with their reaction to bases; to develop speaking and listening skills.

Note: As explained in the Color Capers unit, certain juices contain what is called an *indicator*. This is a chemical which causes the juice to turn different colors when it is mixed with an acid or base. One of the juices in this activity has an indicator. In this unit, children experiment further with acids and bases using different juices than in Color Capers.

WHAT we will need:
    Clear plastic cups
    Small containers
    Small spoons

Small pitchers
Baking soda (several boxes)
Lemon juice
Juice (apple and cranberry)
Popsicle sticks
Trays
Newspaper
Puppet

HOW we will do it: To prepare, spread several layers of newspaper over your table and set out trays. This experiment frequently results in overflowing, so be prepared. Put a plastic cup and a Popsicle stick on each tray. Arrange containers of baking soda, spoons, and pitchers of both juices so that each child will have access to them.

During an Attention Getter time, take your puppet out and use its personality to facilitate a discussion of the following information: that the baking soda is called a *base*, and that an *indicator* is a chemical which changes color when it is mixed with a base. Ask the children to predict which one of the juices has an indicator in it, and encourage them to mix the substances to find out. Use the puppet to ask your students about what they are doing and discovering. What happens to the cranberry juice when it is mixed with baking soda? (It changes color.) Does the apple juice react to the baking powder? (Of all the juices, apple juice has the least amount of acid in it.) What does the lemon juice do? (It foams furiously. When the acid of the lemon juice mixes with the baking soda base, it makes carbon dioxide.) Invite the children to taste the juices. Does one taste like it has more acid in it than the others? Hint: Which one tastes most sour? Which juice has the indicator in it?

Developmental differences: Three- and young four-year-olds will be more interested in mixing, pouring, and stirring, but the discoveries they make during this process will help them understand concepts they are introduced to later. Older children are more likely to be curious about which juice has the most acid in it, and which one contains an indicator.

Making Lemon Soda Pop (Part 2)
Science/Math/Language/Fine Motor

WHY we are doing this project: to give children further opportunity to experiment with an acid and a base by making their own lemon soda pop; to familiarize children with measurements; to develop reading, speaking, and listening skills; to develop fine motor skills through a squeezing activity.

WHAT we will need:
Lemons cut in half (two halves for each child)
Baking soda
Bowl of cold water
Ice cubes
Honey
Teaspoons
½ teaspoons
Tablespoons
½ cup measuring cups
¼ cup measuring cups
Large, clear plastic cups
Popsicle sticks
Recipe signs (provided on page 230; photocopy and enlarge for your use)
Puppet
Orange/lemon squeezer (electric or manual)
Large bowl
Trays

HOW we will do it: To prepare, make recipe signs using the provided format or create your own. If your measuring utensils are similar in size and shape to the symbols in the text, then just photocopy them or trace them onto the chart; otherwise make your own. Use a permanent marker to write the measurements on the measuring utensils. This makes it easier for children to differentiate between them and to familiarize themselves with the relative amounts.

Put your lemon halves on the activity table and place your squeezer next to them. An electric one is much easier for the children to use than a manual one, but if you only have a

Juice of one 1. lemon.

One half ½ cup of cold water.

One quarter ¼ cup of cold water.

Three 3 teaspoons of honey

Stir everything with your popsicle stick.

One half ½ teaspoon of baking soda.

manual one, you can help children who request it by gently placing your hand over theirs and helping them press down on the lemon half.

Place a container of baking soda, a bowl of water, and a small bowl of honey on the table with the appropriate ingredient signs and measuring utensils next to them. During an Attention Getter time, ask the children how many of them like lemon soda pop and whether or not they would like to make some. Go around the table and with the children, discuss each ingredient and each ingredient sign. Make sure you clearly name each measuring utensil, and if you like, compare it to bigger and smaller ones before putting it back next to the ingredient. (Example: hold up a 1 cup measuring cup and say: "This is a whole cup, but today we're only going to use three-quarters of

a cup. That's why we have this ½ cup measuring cup and this ¼ cup measuring cup." Pour water from the ½ and ¼ cup measuring cup into the 1 cup measuring cup so that the children can see how the amounts relate to each other. [Point to the markings on the utensils as you do this.])

Invite the children to take a plastic cup and a Popsicle stick, and to mix the ingredients together according to the recipe sign. Show the children students the ice and tell them that if they like cold lemon soda pop they can put ice in their cups after they make their drink. The amount of juice in lemons varies, so have extra lemon juice and honey on hand for children who need a little more of one or the other. Make sure that when the children add the baking soda, they keep the cups on the trays, because the liquid often overflows. Discuss this step during Attention Getter time.

When the children begin to make their lemon soda pop, take out your puppet and use its personality to react to the bubbling and frothing of the lemon juice and baking soda. (For example, "Look out!! It's out of control—run for your lives!" and then when the frothing subsides: "Whew! That was a close one—I thought we were all going to be swept away." Be creative and have fun with your puppet.) Invite the children to drink their lemon soda pop. How does it taste? Does it taste the same as fizzy lemon soda pop you buy in a store? Does it taste better or worse?

Tip: Save all squeezed lemon halves for the Lemon Peel Tower.

Lemon Soda Pop Bottles and Labels
Language/Math/Art

WHY we are doing this project: to build on the experience of the previous activity; to develop all components of language arts: reading, writing, speaking, and listening; to facilitate creative expression.

WHAT we will need:
Small, plastic soda bottles (½ liter [16 oz.] size)
Markers
Pens
Crayons
Glue sticks
Funnels
Paper rectangles or sticky labels (25 cm x 7.5 cm [10" x 3"])

HOW we will do it: Begin collecting the plastic soda bottles several weeks ahead of time. Ask friends, neighbors, and parents to help. Clean all of the bottles thoroughly with hot,

soapy water, and rinse thoroughly with cold water. To remove the labels, soak the bottles in hot water and scrub them off.

Decorate a sample lemon soda pop bottle. Some options in making your label: draw a lemon, lemonade, lemon tree, lemon drops; write the ingredients; make up a name for your brand of lemon soda pop—be creative! If you have used a sticky label, smooth it onto your bottle; otherwise, use a glue stick.

If you need to make more lemon soda pop to put in your bottles because you drank what you made in the previous activity, an option is to use three tablespoons of commercially prepared lemon juice instead of the juice from fresh lemons, which can be expensive.

Use a funnel to pour your soda pop into your bottle. Have the funnels and bottles available at the table where the children will be mixing up their soda pop. Set out all the label-making materials on another table.

During an Attention Getter time, show the children your homemade soda pop in its bottle and read all the words on your soda pop label. Ask your students what they see in the room that will help them make their own. While the children are working on their labels, take story dictation, spell words, support invented spelling or scribbling, or write words out on a separate piece of paper to be copied, depending on the needs and requests of your children. As they finish working on their labels, ask them to tell you about it.

Lemon Peel Tower
Sensory/Small Group Activity

WHY we are doing this project: to provide children with a sensory and manipulative experience using squeezed lemon halves; for kindergartners, to help them understand the meaning of concave and convex; to practice rational counting; to promote cooperation as a group, through a group counting activity.

WHAT we will need:
    Squeezed lemon halves (from lemon
        soda activity)
    Sensory tubs or table
    Yellow construction paper
Preparation:
    Scissors

HOW we will do it: To prepare, cut the yellow construction paper into a lemon shape, and tape it on the wall. Put all the lemon peels in the sensory tub or table. During an Attention Getter time, show the children the materials. Demonstrate how, if you put one lemon half with the open or concave side down, you can build a tower by putting other lemon halves on top, one after another.

If you work with older preschoolers or kindergartners, point to the inwardly curved side of the squeezed lemon half, and ask the children if it reminds them of a cave. Let them know that that is the *concave* side of the lemon. Point to the outwardly curving side of the lemon half, and explain that that is the *convex* side. If you have a bowl, an old contact lens, a spoon, or anything else that reinforces these concepts, use these materials in your explanation.

As a group, use all of your lemon halves to build up one tower, and then together, count all the lemon halves. Write the number you count on the paper lemon on the wall. Leave the lemon peels in the sensory table or tubs for the children to play with independently.

Lemon Soda Song
Music/Movement/Gross Motor/
Language/Multicultural/Anti-Bias

WHY we are doing this project: to build on previous activities; to help children enjoy using their singing voices; to reinforce, through music and movement, the reaction of an acid and a base when they are mixed together; to create multicultural, anti-bias awareness; to provide the opportunity for children to develop imagination and verbal skills through use of flannel board materials.

WHAT we will need:
    Flannel board
    Felt
    Glue
    Flannel board shapes (provided on
        page 233; photocopy and enlarge for
        your use)
    Song: "LEMON SODA SONG"
        (to the tune of "Pop Goes the Weasel")

"LEMON SODA SONG"
Lemon juice and baking soda,
frothing and a-foaming,
Rising up, they bubble and fizz,
Whoops!! They're overflowing!

HOW we will do it: To prepare, color your flannel board shapes and glue them onto felt. If you want them to last longer, cover them with clear contact paper on the non-felt side. When the children are gathered during an Attention Getter time, use the pieces while you sing the song. Do this several times until the children know the words and can sing it with you. If you like, have the children take turns putting the pieces on the board when that part of the song is sung. If you have a large group, have three children come up at a time, and give each child one piece. Set the materials out for free play time, and invite the children to play with the flannel board story during this time.

Next, stand up and spread out, and sing the song with gestures instead of the flannel board. For "Lemon juice and baking soda," pretend to squeeze a lemon with your hand and to spoon baking soda into a container. For "frothing and a-foaming," move your hands to create an image of something foaming in a mass of bubbles. For "Rising up, they bubble and fizz," move your hands upward and outward. For "Whoops!! They're overflowing!" spread your arms out and make your face look surprised and alarmed. Encourage the children to join you.

Last, for gross motor development, crouch down on the floor. For the first line of the song, bring your hands together from opposite directions as if one is lemon juice and the other is baking soda, and intertwine your fingers. For the rest of the song, slowly rise up as if you are frothy bubbles that are rising in a glass, and then use your arms and the rest of your body to spread out and "overflow" when you reach a standing position.

Yeast Feast

Science/Math/Sensory

WHY we are doing this experiment: to help children understand that yeast is a plant which cannot make its own food and, therefore, must be given food; to help children understand what yeast needs to grow; to familiarize children with spoon and cup measurements; to provide a sensory experience.

The facts of the matter: Yeast are one-celled plants. Yeast cannot use sunlight to make its own food, the way green plants can. When yeast feed off sugar, they give off alcohol and carbon dioxide.

WHAT we will need:
  Large bowl of flour
  Small bowls (one for each child)
  Packages of yeast
  Sugar
  Two containers (for sugar and yeast)
  Popsicle sticks
  Pitchers of warm water
  Two ½ cup measuring cups
  One teaspoon
  ¼ teaspoon
  Ingredient signs (provided on pages 235–238; photocopy and enlarge for your use)
  Construction paper
  Markers

HOW we will do it: To prepare, use the sample ingredient signs in the text and your construction paper to make ingredient signs. Fold the construction paper so that each sign will be self-standing.

Place the large bowl of flour, a pitcher of warm water, and the containers of sugar and yeast on the activity table and use the ingredient signs to identify each one. Put one ½ cup measuring cup in the flour, another one next to the warm water, the teaspoon in the sugar, and the ¼ teaspoon in the yeast. Have the containers and Popsicle sticks nearby so the children can mix their yeast feasts.

During an Attention Getter time, show the children some packages of yeast, and open them. Pour some yeast into each child's hand so that everyone has some to examine. Show the children the materials on the activity table, and together, read/interpret the ingredient signs. Encourage the children to follow the instructions, and then place the bowls in a warm place. Ask them to predict if the contents of their bowls will be different in any way when you check them again.

Together, as a group, prepare another bowl of yeast, warm water, and flour, but no sugar. Check the yeast feasts in an hour or so. What happened? What does the sugarless yeast bowl look and smell like? What does this tell us about yeast? Encourage the children to play with their yeasty dough, and to smell it. If you like, conduct another experiment with yeast and different temperatures of water. What are the ideal conditions for yeast to grow?

234

½

Take one half cup of flour.

Fold on the dotted line for a self-standing ingredient sign. Above the word "water" draw whatever container you are using to hold your water.

½

½

Take one half cup of warm water.

Fold on the dotted line for a self-standing
ingredient sign.

1/4

Take one-quarter teaspoon of yeast.

Fold on the dotted line for a self-standing ingredient sign.

1

Take one teaspoon of sugar.

What Is Osmosis?
Science

WHY we are doing this project: to enable children to observe osmosis; to develop reading and writing skills; to help children become familiar with measuring time.

WHAT we will need:
>Clear plastic cups
>Raisins
>Water
>Small pitchers
>Strainers (as many as possible)
>Newspaper
>Sticky labels
>Large, empty tub
>Magnifying glasses
>Large piece of pale-colored
>>construction paper
>Paper
>Markers
>Crayons
>Pens

Demonstration:
>Grape
>Raisin

HOW we will do it: Spread newspaper out on the activity table, and set out the cups, pitchers of water, and raisins. Write each child's name on a sticky label (unless your children can do this for themselves), and place these on the activity table with the strainers, magnifying glasses, and empty tub. On a table nearby, set out the paper and writing/drawing utensils.

During an Attention Getter time, show the children the grape and the raisin, and ask them if they know that they are the same fruit. What is the difference between them? (One has water in it, one has been dried.) Ask the children if they remember what other hydrated and dehydrated foods the group has talked about. Show the children a pitcher of water and ask them to predict whether it is possible to put water back into a raisin. Ask the children what they see in the room that will help them conduct this experiment. Let them know that they will need

to leave their raisins in the water for quite a while (about an hour). Look at a clock and decide together where the hands must be before you can pour the water and raisins out. If you like, draw a picture of what the clock will look like when that much time has passed, so that the children can compare the picture to the clock. (Some children will probably dump out their raisins and water before an hour has passed. Compare their raisins to the ones which have been in water for an hour. What differences do they notice?) Show the children the sticky labels with their names, and invite them to put their own names on their experiment cups.

After the designated time has passed, encourage the children to pour the contents of their experiment cups through a strainer, and to examine the raisins. Remind the children that they can use the magnifying glasses to do this. What happens when they squeeze the raisins? How do they look different from the regular raisins? What happens when a regular raisin is squeezed? Explain that water will move to a place where there is less water. Water will actually pass through the skin of a raisin because of *osmosis*. Write the word *osmosis* on the construction paper and tape it to the wall. Say the word together. Ask the children to describe how the raisins looked and felt before the experiment, and how they looked and felt after the experiment. Show them the paper and writing/drawing materials and invite them to make a "before" and "after" record. Use the word *osmosis* as you discuss the results of the experiment together.

The Amazing Pepper Trick
Science

WHY we are doing this project: to allow children to experiment with and observe the effects of static electricity.

Electricity is far too complicated a subject to explain to young children, but this activity creates an awareness of its presence around us, and helps children understand that something can become charged with electricity through friction.

WHAT we will need:
    Plastic spoons and/or forks
    Black pepper grains
    Pepper shakers
    Salt
    Salt shaker
    Tissue paper
Demonstration:
    Balloon

HOW we will do it: On an activity table, lay out the plastic spoons and shakers. Inflate the balloon.

During an Attention Getter time, turn a light on and off, and ask your students if they know what powers the light. If the children do not mention electricity, tell them that this is what powers the lights. Ask them about all the other things at home or school that work electrically. Show the children the electrical outlets in the room and talk about why it is dangerous to put a finger in one. If possible, go to the window and point out the power lines through which the electrical current travels. Tell the children that there is also electricity in the room. Ask them to predict what will happen if they rub the balloon against their hair and then try to stick it onto their arm or stomach. (Many children have already had experience with this phenomenon.) Let the children take turns trying this as you explain that *static electricity* is all around us. When the children rub the balloon against their heads, the friction charges the balloon with the same electricity that was in their hair.

Show the children the plastic utensils and pepper on the activity table. Ask them to predict what will happen if they rub the spoons and forks against their hair and try picking up the pepper. Caution your students against breathing in any pepper grains, and then invite them to conduct this experiment. What happens? Encourage the children to try the same experiment with salt granules. Ask your students to hypothesize about why static electricity will cause the spoon to pick up pepper, but

not salt. When appropriate, explain that the salt grains are heavier than the pepper grains, and that the spoon's electricity is not strong enough to pick them up. Put small scraps of tissue paper out and then invite the children to go around the room and see if their charged utensils will pick anything else up.

Science kits: Collect the small paper packets of salt and pepper from fast food restaurants. In sandwich bags or small boxes, put a packet of each and a plastic fork and/or spoon. Set these kits out for the children to use independently.

Cornstarch Goo
Science/Sensory

WHY: we are doing this project: to enable children to become familiar with the properties of starch, in particular, the texture of cornstarch; to provide a sensory experience.

The facts of the matter: Explain that the cornstarch is made of small grains and granules, and that only heat makes them burst open so that they dissolve in water.

WHAT we will need:
    Cornstarch (several large boxes)
    Containers (for cornstarch)
    Spoons
    Small pitchers containing small
        amounts of cold water
    Food coloring (small containers)
    Eye- or medicine droppers
    Tubs or sensory table
    Popsicle sticks

HOW we will do it: This project does not work if there is too much water mixed with the corn-starch, so control the amount of water you provide. You will know when you have added the correct amount, because the "goo" will have the consistency of drying mud rather than milk. Put the containers of cornstarch, small amounts of water, and Popsicle sticks near the tubs or sensory table. Ask the children to predict whether or not the cornstarch will dissolve in the water. Encourage them to explore the materials. What do they notice? (It makes a muddy, gooey type of substance.) Encourage further sensory exploration: what happens when you squeeze the goo in your hand? Can you draw something in the goo and keep the shape? (The goo slowly refills any space you make in it.) After a while, put out the food coloring and eyedroppers so that the children can color their goo.

Kitchen Kaboodle
Dramatic Play/Language

WHY we are doing this activity: to promote child-to-child interaction and cooperation; to develop speaking and listening skills; to allow children an opportunity to re-enact real-life situations through fantasy dramatic play; to enable children to work through emotions.

WHAT we will need:
Play kitchen furniture (including a table and chairs)
Dishes
Children's aprons
Recipe books

HOW we will do it: If you do not have play kitchen furniture, paint and decorate boxes to simulate a kitchen. Provide the children with play dishes, silverware, pots, pans, and so forth. Encourage the children to explore the materials and, if appropriate, pretend to be a guest arriving for a meal, or create whatever role and situation you like.

Literature

Symbol Key: *Multicultural
+Minimal diversity
No symbol: no diversity or no people

Asch, F. (1976). *Good lemonade*. New York: Franklin Watts.* (You may wish to skip page 8 when you read this book, as it contains a sexist picture of girls in bikinis selling lemonade.)

Brown, M. (1975). *Stone soup*. New York: Charles Scribner's Sons. (This classic book features carrots, potatoes, and cabbage.)

De Paola, T. (1989). *Tony's bread*. New York: G. P. Putnam's Sons.

Erlback, A. (1994). *Soda pop*. Minneapolis, MN: Lerner.

Florian, D. (1992). *A chef*. New York: Greenwillow Books.*

Food and the kitchen. (1993). Washington, D.C.: Smithsonian Institute. (This book has many ideas for activities with food.)

Mitgutsch, A. (1986). *From lemon to lemonade*. Minneapolis, MN: Carolrhoda Books.

Nottridge, R. (1993). *Sugars*. Minneapolis, MN: Carolrhoda Books.*

Sobol, H. L. (1984). *A book of vegetables*. Northbrook, IL: Dodd, Mead.

Extenders

Science/Cooking: After you conduct the hydration experiment, make soup from a dried soup packet. Make sure the children get a good look at the dried soup mix. Together, try to identify the vegetables they see. After you make the soup, how have the vegetables changed?

Science: After you find out that the acid in cola will clean a penny, see if other acids, like vinegar or lemon juice, will do the same thing.

Sensory/Language: After making your lemon soda pop, compare the way it tastes with store-bought soda. Read the ingredients of the commercial soda and compare it to the ingredients of your homemade soda. If you like, make language charts of each.

Science/Cooking: After doing the yeast feast experiment and reading *Tony's Bread*, pick out a bread recipe that uses yeast and make bread with the children.

SOAP SCIENCE

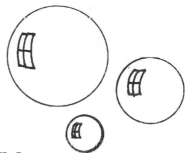

Attention Getter: A fun way to begin this unit is to invest in a few shaped soaps (animals, seashells, flowers, etc.), and let the children examine them. If you do not have any shaped soaps, kick off the activities by asking the children to close their eyes and smell a bar of soap. Can they guess what it is? Or bring in a selection of different bar, liquid, and powder soaps to discuss and compare. Ask the children if they can guess what you will be working with over the next few days. A safety precaution: remind the children before every activity that it is important not to touch or rub their eyes while using soap.

Comparing Soaps
Science/Sensory/Language

WHY we are doing this project: to facilitate scientific observation of soap in its different forms; to provide children with a sensory experience; to develop speaking, listening, reading, and writing skills.

WHAT we will need:
Liquid dish soap
Soap leaves
Powdered laundry soap
Ivory Snow flakes
Bar soap
Pitchers of water (warm and cold)
Tub of cold water
Forks
Spoons
Funnels
Aquarium tubing (available at pet stores)
Small containers
Newspaper
Tubs or sensory table
Paper towels
Butcher paper
Markers

HOW we will do it: To avoid a catastrophic mess, put small amounts of each kind of soap into the containers. Spread plenty of newspaper under your work area. Pin the butcher paper up on the wall at the children's level. Put all the materials in the sensory table and encourage the children to explore them.

As they touch and use the different soaps, ask them how each one feels. If a discussion is slow to get started, introduce some descriptive words into the conversation; *gritty*, *slimy*, and *soft*. Encourage observations. At the top of the butcher paper, write: "How do different soaps feel and look?" If you work with younger children, write down their comments. Use quotation marks and write their names next to their words. Use alternate colors of markers for each child's comment so your students can distinguish individual sentences. If you work with

older children, invite them to write their own comments and/or draw pictures on the chart. At the end of the session, read the chart together.

Making Bubbles
Science/Math

WHY we are doing this project: to facilitate cooperation as a group and to practice rational counting with cup measurements.

WHAT we will need:
1 cup measuring cup
½ cup measuring cup
Large container
6 cups water
Joy liquid detergent (2½ cups)
3 cups glycerine (available at drugstores and some supermarkets)
Large spoons
Wire bubble blowers (instructions below)

HOW we will do this: Ahead of time, twist wire into bubble blowers by wrapping each piece around a cup to form a round circle. Make this bubble liquid together as a group, after the introductory Attention Getter discussion. Tell the children how many cups of each ingredient you need, and have them count each cup you pour into the container. If possible, have the children take turns pouring a cup of an ingredient into the mixture. Let them use the large spoons to mix everything together. Pass around the bubble blowers and invite the children to dip them into the bubble mixture and blow.

244

Making a Bubble Holder
Science/Fine Motor/Crafts

WHY we are doing this project: to develop the fine motor muscle group; to enable children to examine bubbles closely.

There are several ways to make a bubble holder, so choose the method which utilizes the materials that are easiest for you to obtain. Or, if you like, make all the bubble holders and compare how well they work.

WHAT we will need:
   Plastic cups
   Spools
   Pencils
   Wire
   Small funnels
   Bottles
   Magnifying glasses
Preparation:
   Scissors
   Sharp knife

HOW we will do it: To make a bubble holder from a plastic cup, turn the cup upside down and use a sharp knife to punch a horizontal slit in the side of the cup, directly beneath the cup bottom. Then use scissors to cut the bottom out. Bubbles can be blown through the cup and then placed on the rim.

To make a bubble holder with a spool, insert a pencil in the hole of the spool, and wrap one end of a piece of wire around the pencil. Wrap the other end around a glass or round container to get the best circular shape you can, and then remove it. The spool will hold the pencil upright and the wire will remain horizontal. To use a funnel for a bubble holder, simply turn it wide side up, and put the narrow end in a bottle.

Make sure all the bubble holders are dipped into bubble liquid before transferring bubbles to them; dry holders will pop the bubbles. Blow bubbles through the cup, funnel, or wire and then set the holders down to examine the bubbles, or use a bubble wand and gently transfer the bubbles to soapy holders. Children can gently transfer bubbles to the holders, or catch bubbles with them. Show them the magnifying glasses and encourage them to use them to examine the bubbles closely.

Bubble Palace: It Takes Air to Make Bubbles
Science

WHY we are doing this project: to allow children to understand how the force of air is necessary to make bubbles.

WHAT we will need:
   Bubble liquid
   Straws
   Shallow containers
   Food coloring

HOW we will do it: Set out the containers and put a little bubble liquid and food coloring in each one. Place a straw next to each container. Invite the children to blow into the liquid through the straws and see what happens. If you work with three- and young four-year-olds, have the children practice blowing out through the straws instead of sucking in. Talk about what will happen if they suck up the soapy liquid through their straws.

Ask: "Do you think you can make a bubble without air or wind?" Invite the children to try. When they begin to use the straws to make bubbles, invite them to see how high they can build up their bubble palaces. Explain that the children's breath is forced through the straw and into the soapy liquid, where the air and the force combine to make bubbles.

More Proof That It Takes Air to Make Bubbles

Science/Gross Motor/Cognition

WHY we are doing this project: to provide children with another method to discover that it takes air and force to make bubbles; to develop large muscles; to help children understand how the gears in beaters work.

WHAT we will need:

Manual rotary eggbeaters
Whisks
Forks
Large slotted spoons
Tubs or sensory table (filled with water)
Liquid soap
Small containers (for liquid soap)
Eyedroppers
Spoons
Newspaper
Large pitchers of cold water
Large empty tub

HOW we will do it: To prepare, spread several layers of newspaper under your work area. Set out your tubs of water with the manual rotary beaters and whisks. Use the large pitchers of water for refills, and the large empty tub for dumping soapy water. Young children can often have great difficulty operating manual rotary beaters because they are large and cumbersome, so use your own judgment about whether or not to provide these with the other materials.

During an Attention Getter time, ask them to predict what will happen if they mix the water with soap by using the beaters, whisks, and slotted spoons. Encourage them to conduct this experiment. Remind the children of what they learned when they used the straws with soapy water in the previous experiment and, using this information, encourage your students to hypothesize about why beating or whisking the soap and water results in bubbles. (The motion of the beaters forces air into the soapy liquid, and this makes bubbles.) Compare the bubbles made with the beaters to the bubbles made with the straws. Do they look the same? Why? (Beaters force more air into the soapy water and make many more bubbles. This is why the bubbles appear to be much frothier and foamier.)

At the end of the day or the session, talk about your findings. What did the children notice about which tool made the most bubbles the fastest? Demonstrate the manual rotary beater and discuss what makes the beaters turn around.

Bubble-Making Song

Music/Movement/Cognitive

WHY we are doing this activity: to musically reinforce the process involved with making bubbles; to help children enjoy using their singing voices; to develop cognition through memorization of words and related actions.

WHAT we will need:

Song: "BUBBLE-MAKING SONG"
(to the tune of "The Grand Old Duke of York")

"BUBBLE-MAKING SONG"
I take my bubble wand
and dip it in my soap,
wind is blowing,
bubble's growing,
and away it floats.
First it floats up high,
then it floats down low,
finally that old bubble bursts;
I wonder where it goes!

For "I take my bubble wand and dip it in my soap," pretend to be holding a bubble wand and dipping it into liquid soap. For "wind is blowing, bubble growing," blow air with your lips and then use your hands to simulate a growing bubble. For "First it floats up high, then it floats down low," cup your hands to simulate a bubble, and move your hands slowly up and then slowly down. For "finally that old bubble bursts," make a tight fist, and then suddenly open all your fingers wide. For "I wonder where it goes!" put your hands out in a questioning gesture.

Sing the song and do the motions until the children have learned them. When the song is very familiar to the children, try a variation of it. Agree to leave out the word "bubble," "float," or both when you sing the song. Can everyone remember not to sing those words?

Soap Boat
Science

WHY we are doing this project: to enable children to observe that soap breaks up the water molecules which create surface tension.

WHAT we will need:
  Half-gallon cardboard milk cartons (one
    for every four children)
  Boat pattern #1 (provided below;
    photocopy and enlarge for your use)
  Water
  Liquid soap
  Small containers (for liquid soap)
  Eyedroppers
  Tubs or sensory table (filled with water)
  Newspaper
Preparation:
  Skewer or needle
  Fingernail scissors
Demonstration:
  Two small containers
  Water
  Black pepper
  Liquid soap
  Magnifying glass
  Water refills

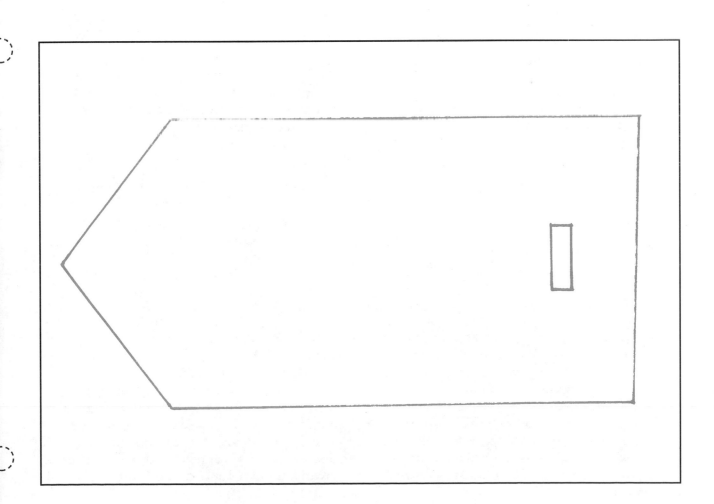

HOW we will do it: To prepare, use the provided boat pattern to cut flat, rectangular boats out of milk cartons. To make the rectangular hole, use a skewer or needle to poke a starter hole, and then use fingernail scissors to cut out the rest. This can be time-consuming, but children really get a kick out of watching the boats be propelled by soap power. Ask friends or parents to help you prepare one boat for each child.

On the day of your activity, spread out plenty of newspaper layers on the floor, under the project. Set out tubs of water or fill the sensory table. Put the boats, containers of liquid soap, and eyedroppers out on the activity table.

During an Attention Getter time, have the children lie on their stomachs in a circle, so that they can see your demonstration. Fill a small container with water and ask the children to predict what pepper will do when you sprinkle it into the water. After the children have made their predictions, sprinkle some pepper in your hand, and then drop it onto the water. What does the pepper do? Pass around the magnifying glass and encourage each child to notice how all the pepper grains sit on top of the water. Tell them that water has *surface tension* because the water molecules cling together. Ask the children if they have ever seen insects sitting on top of the water in a puddle or a pond. Insects can stand on water because of the surface tension. Drop several drops of liquid soap in the other container of water and stir in the soap with your finger. Ask the children to predict what will happen when you sprinkle pepper into this water, and then do so. What happens to almost all of the flakes? Why did they sink? Tell the children that the soap broke up the water molecules so that they spread apart and destroyed the surface tension. This is why the pepper sank instead of staying on top of the water.

Show the children the boats, and ask them to predict what will happen if they lay them on top of the water, and then use the eyedroppers to put drops of soap in the rectangular holes. Encourage the children to conduct this experiment. Remind them of the pepper experiment. Why do they think the boats move? If necessary, explain that when the soap breaks the water molecules apart, behind a boat, it pushes the boat forward. Encourage observations and discussion.

Note: In order for the experiment to work each time, everything must be washed free of detergent, and you must use fresh water. For this reason, if you do not have a sink in your activity room, use shallow amounts of water in your tubs to minimize the amount of refill water you have to keep on hand. Use one tub of clear water for children to wash their hands in when they want to try the experiment again.

Developmental differences: Three- and young four-year-olds may be more interested in floating and sinking the boats, splashing the water, and squeezing the eyedroppers. In the process of this sensory exploration, they are still likely to observe the effect of soap on the water and on the boats. Older children will be more likely to explore the materials with the specific goal of observing the soap's effects.

Another Soap Boat
Science

WHY we are doing this project: to enable children to experiment with another design of soap boat and to observe how it compares with the first boat design.

WHAT we will need:
Half-gallon cardboard milk cartons
Boat pattern #2 (provided on page 249; photocopy and enlarge for your use)
Tubs of water
Liquid soap detergent
Small containers (for the detergent)
Popsicle sticks

HOW we will do it: Use pattern #2 in the text to cut out flat, triangular boats from the milk carton sides. Fold the middle flap up so that the boat looks like the smaller diagram on the pattern. Fill the tubs with water, and put the detergent in the small containers with the Popsicle sticks beside it. Ask the children to predict if these soap boats will react to soap in the same way that the other ones did. Encourage the chil-

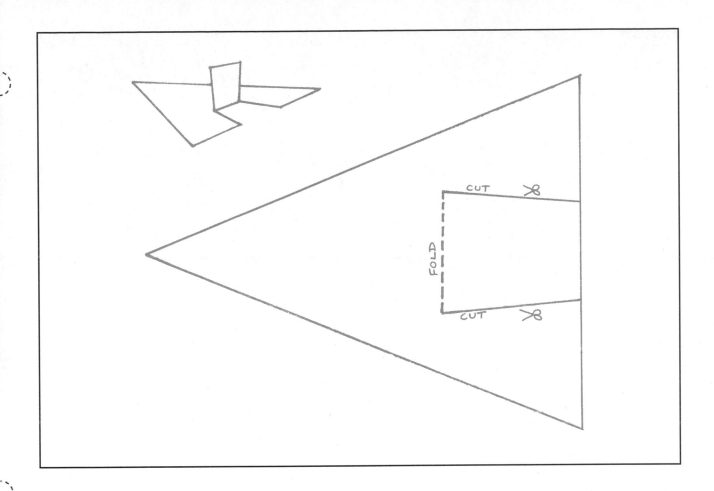

dren to set a boat on the water, and to touch the water space in the back of the boat with a Popsicle stick dipped in detergent. What happens? (The detergent reduces the surface tension in the back of the boat, so it is pulled along by the stronger surface tension in the front.)

Invite the children to put both types of boats side by side and to predict, and then compare, which one is pulled the farthest. To explore further, make both types of boats in different sizes, again, to compare which travels the farthest and the fastest.

It's a Shipwreck!
Science/Art

WHY we are doing this experiment: to provide children with a fun way to experiment with surface tension and soap's effect on it; to facilitate artistic expression.

WHAT we will need:
    Zinc metal (used for window screens)
    Construction paper (white and brown)
    People pattern (provided on page 250;
       photocopy and enlarge for your use)
    Tub of water
    Popsicle stick
    Eyedropper
    Small container of liquid soap
    Markers
    Crayons
    Children's scissors

HOW we will do it: Zinc screening is available at hardware stores. To make a raft, start with a zinc rectangle about 12.5 x 7.5 cm (5" x 3") and fold all sides so that the edges are turned up like a box lid. Your corners will poke out, which is fine, although make sure none of the corners are jagged. Put the raft, a tub of shallow water, the container of liquid soap, eyedropper, and Popsicle stick on one activity table. Use the pat-

tern in the text to cut out little people from brown and white paper. Put these on another activity table nearby, along with extra brown and white paper, crayons, markers, and children's scissors.

During an Attention Getter time, pass the raft around so that the children can examine it. Even though it has holes, do they think it will float? Encourage predictions. Show your children how to place the raft gently on the surface of the water. What stops it from sinking? (The water's surface tension.) Gently place a few paper people in the raft, and show the children the Popsicle stick, eyedropper, and liquid soap. Ask them to predict what will happen to the raft when soap is dropped on it, but first, show them the rest of the paper people with the art materials, and encourage them to make their own paper sailors. Have water refills handy, as well as a large empty tub for dumping used soapy water. Make several rafts if possible, but

if you only have one raft, make a sign limiting the number of children who may explore the materials at any one time. Encourage the children to verbalize their findings as they conduct this experiment.

Developmental differences: Three- and young four-year-olds may be more interested in engaging in dramatic play with the sailors and boats. If you like, conduct the experiment yourself and see if any children become interested. Older children are likely to be curious about how the soap affects the surface tension and, therefore, the boats.

Soapy Spiral
Science

WHY we are doing this project: to provide children with another fun way of exploring surface tension.

WHAT we will need:
>Spiral patterns (provided below; photocopy and enlarge for your use)
>Cardboard milk cartons
>Water
>Liquid soap
>Eyedroppers
>Small containers
>Tubs of water

HOW we will do it: To prepare, use the spiral pattern in the text to cut out spirals from milk cartons. Set them out beside the tubs of water. Put liquid soap and eyedroppers in the small containers.

Ask your students to predict what will happen if they drop the spirals in the water, and use the eyedroppers to drop soap into the spiral centers. Invite your students to conduct this experiment. What happens? (When the surface tension inside the spiral is weakened, the stronger surface tension outside the spiral makes it spin.)

Stream Squeeze
Science/Sensory

WHY we are doing this project: to provide children with a fun, sensory-oriented way of exploring water surface tension and soap's effect on it.

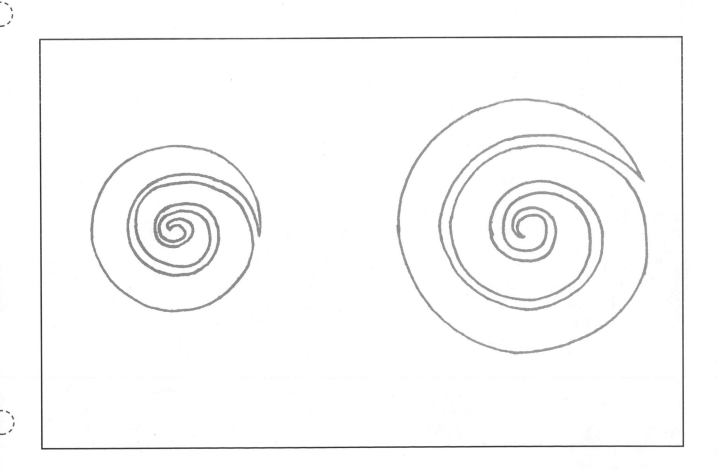

WHAT we will need:
  Small coffee cans
  Clean water
  Small container of liquid soap
  Eyedropper
  Tubs or sensory table
  Plastic bowls with flat bottoms
  Small pitchers
Preparation:
  Hammer
  Sharp nail

HOW we will do it: To prepare, use the hammer and nail to punch three holes, close together in a row, about half an inch from the bottom of each coffee can. In the empty tub or sensory table, turn the bowls upside down and put the tins on top.

Invite the children to cover the holes with their fingers while they fill the tins with pitchers of water. Ask the children to predict, when they take their fingers away, whether the water will run out of all the holes. As they conduct the experiment, ask them to try to squeeze the three streams into one. Why are they able to do this? (The surface tension of all three streams combines to keep them together as one.) After the children have explored this thoroughly, put the liquid soap and eyedroppers out. Ask them to predict whether or not this experiment will work when soap is mixed with the water. Encourage the children to verbalize their findings, and to hypothesize about why the experiment does not work with liquid soap in the water.

Developmental differences: Three- and young four-year-olds will have fun pouring, splashing, and feeling the water, as well as filling containers with the water that streams out of the coffee can. Provide small containers for this kind of sensory exploration. If you like, squeeze the streams together yourself, and see if any children become interested in this experiment. Older children tend to be more fascinated with the phenomenon of squeezing the three streams into one, and with what happens when soap is added.

The Exploding Triangle Trick
Science

WHY we are doing this experiment: to provide children with a dramatic way of observing how soap weakens surface tension; to develop self-esteem and a sense of autonomy through use of a one-person work station.

WHAT we will need:
  Shallow tub of water
  Water refills
  Tub for emptying used water
  Three 10 cm (4") straws
  One Popsicle stick
  Small container of liquid soap
  "One person may be here" sign
    (provided on page 3; photocopy and
    enlarge for your use)
  Newspaper

HOW we will do it: To prepare, spread several layers of newspaper underneath your activity area. Pour a shallow amount of water in the tub, set all other materials beside it, and pin up your "One person may be here" sign.

During an Attention Getter time, read or interpret the sign together. Show the children how to use the Popsicle stick to arrange the straws into a triangle in the water. What will happen if they dip a Popsicle stick into the liquid soap, and then dip it into the middle of the triangle? Encourage predictions and then invite them to find out. Explain that every person who conducts the experiment will have to have clean water. Show them where the refills are, and the empty tub in which used water can be dumped.

Ask your students to hypothesize about why the triangle explodes. When the surface tension in the middle is broken up, the stronger surface tension on the outside pulls the straws apart. After a while, provide an eyedropper. Experiment with dropping different amounts of liquid soap into the middle.

Developmental differences: Three- and young four-year-olds will enjoy splashing and stirring soap into the water with the straws and Popsicle sticks. If you like, conduct the exploding triangle experiment yourself and see if any children become interested. Older children are likely to be more interested in how the straws "explode" when soap is added to the water.

Soap and Light: Making Rainbow Bubbles
Science

WHY we are doing this project: to enable children to observe how light reacts to bubble film.

The facts of the matter: As the walls of a bubble become thinner, white light rays no longer pass through the bubble. Instead, the light is reflected back, either from inside the soapy film or from the outside. When this happens, the colors of the spectrum appear. The colors will change by disappearing and reappearing as the bubble constantly stretches into thinner and thicker film. This explanation may be too involved for young children, but they will enjoy seeing the colors of the spectrum as the bubble film reflects the white light.

WHAT we will need:
Bubble liquid:
6 cups water
2 cups clear dishwashing liquid
   (Joy is recommended)
1 to 4 cups glycerine
Metal coat hangers
Bubble blowers
Bubble holders
Shallow containers
Pliers
Flashlights

HOW we will do it: Mix together the ingredients for the bubble liquid and pour it into the shallow containers. Unbend the coat hangers, and use the pliers, if necessary, to reshape them into bubble blowers. Spread several layers of newspaper under your work area. Show your students the flashlights and invite them to pre-

dict what they will see if they shine light into bubble film. Invite them to use the materials to make bubbles and to conduct this experiment. Mention to the children that they may need to ask each other for help; it might be difficult to hold a bubble blower and a flashlight at the same time. Encourage your students to verbalize their findings.

Super Bubbles
Science/Gross Motor

WHY we are doing this experiment: to enable children to discover that soap makes water elastic; to develop the large muscle group.

The facts of the matter: Soap forces water molecules apart, and this makes water more elastic and "stretchable."

WHAT we will need:
Bubble mixture (several batches)
Wire coat hangers
Hula hoops (if possible)
Straws
String
Large tubs
Trays
Windy day
Preparation:
Pliers

HOW we will do it: Mix up your bubble liquid and put it in the large tub and trays. Untwist the wire coat hangers, and twist them around a cooking pot into large, circular bubble blowers. You will probably need pliers to help you with this. Be sure to leave a handle sticking out from the circle. If you have any hula hoops, these work well as bubble blowers too. To make rectangular super bubble blowers, feed long lengths of string through four straws, and tie the ends together. Slide the straws so that each side is even, and the bubble blower can be held in a rectangular shape.

Put all the materials outside, preferably on a windy day, and encourage the children to use them. Explain that soap makes water molecules move apart, and that this makes the water more "stretchable." Thus, it is possible to blow giant bubbles.

Bubble Blow-Up
Science

WHY we are doing this project: to enable children to experiment further with the elasticity of bubble film; to enable children to discover that the wall of a bubble is so elastic that it will stretch around a straw opening without bursting; to facilitate cooperation between children.

WHAT we will need:
    Bubble wands (regular size)
    Bubble solution
    Straws
    Small containers
    Paper towels

HOW we will do it: To prepare, put some bubble solution in the small containers, and set out the materials on the activity table so that all children will have access to them. During an Attention Getter time, make a bubble on a bubble wand so that the bubble hangs upside down. Ask a child to hold the wand for you in that position. Take a straw and dip it into the bubble solution, making sure the children notice this step. (A dry straw will burst the bubble.) Ask the children to predict whether, when you gently and slowly insert the straw into the upside down bubble, the bubble will burst. Ask them to predict what will happen if you put the straw in the bubble and blow. Ask the children if they see anything in the room that would help them conduct these two experiments, and invite them to do so.

If you work with three- and young four-year-olds, practice blowing out through the straws instead of sucking in. Before the children approach the table, caution them not to

share their straws. Also, say, "I had to ask someone to help me do this experiment, because I couldn't hold the wand very easily while I put the straw into the bubble. When you do this experiment, you may have to ask a friend to help you, and then maybe you can help your friend in the same way."

Depending on your goals for this activity, another option is to spread soapy water on a table surface, and let the children experiment there. This method doesn't require cooperation between students; however, by using this method, we have managed to inflate bubbles to amazing sizes.

Encourage the children to verbalize their findings as they experiment. Ask them if they remember what they learned in the previous activity about how soap makes water more "stretchable." Using this information, ask your students to hypothesize why a bubble does not burst when a wet straw is put inside it. (The bubble wall stretches and bends to let the straw in.) Ask them to hypothesize why the bubble gets bigger when air is blown into it, instead of bursting right away.

More Bubble Tricks
Science

WHY we are doing this activity: to allow children to discover that soap keeps water (and therefore bubbles) from drying out; to provide children with more fun ways of observing that soap makes water elastic.

WHAT we will need:
    Small containers
    Bubble solution
    Bubble wands
    Straws
    Paper towels

HOW we will do it: Set out all materials, and encourage the children to try these experiments:

Catching bubbles and observing a floating bubble land: Ask the children to try to catch a bubble with dry hands. What happens? What happens when a bubble lands on a dry surface? Spread bubble liquid onto a table and encourage the children to blow bubbles over its soapy surface. What happens when the bubbles land on it? Ask the children to hypothesize about the reason for the difference in reactions when a bubble lands on a dry and wet surface. (A dry surface makes a bubble pop right away, but soap keeps the bubble from drying out, so it lasts longer.) Invite the children to put bubble liquid on their hands and to predict whether a bubble will burst if they try to catch it. Invite them to conduct this experiment. (Sometimes the impact of the landing bubble will cause it to burst, even on a soapy hand, but other times the bubble will land on a soapy hand and stay intact for several seconds.)

Blowing a bubble within a bubble: Slick down a table surface with bubble liquid. Encourage the children to blow bubbles so that they land on the soapy surface. Invite them to dip a straw into bubble liquid, insert the straw into a large bubble, and blow a new, smaller bubble inside. If you provide several containers of bubble liquid, each with a different food coloring mixed in it, this experiment can be especially interesting.

Bubble squeeze: Show the children how to hold a bubble wand in each hand, and gently blow a bubble through one of the wands (without blowing it off). Ask them to predict what will happen if they dip the empty wand into bubble liquid, put it on the other side of the bubble, and squeeze. Encourage your students to verbalize their observations.

What happens when they gently and slowly pull the wands away from each other? (The bubbles stretch and change shape.) What happens if they slide a soapy wand over a bubble that is already sitting on another bubble wand?

Grating Soap
Gross Motor/Sensory

WHY we are doing this activity: to provide a sensory experience for children and to develop the large muscle group.

WHAT we will need:
  Soap bars
  Freestanding graters
  Tubs of water
  Paper towels
  Play dishes

HOW we will do it: Set all materials on an activity table. Invite the children to grate soap and use it in water to clean the play dishes, or wash plastic toys. What does the grated soap feel like, compared to bar soap? What happens to them both in water? What do the children notice about the difference in the kinds of bubbles they make?

Soap Boxes: Math Kits
Math

WHY we are doing this project: to practice rational counting and, for older preschoolers and kindergartners, subtraction.

WHAT we will need:
  Small, shaped soaps
  Three boxes with lids to hold collections
    of soaps
  Blank sheets of paper
  Writing sheets (format provided on
    page 256; photocopy and enlarge
    for your use)
  Small pencils

HOW we will do it: Many gift shops have a large variety of small, shaped soaps that cost about $.35 to $.85. Buy enough of these to put a

How many soaps are in the box? _____ Take three soaps away. How many are left? _____

How many soaps are in the box? _____ Take soaps away. How many are left? _____

Use this sample to draw pictures that represent the box and soaps you are actually using, as well as the number of soaps you want taken away. Include the subtraction problem only if you are working with older preschoolers or kindergartners.

small collection in each box. Make several copies of the writing sheet, and put one of these (or blank sheets of paper that are the same size) with a pencil in each box. Keep spares handy so that you can replace used sheets with blank ones as the children use the materials.

Set the soap boxes out on the floor or a table. During an Attention Getter time, show one to the children and ask them to guess what is inside. Take out the writing sheet, and together, read or interpret what it says. As a group, count the number of soaps in the box, and on the blank piece of paper or writing sheet, write down the number you counted. With kindergartners, read/interpret the subtraction problem and have the children help you count the number of soaps to take away. Count the soaps that are left, and write this number on the blank paper or writing sheet. After your demonstration, change the number of soaps in that box so that the math problem will be a new one. Invite the children to explore the soap boxes, and replace paper as necessary.

Soap Match
Math

WHY we are doing this activity: to facilitate a matching exercise; to provide a math experience for younger children; to promote self-esteem through use of a one-person work station. (For younger preschoolers.)

WHAT we will need:
Collection of shaped soaps
Butcher paper
Dark-colored marker
Basket
"One person may be here" sign
(provided on page 3; photocopy and enlarge for your use)

HOW we will do it: To prepare, arrange your soaps on the paper. Trace around them with the marker. If you have more than one soap of the same shape, make sure they are different colors and shade the corresponding outline in the corresponding color. Put the soaps in a basket, next to the butcher paper. If you are going to be using this activity again, draw your outlines on poster board and cover with contact paper.

During an Attention Getter time, show the children the materials you will be using, and discuss the "One person may be here" sign. Invite your students to match the soaps to their outlines.

Soap Book
Science/Language/Art/Fine Motor

WHY we are doing this project: to reinforce the fact that soap comes in many different forms; to develop the small muscle group; to facilitate creative expression; to develop all components of language arts: reading, writing, speaking, and listening.

WHAT we will need:
    Construction paper
    Family/home magazines
    Soap and bubble pictures (provided below; photocopy and enlarge for your use)
    Scissors
    Glue
    Small containers for glue
    Markers
    Crayons
    Pens
Preparation:
    Stapler

HOW we will do it: Begin collecting family/home magazines several weeks ahead of time. Ask friends, family, and other parents to help. To make one blank soap book, put two pieces of construction paper on top of each other, and fold into equal halves. Staple along the fold.

Color in the provided soap and bubble pictures. Affix these to the cover and print: "The Soap Book." Make one of these books for each child. Leave several covers blank for children who want to design their own.

Leaf through the magazines, and tear out photographs of bar soap, liquid soap, dishwashing liquid, and powdered detergent. Ahead of time, make a sample soap book by gluing some of these pictures onto the pages of your book and writing words. (Example: "This is the kind of soap I use to wash my clothes. It feels gritty when I touch it." "This bar of soap is a pretty color. Lilacs are flowers that are the same color.")

Set out all materials on the table so that all children will have access to them. During an Attention Getter time, show the children your sample soap book and read it to them.

Ask your students if they see anything in the room that will help them make their own soap books. If you work with young preschoolers, take story dictation. If you work with older children, spell words, support invented spelling, or write words down on separate pieces of paper to be copied, according to what the children request. When the books are completed, ask the children to read them back to you, tell you about them, or read the books to them. Ask if you can put them out on your bookshelf with your other books.

Bubble Art
Science/Art/Sensory

WHY we are doing this activity: to enable children to see that soap, force, and air make millions of tiny bubbles; to allow children to express themselves artistically with different materials; to provide them with a sensory experience.

WHAT we will need:
   1 cup Ivory Snow flakes
   1 cup water
   Food coloring (variety of colors)

Small containers
Paper
Large bowl
Newspaper
Magnifying glass
Preparation:
   Electric beater

HOW we will do it: Spread several layers of newspaper under your work area. Use the electric beater to whip the water and soap flakes until the mixture is thick. If you like, have the children help you do this. Put some of the mixture into the small containers and to each one add some food coloring. Encourage the children to examine the mixture with the magnifying glass. What do they see? Ask them how many bubbles they think there might be in the mixture. Encourage the children to finger paint with the soapy mixture. When the pictures dry, what do the children see (tiny bubble prints from dried bubbles)?

Bubble Prints
Science/Art

WHY we are doing this project: to enable children to see that burst bubbles leave prints behind; to facilitate creative expression; to facilitate cooperation through a group project. (This project makes gorgeous paper!)

WHAT we will need:
   Bubble mixture
   Food coloring
   Bubble blowers/wands
   Butcher paper (white)
   Small containers
Preparation:
   Masking tape

HOW we will do it: To prepare, use masking tape to secure butcher paper over your activity table, so that the entire surface is covered. Put bubble mixture into each small container and add a different color of food coloring to each one. Use various bubble blowers and wands, for example, fly swatters with lattice-style plastic, twisted wire, and plastic six-pack bottle holders.

Set all the materials out in the middle of the table, on top of the butcher paper, and encourage the children to blow bubbles over it, so that they burst on the paper. As the children do this, watch the paper get prettier and prettier. If you like, provide certain combinations of colors, such as: brown/orange/yellow, purple/pink/turquoise, or green/blue/aquamarine. Make turquoise by adding a little bit of green to blue. Make aquamarine by adding a little bit of blue to green. When the bubble-print picture is finished, hang it up on the wall, or cut it into pieces and use it as gift wrap for presents the children make.

Painting Soap
Art

WHY we are doing this project: to facilitate creative expression and to develop fine motor skills.

WHAT we will need:
Bars of soap
Water-based paints
Fine paintbrushes
Newspaper
Small containers of water
Small tub of water

HOW we will do it: Spread newspaper out on your work surface, and put all materials on the table. Invite the children to paint the soaps, and sit down and paint one yourself. Show the children how to wash the soaps in the small tub of water when they want to paint a new design on the same bar of soap.

Laundry Day
Dramatic Play/Language/Gross Motor/
Multicultural/Anti-Bias

WHY we are doing this activity: to give children the opportunity to work through emotions during pretend play; to facilitate social interaction between children; to help children develop conversational skills and the ability to put their ideas into words; to help children develop awareness of diverse cultures and gender roles.

WHAT we will need:
Large tubs or sensory table
Ivory Snow flakes
Miniature boxes of soap detergent
Dolls' clothes and dress-up clothes
Clothes rack
Clothes wringer (if possible)
Clothespins
Newspaper
Magazines (including *National Geographic*)
Clean-up:
Mop

HOW we will do it: Spread many layers of newspaper under your "laundry" area. You can buy miniature boxes of laundry detergent at variety stores, sometimes as promotional samples, or in vending machines at laundromats. Replace the detergent in them with Ivory Snow flakes. Fill several of your tubs with cold water for rinsing. Put all of the clothes in another tub. If you can find an old-fashioned laundry wringer, children love using these.

Leaf through your magazines, including *National Geographic*, for photographs of people washing clothes, and tape these on the walls around the laundry area. Aim for a collection of photos that is culturally diverse and, if possible, in opposition to gender stereotypes. Invite your students to explore the materials. Children absolutely love this dramatic play, but it does tend to get messy, so be prepared with your mop when it is all over.

Literature

Symbol key: *Multicultural
              +Minimal diversity
              No symbol: no diversity or no people

Bell, J. L. (1993). *Soap science*. Redding, MA: Addison-Wesley.

Sutherland, H. A. (1988). *Dad's car wash*. New York: Atheneum.

The following books feature bubbles:

   Woodruff, E. (1991). *Show and tell*. New York: Holiday House.

   Woodruff, E. (1990). *Tubtime*. New York: Holiday House.

Extenders

Music: Here is a good song to sing when you make the super bubbles outside.

To the tune of "Oh my darling Clementine":
     Super bubble, super bubble,
     watch me blow it in the air,
     wind is blowing, bubble's floating,
     whoops it burst, right over there!

Language: If you choose to hang the bubble-print paper on the wall, ask the children later if they remember how they made it, and write their comments on the top, bottom, and sides of the paper. If you cut the paper into gift wrap, make gift tags too. Take dictation for the gift tags, or if you work with older children, have them write their own words. You could give shaped soaps or the painted soaps as gifts.

Science: This is an extender for the whipped-soap painting. Use an electric mixer, soap, and cold and warm water to see if the same amount and kinds of bubbles are produced. Does the force created by the electric mixer make a difference?

Dramatic Play: Put containers for various types of soaps (e.g., dishwashing liquid, Ivory Snow flakes, soap bars, and soap leaves) in your housekeeping area or in a dramatic-play store.

AIR AND WIND

The air in a room cannot be seen, felt, heard, tasted, or smelled by children, although it is all around them. This can make understanding the properties of air rather difficult for young children to grasp, especially three- and young four-year-olds. The impact of wind, on the other hand, or air in motion, *can* be seen, felt, heard, and sometimes even smelled. Wind is tangible; it makes air real. For this reason, air and wind have been combined in this unit, which begins with the projects that explore wind. Wind science experiments are provided first, air science experiments are next, and the other curriculum areas which involve both air and wind are described last. You know best what the cognitive level and abilities of your children are. Read over the activities, and decide which ones you think will be most meaningful to them, and in what order and combination they should be facilitated. If you live in a region with distinct seasons, you may want to do this unit in the fall, when there tends to be more wind, or on hot, windy summer days. For the experiments that involve going outside, talk to the children first about what clothes they need to put on before they go out to pin up their wind streamers, Vaseline cards or other wind devices (jacket, sweater, regular clothes—depending on temperature and time of year). Have fun!

Attention Getter: Go to a window with the children, and look out. Ask your students if they can see any clues that there is moving air outside. Even on a day that is not particularly windy, you will often see the tips of leaves and branches fluttering in a breeze. Ask: "What do we call moving air?" Try to spot more clues that air is moving outside.

Gather the children together again and show them an inflated balloon which has not been tied off. Ask if they know what is inside the balloon. Most children will know that it is filled with air. Tell the children that you want them to feel the air inside the balloon. Walk around the group and gently press the balloon down on the children's legs or arms. Explain that even though what the children feel on their skin is the balloon, the pressure they feel is from the air inside. Release a little air on each child's skin. Ask the children what they breathe in and out, and what is all around us. Ask them if they can see the air in the room. Ask the children to guess what you will be talking about and working with over the next few days.

PART 1:
Experiments with Wind

Air in Motion
Science/Sensory

WHY we are doing this project: to enable children to see and feel how much force air (wind) can have; to familiarize children with how pump and suction devices work; to build feelings of competence with tools; to provide a sensory experience involving air in motion.

WHAT we will need:
Medicine droppers
Basters
Squeeze bottles
Bicycle pump
Plastic foot pump (for inflating inner tubes, rubber boats, etc.)
Any other devices that create a flow of air
Feathers (just a few)
Ping-pong ball
Kleenex scrap
Marble
Paper clip
Tray

HOW we will do it: Put the non-wind-making materials on a tray. Put the tray and all other materials on your activity table. Plan on leaving them there for several days, or for the duration of the unit. During an Attention Getter time, encourage the children to squeeze air out of the basters, droppers, and squeeze bottles, and to pump air out with the bicycle pump. Ask them to predict whether or not they can use these "wind makers" to move the items on the tray (e.g., feather, Kleenex, marble). Invite the children to direct the air flow toward their skin when they squeeze air out. A medicine dropper has to be directed toward your cheek in order to be felt—the impact is too soft to be detected by the epidermal nerve endings in your hand or arm. As the children conduct their experiments, ask them which tools create the strongest force of air. Can any of them move the marble? Encourage discussion.

Breath is Air in Motion
Science

WHY we are doing this project: to enable children to understand that breath is air in motion.

Safety precaution: Be sure to caution the children beforehand not to suck air in through the straws. You may want to distribute straws to your students and have them practice blowing out. Make a point of differentiating between this and sucking in. With three- and young four-year-olds, you may decide to demonstrate the experiment yourself rather than have them do it.

WHAT we will need:
Small, clear plastic soda bottles
Confetti
Straws
Preparation:
Funnel

HOW we will do it: Begin collecting the plastic soda bottles well ahead of time. Ask parents, neighbors, and friends to help. To prepare a bottle for this activity, insert a funnel into the opening and pour a little confetti into the bottle. To make your own confetti, use a hole puncher to punch out circles from paper. Put the prepared bottles on the activity table.

During an Attention Getter time, show the bottles and the straws to the children, and ask them to predict what will happen to the confetti when they blow into the bottles. Before the children conduct the experiment, ask: "Is it okay to share your straw with somebody else? What would happen if you have a bad cold, and someone else puts their mouth on your straw?" Discuss.

When the children blow into the bottles, encourage observations. What happens to the confetti? Why?

Another Way to Prove That Breath Is Air in Motion
Science

WHY we are doing this activity: to prove, using another method, that breath is air in motion; to develop fine motor skills.

WHAT we will need:
Empty thread spools
Straight pins with plastic heads
Modeling clay
Ping-pong balls
Bendable straws
Sticky labels
Pens

HOW we will do it: Make a demonstration sample ahead of time. Put some modeling clay on the top of a spool, and then stick four pins into the clay, equidistant from each other, in a circle. Insert the short end of your bendable straw into the bottom hole of the spool. If you work with three- and young four-year-olds, write each child's name on a sticky label and have them ready for labeling the children's projects. If you work with older preschoolers or kindergartners, put the blank labels and pens on the activity table so that your students can write their own names.

During an Attention Getter time, place a ping-pong ball on top of the pins. Ask the children to predict what will happen to the ping-pong ball if you blow through the straw. Let the children know that if they would like to make their own ping-pong-ball blower for this experiment, the materials are on the activity table. Show the children the pins, and talk to them about being careful with the sharp ends.

Once the projects are completed, ask the children to predict what will happen to the ping-pong ball if they blow softly through the straw, and what will happen if they blow harder. Invite them to conduct this experiment. What happens? Which method raises the ball the highest? Which method keeps the ball supported on air the longest? Why do they think this is? Invite the children to breathe in as far as they can, and to breathe out as far as they can. Explain that our lungs can only take in a certain amount of air with each breath. Using this information, ask the children to hypothesize why the ping-pong ball floats on air longer when they blow softly, and why it rises higher when they blow harder.

Wind Poem
Language/Gross Motor/Creative Movement

WHY we are doing this activity: to help children appreciate poetry; to expand vocabulary; to develop reading skills; to enable children to use their bodies and voices creatively; to develop the large muscle group; to stimulate interest in the science experiment (What Makes the Wind?) that follows.

WHAT we will need:
Butcher paper
Markers
Poem chart pictures (provided on
    page 265; photocopy and enlarge for
    your use)
Glue stick
Poem: "THE WILD WIND"

"THE WILD WIND"
I went walking one fine day,
The wind was strong that gusty day.
It blew my hair right in my face,
leaves whirled and swirled 'most
every place.
I listened to it howl and wail,
that wild, windy, gusty gale.

HOW we will do it: Use the pictures in the text to make a language chart of this poem. Print the words and leave plenty of room between lines. Make one photocopy of each picture, and glue each one above its corresponding word. Pin the poster on the wall.

During an Attention Getter time, and before you read the entire poem, point to each picture and ask the children to describe what it is. Together, guess, interpret, or read the word beneath it. When you have done this with all the words/pictures, read the poem to the children several times. Explain new words to the children. (A gust is a strong, sudden rush of air or wind. A gale is a strong wind. A wail is a sad, crying sound.) Ask the children if they have ever heard the wind make sounds. What kind? Where were they when they heard the wind's noises? Stand up and spread out, and do these motions as you say the poem:

"I went walking one fine day"—Pretend to be outside walking.

"The wind was strong that gusty day"—Put your head down and pretend to be walking against a very strong wind.

"It blew my hair right in my face"—Pretend to brush your hair away from your eyes, out of your mouth, away from your face.

"Leaves whirled and swirled 'most every place"—Use your arms and hands to simulate leaves whirling and swirling around you.

"I listened to it howl and wail"—Put your hand to your ear, and first make a howling sound and then a wailing sound that the wind might make.

"That wild, windy, gusty gale"—Use your whole body to become a wild wind.

The Wild Wind

1.

I went walking one fine day,

The wind was strong that gusty day.

It blew my hair right in my face,

leaves whirled and swirled 'most every place.

I listened to it howl and wail,

that wild, windy, gusty gale.

The Wild Wind (Writing Center)

Language

WHY we are doing this project: to create interest in the unit's theme and to develop all components of language arts: reading, writing, speaking, and listening skills.

WHAT we will need:
  Blank paper
  Poem picture chart (from previous activity)
  Photocopies of poem pictures
  Lined paper
  Pens
  Markers
  Crayons
  Tape
  Glue sticks
  Scissors
  Blank books (folded, stapled paper)

HOW we will do it: Find a quiet corner to set up a cozy writing center. You may want to put a shelf next to the writing table to hold all the materials. Post the charted poem on the wall above the writing center table. Set out all the materials on the table and shelf. Cut out some of the poem pictures, and leave others uncut. Separate some pictures from their words and leave other words and pictures together.

By supplying a variety of materials and plenty of blank and lined paper, you are providing many options for children: they can copy words from the chart, match words with poem pictures, draw their own pictures and write their own words, write their own words next to pictures, or do something completely different. Depending on the needs of your children, take story dictation, spell words, or support invented spelling or scribbling.

At the end of the day or session, gather together and invite the children to show-and-tell what they made at the writing center.

Developmental differences: Three- and young four-year-olds will enjoy scribbling and drawing. Older children will be interested in writing words.

What Makes the Wind? (Part 1)

Science/Small Group Activity

WHY we are doing this experiment: to enable children to observe that hot air rises (a foundation for understanding what makes wind).

WHAT we will need:
  Strips of lightweight paper
    (about 7.5 cm x 2.5 cm [3" x 1"])
  Lamp

HOW we will do it: Plug in your lamp and remove the shade so that you have easy access to the light bulb. During an Attention Getter time, pass a strip of paper to each child. Show the children the light bulb, and explain that you want them to see what happens to the paper when the air around it is hot. Before you begin, ask: "What could happen if you put your paper right on the bulb? What will happen if you touch the light bulb?" Make sure the children understand that you are going to hold the paper strips above the bulb and not on it.

Gather around the light bulb and switch it on. Encourage the children to hold their paper strips above (but not on) the light bulb. If nothing happens, turn the paper 90°. What happens? Talk about the way the end of the paper floats up. Explain that hot air rises, and that the light bulb heats the air around it. The heated air from the light bulb rises and lifts the paper strip with it. Move on to the next experiment below.

What Makes the Wind? (Part 2)

Science/Small Group Activity

WHY we are doing this experiment: to facilitate an understanding of how the movements of hot and cold air create wind.

WHAT we will need:

- Large, clear plastic container (empty peanut butter containers work well)
- Ice water
- Hot water
- Food coloring

HOW we will do it: To prepare, remove the ice from the ice water. Pour the water into the large plastic container. Add some drops of food coloring to the hot water. Have all materials on hand. When the children are gathered, ask them to gently touch the outside of each container and tell you what kind of water is inside (cold and hot). Tell them that you are going to pretend that the hot water is hot air, and that the cold water is cold air. Let them know that you are going to pour the hot water into the cold, and that you want them to notice how the hot water moves.

Without moving the cold water container, observe what happens for a minute after you pour the hot water in. Encourage comments from the children, and explain that cold air and cold water are heavier, and that hot air and hot water are lighter (Say: "Remember how the hot air from the light bulb moved up and lifted our paper?"). Therefore, cold air and cold water sink downward, and move under hot air and hot water. By doing so, they push the heated air or water upward. Explain that with air, this happens very, very fast. Cold air rushes under hot air and the hot air billows up very quickly. This is what makes the wind that we feel. End the activity by saying and moving to "The Wild Wind" poem.

Wind and Sound: Vibration

Science

WHY we are doing this project: to enable children to discover that wind can cause vibration and that vibration can have sound; to develop fine motor skills.

WHAT we will need:

- Plastic lids
- Yarn lengths (35 cm [14"])
- Masking tape
- Windy day

Preparation:

- Skewer or nail

HOW we will do it: To prepare, use the skewer or nail to poke two holes into each plastic lid. The two holes should be equidistant from each other and the edges. Wrap masking tape around one end of each yarn length to facilitate easy threading through the holes. Put the lids and yarn lengths on the activity table.

Ahead of time, make a sample wind hummer by threading one yarn length through both holes and tying the ends in a knot. During an Attention Getter time, take out the kazoo you made in the Sound Makers unit. Blow on the kazoo, and ask the children if they remember what *vibrate* means. Talk about how your breath, which is air in motion, makes the wax paper move back and forth very quickly. When it *vibrates* like that, it makes a noise. Let the children know that they are going to make something that vibrates in the wind and makes a noise. It is called a *wind hummer*. Show the children the wind hummer you made, and tell them that after they make their own, they will all go outside and find out how they work.

Invite the children to put the wind hummer materials together. Help younger children to thread their lids if necessary, and assist with knot tying.

When the wind hummers are made, go outside and encourage the children to wind their hummers up. Hold a loop of the yarn in each hand, keeping the lid in the middle. Move both hands around and around in large circles, and then pull the yarn tight. Ask the children to listen to the sound of the vibration, and to look at the lid carefully. Can they see the wind vibrating it?

Which Way Is the Wind Blowing? (Part 1)
Science/Art/Crafts

WHY we are doing this project: to enable children to make instruments that indicate wind direction; to facilitate creative expression; to develop fine motor skills.

WHAT we will need:
    Brown paper lunch bags
    Crepe paper (variety of colors, including
        brown and black)
    Yarn
    Tissue paper
    Other collage scraps
    Glue
    Glue brushes
    Paint
    Paintbrushes
    Small containers (for paint and glue)
    Clothespins
    Newspaper
    String lengths (about 45 cm [1½ ft.])
    Hole puncher
Demonstration:
    Hair dryer

HOW we will do it: To prepare, cut the bottoms out of the brown paper bags, and cut the crepe and tissue paper into strips that measure approximately 25 cm x 2.5 cm (10" x 1"). Spread out newspaper on the activity table and arrange the materials so that all children will have access to them. Find a place to string out the yarn, such as a clothesline.

Developmental differences: If you work with three- and young four-year-olds, you will

need to attach string to the wind socks before they decorate them. Punch two holes opposite each other and near one opening of each paper bag. Thread the string through the holes and tie the ends. Older children will be able to do this themselves, although you may want to wrap tape around the ends of the string to make threading easier.

Make a sample wind sock ahead of time. Decorate a prepared bag with the collage materials, and glue crepe paper strips all around the opening opposite the string. Use a clothespin to hang your wind sock from the yarn line, so the glue can dry.

During an Attention Getter time, sit near an electrical outlet and plug in the hair dryer. Show the children your wind sock. Let them take turns holding the sock and using the hair dryer to blow "wind" into it. Encourage them to blow the sock from different directions, and ask the other children how the tissue and crepe paper streamers are blowing. (For example, "Now they're blowing toward the writing center. Now they're blowing toward the door. Now they are blowing toward the climber.")

Show your students the materials on the activity table and invite them to make their own wind socks. Show them how to hang their wind socks from the yarn line to dry.

Which Way Is the Wind Blowing? (Part 2)
Science

WHY we are doing this project: to enable children to use their wind streamers to observe wind direction; to familiarize children with how to use a compass.

WHAT we will need:
    Wind streamers (made in previous
        activity)
    Compass
    Windy day

HOW we will do it: Look around your yard or garden for places children can reach to hang their wind socks. If there are not enough accessible places for every child, make a line with string and tie it up at the children's level (high enough to catch the wind). Provide clothespins so that your students can pin their streamers (by the string handles) to the line. As the children hang up their streamers, ask if they can feel wind on their faces. Can they predict which direction their streamers will be blowing?

Show the children the compass, and point out the letters that indicate north, south, east, and west. Encourage the children to observe how the wind is blowing the streamers and to compare it to the compass. Which direction is the wind blowing?

Developmental differences: Three- and young four-year-olds are not likely to be interested in the compass information. Instead, use landmarks to discuss together which way the wind is blowing (e.g., toward the slide, toward the shed). Older children will be interested in watching the compass dial move.

What Does the Wind Carry? (Part 1)
Science/Language

WHY we are doing this activity: to enable children to discover that the wind carries objects (seeds, dust and earth particles, and other materials).

WHAT we will need:
   String
   Index cards
   Vaseline
   Popsicle sticks
   Pens
   Clothespins
   Small containers
   Magnifying glasses (plastic)
   Windy day

HOW we will do it: If you work with children who are not yet writing their names, write each child's name on an index card. On the activity table, set out small containers of Vaseline and Popsicle sticks. Outside, hang up the string like a clothesline. Put clothespins nearby.

Ahead of time, write your own name on an index card, and use a Popsicle stick to smear some Vaseline on it. During an Attention Getter time, show it to the children. Tell them that you are going to hang it outside where the wind is blowing. Ask the children to predict if the card will look different after it has been in the wind for a while. Will there be anything stuck in the Vaseline? What kinds of things?

Have the children accompany you outside while you attach your Vaseline card to the string line. When you go back inside, show them the materials on the activity table and invite them to make Vaseline cards and to pin them up for their own experiments.

After the cards have been exposed to the wind for a few hours, pass out magnifying glasses and go outside as a group. Walk down the line of cards and ask the children what they see stuck in the Vaseline. Do they see any seeds? (Dandelion seeds are fun to find.) What does this tell us about how seeds travel? Do the children see any particles? Explain that a *particle* is a tiny, tiny piece of something. Repeat the word if you like, while you blink your eyes in time with the syllables, or tap your toes. Are there other things that have been blown onto the Vaseline by the wind?

Encourage the children to use the magnifiers to examine the Vaseline closely. Ask them to take their cards down and bring them inside for the following project.

What Does the Wind Carry? (Part 2)

Science/Language/Art

WHY we are doing this activity: to encourage children to record the results of the previous experiment; to facilitate artistic expression; to develop all components of language arts: reading, writing, speaking, and listening.

WHAT we will need:
Pale-colored construction paper
Small wind pictures (provided below; photocopy one for each child)
Crayons
Markers
Pencils
Pens
Vaseline cards (from previous experiment)
Preparation:
Stapler
Glue stick

HOW we will do it: Make blank books by stacking two or three sheets of paper on top of each other, folding over evenly, and stapling along the fold. On the cover of each, glue a wind picture and write: "What does the wind carry?" Leave several book covers blank for children who want to create their own. Put all materials out on an activity table.

When you come back inside from the Part 1 activity, show the children the blank books and read/interpret the cover together. Sit down at the table and begin to make one yourself, based on what you found in your Vaseline. Draw pictures of what you found and write words about each one. As the children make their books, take story dictation, spell words, support invented spelling or scribbling or write words down to be copied, depending on the needs of your children. When your students are finished, ask them to read or tell you about the books they made.

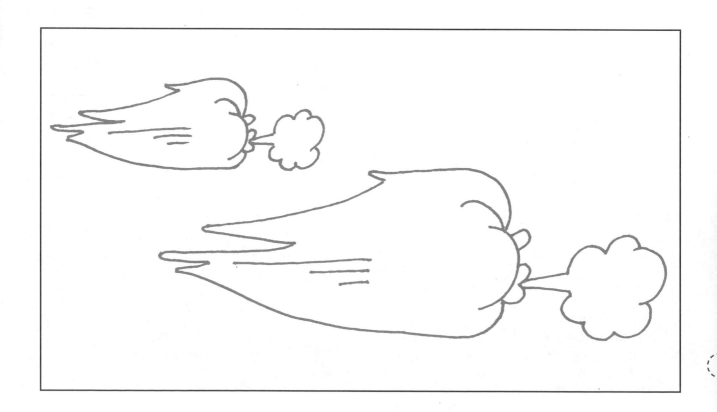

270

Does a Cloth Dry Faster With Wind or Without?

Science/Sensory

Note: The results of this experiment will vary, depending on the time of year. If you conduct it in the fall, the cloth will dry faster indoors, with no air in motion, than outside in cold wind. If you conduct it on a hot, windy summer day, the cloth will dry faster outdoors. Either way, the activity will provide learning experiences for your children. See Extenders for another way to introduce the concept.

WHY we are doing this project: to enable children to compare and understand the relationship between the drying ability of still air, air in motion, warm air, and cold air; to provide a sensory experience (with warm, soapy water and cold clear water).

WHAT we will need:
>   Large tub of cold water
>   Large tub of warm, soapy water
>   Material (handkerchiefs, dolls' clothes, fabric squares, or other things that need washing)
>   String
>   Clothespins
>   Warm, windy day

HOW we will do it: If weather permits, set this entire activity up outside. If you do set up the washing tubs inside, use lots of newspaper on the floor beneath the materials. To prepare, string up a line outside that the children can easily reach, and put the clothespins nearby. Set your tubs of water in a sensory table if you have one; otherwise, put them on an activity table. Put the clothes/handkerchief squares/ fabric scraps nearby. Inside, string up a small line and hang up one wet piece of cloth.

During an Attention Getter time, ask the children to predict which will dry faster—something wet that is hanging in the wind, or something wet that is hanging inside. Show them the wet cloth you hung inside and the dry

clothes and tubs of water. Encourage them to wash and rinse the material and to hang it up on the line.

Be aware that young children tend not to squeeze water out of the things they wash, and that most of what they hang up will be dripping wet. Before you go on to other activities, make sure you squeeze the items which are hanging on the line. In case they are still soapy, hang up at least one piece of material which you have rinsed well and squeezed out.

The time it takes for the items to dry will depend on how soapy they are, the amount and velocity of wind, and the air temperature. Throughout the day or session, periodically encourage the children to check the items indoors and outdoors by touching them. Which ones dry first? Talk about the air temperature indoors and out, as well as which environment has air in motion, and which one has air at rest.

What Is the Wind Doing Today?

Science/Gross Motor/Cognitive

WHY we are doing this activity: to enable children to observe evidence of the wind by seeing its impact on a variety of things outdoors; to develop the large muscle group; to develop cognition by recalling a sequence of events.

WHAT we will need:
>   Rope (optional)

HOW we will do it: If you work with young children who have difficulty choosing partners during walks, use a rope for everyone to hold on to. Before you set out on your walk, talk to the children about what you need to do at sidewalk curbs before crossing the street, and remind them not to pick anything up (like glass or rusty objects).

Explain that you are going to see what the wind is doing today, by looking carefully at everything outside to see if the wind is blowing it. Ask the children what kinds of things you might see above you (e.g., tree branches and leaves, clouds, flags, store banners, awnings) and what you might see below you (e.g., puddles, blades of grass, litter on the ground).

Set out on the walk, and ask the children what things they see that show the wind is blowing. When you get back to home or school, have a group discussion to recall the sequence of the things you saw. If you like, write them down on a chart and invite your students to illustrate it.

PART 2:
Experiments with Air

It's a Trap! (An Air Trap)
Science

WHY we are doing this experiment: to stimulate children to think about the presence of air in materials around them.

WHAT we will need:
   Wool mittens
   Magnifying glasses
   Large containers of water

HOW we will do it: Ahead of time, ask friends, parents, and relatives to lend you wool mittens. You will need one for each child. During an Attention Getter time, ask the children if they think there is any air in a mitten. Show them the containers of water, and ask them to predict what they will see if they crumple a mitten up and plunge it into water. Invite them to conduct this experiment. What comes floating up from the mitten? (Air bubbles.) Ask the children to hypothesize why air bubbles came out of the mitten. (The wool of the mitten

traps tiny air pockets.) If you do not have enough mitten pairs for everyone, demonstrate this experiment yourself and ask the children to watch closely to see what comes out of the mitten once it is suddenly immersed in water. Provide a magnifying glass to each child for this purpose.

What Is in Air?
Science/Small Group Project

WHY we are doing this activity: to enable children to observe the dust particles in air.

WHAT we will need:
   Dark room
   Flashlight or lamp

HOW we will do it: During an Attention Getter time, tell the children that you are going to turn the lights off, and turn the flashlight or lamp on. Ask the children to predict what they will see. Shine the flashlight into the dark room. Ask the children to look closely at the beam of light. What do they notice about what is floating in the air? Introduce the word *particle* again.

Fire Needs Air
Science/Adult Supervised/One-on-One

WHY we are doing this project: to allow children to discover that fire needs air.

WHAT we will need:
   Candle
   Matches or lighter
   Drinking glass

HOW we will do it: This is a project for the teacher or parent to do with children one-on-one. Beforehand, be sure to emphasize that it is *never* okay to use matches or lighters without an adult. Light a candle, and invite the child to put the glass over the candle so that the candle is sealed off from air. Ask the student to predict what will happen. Conduct the experiment and observe what does happen. What does this tell us about what a fire needs to burn?

The Balloon Experiment
Science

WHY we are doing this experiment: to allow children to discover that air expands when it is heated.

WHAT we will need:
    Balloons
    Candle
    Lighter
    Sticks or skewers

    Note: If you work with very young children who are easily frightened, you may want to skip this experiment, as the noise of a bursting balloon is very loud and startling. Some older children are thrilled by the loud bang this activity produces, so use your own judgment. Again, this is a one-on-one project.

HOW we will do it: During an Attention Getter time, tell the children that they may hear loud bangs today because of a science experiment you are going to do with heat and balloons. During a free play time, invite children who are in between activities to conduct the experiment with you. Ahead of time, inflate the balloons and tie the mouth of each one around a stick or skewer. Invite one child to hold a balloon on a stick. What will happen when you hold the lit candle underneath? The children should hold the balloon as far away from themselves as possible. Prepare the children for a loud, sudden noise. When the balloon bursts, explain that the lit candle heated up the air in the balloon and that made the air spread out more. When the air spread out, the balloon could hold no more and it burst. If possible, it is a good idea to do this activity outside because the loud noise is less startling.

Can Air Be a Barrier?
Science

WHY we are doing this experiment: to enable children to discover that air can be a barrier and to develop speaking and listening skills through discussion.

WHAT we will need:
    Plastic cups
    Paper towels (cut in half)
    Large tubs of water
    Newspaper

HOW we will do it: If you have a sensory table, use it for this project. Spread several layers of newspaper underneath your activity area. Set out the tubs of water, cups, and paper towels.
    During an Attention Getter time, take a plastic cup and forcefully push it down into the water, brim side down. Ask the children to watch carefully while you let go of it. When it bounces up, ask the children why they think it did. Invite them to touch the inside of the cup, near the bottom. What do they notice about whether it feels wet or dry? Talk about the air in the container. Did it let the water rush into the cup? Crumple a piece of paper towel and show it to the children. Say: "If I stuff this down into the bottom of the cup, and push the cup into the water, do you think the paper will be wet or dry when I take the cup out of the water?" Rather than conducting this experiment yourself, show the children the materials and encourage them to find out the answer to this question. Encourage discussion of observations

and findings. Ask the children to hypothesize about why the paper in the cup stays dry.

Developmental differences: Three- and young four-year-olds may be more interested in pushing cups upside down into water, and splashing and playing with the water. Older children are likely to become more involved with using the paper in the experiment.

When Air Cannot Get In
Science/Sensory

WHY we are doing this experiment: to enable children to observe that water will not drain out of a hole in an otherwise sealed container.

WHAT we will need:
    Tubs or sensory table
    Clear plastic bottles (or containers with screw-on lids)
    Small pitchers
    Scoopers (e.g., coffee scoopers)
    Funnels
    Water
Preparation:
    Skewer or nail
Optional:
    Food coloring
    Water

HOW we will do it: To prepare, use a sharp object to poke a hole in the side of each bottle, about two inches from the bottom. Put containers, funnels, and pitchers in the tubs or sensory table with plenty of water.

During an Attention Getter time, show the children the hole in one bottle. Fill the container with water, making sure to leave several inches at the top for air to occupy. Hold your finger over the hole while you do this. Screw the lid onto the bottle. Tell the children that you are going to take your finger off of the hole. Before you do, ask them to predict whether or not the water will pour out of it.

Pass the bottle around the group for each child to hold and observe. Why does the water not leak out of the hole? Encourage hypotheses. Explain that because you sealed the top of the bottle, there is no way for new air to get in to take the place of any water that pours out, so the water is trapped there. Ask the children what they think will happen when the bottle is unscrewed. Show them the materials in the tubs or sensory table, and encourage them to find the answer to this question themselves. Ask them to hypothesize why the water pours out as soon as a top is unscrewed. (Air rushes in to replace the water and pushes the water out through the hole.)

PART 3:
Wind and Air: Math, Art, Language, Dramatic Play, Gross Motor, and Music

The Blowing Song
Music

WHY we are doing this activity: to develop an appreciation for music; to help children feel good about their singing voices; to stimulate interest in the theme of the unit.

WHAT we will need:
    Small feathers (or facial tissues)
    Song: "THE BLOWING SONG" (to the tune of "Row Row Row Your Boat")

"THE BLOWING SONG"
Blow, blow, blow, blow, blow
First blow fast and then real slow,
blow so gently then so strong,
Can you blow a feather/tissue along?

HOW we will do it: During an Attention Getter time, pass a feather or Kleenex scrap to everyone. Give the children a few minutes to blow them up in the air, throw them, and touch them. When they have satisfied their curiosity, begin the activity.

Sing the song yourself once, while the children follow the directions of the song. Then have the children put the feathers or tissue aside while they learn the words to the song and sing it with you a few times. Next, divide the group in half. Have one part of the group sing the song while the others follow directions, then reverse roles.

How Far Did I Blow It?

Math/Science

WHY we are doing this activity: to familiarize children with standard units as measurements; to enable children to understand the connection between the weights of different objects and the force of air in motion which is needed to move them; to develop reading and writing skills.

WHAT we will need:
    Cardboard tubes (from plastic wrap and
        foil boxes)
    Photocopies of children's ruler (provided
        on page 276)
    Writing sheets (provided on page 277;
        photocopy and enlarge for your use)
    Blank paper
    Large straws
    Marbles
    Pebbles
    Leaves
    Cotton balls
    Feathers
    Trays
    Pens
Preparation:
    Scissors

    Markers
    Double-sided tape
    Stapler
Demonstration:
    Piece of yarn
    Coin or key
    Paper clip

HOW we will do it: To begin, cut your cardboard cylinders in half, lengthwise. Make copies of the children's ruler. To make the numbers more distinct, trace each mark and corresponding number with a different colored marker. Use double-sided tape to attach the paper ruler to the bottom of each cylinder half. (Double-sided tape is better than glue, because glue can create wrinkles which will interfere with smooth rolling.) When you smooth your paper ruler to the bottom of the cylinder, start in the middle and smooth the paper outward.

If you want to extend the cylinder halves to make them longer, make sure the bottom of the two tubes are level for smooth rolling from one to the other. You may want to join the two edges with glue.

Put one cylinder half and one of each object on each tray. Make copies of the writing sheets, staple the pages together, and place these with the pens on the activity table. Also provide blank paper for children who want to record the results of the experiment in their own way. Younger children will probably not record their results but may use the materials for scribbling and coloring, which is a useful part of their learning experience.

During an Attention Getter time, show the children the materials. Hold up a prepared cylinder half and, together, identify each number on the paper ruler. Make sure the children understand that the number represents centimeters. Using a straw, blow the piece of yarn along a cylinder half. With the children's help, note how many centimeters you blew it. Do the same with the paper clip and the coin or key. Again, note how many centimeters you blew each object. Record your results on a writing sheet or blank piece of paper. For "I blew the ___ the most centimeters," draw a picture of yourself above "I," draw a picture of the object you blew the furthest, and write the word in

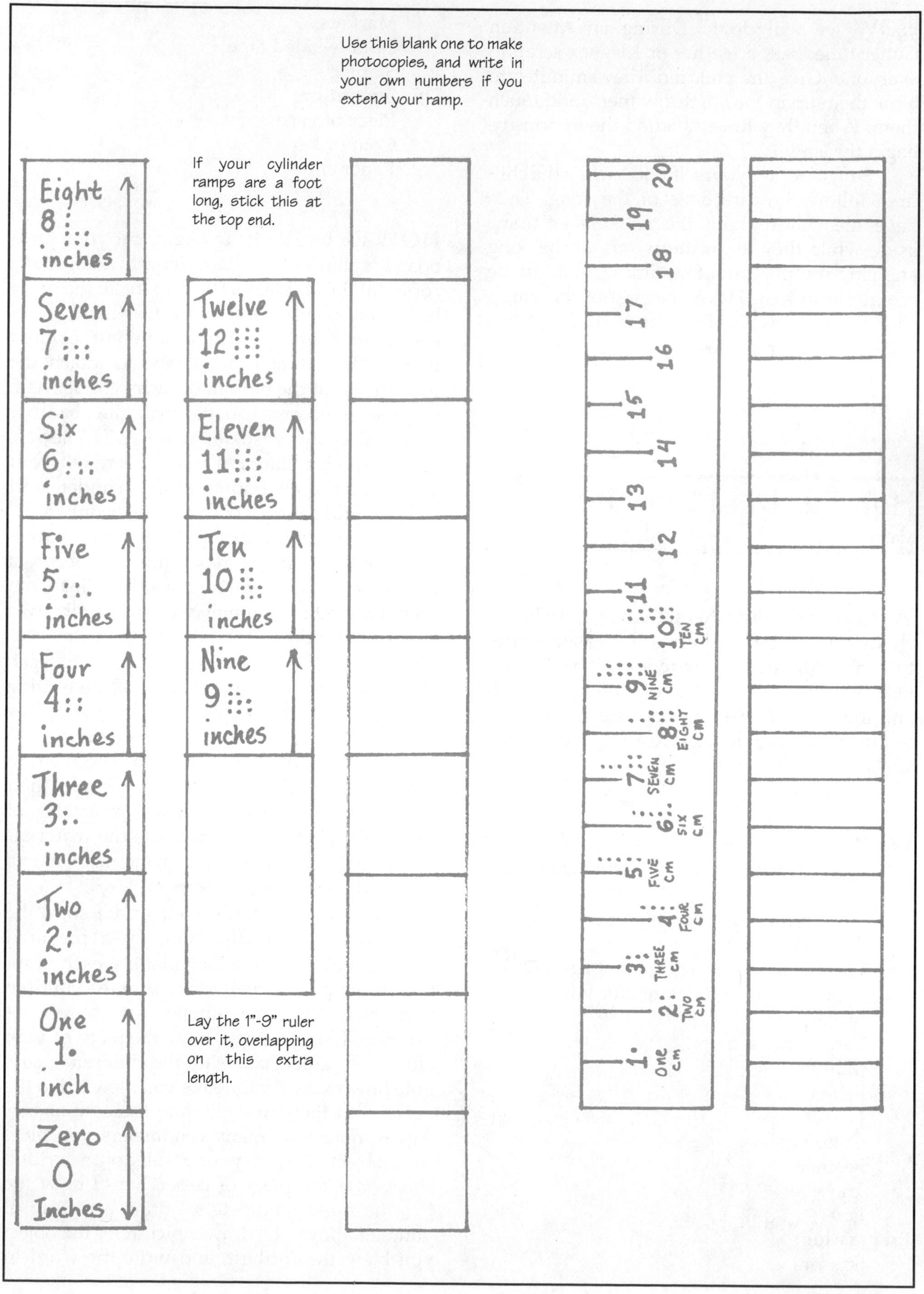

Use this blank one to make photocopies, and write in your own numbers if you extend your ramp.

Eight 8 ⋮⋮ inches	If your cylinder ramps are a foot long, stick this at the top end.		20 19 18	
Seven 7 ⋮⋮ inches	Twelve 12 ⋮⋮ inches		17 16 15	
Six 6 ⋮⋮ inches	Eleven 11 ⋮⋮ inches		14 13 12	
Five 5 ⋮⋮ inches	Ten 10 ⋮⋮ inches		11 10 TEN CM	
Four 4 ⋮⋮ inches	Nine 9 ⋮⋮ inches		9 NINE CM 8 EIGHT CM	
Three 3 ⋮ inches			7 SEVEN CM 6 SIX CM	
Two 2 ⋮ inches			5 FIVE CM 4 FOUR CM	
One 1 inch	Lay the 1"-9" ruler over it, overlapping on this extra length.		3 THREE CM 2 TWO CM	
Zero 0 Inches			1 ONE CM	

276

© 1996 Delmar Publishers

Science Experiment: How far can a marble, a feather, a cotton ball, a pebble, and a leaf be blown?

I blew the marble _____ inches.

I blew the feather _____ inches.

I blew the cotton ball _____ inches.

I blew the pebble _____ inches.

I blew the leaf _____ inches.

I blew the _____ the most inches.

I blew the _____ the fewest inches.

the blank space. Follow the same procedure for "I blew the _____ the fewest centimeters."

Ask the children if they see other things in the room with which they can conduct the same experiment. Ask them to predict which object they will be able to blow the farthest, and which will be blown the least distance. (Before you hand out the straws, discuss the importance of each child using only his or her own straw.) At the end of the session or day, ask the children what they notice about which objects were easy to blow far, and which objects were difficult to blow any distance. How many centimeters were they able to blow the marble? The cotton ball? Compare. Invite your students to hold a light object on one fingertip and a heavy object on another. What does this experience tell them about the force of breath needed to move the different objects? (Heavier objects need forceful air in motion; lighter objects need less force.)

Developmental differences: Three- and young four-year-olds will enjoy blowing the different objects through straws, but will probably not take note of how far they blew them and may not use the cylinder halves at all. Their exploration of the materials, however, will still allow them to make the connection between the weight of an object and the force of air in motion needed to move it. Older children will be more likely to use the tubes and to note how many centimeters an object was blown.

The Air Chant
Music/Rhythm

WHY we are doing this activity: to help children appreciate music; to have fun playing musical instruments; to help children feel rhythm.

WHAT we will need:
Musical instruments (e.g., tambourines, rhythm sticks, or triangles)
Chant: "THE AIR CHANT"

"THE AIR CHANT"
Air air air is around me everywhere;
I breathe it in and breathe it out
through my nose and through my mouth
'cause air air air is around me everywhere.

HOW we will do it: Say this chant a few times while you clap in time to the words. Repeat the chant until the children know the words. Pass out your rhythm sticks or musical instruments and say the chant while you use them. Can everyone stop at the same time? Try saying it very slowly and very quickly. Does everyone still stop at the same time?

Does Air Have Weight?
Math/Science

WHY we are doing this project: to enable children to observe that air has weight; to facilitate comparison of heavier and lighter; to facilitate speaking and listening skills.

WHAT we will need:
Yardstick
Balloons (each a different color)
String
Large tub
Puppet

HOW we will do it: To prepare, blow up the balloons so that they are graduated in fullness, and tie them off. Tie a loop of string around each knot so that the balloons can be hung on the yardstick. Tie a string loop around one balloon that has not been inflated at all.

Put the balloons in a large tub. Tie a long length of string around the exact center of the yard stick and hang it from the ceiling. Secure the string around the yardstick with tape, so that it does not slide out.

During an Attention Getter time, show the children the balloons in the tub and the yardstick balancing scale. Ask the children if they think that air weighs anything. Show them the loops on the ends of each balloon and how the balloons can be carefully hung on the meter stick. Encourage them to explore the materials and take out your puppet. Use its personality to ask questions about the children's discoveries. Why do the big balloons make the yardstick dip lower? Which color balloon seems to be the heaviest? What do they notice about its size? Which balloon seems to be the lightest? Is it also the smallest?

How Many Leaves?
Math/Language

WHY we are doing this activity: to practice rational counting; to facilitate a subtraction exercise (for kindergartners); to develop reading and writing skills; to promote healthy self-esteem and a sense of autonomy through use of a one-person work station.

WHAT we will need:
Cardboard (one panel from a large box)
Colored contact paper
Clear contact paper
Wind drawing (provided on page 280; photocopy and enlarge for your use)
Leaf drawings (provided on page 280; photocopy and enlarge for your use)
Construction paper (green, brown, and orange)

Scissors
Double-sided tape
"One person may be here" sign (provided on page 3; photocopy and enlarge for your use)
Dark-colored marker
Writing sheet (provided on page 280; photocopy and enlarge for your use)
Blank paper
Pens
Tray

HOW we will do it: To prepare, cover your cardboard panel with the colored contact paper. On the top, use the marker to print: "How many leaves is the wind blowing?" Cut out the wind drawing and cover both sides with contact paper. Use the leaf patterns to cut out different colored leaves from construction paper, cover both sides with clear contact paper, and then cut them out. The number of leaves you should make depends on the age of your children and how high they are counting. Put double-sided tape on the backs so they will stick to the board. If you work with kindergartners, write near the bottom of the board: "Take four leaves away. How many are left?" Write the number four and four dots next to the word. Stick the wind and all the leaves on the board, and prop it up against a wall, either on a table or on the floor.

Place the writing sheets, blank paper, and pens on the tray. Set the tray near the wind board, and above it, hang the "One person may be here" sign.

During an Attention Getter time, as a group, read all the signs together, and read/interpret the writing sheet. Invite the children to explore the materials.

I counted _____

leaves 🍁🍂🍃🍂.

4

When I took four leaves away,

there were _____ left.

The Wind and the Sun Have a Contest

Language/Multicultural/Anti-bias

WHY we are doing this activity: to encourage child-to-child interaction and cooperation; to expand vocabulary; to develop speaking and listening skills; to encourage the use of imagination and the expression of ideas.

WHAT we will need:
  Flannel board shapes (provided on
    page 282; photocopy and enlarge for
    your use)
  Scissors
  Felt
  Glue
  Markers or crayons
  Flannel board
  "Two people may be here" sign
    (provided on page 13; photocopy and
    enlarge for your use)
  Story: "THE WIND AND THE SUN
  HAVE A CONTEST" (provided)

HOW we will do it: Cut out the flannel board shapes. Color the pictures and glue them onto felt. Set up your flannel board. After you tell the story, put the materials out for the children to explore. Together, read the "Two people may be here" sign to make sure the children understand what it means.

"THE WIND AND THE SUN HAVE A CONTEST"

Once upon a time there was a little boy named Darnell who was going to his friend's house. [Put Darnell up on flannel board.] It wasn't really that warm a day, so Darnell had his new jacket on. Well, the wind [put up wind] and the sun [put up sun] were both out that day. The sun was shining and the wind was blowing, and suddenly the wind said to the sun, "Don't you wish you were me? I'm so much stronger than you. I blow mighty ships with huge sails so that they can sail in the ocean; I blow so hard that big trees fall; I blow rain and sleet and hail and sometimes I'm so powerful that I make a tornado."

"Stronger than I?" the sun said. "Why, that's ridiculous!"

"All right then," the wind said, "let's have a contest! See that little boy down there? Let's see who can take his jacket off."

"Fine," the sun said. "You go first."

So the wind huffed and puffed and blew, trying to blow Darnell's jacket right off his back, and the wind made a great gusty gale rise up. Leaves flew wildly in the air [put leaves up] and the tree branches were pressed down hard by the power of the wind [put tree up] and a lady's hat went sailing away because that wind was so strong [put lady up and her hat above her]. But no matter how the wind blew, Darnell kept his jacket on, buttoned up tight, and the wind simply could not blow it off, no matter how it huffed and puffed. So finally the wind gave up.

"Huh," the wind said sulkily to the sun, "I bet you can't do any better."

"We'll see!" the sun said with a little smile. And then it shone and shone and shone as hotly and as brightly as it possibly could, and it became so hot that guess what? [Put up picture of Darnell taking his jacket off and let children answer.] And the wind rushed away angrily to blow some nests down from trees and it didn't boast to the sun for a long time after that.

282

Sail Away

Art/Crafts

WHY we are doing this project: to enable children to make their own materials for further exploration of the effects of wind; to facilitate creative expression; to develop fine motor skills; to develop self-esteem by enabling children to make their own toys.

WHAT we will need:

    Popsicle sticks
    Construction paper
    Styrofoam meat trays
    Plasticene or modeling clay
    Toothpicks
    Glue
    Small containers for glue
    Glue brushes
    Toothpicks
    Small boxes
    Spools
    Pirate flag and blank flags (patterns
        provided below; photocopy
        and enlarge for your use)
    Crayons

Preparation:

    Hole puncher
    String
    Sticky labels

Optional:

    Fisher Price people
    Tubs of water
    Cardboard cylinders (from cling wrap
        boxes)

HOW we will do it: Assemble the pirate flags and blank flags (instructions provided with patterns). Set out all the materials for making sailboats on an activity table. The name labels can be affixed to the top of the meat trays in order to identify them.

Make a sample sailboat ahead of time. To use a triangular sail, glue a paper triangle to a Popsicle stick. Press a blob of modeling clay in the center of a meat tray and insert the Popsicle stick into the clay so that it stands up. To make a rectangular sail, glue the short edges of a paper rectangle to two Popsicle sticks. Press two blobs of modeling clay in a meat tray, the same distance apart as the "sail." Insert the Popsicle sticks in the clay so that they stand up. Be cre-

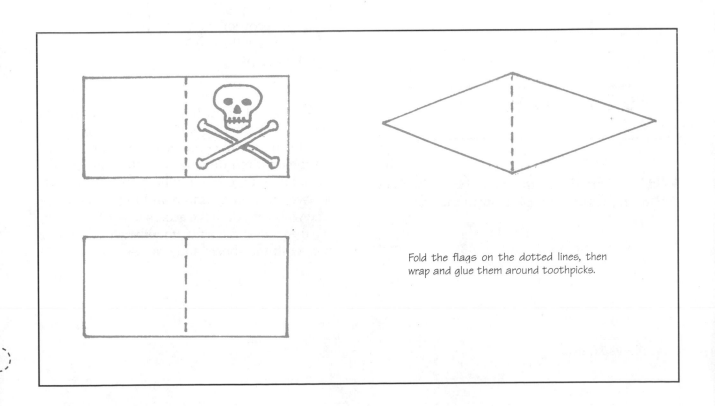

Fold the flags on the dotted lines, then wrap and glue them around toothpicks.

ative with the flags, spools, and small boxes.

During an Attention Getter time, show the children the sailboat you made. Be sure to mention that everyone's boats will look different because people have their own way of creating things. Show the children the materials and invite them to use them. Write their names on the sticky labels unless they can do this themselves.

If you have access to some puddles or small ponds, plan on taking the sailboats there after the glue has dried. Before you go, punch a hole in the upper rim of each meat tray and tie long lengths of string through the hole, so that the children can hold on to the strings and retrieve their boats from the middle of a large puddle or a small pond. Try to take the sailboats out on a windy day.

If you choose to use the sailboats indoors, fill a sensory table or tubs with water, and spread plenty of newspaper underneath. Provide Fisher Price people for sailors and cardboard cylinders for blowing through and creating a "wind."

Note: Some educators and parents feel that pirate skull-and-crossbones symbols promote violence. In my experience, children love the pirate flags, and I personally have never received complaints from parents, but do what you feel comfortable with.

Paint-Blowing Pictures
Art

WHY we are doing this activity: to facilitate artistic expression by using air in motion.

WHAT we will need:
    Paint
    Paper
    Straws
    Small containers
    Spoons
    Newspaper

HOW we will do it: Spread out newspaper on your activity table. Put paint and spoons in the small containers and arrange them on the table, with paper, so that all children have access to all materials. During an Attention Getter time, show the children the materials and hand a straw to each child who wants to make a paint-blowing picture. Before the children approach the table, talk about the importance of not sharing straws. Invite your students to spoon paint onto the paper and to blow it with the straw.

Sheet and Scarf Dance
Gross Motor/Sensory

WHY we are doing this project: to encourage children to move creatively; to develop the large muscle group; to encourage children to feel wind in an unusual way.

WHAT we will need:
    Sheets
    Scarves
    Windy day
    Tape recorder
        (with batteries)
    Music tape

HOW we will do it: To prepare, cut the sheets down to about 3' x 3' for three- and young four-year-olds or, for five- and six-year-olds, 4' x 4'. Take the children outside with the scarves and sheets. Encourage them to hold the fabric with one, two, or more children and to feel the force of the wind. If you have access to a grassy area, turn the music on and, together, do a wind dance with the sheets and scarves.

Hot Air Balloon (Part 1)
Science

WHY we are doing this project: to enable children to see that helium weighs even less than oxygen; to enable children to observe how this manifests itself in balloons; to stimulate interest in the dramatic play which follows.

WHAT we will need:
  One helium-filled balloon
  One regular balloon

HOW we will do it: You can buy a helium-filled balloon at a florist's shop. Make sure you tie a very long string onto it, so that when it floats up to the ceiling, children can easily retrieve it. During an Attention Getter time, show the children the two balloons and ask them to predict if they will float in the air in the same way. Let both balloons go. Encourage discussion about what happens. Explain that the balloon which rises and stays in the air is filled with *helium*. Say this word together several times. If you work with three- and young four-year-olds, say it as you blink your eyes, pat your head, or tap your toes. Explain that the air around us is mostly *oxygen*. Repeat this word in the same way. Explain that helium weighs even less than oxygen, which is why the helium balloon rises to the ceiling while the oxygen balloon falls to the floor. Before you let the children explore the balloons, have a discussion about taking turns, and about being gentle with the balloons. You may want to use a puppet to make this talk more interesting to your students. Also, discuss with the children what should be done with the rubber pieces of a burst balloon (they should be picked up and thrown away).

Hot Air Balloon (Part 2)
Art

WHY we are doing this project: to facilitate artistic expression; to encourage cooperation through a group effort; to develop healthy self-esteem by enabling children to make their own props for dramatic play.

WHAT we will need:
  Book: Wade, Alan, *I'm Flying*
  Butcher paper (cut into squares, 1½' x 1½')
  Newspaper
  Paint (variety of colors)
  Shallow containers
  Large paintbrushes
  Helium balloon
Preparation:
  Masking tape

HOW we will do it: Spread several layers of newspaper on the floor, and lay the butcher paper squares on top. Set out the shallow pans of paint and paintbrushes on the newspaper as well.

During Attention Getter time, read *I'm Flying*, by Alan Wade. Let a child hold the helium balloon and pass it to the next child when you turn a page of the book. When the story has been read, ask the children if they remember what kind of gas is in the balloon they have been passing around. If necessary, remind them that it is called *helium*. Ask the children what kind of gas they think is in a hot air balloon. What would happen if they tried to use a hot air balloon that had regular air (*oxygen*) in it? Why? Bring out a regular balloon to remind the children that a balloon filled with oxygen will sink to the ground. Tell the children that they are going to make their own pretend hot air balloon to display on the wall. Name all the colors of the hot air balloon in the story. Tell the children they will need to paint it lots of colors, and show them the materials on the newspaper. Supervise closely so that you do not end up with paint tracks all over the floor.

When the paintings are dry, invite the children to help you tape them together to form a large square. Cut a hot air balloon shape out of the square. Tape it to the wall.

Hot Air Balloon (Part 3)
Dramatic Play

WHY we are doing this activity: to facilitate child-to-child interactions; to help children develop imagination and the ability to express ideas.

WHAT we will need:
> Large appliance box
> Yarn
> Cardboard cylinders (to simulate telescopes)
> Toilet paper rolls (glued or stapled together to simulate binoculars)
> Picnic basket (improvise!)
> Hot air balloon (from previous activity)

Preparation:
> Exacto knife or sharp blade

HOW we will do it: Obtain the cardboard box from a store that sells large appliances. Using the Exacto knife or blade, cut the cardboard box down to simulate the basket of a hot air balloon. Leave four posts—a margin of several inches at each side of each corner. Tie or tape yarn to the end of each cardboard post. Tape the ends of all four lengths to the bottom of the paper hot air balloon or the wall. If your box is a big appliance box, the yarn should be well above the children's heads. In between the posts, cut the box down far enough so that the rim will be at the children's waist level.

Arrange the other props inside it. Encourage the children to explore. Every now and then you might want to say something like: "Hold on tight! Here comes a big gust of wind—whoooo!"

Literature

Symbol Key: *Multicultural
              +Minimal diversity
              No symbol: no diversity or no people

Ardley, N. (1991). *The science book of air*. San Diego, CA: Harcourt Brace.

Branley, F. M. (1962, 1986). *Air is all around you*. New York: Thomas Y. Crowell.*

Davies, K., & Oldfield, W. (1989). *My balloon*. New York: Doubleday.*

Dorros, A. (1989). *Feel the wind*. New York: Thomas Y. Crowell.+

Paulsen, G. (1993). *Full of hot air*. New York: Delacorte Press. (This book has excellent photographs for discussion.)

Schmid, E. (1992). *The air around us*. New York: North-South Books. (Color in diverse skin shades yourself.)

Wade, A. (1990). *I'm flying*. New York: Alfred A. Knopf.

Ziefert, H. (1986). *My sister says nothing ever happens when we go sailing*. New York: Harper & Row. (This book has a very interesting design. Shade in diverse skin colors yourself.)

Extenders

Science/Sensory: Bring in some plastic bubble packing. Let the children explore it and pop the air pockets. Is it possible to sink the plastic bubble packing in water? What is it used for? Why?

Math/Science: After the "How Far Did I Blow It" activity, use some blocks to prop up the cylinders like ramps. Is it still possible to blow any of the objects some distance up the ramp?

Math: If you can obtain several meter sticks, put them end to end across the length of your living room or classroom, and invite the children to see if they can blow a feather all the way along them. Together, count how many meters the feather travels as children take turns blowing it. On butcher paper, write: "We blew the feather _____, " and write down the measurements. Tape the chart on the wall at the children's eye level.

Gross Motor: Cut long crepe or paper streamers and take the children outside on a windy day. On a grassy patch, run in a circle while you hold your streamers. Play "Red Light Green Light"—stop for red and run for green. Vary the game by saying, "Change direction!" every now and then.

Science: Let the children take turns flying a kite on a windy day.

Science: To extend the cloth-drying experiment, hang two wet cloths indoors. Let the children take turns using a hair dryer to dry one of the cloths. Let the other dry naturally. Which dries faster? Experiment further if you like with the hair dryer settings: cool, warm, hot, low air flow, and high air flow.

GOOD GRIEF! IT'S GRAVITY!

Gravity is another scientific concept which even adults have difficulty understanding. The intention of this unit, though, is to provide activities which allow children to observe the pull of gravity, and to observe its effects and impact on objects through hands-on exploration. These types of child-initiated projects are meaningful to children and make them aware of a natural force that affects them every day.

Attention Getter: Hang a piece of butcher paper on the wall, and have a marker ready. Put ten paper clips in a clear container. Get your puppet out, and gather the children together. Shake the container and pass it around, so that the children can see the clips inside. Say: "I'm going to throw everything in this container up in the air." Have your puppet say: "Oooh, I wonder how many of them will land on the ceiling and how many will land on the floor?" Ask the children what they think. Toss the contents into the air. As a group, count how many paper clips

landed on the ceiling, and how many landed on the floor. Have your puppet ask why they all fell to the floor. Why do things never float off the ground? Ask the children what they think. Write the word gravity on the butcher paper. If you work with young children, repeat the word several times while you blink, tap, or pat parts of your body. Explain that gravity is the force that pulls everything toward the center of the earth. We cannot see gravity working, but we can feel it. Ask the children to guess what you will be talking about and working with over the next few days.

The Gravity Song
Music/Movement

WHY we are doing this activity: to create interest in the unit; to develop the large muscle group; to help children enjoy singing.

WHAT we will need:
> Song: "THE GRAVITY SONG" (to the tune of "Twinkle Twinkle Little Star"

> "THE GRAVITY SONG"
> Imagine what the earth would be
> if we had no gravity!
> We'd float here and we'd float there,
> our bodies flying everywhere.
> Instead our bods stay on the earth;
> It's gravity that holds us firm.

HOW we will do it: Sing the song a few times until the children are familiar with the words. Spread out and combine movements with the words. For "Imagine what the earth would be if we had no gravity!" put your hand on your chin as if you are thinking hard. For "We'd float here and we'd float there, our bodies flying everywhere," pretend to be floating in the air. Try to imagine what it would be like not to feel the weight of your body. For "Instead our bods stay on the earth," give a little jump and land with both feet firmly on the ground. For "It's gravity that holds us here," pat the ground.

After you sing the song and perform the actions, spread out and encourage the children to jump as high as they can. Then ask: "Did you feel gravity pull you back to the ground when you were high in the air?"

Gravity, Distance, and Force
Science

WHY we are doing this experiment: to enable children to discover that gravity causes objects to increase in force the farther they fall; to familiarize children with the centimeter as a standard unit of measurement.

WHAT we will need:
> Three buckets
> Wet sand
> Three hard balls (all the same size)
> Climber
> Wooden spatulas
> Tub of water
> Paper towels
> Plastic rulers (with centimeter measurements)
> Erasable markers
> Damp cloth
> Tray

Preparation:
> Marker
> Paper

HOW we will do it: In this activity the children will drop a ball into a bucket of wet sand from three different heights. They will be able to observe how much deeper the imprint in the sand is when a ball falls a greater distance. Set up this activity according to what equipment you have available. Place a bucket of wet sand in front of two objects of different heights, such as a climber and a stepstool. For the shortest distance, simply place a bucket of wet sand on the floor for the children to use while standing in front of it. Arrange everything so that the buckets of wet sand are all in a row. This facilitates easy comparison of the imprints the balls make. To make an activity sign, draw a thick line and write: "Drop your ball from this height." Draw a ball above the word.

Post the activity signs at the height from which each ball should be dropped and read/interpret them with the children during an Attention Getter time. When you supervise the activity, be ready to hand the ball to children on the climber so that they do not have to climb it with only one free hand. Put the plastic rulers, damp cloth, and erasable markers on the tray and place it nearby. Set out the tub of water and the paper towels.

During an Attention Getter time, take a ball and drop it into the bucket on the floor. Encourage the children to examine the imprint it makes in the wet sand. Show the children one of the rulers and the centimeter markings. Stick the ruler into the imprint, and decide which marking it reaches. Wipe the sand off the ruler and draw a thick line to make that marking more visible. Say: "When you drop the balls in the other buckets, you can stick the ruler down into the mark the ball makes, and see if it's different than what we measured for this one. Do you predict that it will be different, or do you predict that the imprints will be the same?"

Show your students the signs next to the other two buckets of wet sand and read or interpret them together. Show them the wooden spatulas and explain that the children can use them to smooth the sand before the next person drops a ball. The tub of water and paper towels are for cleaning the balls when necessary. Talk to the children about how many people can use a ball and bucket of sand at one time. (One.) Invite the children to conduct the experiment and to compare the imprints each ball makes in the sand. Encourage them to express their observations as they experiment. Which ball creates the deepest imprint? Invite their hypotheses about why this is so. When appropriate, explain that gravity pulls all the balls down. The ball which falls the farthest gathers the most speed and lands with the most force.

Developmental differences: Three- and young four-year-olds are likely to be more interested in sensory exploration of the wet sand and in throwing and rolling the balls. Conduct this experiment yourself and see if any children become interested. Older children are likely to be interested in comparing sand imprints.

Paint Plops
Art/Science

WHY we are doing this project: to provide children with an experience of gravity and an opportunity for artistic/creative expression.

WHAT we will need:
    Newspaper
    Very small sponges
    Small containers of water
    Shallow containers of paint
    Shirt boxes
    Paper
    Children's smocks

HOW we will do it: Spread several layers of newspaper over an activity table and put all materials on the table. Put pieces of paper in the shirt boxes. If you do not have small sponges, buy large ones and cut them with scissors. Cutting the sponges into pieces approximately 2.5 cm x 2.5 cm (1" x 1") ensures that you keep reasonable control over paint splatters. Reserve some sponges for the second part of the activity.

During an Attention Getter time, show the children the paper in the shirt boxes. Immerse a sponge in water (to give it weight for greater impact), dip it into paint, hold it over the paper, and ask the children to predict what they will see if the sponge is dropped. Invite the children to conduct this artistic experiment. Provide them with the dry sponges, and ask them to find out what happens if they dip a sponge in paint without soaking it in water first, and then let it fall onto the paper. Ask the children if they remember what they learned in the previous activity, about how heavier objects land with greater force. Using this information, encourage the children to hypothesize about why there is a difference in the paint plops made by a wet and dry sponge.

Gravity Is a Constant
Science/Sensory

WHY we are doing this experiment: to enable children to observe that marbles of different weights fall at the same speed from the same height; to enable children to see that although they may fall from the same height, the heavier marble lands with greater impact; to encourage children to use the sense of hearing; to facilitate a sensory experience with Playdough.

WHAT we will need:
Large marbles
Small marbles
Cookie sheets
Playdough
Rolling pins and other Playdough toys
Small containers
Vinyl tablecloth
Tub for Playdough and Playdough toys

HOW we will do it: Set up as many experiment centers for this project as you wish. Spread the tablecloth on the floor and place the cookie sheets on it. Next to each sheet, place a small container holding a large and a small marble. Put the Playdough and Playdough toys nearby.

During an Attention Getter time, pass a large, heavy marble and a smaller, lighter marble around the group so that each child can feel their relative weights. Hold both marbles over a cookie sheet and say, "If I hold both of these marbles at the same height, like I'm doing now, and drop them at the same time, from the same place, do you think one will land before the other one?" Encourage discussion, but do not drop the marbles. After you have talked about it as a group, invite the children to discover the answer to the question by conducting the experiment themselves. Ask them to listen carefully when they drop the marbles to see if they make different sounds when they land. Show your students the Playdough. Invite them to roll Playdough out on the cookie sheets, and drop both marbles onto it. Will both marbles make the same marks in the Playdough? As the children conduct the exper-

iments, encourage them to express their observations. Do marbles of different weights fall at different speeds from the same height? Does the heavier marble land with more force (leave a deeper imprint)?

Does Gravity Treat Them the Same?
Science/Language/Math

WHY we are doing this experiment: to enable children to discover that even though objects have different weights, gravity draws all of them toward the center of the earth; to familiarize children with heavy/light comparisons using weighing scales; to develop reading and writing skills.

WHAT we will need:
Three large tubs or buckets
Three long cardboard cylinders (from cling wrap or foil boxes)
Empty yogurt cartons (or other small containers)
Pom–pom balls
Cotton balls
Small stones (roughly the size of the other objects)
Rubber balls
Marbles
Writing sheets (provided on page 293; photocopy and enlarge for your use)
Blank paper
Pens
Crayons
Balancing scales
Preparation:
Tacks
String
Hole puncher
Demonstration:
Piece of sponge
Key
Large potato (or other heavy object)

Science Experiment: with Gravity

Does gravity make it fall! into the bucket?

YES ✓ or NO ✗

	YES	NO
Cotton ball		
Marble		
Pom pom Ball		
Stone		
Rubber ball		

Science Experiment with Gravity

Does gravity make it fall! into the bucket?

Here is a blank writing sheet in case you use different materials for this experiment. Write in the words and draw symbols to represent them.

YES ✓ or NO ✗

	YES	NO

HOW we will do it: In this activity you will need to set up three experiment centers (chutes), using the same materials for each. First punch a hole in each end of the cardboard cylinders, on the same side.

Take two lengths of string, and tie each one through a hole. Secure each cylinder to the ceiling so that (1) each chute hangs down low and is accessible to the children, and (2) the chutes are at angles. Experiment to find out which angle will ensure that even the cotton balls roll smoothly down the cylinder. Position the tubs or buckets underneath each chute so that the objects fall into them.

Place all the objects in cartons or containers. Put all the containers on a nearby activity table with the balancing scales, writing sheets, blank paper, crayons, and pens.

For younger children: During an Attention Getter time, pass the sponge, key, and potato around to each child in the group, and ask them to notice which object feels lightest and which feels heaviest. Show the children the weighing scales and weigh the objects against each other. What do the scales tell us about the weight of each object in relation to the others? Show the children the chutes and tubs, and ask them to predict whether gravity will pull light objects as well as heavy objects into the tub, or whether it will treat the objects differently. Drop the key, sponge, and potato down a chute, and after each one lands, use a writing sheet or blank piece of paper to record whether gravity pulled it into the tub. Write a "yes" or "no" in the appropriate space and draw a check or an "X" mark, depending on what the object does. Pass around one of each of the other objects the children will be dropping down the chutes. Ask them to notice the weight of the objects and to predict how gravity will treat each thing when it is dropped into a chute. What do the children think about whether gravity will pull heavy objects into the tubs? What do they think about whether gravity will pull the light objects into the tubs? Invite your students to experiment with the materials and to express their observations.

Older children: During an Attention Getter time, invite the children to hold the objects and compare their weights. Show them the scales, chutes, and blank paper and writing sheets for recording results. Ask them to predict whether gravity will pull both the light and heavy objects into the tubs. Invite them to conduct an experiment to find out, and encourage your students to verbalize their discoveries. What does this tell us about gravity? (It treats heavy and light objects the same.)

Gravity and Distance
Science/Math/Language

WHY we are doing this project: to enable children to explore the relationship between gravity, the steepness of a ramp, and the distance a toy car rolls; to familiarize children with centimeters as standard units for measuring; to facilitate rational counting.

WHAT we will need:
Three shoe boxes
Poster board
Toy cars
Rulers or measuring tapes
Double-sided tape
Masking tape
Tray
Kindergartners:
Writing sheet (provided on page 295; photocopy and enlarge for your use)
Blank paper
Pens
Crayons
Preparation:
Exacto knife
Scissors

HOW we will do it: To prepare, cut away one end and side of each shoe box. Most shoe boxes for adult shoes measure 19 cm x 32.5 cm (7½" x 13"). Using the Exacto knife, cut three horizontal slots in the remaining end of the box so that each slot is about 2.5 cm (1") away from the others. The slots begin flush with the open side, and extend 9 cm (3½") into the box. (See illustration or activity sign).

For each box, cut a rectangle from poster board that measures 19 cm x 34 cm (7½" x 13

Science Experiment
with Gravity and Distance

Apply a scribble of color above each ramp description (highest, middle, lowest) which corresponds to the color you applied around each slot.

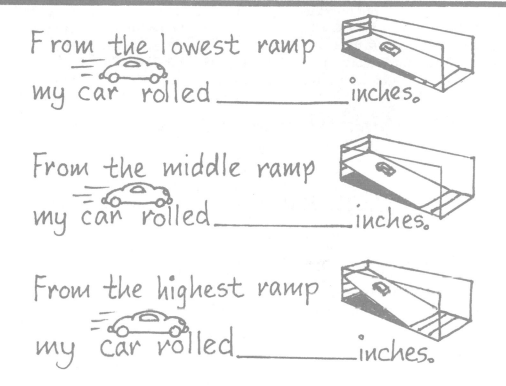

From the lowest ramp my car rolled_____inches.

From the middle ramp my car rolled_____inches.

From the highest ramp my car rolled_____inches.

½"). At one end of the rectangle, about 2.5 cm (1") away from the edge, cut a notch that also measures 9 cm (3½") so that the ramp can be inserted into the slots. Cut the notches in the box and ramp so that the ramp fits snugly into each slot. Color the area around each slot a different color: one red, one brown, and one black. Inside the box, next to each slot, use the corresponding colored marker to write: "Highest ramp," "Middle ramp," and "Lowest ramp."

Stick several strips of double-sided tape on the floor of the ramp box, at the opposite end of the slots. This helps secure one end of the ramp to the floor of the box while the other end is inserted into the slot.

Place the ramp boxes on the floor with toy cars. Place the tape measures (or rulers) and masking tape strips on the tray. Use a marker to enhance the numbers and lines on your rulers. (One way of doing this is to put a strip of sticky label paper along the inch side of the ruler, and

write bigger numbers and lines indicating the centimeter measurements.)

If you are working with kindergartners, set out copies of the writing sheet with a scribble of the appropriate color next to each ramp symbol, to correspond with the colors around each slot on the ramp box. Put the writing sheets, blank paper, pens, and crayons on the tray with the ruler and masking tape.

During an Attention Getter time, give one child a masking tape strip. Position the box so that it aims toward empty floor space. Slide the ramp into the lowest slot, and roll a toy car down it. Ask the child to put the masking tape strip on the floor where the car stops rolling. Say: "Let's measure how far the car rolled down this low ramp." Have the children help you while you use one of the tape measures or rulers, and together, as a group, count how many centimeters the car rolled. Read or interpret a writing sheet together. Next to the symbol for the lowest ramp, write down the number of centimeters the car rolled. Let the children know that if they want to record the results of the experiment in their own way, they can use the blank paper, pens, and crayons to do so.

Without actually putting the ramp in the next highest slot, lift the ramp up to it and ask, "Is this ramp higher or lower than the one I just used? Do you think the car would travel faster or slower down this ramp? Do you think it would travel the same distance as it did on the low ramp?" Invite the children to explore the materials and find out, and to discuss their findings.

Making Ramp Boxes
Art/Crafts

Some children get very excited about using the ramp boxes and toy cars and spend quite a bit of time rolling objects down the ramp, over and over again. If, during the previous activity, you notice that your students are very engrossed in it, consider doing this project so that they can make their own ramp boxes to take home.

WHY we are doing this project: to facilitate artistic expression; to develop fine motor skills; to develop self-esteem by enabling children to make their own experiment tools.

WHAT we will need:
    Shoe boxes (adult size)
    Tissue scraps
    Glue
    Small containers for glue
    Glue brushes
    Newspaper

HOW we will do it: Several weeks ahead of time, begin collecting shoe boxes. Shoe stores may have spare boxes from display shoes, and you can ask other parents, friends, family, and neighbors to help you save them. Make sure you specify that you need adult-sized boxes.

To prepare, cut one side and one end away from each box. Cut the slots in the box *after* the

children decorate the boxes, otherwise the children may inadvertently put glue in the slots. Spread newspaper over a work surface, and put glue in the containers. Put all materials out on the table so that the children will have access to them.

Ahead of time, take one of the ramp boxes you used in the previous activity, and glue tissue scraps to the outside of the box. You do not have to cover the whole box—the idea is to have a sample to show the children.

During an Attention Getter time, ask the children what they see in the room that will help them make their own ramp boxes for rolling things. Let them know they can take their ramp boxes home. Show them the one you began decorating. Tell the children that you wanted to make the ramp box nicer to look at, so you glued tissue scraps on the outside. Invite the children to decorate their own.

After the ramp boxes dry, ask parents or friends to help you cut out the ramps and notches for the ramp boxes, and then return them to the children to take home.

Balancing Blocks
Science/Manipulative

WHY we are doing this project: to provide children with a fun way of exploring the concept of *center of gravity*.

Center of gravity: the point in an object around which its weight is evenly distributed or balanced.

WHAT we will need:
    * Eight blocks (all the same size)

*Depending on the thickness and size of your blocks, you may need fewer. Use the number of blocks that work.

HOW we will do it: Stack the blocks on top of each other, on a table near the edge. Be sure the table is on a carpeted area. Move the top block so that it juts off the edge of the stack to the maximum amount it can without falling. Pull out each block underneath in the same way.

During an Attention Getter time, point out the leaning tower of blocks and encourage the children to play with them by experimenting with how far the blocks can be slid out before they fall.

In this experiment, the overhang of each block must diminish from the top down, because with each block that is moved, a greater number of blocks above it is influencing the pile's center of gravity.

Gravity Defiers
Science/Sensory

WHY we are doing this activity: to enable children to experiment with materials which involve forces stronger than gravity; to provide sensory experiences; to familiarize children with suction and magnetic attraction.

The facts of the matter: *Magnets* have the property of attracting iron or steel. If the magnet is strong enough, its magnetic force is more powerful than gravity, which means that it can pull objects up onto it even though gravity is pulling them down. In addition, the magnet can hang sideways on an iron or steel surface without falling off.

Suction, which is at work in a baster or medicine dropper, functions because of the vacuum that is created. When the rubber bulb is squeezed, all the air is forced out. This creates a vacuum which, combined with the pressure of the surrounding liquid, forces the liquid to rush up, against the pull of gravity, into the dropper or baster when the rubber bulb is released.

Suction is also at work in a rubber suction-cup soap holder. Vacuums or partial vacuums are created in the small concave cavities which, combined with the external atmospheric pressure, cause the pad to adhere to a surface against the pull of gravity.

WHAT we will need:
Cookie sheets
Magnets (of different strengths)
Paper clips (or other light objects which are attracted to magnets)
Steel marbles (or other heavy objects which are attracted to magnets)
Rubber soap pads (the kind with small suction cups)
Basters
Eye- or medicine droppers
Plastic bowls or containers (of varying sizes)
Tubs or sensory table
Water
Activity signs (provided on page 298; photocopy and enlarge for your use)

HOW we will do it: One of the strongest magnets available is a *cow magnet*. A cow magnet is implanted in the first stomach of a cow so that any metal objects the cow inadvertently eats will not pass through to other intestinal passages and cause damage. If possible, contact a farmer, slaughterhouse, or dairy about obtaining these; they provide a wonderful contrast to weaker magnets.

To prepare for the activity, prop some cookie sheets against a wall, and set out the magnets, paper clips, and other objects nearby. Place the rest of the cookie sheets and all other materials in the tubs or sensory table. Post the activity signs near the materials.

During an Attention Getter time, ask the children to name each material and to predict whether it will be stronger than gravity. Invite them to conduct experiments with the magnets, basters, medicine droppers, and suction-cup soap pads to see how and when they work against gravity. As the children explore the materials, discuss what they discover.

Some questions to facilitate discovery and discussion:

Magnets: How close does a magnet have to be to an object to be stronger than gravity? Which is stronger in pulling a steel marble— gravity or magnetic force? Does the type of magnet make a difference (stronger or weaker magnet)?

Basters and Medicine Droppers: What happens when you put a medicine dropper or

Can the suction of a dropper or baster be stronger than gravity?

Can the suction of a soap pad be stronger than gravity?

Here is a sample of what your sign could look like. There are no pictures of magnets or objects in this one, so that you can draw pictures that prepresent the actual size and shape of your magnets and metal objects.

Can a magnet be stronger than gravity?

baster in water without squeezing the plastic holder? (Nothing: gravity keeps the water in the container.) What happens when you suck water up into a dropper or baster and shake it? Does the water come out? (Yes—the motion, combined with gravity, is stronger than the air pressure that kept the water in the dropper/baster at first.) What happens when you suck water up and quickly squeeze and release the rubber bulb? (Drops will be on the verge of falling and will then be sucked up again.)

Suction: Let the children know they have to push down on the rubber soap pads to adhere the tiny suction cups to a cookie sheet or other surface. Is there a difference if the soap pad is wet or dry? What happens if you turn a cookie sheet so that the soap pad is hanging upside down? Does it come off? What happens if you shake the cookie sheet? (That's how strong suction is!) Encourage the children to stick the soap pads onto the inside of a bowl or container. Does the suction work on a curved surface? Is it still stronger than gravity?

Another Gravity Defier
Science/Sensory

WHY we are doing this activity: to enable children to discover that air pressure can be a more powerful force than gravity; to provide a sensory experience with straws and water.

The facts of the matter: When you put your finger over one end of a straw full of water, you are trapping the small amount of air inside it. The air pressure outside the straw is stronger than the air pressure inside the straw. This keeps the water in the straw, against the pull of gravity.

WHAT we will need:
> Clear straws
> Tubs or sensory table
> Water
> Food coloring
> Newspaper

HOW we will do it: To prepare, cut the straws into a variety of lengths. Spread several layers of newspaper underneath the tubs or sensory table. Put water, straws, and some food coloring into the tubs. During an Attention Getter time, pick up a straw and plunge it into a tub of water. Put a fingertip over one end of the straw while it's still in the water, and say: "If I keep my fingertip on the end of this straw, take it out of the water and hold it straight up, do you think the water will run out?" Rather than demonstrate yourself, encourage your students to explore the materials and find the answer for themselves. Is there a difference in how this works with a short straw and how it works with a long one? Invite the children to lift and tap the end of the straw quickly while it is full of water (water will quickly drip out when the finger is lifted and stop while the finger seals the end of the straw). They will see, over and over again, that the pressure of the trapped air inside the straw exerts a force that is stronger than gravity.

And Yet Another Gravity Defier
Science

WHY we are doing this project: to expose children to one more force which can be stronger than gravity: absorption.

WHAT we will need:
> Strips of paper towels (about 5 cm x 12.5 cm [2" x 5"])
> Variety of small containers
> Water
> Food coloring
> Trays or pans
> Small pitchers

HOW we will do it: To prepare, add food coloring to small pitchers of water, and set them on the activity table. Place one container and one strip of paper towel on each tray or pan. Have plenty of spare paper towel strips on hand.

During an Attention Getter time, pour a little colored water into a container, and hold a paper towel strip above it. Ask the children if they remember the experiments you did with absorption during the fluid unit. (If they do not remember what *absorb* means, remind them.) Ask the children to predict which will be stronger: absorption or gravity. Invite the children to pour water into the containers, dip strips of paper towel into the containers, and to verbalize their observations as they conduct the experiment. How high does the water climb on the paper towel strips? Does it climb quickly or slowly?

The Funnel Illusion
Science

WHY we are doing this project: to allow children to experiment with an optical illusion involving gravity.

The facts of the matter: The illusion is possible because as the funnels move, the sides slope upward even though the center of the funnels go down the upward track. If you look directly into the spouts you can see this more clearly.

WHAT we will need:
> Two funnels (the same size)
> Tape
> Two meter sticks (or two yardsticks)
> Blocks (or books)

HOW we will do it: To prepare, tape the two funnels together, widest opening to widest opening. Arrange the blocks in two stacks of different heights. Lay the meter sticks on the stacks so that the ends on the lower stack are closer together than the ends on the higher stack.

Try rolling the funnel piece on the tracks. Adjust the meter sticks accordingly to accommodate it. Encourage the children to roll the funnel piece on the track. It looks like it rolls uphill!

Gravity and Balance
Science

WHY we are doing this experiment: to help children understand the concept of *center of gravity*; to develop self-esteem and a sense of autonomy through use of a one-person work station.

Center of gravity: the point in an object around which its weight is evenly distributed or balanced.

WHAT we will need:
> Symmetrical clown (provided on
>> page 301; photocopy and enlarge for your use)
> Two soda bottles (of equal size)
> Wet sand
> String
> Glue
> Markers or crayons
> Small metal nuts
> Poster board
> "One person may be here" sign
>> (provided on page 3; photocopy and enlarge for your use)

HOW we will do it: To prepare, cut the clown shape out of poster board. Color the clown. Cut a small notch on the clown's nose. Glue each nut onto the space indicated on the clown. Fill the soda bottles half full with wet sand. Tie a length of string between the nozzles of each one to make a "tightrope." Put all the materials on the table and post the "One person may be here" sign.

During an Attention Getter time, show the children the clown and the tightrope, and ask them to predict if she will balance on the tightrope. Show them the notch on her nose. Discuss the "One person may be here" sign. Invite your students to conduct the experiment. What happens when they push the clown very, very gently. Does she fall off? Ask the children to hypothesize about why the clown stays balanced, even when she is gently pushed. Ask your students what they notice on the hands of the clown. Explain that these pull the clown

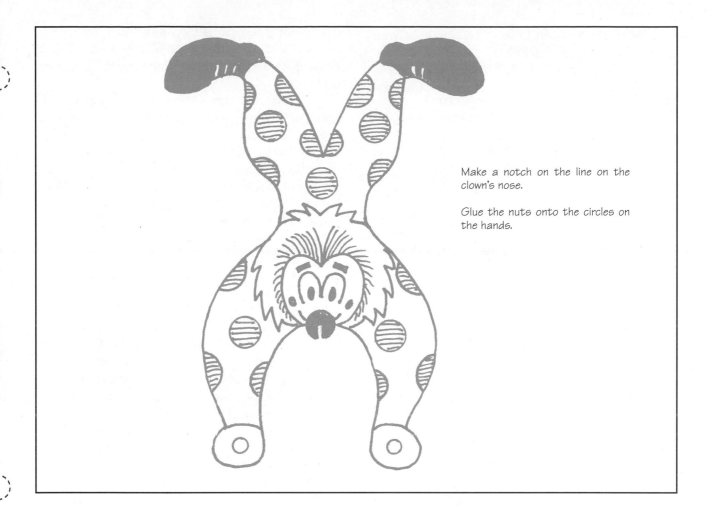

Make a notch on the line on the clown's nose.

Glue the nuts onto the circles on the hands.

down onto the string. The small nuts are the same weight and, because they are in exactly the same place on both sides of the clown, they are evenly balanced. They pull the clown onto the tightrope and let her balance there on her *center of gravity.* If you like, make a clown with a metal nut on only one hand, and let the children compare this to the balanced clown.

Tip: Do not worry if your clown is not completely straight and erect when balancing. Balance and center of gravity are still demonstrated even if your clown totters a little!

The Island Children and Gravity
Language/Multicultural

WHY we are doing this project: to reinforce the connection between gravity and balance; to develop listening and speaking skills; to create multicultural awareness; to develop imagination, expand vocabulary, and encourage verbal expression through children's use of flannel board materials.

WHAT we will need:
Flannel board
Felt
Scissors
Glue
Markers or crayons

Clear contact paper
Flannel board shapes (provided on
  page 303; photocopy and enlarge
  for your use)
"Two people may be here" sign
  (provided on page 13; photocopy and
  enlarge for your use)
Story: "THE ISLAND CHILDREN
  AND GRAVITY" (provided)

HOW we will do it: Color the pieces, glue these pieces onto felt, and cover with a sheet of clear contact paper. Then cut each piece out along the outlines. Set up the flannel board and tell the story.

"THE ISLAND CHILDREN AND GRAVITY"

Once upon a time there were two islands in the middle of the ocean. [Put up islands.] Three children lived there: Binh, Carla, and Azeem. [On island nearest you, put up children.] A Very Grand Wizard ruled these islands. [Put up wizard on same island.] He lived in a big tower [put up tower on same island] and had a book called the Book of Magic [put up book on island nearest you], which he guarded very carefully because there were some very powerful spells in it. The children there were very happy, and played together almost all day, every day.

But there was just one problem. Although the children lived on one island with the Very Grand Wizard, all their food grew on the other island. [Put fruit tree on the other island.] There were stepping stones and planks connecting one island to the other [put planks up between islands], and every day the children had to walk along the planks, balancing carefully. Then they had to pick the fruit off the trees, and go back to their own island, carrying the fruit in their hands, and again, balancing on the planks very carefully. Well, maybe you think this wasn't so bad, but here's what made it so scary. The water around the islands was infested with sharks. [Put up the sharks.] This was what made balancing on the planks so very frightening, especially when the children were holding fruit in both hands on the way back. One day, when the sharks had been snapping at them

particularly ferociously on their way across the planks, they decided to ask the Very Grand Wizard to use his magic to make things easier for them.

"Hmmm," the Very Grand Wizard said, looking through his magic book, "How about a spell to get rid of the sharks?"

"That would be splendid!" Carla said. (She liked to use words like "splendid.")

[Put book up near wizard.] So the Very Grand Wizard made all sorts of strange gestures and muttered and mumbled something that sounded like:

Hocus pocus pickus park
We've got a problem with those sharks,
Get rid of them, they make things tough.
Abracadabra and all that stuff.

And then the Very Grand Wizard brandished his magic wand [move wizard's wand arm] and everyone waited for something Very Grand to happen. But nothing did, and when the children looked at the ocean [move children as if they're looking at ocean], they could see that the sharks were still there. It was very disappointing.

Now the truth is, if you're a wizard or a witch, you have to practice your magic spells all the time if you want to be really good at doing magic. And lately the Very Grand Wizard had forgotten all about practicing his magic because he'd begun to think that instead of being a Wizard, it would be much more fun to be a librarian [put up wizard's thought bubble—librarian picture] and to use that little wand to pass over the books and hear the computer make that little beep, and then to use the stamper to stamp inside every book. He thought this would be so much fun that every day when he woke up he played library from early in the morning until late at night, and forgot all about doing magic. Well, when he saw that his shark spell hadn't worked, he said, "This is terrible! My magic doesn't work anymore! What am I going to do? I must go speak to the Very Very Very Grand Magician at once and get some advice." And he said to the children, "She lives far away, so I'll be gone for a while. Be good, and whatever you do, DON'T GO NEAR MY MAGIC BOOK!"

The Very Grand Wizard was secretly afraid he wouldn't even be able to make his flying spell work, but luckily, when he said:

Use this silhouette to cut shapes out of three different colors of felt, one representing each child.

Enlarge these shapes on a photocopier.

HOW TO TAKE
GRAVITY AWAY.

EVERYTHING
YOU ALWAYS
WANTED TO KNOW
ABOUT MAGIC
AND
WERE AFRAID
TO ASK.

Hunckle Crunckle Abidee Abiday,
Up up I leap and fly far away!

—luckily, when he said those words, the magic worked, and he went soaring away in the air. [Put wizard up in the air, move him as if he is flying, and gradually move him off the flannel board.]

Well, I don't know who it was who first had the idea, (I think it was Binh) but one of the children said, "I bet if we look in the magic book ourselves, we can find a spell to fix our problem." They all looked at each other. They knew they shouldn't go near the magic book, but they were so very tired of balancing along those planks with sharks snapping at their heels. So they decided to do it. Well, they leafed through the book and guess what they found? [Put open book up.] A page that said, "How to take gravity away."

"Hey!" Azeem said, "That would do the trick—if there was no gravity, we could just float over to the other island. We wouldn't have to worry about sharks or balancing on planks, or anything—we could just float over everything."

The children looked at each other again, sort of scared to try it, but very excited and curious too. And they thought it would be awfully fun to have no gravity and to be weightless and float everywhere. So, all together, they said the magic spell to take away gravity:

Hocus pocus abilee abilone,
Take gravity away from our island home!

And guess what happened? The magic spell just happened to work, and instantly, in a flash, everything was topsy-turvy, floating in the air. [Move all pieces around on the board as if they are floating.] The children floated around and around and upside down, completely weightless and directionless because now there was no gravity. They couldn't float over to the island with the fruit tree, because every time they tried to move in that direction, they went shooting off in another. "This is awful!" one of the children shouted to another. "What are we going to do?"

Luckily the magic book happened to be floating very near Carla, and ever so carefully, so as not to make it go shooting away, she put out her hand and was able to take the magic book quickly, and read the spell that would put gravity back:

What a bad idea this whole thing was,
Our island needs gravity back, it does
So right away, right now, today
Put gravity back without delay.

The children crossed their fingers, hoping and hoping the spell would work, and guess what? In a flash, in one split second, everything was back to normal. It took a while for the children to recover, but after a while, Azeem said, "Hey, why don't we just build a good, big, strong bridge? I'm tired of messing around with magic." So that's what they decided to do and when the Very Grand Wizard came back, he saw the beautiful bridge the children had built. [Put up bridge.] As for him, he decided to follow the advice the Very Very Very Grand Magician had given him, and he built a library on the island, and when the children came to borrow books he got to pass a little wand over the books and hear the computer beep and then he got to stamp the inside of every book and he was as happy as any Wizard has a right to be. They all lived happily ever after except for the sharks, who could only watch the children cross over the strong bridge high above them without any hope of even getting a little nibble. And that's the very end of that story.

VOCABULARY:
Infested
Leap
Splendid
Leafed
Strange
Instantly
Gestures
Advice
Brandished
Nibble
Disappointing
Ferociously

Explain and discuss the vocabulary words over time, through several tellings of the story. After telling it the first time, let the children know they can use the flannel board materials to retell the same story or to make up new ones. Discuss the "Two people may be here" sign.

304

Balancing Act

Science/Gross Motor

WHY we are doing this experiment: to build on interest created in the flannel board story; to allow children further exploration with the relationship between gravity and balance; to develop physical coordination; to develop the large muscle group.

WHAT we will need:

Balancing beam
Four plastic half-gallon containers with handles
Wet sand
Tub
Scooper for sand
Four rocks (roughly equal in size and weight)
Four stones (roughly equal in size and weight)
Feathers
Cotton balls
Strawberry baskets
Plastic grocery bags
Gym mat
Newspaper
Meter or yardstick

Preparation:

Scissors/Exacto knife

HOW we will do it: To prepare, set up the balancing beam on the gym mat, and place a small table nearby. Cut away the top opening of each plastic container so that the handle remains intact, while allowing the children to easily scoop or place wet sand or rocks inside. Cut the handles from plastic grocery bags, leaving extra strips of plastic on each end for tying around the strawberry baskets.

Secure the handles to the baskets, and place them on the table. Put the wet sand and a scooper in the tub and place it on the table. Set all other materials on the table as well. After telling the flannel board story, point out the balancing beam and materials to the children.

Invite them to experiment with walking across the beam while holding a basket in both hands. Brainstorm with the children to come up with some of the options. For example, they could hold two big containers in their hands and put the same amount of wet sand in them. They also could hold a small basket in one hand, with only one feather in it, and hold a big heavy rock in a big container in the other hand. Or they could walk across the beam with nothing in their hands.

Ask the children to predict, with each suggestion they make, whether it will be easy or difficult to balance as they walk across the beam. Invite them to compare walking along the beam with their hands at their sides to crossing the beam while holding the meter stick. Ask the children if they have ever seen a tightrope walker. What do tightrope walkers sometimes use to find their center of gravity?

Supervise the activity while the children explore the materials, and encourage them to discuss their discoveries. What makes it easiest to balance while walking across the beam? What makes it hardest? Ask the children to hypothesize about why this is so. Explain that air holds light things up (like feathers), in resistance to gravity. As gravity pulls heavy things down toward the ground, they feel very heavy when they are held. How do these two things affect balance?

Island Children
Dramatic Play/Language

Low balance beam
Gym mats
Play furniture
Baskets

WHY we are doing this activity: to provide children with more hands-on experience with gravity and balance; to give children an opportunity to act out real-life situations through fantasy play; to enable children to work through emotions in fantasy play; to develop speaking and listening skills; to promote child-to-child interaction and cooperation.

HOW we will do it: Using the play furniture, set up a housekeeping area on one "island." Set up the balance beam on a gym mat so that the "islands" are connected. Encourage the children to explore the materials and caution them to walk carefully on the balance beam.

WHAT we will need:

Two areas that simulate islands (e.g., gym mat, climber, large appliance box, carpet, floor section taped off with masking tape)

Literature

Symbol Key: *Multicultural
+Minimal diversity
No symbol: no diversity or no people

Arnold, T. (1987). *No jumping on the bed*. New York: Dial Books for Young Readers.

Branley, F. M. (1986). *Gravity is a mystery*. New York: Thomas Y. Crowell.+

Stoll Walsh, E. (1993). *Hop jump*. San Diego, CA: Harcourt Brace.

Wiesner, D. (1988). *Free fall*. New York: Mulberry Books.

Extenders

Science: After you conduct the initial experiment with balls and wet sand, give the children balls of varying sizes. Let them explore and discover comparative sand imprints of different-sized balls from different heights.

Science/Manipulative/Gross Motor: After you conduct the initial chute experiment, give the children cardboard cylinders, plasticene, and blocks and invite them to make new chutes with these materials. Provide marbles, rubber balls, and toy cars to use with the chutes. Other options: Provide plank-like blocks, cookie sheets, and ping-pong balls. Be creative!

Language: Before the children drop the large and heavy marbles onto the cookie sheets, make a chart of their predictions in response to the questions: "Do you think one marble will land before the other one, or will they land at the same time? If you think they will land at different times, which one do you think will land first?"

Language/Science: Acquire some of the space books listed in Unit 17, and with the children, discuss the pictures of astronauts floating in space and in spaceships without gravity. What would that feel like?

SEED-SATIONAL

Beans are included in this unit in a separate section, since they are technically seeds. However, they lend themselves to many interesting activities of their own. You may want to do this unit in spring or summer, when you can find seeds in abundance outdoors. Several weeks ahead of time, start gathering a seed collection that could include: winged seeds, grass seed stems, white dandelion heads, chestnuts, or wild birdseed.

Attention Getter: For this Attention Getter, you will need a small potted plant, an empty pot, some potting soil, a small paper cup of water, a large spoon, and seeds (marigold or zinnia work well), as well as butcher paper and two markers that are different colors. Pin your butcher paper on the wall. When the children are gathered, show them the potted plant, and invite them to touch the leaves and the stem gently. Ask: "What do plants grow from?" If or when the children say "seeds," show

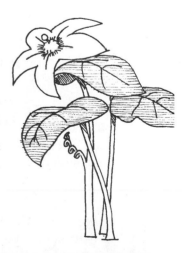

them the seeds and ask them to help you plant them in the empty pot. Have each child put a spoonful of soil into the pot. Encourage the children to touch the potting soil if they would like to. When the pot is half full, sprinkle the seeds in, and then have the children continue to spoon soil over them. Water the seeds and together, find a sunny spot (but not too sunny) for the seeds to grow. Ask: "What do you think will grow from the seeds?" Encourage all kinds of predictions (make some yourself if necessary, to get the ball rolling: e.g., A vegetable? A flower? A tree? What color will it be? How big?). Write each prediction down on the butcher paper, using alternate colors of markers as well as quotation marks to make individual sentences easier for the children to identify.

Nurture the plant and check it every day. As the plant grows, invite the children to draw pictures of it, and name the plant. Use the drawings to create a class book if you like, and compare them to the chart. Did the plant turn out to be what the children predicted?

PART 1: Seeds

The Star in the Apple
Math/Language/Small Group Activity

WHY we are doing this activity: to stimulate interest in seeds and in the next project; to practice rational counting; to develop listening skills; to facilitate group cooperation.

WHAT we will need:
 Butcher paper
 Markers
 Apple
 Sharp knife
 Story: "THE STAR IN THE APPLE"
  (provided)

"THE STAR IN THE APPLE"

nce upon a time there was a little star who shone very fiercely and brightly up in the galaxy. At night, when this lit-

tle star came out, she used to stare and stare at the earth and wish that she could visit it. So one night, even though she knew it was naughty, she fell down to the earth and began to look around. Well, Mother Moon was also shining brightly that night, and she checked to make sure all her family was there, and guess what? She found that the little star was missing. So she sent a beam of moonlight down to the earth to look for the little star. But the little star was having fun and didn't want to be found, so she hid behind the trunk of an apple tree, but the moonbeam followed her. She hid in the leaves of the apple tree, but the moonbeam followed her there too. So then she hid inside an apple.

The moonbeam said, "Little star, won't you come back up to the galaxy with me? Mother Moon and all the other stars and planets miss you dreadfully." So the little star came out of the apple and traveled on the moonbeam's back up into the sky, and right beside Mother Moon, she shone fiercely and brightly all night long.

HOW we will do it: Pin up the butcher paper, and as you tell the story, use the markers to draw pictures. At the end of the story, take the apple and the knife and say, "Now I've heard that when the little star came out of the apple, she left her shape behind, in the middle of the apple. Do you think that could be true? Shall we cut this apple open to see?" Cut the apple horizontally instead of from top to bottom. What do you see? As a group, count the number of seeds in the star of the apple.

Do You Seed Them?
Science/Sensory

WHY we are doing this project: to help children understand that most plants make seeds so that new plants can grow; to allow children to discover that seeds come in many different shapes and sizes and that different plants store seeds in different ways; to provide a sensory experience.

The following list is comprised of suggestions; use whatever seeds you can find or have handy. Try to make the collection as varied as possible. To find the seeds in pinecones, choose new cones which have scales that are closed up and close together. The scales will separate if you put them in a warm oven. (The seeds are in between the scales.) Provide shelled (or hulled) as well as unshelled (unhulled) seeds and nuts so that the children understand that the former comes from the latter.

WHAT we will need:
> Trays
> Magnifying glasses
> Plastic knives
> Paper towels
> Small Styrofoam meat trays
> Chestnuts
> Pinecones
> Grass seeds
> Burrs
> Winged seeds
> Apple
> Orange
> Tomato
> Nectarine
> *Avocado
> Sunflower seeds
> Peanuts
> Pumpkin seeds
> Birdseed
> Variety of nuts
> Cucumber
> Melon
> Corn
> Corn on the cob (fresh)
> Popcorn kernels
> Feed corn
> Kiwi fruit
> Pea pods
> Green beans

Preparation:
> Nutcracker
> Knife

*Caution: Do not cut the avocado seed open, as these seeds contain a toxic substance.

HOW we will do it: To prepare, use the nutcracker to shell some of each kind of nut, making sure to leave a sample of each unshelled. Use the knife to cut open the fruits and vegetables, and to cut them into segments or pieces. If you cut the apple horizontally instead of vertically, you are more likely to leave the seeds intact.

Put all the seeds on trays in categories (e.g., all types of corn together, all other vegetables together, all nuts together, all fruits together). Put the birdseed on the small Styrofoam meat trays. Place the magnifying glasses, paper towels, and plastic knives on the activity table with the seeds.

During an Attention Getter time, ask: "Can you think of some things which have seeds in them?" Encourage the children to describe how they noticed this type of seed. Show them the seed table, and encourage them to explore the materials. As they do this, encourage discussion. Some observations which may trigger discussion: Nuts have hard cases around them; other seeds do not. Many vegetable seeds are inside the vegetable. Often the seeds are arranged in a pattern. Notice the different amounts of seeds; there is only one seed in each nut shell. Apples and oranges may have five to twenty seeds, but the seeds in a melon are almost too many to count. The flesh of a fruit which is close to the seeds may be slightly different than the rest of the fruit. (It is often more pithy, such as in cucumbers and melons. Ask the children to hypothesize about why this is. [The pithier flesh protects the seeds.]) Encourage your students to notice the different sizes and shapes of the seeds, and invite them to touch and smell all the materials.

How Do Seeds Travel?
Science

WHY we are doing this activity: to enable children to observe the forces that spread seeds from their place of origin to the place where they grow; to develop speaking and listening skills.

WHAT we will need:
> Winged seeds
> White dandelion heads (one for each
>   child)

Grass or weeds with seed heads and
   burrs
Stems with seeds that have hooks or
   barbs
Hair dryer
Woolly mitten or sock
Nylon stocking
Magnifying glasses

HOW we will do it: Put all the seeds on an activity table. Plug the hair dryer into an outlet some distance away from the seed table, so that one child does not accidentally blow all the seeds off all the dandelion heads (I speak from experience!). During an Attention Getter time, point to the seeds and ask: "How do you think seeds travel? How do they get from the plant where they start out as seeds, to the place where they grow into new plants?" Encourage expression of ideas.

Show the children the seeds with hooks and barbs. Give them the opportunity to examine them closely. Say: "These barbs and hooks are very sharp, and if you touch them with your finger, they might hurt. But if you put one of these (point to the mitten, sock, or nylon) over your hand and rub it against the seeds, you'll see something happen that will show you one way that seeds travel." Point to the white dandelion heads and say, "There is one of these for each of you. You can either blow on it to see what happens, or take it over to the hair dryer which you can use, pretending it is the wind. That will show you another way that seeds travel." If you work with very young children ask: "Is it okay to take more than one dandelion head? What will happen if one person takes two?" (Someone will not get one.) Show the children the winged seeds and invite them to throw them up in the air, or blow them into the air.

After the children have experimented with the materials, gather them together at the end of the day or session, and review all the ways that seeds travel. Also mention that animals eat plants that have seeds in them, and when the animals get rid of their waste, the seeds come out whole and begin to grow.

Growing Seeds
Science/Sensory/Art

WHY we are doing this project: to build interest in the unit by enabling children to grow plants from their own seeds in a creative way; to allow them to observe how sprouts emerge from soil and grow bigger every day.

WHAT we will need:
   Bird- or grass seed
   Regular-sized paper cups
   Markers
   Potting soil
   Spoons
   Water
   Eye- or medicine droppers
   Newspaper

HOW we will do it: Spread several layers of newspaper over an activity table. Put out the materials so that all children will have access to them.

During an Attention Getter time, take a cup and say, "I thought of a funny way to plant some seeds today." Draw a face on a cup. Say: "This is just the way I'm drawing my face. Everyone will draw a different kind of face, because we are all different and have our own way of doing things." Fill your cup with soil and say, "If I plant some seeds in my cup, what do you think they'll look like when they grow?" (Hair.) Say: "I want the plants that grow from these seeds to look just like hair, so I'm going to make sure I sprinkle the seeds all over the top of my cup, even around the edges." Put a layer of soil on top of the seeds, and then use a medicine dropper to water them. Explain to the children that you are watering the seeds that way because you want to make sure they do not get too much water. Too much water is just as bad for plants as not enough. Put your cup on the shelf or table you have set aside for this purpose, and invite the children to make their own seed faces.

Leave small containers of water and the medicine droppers beside the plants. Encourage the children to check and water them every day. Make this a daily ritual so that you can notice and discuss the first signs of sprouts. Make a point of noticing how a sprout unfurls from its seed shell, and what happens to the shell as time passes.

When the "hair" grows in, and the plants become quite tall, cut the hair. Feed it to a rabbit if you know of a deserving one. You may choose to transplant the plants to a field where they can grow even bigger, or let the children take their faces home.

What Does a Seed Need?
Science/Language

WHY we are doing this project: to enable children to see that a seed needs both air and water in order to grow; to develop reading and writing skills.

WHAT we will need:
Styrofoam egg cartons
Birdseed
Small cups
Water
Paper towels
Writing sheet (provided on page 314; photocopy and enlarge for your use)
Blank paper
Pens
Crayons
Markers
Eye- or medicine droppers
Sticky labels
Preparation:
Scissors

HOW we will do it: Cut the Styrofoam egg cartons into sections of three egg cavities each. Put water into the small cups, and put all materials on the table so that the children will have access to them.

During an Attention Getter time, ask the children what a seed needs to grow. After you discuss their ideas, say: "Today we are going to do an experiment to see if a seed really needs both air and water to grow." Pour water into one section and drop a seed in. Show the children that the seed is now surrounded by water. Put one dry seed in another section with nothing else and show this to the children. Fold a small piece of paper towel and stuff it into the bottom of the last section. Use an eye- or medicine dropper to moisten it, and drop a seed on top. Show this to the children. Say: "I don't want to put too much water on this paper towel, because I want to make sure this seed has air *and* water." Point to each section again, and say: "This seed is covered in water. It has no air. This seed has lots of air, but no water. This last seed is on a wet paper towel. It has water underneath it, and air above it."

Ask the children to predict whether, and how, each seed will grow. Let the children know that you are going to record the results of the experiment every day. On a blank piece of paper or writing sheet, under "Day One," write some observations for each seed. (For example, "This seed hasn't changed.") Use the crayons or markers to draw a picture of what each one looks like. Ask the children if they see anything in the room which would help them conduct this experiment for themselves. Invite your students to write their names on the sticky labels to identify their materials. Keep the writing sheets, blank paper, and pens, crayons, and markers near the experiment for its duration, so they can record observations and results. After a week, what do the children notice about the seeds? Which seed grew the most? What does this tell us about what seeds need? (The seeds in the water will sprout a little, but because of lack of air, they will stop growing at a certain point.)

Science Experiment:

What does a seed need? How my seeds change:

Make photocopies, and next to "Day" write in the number of the day.

Day ☀ ☾ _____ Seed with NO air and NO water.

Day ☀ ☾ _____ Seed with water and NO air.

Day ☀ ☾ _____ Seed with water and air.

Science Experiment:

These blank writing sheets can be used in case you use containers other than egg cartons.

What does a seed need? How my seeds change:

Day ☀ ☾ _____ Seed with NO air and NO water.

Day ☀ ☾ _____ Seed with water and NO air.

Day ☀ ☾ _____ Seed with water and air.

How Do Plants Take Up Water?

Science

WHY we are doing this project: to help children understand how growing seeds, sprouts and plants take up water; to help children understand what the *xylem* is; to develop speaking and listening skills.

The facts of the matter: Xylem is a tissue that conducts water and mineral salts in stems, roots, and leaves. In celery, this happens when air presses down on the water around a stalk and the cells in the celery draw the water up inside the stalk. The narrower the xylem tubes are, the higher the water will rise. Hundreds of hollow cells in the pipelines comprise xylem.

WHAT we will need:
    Celery stalks with leaves
    Celery seeds
    Clear plastic cups
    Small pitchers of water
    Red food coloring
    Sticky labels
    Pens
    Magnifying glass

HOW we will do it: Cut the celery off at the base of the bunch. Place the celery stalks, cups, labels, and pens on an activity table. Add red food coloring to the pitchers of water. Clear away a surface on which the experiment can be left for some time.

Say to the children: "When seeds are growing, and as they become plants, how do they get water from the ground?" Encourage the children to express their ideas. Pass the celery seeds to the group and say, "These are the tiny seeds which have to grow to become celery plants." Then pass around the magnifying glass and a celery stalk and ask the children to examine the inside of the celery. What do they see? Explain that there are *pipelines* in the celery which are called *xylem*. Ask the children what these pipelines might have to do with a plant getting water. Show your students the colored water, and ask them to predict what will happen if they leave the celery stalks in the water.

Invite the children to conduct the experiment and to use the labels to put their names on their cups. Decide to check your experiments in an hour. Talk about what the clock will look like then, or draw a picture of what the clock will look like in one hour for the children to compare as time passes.

When your students check the experiments, ask them what they notice about the celery stalks. Look at the bottoms of the stalks, where they were cut. You should be able to see red spots, in a row, across the stalk of the celery. These are the xylem. Invite the children to peel off the outer strands and to see how far up the stalk the xylem carried the water. Invite them to put new stalks in the red water and leave them there several days. After this time has passed, what do the children notice? (Leaves will take on a red tinge.) Even though the cells and the pipelines in celery are so small, they are strong enough to pull water all the way up through the stem to the leaves at the top.

Root Power

Science

WHY we are doing this experiment: to enable children to see that the roots of seeds are very strong in their search for nourishment.

WHAT we will need:
    Eggshell halves (as intact as possible,
      to serve as soil cups)
    Soil
    Seeds
    Egg carton
    Sticky labels or masking tape
    Small containers for water
    Eye- or medicine droppers
    Small plastic spoons
    Magnifying glasses

HOW we will do it: Ahead of time, start collecting eggshells by asking friends, neighbors, family, and parents to save them for you. The eggshells need to be able to hold soil and seeds.

To prepare, put all materials on the activity table. Stick the labels or masking tape strips around the edge of the table. During an Attention Getter time, remind the children of the What Do Seeds Need? experiment. Sprouts began to grow from the top of the seeds, but did the children notice what grew from underneath the seeds? Tell them you want to conduct an experiment to find out how strong seed roots are. Use a spoon to put some soil in an eggshell. Say: "I'm doing this very gently, and being very careful with the eggshell, because I don't want it to break." Drop some seeds into the soil, and cover them with a little more soil. Use the medicine dropper to water the seeds. Place the eggshell in an egg carton and label that cup with your name.

Ask the children to predict what will happen to the eggshell as the seed grows. Invite them to conduct this experiment for themselves. Three- and young four-year-olds may need help preparing the experiments without breaking their eggshells.

It may take as long as three or four weeks before you begin to see roots breaking through the shells. At this time, discuss what the children observe. What does this tell us about the strength of roots? Why did the roots break through the shells? (They seek out water for the plant.) Provide your students with magnifying glasses for examining the roots.

Nature Walk
Science/Gross Motor

WHY we are doing this activity: to enable children to observe places outdoors where roots have cracked or broken cement, asphalt, or other materials; to develop the large muscle group.

WHAT we will need:
Rope
Nice day
Optional:
Polaroid camera

HOW we will do it: If you do not want to deal with matching the children with partners, have them all hold on to the rope. Before you set out for your walk, have another look at the roots which have broken through the eggshells in the previous activity. Say to the children: "We are going to go for a walk to see if we can find other places where roots have broken something up. Where do you think we should look?" If necessary, suggest sidewalks, the road beside curbs, and the walls of buildings. (You may also decide to look for places where seeds have been blown and begun to grow, such as the cracks between sidewalk sections and cracks in walls.

When one of you spots an example of strong roots breaking up cement or stone, make sure everyone gets a chance to take a look, and if you have a camera, take a photograph. Did you find any roots in very odd or unusual places? Talk about your findings later in the day when you are back at school or home, and examine the photographs to remind you of the sequence of your discoveries.

Terrific Tropism (Part 1)
Language/Math/Small Group Project

Tip: Begin this project several weeks before you facilitate Part 2.

WHY we are doing this activity: to develop speaking, listening, and reading skills and, for kindergartners, to develop writing skills; to practice rational counting; to facilitate group cooperation; to help children develop problem-solving skills; to promote self-esteem by enabling children to take responsibility for gathering their own materials for an experiment.

WHAT we will need:
   Butcher paper (two large pieces)
   Markers (two different colors)
   One shoe box (children's size)
Kindergartners:
   Paper
   Pens
   Envelopes

HOW we will do it: Pin two pieces of butcher paper up on the wall, side by side. During an Attention Getter time, show the children the shoebox and say: "In a few weeks, we are going to do a seed growing experiment that uses small shoe boxes like this one. The problem is, I only have one shoe box, and there are a lot more of us. I wonder how many of us there are all together?" As a group, count all the children. If some children are absent that day, remind your students who they are, and remember to include them in your final count. On top of the butcher paper, write: "There are ___ of us, but only one (1) shoe box." Draw a picture of a shoe box above the word. Draw a group of faces above the word "us." Color in skin shades which reflect the skin shades of your group.

Ask: "How do you think we could get more shoe boxes so that everyone could have one for the experiment?" Write down the children's ideas, alternating the color of each sentence to make it easier for the children to distinguish them. Use quotation marks and write children's names after their comments. If or when the idea of asking for the help of friends and family is mentioned, suggest that you write a letter to explain what you need and why you need it.

On the second piece of butcher paper, take dictation from the children in regard to what a letter to friends and family should say. Afterward, if you work with kindergartners, point out the paper and pens and say, "We've just come up with a few ideas of what our letters could say. If you'd like to write your own letter to ask your mother or father or a friend to save small shoe boxes for you, you can use the paper, envelopes, and pens to write it."

If you work with three- and young four-year-olds, incorporate the dictated comments into a letter for the children to take home. Make photocopies and during another Attention Getter time, read the letter to the children again and give each child one to take home or to a friend.

Terrific Tropism (Part 2)
Science

WHY we are doing this experiment: to enable children to observe that plants grow and turn in response to external stimulus (sunlight).

WHAT we will need:
   Plastic yogurt containers (the smallest
      size possible—4.4 oz. or 6 oz.)
   Plastic lids from (8 oz.) yogurt containers
   Trays
   Soil
   Raw sunflower seeds (unshelled)
   Spoons
   Sticky labels or masking tape
   Small containers of water
   Medicine droppers
   Children's shoe boxes with lids
   Cardboard
   Duct tape
Preparation:
   Skewers
   Scissors

HOW we will do it: For this experiment, you will need to make a "tropism box" for each child, as well as one sample for demonstration. The writing sheet provided for Part 3 of this activity includes an illustration that will help you visualize how to assemble the boxes.

To prepare one tropism box: You will need to cut a square opening that measures 5 cm x 5 cm (2" x 2") out of one short end of the shoe box. Hold the box so that you can see into it. This square should be positioned about 5 cm (2") from the left corner of the box. Use the skewer to make a starter hole before you cut.

Measure the depth and width of the box. Add 5 cm (2″) to the width measurement. Cut two pieces of cardboard according to these dimensions.

About 7.5 cm (3″) from the edge of each cardboard piece, cut out a square opening the same size as the one in the end of the box.

Fold down flaps that measure 2.5 cm (1″) on both ends of the cardboard pieces. Fold them several times and press down hard so that the corner is firm. With the flaps pointing down, wedge one piece horizontally into the shoe box, one-third of the way down. Be sure that the hole in the top of the box is opposite the hole in the cardboard. Secure the flaps with duct tape. Wedge the other cardboard piece into the box two-thirds of the way down. The hole in this piece should be in line with the one in the top of the box, and opposite the one in the piece above it. Secure the flaps with duct tape.

The tropism box will need to stand on end with the lid on the front. To facilitate this, cut the rim off one short end of the lid. Fit the lid onto the front of the box, with the missing rim at the bottom. Secure the top rim to the roof of the box with duct tape. This will allow you to swing the lid open and up to view the inside of the box.

Enlist the help of friends, family, and other parents to make enough tropism boxes for each child.

Use the skewer to poke holes in the bottom of each yogurt container for drainage. (The lids from the larger yogurt containers will be placed under the "planting pots" to catch the excess water.)

Set up a table or countertop near sunlight where the experiment can be left for several weeks and where there is enough space for all the tropism boxes.

When you are ready to do the experiment, put all materials out on an activity table. During an Attention Getter time, ask, "Why do you think plants grow up, out of the ground, instead of down in the ground toward the center of the earth?" Encourage comments. Talk about the fact that plants grow toward sunlight, and tell the children that this is called *tropism*. Say this word several times, and if you work with three- and young four-year-olds, blink your eyes, tap your nose, or tap your foot on the floor in time to the syllables. Show the children a tropism box

and make sure they see the holes in the shelves inside, as well as the hole in the top end. Since we know plants grow toward sunlight, what would happen if a seed was planted in a tropism box? Encourage predictions.

Prepare your own tropism experiment. Spoon some soil into a yogurt container, plant a seed, and place the container on the bottom of the box, underneath the lowest hole. Use a medicine dropper to water the seed. Fit the shoe box lid over the front of the box, put the box on a tray, and place the tray on the designated table or countertop. Ask your students if they see anything in the room that will help them conduct this experiment for themselves.

Show the children how the bottoms of the yogurt containers have holes. Ask them why they think the holes are there. (For drainage, or so the seed does not stay too wet.) Show them how a bigger plastic lid can be placed under the planter and ask why it might be a good idea to use one. Instruct your students to plant one sunflower seed each—the small containers are not big enough for the roots of more than one plant.

Encourage the children to use the sticky labels or masking tape for name labels. If the boxes do not stand solidly on one end, use duct tape to secure them to the table.

Put the small containers of water and medicine droppers on the table beside the tropism boxes so that children can easily water the plants.

If you like, designate a certain time each day for checking the plants. As the sunflower sprouts begin to emerge and grow, what do the children notice about the direction they are growing? As weeks pass, how do the sunflower plants react to the holes? As necessary, remind them that *tropism* means that plants grow and turn in response to things around them, like sunlight. Using this information, ask the children to hypothesize about why the sunflower always grows toward the holes. See the next activity for how to record observations and results of this experiment.

Terrific Tropism (Part 3)
Science/Language/Art

More Proof of Tropism
Science

WHY we are doing this activity: to facilitate scientific recording of experiment results; to develop reading and writing skills; to facilitate artistic expression; to develop fine motor skills.

WHAT we will need:
> Observation sheet (provided on page 320; photocopy and enlarge for your use)
> Blank paper
> Crayons
> Pens
> Pencils
> Markers

HOW we will do it: To prepare, make observation books by combining and stapling several copies of the observation sheets provided. Make several blank books as well. Place all materials on a table near the tropism boxes.

Show the children an observation book and read the title. You may choose to wait to do this until sprouts have emerged from the seeds. On the first page, draw what you see in your box. Write some words next to it about your observation, for example, "A plant has started growing from my seed, but it hasn't grown up through the hole yet." Explain to the children that their pictures and words will be different, because we all have our own ideas and our own ways of doing things.

Invite the children to use the blank paper or observation books to record the results of their experiments. Leave these materials beside the experiment table for its duration. As the children work on their observation books, help with spelling, take dictation, write down their words for them to copy, or support invented spelling as needed. If you like, before the children take their sunflowers home, have a show-and-tell of observation books.

Developmental differences: Three- and young four-year-olds will use the books or blank paper for scribbling. Older children will be likely to draw pictures of what they see and to record observations.

WHY we are doing this experiment: to prove that tropism is also at work when a seed grows around an obstacle, such as a stone.

WHAT we will need:
> Plastic cups
> Soil
> Spoons
> Seeds
> Small stones
> Small containers of water
> Medicine droppers

HOW we will do it: To prepare, put all materials out on an activity table so that your students have access to them.

During an Attention Getter time, put soil in a cup, plant a seed or two, cover with more soil and put a stone directly on top of the spot where you planted the seeds. Be sure the children can clearly see what you are doing. Ask: "Do you think the stone will stop the seed from growing?" Encourage predictions. Let the children know that if they would like the answer to this question, they can conduct the experiment for themselves with the materials on the table. Leave the small containers of water and medicine droppers near the planted seeds so that the children can water them every day. As sprouts begin to emerge, ask the children if they remember what *tropism* is and what they observed in the previous experiment (which may still be in progress). Using this information, ask the children to hypothesize about why the seed sprouts grow around the stones.

© 1996 Delmar Publishers

Tropism Experiment:

Day _____

Seed–Sational
Science/Sensory

WHY we are doing this project: to enable children to discover that many seeds are good to eat and to provide a sensory experience.

For this project, try to provide as large a variety of edible seeds as possible. For the purposes of comparison, provide salted, unsalted, raw, and roasted seeds when possible.

WHAT we will need:
Sunflower seeds
Pumpkin seeds
Peanuts
Popcorn kernels
Oil popcorn popper

HOW we will do it: Make sure the children sit down while they sample the seeds. Which ones are their favorites? What kind of plant does each one come from? What kinds of animals eat these seeds? What seeds do they eat at home? Use the oil popper to pop the corn kernels. Explain that when a popcorn kernel is heated very quickly, the water inside the kernel evaporates into a gas. This puts a lot of pressure on the kernel from the inside, and makes the hard skin burst. Then the rest of the gas makes the softer parts of the kernel billow into the white, soft part that tastes so good.

"The Pumpkin Seed"
Big Book
Language/Small Group Project

WHY we are doing this project: to stimulate interest in the pumpkin projects which follow; to develop listening and reading skills.

Pumpkins lend themselves to many wonderful seed activities. Kick off your pumpkin seed exploration by making this big book.

WHAT we will need:
Book: Krauss, Ruth, *The Carrot Seed* (paperback edition)
Large pieces of orange poster board
Pumpkin patterns (provided on page 322)
Scissors
Glue
Two key rings
Two markers (brown and black)

HOW we will do it: In this project, you are going to make a big book by adapting *The Carrot Seed* to become "The Pumpkin Seed." Cut out seven identical pieces of orange poster board in the shape of a pumpkin, including a stem at the top. Cut out the cover of *The Carrot Seed*, minus the title, and glue it onto the front page. Using the black marker, print "The Pumpkin Seed" above the illustration.

Go through the book, and use the brown marker to draw a round pumpkin shape around each small carrot sign in the illustrations, so that each sign shows a pumpkin instead of a carrot. (This works perfectly. From a distance no alteration is visible.) Tear or cut each page out, cut off the text, and glue it onto a page of your big book. On each big book page, use the black marker to write the original text in large print, but substitute the word "pumpkin" for "carrot."

On the last two pages, you will need to change the carrot into a pumpkin. Use the patterns provided to make a pumpkin stalk and pumpkin. Use green paper for the stalk and orange paper for the pumpkin. Cut out the pictures from the last two pages of *The Carrot Seed*. To put a pumpkin in the wheelbarrow instead

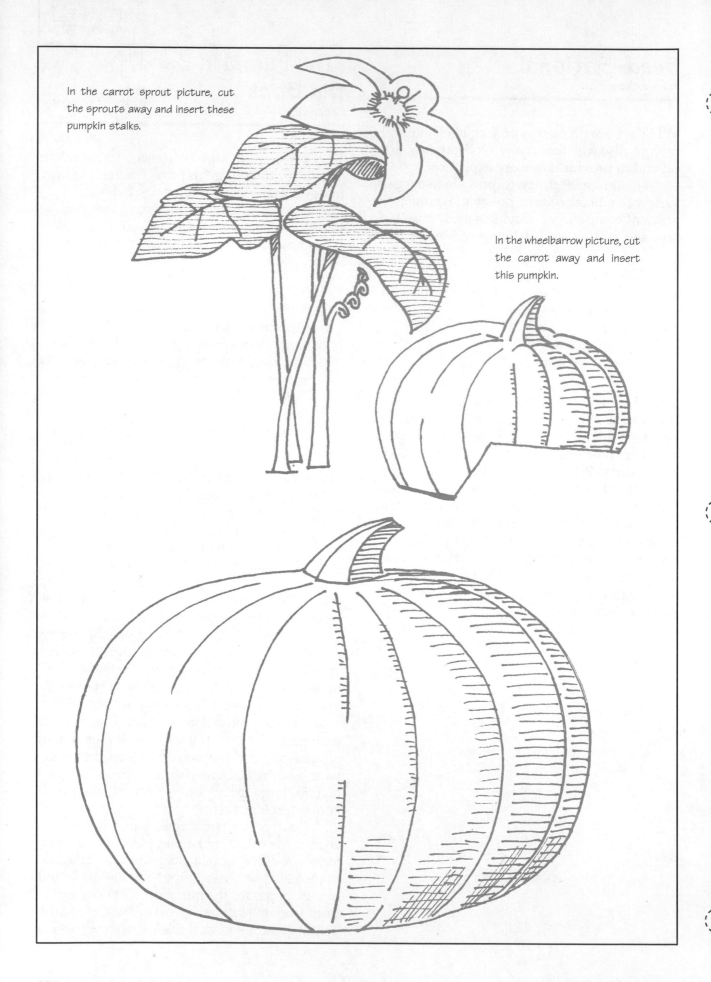

In the carrot sprout picture, cut the sprouts away and insert these pumpkin stalks.

In the wheelbarrow picture, cut the carrot away and insert this pumpkin.

of a carrot, cut the carrot out of the wheelbarrow and glue the pumpkin in its place. Glue these altered illustrations onto the blank pages you find in *The Carrot Seed* book, then glue these pages into your big book.

To make the big book more sturdy, have it laminated. Read the big book to the children. Ask: "Was the boy's father right when he said the seed wouldn't come up? Was his mother? His brother? Have you ever been told that you couldn't do something when you knew that you could? Have you ever been told that something wouldn't happen, and then found that it did?" After the discussion, put the big book on the floor with some cushions around it so the children can examine and read the book themselves.

Pumpkin Play (Part 1)
Science/Sensory

WHY we are doing this activity: to enable children to closely examine the seed pattern in a pumpkin; to provide a sensory experience; to develop speaking and listening skills.

WHAT we will need:
  Large pumpkin
  Tubs or sensory table
  Newspaper
  Butcher paper
  Marker
Preparation:
  Sharp knife

HOW we will do it: To prepare, pin a piece of butcher paper on the wall and at the top print: "How many seeds does our pumpkin have? We predict that it has___ seeds." Draw a picture of seeds above the word "seeds," and likewise, a picture of a pumpkin above that word. During an Attention Getter time, spread newspaper on a table and put the pumpkin on top. Gather the children around, and together, read/interpret

the poster heading. Cut the pumpkin open. Invite the children to reach in and touch the inside. Let them examine the seeds and guess how many there might be. Write down the children's guesses. Write their names next to their predictions. Put the pumpkin pieces in the tubs or sensory table and let the children explore them.

Pumpkin Play (Part 2)
Math/Small Group Project

WHY we are doing this activity: to practice rational counting above ten; to familiarize children with cup measurements; to facilitate group cooperation.

WHAT we will need:
  Pumpkin (from previous project)
  Chart (from previous project)
  Marker
  Three 1 cup measuring cups
  Piece of paper
  Pencil

HOW we will do it: After the previous activity, throw out all parts of the pumpkin except the seeds. Wash them thoroughly and let them dry. Use the same chart from that activity to write, after the estimates you recorded, the words: "We count _____ seeds in our pumpkin." "We got ___ cups of seeds from our pumpkin." Draw the same symbols for this sentence as you drew for the heading of the previous project.

When you are ready to begin the project, have the children wash their hands, and facilitate the exciting discussion about what happens if they sneeze or cough on food. (They will be eating these seeds in the following activity.)

Gather the children together, and read again the predictions of how many seeds are in the pumpkin. Together, read/interpret the new headings. Say: "Let's count all the seeds together, and find out exactly how many there are."

As you count, let the children take turns taking each seed that is counted and dropping it into the measuring cup. Every time you stop to give another child his or her turn, use the paper and pencil to write down the last number you counted so that you do not lose track.

After all the seeds are counted, write the number down in the blank space of the first sentence (or have one of the children do this). How close is the number to your predictions? Look at the measuring cups. How many cups of seeds are there? Write the number down in the blank space of the second sentence. Leave the chart up for several days.

Pumpkin Seed Treat
Sensory/Small Group Project

WHY we are doing this activity: to build self-esteem by enabling children to prepare their own snack; to provide a sensory experience.

If you do not have enough pumpkin seeds for all your children to eat from one pumpkin, buy additional pumpkins and prepare the seeds for this project.

WHAT we will need:
    Pumpkin seeds (from previous activity)
    Vegetable oil
    Cookie sheets
    Basting brushes
    Small container for oil
    Spoons
    Puppet

HOW we will do it: Put the cookie sheets, container of oil, and basting brushes on the activity table. Take out your puppet and talk together about the seeds. Take some seeds in your hand and have your puppet sneeze right on them. Then have a discussion along these lines: "Oh, Alexander! You sneezed right on my seeds!" To the children: "Do you think I want to eat these seeds no that they have Alexander's

germs all over them? Maybe Alexander has a cold. What will happen if I eat my seeds now that he's sneezed on them?" Have a discussion about covering mouths during sneezing around food, as well as keeping fingers out of eyes, ears, and nose. Be creative and use your puppet for this discussion, then have it say goodbye so that your hands are free for the project. (Maybe your puppet is sleepy, has to go take a nap, and will come back after the snack is prepared.)

Let your students take turns brushing the bottom of the cookie sheets with oil, and then using the spoons to scoop the seeds onto the sheets. Make sure the seeds are spread as evenly as possible.

Bake the seeds in a 250°F oven for one hour, so that they will dry out completely. Shake the pan periodically to reposition the seeds. Turn the oven up to 350°F for a few minutes until the seeds brown, and then take them out to cool. Salt the seeds if you like, and when they are cool, have a delicious snack.

Making Bird Feeders
Nature/Craft

WHY we are doing this project: to help children understand that birds use seeds for food and to enable children to observe birds more closely.

WHAT we will need:
    Half-gallon milk cartons
    Wild birdseed
    Twine
    Long sticks
Preparation:
    Scissors
    Exacto knife
    Skewer

HOW we will do it: Depending on how many milk cartons you wish to collect, you may choose to make one bird feeder as a group, or you may give each child the opportunity to make one.

To prepare a milk carton, use the Exacto knife and scissors to cut out two opposite sides of each milk carton. Leave a border of about 6.5 cm (2½") all around the cut-out. Use the skewer to poke a hole through the bottom borders. Make the holes big enough for the sticks to push through.

Invite the children to push the stick through. This will be the birds' perch. Let the children fill the bottom of the milk carton with wild birdseed. Help them take twine and string it through the top of the carton.

Tie the ends into a knot, and string the feeder outside your classroom or home window and watch your feathered visitors chow down. If the children each make their own, let them take their bird feeders home.

PART 2:
Beans

Bags of soup beans are available in supermarkets. These are perfect for bean activities, as they provide a nice variety of beans that are different shapes, sizes, and colors.

Beans Are Seeds
Science

WHY we are doing this experiment: to enable children to discover that a new bean plant will grow out of a bean; and that it is, therefore, a seed.

WHAT we will need:
    Uncooked dried kidney beans
    Small, clear plastic containers
    Paper towels (several rolls)
    Small containers of water
    Small basters
    Sticky labels

HOW we will do it: Place all materials on an activity table. During an Attention Getter time, show the children a variety of beans. Give them a chance to hold some in their hands, and notice their different sizes, shapes, and colors. Ask: "If you plant a bean, do you think anything will grow?" Encourage predictions. Prepare an experiment yourself by stuffing a container full of paper towels. Make sure one towel lays flat against the inner surface of the container. Use the baster and water to soak the towels, but make sure they do not absorb so much water that they collapse in a sodden heap at the bottom of the container. Take a kidney bean, and position it between a paper towel and the inside of the jar so that the bean is visible from the outside. Write your name on a sticky label and put it on your container. Ask the children if they see anything in the room that will help them conduct this experiment for themselves. You may need to help three- and young four-year-olds position their paper towels so that a bean will stay lodged between the paper towel and the inside of the container.

After a few days, what do the children notice? What does this tell them about whether or not a bean is a seed? Peel the skin off a kidney bean (this is easier to do with a bean that has soaked in water for a while). Pull apart the two halves and tell the children that this is called the *cotyledon* (rhymes with mottle Eden). Explain that this is what feeds a tiny new bean plant when it first begins to grow.

Bustin' Beans
Science

Note: A few days before you facilitate the following activity, put a few kidney beans into two containers. Fill one with water and leave the other one dry.

WHY we are doing this experiment: to enable children to observe that beans absorb water, and that this causes them to expand with such force that they will crack open a sealed plastic container.

WHAT we will need:
- Small, clear plastic containers with lids (such as empty peanut butter containers)
- Variety of dried beans
- Small pitchers of water
- Trays
- Newspaper
- Scoopers or spoons
- Sticky labels
- Pens

HOW we will do it: Spread newspaper over a work area and set all materials on an activity table. Bring out the beans you prepared ahead of time and ask the children to examine them. How are they different? (The beans in liquid absorbed the water, expanded, and split their skins.) Ask your students to compare the size of both sets of kidney beans. Tell the children that when something *expands*, it gets bigger.

Fill a container with beans, and cover them with water. Screw the lid on. Ask the children to predict what will happen if the beans and water are left in the sealed container. Ask your students if they see anything in the room that will help them conduct this science experiment for themselves. Show the children the sticky labels and pens for labeling their experiments and the trays on which they can set them.

After a few days, what happens? After the children have finished examining the cracked containers, invite them to pour out the beans and look at them carefully. Have any begun to sprout?

How Many Beans Are Buried?
Math/Sensory

WHY we are doing this activity: to practice rational counting and to provide a sensory experience. For kindergartners: to develop reading and writing skills and to facilitate subtraction.

WHAT we will need:
- Book: Briggs, Raymond, *Jim and the Beanstalk*
  - or: Biro, Val, *Jack and the Beanstalk*
- Tins or boxes with lids
- Potting soil (or sand or flour)
- Variety of beans
- Large strainers and sifters
- Tubs or sensory table
- Writing sheets (provided on page327; photocopy and enlarge for your use)
- Blank paper
- Pens
- Spoons

Note: If your soil cannot be sifted through your strainers, try sand. If neither of these pass through the mesh of your strainers, use flour instead.

HOW we will do it: Put potting soil and several beans in each tin or box. The number of beans you put in each container should be determined by how high your children are counting. Make sure the beans are well-mixed in the soil.

Put the boxes and tins in the tubs (or sensory table) with the sifters and strainers. On a table nearby, put blank paper, writing sheets, and pens.

During an Attention Getter time, read the children one of the beanstalk books. After you have had a chance to discuss the story, show the children one of the prepared boxes and pass it around. Ask them to guess what is inside. Open the container and dump the contents into a strainer. Ask: "Do you think there's only dirt in this box?" Start sifting and have the children help you count the number of beans you find.

Show the children a writing sheet, and together, read or interpret what it says. On blank paper or on a writing sheet, write down the number of beans you counted. If you work with kindergartners, have a child take away the number of beans the writing sheet specifies. Together, count how many are left and write that number down. Invite the children to explore the materials themselves.

Math kits: Gather some large food storage bags, spoons, and several small strainers.

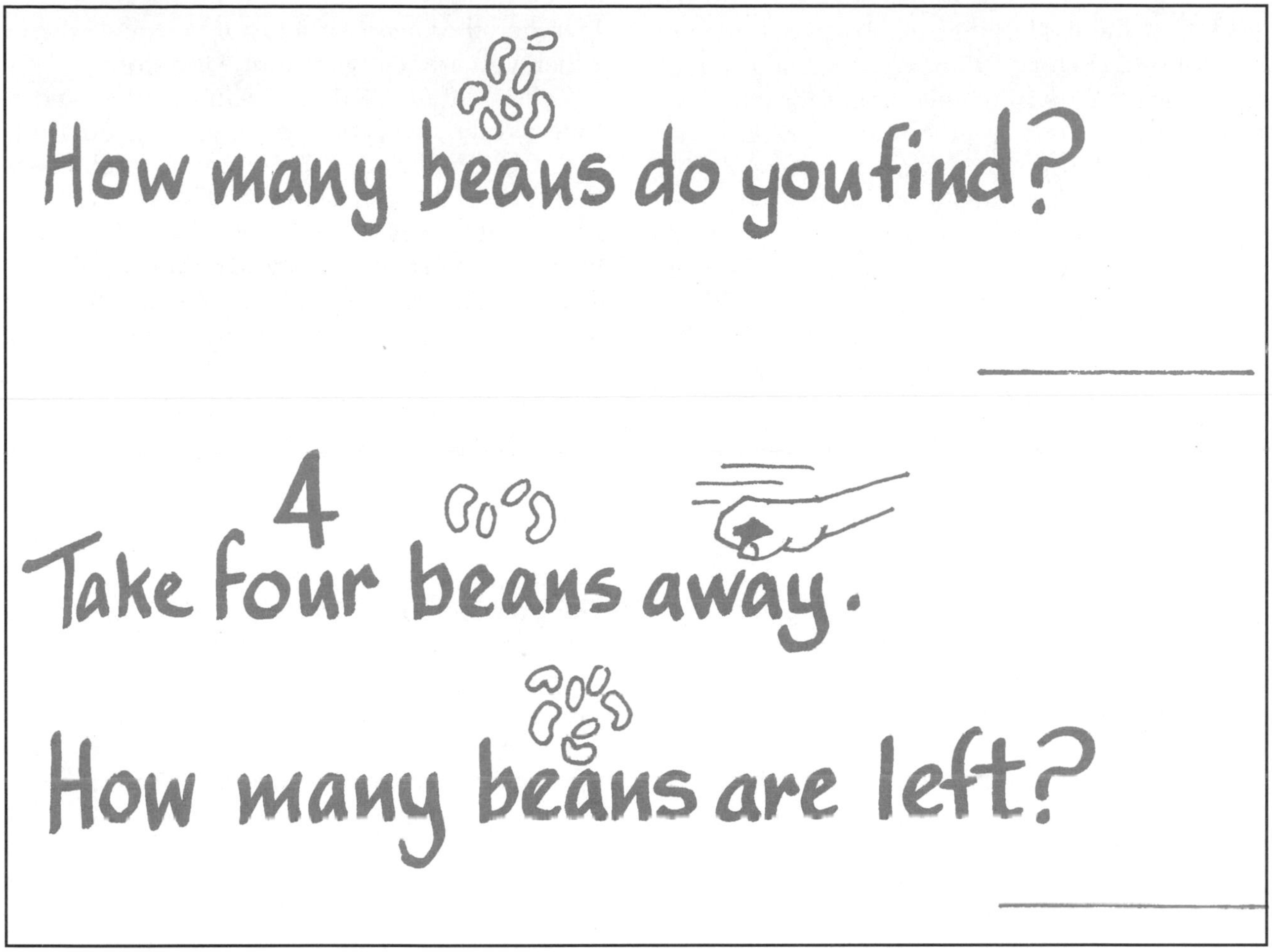

How many beans do you find?

_____

4
Take four beans away.

How many beans are left?

_____

Put one strainer and one spoon in each bag, along with a box or tin in which small beans and soil have been mixed. Put these math kits in a sensory table for the children to explore independently.

Making Bean Soup
Dramatic Play / Language / Anti-Bias

WHY we are doing this activity: to facilitate child-to-child interaction; to help children work out real-life conflicts and emotions through dramatic play; to develop speaking and listening skills; to foster confidence in expressing ideas; to create awareness of non-traditional families as well as non-traditional gender roles.

WHAT we will need:
> Children's kitchen furniture (including small table, chairs, and tablecloth)
> Soup pots and pans
> Large spoons
> Dishes
> Recipe books
> Chef hats
> Children's aprons
> Dried beans (kidney, navy, and lima beans)
> Three bowls
> Three scoopers or small cups
> Story: "MAKING BEAN SOUP" (provided)

Clean-up:
> Broom
> Dustpan
> Hand brush

HOW we will do it: Set up the play kitchen. The following story stimulates interest in this dramatic play area and encourages the children to use the beans in pretend cooking. Sort the beans into separate bowls and put a scooper or small cup in each one. Have a big pot and spoon available when you tell the story, and make sure every child gets a turn at either pouring the beans or stirring them. If you have a large group, add more bean varieties, bowls, and scoopers to stretch the story, long enough for everyone to get a turn.

"MAKING BEAN SOUP"

Once upon a time, there was a family who was very hungry, and the only thing to eat was beans, so they decided to make bean soup. There were two Dads in this family, and one of the Dads poured some water into their soup pot. [Pretend to pour water into your pot.] The other Dad said, "I think kidney beans would be good in this bean soup." So he poured in some kidney beans [have a child scoop some kidney beans into the pot] and began to stir them. [Pass the pot along so the next child can stir the beans.]

After the beans had cooked a while, the Dad gave everyone a taste of the bean soup. "Mmmmm," everyone said, licking their lips. But one of the children said, "Oooh, yuck. I won't try any bean soup." And no matter how good everyone told her it was, she wouldn't try any.

Well, the other Dad suddenly remembered that they had some navy beans in the cupboard, and he thought those would be good in the soup, so he poured some in [have a child scoop some navy beans into the pot] and then he stirred and stirred those beans into the soup. [Pass pot so the next child can stir.] After those beans had cooked a while, everyone tried the beany broth and said, "Mmmmmm," and licked their lips. But the same child again said, "Ooooh, yuck. I won't try any bean soup." And no matter how good everyone told her it was, she wouldn't try it.

Well, then the other Dad suddenly remembered that there were lima beans in the cupboard, and thought those would be good in the bean soup. [Repeat everything as above.

Include other bean varieties if you have them. When you are ready, continue the story.]

Well, after all those beans had cooked a long while, everyone tried that good, hot, beany broth and said, "Mmmmm," and licked their lips. But that same child was just opening her mouth to say: "Oooh yuck, I won't try any bean soup," when guess what happened? One of the Dads was holding a big spoonful of that bean soup where it was cooling so that he could eat it, when he tripped, and that beany broth spilled off his spoon, went flying through the air, and dropped right into the open mouth of that child! Well she was so surprised that she swallowed that soup before she knew it. She moved her tongue around her mouth. She said, "Hmmm," [move your mouth around and look like you are concentrating hard on what the soup tastes like] and she said, "Ooooh," and finally she said, "You know, that's pretty good. May I have some more, please?" And as it happened, the bean soup was ready to eat just then so they filled up their bowls, and the soup was so delicious that everyone had three big bowls of that hot beany broth and that's all there is to that story.

After you tell the story, put the pots, scoopers, and bowls of beans in the dramatic play kitchen and invite the children to participate. Beans do get on the floor, but they are easy to sweep up.

Sorting Beans
Math

WHY we are doing this project: to facilitate a sorting exercise for young children; to facilitate rational counting and subtraction for kindergartners.

WHAT we will need:
    Sorting trays
    Mixed beans
Kindergartners:
    Writing sheets (provided on page 329;
        photocopy and enlarge for your use)

Sorting the beans.

Use each blank space to draw or glue each kind of bean, and to write the name of it.

Sample:
There are _____ kidney beans.

There are _____.

There are _____.

There are _____.

There are _____.

When I count all the beans together,

I count _____ _____.

When I take away _____ beans,

there are _____ left.

Blank paper
Pens
Yogurt containers with tight-fitting lids
(the kind with bendable plastic lids
seal more tightly)

HOW we will do it: If you work with three-
and young four-year-olds, tell them the nail sorting story provided in the Woodworks unit, but
substitute beans for nails. This reminds children
of what sorting trays are for and how they can be
used, and stimulates interest in the project.

If you work with kindergartners, make
several copies of the writing sheet. You can
either draw a picture of each kind of bean before
you make the copies, or glue each kind of bean
onto each sheet. If you draw pictures, choose
beans that are very distinct in shape and size, so
that they will be easily recognizable on the writing sheets (e.g., lima, kidney, black-eyed pea,
black bean. These are fairly easy to represent
with black and white line drawings). Put a mixture of beans in each yogurt cup, making sure
that the total number is not higher than your
children can count, and fasten the lids on. Put
these bean containers on an activity table beside
the blank paper, writing sheets, and pens.

During an Attention Getter time, spill the
contents of one container out on the floor, and
help them, as a group, sort them. Show the children the writing sheet and help them read or
interpret each part. Together, count each kind
of bean and on a blank piece of paper or writing sheet, print the number of each kind of bean
counted. Together, read the subtraction problem
on a writing sheet. Take away that number of
beans, count the rest, and write down the number. As a group, count the total number of beans
and write that number down. Encourage exploration of the materials on the activity table.

Seed Collage
Art/Fine Motor

WHY we are doing this project: to facilitate
creative expression using beans and other
seeds; to develop fine motor skills.

WHAT we will need:
Beans (all kinds)
Seeds (all kinds)
Construction paper
Glue
Small containers for glue
Small containers for beans and seeds
Glue brushes
Newspaper

HOW we will do it: Spread newspaper out on
an activity table, and put the glue in the containers. Put the beans and other seeds in the
rest of the containers and arrange all materials
so that children will have easy access to them.
Nothing else is needed; the children will know
what to do!

Bean Bag Toss (Part 1)
Gross Motor

WHY we are doing this activity: to develop
hand-eye coordination; to develop the large
muscle group.

WHAT we will need:
Variety of beans
Old socks
Small Ziplock freezer bags
Glue
Sewing kit
Large tubs
Masking tape

The Polaroid Education Program in association with

The National Parks and Conservation Association

Presents

imagine A Green Tomorrow
A Visual Learning Environmental Project Guide

How do you begin when you want to make a change? Whether you want to preserve a small piece of natural beauty, stop the fouling of a vital waterway or revive a desolate vacant lot, you begin with a vision. Visions, in your mind's eye, are filled with images. The images we create, with tools like Polaroid instant photography, can fuel our imagination. The images of our imagination can lead us to take action, moving us toward the realization of our vision.

Imagine A Green Tomorrow

is a project guide for students and teachers.
It is filled with ways to use the techniques
of visual learning: exploring, recording,
expressing, communicating, motivating,
and imagining. The projects provided in the
Guide link students to national, state, and
local parks, and historic sites. They are designed to help students link vision with action,
to make a difference in their communities.

Imagine A Green Tomorrow:

A Visual Learning Environmental Project Guide

Developed and written by
Tom Crockett and Phillip Seymour

Polaroid photography by
Tom Crockett and Phillip Seymour

Imagine The Future

Aim: Photography is used to encourage students to consider what the environment will be like in the future. Students are challenged to analyze both their present and future environments to understand the impacts of their actions and choices. They are also challenged to define "environment."

Activity: Each student takes two photographs which represent the following:

1. What would the *worst* environment of the future look like?

2. What would the *best* environment of the future look like?

Use these photos as a springboard for discussion. Each of the students might ask "<u>How</u> can I help make the best environment photo come true?" Have the students keep records of their photographs and accompanying comments. As they proceed throughout the activities encourage them to go back to their records for comparisons. Record projected and actual goals as well.

Product/Action: Some of the answers to the "how" question will be discovered in the projects described in this booklet. By using visual images to explore, record, express, communicate, motivate and imagine, students can work for a better, greener tomorrow.

Materials: Polaroid camera, 600 HighDefinition Film, booklet for record keeping.

An introductory Activity

Environmental Study Project

Aim: The camera is used as a tool to help students focus their attention by encouraging active observation. Students learn about their environment and the relationships which form an ecosystem, while learning research and observation skills.

Activity: Select a specific ecological site to study. An ecological site could be a hillside, tidal pool, pond, grass plain or even an overgrown vacant inner city lot. Parks often provide good sites for study. Park service personnel can provide valuable information and ensure that important features are not overlooked on a visit. Research and photograph the various elements of the site, paying specific attention to the interrelationships found. Photograph overall views as well as details. Consider photographing plants, insects, animals, landforms and manmade structures.

Product/Action: The final product could take the form of a report with accompanying photographs. This report could be made for display in the school or in area businesses to spread awareness to local residents. It can also serve as a catalyst for community activity around and support for the ecosystem.

Materials: Polaroid camera, 600 HighDefinition Film, notebooks and pens, display materials, such as large oaktag sheets, easels, folding display boards, etc.

i can explore my world.

Aim: Older students use photography to teach younger students about the environment. In this manner, students are encouraged to share their acquired knowledge and increase environmental consciousness.

Activity: Select a park in your area and contact the park ranger or supervisor. Ask the ranger to help you and your students mark off or select an area as large or as small as you choose. This may be done by selecting existing boundary features, such as streams, ponds, walls or fences, or by cordoning off an area with stakes and twine. Students should document with photographs each species of plant or animal they find. Back in the classroom, research the findings; brief captions or descriptive text should accompany each photograph. Many parks have nature centers or visitor stations which can be excellent resources for identifying flora and fauna.

Product/Action: The active component of this project starts with the use of clear plastic sleeves to hold photos and text. Attach the plastic sleeves to wooden stakes to create photo markers for a nature walk. Take younger children on the nature walk, with older students acting as their guides. Reach out further to the community towards senior citizen centers, business groups, or clubs.

Materials: Polaroid camera, 00 HighDefinition Film, twine, stakes, clear plastic sleeves to protect photographs.

i can explore my world.

Economic Interdependence Project

Aim: Cameras and images help students explore the relationship between government, economics, and the environment. Students learn responsibility for their environment and the various means for affecting its change.

Activity: Research and photograph businesses in the community. Examine the relationships between businesses and the environment. Look hard for direct or indirect impacts that various businesses have on the environment. Discuss the kinds of businesses that might be supported or affected by the creation of a large national park or a small local park.

Product/Action: Create a bulletin board to chart or graph businesses based on their economic importance to the community, their necessity, the amount of pollution or waste they generate. Discuss how political decisions which affect the environment are made. What actions can mitigate change when findings indicate a negative business influence on the environment? Is it appropriate to confront a polluter directly or to identify the proper agency whose responsibility it is to correct this problem? What do students believe their roles and responsibilities include?

Materials: Polaroid camera, 600 HighDefinition Film, chart paper, pencils or markers

i can explore my world.

Aim: Using cameras in one of their traditional roles, as tools for documenting change, students learn responsibility for preserving the important public features that help define their community. Simultaneously, they gain historical perspective, experience their own power as agents of change, acquire charting skills, and learn how to share information with others.

Activity: Select a monument, historical site, or a portion of a park that is in need of care and attention. Work with park personnel and/or the responsible person from local government to uncover the history of the community treasure you selected and the problems it faces. These problems could include graffiti, lack of general maintenance, erosion, or garbage pollution. Design an appropriate strategy to provide both immediate and long term solutions to the problems. Once problems and strategies for solving them have been determined, create "before" photographs. These images establish a benchmark against which progress can be gauged.

Product/Action: Maintain a timeline in the classroom using photo-markers to show progress in achieving the plan. The photographs will also motivate students to continue the work. Explore the possibility of displaying the timeline in local business establishments. Create a guide for tours of your chosen treasure. Include research findings, before and after pictures, and copies of historical photographs to draw attention to interesting features. Consider creating tour booklets that can be photocopied and distributed as handouts at the site.

Materials: Polaroid camera, 600 HighDefinition Film, access to a photocopy machine, copy and writing paper, oaktag, poster board, markers and other writing implements.

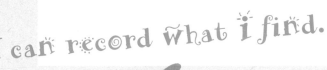

i can record what i find.

Living History Project

Aim: Photography is used to add images to the voices of community members recollecting earlier times in a structured interview activity. Students are encouraged to explore the history of their community with those who have experienced that history first hand.

Activity: In teams, or as a class, students should create a list of interview questions about what their city or town used to be like. If you are focusing on architectural or historic preservation, include questions about growth, expansion, new construction, architectural styles, lifestyles, etc. If you are focusing on environmental protection, include questions about land use, water and air quality, etc. Use the public library as a resource for research regarding the history of the community, a specific building, or park. After compiling their questions, ask students to interview older members of the community to learn about the history of their village, town, or city.

Product/Action: Record the interviews and stories on audio tape and photograph the subjects being interviewed. Photograph specific areas or buildings discussed during interviews. Create tape archives with photographs so that other students might learn about their community. Share this audio/visual archive with others in your city, town, or village.

Materials: Polaroid camera, 600 HighDefinition Film, audio tape recorder, audio tape.

i can record what i find.

Waterways Project

Aim: Imagery can be an important element in expressing an opinion effectively. Photographs are used to document the many ways in which water is made available to us and is used.

Activity: Trace the water which comes out of a tap or drinking fountain as far back as possible to a source. Follow its course after it leaves your classroom (through a drain, down a toilet, out by evaporation, etc.). Collect photographs of every distinct stage water goes through or mode of transportation used. If some stages cannot be captured photographically, take photos which symbolize those stages (for example: pipes of all sizes, water holding tanks, water treatment or sewage processing plants, lakes, rivers, streams, springs, mountain runoff, snow melt, rain, etc.)

Product/Action: Use the photographs to create picture books or, for younger children, large display boards which explain where water comes from and where it goes after we use it. Discuss what role parks and designated conservation areas have in protecting our water supply. Encourage student authors to express their own points of view about conservation and care of our water supply. How do their actions affect our waterways, positively or negatively? Display the books or boards in various parts of the school or in the windows of local banks and shops.

Materials: Polaroid camera, 600 HighDefinition Film, paper, cardboard, glue sticks.

i can express my feelings.

Pollution Point Of View Project

Aim: Visual imagery can reinforce a student's association and identification with the environment. Students use imagery directly to convey attitude and point of view.

Activity: When visiting a park, especially one with a nature center, have students select a plant or animal on which to focus their interest. Write stories about the animals or plants they chose and why they appreciate the park. How are they part of the park? Another approach might be to write stories about types of pollution from the point of view of fish, birds, insects, animals or plants. Illustrate the stories with photographs which also show point of view. Encourage students to be creative in their search for effective point of view photographs. What would bother a bird? What would a fish's view look like?

Product/Action: Display the stories and photographs on a bulletin board. Be creative — design the boards to look like the habitat in which the subjects live.

Materials: Polaroid camera, 600 HighDefinition Film, paper, oaktag, writing implements.

i can express my feelings.

Campsite Camouflage Project

Aim: Help students identify and discuss the impact of visitors on parks or campsites. Gain understanding about the complexity of restoration and the value of low impact planning or use. Communication skills are learned and employed for environmental awareness.

Activity: At a park or wilderness preserve identify areas or damages which show the impact of campers or excessive use. Work to make the site look as though no one had ever camped there or to minimize the physical evidence of use. This can be done by dismantling unofficial fire rings, picking up trash, rescattering cleared debris and brush, raking away footprints with downed branches, and so on. Discuss the type and level of activity necessary to restore the area. Can it ever be completely restored? How can people enjoy these areas and minimize damage?

Product/Action: Document this process with before and after pictures. Create a display for installation at the entrances to the park to help educate other campers or visitors. Document positive behaviors that illustrate low impact use of the area.

Materials: Polaroid camera, 600 HighDefinition Film, poster board, glue sticks, writing implements.

i can express my feelings.

Enviro-links Project

Aim: Photographs are tools for clearer communication and for understanding the relationship of communities to one another. Students develop geographical perspective through visual and written communication with other students.

Activity: Form photo pen pal links with schools that share environmental concerns. Perhaps other schools are located along a coast or waterway or border an urban or national park. Exchange students' letters and photographs depicting common environmental concerns. Display a map in the classroom. Photographs of landmarks from the community could serve as visual cues for others who see the map. Capture environmental concerns photographically, keeping some pictures for your map and trading other pictures with photo pen pals. Collectively, these photographs help form a geographical understanding of the area being viewed and appreciation for the concerns of those who live within the area.

Product/Action: Use photographs as a focal point for developing a strategy to address shared concerns. Make photocopies of photographs to use in joint proposals to local governments with suggested solutions to environmental problems.

Materials: Polaroid camera, 600 HighDefinition Film, research data on government agencies, paper, writing implements.

i can communicate what i feel to others.

Endangered Views Project

Aim: Students "adopt" a view site and explore the concepts of restoration and the means available to communities to begin a restoration activity.

Activity: Select an historic building, a park, a natural site that is in danger of being lost or destroyed. Document the site with photographs.

Product/Action: Determine whether the site is worth preserving. How would student citizens go about restoring historical and/or public sites? What can local government do? What agencies do they need to target? How could they go about generating public awareness and support? Students should work out their entire strategy. Create photo flyers as part of the preservation campaign; use images and text to describe how it would look or feel if the site were lost. Use sketched images of what a restored site would look like. Include these sketches in the flyers. Challenge students to plan interviews with local government officials. Schedule those interviews and file reports on the results. How else can students be proactive?

i can communicate what i feel to others.

Don't forget to look for community success stories. Celebrate efforts that have succeeded in preserving an irreplaceable view, park, or historical site as a counterpoint to the work that remains to be done.

Materials: Polaroid camera, 600 HighDefinition film, paper, drawing tools.

Special Places Photo Exhibit Project

Aim: What we value may differ from those things that are important to people from other cultural backgrounds. Photographs communicate and share the things we value with others. Students are asked to identify and share their emotions, thoughts and ideas.

Activity: American Indians and people from other cultures believe some spaces or sites are special and sacred. Research famous sacred sites like Stonehenge, Anasazi ruins, Cahokia, Wounded Knee, Mesa Verde. Discuss the qualities that might define a sacred site for your students. Many parks commemorate places that were special or sacred to early inhabitants. Do you have any parks with sacred sites in them in your area? Ask students to find and photograph their special space, the place where they feel secure and energized. What makes this place so special? What do they feel when they visit this place? How do they feel?

Product/Action: Install a photo exhibit to call attention to the importance of our special places. Create a class book of special place photos. Write poems or stories to go with the photo. Will students share their feelings about these space

Materials: Polaroid camera, 600 HighDefinition Film, paper, and writing implement

i can communicate what
i feel to others.

Planting Project

Aim: Photographs serve to motivate change. Students learn to take action on environmental concerns.

Activity: Organize a tree or shrub planting campaign. Contact local park rangers or officials who can help identify sites which might be enhanced by the planting of trees, shrubs, or flowers. Small community parks can often benefit greatly from community volunteer effort. Find government agencies that might help you in this project. Make a case for planting based on aesthetics, environmental health, or erosion control. Discuss the benefits of these efforts to the community and to the volunteers. What would the world look like without plants or flowers?

Product/Action: Encourage students to keep a personal commitment journal and record the planting they have done with photographs and written documentation. Lead and motivate others by setting an example.

Materials: Polaroid camera, 600 HighDefinition Film, blank books, scrapbooks or journals.

i can motivate for change.

Patterns Of Nature Mural Project

Aim: Through the use of instant photography, isolated details are employed in the construction of large scale compositions. Environmental themes encourage aesthetic and artistic growth and understanding.

Activity: Photograph several solitary elements in natural or manmade settings that emphasize color, pattern, shape, and so on.

Product/Action: Create a photographic mural using various elements found in nature: interesting patterns, colors, textures, shapes, and forms. Have students work collaboratively to show how a new vision can emerge from smaller, singular pieces. Allow the mural to grow out of photographs taken during the year for other classroom purposes. Designate a different pattern artist on a regular basis to rearrange the mural photos to create new patterns or images.

Materials: Polaroid camera, 600 HighDefinition Film, glue sticks.

i can imagine a green tomorrow.

Flower Painting Project

Aim: Photographs and art supplies are employed to help communicate a vision of change. This activity encourages artistic expression through environmental awareness.

Activity: Plan a wildflower garden by photographing a site that could be enhanced by a splash of natural color. Attach the photo to a larger sheet of paper and draw, paint or color in the flowers as they will look when they bloom. Expand the image off the photograph and onto the page. Experiment with different materials such as fabric paints, sequins, colored glues, or even natural materials such as berries or dried flowers in a collage over the photo.

Product/Action: If student have a chance to actually create a wildflowe garden, document it with photographs and have an art exhibit comparing their original visions to the garden itself.

Materials: Polaroid camera, 600 HighDefinition Film, art supplies, fabri paints, sequins, permanent markers.

i can imagine a green tomorrow.

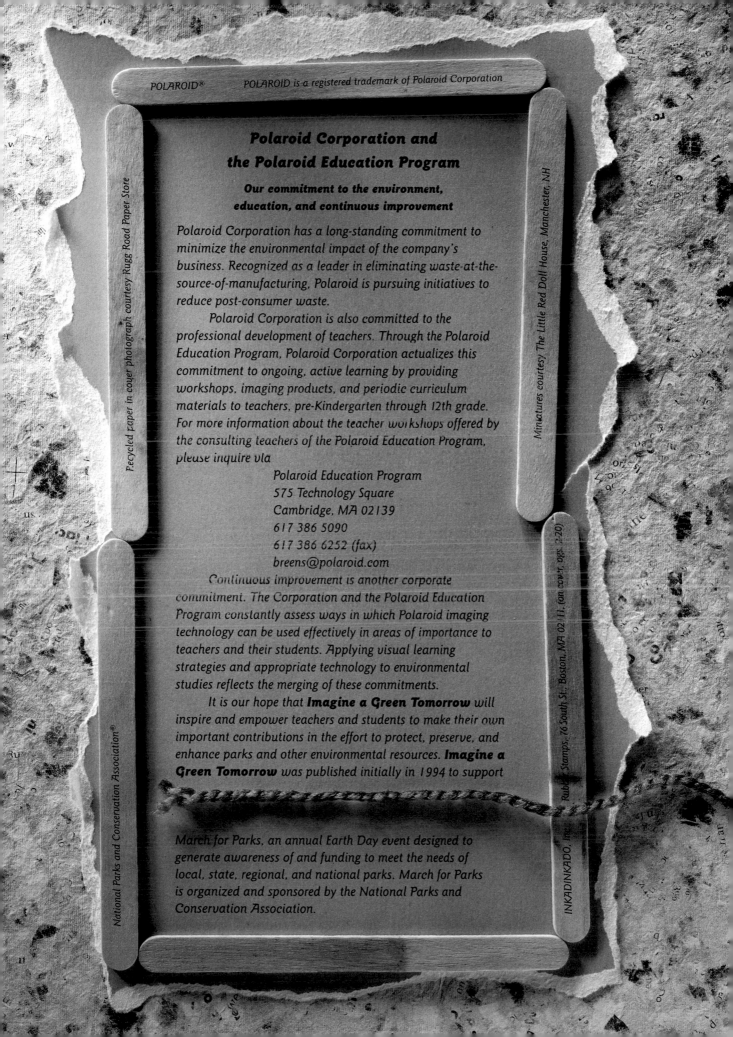

POLAROID®   POLAROID is a registered trademark of Polaroid Corporation

Polaroid Corporation and the Polaroid Education Program

Our commitment to the environment, education, and continuous improvement

Polaroid Corporation has a long-standing commitment to minimize the environmental impact of the company's business. Recognized as a leader in eliminating waste-at-the-source-of-manufacturing, Polaroid is pursuing initiatives to reduce post-consumer waste.

Polaroid Corporation is also committed to the professional development of teachers. Through the Polaroid Education Program, Polaroid Corporation actualizes this commitment to ongoing, active learning by providing workshops, imaging products, and periodic curriculum materials to teachers, pre-Kindergarten through 12th grade. For more information about the teacher workshops offered by the consulting teachers of the Polaroid Education Program, please inquire via

Polaroid Education Program
575 Technology Square
Cambridge, MA 02139
617 386 5090
617 386 6252 (fax)
breens@polaroid.com

Continuous improvement is another corporate commitment. The Corporation and the Polaroid Education Program constantly assess ways in which Polaroid imaging technology can be used effectively in areas of importance to teachers and their students. Applying visual learning strategies and appropriate technology to environmental studies reflects the merging of these commitments.

It is our hope that **Imagine a Green Tomorrow** will inspire and empower teachers and students to make their own important contributions in the effort to protect, preserve, and enhance parks and other environmental resources. **Imagine a Green Tomorrow** was published initially in 1994 to support

March for Parks, an annual Earth Day event designed to generate awareness of and funding to meet the needs of local, state, regional, and national parks. March for Parks is organized and sponsored by the National Parks and Conservation Association.

Recycled paper in cover photograph courtesy Rugg Road Paper Store

Miniatures courtesy The Little Red Doll House, Manchester, NH

National Parks and Conservation Association®

Rubber Stamps, 76 South St., Boston, MA 02111, (on cover, pgs. 2-20) INKADINKADO, Inc.

Polaroid
Education
Program

NATIONAL PARKS AND CONSERVATION ASSOCIATION

Est. 1919

Polaroid Education Program
575 Technology Square, Cambridge, MA 02139
Telephone (617) 386-5090

HOW we will do it: To make one bean bag, pour beans into the bottom of an old sock, and cut it off at the point which will make the bean bag the size you desire. Sew the sock ends together.

It is nice to make transparent bean bags out of Ziplock bags to provide some variety. Fill the Ziplock bags about three-quarters full, squeeze glue along the zippered seams, seal, and let dry.

To begin the activity, put masking tape on the floor to indicate where the children should stand. Place the bean bags near this line. Set the open tubs some distance away, depending on the age and gross motor capabilities of your children. Encourage the children to toss the bags into the tubs, and sincerely praise all efforts.

Bean Bag Toss (Part 2)
Music/Movement

WHY we are doing this project: to develop listening skills; to develop hand-eye coordination; to develop an appreciation for music.

WHAT we will need:
Masking tape
Bean bags (from Part 1)

Music (on a tape recorder or record player)
Beans
Fabric or Ziplock sandwich bags

HOW we will do it: Put "X"s of masking tape on the floor in the shape of a circle, at about three-foot intervals. Make one for each child. Ask everyone to sit on an "X" and to pretend that each "X" is a little island surrounded by water. (Having specific spots to sit on ensures that the children are a distance away from each other, and must throw the bean bag instead of handing or pushing it.) Take a bean bag, and tell the children that when they hear the music, they are going to pretend the bean bag is very, very hot. When you say this, pretend the bean bag you are holding is burning your hands. Then tell the children that when the music stops, they are going to pretend that the bean bag turns to ice and freezes the person holding it into ice.

Put the music on and toss the bean bag to the child next to you. When the music stops, can the person holding it remember to freeze like ice? When the music is on, can children throw the bag quickly because it is too hot to hold? After a while, let the bean bag go around the circle without stopping the music. How quickly does the bean bag make one complete round? Can you play the game with more than one bean bag?

Literature

Symbol Key: *Multicultural
             +Minimal diversity
             No symbol: no diversity or no people

Berenstain, S., & Berenstain, J. (1990). *The Berenstain bears and the prize pumpkin*. New York: Random House. (This story is a little long for three- and young four-year-olds.)

Biro, V. (1989). *Jack and the beanstalk*. New York: Oxford University Press.

Branley, F. M. (1988). *The sun: Our nearest star*. New York: Thomas Y. Crowell. (Excellent photographs of a bean-growing experiment.)

Briggs, R. (1970). *Jim and the beanstalk*. New York: Coward-McCann.

Burhe-Wiener, Kimberly. (1992). *The maybe garden*. Hillsboro, OR: Beyond Words.

Gibbons, G. (1991). *From seed to plant*. New York: Holiday House.+

Jennings, T. (1981). *Seeds and seedlings*. Chicago: Children's Press. (This book has some excellent pictures that you can look at and discuss with children.)

Titherington, J. (1986). *Pumpkin pumpkin*. New York: Greenwillow Books.

Wilkes, A. (1992). *My first garden book*. New York: Alfred A. Knopf.

Extenders

Science: Try growing seeds and beans in a variety of materials: sand, soil, paper towels, Styrofoam, water. Which ones support the most growth?

Cooking: Find a favorite bean soup recipe and make it with the children. Make sure your students have a chance to compare raw beans with cooked ones. How does heat change the beans?

Nature/Gross Motor: Go for a nature walk to collect seeds. Give the children paper bags and encourage them to look for seeds to put into their bags. When you get back to home or school, have a show-and-tell of seeds.

Sensory: Put beans, wild birdseed, and/or unpopped corn kernels in tubs or a sensory table with scoopers, bowls, containers, and funnels.

OUTER SPACE

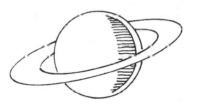

Facilitating a unit on outer space is a challenge, because it is hard to keep activities hands-on and child-initiated when the unit focuses on something—the solar system—that children cannot touch, visit, see, or experience directly. This unit, like the others, is designed to be as hands-on as possible, and I have to say my students have always enjoyed it tremendously.

One thing that helps immensely is to create a "space environment" in your home or classroom, as much as is feasible. Before you begin the unit, put space posters up on your walls and play "spacey" music. Be creative!

Another important aspect of this unit is to help children feel that everyone has an equal opportunity to choose a career as an astronaut or in space technology. This can be very difficult to do since there are few photographs available of astronauts and space scientists who are not white men. For this reason, I have included a clip art section in this book which provides pictures you can use to enlarge by photocopier and post on your walls to create a multicultural, anti-bias environment for this unit. Cut out diverse faces from magazines to glue into the astronaut helmets. Another way you can combat societal bias during your pretend spaceship journeys is to give every child a turn as Mission Leader.

Attention Getter: See the list of books on outer space at the end of this unit, and check out a few of them, or others, from the library. Try to find books with actual photographs of outer space (or at least very realistic drawings). Leaf through the books with the children, and discuss what you see. Identify planets, stars, the moon, planet Earth, satellites, and so forth. Ask the children to guess what you will be talking about and working with over the next few days.

NASA Outer Space Kits
Science/Multicultural/Anti-Bias

WHY we are doing this project: to obtain excellent posters, pictures, booklets, and information about outer space and space technology; to help all children feel that a career in space science is open to them.

WHAT we will need:
    This address:
    NASA Publications
    250 E Street, Southwest
    Washington, DC 20024
    1-202-358-1110

HOW we will do it: To make sure you get your NASA kit in time, write or call about one month before facilitating the unit. Be sure to specify that you want the kit designed for the lowest grades (preschool to kindergarten).

I do not know how frequently NASA develops new materials or changes the contents of the kit, but you may want to specifically request the materials below.

The "NASA Superstars of Science" poster portrays and describes the work of scientists from diverse races and backgrounds. Another wonderful poster (although I could do without the Native girl's headband) is titled, "There is a new world for all of us," and shows children of different races in astronaut suits, floating above the earth. Also excellent is a poster called "Spacesuit," which names and describes the function of every component of a space suit. (A booklet is available which elaborates on this.) "Rockets" and "Aboard the Space Shuttle" were also included in the kit I received, as well as some fantastic 20 cm x 25 cm (8" x 10") photographs of planets, rockets, and astronauts. An "Information Summaries Source List" provides addresses for other space-related organizations. The kit also included books with activities, although many of these are not developmentally appropriate for young children. However, if you need some excellent posters for the walls while you do this unit, as well as some good information, then order a kit. Our tax dollars at work—the kit is free!

Earth Is Not Alone
Science/Small Group Activity

WHY we are doing this project: to familiarize children with the planets; to help them remember the planets' names; to help them understand the size of Earth in relation to the other planets; to familiarize children with ordinal numbers; to help them remember that our sun and the nine planets which revolve around it comprise the solar system.

WHAT we will need:
    Poster of the solar system
    Poem: "THE PLANET POEM"

"THE PLANET POEM
Mercury's closest to the sun,
Pluto is the farthest one.
From the sun, just where is Earth?
When you count them, it is third.

HOW we will do it: In poster shops, it is usually easy to find some excellent charts that show the planets of the solar system. Try to find one that uses bold colors, aims for realism in terms of the colors of the planets, and that, ideally, has fairly large type to identify each one. There are two layouts: one shows the planets in a line from the sun. This is the kind you need for this activity so that the children can clearly see that Earth is third closest to the sun. However, I also recommend that you buy a poster that shows the planets around the sun, so the children understand that this is how the planets are positioned, and are not in a straight line.

Pin up the poster on the wall and discuss it during an Attention Getter time. Let the children know that, together, the sun and nine planets are called the *solar system*. *Sol* is the Latin word for sun. Explain that even though the poster makes the planets look very close together, they are actually millions and millions of miles apart. From the sun, the planets are: Mercury, Venus, Earth, Mars, (Asteroids,) Jupiter, Saturn, Uranus, Neptune, and Pluto. Say the above rhyme several times until the children know the words. Together, count the planets on the poster, starting with Mercury, which is closest to the sun. Which one is third? Compare its size to the other planets. What do the children notice about whether it is the biggest? What do they notice about whether it is the smallest? Use the poster as a backdrop for the following activities.

Making Space Helmets
Art/Fine Motor

WHY we are doing this project: to prepare for the dramatic play activity to follow; to facilitate creative expression; to stimulate interest in the unit.

WHAT we will need:
Large, brown paper grocery bags
Aquarium tubing (3 mm-6 mm [⅛"-¼"] in diameter)
Crayons
Markers
Poster (used in previous activity)
Picture of astronauts (provided on page 336; photocopy and enlarge for your use)
Preparation:
Scissors
Cardboard
Glue
Exacto knife
Wooden cutting board

HOW we will do it: To prepare, cut your grocery bags down so that children can wear them on their heads. Cut a window out of each one.

In the following activity, the children will make "air packs," which will then connect to the space helmets with aquarium tubing. You will need to create a stiff opening in each helmet into which the tubing can be inserted. To do this, cut out cardboard squares about 7.5 cm x 7.5 cm (3" x 3"). Glue one cardboard square securely to each helmet, at the front and near the bottom.

After the glue has dried, lay one of the bags down on the wooden cutting board, with the cardboard square facing out.

In the center of the square, from the inside of the paper bag, cut a cross (+) in the center, leaving a wide margin of cardboard around the cross. Use an Exacto knife or razor blade to do this. When the tubing is inserted later, the cross will hold it securely in place. Prepare enough helmets for all the children, as well as one sample for yourself.

During an Attention Getter time, tell the children that they are going to take a trip to outer space, and that they will have to start preparing for it. Point to the poster of the planets, and say, "Do you think these planets have air around them, like the air we breathe?" Explain that the other planets have gases around them that human beings cannot breathe. Show the children the picture in the text of the astronauts, and notice how they are all wearing space helmets. Explain that the hel-

Photocopy these pictures on a photocopier

mets protect the astronauts from breathing harmful gases.

Put your own "space helmet" on, and tell the children that you made it, and that, when you wear it, you pretend that the window is covered with plastic, like astronauts' real helmets. Set out the prepared bags, crayons, and markers and invite the children to decorate their own space helmets.

Making Life–Support Systems
Art/Fine Motor

WHY we are doing this activity: to stimulate interest in the unit; to develop self-esteem and a sense of autonomy by enabling children to

make their own props for dramatic play; to prepare children for the Traveling in Outer Space activity.

WHAT we will need:
Plastic gallon jugs (two for each child)
Aquarium tubing (from previous activity)
Control panel illustrations (provided on page 337, photocopy and enlarge for your use)
Construction paper
Glue
Small containers for glue
Glue brushes
Crayons
Masking tape
Children's scissors
Preparation:
Scissors
Rope (several pieces, 1'8" each)
Duct tape

HOW we will do it: To prepare one "life-support system," glue two gallon jugs together. The handles should extend out to the left and right of the pair. Even after the glue dries, it is easy to pull the jugs apart again. Wind duct tape around the two containers to attach them more securely.

Loop a separate length of rope through each handle, and tie the ends together. The children will put their arms through the loops so that the air packs hang on their backs like backpacks.

Children enjoy having the life-support systems as props for this unit; it really adds a dimension to the dramatic play, and to the Traveling in Outer Space activity below. However, there is quite a bit of preparation involved. One alternative is to prepare three or four packs and have the children decorate them as a group project. Let the children take turns using them during dramatic play and omit them from the following activity. If you do want all the children to have the opportunity to make their own, enlist friends, family, or parents to help you with the preparation.

On the activity table, set out the glue, glue brushes, prepared air packs, the copies of air control panels, construction paper, children's scissors, and crayons.

During an Attention Getter time, point to the life-support system on the NASA poster of an astronaut's equipment. Ask the children what they think it is for. Discuss with the children the other parts of an astronaut's life-support system. Connect a sample helmet and life-support system with the aquarium tubing and put them on. Explain to your students that if you are going to explore space, you will need them both. Ask them if they see anything in the room that they can use to make their own life-support systems. Encourage them to be creative with the markers and crayons. Help them to secure one end of the tubing to the jugs with masking tape and to poke the other end through the cross in their space helmets.

Making Space Glasses
Art/Crafts

WHY we are doing this activity: to facilitate artistic expression; to develop fine motor skills; to help children understand that the sun is so bright it can damage our eyes (therefore, we must never look at it directly).

WHAT we will need:
Cardboard
Pattern for space glasses (provided on page 339; photocopy and enlarge for your use)
Acetate papers (different colors)
Thick rubber bands
Glue
Small containers for glue
Glue brushes
Space stickers
Crayons
Markers
Aluminum foil scraps

Preparation:
Scissors and/or Exacto knife
Stapler

HOW we will do it: Use the pattern provided to cut the frames for space glasses out of cardboard. Ask one of the children to model for you, so that you can determine whether you need to make the frames bigger or smaller. You will be stapling the ends of cut rubber bands to the sides of the glasses, so keep in mind that the elastic must stretch a little to secure the glasses on each child's head.

Use the scissors and/or Exacto knife to cut a window out of the glasses, as shown in the pattern. Cut out rectangles of acetate paper, just slightly smaller than the glasses. Glue the acetate to the back of the glasses. Trim off the excess acetate that extends below the curve of the glasses, where they rest on the children's noses. Cut each rubber band once. Staple one end of the band to each side of the glasses, as indicated on the pattern. Prepare enough glasses for all the children, as well as a sample pair for yourself.

Put all the materials on the activity table so that the children have access to them.

During an Attention Getter time, show the children a picture of the sun from one of the outer space books. Ask: "What do you think would happen if you looked right at the sun for a few seconds? (You can damage your eyes.) Say: "We're going to visit the sun on the space trip we're going to be taking, so we will need space glasses to protect our eyes." Put on your own glasses. Ask the children if they see anything in the room that they could use to make space glasses. Invite them to be creative with the stickers, crayons, markers, foil, and glue.

Traveling in Outer Space
Science/Dramatic Play/Movement/Small Group Project

WHY we are doing this activity: to help children learn how the planets are different and to stimulate interest in the unit.

To keep your curriculum child-initiated, give children a choice about participating in this activity. If some would rather not, provide a space with toys and projects for them to use while you do this activity with those who want to join you.

WHAT we will need:
Space helmets, space glasses, and life-support systems (from previous activities)
Long rope
Chairs
Space poster
Calculators
Flashlights
One orange
Long skewer
Paper bag

HOW we will do it: Arrange the chairs to simulate a spaceship. Skewer the orange and hide it in a paper bag. Tell the children that you are going to take a trip to all the planets, so you will need your space helmets, space glasses, and life-support systems. Encourage your students to put on their equipment, and put a helmet on yourself. Pretend to climb into special space suits that will keep you warm on very cold

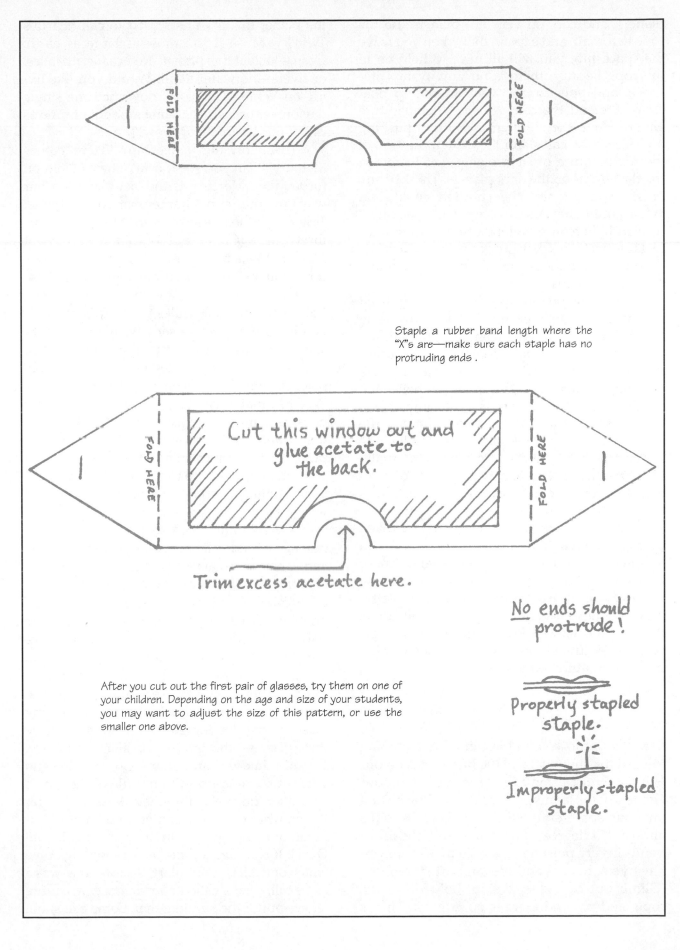

FOLD HERE

FOLD HERE

Staple a rubber band length where the "X"s are—make sure each staple has no protruding ends.

Cut this window out and glue acetate to the back.

FOLD HERE

FOLD HERE

Trim excess acetate here.

No ends should protrude!

Properly stapled staple.

Improperly stapled staple.

After you cut out the first pair of glasses, try them on one of your children. Depending on the age and size of your students, you may want to adjust the size of this pattern, or use the smaller one above.

planets, and cool on very hot planets. Tie the rope to a chair, and explain that when you leave the spaceship, you will all have to hold on to the rope because there is no gravity in outer space, and you do not want anyone to float away. Pretend the calculator is a temperature gauge. Have the children take turns pushing buttons on the calculator to get an indication of the temperature of each planet. Let them use the flashlights on the dark planets. Think of any other "space tools" the children could use. What could they use to steer the spaceship? (Pretend intercoms, pretend cameras for photos to take back to Earth, rocks scattered on the ground as samples—whatever makes it more fun and more real.)

Sit in the spaceship (but not in the front row of chairs—let the children take turns being the leaders of the mission) and ask the children to get ready for takeoff. Together, do a countdown and "blast off." Hold on tight—you are traveling more than 17,000 miles per hour.

Note: What follows is an example of a guided space trip. Feel free to improvise. Be aware that the monologue does not include comments from children. When you actually facilitate this activity, encourage plenty of comments, verbal interactions, and participation as you and the children take the trip together.

Although the following is an unbroken passage about all nine planets, it is a good idea to spread the information over several "space trips" during the unit. You may choose to take one every day, as part of an Attention Getter time. If you visit only a few planets each time, the children will be less likely to confuse the planets because of too much information being introduced at the same time.

TRAVELING IN OUTER SPACE

(After countdown and blastoff) "We are going toward the sun now, and the first planet on our way is Venus. I think I see it out the window. Get ready for landing! Press the cooling button on your space suits—the surface of Venus is almost 900 degrees. Boy, that's hot! The air of Venus is very poisonous, too, so make sure you have your helmet and life-support system on. (Climb out of the spaceship, hold on to the rope, and pretend there is no gravity.) This is the planet that scientists used to call "Earth's Twin" because it is almost as large as earth. Gosh—look at this planet! No oceans, no lakes, or rivers—no water at all. Would you like living on Venus? Did you know that one single day on Venus lasts the same amount of time as 243 of our Earth days? Wow!"

(Back on the spaceship) "Here comes Mercury!! Can you see it down there? Hold on for landing. Mercury is the last planet on our way to the sun. Remember our rhyme: "Mercury's closest to the sun, Pluto is the farthest one." (Climb out onto the surface of Mercury.) Watch out for all these round holes—don't fall in one! There are billions of these craters on Mercury. The biggest one here, Caloris Basin, is 800 miles wide. This planet is nothing but a rocky desert. We're on the dark side of it, away from the sun. This side of Mercury can reach 360 degrees below zero. No place on Earth, not even the North Pole, gets even half that cold. Mission Leader Nicki, what does our temperature gauge say that Mercury's temperature is right now?" (Encourage child to punch buttons on calculator.)

(Back on the spaceship) "Oh my gosh, we're coming up to the sun now. I'm sure glad we have a super spaceship, because if you were on a spaceship that took two days to get to the moon, it would still take you a year to get to the sun—that's how far away it is. But our spaceship traveled the whole 93 million miles in just a few minutes. Put on your space glasses—you don't want to damage your eyes. The sun is the only star in our solar system. Even though we see other stars in the sky at night, none of them are in our solar system—they're all much, much farther away. Oh, the ship is getting closer. Wow! It's such a bubbling, boiling, raging mass of hot, glowing gases. I'm so glad I have these glasses—the light is so brilliant and fierce. I don't think we can get any closer to the sun without burning up—the middle of the sun is 25 million degrees Fahrenheit. Mission Leader Roger, what does the temperature on our temperature gauge show? Oh my gosh!! Look out!! Duck!! It is a huge tongue of gas shooting out—watch out! All stations alert! Whew—that was a close call. That's called a *prominence*, when fire shoots out of the sun like that. Some can shoot out 367,000 miles from the sun. That's the same as if you traveled around the center of Earth fifteen times. That was too close for comfort—we better get out of here. Mission leader, what should we do now?"

(Back on the spaceship) "Now we're traveling away from the Sun, in the other direction, back past Mercury, back past Venus, past Earth (wave out the window). Hi, everyone on Earth! We're exploring the planets in the solar system. We won't be back for a while. There's our moon. People from Earth have been on the moon. Now we're coming to Mars. (Out on the planet.) Mars is only half the size of Earth. See all this rust, or iron oxide, on the ground? (Kick the floor.) That's the reason Mars looks red from far away. There used to be rivers on Mars, but aren't anymore. Does anyone see any dried-up river beds? Oh, I think I see Mons Olympus. See that gigantic volcano over there? It's three times higher than Earth's highest mountain. Oh my gosh, everyone, hold on tight to the rope! (Raise your voice as if you're shouting over the wind.) The wind on Mars can blow with terrific speeds and cause huge dust storms—I think that's what we're in now. Mission leader, should we head back to the spaceship or keep going? "

(Back on the spaceship) "Now we're headed toward the giant planets. Mercury, Venus, Earth, and Mars are very small compared to the other planets. I think I see Jupiter up ahead. It's the fifth planet, but it's not really a planet, because it has no ground to stand on. It's a giant ball of gas. Look at all those swirling storms. Ooh, look at that flash of lightning! See that big red spot? Scientists think that that red spot is a huge, mammoth storm that's so big, it could swallow up three Earths. Jupiter is 1,300 times bigger than Earth, and it takes Jupiter twelve of our years to travel once around the sun. Scientists sent a robot called Voyager to come and take pictures of Jupiter."

"Oh, now we're coming up to Saturn. I can tell it's Saturn because of the rings around it—the rings are made of thousands and thousands of chunks of rock and ice, all floating around it. Does any astronaut want to venture out of the safety of our spaceship to get a rock sample? Saturn is another giant ball of gas. The outside

of the gases can get horribly cold, and the center of Saturn's gas ball is horribly hot. Saturn is 800 times bigger than Earth."

"Saturn was the last planet that Earth robot ships have taken pictures of. Now we are traveling where no astronaut or robot has ever traveled before. I'm kind of scared—how about you? Oh—this greenish blue planet is Uranus. It's another gas giant and it is 300 times bigger than Earth. (Take out the skewered orange. Tilt it a little, but with the skewer running vertically, to simulate Earth's axis and the way it revolves. Say: "This is how Earth turns. This part (point to the skewer) is something I put in the orange to show you what an *axis* is—it means the line we would see if we drew one from the North Pole, the top of planet Earth, to the South Pole, the bottom of planet Earth. But this is how Uranus turns. (Turn the orange so that the skewer is horizontal and roll the orange in this position.) It takes Uranus eighty-four Earth years to move around the sun."

"Now we're coming to Pluto. Sometimes Pluto is farthest away from the sun of all the planets, and sometimes it's closer than Neptune. It must be closer than Neptune right now, because we've come to it first. That's because it moves around the sun in a very odd way—sometimes it swings way out into space, away from the sun, and sometimes it moves much closer to the sun. Wow, look at all that ice and snow—I guess Pluto is just one big frozen snowball in outer space. Mission Leader, should we explore it?"

"Now we're coming to the last gas giant in our solar system, Neptune. I know this is Neptune because of the pale blue color. Neptune is 300 times bigger than Earth. What observations do you have of Neptune, astronauts?"

And head back to Earth.

What Would Happen to the Planet Earth without Gravity?

Science/Sensory

WHY we are doing this project: to enable children to experiment with the force of gravity; to help them understand that the gravitational pull of the sun (and the moon) affects the position of Earth in the universe.

WHAT we will need:

Pillowcases

Large, heavy balls

Activity sign (provided below, photocopy and enlarge for your use)

Large tub

HOW we will do it: Put one ball in each pillowcase, and put these "gravity balls" in a tub, near a large open space. (It may be outside). Post the activity sign nearby.

During an Attention Getter time, point to the space poster and remind the children that all the planets move around the sun, and that gravity is the force which makes this happen.

Ask the children what they think would happen to our planet Earth if there was no gravity and if Earth did not travel around the sun. Show the children the gravity balls and the activity sign. Together, read/interpret what the sign says. Ask the children to predict what will happen when they follow the sign's suggestions. Ask the children what will happen if they let go of a ball when another child is standing nearby. Discuss how this can be prevented. (For example, "Make sure there is wide, open space around you before you swing your ball, and

Stand in an open space.

Swing the gravity ball around and around.

Then let the gravity ball GO!!

What happens?

What does it feel like?

that no one else is near you.") Invite them to conduct the experiment by swinging the gravity balls around and around, and then letting them go, as the sign suggests. What happens?

Afterward, point to the sun on one of your posters of the universe. Say: "The sun has gravity, and pulls on Earth. This keeps Earth circling around the sun. This is why all the other planets circle around the sun, too, and why they also have gravity. (Point to the moon.) Even the moon has gravity and pulls on our planet. The pull of the moon makes the water in the sea rise and fall." Encourage observations and descriptions of the children's experience with the gravity ball.

Other ideas you may wish to introduce: Without gravity, planets would have no pattern or predictability to their movements. Planets might collide, or move far away, out of reach of the sun and its light and warmth. Talk about this together. What would planet Earth be like to live on, if this happened? (Make sure the children know that you are just imagining this scenario—it is not likely to ever really happen.)

Rocket Launcher

Science

WHY we are doing this project: to help children understand that there are many different gases; to enable children to make a gas (carbon dioxide) and to see visible evidence of it; to enable children to launch a "rocket ship" which they can pretend is soaring into outer space.

The facts of the matter: The combination of baking soda, which is a base, and vinegar, which is an acid, makes carbon dioxide gas.

CAUTION: Depending on the size of your bottle and the proportions of baking soda and vinegar used, the corks can pop out of the bottles with great force. Depending on the ages of your children, make this project safe by doing either (or both) of the following: Experiment first with your bottles and safe amounts of baking soda and vinegar, which push the corks up with less force, and then make measuring signs suggesting how much of

each material the children should use; or, during an Attention Getter time, discuss with the children how important it is to stand three or four steps back as soon as they put the corks in the bottles.

WHAT we will need:
    Small, clear plastic soda bottles
    Funnels
    Tubs or sensory table
    Two ½ cup measuring cups
    Baking soda (two boxes)
    Small pitchers of vinegar
    Corks
    Paper towels (cut in 12.5 cm [5"] squares)
    Thumbtacks
    Streamers (strips of crepe or tissue paper
       cut in lengths that are 10 cm x 5 mm
       [4" x ¼"])
    Spoons
    Small bowls (for the baking soda)
    Tubs of water (for rinsing bottles)
    Newspaper
    Book: Baird, Anne, *The U.S. Space Camp
       Book of Rockets*
Demonstration:
    Cup
    Baking soda
    Vinegar
    Tray

HOW we will do it: To prepare, attach the streamers to the corks using thumbtacks. Spread several layers of newspaper on your activity table and set out all materials so that the children will have access to them. If you are working with three- and young four-year-olds who are still mastering pouring, you may prefer to do this project in tubs or a sensory table to minimize your clean-up.

During an Attention Getter time, ask the children: "How do astronauts travel to outer space? What takes them there?" Encourage comments. Together, look at and discuss the photographs in *The U.S. Space Camp Book of Rockets*. Encourage the children to describe what they see.

After you have looked at pictures of space rockets, tell the children that today you are going to launch a space rocket yourselves, and that in order to launch it, you are going to use the power of a gas. Ask: "Do you remember what a gas is?" (If necessary: "A gas is not hard, like this table or chair or the floor, and it is not something wet and pourable like milk or water or juice. One example of a gas is the air we breathe.") "We are going to make another gas, now, and it's called carbon dioxide."

Have the children identify the baking soda and vinegar. Ask the children to predict what will happen when they are mixed. Put the tray under the cup, and have children take turns putting small spoonfuls of soda into it. Then have one child pour some vinegar into the cup. What happens?

The paper towel squares in this project are designed to delay the reaction of the baking soda to the vinegar for the time it takes the children to put the corks in the bottle tops. However, this can be problematic for young children who find it difficult to roll something up, like a pile of baking soda in paper. If you think this will be the case for your children, there are several options: make the baking soda packages yourself by rolling ½ cup soda up in a paper towel square and twisting the ends. Make sure the rolls are narrow enough to fit through the bottle opening. Make several of these and put them out with the other materials.

Another option is to cut toilet paper rolls in half lengthwise and line each one with a paper towel square. The curve of the toilet paper may help some children roll up the baking soda packages. You may also provide sticky tape strips to help them seal the rolls.

Show the children one of the corks with the streamers attached. Say: "This is our space rocket. Which planet is it going to travel to?" Prepare a baking soda package and put it into a bottle. Measure ½ cup vinegar and say: "Do you remember what happened when we mixed the baking soda and vinegar? What do you predict will happen to our rocket (point to the cork with the streamer) if I pour vinegar inside our launcher and put the rocket in the bottle opening?" Invite the children to conduct the experiment for themselves. What happens? If necessary, remind the children that the vinegar and baking soda make a gas called carbon dioxide. Using this information, ask the children to hypothesize about why the rocket shoots up after the vinegar is poured into the launcher.

What Do Other Planets Look Like? Making a Spacescape
Art/Crafts

WHY we are doing this project: to stimulate children to imagine what other planets look like; to develop creative expression; to develop fine motor skills; to create interest in the experiment that follows.

WHAT we will need:
Markers
Crayons
Space magazines
Construction paper (black and brown)
Paper shapes (provided on page 345)
Spools
Small plastic aquarium plants
Nontoxic spray paint (silver, gold, and red or orange)
Small stones
Toilet paper rolls
Pipe cleaners
Shallow boxes and lids
Small jewelry boxes
Aluminum foil
Acetate papers
Foil star stickers
Dead coral (small pieces [available in nature stores])

HOW we will do it: The preceding list is comprised of suggestions. The items you collect will depend on your budget and your time. Feel free to substitute items or additional items as appropriate to your circumstances. There are a number of ways to prepare this activity, depending on how much time you wish to devote to it.

Children can make their spacescapes on box lids without backgrounds, or you can cut the sides of boxes down and fit lids onto them so that the spacescapes have backgrounds. You can glue black paper onto the base and background of each box, or leave the boxes the way they are. Do what works for you.

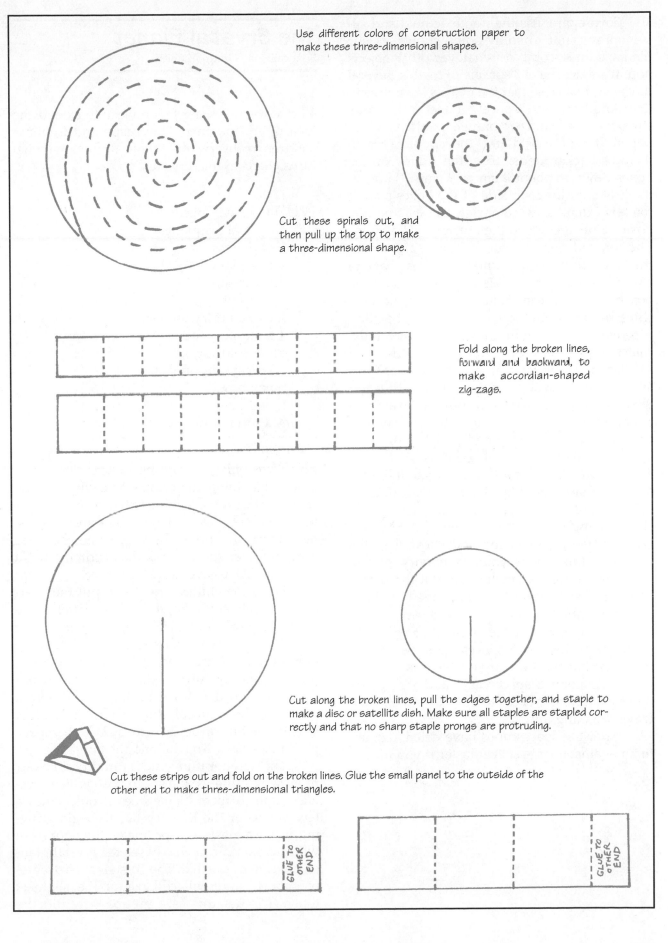

Use different colors of construction paper to make these three-dimensional shapes.

Cut these spirals out, and then pull up the top to make a three-dimensional shape.

Fold along the broken lines, forward and backward, to make accordian-shaped zig-zags.

Cut along the broken lines, pull the edges together, and staple to make a disc or satellite dish. Make sure all staples are stapled correctly and that no sharp staple prongs are protruding.

Cut these strips out and fold on the broken lines. Glue the small panel to the outside of the other end to make three-dimensional triangles.

GLUE TO OTHER END

GLUE TO OTHER END

To prepare, use the nontoxic gold and silver spray paint to spray some spools, plastic plants, stones, coral, or whatever other objects you want to make "spacey." Do this several days in advance so that the objects have time to dry. Another very "spacey" effect is to spray streaks of red and/or orange paint on black paper. If you would like the spacescapes to include backgrounds, trim the edges of the boxes down to about 8 cm or 9 cm (3") and fit the lids onto the long side of the boxes so that the lids extend upward at right angles from the boxes. Glue the lids to the outside of the boxes. The sprayed black paper can then be glued onto the lids to form backgrounds. (You may have to cut the corners of the lids to fit them onto the box bases.) You can make rudimentary spaceships by decorating toilet paper rolls, bending pipe cleaners, and gluing them underneath the rolls to make "legs" or landing apparatus.

Make a sample spacescape ahead of time. When you are ready for the children to begin the activity, put all materials out on the activity table. Some space magazines have drawings and articles about imagined societies or landscapes on planets in far-off galaxies. *Astronomy* and *Sky and Telescope* are two possibilities. Try to find magazines like these, and during an Attention Getter time, show the pictures to the children and encourage comments. Afterward, take out your spacescape and show it to the children. Talk about your imaginary planet. Ask the children what the name of the planet might be, and if you like, talk together about the imaginary galaxy it is in. Ask the children if they see anything in the room that will help them make their own spacescapes. Be sure to mention that the sample you have is just one way of making a spacescape, and that theirs will look different because they have their own way of making things.

After the spacescapes have dried, display them against a large space poster if you like.

The Crystal Planet
Science/Small Group Activity

WHY we are doing this project: to extend the idea of an imagined spacescape and to allow children to observe the chemical reaction which turns charcoal into crystals.

WHAT we will need:
Charcoal briquettes
¼ cup water
Large plate
Tablespoon
¼ cup salt
¼ cup laundry bluing
1 tablespoon ammonia
Food coloring
Medicine dropper
Small bowl
Space poster
Masking tape

HOW we will do it: During an Attention Getter time, after doing the previous activity, tell the children that you are going to try to grow a crystal planet. Ask: "Do you think there are any crystal planets in another galaxy, somewhere far away in outer space?" Ask the children what it would be like to live in such a place.

Have the children help you put the charcoal briquettes in a bowl. Mix the water, laundry bluing, salt, and ammonia, and pour it over the charcoal. The charcoal pieces should be only partially immersed in the solution. Have the children take turns using a medicine dropper to place drops of food coloring at different places on the charcoal. Put the bowl in a place where it will not be disturbed. Use the space poster as a backdrop, behind the bowl.

The temperature and humidity in your room will influence the speed with which crystals begin to form. Sometimes it only takes a few hours for the first crystals to begin growing. Make a masking tape line on the floor from which children can clearly see the crystal planet, but cannot touch it. The crystals are extremely delicate and will collapse at the slightest touch. Discuss this as a group. Why did the crystal planet start to grow? As appropriate, explain that the charcoal briquettes are full of tiny spaces, and that the water seeped into these spaces. Soon the water in the bowl begins to dry up because the air makes the water into vapor, and the vapor mixes with the air. (Evaporation.) The salt in the water is left behind and forms tiny crystals on anything solid. When water evaporates from the ends of the first small crystals, new crystals grow on the old, which is why the crystals "grow."

Brainstorm with the children together to come up with a name for your crystal planet. Ask: What galaxy is it in? How do you get there? What kinds of creatures might live on a crystal planet?

The Sun and the Planets
Music/Movement/Gross Motor/Small Group Activity

WHY we are doing this activity: to help children "feel" music; to help children understand that the planets revolve around the sun; to develop listening skills; to develop imagination.

WHAT we will need:
    "Spacey" music (see suggestions below)
    Books with realistic pictures or
        photographs of planets
    Tape recorder
    Large, open space
    Flashlights
    Crepe paper (red, green, and blue)
    Tape
    Coffee can with sand

HOW we will do it: In this activity, you are going to create a space-like environment in which children can "revolve" around the sun. To prepare, use the tape and crepe paper to cover the flashlights, so that when they are switched on, their light will be different colors. Arrange them in different places around the room. In the coffee can, place one flashlight which has no crepe paper covering and put this in the middle of your room to be your "sun."

There are some wonderful "space" music tapes on the market right now (sometimes called "New Age" music). One of my favorites is "Astral Journey" by David and Steve Gordon, produced by Sequoia Records, Box 280, Topanga, CA 90290. This is an excellent tape and ideal for this activity. "Celestial Suite" is also produced by these same artists.

Designate certain toys and a certain area for use by children who do not wish to participate in this activity.

When you are ready to begin, take your books or magazines and look at the photographs and pictures of planets in outer space. Ask: "What do you think it sounds like in space? Do you think the planets revolve around the sun quickly or slowly? Do you think there's any life in outer space?" Tell the children that you are going to pretend to be the planets. Turn all overhead lights off, and all flashlights on. Ask your students to guess what the flashlight in the middle of the room is supposed to be. Turn on your space music and revolve around the "sun" as lazily and slowly as planets would in outer space. After a minute or two, ask the children which planets they are. Next, ask the children to imagine that they are astronauts who are exploring outer space. They are the only ones on their space mission who are brave enough to climb out of the spaceship to do this. Cords connect them to the spaceship, but they are slowly floating in outer space. After a few minutes, ask them to imagine that the gravity of a strange new planet is starting to pull them toward it, closer and closer. They land on the surface. It is a planet in another galaxy, and it is the strangest, oddest place they have ever seen. Invite them to explore the strange planet. If you like, take this activity in other directions of your choice. One nice option is to invite the children to lie down and listen and relax to the music for a few minutes.

What Is a Meteor?
Science/Sensory

WHY we are doing this experiment: to help children observe how craters are formed by meteors; to help them understand what meteors are; to provide a sensory experience.

WHAT we will need:
- Any book on outer space that describes meteors
- Dirt
- Small pitchers of water
- Spoons (large and small)
- Medicine droppers
- Popsicle sticks
- Pebbles
- Stones (large and small)
- Smocks
- Tubs
- Soapy water and paper towels (for clean-up)

HOW we will do it: There is no doubt that this activity can get messy, but children do love it, and it demonstrates in a very fun, hands-on way the impact meteors have on Earth's surface.

To prepare, set out the dirt, stones, tubs, smocks, and pitchers of water in an outside space which you do not mind becoming messy.

During an Attention Getter time, take out your book which features meteors, point to the pictures, and explain: "Sometimes chunks of rock and metal shoot across outer space. When they are out in space, they're called *meteoroids*, but when our planet Earth's gravity pulls them into our sky, they're called *meteors*. They travel so fast, and are sometimes so big and heavy, that when they hit the Earth they make *craters*. One of the biggest craters is in Arizona. It is called the Barringer Crater, and it is almost one mile wide. When a meteor hit that spot, 20,000 years ago, it blasted 400 million tons of rock into the air." Reassure your children that meteors do not crash onto Earth very often, especially not big ones, and that this is not something they have to worry about.

Tell the children that you are going to do an experiment which will show you how meteors make craters. Show them the materials you set out. Ask them to predict what will happen if they make a wet muddy mixture in the tubs with the dirt and water, and then throw mud balls or stones into it. Before you invite them to conduct this experiment, ask: "Is it okay to throw a stone or mud ball at another person? What could happen if you did? Where is the *only* place that it is okay to throw a stone or mud ball?" As the children conduct the experiment, encourage them to observe and verbalize what happens. (If the mud is too thick, they may have to pick the object out before observing the crater, which is why small amounts of water, and small dispensers like medicine droppers and spoons, are recommended.)

Describe meteor showers to the children. (A meteor shower is hundreds of meteors falling in one hour, all coming from the same direction.) Again, reassure your students that this is a rare occurrence, and not something they should worry about. Invite the children to discover the impact of a shower of small pebbles on the mud.

Three, Two, One, Blast Off!
Dramatic Play/Language/Art

WHY we are doing this activity: to stimulate expression of ideas, imaginative play, and child-to-child interaction; to facilitate creative expression.

WHAT we will need:
- Refrigerator box
- Posters of galaxies or the Milky Way
- Steering wheel
- Computer keyboard
- Flashlights
- Chairs
- Duct tape
- Markers

Paper
Glue sticks
Children's scissors
Space theme stickers
Book describing rockets and spaceships
Preparation:
Exacto knife
Markers

HOW we will do it: Obtain an empty refrigerator box from a store that sells large appliances. Using the Exacto knife, cut a door in one side of the box and windows with flaps which can be open or shut in two other sides. Since the box is doubling as a spaceship, you may want to cut circular windows like portholes. (More difficult to cut out, granted, but anything for realism!)

The items listed are just suggestions; if you can think of additional or substitute items, use them to create a rocket ship that will feel as real to the children as possible. In our spaceship, we used duct tape to secure a flashlight onto the ceiling, and put a poster of the galaxy in front of the steering wheel, to simulate the view into outer space. Whatever you can find to simulate a control panel—calculators, computer keyboards, or Fisher Price toys with knobs and levers—will greatly enhance the activity.

On the first day of this activity, ask the children for suggestions about what the rocket ship should be called. Write the name on the outside of your rocket ship. Display the book on rockets and spaceships, and make a point of observing the letters, words, and symbols on the outside of the spacecrafts. Discuss these with the children and encourage their comments. Show them the paper, scissors, markers, glue sticks, and stickers. Invite them to use these materials to create a spaceship exterior.

Put the space helmets, life-support systems, and space glasses out near the spaceship, then stand back and enjoy!

Night Sky
Sensory

WHY we are doing this project: to provide children with a sensory experience which utilizes the theme of the unit.

WHAT we will need:
Empty cereal box
Flashlight
Sturdy paper plates (cardboard squares about 21 cm [8"])
Preparation:
Scissors
Exacto knife
Skewer

HOW we will do it: In this project, you will be punching small holes into the bottom of a cereal box, and securing a flashlight inside. When the flashlight is turned on in a dark space, and the light shines through the holes, the effect simulates a starry sky.

To begin, use the scissors, skewer, and Exacto knife to punch holes into the bottom of the box. Star shapes produce a wonderful effect, but are quite difficult to cut. Next, fold the paper plate or cardboard in half, and make a small horizontal cut. Then fold it the other way and make another horizontal cut so that your cuts form a cross (+) in the center. Push the flashlight through it. Bend the edges of the plate or cardboard so that you can wedge it into the box. (Because the sizes of flashlights and cereal boxes vary, you may have to experiment with the best way to secure your flashlight in your box.)

Make several of these and create a dark space; You may be able to use your refrigerator box for this purpose. Invite the children to use them.

Moonshine
Science/Language

Note: This project requires parent participation.

WHY we are doing this project: To encourage children to observe the moon and to develop language skills.

    Tip: It is better to do this activity during winter if possible because in summer, the moon may not be visible until after bedtime. If the moon is visible during school hours, take the children outside to observe it.

WHAT we will need:
    Book: Asch, Frank, *Moongame*
    Paper
    Pens
    Markers
    Butcher paper

HOW we will do it: Put your butcher paper up on the wall and have a marker handy. During an Attention Getter time, read *Moongame*. Afterward, ask the children to tell you about a time when they saw the moon. Tell them that you have some important homework for them to do. You would like them to observe the moon. Ask: "When do you think would be the best time for getting a good look at the moon?"

    There are several variations on this activity. You may ask your students to look at the moon for one night only, and then to describe their observations the next day during group discussion. You may ask parents to take story dictation from the children describing their observations. You may ask the children to observe the moon over a week or so and to draw pictures of what they see so that they can observe how the moon appears to change shape. If the children record their observations with words and drawings, have a group show-and-tell of their work. If you work with three- or young four-year-olds, have only three or four children show-and-tell their work at one time.

    Whichever option you choose, write a letter to parents explaining what you are doing and asking for help with this special homework assignment. Take dictation and write the children's words for the letter on the butcher paper.

If you work with kindergartners, they may want to write their own individual letters. If necessary, send your own letter with the children's. Include a suggestion that children notice whether there is any light in their yard or house that comes from the moon.

Observatory
Science/Dramatic Play/Language

WHY we are doing this activity: to enable children to understand what astronomers do and the tools that they use; to expand vocabulary; to facilitate imaginative play and child-to-child interactions.

WHAT we will need:
    Cardboard poster tubes
    Chairs
    String
    Packaging tape
    Graph paper
    Pens
    Markers
    Table
    Chairs
    Measuring devices (found in geometry sets; e.g., ruler, protractor)
    Computer monitor and keyboard (if possible)
    Play bed, table, chairs, dishes—astronomers' living quarters
Optional:
    Black construction paper
    Photographs of planets from astronomy magazines
    Star-shaped stickers

HOW we will do it: In this activity, you are going to set up a dramatic play observatory. Make telescopes out of the cardboard poster tubes. Remove the plastic ends so children can look through them. If you like, make them look a little more real by wrapping them in aluminum foil or construction paper. Attach the tubes to the backs of chairs, at angles, using string and/or tape, or hang the "telescopes" from the ceiling with string.

Either position your telescopes near windows so that when the children look through them, they see the sky, or aim them toward a sky picture pinned up on the wall. You may wish, as a group, to make your own picture of the sky or solar system to place in front of the telescope. To simulate a night sky, put photographs of planets, star stickers, or whatever else you like, onto black construction paper.

Put the table and chairs near the telescopes. Put the graph paper, rulers, pens and markers on the table. Set up the computer and monitor nearby. Depending on the computer and programs you have available, you may decide to have the children enter their data with the computer on, or you may leave it switched off and simply let the children pretend while typing on the keyboard.

In another part of the "observatory," use the play furniture and dishes to set up the astronomers' living quarters.

Look through your astronomy magazines to find a drawing or photograph of a telescope. During an Attention Getter time, show the telescope to the children and ask them what they think it might be for. Let the children know that people who look into the sky to learn about planets, stars, meteors, and comets are called *astronomers*. Astronomers study *astronomy*. Say these words several times and pat your head, blink your eyes, or tap your feet on the floor in time to the syllables. Show the children the dramatic play area and let them know it is the "observatory." Explain that an *observatory* is where astronomers study the sky. Show the children the play furniture in your observatory and ask them why they think astronomers might need a place to sleep and eat while they work. Discuss the work that astronomers do; for example, predict what will happen in the sky, *chart* the paths of planets, or take photographs or draw pictures of the planets to learn about their size and position. Show the children the materials on the table for these purposes and invite them to explore. Use the new vocabulary words as much as you can during the day: *astronomer, astronomy, observatory, chart*.

Space Books
Science/Language/Art

WHY we are doing this project: to develop all language arts skills: reading, writing, speaking, and listening; to expand vocabulary; to teach children about other things connected with space technology.

WHAT we will need:
    Space magazines (e.g., *Astronomy,*
        Sky and Telescope)
    Paper
    Glue sticks
    Children's scissors
    Markers
    Crayons
Preparation:
    Stapler
    Scissors
Optional:
    Puppet

HOW we will do it: To prepare, take two or three sheets of paper stacked on top of each other, and fold them in half. Staple twice along the fold to make a blank book. Make one of these for each child. If you work with three- and young four-year-olds, cut out some magazine pictures (e.g., asteroids, comets, meteoroids, space robots, satellites, rocket ships, astronauts, telescopes, constellations, and planets). Older children can do this themselves. Put out all materials, and include blank sheets of unstapled paper.

Make a sample space book ahead of time by gluing pictures in your book and writing about them. Examples: (Realistic magazine drawing of red planet.) "This planet looks spooky. It is red, like Mars. It looks cold and lonely to me." (Drawing of spaceship.) "This is the kind of spaceship I'd like to travel in. In the refrigerator, I drew my favorite food: grape juice and potato chips. I would eat them in outer space."

During an Attention Getter time, read your book to the children. Ask them if they see anything in the room that would help them make their own space books. As the children use the materials, reinforce the names of the space-related objects in the magazine pictures through conversation, or use your puppet to do this. Take story dictation, write down words to be copied, spell words, or support invented spelling, depending on the needs of your children. As and when appropriate, explain the new things in the pictures.

At the end of the day or session, or even the next day, have a show-and-tell of space books.

Space Math
Math/Multicultural/Anti-Bias

WHY we are doing this project: to practice rational counting and subtraction; to facilitate sorting into sets; to create multicultural, anti-bias awareness; to develop self-esteem and a sense of autonomy through use of a one-person work station.

WHAT we will need:

Large cardboard panel (from large appliance box)
Black paint (or black contact paper)
Clear contact paper
Cardboard
Space shapes (patterns provided on page 353; photocopy and enlarge for your use)
Double-sided tape
Writing sheets (provided on page 354; photocopy and enlarge for your use)
Blank paper
Pens
Crayons
"One person may be here" sign (provided on page 3; photocopy and enlarge for your use)

Preparation:

Scissors

HOW we will do it: To prepare an "outer space" board, cut off the ragged ends of the cardboard panel. Paint it with black paint, or cover with black contact paper, then cover again with clear contact paper. Prop the board against a wall.

Make several copies of the shapes provided, and color them. If necessary, ask friends or parents to help you with this. Using double-sided tape, stick all the shapes to cardboard, cover on both sides with clear contact paper, and cut them out. Put a few strips of double-sided tape on the back of each shape, and stick them to the black "outer space" board. Put copies of the writing sheet, blank paper, crayons, and pens near the board. Post the "One person may be here" sign on the wall above it.

During an Attention Getter time, show the children the board. Together, as a group, begin to sort the different shapes by grouping them in different places on the board, but do not finish this process. (Leave that for the children to do.) Together, read/interpret a writing sheet, and discuss the "One person may be here" sign. Show the children the blank paper, and let them know that if they like, they can use this to record the number of shapes they count. Encourage exploration!

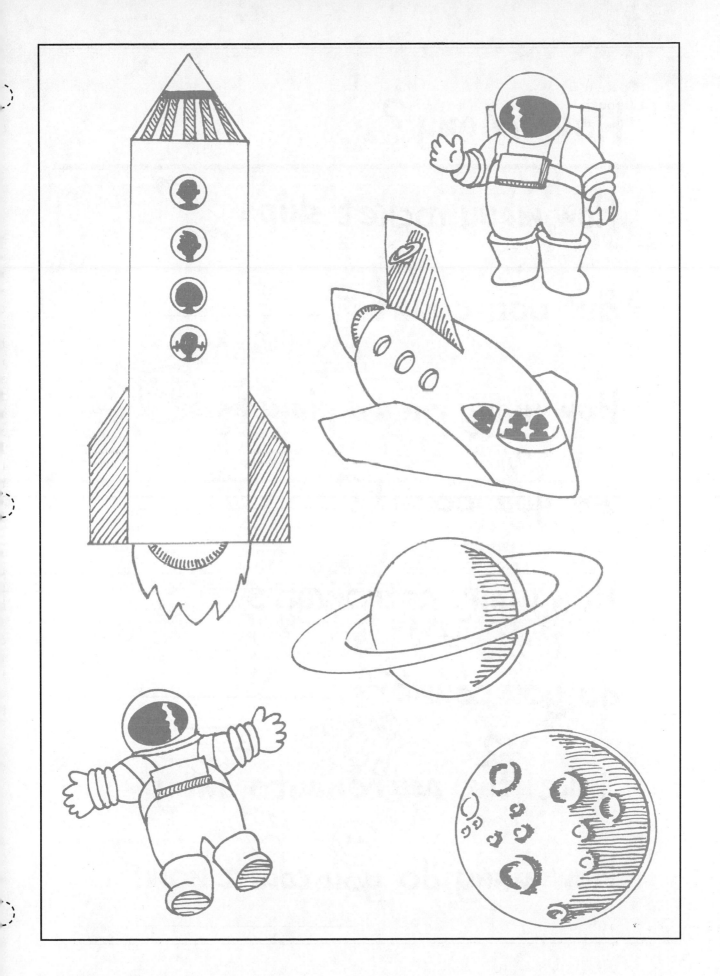

How Many?

How many rocket ships

do you count? _____

How many ringed planets

do you count? _____

How many astronauts

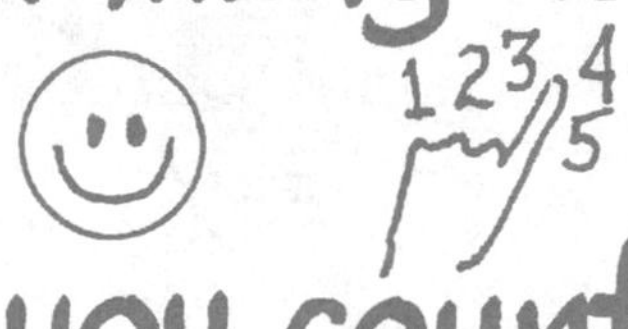

do you count? _____

2:
Take two astronauts away.

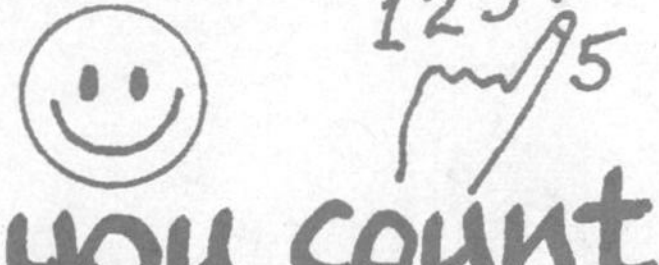

How many do you count now?

_____

354

Literature

Symbol Key: *Multicultural
+Minimal diversity
No symbol: no diversity or no people

Asch, F. (1984). *Moongame*. New York: Simon & Schuster.

Baird, A. (1994). *The U.S. Space Camp Book of Rockets*. New York: Morrow Jr. Books.

Cole, J. (1990). *The magic school bus lost in the solar system*. New York: Scholastic.*

Cother, J. (1990). *Sky above, earth below*. New York: Harper & Row.

Fernandes, K. (1991). *Zebo and the dirty planet*. Buffalo, NY: Annick Press.*

Fradin, D. (1984). *Skylab*. Chicago: Children's Press.

Hansen, R., & Bell, R. A. (1985). *My first book of space*. New York: Simon & Schuster. (Excellent photographs.)

Ride, S., & O'Shaughnessy, T. (1994). *The third planet*. New York: Crown. (Good reference picture book.)

Extenders

Language: After the children make their spacescapes, encourage them to make up names for their planets. Take story dictation or have the children write about their planets. Ask open-ended questions to get the ball rolling: Who or what lives on your planet? What kind of air or gas surrounds your planet? What grows on your planet? What kind of lightness, darkness, warmth, and cold are on your planet?

Language/Cognitive: To add language development to the Space Math activity, print the name of each object on cardboard rectangles. Place a reduced picture of the object beside the name. Cover the name cards with contact paper and put double-sided tape on the back. Invite the children to match each word with the object it names.

Art: Borrow a book from the library about rocket ships and, as a group, look through it together. Tape several pieces of butcher paper together and cut one long rocket shape. Encourage the children to paint and/or draw on it. Cut slashes in several pieces of colored acetate and glue them under the tail of your rocket ship to simulate fire explosions from blastoff.

    Another variation is to decorate two identical rocket ship shapes, staple or glue them together, stuff the inside with newspaper, and hang it from your ceiling. If you do this, staple the middle edges together first, before you fill that section with stuffing. Then staple the remainder, moving toward the ends as you stuff.

DIGGABLE DIRT

Attention Getter: Use a large plastic jar (an empty peanut butter container works well) and build up layers of whatever different kinds of dirt or ground materials you have access to. For example, the first layer might be gravel, the second might be earth you dug up in a forest, the third might be potting soil, and the fourth might be a sample from the sandy shore of a lake or pond. Put the lid on, and punch breathing holes in it, because, invariably, there will be insects in dirt samples.

When the children are gathered, pass the jar around and ask each child to examine each layer. Say: "What's in dirt? What kinds of dirt are there?" Small stone pieces, rotting leaves and wood, pebbles and soil granules are all in dirt—as well as plenty of insects. Discuss the children's observations of the samples in the jar, and ask them to guess what you will be talking about for the next few days. Tell the children that *soil* is another word for *dirt*. Say this word together several times. Put the jar on a science table as an exhibit for the duration of the unit.

How Many Layers?
Science

WHY we are doing this experiment: to enable children to separate the different materials in dirt.

WHAT we will need:
- Tubs or sensory table
- Large empty plastic containers (peanut butter or mayonnaise containers)
- Pitchers of water
- Dirt
- Strainers
- Magnifying glasses
- Small bowls
- Spoons
- Activity sign (provided on page 359; photocopy and enlarge for your use)
- Newspaper
- Timers
- Pumps from pump bottles

HOW we will do it: To prepare, spread several layers of newspaper underneath your work surface. Put all materials in the tubs or sensory table. If you do not want a lot of insects in your home or classroom, you may want to mix up your own dirt for this project by combining sand and pebbles with potting soil and some mulch. If you dig up several pounds of dirt from the ground, you are going to have some long-term problems with insect life. Bagged potting soil and mulch are relatively insect-free and can be bought at plant nurseries.

Post the activity sign beside the materials. During an Attention Getter time, read/interpret the sign as a group. Ask the children to predict what will happen when they follow the sign's suggestions. The most important part of this experiment is *time*. Young children have a hard time waiting for anything, so if your students cannot wait for the contents of their own containers to settle into layers, you can demonstrate this with one container which they can then look at. It is worthwhile though to help the children wait by stressing that aspect of the activity sign, holding up the timers, and talk-

ing about their use. Or, instead of using timers, ask the children to count to a certain number after they shake the dirt and water in their containers. How many layers can they see when the dirt settles? Are there any *floaters*—bits of bark, root or leaves which float on the surface? Invite your students to pump the water out with the bottle pumps and then spoon the layers into bowls.

As a variation, invite the children to pour dirt water through strainers. What is left behind in the strainer?

Soil Samples (Part 1)
Language

WHY we are doing this experiment: to develop self-esteem by enabling children to collect their own materials for a science experiment; to develop all components of language arts: speaking, listening, reading, and writing skills; to help children organize their thoughts in a letter format.

WHAT we will need:
- Butcher paper
- Markers
- Plain paper
- Pens
- Envelopes
- Small plastic containers with lids (four or five for each child)
- Paper bags
- Sticky labels

Preparation:
- Skewers

HOW we will do it: Start collecting the small plastic containers several weeks ahead of time. Use the skewer to poke a few holes in each lid.

When you are ready to begin this activity, pin up the butcher paper on a wall, near the place where you gather for Attention Getter time. Show the children the plastic containers, labels, and bags. Tell them that you are going to give them a homework assignment. Ask them

Science Experiment
with Dirt:

Spoon dirt into container.

Pour some water in.

Screw the lid on tightly.

Shake hard.

What happens to the dirt?

to collect soil samples from around the place where they live. Say: "I'm going to give each one of you a bag with five of these containers in it. Can you guess what these containers are for?" (For the soil samples.) Once again, you do not want your home or classroom crawling with insects, so emphasize that the soil samples should be small amounts. Show your students the labels. Say: "I'm giving you all a sticky label for each container, so that you can write down where you got your soil sample. Who do you think we could ask to help you collect your soil samples?" (Parents, grandparents, babysitter.) Write down the children's answers. Other questions to ask: "Where could you look for soil samples?" (In the backyard, in the front yard, the park that we play in, my friend's house, my Grandma's house.) Make sure the children know they must ask permission to dig a sample from someone else's garden. Then say, "Let's write a letter to ask our families for help. What are the things we want to say in our letter? What day should we say the soil samples need to be ready by?"

If you work with three- and young four-year-olds, write the dictated letter on the butcher paper and, later, copy it on a regular-sized piece of paper. Photocopy and distribute to family members. If you work with older preschoolers and kindergartners, show them the blank paper, pens, and envelopes after you read all their comments from the butcher paper. Invite them to write their own notes. If you feel it is necessary, you can still send a little note home with the children's letters, just for clarification.

Soil Samples (Part 2)
Science/Sensory

WHY we are doing this project: to help children understand that there are many different kinds of soil; to enable children to compare soil in terms of color, content and consistency; to develop observation skills; to develop speaking and listening skills; to provide a sensory experience.

WHAT we will need:
  Soil samples (from previous activity)
  Newspaper
  Magnifying glasses
  Frozen dinner trays (or other
    segmented trays)
  Strainers
  Colanders
Insect control:
  Container of dirt
  Plastic cup
  Piece of cardboard

HOW we will do it: Spread newspaper out on an activity table, and put out the segmented trays and magnifying glasses. Before the children dump out the contents of their containers and compare them, gather together and ask the children to tell the group where they collected some of their samples. Ask them to predict how their soil samples will be the same or different. Then invite your students to pour out their soil samples in the trays and to use the magnifying glasses to examine and compare them. What different colors are there? How does each one feel? How does each one smell? How is each sample different or the same? Do they see sand, wood shreds, stones, small, fine particles, and large clods? Which soils can be sifted through strainers and colanders and which cannot? Encourage exploration and comments.

If you find insects in the samples, the easiest way to capture them is to put a cup over each stray insect, and then slide a piece of cardboard underneath. Tip the insect into your container of dirt, and, after the activity, deposit it outside. If you like, invite the children to look into the container without touching it.

Developmental differences: Three- and young four-year-olds very much enjoy holding, squeezing, and sifting dirt with their fingers. Through this kind of sensory exploration they will discover how their soil samples feel different or the same. Older children are likely to be interested in comparing their soil samples in terms of appearance and content, in addition to sensory exploration.

How Much Humus?
Science

WHY we are doing this experiment: to teach children that humus is decayed plant and animal matter; to expand vocabulary; to enable children to find out if their soil samples contain humus.

WHAT we will need:
- Styrofoam meat trays
- Containers of water
- Tablespoons
- Medicine droppers
- Soil samples (from previous activity)
- Masking tape or sticky labels
- Pens

Demonstration
- Sand
- Dirt with bark, root, and/or plant pieces (humus)
- Bark piece
- Dead leaves

HOW we will do it: Several weeks ahead of time, make some humus by gathering bark, root, and leaf pieces. Put them in a container with enough water to keep them damp, to speed up the decomposition process. Add no water for the last two or three days before the activity. You may be able to get some bark chips from a park or playground for your humus. Use a sharp knife or saw to break down or shred the chips. Or you may find a spot underneath trees where the soil is rich with bark, root, and leaf pieces.

When you are ready to do this activity, spread several layers of newspaper on your activity table. Set the meat trays, water, spoons, and medicine droppers on the table. Have the masking tape or sticky labels available to label the trays.

During an Attention Getter time, pass around your humus and encourage the children to examine it. Explain that some soil has *humus* in it. *Humus* is the rotting parts of plants and animals—things like rotting leaves, bark, roots, and dead animals. Introduce the follow-

ing new words when the children are ready for them: *decay* and *organic*. *Decay* is another word for rotting. *Organic* means that a thing comes from something that used to be alive, like a plant or an animal.

Spoon some sand and some humus onto a meat tray in separate piles. Use a spoon or medicine dropper to soak both soil samples with water. Ask the children to predict which one will dry first. Ask your students if they see anything in the room that will help them conduct this experiment for themselves. (The samples which stay wet the longest have humus in them because humus absorbs water and stays wet for a long time.) Show them the masking tape or sticky labels for naming their experiment trays. Check your samples the next day. Which ones are still wet? Why?

Making Humus
Science

WHY we are doing this project: to help children understand one way in which dirt is made.

Note: This is a long-term project, so you will need to find a place to leave your containers for several months.

WHAT we will need:
- Cut-up vegetable and fruit skins
- Sand
- Crushed eggshells
- Peat moss
- Moss
- Stone
- Small plastic containers with lids
- Water
- Masking tape or sticky labels
- Medicine or eyedroppers
- Small shallow containers of water

HOW we will do it: Ahead of time, ask the children and their parents to save vegetable peel scraps and fruit skins. When you are ready to do the activity, put all the materials out on the table.

During an Attention Getter time, tell the children that you are going to try to make your own dirt. Invite the children over to the activity table and encourage them to touch each material as you all identify it. Before you identify the peat moss, show your students your piece of actual moss. Explain that peat moss has rotten or decayed moss in it. Also show the children the stone and let them hold it while you ask what sand comes from. (Stones that are repeatedly broken.) Show the children the empty containers and invite them to make a mixture of the materials. Ask them to predict what will happen if they leave their mixtures in the containers for several months. Label the containers with the masking tape or sticky labels. Ask the children what they could use the medicine droppers and water for. Ask them to predict whether the materials will rot faster with water or without and, also, whether the humus will be produced faster in a container with a lid or without one. Let the children choose whether or not to add water or to use a lid. Every few weeks, check on the contents of the containers and ask the children what they observe. Use the words *decay* and *decompose* as you discuss how the vegetable and fruit skins are rotting. When you feel you have something in which a seed might grow (usually several months, but sometimes more, depending on the warmth and humidity of the room) see if it will!

Soil Sample Collage
Art/Language/Sensory

WHY we are doing this activity: to enable children to categorize soil samples; to develop fine motor skills; to develop all components of language arts: reading, writing, speaking and listening; to develop creative expression.

WHAT we will need:
    Soil sample collections
    Cardboard
    Glue

    Containers for glue
    Glue brushes
    Strainers
    Sifters
    Colanders
    Spoons
    Pens
Preparation:
    Scissors

HOW we will do it: To prepare, cut out cardboard pieces on which each child can glue a soil sample collage. Put all other materials out on the activity table. Invite children to spread glue on their cardboard, and then sprinkle, drop, sift, or strain soil samples onto it. As the children work on their collages, take story dictation about where they found each sample, or if you work with kindergartners, help them write this for themselves. After the collages are dry, display them on the wall. How many different colors of samples do the children see?

Erosion
Science

WHY we are doing this experiment: to allow children to observe that plant roots hold soil in place and that unplanted soil is easily eroded; to expand vocabulary.

WHAT we will need:
    Two aluminum pans
    Soil
    Bird- or grass seed
    Large sensory table (must accommodate both pans)
    Blocks
    Spray bottles (on hard stream setting)
    Watering can
    Hair dryer
    "One person may be here" sign (provided on page 3; photocopy and enlarge for your use)

HOW we will do it: About two weeks ahead of time, put soil in one of the pans and plant grass or birdseed evenly throughout. Water and nurture the seeds until they are several centimeters high.

When you are ready to facilitate the experiment, put soil in the other pan. The soil should be dry, loose, and fine. Spread several layers of newspaper under the sensory table, and make sure it is near an electrical outlet. Put both pans in the sensory table and prop each one up on blocks so that the same end of each pan is tilted.

Put your spray bottle nearby and post your "One person may be here" sign.

During an Attention Getter time, show the children the experiment. How are the two pans different? Squirt the bottle into a sink so the children can see the water stream it produces and ask them to predict what will happen to the soil in each pan when the water is squirted on it. Pour water from the watering can and ask for predictions on how that water stream will affect the soil. Discuss the "One person may be here" sign. As the children conduct the experiment, discuss what happens to the soil in each pan and ask them to hypothesize why. (When dirt has no plants in it, water can easily wash soil away.) This is called *erosion*. Water *erodes* the dirt. Use these words as often as you can during the discussion.

After the soil in each pan has dried (perhaps by the next day), put the two pans out again, but this time plug in a hair dryer and set it nearby. Before the children use the hair dryer, find out which setting will blow the soil away but minimize mess. Ask the children to predict what will happen when they blow the hair dryer on each pan. After the children have discovered and discussed the results of this experiment, ask them what might erode the soil outside by blowing it away. (The wind.) Also ask: "When forests are chopped down and burned, what could happen to the dirt, since plants and trees do not grow in it anymore?" Explain that when rain forests are chopped down, the soil is eroded because the roots of the plants and trees are no longer there to hold the dirt in place.

What Lives in Dirt?
Science/Nature/Gross Motor

WHY we are doing this project: to enable children to observe the variety of insect life in the ground; to help children respect other creatures; to develop gross motor muscles through walking, crouching, and digging.

WHAT we will need:
Magnifying glasses
Shovels or large metal spoons
Nice, warm day (in the winter, earth is
   too hard to dig)

HOW we will do it: Before you go outside to turn soil over, discuss with the children the importance of using their *eyes* and not their fingers or hands to learn about the insects, because it is easy to hurt or damage insects when they are handled. Show the children the shovels and large metal spoons. Ask them what they could do with these tools. If necessary, suggest that they gently dig up some earth, and ask them to predict what they will see when they do this. Show your students the magnifying glasses and explain that these will be used to get a better look at what they observe.

When you are outside and each child has turned over a clod of earth, ask them what they see. How many different insects do they observe? (Typically, you may see earwigs, worms, beetles, and ants, among others.) You may discover some grubs. Grubs have three pairs of legs and are fat and white. They make good food for shrews and moles, which are small, furry animals that burrow underground. Grubs change into beetles if they are not eaten. If you see worms, explain that there is air in the earth, but when it rains, the rain takes the place of the air in the ground. The worms cannot breathe, so they come up to the surface of the earth to get air again.

Later, at the end of the session or day, encourage the children to recall and describe the sequence of events in this activity and what kinds of things they observed.

See the literature list for books about underground creatures and worms.

Eating Dirt and Worms
Snack/Gross Motor/Small Group Project

WHY we are doing this project: to reinforce the unit theme; to develop self-esteem and a sense of autonomy by enabling children to make their own snacks; to promote cooperation as a group; to develop the large muscle group by crushing cookies.

It is fun to make this snack right after the previous activity in which you observed insect life in soil.

WHAT we will need:
> Gummy worms
> Chocolate pudding
> Crushed Oreo cookies
> Small, clear plastic cups
> Spoons
> Rocks
> Freezer storage Ziploc bags
> Small bowls
> Masking tape strips
> Pens

HOW we will do it: You may choose to make the chocolate pudding with the group. Open up the Oreos and scrape the sweetened lard off. Put the cookies in the Ziploc bags. Double-bag each batch. Invite the children to take turns smashing the cookies with the rocks.

Put the cookie crumbs in bowls with spoons. Set the bowls on an activity table with bowls of pudding, spoons, and the gummy worms. Place a plastic cup in front of each chair.

Ahead of time, make a sample dirt and worms snack yourself. Put one gummy worm at the bottom of your cup, spoon chocolate pudding into your cup, then sprinkle the crushed Oreos on top. Tuck another gummy worm into the "dirt," with its head poking over the side of your cup.

During an Attention Getter time, tell the children that you are going to have dirt and worms for a snack. Say: "Doesn't that sound delicious?" Have fun with the children, and then show them your real dirt and worms snack, and explain how you made it. Can the children see the worm at the bottom through the plastic? Invite them to use the materials on the activity table to make their own snacks.

Use the masking tape strips and pens to put name labels on each snack. If you work with older children, encourage them to do this for themselves. Let the dirt and worms chill in the refrigerator for a little while, then enjoy your snack!

What Helps Seeds Grow Fastest?
Science/Language

WHY we are doing this project: to enable children to conduct a scientific experiment which compares how quickly or slowly seeds grow in different growing bases; to develop reading and writing skills.

Note: The soil samples listed below are available at any good nursery. Whatever variety you choose, be sure you include potting soil in the experiment, because it is too heavy for seeds to sprout in and it is important for the children to observe this. Peat moss lightens soil up, allows air in, and permits roots to move more easily. Vermiculite has the same purpose, and consists of tiny Styrofoam beads. Compost is cow manure, but when it is purchased at nurseries, it does not have a strong odor.

WHAT we will need:
> Potting soil
> Two of the following: sand, vermiculite, compost, peat moss
> Seeds (one kind)
> Styrofoam meat trays
> Three large tubs
> Small shovels
> Construction paper
> Sticky labels
> Small yogurt containers (three per child)
> Small containers of water
> Medicine droppers
> Observation books (pages provided on page 365; photocopy, enlarge, and assemble per instructions)

Science Experiment

with Dirt :

Which kind of dirt helps seeds grow fastest?

Observation Book

Day _____

One **1**·

This is a sample page for your observation book. Make a page for every day of the experiment. You may choose to write names (e.g., "Monday," "Tuesday") rather than numbering the days. Leave plenty of room for children to draw what they see in their cups as well as write words underneath if they wish.

Vermiculite   Potting Soil   Peat Moss   Sand   Compost

Here's what I see: _____

_____

_____

_____

Blank paper
Crayons
Pens
Rulers
Small bowls
Preparation:
Skewer

HOW we will do it: To prepare the yogurt containers, punch a few holes in the bottom of each one with a skewer (for drainage). Pour one growing material in each tub and set them on the table. On construction paper, print the name of each growing material, and pin it up on the wall, above the tub that holds that material. Draw a picture of each one underneath the name. Make many name labels of each one, so that all children can identify their three samples. Put the labels on the edge of the table, in front of the tub that holds that growing material. Put the seeds in containers beside each tub. A long, narrow table works well for this part of the experiment, because children can fill a container with a growing base and plant a few seeds, then continue along the table to do the same at the next tub, and so on to the end.

The experiments need to be left for at least one week on a table near a light source. On this table, place containers of water and medicine droppers for watering. Rulers should also be placed on this table. Some older children may be ready and able to use the rulers to measure growth, and even younger children may hold rulers up to their sprouts.

On a table near the experiment, set out the observation books, blank paper, crayons, and pens. These should be left out for the duration of the project, so that children can check on their experiments and add to their observation books at any time.

During an Attention Getter time, take the children down the line of tubs which hold the different growing materials. Read the names and encourage the children to touch and even smell each growing material. What is vermiculite? Which growing material is heaviest and which is lightest? Have the children wash their hands after this exploration, especially if compost is one of the samples. Show them the trays of empty containers and all the other materials. (It is difficult to tell when vermiculite is wet, so make sure the seeds in this growing base are not over-watered.) Ask them to predict in that growing material the seeds will grow fastest and highest. Ask the children if they see anything in the room which would help them conduct an experiment to find out. Show them the rulers and have them examine the centimeter markings. Ask your students how they could use the rulers in the experiment.

Before the children prepare their experiments, hold up an observation book and, together, read/interpret what it says. Show the children the blank paper, crayons, and pens, and invite them to record their observations, day by day, with any of these materials.

After a few days, examine the experiments. Which growing bases support the most and least growth? Are the results the same for everyone's experiments? Set out small bowls containing each kind of growing base and invite the children to hold each one in their hands, paying special attention to the weight of each one. Using what they notice from this experience, ask your students to hypothesize about why the least growth occurred in the potting soil. (Compost is cow manure. It has a lot of nutrients in it and is very rich. Peat moss and vermiculite lighten up soil—they make it looser so that there is air in the dirt, and so that roots can easily move in their search for water and nutrients.) After about a week, have a show-and-tell of observation books.

Weighing Growing Materials
Science/Math/Sensory

WHY we are doing this project: to enable children to weigh the growing materials and further explore their different weights; to enable children to discover that water adds weight to dirt.

WHAT we will need:
Tubs or sensory table
Growing materials (used in previous activity)

Measuring cups
Spoons
Balancing scales
Small, half-full pitchers of water
Spoons
Small scoopers

HOW we will do it: This activity can get quite messy, so you may want to set it up outside. Otherwise, put many layers of newspaper under your work area. Set all materials in or beside the sensory table or tubs. Ask the children to predict what will happen if they put an amount of vermiculite (or other material) on one side of the scales, and the same amount of potting soil on the other side. Encourage them to suggest other combinations they can weigh against each other and to predict what they will observe. Invite the children to conduct weighing experiments. Which materials are heaviest and which are lightest? Remind the children of the previous experiment and ask them to hypothesize about how and why the results of the two experiments are related. When appropriate, provide small pitchers of water, scoopers, and spoons. Does water change the weight of the materials?

    Developmental differences: Three- and young four-year-olds enjoy sensory exploration of different growing materials and how they feel when mixed with water. Through this exploration, they will feel the different weights of the materials. Older children are likely to use the scales to compare the weights of the materials.

Gardening Tools
Science/Gross Motor

WHY we are doing this activity: to familiarize children with tools that are used to prepare soil for planting; to provide a gross motor exercise.

WHAT we will need:
    Patch of ground at your home or school
    Children's-size shovels, hoes,
        rakes, and trowels
    Seeds

HOW we will do it: If you can find a patch of ground to use for this activity, you can start a class/group collective garden. You can either order the tools from toy or school supply catalogs, or visit a nursery or a variety/hardware store with a gardening section to see if you can find tools your children will be able to use without difficulty. Dig up and loosen the soil of your garden a little before the children work in it; otherwise, it may be too hard for them and they may become frustrated. Name and demonstrate the use of each tool before the children work with it. (A hoe is used to dig out weeds and to loosen soil. Trowels are for digging holes and loosening soil.) To prepare your garden, remove all weeds and aerate the soil by loosening it. Consult with a nursery to find out what is likely to grow well and quickly in your part of the country, and how best to nurture it. (In areas with adequate sunshine, sunflowers are fun to plant.) If you do not have the space for a garden, your children will have fun with the tools in a sandbox.

Mudworks
Science/Sensory

WHY we are doing this activity: to enable children to discover that mixed water and dirt make a muddy substance which sticks together, and to compare this to mixed water and sand.

WHAT we will need:
    Bowls
    Sand
    Dirt
    Small pitchers of water
    Tubs or sensory table
    Newspaper
    Popsicle sticks
    Spoons
    Activity sign (provided on page 368;
        photocopy and enlarge for your use)

HOW we will do it: To prepare, spread several layers of newspaper under your work surface. Put separate bowls of sand and dirt and all other materials in the tubs or sensory table. Post the activity sign on the wall by the activity table.

During an Attention Getter time, read/interpret the activity sign together. Ask the children to predict what they will observe when they follow the sign's suggestions. Ask them if they see anything in the room that will help them conduct an experiment to find out. Students can use the Popsicle sticks to stir the water and sand or dirt together. While your students are exploring the materials, discuss their findings. Which material makes a puddle and which does not? Ask them to hypothesize about why this is so. Invite the children to try to make balls of each material. Which one sticks together? Why? (Grains of sand are small stone particles. Water runs through them, but particles of dirt stick together.)

Mud Sculpting
Art/Sensory

WHY we are doing this project: to facilitate creative expression; to provide a sensory experience.

WHAT we will need:
    Mud
    Styrofoam meat trays
Clean-up:
    Hose

HOW we will do it: This is an outdoor activity. Invite the children to sculpt the mud into interesting shapes. Ask them to put their shapes on Styrofoam meat trays to dry for a few days. To clean up, spray the hose over the muddy area.

Make a hollow in a pile of dirt and a pile of sand. Pour a little water in both. What happens? _____

Volcano!

Science/Sensory/Small Group Project

WHY we are doing this activity: to give children another opportunity to see how vinegar and baking soda react to each other; to provide children with a sensory experience using wet dirt.

WHAT we will need:

>   Plastic bottle (16 oz.)
>   Red food coloring
>   Vinegar
>   Baking soda
>   Wet dirt
>   Tub
>   Volcano pictures

HOW we will do it: To prepare, put several heaping tablespoons of baking soda in the bottle. The more baking soda and vinegar you use, the more dramatic the effect will be. Put the bottle in the tub, and add red food coloring to the vinegar. Have a tub of wet dirt available.

During an Attention Getter time, ask the children if they know what a volcano is. Show the pictures of volcanoes to your students and discuss them. Let the children know that you are all going to make a pretend volcano. Together, mold the wet dirt all around the base of the bottle until it looks like a mountain. Pour vinegar into the bottle and stand back while the red lava surges out! If you have enough materials, let the children do this as a child-initiated project.

Growing in the Earth

Music/Movement/Gross Motor/Small Group Activity

WHY we are doing this activity: to help children express themselves physically through music; to develop the large muscle group; to help children enjoy music; to encourage creative exploration with music.

WHAT we will need:

>   Tubs of cool, dry dirt
>   Soft, relaxing music

HOW we will do it: This is a guided imagery activity, so you may want to designate a space and some toys for children who do not wish to participate.

Before you begin, pass around the cool dirt, and invite the children to plunge their hands into it with all their fingers spread apart. Can they feel it between their fingers? If you have the time and energy, you may also choose to let the children step into the tubs of dirt with their bare feet.

Have everyone spread out on the floor, and put on the soft, relaxing music. To begin, curl up tight and guide the activity along these lines:

"Imagine that you're a little seed that's just been planted. You're resting on soft, dry earth, but are waiting for something you need to grow. What do you think it could be? (Water, sunlight.) You just got a nice sprinkle of water, and the sun is shining so warmly on you, that you begin to uncurl a little sprout on top (begin to unfold one arm) and a little root starts to grow underneath (begin to uncurl one leg). Your roots grow a little bigger and a little longer every day. Remember how the dirt felt between our fingers? Imagine now that your roots are spreading and growing in the good, rich dirt and that's just how it feels. Now imagine that the seed you used to be is growing into a beautiful flower and your petals are opening up to hug the sunshine." (Let children move creatively in their own way.)

Try this variation: Stand together closely and tell the children that now you're going to pretend to be the roots of a tree. Say: "Did you know that the roots of a tree can grow many, many feet away from the tree? Let's imagine that we're the roots of a huge tree now, and we're slowly growing and spreading out into the earth that the tree is growing in. We're searching for water to soak up, to carry up our trunk, through our branches, to all the leaves including the highest ones, at the very top." Lie on the ground and slowly stretch and creep as roots might do.

For the last variation, pretend to be a little shrew, scraping and scrabbling a tunnel in the dirt, snuffling and sniffing for nice, fat, white grubs to eat.

The Archaeologists and the Bone

Language/Multicultural/Anti-Bias

WHY we are doing this activity: to teach children what archaeologists do; to expand vocabulary; to encourage children to use words and imagination to make up their own stories; to encourage children to trust their own judgment; to create multicultural and anti-bias awareness.

WHAT we will need:
> Flannel board shapes (provided on
> > page 371–372; photocopy and enlarge
> > for your use)
> Flannel board
> Felt

Preparation:
> Scissors
> Glue
> Clear contact paper
> Markers or crayons
> Story: "THE ARCHAEOLOGISTS AND
> > THE BONE" (provided)

HOW we will do it: To prepare, color the flannel story shapes in the text and cut them out. Glue them onto felt, cover with clear contact paper, and cut them out. Gather the children together and use the flannel board pieces to tell the following story:

"THE ARCHAEOLOGISTS AND THE BONE"

Once upon a time there were two archaeologists. *Archaeologist* is a hard word to say. Try AR-KEE-AWL-OH-GIST. [Repeat several times. If you work with young preschoolers, pat your head, blink your eyes, or tap your toe while you say the syllables.] What is an archaeologist? Well, it's someone who digs and sifts carefully through dirt to try to find things that tell us about people or animals who lived a long, long time ago. What kinds of things do they find? Bones. [Put up bone picture.] Fossils. [Put up fossil picture.] Fossils are plants or animals that have turned to stone. Archaeologists also find very old dishes and jewelry sometimes. [Put up dish and jewelry picture.] Sometimes they even find gold. [Put up picture of gold.] But they don't find gold very often. Mostly they find bones and fossils of plants and animals that lived a long time ago, as well as the kinds of every day things that ordinary people used thousands of years ago. [At the top of the board, put picture of people from long ago.]

Well, anyway, like I started to say, once upon a time there were two archaeologists, Dr. Jane P. Digalot, and her assistant, Dr. Seymour Scrabble. And one day, when they were digging and sifting oh-so-carefully through the dirt, so as not to break or disturb anything they found in the dirt—well, guess what they found? [Put up huge bone and let children answer.] A huge bone! What kind of animal could it have belonged to? It was larger than any bone of any animal on earth. Well, Dr. Jane P. Digalot and Dr. Seymour Scrabble got very, very excited, and dug and dug and dug some more, but much to their disappointment, they didn't find anything else. Why do you think they kept digging? What were they looking for? [More bones to tell them more about the animal the huge bone belonged to.]

Well, a group of other archaeologists came to visit the dig, which is what a place is called when archaeologists are working there—a dig—[put up group of other archaeologists] and they all gave their opinion.

"You're wasting your time," they said. "You're not going to find any more bones. The first one you found was obviously washed away by a river, thousands of years ago, and that's why you only found that one bone. You won't find any more bones digging around here." [Put up river picture.] That's what all those archaeologists said, and then they went away again.

But Dr. Digalot and Dr. Scrabble didn't find any signs at all that there had been a river to carry that bone to the spot where they'd found it. And no matter what the other archaeologist said, they had a strong feeling that some huge animal, maybe a dinosaur, had died in that spot and that there must be more bones. So they kept digging and kept digging, and one day, when they were getting very tired and wondering if it was all worth it, Dr. Scrabble found something.

"Over here, over here!" he shouted to Dr. Digalot. So they both excavated—which is another word for digging things out of the earth—and they excavated for many days, and when they were all done, guess what they had? [Put up picture of reconstructed dinosaur bones and let children answer.] What do you think of that? They decided that long, long ago when the dinosaurs were alive, another dinosaur had carried that one huge bone away from the other bones, probably to eat the meat that had been on it. Dr. Jane P. Digalot and Dr. Seymour Scrabble were glad they had not listened to the other archaeologists, and I am too.

VOCABULARY:
Archaeologist
Fossil
Excavate

After you tell the story and discuss it, show your students where the flannel board and pieces will be and invite them to use the materials.

Archaeologist Play
Dramatic Play/Sensory/Multicultural/Anti-Bias

WHY we are doing this activity: to promote child-to-child interaction; to develop speaking and listening skills; to help children feel confident about expressing ideas; to create multicultural and anti-bias awareness; to help all children feel that a career as an archaeologist is open to them.

WHAT we will need:
Campsite:
Tent (construct your own makeshift tent if you do not have a real one)
Dishes
Maps
Notebooks
Pens
Blankets
Archaeology pictures (provided on pages 371–372; photocopy and enlarge for your use)
Excavation:
Large shallow tubs
Sand
Semi-precious stones, shells (Tiger's eye, abalone shell, polished stones, etc.)
Large beef bones
Any small, old-looking objects
Colanders

HOW we will do it: To prepare, post the archaeology pictures around the walls of the room. If you have time, color them. Pitch your tent and put all the campsite materials beside it. Put the sand, colanders, stones, and shells in the shallow tubs, on the floor near the tent. This is the "excavation site." Invite the children to play with the materials. They can sift sand in the colanders to discover the *artifacts* (bones, stones, and shells) that you have buried in it. Show them the pens and notebooks that they can use to keep a record of the artifacts they find.

© 1996 Delmar Publishers

373

Literature

Symbol Key: *Multicultural
                      +Minimal diversity
                      No symbol: no diversity or no people

Aliki. (1972). *Fossils*. New York: Harper Trophy.*

Aliki. (1981). *Digging up dinosaurs*. New York: Harper Trophy. (This book is perfect for reading in conjunction with the flannel board story and dramatic play. Shade in diverse skin colors yourself.)

Aliki. (1988). *Dinosaur bones*. New York: Harper Trophy.+

Cavies, B. (1993). *Compost critters.* New York: Dutton's Children's Books.

Glaser, L. (1992). *Wonderful worms*. Brookfield, CT: The Millbrook Press.

Rius, M., & Parramon, J. M. (1987). *Habitats: Life underground*. Hauppauge, NY: Barron's Educational Series.

Soutter-Perrot, Andrienne. (1993). *The earth*. Columbus, OH: American Education.

Stille, D. R. (1990). *Soil erosion and pollution*. Chicago: Children's Press.

Extenders

Language: To extend the Soil Samples activities, make a language chart that describes how the samples are different in terms of color, texture, and content.

Science: After experimenting to see how quickly the seeds grew in potting soil, vermiculite, peat moss, and so forth, have the children mix combinations of these to see how seeds grow in them.

Sensory: Buy clay from a school supply store and let the children make coil pots or other shapes. Some clay from school supply stores can be air-dried, but some mixtures are synthetic and are not authentic clay.

FAT–TASTIC

Attention Getter: Gather the following materials: margarine, cooking lard, a tub, a smooth ball, vegetable oil, a tub of warm soapy water, and paper towels. Cover the ball in vegetable oil and put it into the tub. When the children are gathered, pass the tub around and invite the children to try to pick it up. Is it easy? Why not? Show the children the bottle of vegetable oil, and tell them that when people bake, they often grease their pans with vegetable oil first. Using their experience trying to pick up the oily ball, ask the children why they think this is hard. Show your students the lard and margarine and say: "If we melted this lard and this margarine down, they would be oily liquids, like this vegetable oil. The margarine, the oil, and the lard are all different kinds of fat. Lard is animal fat. The margarine and the oil are vegetable fat, pressed out of safflower or sunflower seeds. Butter is the fat that comes from milk." Ask the children to guess what you are going to talk about for the next few days. Have them

wash their hands with the clean, soapy water, and then give them small smears of margarine and lard to explore with their hands and fingers. How does each one feel? Explain that oil is fat in a liquid state and that the margarine and lard are fat in a solid state.

Fat Floats
Science/Sensory

WHY we are doing this project: to provide children with a hands-on opportunity to discover that fat floats.

WHAT we will need:
    Dollops of margarine
    Dollops of lard
    Vegetable oil
    Medicine droppers
    Clear plastic cups
    Tubs
    Cold water
    Trays
    Small pitchers
    Small containers for vegetable oil
    Newspaper
    Warm, soapy water
    Paper towels

HOW we will do it: Spread many layers of newspaper underneath the work surface. Set the warm, soapy water and paper towels near the experiment activities, but not so near that the children might drop fat into the water. The soapy water and towels are for cleaning hands.

Put the clear plastic cups and medicine droppers on a tray with the small containers of vegetable oil. Place the small pitchers of water nearby. Have some empty tubs available in which experiments can be dumped when children want to begin new ones.

Pour cold water into the other tubs and set the dollops of lard and margarine nearby. Ask the children to predict what will happen when they put the fats in the water. Ask them what they see in the room that will help them find out. As your students conduct the experiment,

ask them what they notice about whether it is possible to sink the fat dollops. What do the vegetable oil drops do in the water? (Immediately float to the surface.) Is it possible to keep oil drops at the bottom of a cup filled with water? (Fat weighs less than water, so it floats.) What happens when one oil droplet meets another one in the water? Encourage verbalization of comments.

Oil (Liquid Fat) Repels Water
Science

WHY we are doing this experiment: to provide children with a hands-on method of discovering that fat repels water.

WHAT we will need:
    Wax paper
    Water
    Vegetable oil
    Small containers (for oil and water)
    Medicine droppers
    Toothpicks
    Food coloring
    Trays

HOW we will do it: To prepare, put a tray in front of each chair at an activity table. Put a sheet of wax paper and a toothpick on each tray. Add food coloring to the small containers of water and arrange these and the containers of vegetable oil so that all the children have access to them. Ask the children to predict what they will observe if they drop both colored water and oil onto the wax paper. Invite them to conduct this experiment. Do the two fluids mix? Does this result change when they use toothpicks to stir the oil and water together? Explain that fat molecules are drawn to other fat molecules, and water molecules are drawn to other water molecules. *Molecules* are tiny, tiny particles. *Repel* means to push away. Using this information, ask your students to hypothesize about why the oil and water cannot be mixed very easily.

More Proof That Oil and Water Do Not Mix (Part 1)

Science/Sensory

WHY we are doing this experiment: to provide children with another fun method of proving that water and oil do not mix.

WHAT we will need:

Small plastic containers with lids
Tall plastic bottles with caps
Small pitchers of water
Food coloring
Funnels
Vegetable oil
Tubs or sensory table
Newspaper

HOW we will do it: Spread many layers of newspaper underneath your work area. In the tubs or sensory table, provide separate, small pitchers of oil and of water. Add the containers, bottles, lids, caps, and funnels. It is nice to have tall, narrow bottles as well as wider, shorter containers because this allows children to see that even though the container shapes change the thickness of each layer, the water and oil still separate. This is especially interesting to observe in Part 2 of this project.

During an Attention Getter time, ask the children if they have ever seen their fathers or mothers make salad dressing. How did they make it? Ask the children what they see in the room that will help them make their own water and oil mixtures. Ask them to predict whether the water and oil will mix if their containers are shaken hard. Also ask: "What will happen if you shake your oil and water and the lid of your container has not been screwed on properly?" As the children conduct the experiment, ask them what they observe. What do they notice about whether the water and oil stay mixed?

More Proof That Oil and Water Do Not Mix (Part 2)

Science/Sensory

WHY we are doing this part of the experiment: to provide children with an opportunity to see how other materials settle, float, or sink when mixed with oil and water.

WHAT we will need:

Oil and water mixtures (from previous activity)
Small bowl of coarse ground pepper
Small bowl of crushed red pepper
Bowl of ketchup
Bowl of mustard
Mustard seeds
Small pitcher of red vinegar

HOW we will do it: Invite the children to add all or some of the above to the oil and water mixtures they made in the previous activity. Ask them to predict what will happen to the new materials when the children screw lids and caps on and shake their containers hard. Do the pepper flakes sink or float? What happens to the ketchup and mustard? How many distinct layers can the children count in their containers after everything settles? If you like, add small pitchers of water to which green or blue food coloring has been added.

Lard and Margarine (Solid Fats) Repel Water

Science/Language

WHY we are doing this experiment: to provide children with a hands-on method of discovering that solid fat also repels water; to develop speaking and listening skills; to develop reading skills.

WHAT we will need:

    Pats of margarine (on individual wax
        paper pieces)
    Spray bottles on "mist" setting
    Water
    Dark-colored plastic plates (and/or
        cookie sheets)
    Large plastic garbage bags
    Activity sign (provided below; photocopy
        and enlarge for your use)
    Newspaper
    Puppet

HOW we will do it: Spread newspaper out on the activity table and put the dishes on top. Dark-colored plates work best because the margarine is light-colored and the children can more easily observe where the grease adheres and where it is repelled. Set a plate in front of every chair at the activity table. Cut squares out of the plastic bags, which will cover half of the plates. Plastic garbage bags work best because they are heavy enough to lie down flat (especially new, unused bags). Do not put too much water in the spray bottles. Put one margarine pat beside each plate. Put all other materials out on the table so that all children will have access to them.

Make an activity sign based on the sample provided and pin it up near the activity table. During an Attention Getter time, interpret/read the activity sign. Ask your students to predict what they will see when they follow the sign's suggestions. Invite them to do so. Take out your puppet and use its personality to ask the children what they are doing. Can the margarine be spread on the wet part of the dishes? How about the dry part? Ask the children if they remember how oil and water reacted to each other in the previous experiment. Using this information, ask them to hypothesize about why margarine cannot be rubbed onto the wet part of the dishes and pans.

Science Experiment with Grease and Water:

Alter this sign to reflect your materials.

Put plastic on one half of a plate or cookie sheet. Spray water on it. Take away the plastic. Now try to smear margarine on both sides. What happens?

Making a Water Magnifier with the Help of Grease

Science

WHY we are doing this experiment: to enable children to observe how a greased, looped paper clip will hold a drop of water (the fat repels the water and exerts pressure, which holds the drop in place).

WHAT we will need:

Metal paper clips
Margarine
Sensory table or tubs
Small containers for margarine
Small measuring cups or coffee scoopers
Bowls of water
Medicine or eyedroppers
Small letters and shapes page from
    Magnificent Magnifiers unit
Small paper towel squares
Warm soapy water

Preparation:
Pencil

HOW we will do it: To prepare, unbend one paper clip for each child, and rebend it around a pencil to form a loop with a handle. Make sure the upper part of the loop actually touches the lower part where they cross, so that the circumference will hold a drop of water.

Put the metal loops, small scoopers, bowls of water, and eyedroppers in the sensory table or tubs.

Make photocopies of the tiny shape, letter, and number page from the Magnificent Magnifiers unit, and put these on an activity table near the other materials.

During an Attention Getter time, hold up one of the paper clip loops and, using your fingers, grease it thoroughly with margarine. Ask your students to predict what will happen to a water drop if it is dropped onto it. Ask the children if they see anything in the room that will help them conduct this experiment. Invite them to do so. What happens? Do water drops fall through the greased metal loops? (Because the grease repels the water, it pushes out on the water, and this pressure keeps the water drop wedged in the middle of the loop.)

Tip: Encourage the children to turn the metal loops so that the overlapping part is on top, and gently pour streams of water over them.

Invite your students to use their water-drop magnifiers to examine the sheets of tiny shapes and letters.

After they have explored the materials for a while, invite the children to wash their greasy loops in the warm soapy water, dry them with paper towels, and hold them under a stream of water. Will an ungreased metal loop hold a water drop?

What Dissolves Grease?

Science/Sensory

WHY we are doing this experiment: to enable children to observe the effects of cold water, warm water, and liquid soap on grease.

WHAT we will need:

Tub of cold water
Tub of warm water
Tub for dishes
Children's play dishes
Pats of margarine
Liquid soap
Vegetable oil
Small containers (for soap and oil)
Medicine droppers
Spoons
Newspapers

HOW we will do it: Spread many layers of newspaper underneath your work surface. If you have a large sensory table, put all the tubs inside it. Place the margarine pats, vegetable oil, and some spoons beside the tub of play dishes, and the liquid soap, spoons, and medicine droppers beside the tubs of water.

During an Attention Getter time, ask the children if they have ever had grease on their hands. How did they get it off? Ask them if they've ever washed greasy dishes or seen their parents wash greasy dishes. Encourage observations, and then show the children the materials and encourage them to explore. As they do, ask: "What do you notice about whether the cold or warm water takes the grease off the dishes faster? What happens when the liquid soap is added?" Warm water and liquid soap make fat molecules move apart from each other. They *dissolve* the grease.

Developmental differences: Three- and young four-year-olds tend to become engrossed in the sensory aspect of this activity. Through their exploration, they will discover that oil or margarine stays on their hands in cold water and comes off in warm, soapy water. Older children tend to enjoy sensory exploration and also enjoy observing what happens to the oil and grease on the dishes.

Fat Makes Paper Transparent

Science

WHY we are doing this project: to enable children to observe that as fat saturates paper, the paper becomes transparent; to develop reading skills with an activity sign.

The facts of the matter: The fat of margarine soaks into the spaces between the fibers of paper. As it soaks in, or saturates, the paper becomes transparent because the fat transmits light, so the light is conducted directly through the paper.

WHAT we will need:
  Construction paper
  Regular white paper
  Newspaper
  Brown paper bags
  Kitchen parchment paper
  Margarine pats
  Small containers for margarine
  Small pictures, letters, and numbers page
    from Magnificent Magnifiers unit
  Tub of soapy water
  Paper towels
  Activity sign (provided below; photocopy
    and enlarge for your use)

HOW we will do it: Kitchen parchment paper is available in supermarkets. To prepare, cut all the paper samples into squares measuring about 7.5 cm x 7.5 cm (3" x 3"). Put pats of margarine in the small containers, and make an

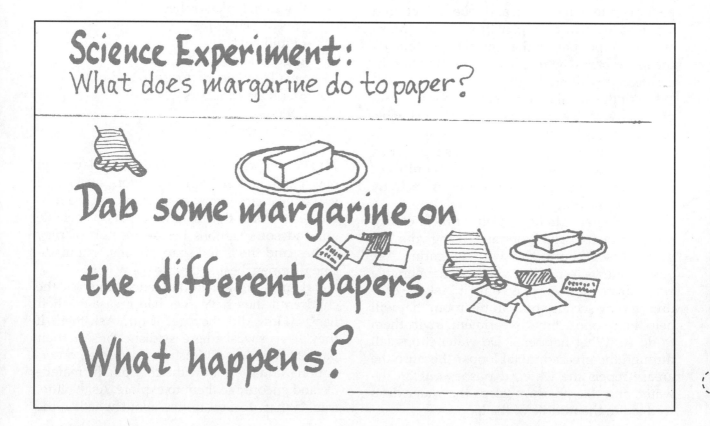

Science Experiment:
What does margarine do to paper?

Dab some margarine on the different papers. What happens?

activity sign based on the sample in the text. Post the sign near the work surface. Make photocopies of the shapes, numbers, and letters page from the Magnificent Magnifiers unit. The purpose of these is to provide something children can examine through their transparent papers.

During an Attention Getter time, read/interpret the activity sign together. Ask the children to predict what will happen to the papers when the fat is rubbed on them. Ask your students if they see anything in the room that will help them conduct this science experiment. As they follow the sign's suggestions, ask them to notice which paper the fat of the margarine makes most transparent and which paper becomes least transparent. Ask them to notice the thickness of the papers. Is there a connection? Explain that *saturate* means to soak in until there is no room for more, and ask your students if they can think of other ways to use this word. Then ask them to notice how the transparent spot spreads when they rub margarine into the paper.

How Much Fat Is in Meats?
Science/Language

WHY we are doing this experiment: to enable children to compare the fat content of a variety of meats; to develop speaking, listening, reading, and writing skills.

WHAT we will need:
Kitchen parchment squares (7.5 cm x 7.5 cm [3″ x 3″])
Small pieces of bacon (cooked and uncooked)
Salami slices
Summer sausage slices
Hot dog slices
Small containers (for meat samples)
Butcher paper
Markers
Scotch tape
Chart headings (provided below; photocopy and enlarge for your use)

HOW we will do it: Arrange all materials on the table so that all children will have access to them. Prepare the headings for a language chart, and pin it up near the experimentation area.

During an Attention Getter time, explain to the children that they can press the paper squares down onto the meat slices and see how large the transparent spots are when the paper soaks up the fat from the meat. (Make sure you discuss the fact that the children should never eat raw meat.) Ask the children to predict which meat will cause the most and least fat to saturate the paper.

After the children have conducted the experiment, read/interpret the headings on the language chart together. Have the children tape a sample of a grease-spotted paper from each meat under the corresponding heading. Together, as a group, look at and compare the size of the grease spots and the degree of transparency.

Note: Some of this will be determined by how hard the paper was pressed onto the meat sample. For the purposes of the language chart, you may want to make your own grease spots on paper so that you can be sure the same amount of pressure was applied to all the meat samples and that the results are more accurate.

As the children discuss the fat contents of the different meat samples, record their observations on the chart or have them write their words on the chart themselves. Use alternate colors of marker for each observation so that individual sentences can be more easily identified. Use quotation marks and write the children's names after their comments. Ask the children to look at each meat sample. Can they tell just by looking which one has the most fat? Does this correspond with the results of the paper test?

The Food Pyramid
Social Studies /Small Group Project

WHY we are doing this: to make children aware of healthy eating habits; to develop observation skills; to develop cognition by classifying food groups.

WHAT we will need:
>   Food pyramid chart (providedon page 382;
>   photocopy and enlarge for your use)
>   Home and food magazines

HOW we will do it: Pin the food pyramid chart up on the wall near the place where you will be gathering, and have your food magazines available.

During an Attention Getter time, point to each part of the food pyramid and, together, discuss the amounts and types of foods that should be eaten. Leaf through the home and food magazines as a group, and when you come to a food type, have the children say which food group it belongs to. Do the children think that that food is high in fat or low in fat? You may also choose to discuss high sugar content/low sugar content foods and where they fit into the food pyramid.

Fat Means Nonstick
Science/Math/Small Group Project

WHY we are doing this project: to enable children to observe that fat acts as a lubricant; to practice rational counting; to familiarize children with spoon and cup measurements.

WHAT we will need:
>   Three ripe bananas
>   Two eggs, well beaten
>   2 cups flour
>   ¾ cup sugar
>   1 teaspoon salt
>   1 teaspoon baking soda
>   Large bowl
>   Muffin tins
>   Margarine
>   Wax paper squares
>   Food coloring
>   Butter

HOW we will do it: Before you begin, remind the children about not sneezing or coughing on food and dishes while cooking, and about

What to eat every day.

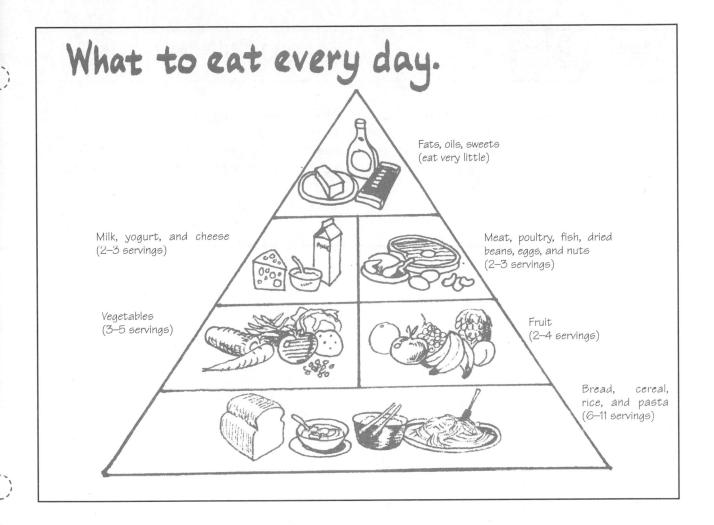

Fats, oils, sweets
(eat very little)

Milk, yogurt, and cheese
(2–3 servings)

Meat, poultry, fish, dried
beans, eggs, and nuts
(2–3 servings)

Vegetables
(3–5 servings)

Fruit
(2–4 servings)

Bread, cereal,
rice, and pasta
(6–11 servings)

keeping fingers out of mouths, eyes, noses, and ears. Pass the muffin tin around and invite each child to use a wax paper square and some margarine to thoroughly grease one muffin section in the tin. Leave one muffin section ungreased.

Preheat your oven to 350°F. In a large bowl, mix the bananas and eggs together. Let the children take turns stirring. Then let some children take turns measuring out the flour, sugar, salt, and baking soda and pouring them into the wet mixture, while other children continue to stir.

Make sure all the muffin sections (except one) are thoroughly greased, including around the rims and tops. When children fill the pans, batter tends to get everywhere. Ask your students to spoon the mixture into the muffin sections. Add some food coloring to the muffin batter in the ungreased section so that you will be able to easily distinguish it. Bake the muffins for forty minutes or until firm and brown.

(Baking time varies, depending on your oven.) Test for doneness by inserting a metal knife into one muffin. If it is clean when you remove it, the muffins are ready. If some sticky batter clings to the knife, more baking time is needed.

After the muffins have cooled, turn the pans upside down and have the children watch as you shake them. Which ones fall out easily? Which muffin stays in the pan? Remind the children of how they greased the pan and how only one muffin section was ungreased. Ask the children to hypothesize about why the muffin in the ungreased section is difficult to pry out. If you like, spread butter on your warm muffins. Enjoy!

Pressing Oil
Science/Gross Motor

WHY we are doing this project: to help children understand where vegetable oil comes from; to help them understand that this fat can be pressed out of nuts, olives, and seeds; to develop the large muscle group.

WHAT we will need:
Black olives (pitted)
Shelled peanuts
Shelled walnuts
Clear, plastic freezer storage bags
   (Ziploc)
Rolling pins
Safflower oil
Safflower seeds (available at pet stores)
Olive oil
Jar of peanut butter with oil at the top
   (try an all natural peanut butter)

HOW we will do it: Put the bottles of oils, safflower seeds, olives, peanuts, and peanut butter on an exhibit table for the children to examine. Position the source material in front of the corresponding container (e.g., a peanut in front of a jar of peanut butter, an olive in front of a can of olives). Put the nuts and olives in double bags and seal them. Put them on the table with the rolling pins.

During an Attention Getter time, have the group identify each kind of oil and the kind of seed, nut, or vegetable it came from. Be sure the children know that the glass bottles should be left exactly where they are and not be picked up or carried away. Show your students the materials on the activity table and invite them to pound the nuts or olives, and then to roll the rolling pins over the bags using as much pressure as they can. Leave the materials out for several days, but refrigerate the bags in between times. Eventually, the inside of the bags will become coated with the oil from the nuts.

Making Butter
Science

WHY we are doing this project: to help children understand that there is fat in milk; to enable them to observe that butter is milk fat; to help them understand what *coalesce* means.

WHAT we will need:
Three cartons of whipping cream
Three plastic containers with lids
Heavy steel balls or marbles (six)
Small plastic spoons
Crackers
Optional:
Timer
Popsicle sticks

HOW we will do it: Put two marbles in each container. During an Attention Getter time, ask the children if they know what butter is made from. Show them your cartons of cream and, if you like, use the plastic spoons to give everyone a small taste of the cream. Do the children think it tastes like it has a lot of fat in it? Tell the children that you are going to make butter. Show them the containers with the marbles in them and let them take turns pouring one carton of cream into each container. Let the children know that once they start shaking the containers, everyone has to take turns to keep shaking them until the butter is made. Encourage the children to move the containers in a figure-eight motion. If necessary, use the timer to help the children with taking turns. (See the activity directly following this one for a song children can sing while they shake.)

At first, your students will hear the marbles moving, but after a while the fat will begin to coalesce and the cream will be so thick that it will not be possible to hear them. Explain to the children that the fat is *coalescing*. This means that the fat droplets are drawn to each other and form globules. As more and more fat droplets cling to the globules, the globules get bigger and bigger until the butter is completely separated from the buttermilk.

Rinse the butter off, salt it if you like, and let the children use the Popsicle sticks to spread small dabs of butter on crackers to eat.

This Is the Way We Shake the Cream
Music/Movement/Cognitive

WHY we are doing this activity: to develop cognition through memorization of words and actions; to help children feel comfortable using their singing voices.

WHAT we will need:
> Song: "THIS IS THE WAY WE SHAKE THE CREAM" (To the tune of "This Is the Way We Brush Our Teeth")
>
> "THIS IS THE WAY WE SHAKE THE CREAM"
> This is the way we shake the cream,
> shake the cream, shake the cream.
> This is the way we shake the cream,
> and make it into butter.
>
> This is the way we spread the butter,
> spread the butter, spread the butter,
> This is the way we spread the butter
> and eat it with the bread.

HOW we will do it: Pretend to be shaking a jar of cream for the first verse. For the first three lines of the second verse, pretend to spread butter, and for the last line, pretend to eat the delicious snack. After the children have learned the words, can they remember to sing it without saying the word "cream"? The word "butter"? Try it!

Butter Box
Math

WHY we are doing this project: to practice rational counting and subtraction; to develop self-esteem and a sense of autonomy through use of a one-person work station.

WHAT we will need:
> Bowl
> Ice cubes
> Tin box
> Butter squares
> Writing sheet (p0rovided on page 386; photocopy and enlarge for your use)
> Pens
> Blank paper
> "One person may be here" sign (provided on page 3; photocopy and enlarge for your use)

HOW we will do it: To prepare, put the ice in the bowl, and cut butter squares to put in the tin. The number you put in the tin should be determined by how high your children are counting. Then put the tin in the bowl of ice, to keep the butter squares hard. Make several copies of the writing sheet and put these, blank paper, and pens beside the butter box.

During an Attention Getter time, discuss the "One person may be here" sign and read/interpret the writing sheets. Encourage the children to explore the materials and let them know that they may use the blank paper instead of the writing sheets if they'd like. Talk about the fact that the butter squares in the butter box are for counting, not eating.

How many butter squares are in the butter box?

I counted _____ butter squares.

Take three butter squares away.

How many are left? _____

Crunkle and the Carrot Juice

Language/Anti-Bias/Social Studies

WHY we are doing this project: to develop speaking and listening skills; to help children become critical thinkers; to help children become aware of the hidden messages in advertising.

WHAT we will need:
Flannel board shapes (provided on pages 387-389; photocopy and enlarge for your use)
Flannel board
Felt
Scissors
Glue
Clear contact paper
Markers or crayons
"Two people may be here" sign (provided on page13; photocopy and enlarge for your use)
Story: "CRUNKLE AND THE CARROT JUICE" (provided)

HOW we will do it: To prepare, color in the flannel board shapes in the text. Ask friends, family, or parents to help you with this if you are short on time. Glue the shapes onto felt, cover with clear contact paper, and cut them out. Set up your flannel board and tell the following story to the children.

"CRUNKLE AND THE CARROT JUICE"

As you probably know, rabbits love carrots. Well, there was once a rabbit by the name of Crunkle who made carrot juice and sold it to all the rabbits for miles around. [Put up standing Crunkle.] Now there

Enlarge these drawings on a photocopier.

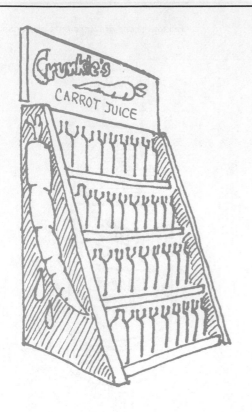

Everyone likes a rabbit who's fat and plump and happy!

Fatten yourself up! with Crunkle's CARROT JUICE

Everyone likes a rabbit who's thin and skinny and sleek!

Skinny Rabbits Drink Crunkle's CARROT JUICE

NEW! IMPROVED!

Everyone likes a rabbit who's not too fat and not too thin

Get that "just right" feeling with Crunkle's CarrotJuice

Totally NEW Formula

was one thing that Crunkle wanted more than anything else in the world, and that was to be rich, rich, rich. But in order to be rich, rich, rich, he knew he'd have to sell a lot more carrot juice. [Put up bottle of Crunkle's carrot juice and picture of Crunkle thinking.]

"Hmmmm," he thought. "How can I make those rabbits want to buy more of my carrot juice?" And he thought and he thought and he pondered and cogitated until his thinker was sore from thinking but finally he had what he thought was a wonderful idea. He made a big poster and it said: "Everyone likes a rabbit who's fat and plump and happy!! Fatten yourself up with Crunkle's carrot juice!" And he put this poster up beside his carrot juice. [Put up the poster and bottles of carrot juice and standing Crunkle.] The other rabbits came by and looked at the poster.

"Step right up, folks!" Crunkle said. "Be the most popular rabbit in your warren! You can see what the sign says plain as day—everyone likes a rabbit who's plump and fat and happy and Crunkle's carrot juice will fatten you up in no time!! There it is in writing, so it must be true!! Buy one bottle of Crunkle's famous carrot juice and be amazed by the results!!" Well, the other rabbits looked at each other and talked and wondered and didn't quite know what to think. But they all knew they wanted the other rabbits to like them.

"Everyone likes a fat, plump, happy rabbit," they thought. "Maybe that Crunkle's carrot juice really will help me." And before you know it they were all buying a bottle. And when they were gone [take group of rabbits down] Crunkle looked at all his money and then he laughed and skipped all the way to the bank.

"Hee hee!" he laughed, "I'm going to be rich, rich, rich!" [Put up Crunkle on his way to the bank.]

Well, all the rabbits had a bottle of Crunkle's carrot juice now, so nobody bought any more for a while. Do you think Crunkle was happy about that? [Let children answer.]

"Hmmmm," he thought. "How can I make those rabbits want to buy my carrot juice again?" And just like before, he thought and he thought and he pondered and cogitated until his thinker was sore from thinking, but once again he had what he thought was a wonderful idea. He made a new poster, and this one

said: "Everyone likes a rabbit who's thin and skinny and sleek! Skinny rabbits drink Crunkle's new improved carrot juice!" And he put *that* poster up beside his bottles of carrot juice. [Put up poster and bottles of carrot juice and standing Crunkle.]

Well, pretty soon the other rabbits came by again [put up group of rabbits] and Crunkle said, "Step right up folks—don't be shy!! The poster says it plain as day: 'Everyone likes a thin, skinny sleek rabbit and skinny rabbits drink Crunkle's carrot juice!' There it is in writing, so it must be true! Buy a bottle of Crunkle's new, improved carrot juice and be amazed by the new, improved results."

Well, the rabbits looked at the new poster and they talked and they wondered, and pretty soon they began to think: "I really want the other rabbits to like me. I wonder if Crunkle's carrot juice really will make me thin and skinny and sleek. Maybe I'll just buy one bottle of this new improved stuff and try it." And they did. And when they were gone [take group of rabbits off the board and put blank picture up] Crunkle looked at all of his money and laughed and skipped all the way to the bank again.

"Hee hee!" he laughed, "I'm going to be rich, rich, rich."

Well, do you think Crunkle was satisfied? Not him—he began to think of another dastardly plan. [Put up thinking Crunkle.] Just like before, he thought and he thought and he pondered and cogitated until his thinker was sore from thinking, but once again he had what he thought was another wonderful idea. He made a *third* big poster, and this one said: "Everyone likes a rabbit who's not too fat and not too thin! Get that "just right" feeling with Crunkle's totally new formula carrot juice!" And just like before, he put the poster up beside his bottles of carrot juice. [Put up third poster beside bottles of juice.]

Well, the other rabbits came by, and Crunkle said, "Step right up, folks! Get your totally new formula Crunkle's carrot juice. Nobody likes a rabbit who's too fat or too thin!! Crunkle's new formula carrot juice will give you that 'just right' feeling!"

But this time, just as the other rabbits were thinking that they should buy a bottle, one of the rabbits (her name was Cotton Top) said to them, [put up rabbit with blue bow] "You know, I've bought two bottles of Crunkle's carrot juice already and I'm exactly the same now as I was before. My bunny friends and family didn't care if I was fat, and they didn't care if I was thin, and they didn't care if I drank Crunkle's carrot juice, and they didn't care if I didn't drink it. I'm not buying any more of your stupid carrot juice, Crunkle. I'm going down to the lettuce patch to play tag with my friends." And off she hopped to do just that. [Take Cotton Top off the board.]

Well, all the other rabbits began to think about it, and realized that Cotton Top was right, because the same thing was true for them. None of their friends and family had cared if they were fat and none of them had cared if they were thin and nothing had changed whether they drank Crunkle's carrot juice or not. And the more they thought about that, the angrier they got at Crunkle.

And Crunkle said, "Now, now, folks, no need to get riled up. A rabbit's got to make a living, doesn't he?" But the rabbits were too angry at themselves and at Crunkle to listen to his excuses, so they made him pack up every last bottle of his Crunkle's carrot juice and take them all away. And because he couldn't sell a single bottle any more, he packed everything up and left town [put up ashamed Crunkle] and the last I heard of him he was trying to sell cabbage juice out by Bobtail Bluff. As for the rest of the rabbits, they went down to the lettuce patch too, and played tag until the sun went down and that's the end of that story.

Questions for discussion:

• Do you think it was true that everyone liked rabbits who were plump and fat? Thin and skinny? Think about the people you like. Why do you like them?

• When Crunkle's posters said the carrot juice was "new and improved" and a "totally new formula," do you think the carrot juice was really better or different? Why did Crunckle say it was new and improved?

• One of the posters said: "Everyone likes a rabbit who's thin and skinny," and Crunkle said, "There it is in writing so it must be true." Do you think he was right? If something is in writing, is it always true? Is everything on the

television true? (Lead into a discussion of things seen on television that are not true.)

• When Cotton Top said that her friends and family didn't care if she was fat or thin or if she drank Crunkle's carrot juice or not, the other rabbits realized the same thing was true for them. The story says they got mad at Crunkle and they got mad at themselves. Why do you think they were mad at themselves?

VOCABULARY:
Cogitate
Satisfied
Ponder
Dastardly
Amazed
Realize
Results
Warren
Sleek

After telling and talking over the story, discuss the "Two people may be here" sign. Leave the flannel board and the pieces out for the children so that they can retell the original story as well as make up new ones.

What Is Real?
Social Studies/Anti-Bias/Small Group Activity

WHY we are doing this activity: to make the children aware that all bodies have body fat and that it is a natural, normal part of all bodies; to make children aware of the function of body fat; to make children aware of body fat standards, especially for women, which are imposed by the media, and to encourage children to question them; to help children critically examine media images and messages in general; to develop observation skills.

Food for thought: In the 1950s, the average female model weighed 8 percent less than the average woman. Today, the average female model weighs 22 percent less than the average woman. Only one in every 80,000 women has the body type of the average model. Although there are many more sexualized images of women than of men in the media, men too are confronted with "perfect" body images.

WHAT we will need:
Fashion magazines
Photojournalism magazines
(e.g., Sunday newspaper supplements, *Life* magazine)
Barbie photograph (from a toy catalog)

HOW we will do it: Leaf through the magazines and cut out two kinds of photographs: those that feature posed, glamorized models and those that are slice-of-life photos of real people in action. Tape the former group of photographs and the Barbie picture on one side of a wall so that they will be clearly visible to the children. Do the same with the latter group of photos on another part of the wall.

Explain to the children that the fat in our bodies is stored energy. If we are in a very cold place, our body fat helps keep us warm. If for some reason we cannot get any food for a long time, our bodies use up our body fat to give us energy. Everyone has body fat. Body fat is a normal, natural part of everyone's body.

Together, talk about the photographs of the "real" people and compare them to the fashion models. How are they different? (Models are almost always posed; "real" people are often photographed in action. Female models are usually much thinner than real women and wear much more makeup. Female models are often wearing skimpy or tight clothes which reveal a lot of their bodies, clothes that are rarely seen on real women.) Compare the body of the Barbie doll to the pictures of real women. (Barbie doll: huge eyes, tiny nose, tiny waist, large bust, exaggeratedly long legs.) Ask the children if they know any real women whose bodies look like this. If you like, use a Ken doll to make the same comparison to real men.

Ask the children what they notice about the skin color of most of the models. Do most of the people in the world have white skin? Discuss these issues with the children. Remind them of the flannel board story about Crunkle. Did it matter to their friends and families how the bunnies looked and whether the bunnies were fat or thin? Ask: "Do you think your friends and your family love you for how you look, or for the special person that you are?" Discuss.

Oil Art
Art

WHY we are doing this project: to facilitate creative expression.

WHAT we will need:
Large shallow pans
Water
Vegetable oil
Tempera paint
Medicine droppers
Small containers (for colored oil)
Construction paper
Newspaper

HOW we will do it: To prepare, spread many layers of newspaper on the work surface. Put water in the shallow pans and set them on the activity table. Mix the oil and tempera paint well and put it in the small containers with medicine droppers. Find a surface where the pictures can dry and spread newspaper there as well.

When the children are ready to do the activity, invite them to use the medicine droppers to put drops of colored oil into the water. Encourage them to float pieces of paper on the top of the water for a few seconds and then to take them out. Let them dry on the surface you have designated for this purpose. The pictures will not dry completely because of the oil, so when you are ready to put them on the wall, hang them above the children's reach, but where they will still be visible.

Kitchen Play with Fat: Oil and Grease

Dramatic Play/Language

WHY we are doing this activity: to promote child-to-child interaction; to enable children to act out real-life situations through fantasy play; to develop vocabulary as well as speaking and listening skills.

WHAT we will need:
Kitchen dramatic play area
Empty margarine tubs
Empty margarine boxes
Empty lard containers (e.g., Crisco)
Empty plastic vegetable oil bottles
Measuring cups
Measuring spoons
Recipe books
Aprons
Muffin pans

HOW we will do it: Add the empty containers and cooking materials to a kitchen dramatic play area. Encourage the children to explore and play.

Birds Like Fat, Too!

Nature/Crafts

WHY we are doing this activity: to help children discover that fat is sticky and that seeds will adhere to it; to develop fine motor skills through crafts.

WHAT we will need:
Fairly large pinecones
Softened suet or lard
Wild birdseed
Shallow pans for seeds
Popsicle sticks
Twine

HOW we will do it: Put all materials out on the activity table. Encourage the children to use the Popsicle sticks to spread and poke suet or lard in between the scales of the pinecones and to then roll the pinecones in the pans of wild birdseed. Help your students wrap twine underneath the top scales of the cones so that you can hang them in trees. Try to hang them near a window so that you can watch your feathered visitors.

Literature

Symbol Key: *Multicultural
   +Minimal diversity
   No symbol: no diversity or no people

MacDonald, E. (1989). *Miss Poppy and the honey cake*. New York: Dial Books for Young Readers. (Butter is used to make the honey cake in this book. On the inside of the front and back covers, there is a recipe for honey cake which includes instructions about how to grease the pan.)

Seuss, D. (1984). *The butter battle book*. New York: Random House.

Thomas, M. (1972). *Free to be you and me*. (Cassette). Bertelsmann Music Group Co. New York: Arista Records. (This excellent tape includes songs which encourage children to examine advertising messages critically.)

Wake, S. (1990). *Butter*. Minneapolis, MN: Carolrhoda.

Extenders

Social Studies: Play the tape: *Free to Be You and Me*. Discuss with the children the issues this tape raises and sing the songs together. Carol Channing and Marlo Thomas are just two of the artists who make contributions. *Free to Be You and Me* is available on tape, CD, and video, and can be purchased at many children's book and toy stores.

Science: When the children experiment with how fat makes paper transparent, provide them with some warm, melted margarine to drop onto paper. Does the temperature affect the speed or degree of transparency of the paper? Explain that heat makes molecules move apart, so this makes the fat soak into or saturate the paper even faster.

Science: After you make the water magnifiers using grease, invite the children to try the same experiment with warm water or warm, soapy water. Why does it not work?

Language: Have children look through food magazines and cut out food pictures to make their own food pyramids. Take story dictation, support invented spelling, or spell or write down words to be copied, as appropriate.

Social Studies/Nutrition: After you introduce children to the food pyramid, bring in samples from each food section. Have the children taste each one and categorize which part of the pyramid it belongs to.

MARVELOUS MOTION

Attention Getter: Put some ball bearings or marbles in tins with lids. When the children are gathered, let them take turns moving the tins. Are the objects inside still or moving? How can they tell? If you like, have the children guess what is inside the tins and then let them take the lids off. Explain that when something is moving, it is in *motion*. Say the word *motion* several times as you pass the tins and ball bearings around the group so that each child can feel the ball bearings roll around in the containers. Ask the children to guess what you will be talking about and working with during the next few weeks.

Marble Mania
Science

Square or rectangular boxes
Activity sign (provided below; photocopy and enlarge for your use)

WHY we are doing this experiment: to help children experiment with centripetal and centrifugal force; to develop reading skills through an activity sign.

The facts of the matter: *Centripetal force* is the force that pushes an object toward the center of a circle. *Centrifugal force* is the force by which an object pushes outward, away from a center. With marbles and bowls, the centrifugal force causes the marbles to climb to the widest part of the bowl, the sides at the top, which is also the part furthest from the center of the circle the marbles are moved in when the bowl is manually moved around and around.

WHAT we will need:
    Ball bearings or marbles
    Large plastic bowls

HOW we will do it: To prepare, post the activity sign on the wall near the spot where your materials will be. Put all materials out on the activity table. Marbles are going to be rolling everywhere during this activity, but children do enjoy it. If you want to try to contain the marbles, designate a particular area for this experiment and, if you like, try to block it off a little with furniture, or by taping cardboard box borders around the perimeters.

During an Attention Getter time, read/interpret the activity sign together. Ask the children to predict how the marbles will react when the bowls are rolled around. Ask them if they see anything in the room that will help them conduct this experiment. Invite them to do so. Why do the marbles climb the sides of the bowls and shoot out? (The sides of the

Marble Experiment:

Put some marbles in a bowl, and move the bowl around in a circle. What happens to the marbles?

bowls push the marbles toward its center, but the weight of the marbles push them out toward the sides of the bowls. When the children move the bowls around and around, this makes the marbles move away from the bowls' centers, too.) Does the same thing happen when the marbles are rolled in the square or rectangular boxes?

More Centrifugal Force
Science

WHY we are doing this experiment: to provide children with more hands-on experience with centrifugal force.

WHAT we will need:
  Small buckets with handles
  Water
  Paper towels
  Hot, sunny day

HOW we will do it: Encourage the children to fill the buckets half full of water, and to swing them over their heads, vertically, as hard and as fast as they can. Does the water fall out? Remind the children that centrifugal force pushes things out, away from the center of the circle. The force of the circular movement they make with their arms forces the water out, toward the bottom of the buckets. Have paper towels on hand in case there are some accidents!

How Do Ball Bearings Work?
Science

WHY we are doing this project: to enable children to discover, through hands-on experimentation, that friction caused by rolling is less than sliding friction; to develop self-esteem and a sense of autonomy through use of a one-person

work station; to develop a sense of mechanical competence; to develop reading skills.

WHAT we will need:
  Four coffee cans (all the same size)
  Ball bearings (all the same size, about twelve)
  Red and brown contact paper (or construction paper)
  Activity sign (provided on page 398; photocopy and enlarge for your use)
  "One person may be here" sign (provided on page 3; photocopy and enlarge for your own use)

HOW we will do it: To prepare, make both signs and pin them up on the wall near the work table. For this experiment, you can use ball bearings (available in hardware stores) or steel marbles (available in toy stores). Ball bearings in hardware stores vary in size and price; typically, they range from $.07 to $.28 each.

Cover two of the cans in brown contact or construction paper and the other two in red. Turn one brown coffee can upside down on the table, and line the ball bearings around the rim. Put the other brown coffee can on top of the ball bearings, right side up. Turn one red coffee can upside down on the table and put the other red coffee can on top of it, right side up.

During an Attention Getter time, read/interpret the signs together. Ask the children to predict which can will be easiest to slide and move over the can underneath. As the children take turns experimenting, ask them about the results. Why is the coffee can on the ball bearings so much easier to turn and slide? Rub your hands together and ask the children if they remember that two things rubbing together make *friction*. There is much less friction when one coffee can rolls on ball bearings than when two coffee cans rub against each other, because the ball bearings roll. Ball bearings are often used in cars and other machines that move.

Slide one red coffee can over the other.

Slide one brown coffee can over the other.

Which one slides easiest? Why?

Kinetic Energy

Science

WHY we are doing this experiment: to enable children to experiment with kinetic energy through hands-on exploration.

Definition: *kinetic*: of or resulting from motion

WHAT we will need:
Cardboard cylinders (from cling wrap boxes)
Marbles (large and small)
Double-sided tape
Blocks

HOW we will do it: To prepare, cut the cardboard cylinders in half, lengthwise. Use blocks to make a number of ramps with a wide variety of lengths and heights. Each ramp should consist of a long flat part, secured to the floor with double-sided tape, and a lifted ramp, secured on one end to the flat ramp, and on the other end to the blocks that support it. Use double-sided tape for this purpose also. Line up four or five marbles in the end of each ramp. Reserve one marble near the top of each ramp.

During an Attention Getter time, put one marble at the top of a ramp. Ask the children: "If I let this marble roll down the ramp, do you think anything will happen to these other marbles? What do you think it will be?" Encourage the children to express their predictions. Put the marble back down on the floor without dropping it down the ramp, and invite your students to use the materials to find out if their predictions are true. As they roll marbles down the ramps, what happens to the other marbles sitting at the bottom? Why?

The facts of the matter: Because the marble that rolls down the ramp is moving, it has energy. When the rolling marble hits the marbles that are standing still at the end of the ramp, the energy of the rolling marble is passed from marble to marble until the one at the very end is pushed off the ramp and rolls away. The still marbles at the end of the ramp move because of the energy, or motion, of the rolling marble. This is an example of kinetic energy.

Developmental differences: Three- and young four-year-olds will enjoy rolling marbles down the ramp. Conduct the kinetic energy experiment yourself and see if any children become interested. Older children will also enjoy using the ramps and marbles, as well as conducting and observing the results of the experiment.

Marble Count
Math

WHY we are doing this project: to use motion to practice rational counting and subtraction; to develop self-esteem and a sense of autonomy through use of a one-person work station.

WHAT we will need:
   Marbles or steel ball bearings
      (large and small)
   Two coffee cans (one large with plastic lid
      and one small)
   Long cardboard cylinders (from cling
      wrap boxes)
   Brown and red contact paper (or con-
      struction paper)
   Twine, books, or blocks (to hold up
      ramps)
   Writing sheets (provided on page 400;
      photocopy and enlarge for your use)
   Pens
   Blank paper
   "One person may be here" sign
      (provided on page 3; photocopy and
      enlarge for your use)
Preparation:
   Scissors
   Double-sided tape

   Glue
   String
   Putty
   Exacto knife

HOW we will do it: To prepare, cut the cylinders in half, lengthwise. In this activity, the children are going to count marbles as they roll them down the cylinder ramps into a coffee can. (The falling marbles make a very satisfying clunking noise as they hit the metal of the can.) Put all the marbles in the small can. Use the Exacto knife to cut a hole in the plastic lid of the large can. Make the hole big enough for marbles to pass through. Use the blocks or books to prop up the ramp at an angle, and use putty or double sided tape to secure the lower end over the coffee can hole.

You can make the ramp as long as you wish. It is fun to make a super-long one, but to do this you need adequate space to create an effective angle. Glue the ends of the cardboard ramps together. You can either hang your ramp with string secured to the ceiling with tacks, or prop the ramp up with blocks. You may need to use putty or double-sided tape to help secure the ramps.

During an Attention Getter time, show the children all the marbles, and ask them to predict how many there are. Look at the writing sheets and together, read/interpret them. Show the children the pens, and let them know they can also use the blank paper to record the marbles they count, if they would like. Talk about the "One person may be here" sign.

Developmental differences: Three- and young four-year-olds will be most interested in rolling the marbles down the ramps, into the cans. If you like, count their marbles out loud while they do this. They may use the blank or writing sheets for scribbling. Older children are likely to count the number of marbles rolled down the ramp and to record the number they count.

Roll the marbles into the brown can. How many marbles do you count?

$3 \therefore$ Take three marbles away. How many marbles are left?

Powerful Pulleys
Science/Fine Motor

WHY we are doing this project: to enable children to discover that the energy of one motion can be harnessed to cause another motion; to develop fine motor skills; to provide experience with manipulatives.

WHAT we will need:
    Wood (flat, square piece about
        25 cm x 25 cm [10" by 10"])
    Spools
    Finishing nails (available at
        hardware stores)
    Strong rubber bands
Preparation:
    Hammer
    Pliers
    Pencil

HOW we will do it: For this project, you will need to make a pulley board. The spools will rotate on finishing nails, which have been hammered into wood and are connected to each other by rubber bands. When the children turn one spool, the others will turn also.

Stretch the rubber bands and decide how far apart the spools should be. Mark the places with pencil. The rubber bands, when stretched around two spools, should not be so tight that the rubber bands are in danger of breaking, but they must be snug enough to function. Hammer a finishing nail into each spot you marked with the pencil. Finishing nails are better for this project than regular nails, because the heads are minimal; this enables children to slide the spools on and off the post. This way, they can rearrange the pulley board in any way they would like. This provides a good fine motor exercise. On two, three, or more spools, hammer one nail into the top of the spool, and use the pliers to bend it so that it can be used as a handle to turn the spool. Make as many of the pulley boards as you wish, and put them out for the children to explore. (They love them!) As the children use the boards, ask them about what they see happening.

More Pulley Play
Science

WHY we are doing this project: to enable children to discover that a pulley makes lifting easier; to develop reading skills with an activity sign.

WHAT we will need:
Wire clothes hanger
Spool
Strong twine (or thin rope)

Two small buckets with handles
Potatoes or rocks (six, roughly the same size)
Plastic margarine tub lid
Activity sign (provided below; photocopy and enlarge for your use)
Red and black construction paper
Tape
Preparation:
Scissors or Exacto knife
Pliers

HOW we will do it: To prepare, unbend the hanger and thread the spool onto it. You may need the pliers to help you untwist it, and then twist it back again.

Find a high place to hang the hanger. Put three potatoes in each bucket. (You do not want the weight of the bucket to pull the hanger out of shape, so only put in as many potatoes as the hanger will accommodate without bending.) Take a length of strong twine (or thin rope), and

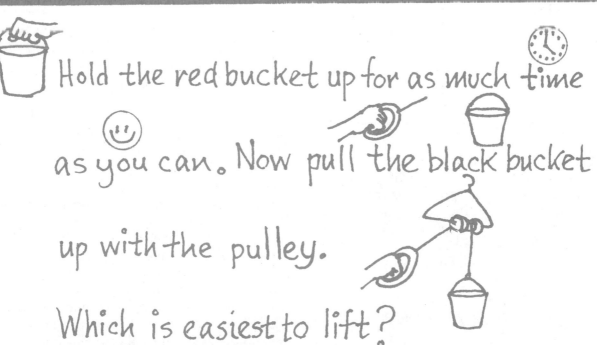

Science Experiment:
Does a pulley help to lift?

Color the squares the appropriate colors.

Hold the red bucket up for as much time as you can. Now pull the black bucket up with the pulley. Which is easiest to lift?

tie one end to one bucket while it is standing on the floor. The twine should be long enough so that the other end is easily reached by children when the twine is threaded over the spool.

Cut the center out of the margarine lid. This is going to be the pulley handle, attached to the other end of the twine. If you can find something (a plastic ring from a game or toy) that is smoother to hold, use that instead. Line up the twine or rope so that it lies on the spool or hanger. (See activity sign)

Cut out two large squares from construction paper (one red and one black). Tape the black one to the bucket attached to the pulley and the red square to the bucket that is standing alone. Put the red bucket of potatoes beside the pulley. Post the activity sign on the wall near the pulley.

During an Attention Getter time, ask the children if they know what a pulley is. Show them the one you made, and together, read/interpret the activity sign. Ask your students to predict which bucket of potatoes will be easiest to lift. When the children explore the materials, ask: "Which bucket of potatoes is easiest to hold up for a long time—the one with the pulley or the one without? Why do you think that is so?" Discuss. (The rolling pulley does part of the work of lifting. Pulleys are used in building. Pulleys help lift large bundles of bricks and heavy planks. Pulleys are also used to unload cargo from ships.)

Levers Also Help Lift
Science

WHY we are doing this experiment: to help children understand that a lever lifts; to allow them to discover, through hands-on experimentation, that when they push down on a lever, an object is lifted up; to help children understand that the point of support on which a lever turns is called the *fulcrum*.

WHAT we will need:
    Rulers (small ones, 15 cm and 30 cm
        [6" and 1'])
    Meter or yardsticks

Blocks
Planks from block sets
Books
Twine
Pencils
Duct tape
Cylindrical objects of diverse diameters
    (e.g., sturdy cardboard tubes, plastic
    containers, cylindrical blocks)
Demonstration:
    Two colors of construction paper
    Little people pattern (from shipwreck
        activity in Soap Science unit)

HOW we will do it: To prepare, use the twine to tie bundles of books and blocks together. The bundles should vary in size and weight, so use small books as well as large, and paperbacks as well as hardcovers. Do the same with blocks. One bundle can consist of one block by itself.

Make a variety of levers by balancing small rulers on pencils or other thin, long, cylindrical objects. Be sure the ruler moves smoothly on the fulcrum or the cylindrical object underneath it. Put yardsticks and planks on the other larger cylinders. In addition, make some levers which use blocks instead of cylinders for fulcrums.

Match the bundles to the levers according to the strength of the plank or ruler and the weight of the bundle. Tie the bundles onto the levers so they do not fall off when the children lift them. If necessary, use duct tape to help secure them. Nearby, set out loose rulers, yardsticks, planks, cylinders, blocks, strips of duct tape, and lengths of twine, so that the children can set up their own levers and bundles.

Use the little people patterns (from the shipwreck activity in the Soap Science unit) to cut out two paper people, each one from a different color of paper. For a demonstration at an Attention Getter time, create a small seesaw with a cylinder and a ruler, and tape a paper person on each end.

During an Attention Getter time, ask the children if they have ever been on a seesaw. Push down on one end of your miniature seesaw and say: "When I push down on this end, what happens?" (The other end rises.) Say: "This is a lever. I push down on one end of the lever, and it lifts the other end." Point to the cylinder on which the lever rests and at the point on which the lever balances, and say: "This part is called the *fulcrum*. The fulcrum is where the lever turns." Say the word several times together as the children take turns pushing down on the miniature seesaw.

Show the children the other levers you set up, and ask them to predict whether or not they will be able to lift the bundles with them. Invite the children to explore the materials. Is there a difference between how a lever on a cylinder works with how a lever on a block works? Which levers lift faster and more easily: those underneath light bundles or heavy bundles? Invite the children to use the loose materials to make their own levers.

Momentum Magic
Science/Gross Motor/Sensory

WHY we are doing this experiment: to enable children to experiment with momentum and to develop the large muscle group.

Definition: *momentum:* the impetus of a moving object, or, a strength or force that keeps growing.

WHAT we will need:
   Large plastic bags with handles
   Rocks (large, medium, and small-sized)

HOW we will do it: Put several heavy rocks in each bag. Encourage the children to put the bags down on the ground and to then twist the plastic handles many times. Ask them to predict what will happen when they pick the bags up again. Invite them to do so. What happens? Are the bags easy to stop once they start untwisting? Do the bags unwind quickly or slowly? What happens when the bags are filled with medium- or small-sized rocks? Experiment with these variations. (The weight of the rocks creates *momentum* as the bags unwind. The weight of the rocks creates a force or motion that grows and grows and is hard to stop.) You may want to repeat this activity at the next day's Attention Getter time, and have the children repeat the word *momentum* several times as their bags unwind.

More Momentum
Science

WHY we are doing this experiment: to enable children to discover that the motion of the fluid inside a raw egg creates momentum.

WHAT we will need:
   Raw eggs
   Hard-boiled eggs
   Small bowls
Preparation:
   Marker

HOW we will do it: Mark each hard-boiled egg with a marker so that the cooked eggs are easy to identify. Put all materials out on the activity table.

During an Attention Getter time, ask the children if they remember what *momentum* means. (Movement that keeps growing.) Invite the children to hold the hard-boiled eggs and to guess whether they are raw or cooked. Do the same with the raw eggs. Ask your students to predict whether there will be a difference in the way that a raw egg spins in a bowl, and the way that a cooked egg spins. Before the children conduct this experiment, talk about how the raw eggs should be handled to keep them intact.

As the children explore the materials, ask them what they notice about which eggs are easiest to stop, once they are in motion. Why do they think this is so? (The fluid inside the raw eggs creates momentum. When the children try to stop the raw eggs from spinning, the fluids inside continue spinning and keep the egg in motion.) Which egg is easiest to spin from a standstill? (The motion of the shell has to be transferred to the fluid of a raw egg, which is why a cooked egg is easier to stop spinning.)

Developmental differences: Three- and young four-year-olds: The temptation to break the eggs will be too much for this age group. Be prepared to facilitate a sensory exploration of both kinds of eggs. Conduct the momentum experiment yourself and see if any children become interested. Older children may be inclined to break open the eggs, but are also likely to be interested in conducting the momentum experiment with eggs that are still intact.

Squeeze Bottle
Science

WHY we are doing this experiment: to enable children to discover that one motion can create a series of motions.

WHAT we will need:
- Plastic squeeze bottles
- Tissue paper
- Small paper cups
- Small containers of water
- Medicine droppers

HOW we will do it: Before you facilitate this unit, start gathering the plastic bottles. They should be the kind that are made out of soft, flexible plastic so that the children can easily squeeze them hard. Put all materials on the activity table.

When the children are gathered during an Attention Getter time, pass the squeeze bottles and encourage the children to squeeze them into their faces. Can they feel the air? What makes it shoot out of the bottles into their faces? (The squeezing motion of the children's hands.) Show your students the materials on the activity table. Sprinkle drops of water from a medicine dropper onto a tissue, and then roll it up into a plug. Pack it into the top of the bottle and put one of the small paper cups on top, upside down. Ask the children to predict what will happen if the bottle is squeezed hard. Instead of demonstrating this, encourage the children to prepare their own experiments and find out.

As they conduct the experiment, discuss the results and the sequence of motions. (Squeezing the bottle makes the air shoot up, which forces the wet tissue paper out, which makes the cup fly off. One motion causes another motion which causes another motion.)

Air and Water in Motion
Science/Sensory

WHY we are doing this experiment: to enable children to discover that with enough force, air in motion can displace water; to facilitate cooperation between children; to develop hand-eye coordination; to provide a sensory experience.

WHAT we will need:
- Sensory table
- Tubs
- Water
- Plastic soda bottles (16 oz.)
- Bendable straws
- Coffee scoopers
- Funnels

Optional:
- Food coloring
- Glitter (or colored sand)

HOW we will do it: To prepare, set up the tubs of water, and put the bottles inside. If you'd like, add food coloring and glitter to the water.

During an Attention Getter time, fill a bottle with water, put a bendable straw inside the bottle, and then turn it upside down and hold it partway under the water.

Ask a child to hold the bottle upside down in position while you hold the straw. Ask the children: "What do you think will happen if I blow through the straw as hard as I can?" Encourage the children's predictions. Say: "I had to ask Miguel to hold the bottle for me so that I could think about holding my straw and blowing into the bottle. What could you say to someone to ask them to hold the bottle when you want to try this science experiment?" Encourage the children to express different ways of asking for help. Also talk about the fact that everyone should use their own straw so that germs are not spread.

As the children use the straws to blow into the upside-down bottles in water, encourage their observations. Why does the water not stay in the bottle? What is pushing it out? What does this experiment tell us about whether air can move water?

Pendulum Play
Science

WHY we are doing this experiment: to introduce children to the motion and principles of pendulums.

WHAT we will need:
> String
> Duct tape
> Washers (various sizes and weights)
> Jumbo paper clips
> Objects of different weights and lengths that can be hooked onto the paper clips: (e.g., pieces of chain bracelets, chain links, key rings with and without keys, unattached keys)

HOW we will do it: To prepare, unbend the paper clips so that they can be used as double hooks. Cut a variety of lengths of string and tie one length to one hook of each paper clip, leaving the other hook free to hold washers. Cut strips of duct tape and stick them onto the edge of the activity table. Put out the washers and the prepared paper clips as well.

Make a sample pendulum by taping one end of the string to the edge of the table and putting an object on the hook on the other end as it hangs down. During an Attention Getter time, ask one of the children to set the pendulum in motion. As the pendulum swings, say: "Back and forth and back and forth," in time to the pendulum's swing. Encourage the children to chant this with you and notice how the distance covered by the pendulum becomes less and less as it slows down. Tell the children that the swinging time of a pendulum is called a *period*.

Show your students the materials on the activity table and encourage them to make their own pendulums. Ask the children about what they discover. Does a pendulum of heavy objects take the same time to swing as one with lighter objects? Does a pendulum with a long string take the same time to swing as one with a short string? What difference does it make when the object at the end of the pendulum is long, like a key or bracelet chain, instead of compact like a washer? Is the motion of the key or bracelet the same as the pendulum's?

Pendulum Rhyme
Music/Movement/Rhythm/Gross Motor

WHY we are doing this activity: to build on the experience in the previous activity; to help children enjoy their singing voices; to reinforce the motion of a pendulum through chanting; to help children feel rhythm.

WHAT we will need:
> Lengths of string (about 37.5 cm [15"])
> Washers
> Rhyme: "PENDULUM, PENDULUM"

"PENDULUM, PENDULUM"
Pendulum, pendulum
swinging to and fro,
first it swings so very fast
and then the swinging slows.

HOW we will do it: Make a pendulum for each child by tying a washer to each length of string. During an Attention Getter time, hand each child a pendulum and start them swinging. Say the rhyme in time to the swinging. Experiment with saying the rhyme quickly and slowly. To make the pendulum swing very fast while you chant quickly, hold the pendulum close to the weight at the end. To make the pendulum swing slowly, hold the pendulum at the top of the string. Stop moving your hand on the last word of the chant and notice how the arc of the pendulum diminishes and eventually slows down to a standstill. When you say the chant quickly and slowly, can everyone keep time together and stop at the same time? As a variation of the chant, sing the words in the tune of the first few lines of the "ABC" song.

For a gross motor exercise, stand up, hold your hands together, and swing your arms as pendulums, in time to the song or rhyme. Try it with both hands loose. Try hanging your head down low and swinging your whole torso like a pendulum. Stand on one leg and swing the other one like a pendulum as you sing the song. Be creative!

Pendulum Pair

Science

WHY we are doing this experiment: to enable children to observe how one pendulum transfers its motion to another.

WHAT we will need:
  String lengths (all the same length)
  Washers
  Duct tape
  Sticks (at least 17.5 cm (7") long)
  Jumbo paper clips
Later part of experiment:
  String in a variety of lengths
  Objects of different weights to hang
    on pendulums

HOW we will do it: Unbend the paper clips and tie these hooks to one end of each string length. Arrange all materials on the activity table as specified in the Pendulum Play activity. The weight at the end of the pendulum is called the *bob*. Make a pendulum pair by taping two pendulums with equally weighted bobs to the edge of the table, about 15 cm (6") apart.

During an Attention Getter time, take a stick and wrap each pendulum string around the stick once about halfway up each string. Ask the children what will happen if you just swing one bob. Will the other pendulum swing too? Rather than demonstrate this, let the children make their own pendulum pairs to find out. What happens? Because they are connected, the motion of the first bob affects the second one and sets it swinging, too. Encourage the children to take the experiment in other directions, by providing a variety of string lengths and differently weighted bobs. What happens if the stick is moved down closer to the bobs? What happens if the bobs are different weights? What happens if the string lengths are different, but the pendulums are still connected? Find out!

Air Boats

Science

WHY we are doing this project: to enable children to discover Newton's third law of motion (for every action, there is an equal and opposite reaction); to provide a novel way for children to experiment further with the force of air and the motion it causes.

WHAT we will need:
  One-quart milk cartons
  Good quality balloons
  Sensory table filled with water (or children's pool)
  Chip clips (clips that keep bags of snack foods closed)
Preparation:
  Exacto knife or razor blade

HOW we will do it: To prepare, cut the milk cartons in half, lengthwise. Glue the pouring spouts back together, and lay each carton down on a table, open side up, to simulate a boat. The top triangular parts of the cartons form the prow of the boats. In the opposite rim of each carton, use an Exacto knife or razor blade to cut a small hole in the middle. It should be just big enough for the opening of a deflated balloon to be pushed through.

Put all materials out near the sensory table of water. During an Attention Getter time, blow up one of the balloons that has been inserted in a boat, and put a chip clip on the end to keep it from deflating. Set the boat in the pool or sensory table of water, and ask the children what they think will happen when you take the clip off. Rather than demonstrate this, encourage the children to prepare their own experiments. Help young preschoolers push the balloon openings through the hole in the milk cartons and blow up the balloons. Either help them pinch the ends of the balloons with their fingers until they are ready to release them, or use chip clips for this purpose. What happens to the boats?

Discuss with the children the "push/push back" law of motion. When there is a push in one direction, it makes a push in the other direction. The air blasts out of the balloon in one direction and makes the boat shoot off in the opposite direction. To test this theory, encourage the children to put their fingers near the end of the balloon after the air is released. In what direction is the air moving? Is it the same direction as the boat?

each have their own and germs are not spread. As the released air from the balloons moves the rockets along the yarn, ask the children if they remember the push/push back law. Encourage them to put their fingers near the opening of the balloon when the air is released. In what direction is the air moving? Does the straw move in the same direction? Discuss.

More Push/Push Back
Science

WHY we are doing this experiment: to give children another opportunity to explore the push/push back law.

WHAT we will need:
  Yarn
  Masking tape
  Strong balloons
  Straws
  Chip clips
  Marker

HOW we will do it: To prepare, string yarn across a long stretch of the room, at a height the children can easily reach. Fix one end securely to the wall. Wind masking tape tightly around the other end of the yarn so that the children can easily thread a straw onto the yarn. Tear off masking tape strips and stick them on the edge of the activity table.

Prepare a rocket: Thread a straw onto the yarn line, inflate a balloon, and tape the balloon to the straw.

Use a chip clip to close the end of the balloon after it is inflated. Ask the children what they think will happen when you take the chip clip off. Rather than demonstrate this, encourage your students to prepare their own experiments. Help young preschoolers inflate their balloons, secure the openings with chip clips, tape the straws onto them, and thread the straws onto the yarn. Use the marker to write children's names on their balloons so that they

The Book of Motion
Language/Art

WHY we are doing this project: to develop all components of language arts: reading, writing, speaking, and listening; to facilitate artistic expression.

WHAT we will need:
  Construction paper
  Magazines (any catalogs, home-improvement magazines, or mechanics publications with photographs of moving parts and machines)
  Glue
  Small containers for glue
  Glue brushes
  Children's scissors
  Crayons
  Markers
  Pens
Preparation:
  Stapler

HOW we will do it: Begin collecting the magazines several weeks ahead of time. Ask friends, neighbors, family, and parents to help you collect them.

Tip: If you see any multicultural, anti-bias photographs in the magazines as you do this project, save them for the Repair Shop activity that follows.

To prepare blank books, lay several pieces of paper on top of each other and fold them over. Staple along the fold. Put all materials out on the activity table.

Make a sample motion book. Write a title on the cover, and "by (your name)." Cut out pictures that interest you of moving parts and machines and glue them into your book. Write a few words about each. Mine is as simple as this: "This is a grandfather clock. It has pendulums a little bit like the ones we played with in class." "This is called a swivel chair. If you sit on it, you can turn yourself around and around on it." "This machine is a bulldozer. The big shovel moves up and down. The person who operates a bulldozer can move the shovel by pushing or pulling a handle. Sometimes I see bulldozers at work when I'm driving." Draw a picture of a moving machine of your own invention. For example, the words under my invented machine say: "I don't know what this machine is, but it has a spring that would be fun to press down. Then the spring bounces back up." Be creative and make your book however you'd like.

During an Attention Getter time, show the sample book to the children. Ask them if they see anything in the room that would help them make their own sample books. Mention that everyone's book will look different because we all have our own ways of doing things. Take story dictation, support invented spelling, spell words, or write them down to be copied, depending on your children's needs.

When the children are finished making their books, have a few children every day show-and-tell their words and pictures.

Repair Shop
Dramatic Play/Multicultural/Anti-Bias

WHY we are doing this project: to promote child-to-child interaction; to provide children with the opportunity to work out real-life emotions through fantasy play; to develop mechanical competence; to create a multicultural, anti-bias play area; to expand vocabulary; to develop speaking and listening skills.

WHAT we will need:
    Broken machines with moving parts

(e.g., clocks, watches, cameras)
    Toy screwdriver and screw sets
    Gear and sprocket toys
    Toy cash register
    Play money
    Signs (provided on page 409; photocopy
        and enlarge for your use)
    Blank paper
    Receipt books
    Pens
    Telephones
    Butcher paper
    Markers

HOW we will do it: Color in the signs provided and pin them up on the walls of your repair shop. Look for multicultural, anti-bias photographs from magazines and put these up on the walls as well. Set up all the materials to simulate a repair shop. If you are using broken machines like clocks and cameras, make sure you remove any rusted or jagged parts.

Pin the butcher paper up on the wall in the repair shop, and during an Attention Getter time, ask the children what the name of the repair shop should be. Print the name on the butcher paper. Invite your students to color and decorate it. Together, read the signs you have posted around the walls. Ask the children what they could use the blank paper and markers for. Invite them to explore the materials. To encourage fantasy play, call the shop to ask how much a repair would cost, or bring something in to the shop to be fixed.

Paint in Motion
Science/Art

WHY we are doing this activity: to allow children to use motion to create art and to facilitate artistic expression.

WHAT we will need:
    Plastic mustard squeeze bottles
        (with adjustable nozzles)
    Paint
    Newspaper

Yarn (or twine)
Thick, strong, rubber bands
Tacks
Newspaper
Large pieces of paper
Duct tape
Exacto knife or scissors
Tub of soapy water
Paper towels
Vinyl tablecloth

HOW we will do it: In this project, you are going to hang bottles of paint upside down. The bottles will be supported by harnesses, made of rubber bands and string, and will swing around when moved. Begin collecting your mustard bottles several weeks ahead of time. In order to control the flow of paint, you need bottles with screw tops, which gradually enlarge the opening.

To prepare, use the Exacto knife or scissors to cut out the bottoms of each bottle so that you can easily refill them with paint when they are in the harnesses. Do not cut off much more than the very bottom. Deep sides prevent paint from splashing out when the bottle is swinging. Twist a rubber band very tightly around each bottle, and tie three or four lengths of string around the band to make a harness.

Secure the strings to the ceiling with tacks. Make sure the bottles are hanging low enough for the children to push them.

Spread the vinyl tablecloth on the floor underneath the bottles and, on top of that, many layers of newspaper. Make sure the openings are closed when you fill the bottles with paint, and make sure the paint is neither too thick nor too runny. When you are ready to facilitate the activity, put paper underneath the bottles, unscrew the openings slightly, and invite the children to swing and push them. When the pictures are dry, hang them up on the walls.

Literature

Symbol Key: *Multicultural
+Minimal diversity
No symbol: no diversity or no people

Ardley, N. (1992). *The science book of motion*. San Diego, CA: Harcourt Brace Jovanovich.*

Barton, B. (1987). *Machines at work*. New York: Thomas Y. Crowell.*

Burton, V. L. (1939). *Mike Mulligan and his steam shovel*. Boston, MA: Houghton Mifflin.

Burton, V. L. (1943). *Katy and the big snow*. Boston, MA: Houghton Mifflin.

Lafferty, P. (1992). *Force and motion*. Boston, MA: Dorling Kindersley Books. (This book has excellent photographs which you can look at and discuss with the children.)

Rockwell, A., & Rockwell, H. (1972). *Machines*. New York: Macmillan.

Extenders

Science/Fine Motor: Introduce the children to tiddly winks and spinning tops. What does it take to make a tiddly wink hop up into the air? Does a spinning top always spin in the same spot?

Gross Motor: Take a walk outside and see how many moving parts of machines you can spot (e.g., wheels of cars, cranes, drills, and jackhammers). How much natural motion (e.g., wind blowing grass, leaves, and puddles) do you see? If you live or teach near a mall, walk through it and see how many moving machines or parts you spot (e.g., exercise bicycles, swinging or revolving doors, swinging pendulums, turning clocks or music boxes).

Math: When you experiment with the air boats and rockets, measure the distance they travel. Inflate the balloons to different degrees, mark the place where each boat/rocket stops moving (after the air is released), and then measure. Is the amount of air in the balloon related to the distance the rockets and boats travel?

FABULOUS FUNGI

Attention Getter: Ahead of time, let some mold grow on a piece of bread. When you are ready to introduce this theme, collect two or three small potted plants, the mold, and a mushroom. When the children are gathered, put the plants to one side in front of the children, and the mold and mushroom to the other side in front of the children. Say: "Take a good look at the plants over here. And take a good look at the mold and the mushroom over here. How are they different?" Encourage observations and let the children gently touch each item.

Facilitate a discussion about fungi and how they are different from plants. Are they the same color? Ask the children to guess what you will be talking about and working with over the next few days. If you like, tell this joke: "Why did everyone invite the mushroom to their party? Because he was a fun-guy!"

The facts of the matter: Plants have roots and leaves and grow from seeds. Plants use sunlight and water to make their own food. Mold and mushrooms are fungi. A fungus cannot make its own food. It must live off something else, dead or alive. (For example, mold grows on bread and mushrooms can grow from dead wood.) A fungus grows from a spore. Spores are so tiny that generally, they cannot be seen.

Growing Molds (Part 1)
Science

WHY we are doing this experiment: to enable children to observe the growth of molds; to develop reading skills.

WHAT we will need:
- Small cups (paper or plastic) (six per child)
- Small plastic trays (or Styrofoam meat trays)
- Masking tape or sticky labels
- Cans of tomato soup
- Small bowls
- Spoons
- Bread crumbs
- Grated cheese
- Soil
- Corn syrup
- Tub of soapy water
- Paper towels
- Plastic wrap
- Labels (provided below; photocopy and enlarge for your use)
- Glue sticks

HOW we will do it: To prepare, you may want to cut the sides of the cups down so that the molds will be more visible when they grow. If you do this, try to cut them down evenly so that your plastic wrap will lay evenly over the tops of the cups when you cover the prepared experiments.

You should have enough cups so that each child can have six. Put the soup in the bowls, and then add the spoons. In other bowls put some bread crumbs, soil, corn syrup, and cheese. Find a dark, warm spot where you can leave the experiments for several days. Display each label next to the material it identifies. Have the tub of soapy water and paper towels available for clean-up.

During an Attention Getter time, ask the children if they think it is possible to grow molds. (A mold is a fungus, because it grows from spores. Spores are too small to be seen, but they are everywhere.) Show the children the materials on the table and ask them how they think they could use the materials to find out if mold spores will grow in tomato soup.

Prepare an experiment yourself by having the children help you put a few spoonfuls of soup into six cups. Show the children the bowl of cheese and then the cheese label. Ask them to read/interpret the label. Ask one of the children to add a small amount of shredded cheese to one of your cups of tomato soup and to use a glue stick to glue the cheese label onto the cup. Ask: "Why is the label useful?" Ask another child to add some bread crumbs to the next cup of soup, and repeat the same process with the appropriate label. After the children help you add corn syrup to the third cup and soil to the fourth, prepare a fifth by scraping your finger on a dirty place on the floor and then sticking your finger into the soup. Your sixth and last cup should contain plain tomato soup. Label all cups, place them on a tray, then write your name on masking tape or a sticky label to put on your tray. Carry the tray to the warm, dark place, and then use a large piece of plastic wrap to cover all the cups. Ask the children to predict whether mold will grow in any of the cups and, if so, which ones.

Invite the children to prepare their own mold experiments. You may need to help the children carry their prepared trays to the designated spot. Have the children use the tub of soapy water and paper towels to wash their hands after touching the floor with their fingers.

Growing Molds (Part 2)
Science/Language

WHY we are doing this project: to facilitate recording the results of a scientific experiment; to develop all components of language arts: reading, writing, speaking, and listening.

WHAT we will need:
    Blank Paper
    Patterns for observation books
        (provided on page 416; photocopy
        and enlarge for your use)
    Pens
    Crayons
    Markers
Preparation:
    Stapler

HOW we will do it: Set up a writing center near the mold-growing area, where you can leave all materials out for the duration of the experiment. Use the stapler and the patterns provided to make observation books for each child. Use a photocopier to reduce the labels on page 416 and glue each label in its corresponding column on your observation sheet. Also, fold and staple sheets of paper to make blank observation books. Put these with the pens, crayons, and markers on the activity table.

During an Attention Getter time, a few days after you prepare the experiments in Part 1 of this activity, hold up an observation book and, together, read/interpret it. In front of the children, check your own experiment, and in a blank or prepared book, draw a picture of each sample of soup and write a few words about each one. You may want to do this on the first day that molds are visible. After you make your observations, remind the children that their observation books will look different, because everyone has a different way of doing things.

Designate a group time every day to check the experiments. Let the children use the writing area during the course of the session or day's activities. As the children work on their books, take story dictation, support invented

Mold Growing Science Experiment

Observation Book

Day _____

BREAD CRUMBS	GRATED CHEESE	DIRT	CORN SYRUP	GERMS FROM THE FLOOR	PLAIN TOMATO SOUP
Inside the cup I see:	Inside the cup I see:	Inside the cup I see:	Inside the cup I see:	Inside the cup I see:	Inside the cup I see:

spelling, spell words or write down words to be copied, according to their needs.

Let the molds grow for as long as you like. Before the children take their observation books home, invite a few children every day to display and talk about their work to the group.

Growing on a Coconut: The Same or Different?
Science

WHY we are doing this activity: to see if new mold cultures (which did not grow on the tomato soup) will grow on a coconut .

WHAT we will need:
Coconut
Magnifying glasses

HOW we will do it: During an Attention Getter time, break open the coconut. It is best to break it into two halves, but I have yet to discover any ideal way of accomplishing this. Tell the children you want to find out what kinds of molds grow on a coconut. First you are going to let it sit out in the air for an hour, in the hope that some mold spores in the air will land on the coconut and start to grow. Ask the children to predict whether they will or not. After an hour or so, close the coconut back up and put it somewhere safe.

If you work with older preschoolers or kindergartners whom you know will not disturb the coconut for several days, put it on your activity table. If you work with younger children, keep the coconut out of their reach for several days, and then put it on the science table once the molds begin to grow. Put the magnifying glasses next to the coconut. How many different molds are there? Are any molds growing which did not grow in the tomato soup? Discuss!

Eating Mold
Science/Sensory/Math/Language

WHY we are doing this project: to help children understand that some molds are edible; to provide a sensory experience through the sense of taste; to familiarize children with cup and spoon measurements; to make children aware of hygienic handling of food; to develop speaking and listening skills through the use of a puppet.

WHAT we will need:
Roquefort cheese (one block)
Crackers
Blender
Celery sticks
Carrot sticks
Puppet
Small dish
Magnifying glass
Small paper plates
Napkins
Dip:
½ cup crumbled roquefort cheese
1 cup yogurt
½ cup mayonnaise
2 tablespoons vinegar
1½ teaspoons honey

HOW we will do it: Before you begin, have all the children wash their hands. Have roquefort slices, carrot and celery sticks, and crackers available on the table for sampling.

Use your puppet to help you facilitate a discussion about why children must not sneeze or cough on the food.

Ask the children: "Did you know that there are certain kinds of molds which are good to eat?" Open up the package of roquefort cheese and encourage the children to examine it. Break a piece of it off and put it into the small dish. Put this dish on the table with the food samples, next to the magnifying glass.

Together, make the dip by putting all dip ingredients into the blender. Let the children take turns filling the cup, ½ cup, tablespoon, and teaspoon with the appropriate ingredients, as well as taking turns to activate and stop the blender. Stop the blender several times and stir the dip as you mix it. Pour it into a bowl, and set it on the table with a spoon in it. Encourage the children to try the "mold dip"! (Show them how to use the spoon to take some dip and put it onto their plates.) Roquefort cheese is not a favorite food of young children and many may choose not to try it, but in this activity you are giving them that choice and demonstrating that mold can be a food. Take your puppet out again and use its personality to ask the children how the mold dip tastes and how they made it.

Fungus Farm
Science

WHY we are doing this project: to allow children to observe how mushrooms grow.

WHAT we will need:
    Mushroom-growing kit
    Magnifying glasses
    Sign (provided below; photocopy and
        enlarge for your use)
    Mushroom

The facts of the matter: The rounded top of a mushroom is called the cap; the gills are the fins underneath. The fleshy part which covers the gills is called the veil. When the veil breaks and the gills darken, the mushroom is ready to release spores. A typical mushroom makes about one million spores per minute, for a period of several days.

HOW we will do it: Mushroom-growing kits consist of mushroom spores in a soil-growing base and are available in nurseries and garden centers in the spring. They range in size and price from $16 for a 9 lb. kit to $22 for a 16 lb. kit, though prices probably vary more widely

Science Experiment:
Fungus Farm

WEIGHT: 9 LBS.
White Button Mushroom
KIT

How do mushrooms grow?

depending on where you live. Mushrooms usually begin to appear anywhere from seven to fourteen days and continue growing over a period of five to six weeks.

If you work in a school that is on a tight budget, ask parents to donate a dollar or so for the mushroom kit. It is well worth the effort because children learn so much from seeing the mushrooms emerge and grow, and derive satisfaction from tending them and taking them home.

Read the instructions on the kit carefully, and follow them. Make sure you put the kit on a very low table so that the children can easily see the surface of the kit, where the mushrooms grow. Make a "Please look but do not touch!" sign and post it near the kit. If you work with very young preschoolers, you may want to put a masking tape line down, to indicate where the children should stand, to make sure that the growth of the mushrooms is not disturbed.

Introduce this activity during an Attention Getter time by telling the children that mold is one kind of fungus and that you are holding another kind behind your back. Invite your students to close their eyes and ask them to pass the fungus around. When the children open their eyes, encourage them to explore the *gills* underneath. Explain that that is where the mushrooms spores are, although they are too tiny to see. Also explain that like mold, a mushroom cannot use sunlight and water to make its own food, the way green plants can.

Show the children the mushroom-growing kit, and discuss the "Please look but do not touch!" sign. Also discuss the many different kinds of mushrooms. Do the children think *all* mushrooms are good to eat? Explain to them that there are many kinds of poisonous mushrooms. Ask: "If you were walking in the forest and you found some mushrooms growing, do you think it would be safe to eat them?" Discuss the fact that it is **never** okay to eat mushrooms you find outside. The only mushrooms you can be sure are safe to eat are the ones you buy in the store.

Show the children the kit and ask them what they think it might be. Introduce the information that the kit will allow them to grow mushrooms that are safe to eat. Use the instructions on the kit to discuss with your students what will need to be done to nurture the mushrooms. Designate a specific time every day to check the mushrooms as a group. Show the children the magnifying glasses and ask them what they could use them for. (To examine the emerging mushrooms.) You can pick the mushrooms at any stage of their development. It is also extremely interesting to pull mushrooms out with the root still attached, so that the children can examine this. As the mushrooms develop, give each child some mushrooms to take home. See the Mushroom Baskets activity for a way to carry them.

A Mushroom Has Many Parts
Science

WHY we are doing this activity: to enable children to observe all parts of a growing mushroom; to expand vocabulary; to develop reading skills.

WHAT we will need:
> Whole mushroom (from mushroom farm in previous activity)
> Diagram (drawn from sample provided on page 420)
> Magnifying glasses
> Trays
> Toothpick
> Fork

HOW we will do it: In this activity, you will need to dig a whole mushroom out of the mushroom farm. Dig very carefully so that the rhizomorph and mycelium (see diagram) remain intact. These root-like strands are very delicate. To begin, use the fork to gently scrape away the soil around the base of the mushroom. Depending on the size of the mushroom, you may find other tools to help you. Use the toothpick to scrape away as much soil as possible, and then gently pull the mushroom up. If you find that your mushrooms are easily uprooted, pull up several so that more than one child at a time can examine whole mushrooms. Set a mushroom and magnifying glass on each tray.

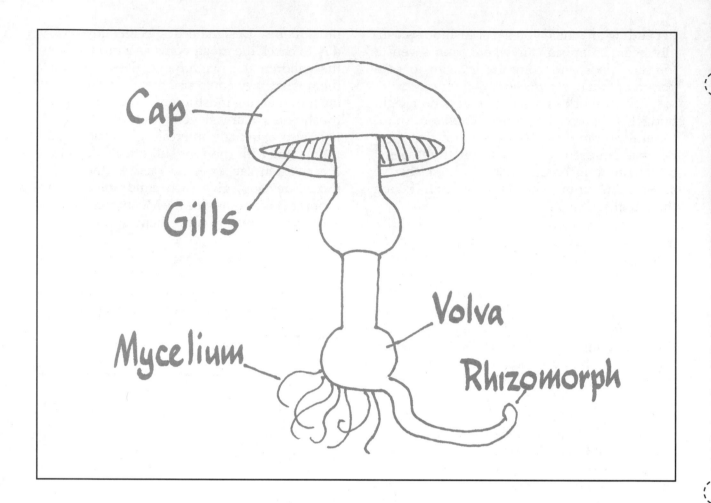

Cap

Gills

Mycelium

Volva

Rhizomorph

Using the illustration provided, make a large diagram of the different parts of a mushroom and post it on the wall near the activity trays.

During an Attention Getter time, go over the chart with the children. Pronounce the names of each mushroom part. Let the children know that if they would like to see these different parts of an actual mushroom, the materials they need are on the trays. Before they approach them, discuss how delicate and fragile the mushroom mycelia are. What will happen if they are rough with the mushrooms?

What Is in a Mushroom?

Science

WHY we are doing this experiment: to enable children to discover that mushrooms have a high water content.

WHAT we will need:
　Thick mushroom slices
　Paper towels
Demonstration:
　Tomato slice
　Paper towel

HOW we will do it: To prepare, cut the paper towels into quarters. Set the mushroom slices and paper towels on an activity table.

During an Attention Getter time, ask the children to predict what will happen if you squeeze the tomato slice between two pieces of paper towel. Conduct this experiment and show the children the paper towel pieces afterward. What came out of the tomato? If the children say, "juice," ask them what they think is in juice. If necessary, explain that the juice is mostly water. There is a lot of water in a tomato. Show the children the mushroom slices and paper towels on the activity table and ask them to predict whether a mushroom has a lot of water in it. What will happen if they squeeze the mushroom slices between two sheets of paper towel? As your students conduct the experiment, ask them about their findings.

More Proof That Mushrooms Contain Water

Science/Sensory/Math

WHY we are doing this activity: to enable children to observe and measure how much water is cooked out of a cup of mushrooms.

WHAT we will need:
- 4 cups sliced mushrooms
- Strainer
- Tablespoon and teaspoon
- Measuring cups
- Colander
- Funnel
- Containers
- Sensory table
- "One person may be here" sign (provided on page 3; enlarge and photocopy for your use)
- One 2-cup measuring cup (plastic)

HOW we will do it: Ahead of time, cook two cups of mushrooms and save the water. The higher the heat, the more the water will evaporate. If you cook the mushrooms on a stove top, do so over medium heat. If you microwave the mushrooms, cover the bowl with plastic wrap so that evaporated water will condense on the underside of the wrap.

To prepare the activity, make an activity sign that says: "How much water in 2 cups of mushrooms?" Draw two cups above the words and mushrooms above that word. Post this and your "One person may be here" sign on the wall near the area where the children will be working. Next to the activity sign, place a two-cup measuring cup filled with fresh, sliced, raw mushrooms, so that your students can compare the size of these with the cooked mushrooms.

In the sensory table, place the cooked mushrooms (in their water), the containers, measuring cups, strainer, colander, and funnel. These straining materials provide children with a variety of ways of separating the mushrooms from their water; the spoons and cups provide two different methods of measuring that water.

During an Attention Getter time, ask the children if they remember the What Is In A Mushroom experiment. What did they find out about what is in a mushroom? Show the children the cup of uncooked, sliced mushrooms, and let them know that you cooked the same amount of mushrooms. Let the children know that if they would like to see what happened to the mushrooms you cooked, the materials are in the sensory table. Read both signs together, as a group, discuss, and invite your students to explore. How are the cooked mushrooms different from the raw ones?

Option: If you'd like, plug in an electric frying pan at the children's eye level and isolate the area with chairs and/or masking tape lines on the floor so that the children can observe from a distance. Saute sliced mushrooms in the pan and, as the children watch, talk about what comes out of the mushrooms as they cook. Have a snack together by eating the mushrooms on toast.

Mushroom Baskets

Art

WHY we are doing this project: to facilitate creative expression; to develop fine motor skills; to develop self-esteem by enabling children to make a functional basket.

WHAT we will need:
- Small brown paper lunch bags
- Cardboard
- Glue
- Small containers for glue
- Glue brushes
- Paper
- Crayons
- Pens

Markers
Collage materials (e.g., bits of yarn, bits
  of paper, stickers)
Construction paper
"Fresh Mushrooms" label (provided
  below; photocopy and enlarge
  for your use)
Newspaper
Preparation:
  Stapler

HOW we will do it: Cut each paper bag down
to about 7.5 cm (3") high. Cut out cardboard
strips about 2.5 cm x 23 cm (1" x 9"). Make several copies of the "Fresh Mushrooms" label in
the text, and cut out blank pieces of paper the
same size so that the children can make their
own labels if they wish. Staple one end of each
cardboard strip to each paper bag to make a
handle. If you work with older children, you
may decide to help them do this for themselves.

Put all materials on the activity table.
Ahead of time, make a sample mushroom basket by gluing collage materials onto it or drawing on it. Pick a few mushrooms from the fungus farm and put them in your basket. During
an Attention Getter time, show the children
your basket and ask them what they see in the
room that would help them make their own.
When each basket is completed, save it until it
is that child's turn to take mushrooms home.

Broiled Fungus Sandwich
Snack/Sensory

WHY we are doing this project: to develop
self-esteem by enabling children to make their
own snacks; to provide a sensory experience.

WHAT we will need:
- Mushrooms
- Two sticks of softened margarine
- Salt
- Bread
- Broiler
- Plastic knives
- Plastic forks
- Bowls
- Paper plates
- Napkins
- Toaster

HOW we will do it: Although this snack tastes wonderful, it does not look too appealing, so you may want to make small amounts. Then if the children like it, you can make more. Take your margarine out of the refrigerator in advance so that it is very soft when the children use it.

Place a bowl and plastic knife in front of each chair, and divide the mushrooms up into the bowls so that each child has roughly the same amount. During an Attention Getter time, ask the children: "Have you ever had a fungus sandwich? Don't you think a nice, juicy fungus sandwich would be delicious?" Have some fun with the children when they respond to this, and then show them your bowl of mushrooms. Begin to slice the mushrooms, and as you do, explain that you are all going to make a broiled mushroom sandwich, but in order to make it, the mushrooms have to be cut up. Show your students the bowls of mushrooms on the table and encourage them to use the plastic knives to cut them. When their mushrooms are cut up into small pieces, give them plastic forks to use to mash squares of margarine into the mushroom pieces. There should be enough margarine in each bowl to hold the mushroom pieces together.

Toast your bread pieces, and then help the children spread their mushroom mixture onto a piece of toast. Broil until the mushrooms are cooked (a few minutes) and slightly burned on top, then salt. Enjoy!

Mushroom Print
Science

WHY we are doing this experiment: to allow children to see spores.

WHAT we will need:
- Large mushrooms, one for each child
- Paper
- Pens

HOW we will do it: In order for this experiment to work, the *gills* of the mushrooms must be exposed. Prepare each mushroom by cutting away any flesh from the underside which covers the gills. Cut the stems flush with the gills. Cut out paper squares that are large enough for each mushroom to sit on. Put all materials on the activity table. Find a place where you can leave the mushroom prints for several days.

During an Attention Getter time, take a mushroom, turn it upside down, and pass it around. Encourage the children to examine and touch the gills. Say: "In between those brown gills is where the spores of the mushroom are. The spores fall to the ground, and if the spores have what they need, they'll grow. Today we are going to do an experiment to prove that there are spores in the mushroom." Write your name on a paper square, put the paper on the table you have designated for the experiment, and put the mushroom on top of the paper. There should be paper under all parts of the mushroom. Invite the children to do the same, and ask them to predict what they will see when they check the paper in two days.

After two days, pick the mushrooms up. What do you see underneath? Notice how the mushroom prints get darker and darker as more days pass. Ask the children to hypothesize about why this is so.

Mushroom Center

Science/Multicultural

WHY we are doing this activity: to enable children to observe that fungi grow in many different shapes and sizes; to familiarize children with foods used in Japanese cuisine.

WHAT we will need:
> Samples of several different kinds of mushrooms (enoki [look like antennae], shitake, portabella, oyster, canary [yellow], and wild)
> Index cards
> Marker
> Magnifying glasses

HOW we will do it: Specialty mushrooms are not cheap, so just buy two or three of each kind. If necessary, ask parents to donate a dollar or two towards the purchase of the mushrooms. Having a variety of fungi for children to directly examine is a very valuable part of this unit and well worth doing. The above list consists of mushrooms available in my local food co-op—your list may be different. Provide as many differently shaped and sized mushrooms as possible.

Put the mushrooms and magnifying glasses out on an activity table. Use the index cards and marker to print signs naming each mushroom type.

During an Attention Getter time, go over the names of each kind of mushroom with the children. Before they examine the fungi, talk about whether it is okay to eat or break the mushrooms. (They are too expensive to replace. If you work with very young children, you may want to put the mushrooms under clear plastic containers.) Show the children the enoki and shitake mushrooms, and explain that they are used quite often in Japanese cooking. Ask the children if any of them have been to a Japanese restaurant. Did they eat any enoki or shitake mushrooms?

Mushroom Writing Center

Language/Art

WHY we are doing this activity: to develop all components of language arts: reading, writing, speaking, and listening skills; to facilitate artistic expression.

WHAT we will need:
> Butcher paper
> Paper
> Markers
> Crayons
> Pens
> Scissors
> Glue sticks

Preparation:
> Adult scissors

HOW we will do it: Make a chart of the mushrooms you provided for the previous activity. If you'd like, ask the children to help you. Draw the shape of each mushroom, color in the appropriate shades, and print the name of each fungus. Put the chart up on the wall by the writing center table, and put all other materials on the table. Photocopy each mushroom drawing and name on the chart, put copies on the table, and have plenty of blank paper available. Cut blank paper into large mushroom shapes.

I have found that my writing centers tend to have more appeal for the children if I am able to set them up in a cozy corner. Dictate, spell, or write out words to be copied, and support invented spelling or scribbling. Children will utilize speaking and listening skills as they work together at the writing center, but you may also want to ask the children to read their work to you, or read their work to them. Some children may create projects that have nothing to do with mushrooms; they will still be developing valuable language arts skills.

Developmental differences: Three- and young four-year-olds enjoy scribbling with pens and crayons and dictating words. Older children enjoy drawing pictures and writing or dictating words.

Mushroom Match

Math

WHY we are doing this project: to develop cognition through a matching game.

WHAT we will need:

 Cardboard panel (from large appliance box)
 Yellow contact paper
 Clear contact paper
 Poster board
 Mushroom patterns (provided below; photocopy and enlarge for your use)
 Markers
 Double-sided tape
 "One person may be here" sign (provided on page 3; enlarge and photocopy for your use)

HOW we will do it: To prepare, cover the panel in yellow contact paper. Use the patterns provided to cut the mushroom shapes out of poster board. Trace a matching outline of each shape onto the board. If you work with kindergartners, make this matching game more challenging by drawing several shapes which are the same, then decorate them differently (e.g., dotted, striped, or small circles).

Cover the board with clear contact paper. Do the same to both sides of each mushroom shape. Put strips of double-sided tape on the board, the shapes, or both. Post the "One person may be here" sign above the board. Discuss this sign during an Attention Getter time. Children instinctively know what to do with these materials.

Mushroom Collage

Art

WHY we are doing this activity: to facilitate creative expression, to develop fine motor skills.

WHAT we will need:
- Construction paper
- Glue
- Small containers for glue
- Glue brushes
- Collage materials (e.g., scraps of fabric, paper scraps, beads, glitter, small macaroni pieces)

Preparation:
- Adult scissors

HOW we will do it: Cut the construction paper into large mushroom shapes and put all materials out on the activity table. Encourage the children to decorate their paper mushrooms in whatever way they would like. When the collages dry, put them up on your walls.

Toady Sittin' on a Big Toadstool

Music/Movement/Gross Motor/Small Group Activity

WHY we are doing this activity: to help children enjoy using their singing voices; to develop cognition through memorization of words; to develop the large muscle group.

WHAT we will need:
- Beanbag, ottoman, or masking tape
- Gym mats
- Song: "TOADY SITTIN' ON A BIG TOADSTOOL" (to the tune of "Froggy Went A-Courting")

"TOADY SITTIN' ON A BIG TOADSTOOL"
Toady sittin' on a big toadstool,
uh huh, uh huh,
thinkin' 'bout jumpin' in the nice cold pool,
uh huh, uh huh,
_____ came and tipped her off,
Toady fell in with a great big plop,
uh huh, uh huh, uh huh.

HOW we will do it: To prepare, put the beanbag or ottoman in the middle of the room, and put gym mats around it. If these materials are not available, make a circle on the floor with masking tape to simulate a toadstool.

Gather the children in the circle, with the "toadstool" in the middle. Sing the song, with a child's name in the blank space. Begin with one child sitting on the toadstool. The next child, who is named in the song, then jumps up onto the toadstool and gently tips the original child off. Before you play the game, talk about ways of tipping. Is it okay to tip hard and roughly? What might happen if students tip other children off that way? Have fun!

Mushrooms in the Kitchen

Dramatic Play/Language

WHY we are doing this activity: to provide opportunities for child-to-child interaction; to enable children to work through emotions and real-life experiences through fantasy play; to develop language skills.

WHAT we will need:
- Play kitchen furniture
- Sliced mushrooms
- Wok set or frying pans

HOW we will do it: Put a wok kit and some sliced mushrooms in your dramatic play area. Toy wok kits can be ordered from school supply catalogs, but you can also give the children small, regular frying pans to use, or toy ones.

Literature

Discuss the photographs in the following books and read selected parts.

Challand, H. J. (1986). *Plants without seeds*. Chicago: Children's Press.

Johnson, S. A. (1982). *Mushrooms*. Minneapolis, MN: A Lerner Natural Science Book.

Selsam, M. E. (1986). *Mushrooms*. New York: William Morrow.

Extenders

Science: Experiment with conditions which prevent mold from growing. In separate experiments, try growing mold without air, moisture, light, or a food-growing base. Try growing it in the refrigerator and in a warm place. Which conditions make a difference to the growth of mold?

Math: Post a big piece of butcher paper on the wall beside your mushroom-growing kit. As a group project, make a mark for every mushroom you pick. Make tally marks in groups of five. When the kit stops producing mushrooms, count all the marks. How many mushrooms did you get from the kit?

Math: After the children have had a chance to examine the mushroom varieties displayed in your mushroom center, use the collection for a one-person work station and invite the children to sort and count the different kinds of mushrooms.

Tater Time

Attention Getter: When the children are gathered, ask them to close their eyes, open their mouths, and stick their tongues out. Tell them you are going to put something on their tongues that is good to eat and that it will give them a clue about what you are all going to talk about during the week. Put a small potato chip on each of the children's tongues. If or when your students guess that they are eating potato chips, ask them what chips are made of, and then ask them to guess what you will be working with for the next few days.

Several activities in this unit utilize potatoes as a material for art or sensory exploration. Because of world hunger, some educators are reluctant to use food for play in early childhood curricula. Other educators feel the experiences with food are very worthwhile. In any case, I have included the activities so that you can choose what is right for you.

A Potato Is Stored Food
Science

WHY we are doing this experiment: to enable children to observe that a potato is stored food that can nourish a growing potato plant.

WHAT we will need:
> Potatoes
> Magnifying glasses

HOW we will do it: Buy some potatoes about a month before you plan on doing this unit, and store them until protuberances begin to grow from the potato eyes. Bring these in, along with a few potatoes with eyes but no growths, and set them on an activity table with magnifying glasses for the children to examine.

During an Attention Getter time, show the children the potato eyes, and then one of the potatoes with a shoot growing from an eye. Emphasize how important it is for the children to be very careful and gentle so that the root does not break off. Pass the potato around the group for the children to hold and examine. Ask: "How can this root be growing when the potato isn't planted in the ground?" Encourage the children to express their ideas. (The potato itself is stored food, and the growing root is fed by the potato until it can find water in the earth.) Show the children the growing potatoes and magnifying glasses on the activity table, and invite them to examine them. Before the children approach the table, talk together about what will happen if the potatoes are handled roughly. (The growing roots will break off.) If you think your students will have trouble with this, make a reminder sign or put the potatoes in or under clear containers.

Growing Potatoes
Science

WHY we are doing this experiment: to enable children to see the initial stages of growth of a new potato plant and to observe how a new plant begins to grow from the original potato.

The facts of the matter: The long white hairs that will grow are roots and the rhizome. The roots extend downward and absorb nutrients. The rhizome swells when the new plant finishes growing and becomes the tuber, or actual new potato. From the same potato eye from which the roots grow, a green shoot will grow upward. This will become the plant stalk from which leaves will eventually emerge.

WHAT we will need:
> Potatoes (one per child)
> Plastic containers (empty peanut butter
>   containers are ideal)
> Toothpicks
> Small pitchers of water
> Masking tape
> Marker

HOW we will do it: You will need a place to leave the potato experiments for at least two weeks. Put the toothpicks, plastic containers, potatoes, and pitchers of water on the table. Tear off masking tape strips for name tags and stick them onto the edge of the activity table. Using the marker, draw a line around each potato at about the one-third mark so the children know where to insert the toothpicks.

Ahead of time, prepare a sample potato-growing experiment. Stick three toothpicks into a potato at equal intervals around the line. Rest the potato on the rim of a container so that approximately one-third of the potato will be in water when the container is filled.

During an Attention Getter time, show the children your experiment. Say: "Remember the roots we saw growing from the potatoes? I was wondering how big those roots would get if they had some water, and whether or not a new potato plant would grow from this potato. So I put toothpicks in the potato right where the line is, so that part of my potato could sit in the water." Show the children the materials on the table, and invite them to prepare their own potato-growing experiments. Ask them to predict what the potato will do. Encourage them to write their names on the masking strips and to label their potatoes.

Potato Observation Books
Science/Language

WHY we are doing this experiment: to enable children to make a daily record of the results of the previous experiment; to develop all components of language arts: reading, writing, speaking, and listening.

WHAT we will need:
   Writing sheets (provided below;
      photocopy and enlarge
      for your use)

Blank paper
Light brown construction paper
Markers
Crayons
Pens
Preparation:
   Scissors
   Stapler

HOW we will do it: To prepare, make several copies of the potato observation sheets provided. Make books out of these, using a blank piece of brown construction paper for the covers. Make one for each child. Also, make some books of blank paper for children who want to create their own observation records. Put the books and writing/drawing utensils on an activity table near the potatoes.

Make a sample observation book. Write a title on the cover and draw pictures on it. Draw and write your observations about your potato in the first space. During an Attention Getter time, show the children your observation book. Together, read/interpret the words on the

Science Experiment:
Potato 🥔 Roots 🥔

Write the appropriate number next to each day, and make as many photocopies as you need. Children can draw, write, or dictate observations.

Day		Day	
I see:		I see:	
Day		Day	
I see:		I see:	

cover and inside the book. Discuss the drawings. Show the children the materials on the table and invite them to start their own observation books, either with the prepared writing sheets or with blank paper. Leave the books out for the duration of the experiment so that children can work on them as and when they choose. After a week or two, have a show-and-tell of observation books by having a few children talk about their books every day.

Growing New Potatoes
Science

WHY we are doing this experiment: to enable children to observe that new potatoes grow from a potato.

WHAT we will need:
    Potatoes with eyes
    Gardening tools
    Plot of earth
    Rulers
    Camera
Preparation:
    Sharp knife

HOW we will do it: You will not see the fruits of this experiment until six to ten weeks after you plant the potato pieces. Even so, it gives children the opportunity to compare the grown potato plant, complete with new potatoes, to the small piece originally planted. If necessary, loosen the dirt of your plot before the children plant their potato pieces. Use a knife to cut pieces of potato, making sure each piece has one or several eyes. During an Attention Getter time, ask the children if they remember what grows out of the potato eyes. Talk again about what you discovered in the Growing Potatoes and A Potato Is Stored Food experiments. Ask the children to predict what will grow from the potato eyes.

Show the children the plot of earth and potato pieces and ask them if they have any ideas about what they could do with them.

Before planting the pieces take photographs of them so that you can compare them to the grown plants, in later weeks. Invite your students to use the gardening tools to plant the potato chunks. They should be planted 12 cm to 18 cm (5" to 7") deep in the ground. When the stalk is about 50 cm tall (20"), the plant has probably grown tiny new potatoes. This can take six to ten weeks.

Check on your plants once a week, and if there has been no rain, water them. When your stalks are the right height, dig one plant up. If you see new potatoes, you can dig up the rest of the plants; otherwise, let them grow for a few more weeks. Shake your plants well to dislodge clods of earth and insects. Ask the children to compare a whole potato plant with the photographs of the original potato pieces. What are all the different parts which grew out of the tiny eyes on the original potato chunks? Invite the children to touch the plant stalk, leaves, roots, and new potatoes.

Potato Discovery Center
Science

WHY we are doing this activity: to enable children to examine, at the same time, a number of potatoes at different stages of growth in the cycle of potato reproduction.

WHAT we will need:
    Potatoes
    Magnifying glasses
    Index cards
    Markers

HOW we will do it: About six to ten weeks ahead of time, plant a few potato pieces with eyes. Three to five weeks ahead, plant a few more. About one week or one and one-half weeks ahead, put a few potatoes in jars of water, as described in the Growing Potatoes activity.

When you are ready to set up the discovery center, dig up the potato plants, making sure you dislodge all clods of earth, and shake the plants well so that insects are left behind. Put these potatoes, the potatoes in jars, and the regular, unsprouted potatoes in your discovery center, along with the magnifying glasses. Use the index cards and markers to label how many weeks each plant grew before it was dug up. Invite the children to examine and compare the potatoes and to discuss their observations.

Potato Badges
Language

WHY we are doing this activity: to develop speaking and listening skills.

WHAT we will need:
Light brown construction paper

Potato shapes (provided below; photo-copy and enlarge for your use)
Double-sided tape or masking tape loops (sticky side out)
Markers

HOW we will do it: Use the potato shape provided to cut out potato badges from the construction paper. Leave some badges blank, and on the rest, write: "Ask me about my potato science experiment!" Use double-sided tape or a masking tape loop to stick one onto yourself. Put the rest of the badges and the markers on an activity table. Stick the tape strips around the edge of the table. If the children do not notice your badge, read it to them and show them the other badges on the table. Encourage children to write their own words on the blank badges if they wish. If necessary, help your students secure their badges to their clothes.

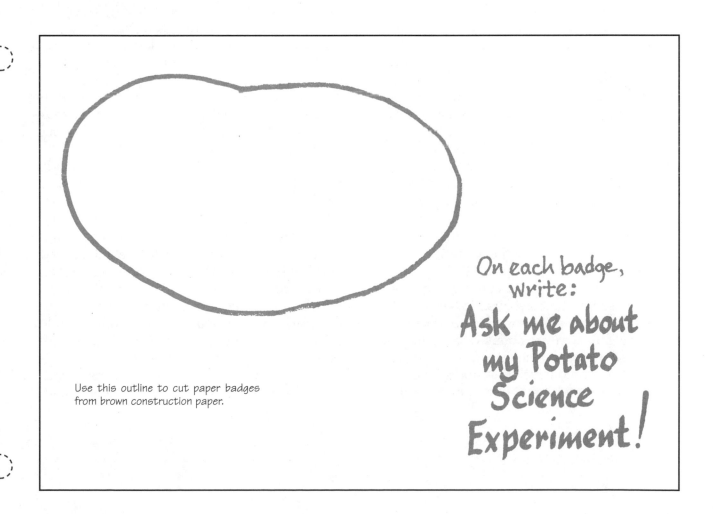

Use this outline to cut paper badges from brown construction paper.

On each badge, write:
Ask me about my Potato Science Experiment!

What is in a Potato?
Science

WHY we are doing this experiment: to enable children to observe that there is sugar (starch) in potatoes.

    The facts of the matter: A starch molecule consists of long chains of sugar molecules.

WHAT we will need:
- Iodine
- Potato slices (raw)
- Medicine droppers
- Small containers
- Potato peeler

HOW we will do it: Put all materials out on an activity table. During an Attention Getter time, explain to the children that the food which is stored in potatoes, and feeds a growing plant, is a type of sugar, also called a *starch*. Show the children the iodine and ask them to notice what color it is. Explain that the children are going to prove that there is starch in potatoes by using iodine. Iodine will turn to a blue-black color when it is put on starch. It is very important that you say: "Iodine is very, very dangerous to taste or drink. We're only going to drop it on our potato slices. We're not going to put the iodine, or the potatoes with iodine, anywhere near our mouths, because that would be dangerous." Discuss this. (The best way to supervise this activity is to sit at the table at where the experiment takes place, so that you can watch the children for the duration of the experiment.)

    Invite the children to conduct the experiment. Discuss their results. What happens when they put iodine on the potato pieces? What does this tell us about what is in potatoes? Use a potato peeler to carve off large pieces of peel onto which the children can drop iodine. Do the children think a potato peel has sugar in it?

Potato Foods (Part 1)
Science/Field Trip

WHY we are doing this activity: to enable children to observe how many different ways there are of using potatoes for food.

WHAT we will need:
- Supermarket
- Money

HOW we will do it: You may want to contact the manager of the supermarket you will be visiting with the children and discuss your plans, especially if you have a large group.

    Before you leave your home or classroom, let the children know that they are going to visit a supermarket to see how many foods they can find in the store that are made out of potatoes. Ask the children how many foods they can think of that you can buy in a store and which are made from potatoes. When you actually enter the supermarket, remind your students to look for bags or boxes or packages of food that might have potatoes in them.

    Go to the produce section first and let each child pick out a small potato to carry as you tour the store. This helps the children make the connection between a fresh potato and the processed foods they will find, which are made out of frozen, dehydrated, fried, or otherwise processed potatoes. Here are some potato foods you might spot and discuss: boxes of potato casseroles (e.g., scalloped, cheddar), potato flakes or powdered potatoes for instant mashed potatoes, frozen hash brown potatoes, frozen french fries, frozen Tater Tots, potato chips, Pringles, and potato sticks. Buy a few of these to take back to your home or classroom. Include dehydrated potato casserole packages, as well as flakes and powder for instant mashed potatoes, so that the children can experiment with what happens to them when water is added. (See the Dried Potatoes activity.)

Potato Foods (Part 2)
Science/Sensory

WHY we are doing this project: to enable children to observe the difference between processed potatoes and fresh potatoes; to discuss relative nutritive value; to provide a taste experience.

WHAT we will need:
  Potato food samples
  Fresh potatoes
  Potato peeler

HOW we will do it: Ahead of time, boil, bake, or roast fresh potato pieces with their skins. Make enough for each child to sample them. Prepare the processed potato foods that require cooking and put these and the other processed samples from the store on a small table for tasting. Put some uncooked samples from each package or box next to the corresponding cooked sample so the children can see how the potatoes changed. If you work with three- and young four-year-olds, you may want to put the uncooked samples in clear plastic cups and tape them shut with packaging tape so that they are not eaten, or discuss with the children which samples can be eaten and which cannot. During an Attention Getter time, show the children the potato samples available for tasting and the original packages from which each one came. Discuss how many samples each student can have. What will happen if someone takes more? (There will not be enough for everyone.) Hold up a fresh potato and ask the children: "How is this potato different from these potato foods? After this potato was dug out of the earth and washed off, do you think anything else was done to it? What about these potato foods we bought in the store? Are they the same as this potato? How are they different?" Talk about the fact that a vegetable that has not been cooked or frozen or dried is called *fresh*. Vegetables that have been cooked or dried or frozen are called *processed*. Pass the fresh potato around the group while you repeat the word *fresh*. Pass a dried potato slice from a casserole package around the group while you say the word *processed*. Ask the children whether they think fresh or processed foods are better. Discuss. Which of these is better for helping your body grow: a fresh potato, or the potato snack junk foods? Discuss.

Using the potato peeler, carve off a potato skin peel for each child to hold. Tell the children that there are a lot of vitamins in potato skins. Ask them if they can think of ways of eating potatoes that include the skins (e.g., baked potatoes, hash browns with the skin on, mashed potatoes with the skin included). Look at your store-bought potato food samples. Does it look like there is any potato skin in any of them? What did people have to do to the potatoes to make each of the processed potato foods you bought at the store? (For example, take the water out; make the potatoes into flour or dried chips or flakes; peel, slice, fry, and salt; peel, dice and freeze.) Tell the children the simple things you did to cook your fresh potato pieces, and the fact that the less you do to food, the better it usually is for your body. When the children try the different samples, ask them if your cooked potato pieces feel different in their mouths than the more processed potato foods. Introduce the word *texture*. As the children try all of the different kinds of potatoes, encourage them to express their observations.

How Much Water Is in Potatoes?
Science

WHY we are doing this project: to enable children to discover that potatoes have a high water content.

WHAT we will need:
  Freestanding graters
  Small- to medium-sized potatoes
    (or large potato chunks)
  Carrots

HOW we will do it: Set out the potatoes and graters on an activity table. Ask the children if they think potatoes have any water in them. Invite the children to grate the potatoes and to squish between their fingers the potato pulp produced by the grater. How does it feel? What does this tell us about what is in potatoes? After the children have squeezed and squished the pulp, put carrots on the table. When carrots are grated, what happens? Invite the children to compare how the potato pulp feels with how the carrot pulp feels. What does this tell us about which vegetable has more water in it?

Tip: Save some of the potato pulp for the following activity.

Dried Potatoes and Water
Science

WHY we are doing this project: to enable children to add water to the various dried potatoes purchased in the Potato Foods activity; to enable them to compare the dried and hydrated textures of the potato foods.

WHAT we will need:
>   Boxes of potato casserole mix (the kind with dried potato slices)
>   Potato flakes
>   Potato powder (for instant mashed potatoes)
>   Medicine droppers
>   Containers of warm water
>   Containers of cold water
>   Containers for mixing potatoes and water

HOW we will do it: Put all the materials on the activity table. During an Attention Getter time, take out the potato pulp from the previous project and encourage the children to touch it again. How does it feel? What does it tell us about what is in potatoes?

Show the children the dried potato foods on the table and ask them how they are different from the pulp. Invite them to mix the dried mashed potato powders with water. Potato slices from casserole packages can be soaked overnight. The next morning, compare the soaking slices to the dried ones. What happened? Invite the children to compare the hydrated potato foods to the fresh potato pulp, and encourage tactile exploration of all materials.

What Grows from a Sweet Potato?
Science/Crafts/Construction

WHY we are doing this project: to promote self-esteem by enabling children to prepare their own materials for a science experiment; to promote cooperation between students by facilitating a group project; to provide fine motor activity; to enable children to observe what happens to a sweet potato as the vine flourishes; to provide recording and measuring opportunities.

WHAT we will need:
>   Two wooden meter sticks for each trellis
>   Popsicle sticks
>   Wood glue (e.g., Elmer's)
>   Glue brushes
>   Butcher paper
>   Paper
>   Markers
>   Pens
>   Rulers
>   Fresh, sweet potato (not kiln-dried)
>   Plastic jar
>   Toothpicks
>   Water

HOW we will do it: The day before this activity, glue two or three Popsicle sticks across both meter sticks like the rungs of a ladder. The Popsicle sticks should be at about 5 cm or 6 cm (2" or 3") intervals. This will form the basis for a trellis. Invite the children to continue gluing Popsicle sticks onto the meter sticks.

The trellis that the children complete will not be as even as a ladder, and in fact, may not even be the shape of a ladder, but having a few Popsicle sticks already glued on will suggest what is needed.

After the glue has dried, ask the children where the trellis could be propped. Explain that you are going to put a sweet potato at the bottom of the trellis and it will need light. Together, prepare a place for the experiment. If possible, place your sweet potato and trellis on the floor or ground. This will make it easier for children to mark the growth of the vine on the chart next to the trellis. Make this chart out of butcher paper, by cutting out a strip which is about 20 cm (8") wide, and as long as the trellis. Post the chart directly next to the trellis. (You may decide to set up several trellises and sweet potatoes, or you may decide to set up only one.) Draw a line around your sweet potato about one-third of the way above the tapered end.

During an Attention Getter time, encourage the children to put toothpicks in the line around the sweet potato, to pour water into the container, and to prop the sweet potato in the container with the tapered end downward, so that one-third of it is covered in water. Ask the children where they should put the sweet potato so that if a vine grows, it will climb the trellis.

A vine may grow for months before the sweet potato collapses in on itself. When the buds and roots begin to appear, move a small table near the chart. Set out the rulers, markers, pens, and paper. Invite the children to mark off, on the chart, the height of the vine as it climbs the trellis, and to measure the height with the rulers. Children can also draw pictures of the sweet potato and vine and record descriptions by using the paper, markers, and pens. How does the vine use the trellis? Encourage the children to examine the tendrils closely to see how they wrap around the sticks. What happens to the sweet potato eventually? When it collapses, you can plant the vine outdoors if you wish.

Potato People
Art/Crafts/Fine Motor

WHY we are doing this project: to facilitate creative expression and to develop fine motor skills.

WHAT we will need:
Potatoes (various shapes and sizes)
Toothpicks
Olive slices (rings)
Carrot pieces (tips and stumps)
Parsley bunches
Celery pieces, some with leaves
Cherry tomatoes, halved

HOW we will do it: Put all materials out on the activity table. Make a sample potato person or animal by pinning vegetable pieces onto a potato with toothpicks. Parsley makes good hair, olive slices and halved cherry tomatoes make good eyes, carrot stumps can be used as legs, and tips can be used as noses. Be creative!

During an Attention Getter time, show the children your potato person or animal, and show them the materials on the activity table. Encourage them to make their own potato creations.

The Spud Fell Out of the Barrel
Music/Movement

WHY we are doing this activity: to develop cognition by memorizing words and connected actions; to develop an appreciation and enjoyment of singing together.

WHAT we will need:
Song: "THE SPUD FELL OUT OF THE BARREL" (To the tune of "The Bear Went Over the Mountain")

"THE SPUD FELL OUT OF
THE BARREL"
The spud fell out of the barrel, the spud fell out of the barrel, the spud fell out of the barrel, and rolled off far away.
It tumbled down a mountain . . .
and hit up against a rock.
It flew into a window . . .
and under a kitchen knife.
It got chopped up in pieces . . .
and went into the soup.
The soup went in my tummy . . .
and was so very good.

HOW we will do it: Explain to the children that *spud* is another name for a potato. Sing the song with the following motions: For "The spud fell out of the barrel," make one arm into a barrel opening and the fist of the other hand into a potato. Have your spud fall out of the barrel, and when you come to "and rolled off far away," make your potato fist turn over and over.

For "It tumbled down a mountain," turn both of your hands over and over each other. For "and hit up against a rock," slap one palm against another. For "It flew into a window," arch your arm to make a window and make your fist fly through it. For "and under a kitchen knife," make chopping motions with the side of one hand and make your other fist fall under it.

For "It got chopped up in pieces," make both hands into knives and pretend to chop. For "and went into the soup," pretend to scoop up the potato pieces and put them into a pot. For "The soup went in my tummy," pretend to eat soup from a bowl with a spoon. For "and was so very good," rub your stomach.

If you like, get a big soup pot to put in the middle of your circle, and use this to throw your imaginary potato pieces into and to eat your imaginary soup from.

Making Mashed Spuds
Science/Math/Cooking/Small Group Project

WHY we are doing this activity: to allow children to observe how hot water changes the texture of potatoes; to provide experience with measuring and counting; to develop self-esteem by enabling children to eat a snack they have prepared themselves; to develop cognition by recalling ingredients and sequence of preparation.

WHAT we will need:
    One potato (half-peeled)
    Several potatoes (peeled and chopped
       into roughly 2.5 cm (1") square pieces
       [for faster cooking])
    Recipe sign cards (provided below;
       photocopy and enlarge for your use)
    Plastic soup bowls
    One tablespoon

One large serving spoon
Forks
Milk
Softened butter (cut into pats)
Salt
Masking tape
Colander

HOW we will do it: On a table, set out the half-peeled potato for the children to examine. Also set out a large bowl for the cooked potatoes, a bowl of milk, a bowl of butter squares, and a bowl of salt. Place the appropriate recipe card behind each one.

Have the uncooked, peeled, and chopped potatoes ready in another bowl. Boil or microwave a pot of water. In order to prevent children from having access to the stove while the water is boiling, put a masking tape line on the floor to indicate where the children may not cross, or block off the area with chairs.

Have the children wash their hands first. Take out a few of the peeled potato chunks and encourage the children to touch them. Leave them out on the table. Let your students know you are going to put the potato pieces into the boiling water. Ask them to predict whether the potato pieces will change in the hot water and if so, how. Before you put the potato pieces in the pot, ask the children to put their hands behind their backs. Scoop out a mug of the hot water. Ask the children if they can see the steam from the water. Why is there steam? Put the potato pieces into the boiling water. When the potato pieces are tender, pour the contents of the pot into a colander over a sink, and then empty the pieces into a large bowl. Take a few chunks out and run them under cool water. Encourage the children to compare the few uncooked chunks with the cooked ones. Leave both kinds out for the duration of free play activities. How did the heat of the boiling water change the potato?

When the rest of the potato chunks have cooled off enough for the children to safely handle them, put them in a bowl with the serving spoon and then place them on the table with the other ingredients. Put the appropriate sign next to the potatoes. Encourage each child to take a plastic soup bowl, go around the table, and take the amount of each ingredient that each sign indicates. Invite them to sit down with a fork, and mash all their ingredients together, and to then eat what they have made. As you eat your snack together, talk about the sequence of events in making your mashed potatoes, to reinforce this for the following language activity. Save the recipe cards you used for this same purpose.

Class Book: Recipe for Mashed Spuds
Language/Small Group Project

WHY we are doing this project: to facilitate group cooperation and interaction; to develop all components of language arts: reading, writing, speaking, and listening; to develop self-esteem through use of a one-person work table.

WHAT we will need:
Light brown construction paper
(large sheets)
Markers
Crayons
"One person may be here" sign
(provided on page 3; enlarge and photocopy for your use)
Preparation:
Stapler
Scissors

HOW we will do it: To prepare, put four or five sheets of construction paper on top of each other, and staple down one side. Cut a potato shape out of the paper, making sure that you do not cut the staples off of the stapled side (in other words, make sure that even after you cut your potato shape, the pages still hold together).

Ask the children if they know what a *recipe* is. Hold up the recipe cards you used in the mashed potato activity. Encourage the children to tell you how they made the mashed potatoes. Say: "A *recipe* tells people how to make something they can eat. I thought we could put our class recipe for mashed potatoes in this book." Take dictation from the children about how they made their mashed potatoes and write their words in the book. When they are finished, read the recipe back to them. Put the book, crayons, and markers at a one-person work table. Discuss the "One person may be here" sign, and let the children know they can take turns illustrating the book. When the book is finished, put it with the rest of your books so that the children may look at and read it.

Mashed Mush

Sensory

WHY we are doing this activity: to facilitate a sensory experience with an unusual play material.

WHAT we will need:
 Prepared instant mashed potato mix
 Tubs or sensory table
 Food coloring (optional)
 Containers
 Spatulas
 Spoons

HOW we will do it: Put the mashed potato mix and the play materials into the tub or sensory table. Add food coloring if you like, and encourage the children to explore.

 Tip: Save some of the uncolored mashed potatoes for the Mashed Potato Art activity.

Potato Count

Math

WHY we are doing this activity: to practice rational counting; to familiarize young children with the concepts of *large*, *larger*, *largest*; to develop self-esteem and a sense of autonomy through use of a one-person work station.

WHAT we will need:
 Potatoes (large, medium, and small)
 Three containers of graduated sizes (e.g., a plastic 900 g (2 lb.) yogurt container, a 1800 g (4 lb.) yogurt container and a basin)
 "One person may be here" sign (provided on page 3; enlarge and photocopy for your use)
 Writing sheets (format provided on page 441)
 Blank paper
 Pens
 Activity sign

HOW we will do it: Fill the containers with potatoes. If you work with younger children who are not counting past ten, adjust the size of the containers and the number of potatoes accordingly. Make writing sheets based on the provided format, but draw symbols that represent the sizes and shapes of the containers you actually use. Set out several copies of these, along with the pens and blank sheets of paper, next to the potatoes. Make an activity sign that says: "How many potatoes?" Draw some potatoes above the word. Post this and a "One person may be here" sign near the activity table.

 During an Attention Getter time, read/ interpret the activity sign and writing sheets together. Show your students the blank paper that can also be used to record the potatoes counted. Discuss the "One person may be here" sign. Encourage the children to explore the materials.

How many potatoes?

Use the blank space to draw in symbols which represent the containers you are actually using.

1 2 3 4 5

I count _____ potatoes in the

large container.

1 2 3 4 5

I count _____ potatoes in the

larger container.

1 2 3 5 4

I count _____ potatoes in the

largest container.

Mashed Potato Art
Art

WHY we are doing this activity: to facilitate creative exploration with color; to develop fine motor skills.

WHAT we will need:
  Instant mashed potatoes
  Medicine droppers
  Small containers
  Water
  Food coloring
  Basin
  Bowl of water

HOW we will do it: Cook the mashed potatoes. Put a small amount in each container, and put the containers in front of the chairs at the activity table. Using food coloring, mix up red, blue, and yellow water, and place all three colors around the table so that the children will have access to them.

Encourage the children to use the medicine droppers and colored water to color their mashed potatoes. What happens when they drop one color on top of another? Tell the children they may dump the colored potatoes into the basin when they want to start a new batch, and that they may use the bowl of water to rinse out clogged droppers.

Potato Prints
Art

WHY we are doing this activity: to facilitate creative expression.
WHAT we will need:
- Potatoes (large and small)
- Paint
- String
- Rubber bands
- Butcher paper
- Shallow pans (for the paint)
- Newspaper
- Paper towels

Preparation:
- Knife

HOW we will do it: Spread many layers of newspaper on an activity surface and spread the butcher paper sheets out on top. Set out shallow pans of paint, so that all children will have easy access to them. The paint should not be too watery or the potatoes will not make good prints. Cut the potatoes in half, vertically and horizontally, and sandwich them between paper towels for a few minutes so that water is absorbed; this produces better prints. To vary the prints the potatoes make, wrap rubber bands around some, string around some, and use the knife to cut grooves in others.

Provide a good variety of different shapes and sizes. Put the potatoes in the pans with the paint, and encourage the children to make potato prints.

Potato Pancakes
Multicultural/Small Group Activity

WHY we are doing this activity: to introduce children to a Jewish tradition.

WHAT we will need:
- Book: Hirsh, Marilyn, *Potato Pancakes All Around: A Hanukkah Tale*

- 6 medium potatoes, peeled and grated
- 2 tablespoons flour
- 2 tablespoons heavy or light cream
- 2 eggs, beaten
- Salt to taste
- 8 tablespoons bacon fat or oil
- One raw, unpeeled potato
- Paper towels
- Electric frying pan
- Chairs or masking tape
- Small paper plates
- Plastic forks
- Napkins

HOW we will do it: Peel and grate the potatoes well ahead of time. Keep the grated potatoes in water to prevent them from turning brown, but be sure you squeeze the water out thoroughly before cooking. You can do this by wrapping the grated potato in strong, absorbent paper towels and squeezing and twisting all the excess water out into the towels. Put all the other cooking ingredients on the activity table. Plug in your electric frying pan, and make a barricade of chairs around it. Depending on your students, you may choose to use a masking tape line that they may not cross.

During an Attention Getter time, read *Potato Pancakes All Around*. There is no large, clear illustration of a potato in this book, so I like to let the children pass a potato around while I read the story. Show the children the cooking ingredients on the table and ask them what they could do with them. Have the children wash their hands and discuss the importance of not sneezing into the food, or putting fingers into mouths, noses, and ears while preparing the pancakes. Show the children the frying pan and the masking tape line or chair barricade. Let them know they may not cross the line, and say: "We're going to cook our potato pancakes in this frying pan and it's going to get very hot. What would happen if you touched it?"

Heat the frying pan. Put the grated potatoes in a bowl and add the flour, cream, egg, and salt. Let the children take turns stirring the mixture. Put about four tablespoons of the mixture in the pan to make each pancake. Cook both sides until browned. Let the pancakes cool a little, then enjoy!

Tater Toss
Gross Motor

WHY we are doing this activity: to develop hand-eye coordination; to develop the large muscle group.

WHAT we will need:
Large tubs or baskets
Small potatoes
Masking tape

HOW we will do it: Set the tubs or baskets at various places around the room. Put a masking tape line down several feet away from each one. The distance between the containers and the tape should depend on the age of your children—further away for older students, closer for younger children. Put several potatoes by each masking tape line. Encourage the children to toss the "taters" into the containers, and sincerely praise all their efforts. Before the activity, you may want to talk about what would happen if a potato were thrown at someone, and how important it is not to do this.

Greengrocer
Dramatic Play/Math/Language/Social Studies

WHY we are doing this activity: to facilitate an understanding of what a greengrocer does; to practice rational counting with pennies and nickels; to develop cognition by distinguishing between fruits and vegetables; to facilitate weighing and comparing; to develop all components of language arts: reading, writing, speaking, and listening.

WHAT we will need:
Balancing scales
Toy cash registers
Pennies and nickels
Potatoes
Other fruits/vegetables: (e.g., carrots, onions, apples)
Produce advertisements from newspaper supplements
Blank "Special" or "Sale" cards (ask your local supermarket to donate some)
Checkbooks and receipt forms (pattern provided on page 444; photocopy and enlarge for your use)
Pens
Markers
Baskets or bags
Children's aprons

HOW we will do it: Set up all materials to simulate a greengrocer's stand. Make several copies of the check patterns provided and cover them with construction paper to simulate checkbook covers. Also make copies of the receipt forms and staple them into a notebook. Post the produce advertisements on the walls around the store and set out blank "special" and "sale" signs with markers.

During an Attention Getter time, ask the children whether a potato is a fruit or a vegetable. Hold up one of each of the fruits or vegetables you will be using in the play greengrocer's, or use photographs, and ask the same question. If there is confusion, tell the children that, generally, fruits are sweet to eat and, generally, vegetables are not. Ask the children if any of them have ever been to a store that sells only fruits and vegetables. Tell them that a person who runs a store like that is called a *greengrocer*. Invite the children to explore the play greengrocery.

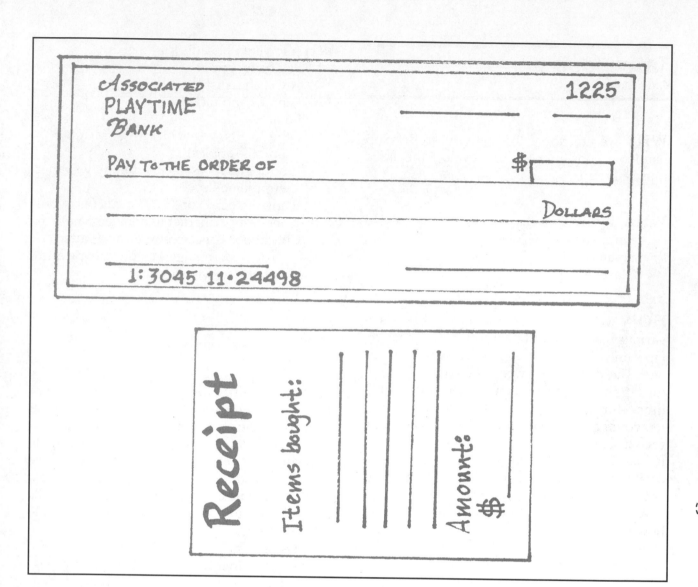

Literature

Symbol Key: *Multicultural
+Minimal diversity
No symbol: no diversity or no people

Brenner, B. (1992). *Group soup*. New York: Viking.

Hirsh, M. (1978). *Potato pancakes all around: A Hanukkah tale*. Rockaway Beach, NY: Bonim Books, Hebrew Publishing.*

Lobel, A. (1967). *Potatoes, potatoes*. New York: Harper & Row. (This excellent book addresses peace and anti-war issues.)

Selsam, M. E. (1972). *More potatoes!* New York: Harper & Row.

Wake, S. (1990). *Vegetables*. Minneapolis, MN: Carolrhoda Books.*

Watts, B. (1987). *Potato*. Morristown, NJ: Silver Burdett Press. (Excellent picture book with good photographs.)

Extenders

Social Studies: If possible, take a trip with the children to the local greengrocer's. Ask the greengrocer to give you a tour of the store so that you can see where fruits and vegetables are sorted and washed. What does the produce arrive in? How many different kinds of potatoes does the store sell? If you do not have a convenient greengrocer's to visit, tour the produce section of your local supermarket, and ask the manager to show you where the produce is delivered, washed, and sorted in the back of the store.

Math: Gather a diverse collection of potatoes: red, white, russet, baking potatoes, new potatoes (if in season), sweet potatoes, and big and small potatoes. Encourage the children to sort them. For younger children, get them interested by telling the sorting story in the Woodworks unit, but substitute the word "potato" for "nail."

Language: When you explore the store-bought processed potato foods, make a language chart of all the potato dishes the children eat at home.

Gross Motor: Play "Hot Potato." Have the children stand a few feet away from each other in a circle, and toss a potato to each other while music is being played. Ask them to pretend that the potato is very hot and they will burn their hands if they hold it for more than a few seconds. Turn the music off suddenly. Who is holding the hot potato? Let that child turn the music off the next time.

WAXWORKS

Attention Getter: You can buy household paraffin wax at most supermarkets. It is often found in the same section as Mason jars and other preserving supplies. Gulfwax brand is sold in boxes that contain four blocks. Cut off about one-third of one block and melt it by putting it in a container and setting the container in boiling water. Mold the wax into a ball and wrap it in clear cling wrap. The wax will harden again. To make it soft for Attention Getter time, put it in a mug of hot water right before the children gather. When you are ready, peel the cling wrap away and pass the wax ball around the group. Encourage the children to squeeze and mold it. What is it? If necessary, explain that it is wax. Is there something else in the classroom which is made of wax? (Crayons, wax paper.) Ask the children if they have ever noticed the wax in their ears. Ear wax helps protect our eardrums by trapping dirt that would otherwise get down inside our ears. Ask the children to guess what you will be talking about and working with over the next few weeks.

Wax Repels Water

Science

WHY we are doing this experiment: to enable children to observe how water and wax react to each other.

WHAT we will need:

Wax paper
Small shallow containers
Medicine or eyedroppers
Small containers of water
Food coloring (blue, red, and yellow)
Newspaper

Demonstration:

Paper towel

HOW we will do it: Spread newspaper out on an activity table. Put wax paper squares in each shallow container and put water on the table so that all children will have access to it. You can either mix up different colors at the beginning of the project, or let the children do this after they have experimented with plain water for a little while. Set out pieces of paper towel on the project table for comparison purposes.

For an Attention Getter time, have a paper towel, piece of wax paper, medicine dropper, and water on hand. Pass the wax paper and paper towel around the group and encourage the children to touch them both. How different do they feel? Suck up some water with the medicine dropper and hold it over the paper towel. Say: "What do you think will happen when I drop this water on the paper towel? Will the towel soak the water up?" Encourage the children to make their predictions and then release the water. Ask the children to predict what water will do on wax paper. Ask them if they see anything in the room that will help them conduct this experiment. As they explore, encourage them to verbalize their discoveries. Ask the children to hypothesize about why beads of water on the wax paper keep their shape. (The wax on the paper pushes away [repels] the water, and the surface tension of the water drops makes them hold their shape.) Encourage the children to make new colors of water beads on the wax paper by mixing the colored water.

More with Wax and Water

Science/Art

WHY we are doing this project: to provide children with an opportunity, through art, to observe again that wax repels water.

WHAT we will need:

Paper
Candles
Paints (not too thick)
Paintbrushes
Newspapers

HOW we will do it: Spread many layers of newspaper on an activity surface, and put all other materials on top. During an Attention Getter time, draw on a piece of paper with a candle. Your drawing will be invisible. Show the children the paints and ask: "If I paint over this picture, what do you think you will see?" Encourage the children to make their own candle and paint pictures to find out. Ask the children if they remember what they learned about wax in the previous activity. Using this information, ask them to hypothesize why the candle drawing shows up after the paper is painted.

Crayons Are Wax

Science/Art/Gross Motor

WHY we are doing this project: to enable children to discover that crayons are made of wax.

WHAT we will need:

Heating or hot plate
Aluminum foil
Kitchen parchment paper
Peeled crayons
Popsicle sticks

HOW we will do it: Encourage your students to make melted crayon pictures by putting a piece of parchment paper on the heating plate and then pressing crayons down on the paper. What happens? The longer the children press the crayon down on the heated paper, the larger a pool of melted wax will grow. To vary this activity a little, crumple up pieces of foil, then flatten them again and invite the children to make melted crayon pictures on the ridged sheets. Cut out aluminum squares and have the children make their pictures on foil instead of paper.

Other variations: Make a melted crayon picture and then press another piece of paper on top. What happens?

Fold paper shapes in half and cut different shaped holes in the paper. Then invite the children to put an intact piece of paper underneath the cut paper and to place both on the heating plate. Use a paper clip to keep the two pieces together. Encourage the children to make a melted crayon picture over the surface of both papers. When you separate the pages, what does the bottom page look like? (Remove the paper clips yourself; they may be hot.)

Crumpled Crayon and Candle Pictures

Science/Art

WHY we are doing this experiment: to enable children to examine how the pure paraffin wax in candles repels water, compared with the diluted wax in crayons; to facilitate creative art.

The facts of the matter: Most candles are made of pure paraffin wax, which is a strong water repellent. Crayons are made of paraffin wax, but also contain stearic acid and powdered, colored pigments. These additives reduce the water-repelling capability of crayons.

WHAT we will need:
   Pans or tubs of water
   Strong paper
   Tall narrow candles (to make
      drawing easier)
   Crayons
   Paints
   Paintbrushes
   Newspaper

HOW we will do it: Spread several layers of newspaper on and underneath a work surface. Place all other materials on an activity table.

During an Attention Getter time, draw one picture with a crayon and another with a candle. Crumple both papers up, immerse in the water, and then gently squeeze out the excess. Gently uncrumple both paper pieces as you say: "I'm unfolding this paper very carefully and slowly because I don't want to tear it." Ask the children if they remember what happened when they painted over a candle drawing. Ask them to predict whether the same thing will happen when they paint over a crayon drawing. Encourage your students to use the materials to conduct this experiment. Three- and young four-year-olds may need help unfolding their crumpled paper. Ask the children to hypothesize why the candle drawings repel water and the crayon drawings do not. Encourage all ideas. As appropriate, explain that candles are pure paraffin wax, and that crayons are made of other things besides wax. This means the wax in the candles is more water-repellent.

Wax Repels Fat

Science

WHY we are doing this experiment: to enable children to discover that wax repels fat.

WHAT we will need:
   Regular paper (or kitchen parchment
      paper, which absorbs fat well and
      leaves clear grease spots)
   Wax paper
   Popsicle sticks
   Margarine (cut into pats)
   Small containers

HOW we will do it: Put margarine pats in small containers and place them on the activity table, along with squares of regular and wax paper and Popsicle sticks.

During an Attention Getter time, pass around a piece of regular paper and wax paper and encourage the children to touch, examine, and compare both. Smear some margarine on the end of a Popsicle stick, and take a piece of regular paper and say: "What do you think will happen when I smear this margarine on this piece of paper?" Encourage predictions. Smear the margarine on the paper and wait a few seconds. What happens? Show the children the grease spot. The paper absorbed the fat. Show your students a piece of wax paper and ask them to predict whether it will absorb fat. Ask the children if they see anything in the room that will help them conduct an experiment to find out.

As they use the materials to experiment, ask: "Does the wax paper absorb the fat?" Invite your students to run their fingers over the greased wax paper. The wax does not soak up fat, so the paper underneath the wax covering cannot absorb it either. If you'd like, let the children experiment with putting margarine and water drops on the same pieces of wax paper. What happens? Why? (The water repels the fat and the wax repels both of them.)

Developmental differences: Three- and young four-year-olds enjoy the sensory aspect of grease and water, and of smearing margarine on surfaces. In the process of this kind of exploration, they will likely become aware of the effects of grease and water on wax paper. Older children are likely to be interested in conducting and observing the results of the experiment.

Some Wax Is Hard; Some Is Soft
Science

WHY we are doing this experiment: to enable children to compare several different waxes for softness and hardness.

The facts of the matter: The harder wax is, the fewer impurities it contains. Most wax is petroleum oil-based. Purer wax has had more petroleum strained out of it until the wax consists primarily of by-product. Beeswax is naturally softer than petroleum-based wax.

WHAT we will need:
- Toothpicks
- Jumbo paper clips (unbent)
- Chapsticks
- Crayons
- Candles
- Beeswax
- Wax from blue cheese
- Sealing wax

HOW we will do it: Set all materials out on an activity table and invite the children to use the toothpicks and paper clips to scratch each kind of wax. Which waxes are hard to scratch? Which ones are easy? How do the easily scratched waxes feel when you squeeze them between your fingers? What about the waxes that are hard to scratch? Discuss!

Can You Sink Wax?
Science/Sensory

WHY we are doing this experiment: to enable children to discover that wax displaces enough water to create buoyancy; to have fun trying to sink different kinds of wax.

The facts of the matter: Whether or not an object floats depends on how much water it displaces. The more water an object displaces, the more of an upward push it receives from the water beneath. Wax displaces enough water to be supported by this "push."

WHAT we will need:
- Large sensory table
- Water
- Candles
- Sealing wax blocks (available in grocery and variety stores that sell preserving and canning supplies)
- Crayons

HOW we will do it: Put all the wax varieties beside a sensory table filled with water. Ask the children to predict whether or not they will be able to sink the wax samples. Invite them to use the materials to experiment. Is it possible to sink any of them? What happens when the children push one of the wax objects all the way down into the water and let go? As the children explore, explain that wax is so light that it pushes water out of the way when it sits in it. This makes the water underneath it push upward, and the upward push keeps the light wax floating.

Molding Wax
Science/Sensory/Art

WHY we are doing this project: to enable children to observe that heated wax is soft and malleable and that cooled wax hardens; to provide a sensory experience; to facilitate creative expression.

WHAT we will need:
  Household paraffin wax
Preparation:
  Pot of boiling water
  Shallow pans (that fit inside pot)
Optional:
  Peeled crayons

HOW we will do it: Boil a large pot of water and put the blocks of wax in the shallow pans. (If you like, wrap the pans in foil first.) Put the pans in the boiling water and melt the wax. When the wax is melted, divide it into other shallow pans so that it cools more quickly. It is important to give the heated wax to the children at just the right time. The wax must be cool enough so that it does not burn them, but still warm and soft enough that it can be easily molded. You may want another adult with you when you do this activity, so that one person can be with the children and one can attend to the wax.

When the wax is ready, encourage the children to squeeze and squish it and to mold it into shapes of their choice. Food coloring is not very effective to use for coloring the wax, but if you melt colored crayons with the wax blocks

and stir the two together you can make colored wax. One fun thing to do is to cover fingertips in the cooled but still liquid wax and, when it dries, peel it off. Are there fingerprints in the wax peelings? Let the children's shapes cool and display them in your home or classroom for the duration of the unit.

Beeswax
Science

WHY we are doing this activity: to enable children to observe beeswax.

The facts of the matter: Bees make six-sided wax cells for storing honey. The sides of the cells can be thinner than $\frac{1}{500}$ of an inch. Bees make wax from glands in their abdomens. They take tiny white wax wafers from this area, chew them in their mouths, and then add them to the honeycomb to strengthen and expand it. Bees eat six or seven pounds of honey for every pound of wax they make.

WHAT we will need:
  Comb honey (available at some supermarkets and at food co-ops)
  Magnifying glasses
  Whole wheat bread
  Butter
  Small paper plates
  Book: Fischer-Nagel, Heiderose & Andeas, *Life of the Honeybee*

HOW we will do it: Put the comb honey and the magnifying glasses on the activity table. During an Attention Getter time, read *Life of the Honeybee* and discuss it. Show the children the comb honey and magnifying glasses on the table and encourage them to examine the honeycomb. What do they see? Talk about the individual wax cells and the honey stored inside. After the comb honey has been out long enough for each child to have an opportunity to examine it, give each child a piece of buttered whole wheat bread with some of the honey on it and break off a piece of the comb for each child to explore. What do the wax cells feel like?

Wax Discovery Center
Science/Language

WHY we are doing this activity: to expose the children to everyday materials that are made of wax, for their hands-on exploration; to develop speaking and listening skills.

WHAT we will need:
- Candles
- Crayons
- Block of blue cheese (with wax covering)
- Chapsticks
- Block of paraffin wax
- Comb honey
- Paper
- Activity sign (format provided below; photocopy and enlarge for your use)
- Puppet

HOW we will do it: Alter the provided activity sign to reflect your materials and post it above the activity table. Put all materials on the table and peel back part of the wax surrounding the blue cheese so that the children can see what the wax covering contains.

During an Attention Getter time, read/interpret the activity sign together. Encourage the children to explore and examine the different kinds of wax. Take out your puppet and use it to discuss the wax items. For example: Puppet (picking up blue cheese): "I'm quite, quite hungry—I'll take a nice big bite of this."

You: "Whoa, Alexander—are you sure you want to eat the wax that's around the cheese? What do you think, children? Should he eat it? Why?"

Puppet: "Who ever heard of someone putting wax around cheese?"

You: "The wax helps the cheese to stay moist, Alexander, so that it doesn't dry out."

Puppet (grabbing a candle): "I think I'll draw a picture."

Science Experiment: Wax

Touch each kind of wax.

Draw on paper with each kind of wax. Which one works best?

You: "Children, what do you think Alexander should use to draw a picture with? Which one has more color in it, Alexander, the crayon or the candle? Why don't you try both and see which one does the best job?"

Seven Candles for Kwanzaa
Language/Multicultural/Small Group Activity

WHY we are doing this activity: to familiarize children with Kwanzaa and the role that candles play in this celebration; to develop speaking and listening skills; to help children feel comfortable with sharing their thoughts.

The facts of the matter: Kwanzaa is an African-American holiday that is celebrated between December 26 and January 1. *Kwanzaa* is a Swahili word which means "first fruits of the harvest." For each day of Kwanzaa, a new candle is lit and placed in the *kinara*, or candleholder. Traditionally, Kwanzaa marks the end of the harvest and the beginning of the new planting season.

WHAT we will need:
    Book: *Seven Candles for Kwanzaa*
    Seven candles

HOW we will do it: Invite the children to sit in a circle on the floor and pass an unlit candle to one child in the group. Read *Seven Candles for Kwanzaa* and have the children pass the candle to the next person every time you turn a page. After reading the story, discuss it. Some ideas: The red candles remind us of the struggles or hard things we have to go through. What kinds of hard things have the children gone through? The green candles remind us to look forward to good things in the future. What are the children looking forward to? Together, count out the seven candles to see how many seven is. Light the seven candles and put them in the middle of the circle, turn the lights down, and invite the children to share their thoughts with the group at that moment. Blow the candles out before the children stand up.

The Candle Crafter
Language/Multicultural

WHY we are doing this activity: to stimulate imagination; to develop speaking and listening skills; to develop multicultural awareness; to help children identify colors.

WHAT we will need:
    Flannel board
    Flannel board shapes (provided on
        page 454; photocopy and enlarge for
        your use)
    Felt
    Spangles or glitter
    Glue
    "Two people may be here" sign
        (provided on page 14; enlarge and
        photocopy for your use)
    Markers or crayons
    Scissors
    Clear contact paper
    Story: "AKIRA AND THE CANDLE
        CRAFTER" (provided)

HOW we will do it: To prepare, color all the flannel board pieces, cut them out, and glue them to felt. If you'd like, cover them on the paper side with clear contact paper to make them sturdier. To make a truly spectacular candle, glue spangles and/or glitter on the felt candle shape.

Tip: There are spangles you can buy that are pink when they reflect the light. They look very attractive on the shell shape.

Set up the flannel board and tell the following story:

"AKIRA AND THE CANDLE CRAFTER"

Once upon a time there was a candle crafter who decided that she was going to make the most beautiful candle that was ever made. [Put candle crafter on board.] She had a huge pot of melted wax which she stirred and stirred to make sure all the wax melted. [Put pot on board.] There was only one

Use a photocopier to enlarge these pattern shapes.

problem. The wax was all white, and the candle crafter wanted the candle to be beautiful, with many colors. So she said to her assistant, Akira, "Akira, please go out and bring me back the most beautiful blue you can possibly find."

Akira went out. It was very, very dark outside. He looked and looked [put Akira on board], and even in the darkness, he could see that the most beautiful blue thing around was the sky, so he reached up and broke a piece of it off and carried it carefully back to the candle crafter. [Put blue patch in Akira's hand and move him back toward the candle crafter.] She thought the piece of sky was indeed a beautiful blue, and put it into the pot with the melting wax. Akira said, "Will you need pink?" The candle crafter said she would, and asked him to get the most delicate pink that he could. Akira looked and looked. He didn't see anything pink. But then, even though it was dark and gloomy, something glistened on the ground, and when he picked it up he saw that it was a beautiful little shell [put shell on the board], and inside the shell was the most delicate pink he had ever seen. He hurried back to the candle crafter, and she looked at it for a long time. "This is lovely, Akira," she said. And she put it in the pot with the melting wax. Do you remember the other color she already had in the pot? [Let children answer.]

Then she said to Akira, "Can you find me the richest, deepest brown that there is?" Akira went out and looked all around. It was hard to see in the darkness. Then something made him look down at his feet, and he saw the rich, good, brown earth everywhere around him. [Put brown dirt in his hand.] He scooped up a cool handful of that earth and brought it to the candle crafter. "Yes," she said, "This is the richest brown I've ever seen." And she added it to the melting pot of wax. Do you remember the other colors she had already added to the wax? [Let children answer.]

They added many more colors. Akira brought her a violet. [Put up violet.] What color did the violet give her? [Let children answer.] Akira then brought her a feather he found that a cardinal had shed. [Put up red feather.] What color did it add to the melting wax? [Let children answer.] Then he brought her a beautiful leaf that the wind carried to him. [Put up leaf.] What color did it add to the wax? [Let children answer.] Last, Akira went out into the soft, downy darkness and found a piece of coal. [Put up patch of black.] What color did it add to the melting wax? [Let children answer.] Finally they were ready to make the most beautiful candle that had ever been. They poured the colored melted wax into a mold, and when it had cooled, guess what they had? [Put up candle.] The candle crafter lit that candle [put up sun/flame] and a beautiful fierce, warm, yellow flame began to burn. That fiery flame burned, hard and fierce, and it gave heat and light to everything. Eggs hatched in the warmth of the candle's flame and plants grew and the water in small puddles and the water in large lakes became nice and warm so that the fat silver fish in them swam slowly and lazily, and all things enjoyed the heat and light that came from that miraculous candle. And that's the story of Akira and the candle crafter and the most beautiful candle in the world.

After you tell the story, put the materials out and let the children know they can use them to retell the story and to make up new ones. Together, read/interpret the "Two people may be here" sign and discuss its meaning.

Candle Collection
Math/Social Studies/Language

WHY we are doing this project: to promote group cooperation; to facilitate ordering, classifying (separating and grouping), and rational counting; to develop speaking, listening, reading, and writing skills.

WHAT we will need:
  Candles (as many as you can collect as a class)
  Sticky labels or masking tape
  Butcher paper
  Markers
  Large tub
  Activity sign and writing sheets (provided on page 456; enlarge and photocopy for your use)

Line up the candles

from fattest to thinnest.

Line up the candles

from longest to shortest.

I counted _____

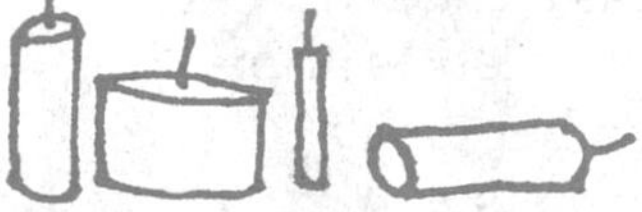

candles in our collection.

HOW we will do it: A week or two before you facilitate this unit, let the children know that you are going to be talking about and working with wax, and that you would like them to start a class candle collection. Pin up a piece of butcher paper on the wall. Say: "Let's write a note to give to our families and friends to ask for help with our candle collection. What could we say?" Take dictation and write down the children's suggestions or have the children write their words down. If you work with kindergartners, you may want to provide them with lined notepaper and pens. After writing down the group's comments, which will give them ideas, encourage them to write their own notes. Some topics to cover: What kind of candles do we want? (Any kind, big and small.) When do we need them by? Who should our friends and families give the candles to? Are we going to keep the candles, or are we just borrowing them? Have the children give their individually written notes to their parents, or write a note from the dictated ideas on the butcher paper, photocopy it, and send it home with the children. If you are a parent at home, send or deliver the notes to friends and relatives.

When you start gathering the candles, use the tub to keep them in. Use sticky labels or masking tape to write names on the candles so that donors get their candles back. Once you have your collection, take it out during an Attention Getter time and encourage a group discussion and exploration of all the different shapes, sizes, and colors of candles. (Discuss the fact that candles should never be lit without the help of an adult.) Together, find out how many ways there are of grouping the candles: (e.g., color, circumference, length, shape). For free play time, consider a variety of activities to facilitate with the candle collection.

Sorting: Find several containers that will hold sorted candles. During an Attention Getter time, tell the sorting story for the nails in the Woodworks unit, but substitute the word "candle" for "nail." Then invite the children to sort the candles themselves. If you like, buy several boxes of birthday candles and encourage your students to sort them by color.

Ordering: Make an activity sign, based on the sample provided, that says: "Line up the candles from longest to shortest" Make another that says: "Line up the candles from fattest to thinnest" Put the candle collection on the floor, perhaps on top of a large piece of butcher paper, to define the activity area. Post the signs nearby. Read/interpret the signs together during an Attention Getter time.

Matching: This is a good math activity for younger preschoolers. On a large piece of butcher paper, trace outlines of various candles, both standing straight up on the paper and lying down. The candles should vary a good deal in size, circumference, and length, so that each outline is distinct and the children can easily match each one to its outline.

Rational counting: Depending on the number of candles in your collection, have the children count them individually or as a group. If the children count them individually, make photocopies of the corresponding writing sheet provided. Set them out with pens, next to the candle collection. Also provide blank sheets of paper for children who prefer to use them to record the number counted.

Math kits: Put birthday candles, a small pencil, and blank paper or a writing sheet (that says, "How many candles do you count?") in a box or tin. Prepare several of these math kits and set them out for the children to use independently.

Candle Dance
Music/Movement/Gross Motor

WHY we are doing this project: to enable children to participate in a quiet, reflective time using relaxing music and candlelight; to facilitate creative movement; to develop an appreciation for music.

WHAT we will need:
  Masking tape
  Candles
  Matches
  Relaxing music

HOW we will do it: Put a masking tape circle on the floor and put the candles in the circle. Before you light the candles, explain to the children that they must not cross the masking tape. Ask: "What would happen if you touched a burning candle?" Explain how dangerous hot wax is.

Have the children gather around the candles, several feet away from the masking tape circle. Dim the lights and draw the curtains. Put on the relaxing music. Here are some movement options to explore: Have the children lie down for a minute or two and imagine they are floating on a cloud, high up in the starry sky at night. Next, have the children sit up with their hands stretched above their heads. Have them imagine that their fingers are a burning flame, on top of a candle. Slowly the candle melts down, lower and lower, until each one is a pool of melted wax on the ground. Imagine that the wax cools a little. What happens? Finally, blow out the candle flames, turn on the lights, and remove the candles. Have the children pair off, with one child pretending to "mold" the wax shape of her or his partner. Then have the children reverse roles. Be creative!

Household Play
Dramatic Play

Add candles to your dramatic play area—put them in special candleholders or on plates. Talk to the children again about how they can pretend to light the candles, but that it is dangerous to light a candle without an adult's help.

Literature

Symbol Key: *Multicultural
+Minimal diversity
No symbol: no diversity or no people

Fischer-Nagel, H., & Fischer-Nagel, A. (1986). *Life of the honeybee.* Minneapolis, MN: Carolrhoda Books.

Gilbreath, A. (1975). *Candles for beginners to make.* New York: William Morrow.

Pinkney, A. D. (1993). *Seven candles for Kwanzaa.* New York: Dial Books for Young Readers.

Teale, E. W. (1961). *The bees.* Chicago: Children's Press.

Extenders

Math: After the activities with the candle collection, make a graph of the results. The graph could show how many candles you have of various colors, how many long, thin candles you have, how many short, fat ones, and so forth.

Field Trip: Visit a candle maker to see how wax is formed into candles.

Art/Crafts: Have the children make their own multicolored crayons by putting broken crayon pieces in muffin pans and melting them in the oven. When the new crayons cool, invite the children to color with them.